COLLINS FIELD

BIRD

OF BRITAIN & EUROPE

Roger Tory Peterson
Guy Mountfort
P.A.D. Hollom

Fifth Revised and Enlarged Edition

In collaboration with
D.I.M. Wallace

HarperCollins*Publishers*

HarperCollins*Publishers*
77–85 Fulham Palace Road
London
W6 8JB

The HarperCollins website address is:
www.**fire**and**water**.com

First Edition 1954
Reprinted eight times
Second Edition 1966
Reprinted four times
Third Edition 1974
Reprinted five times
Fourth Edition 1983
Reprinted five times
Fifth Edition 1993

8 10 9 7

02 03

TO OUR LONG-SUFFERING WIVES

She laments sir … her husband
goes this morning a-birding
SHAKESPEARE – *Merry Wives of Windsor*

ISBN 0 00 219900 9

Printed and bound by Printing Express Ltd., Hong Kong

Contents

Preface to the Fifth Revised Edition	8
The Geographical Area Embraced by the Field Guide	11
How to Identify Birds	12
The Ornithological Societies	19
Checklist of European Birds	20
Topography of a Bird	28

Divers: Gaviidae — 30
Grebes: Podicipedidae — 32
Albatrosses: Diomedeidae — 35
Large Petrels and Shearwaters: Procellariidae — 35
Storm Petrels: Hydrobatidae — 38
Gannets: Sulidae — 40
Cormorants: Phalacrocoracidae — 40
Pelicans: Pelecanidae — 41
Herons and Bitterns: Ardeidae — 42
Storks: Ciconiidae — 46
Ibises and Spoonbills: Threskiornithidae — 47
Flamingos: Phoenicopteridae — 47
Swans, Geese and Ducks: Anatidae — 48
Kites, Vultures, Harriers, Hawks, Buzzards and Eagles: Accipitridae — 69
Ospreys: Pandionidae — 81
Falcons: Falconidae — 81
Grouse: Tetraonidae — 85
Partridges, Quails and Pheasants Phasianidae — 87
Button-quails: Turnicidae — 91
Rails, Crakes and Coots: Rallidae — 91
Cranes: Gruidae — 95
Bustards: Otididae — 96
Oystercatchers: Haematopodidae — 97
Stilts And Avocets: Recurvirostridae — 97
Thick-knees: Burhinidae — 98
Coursers And Pratincoles: Glareolidae — 99
Plovers: Charadriidae — 100
Sandpipers, Stints, Godwits, Curlews, Snipe and Phalaropes: Scolopacidae — 105
Skuas: Stercorariidae — 122
Gulls: Laridae — 125
Terns: Sternidae — 133
Auks: Alcidae — 138
Sandgrouse: Pteroclididae — 141
Pigeons And Doves: Columbidae — 142
Parrots: Psittacidae — 145
Cuckoos: Cuculidae — 145
Barn Owls: Tytonidae — 147

Owls: Strigidae 147
Nightjars: Caprimulgidae 152
Swifts: Apodidae 153
Kingfishers: Alcedinidae 154
Bee-eaters: Meropidae 155
Rollers: Coraciidae 155
Hoopoes: Upupidae 156
Woodpeckers: Picidae 156
Larks: Alaudidae 160
Martins and Swallows: Hirundinidae 164
Pipits and Wagtails: Motacillidae 165
Waxwings: Bombycillidae 170
Dippers: Cinclidae 171
Wrens: Troglodytidae 171
Accentors: Prunellidae 172
Robins, Chats and Thrushes: Turdidae 172
Warblers: Sylviidae 185
Flycatchers: Muscicapidae 203
Babblers: Timaliidae 205
Long-tailed Tits: Aegithalidae 205
Tits: Paridae 205
Nuthatches: Sittidae 208
Wallcreepers: Tichodromadidae 210
Treecreepers: Certhiidae 210
Penduline Tits: Remizidae 211
Orioles: Oriolidae 211
Shrikes: Laniidae 212
Crows: Corvidae 214
Starlings: Sturnidae 218
Sparrows: Passeridae 220
Waxbills: Estrildidae 221
Vireos: Vireonidae 222
Finches: Fringillidae 222
New World Warblers: Parulidae 230
Buntings: Emberizidae 232
Icterids: Icteridae 239

Accidentals 240

Maps 262

Index 308

The Colour Plates

1. Divers
2. Grebes
3. Storm-petrels, Fulmar, Shearwaters
4. Cormorants
5. Miscellaneous Large Lake and Sea Birds
6. Long-legged Marsh Birds
7. Long-legged Marsh Birds
8. Swans and Geese
9. Swans and Geese in Flight
10. Grey Geese
11. Chiefly Grey Geese in Flight
12. Surface-feeding Ducks
13. Diving Ducks
14. Diving Ducks at Sea
15. Diving Ducks at Sea
16. Shelducks And Diving Ducks at Sea
17. Saw-bills and Stiff-tails
18. Vagrant Waterfowl
19. Ducks in Flight from Above
20. Ducks in Flight from Above
21. Ducks Overhead
22. Ducks Overhead
23. Vultures
24. Harriers and Kites
25. Harriers and Kites In Flight
26. Buzzards and Hawks
27. Buzzards and Small Eagles Overhead
28. Eagles
29. Eagles and Osprey Overhead
30. Falcons
31. Falcons and Accipters Overhead
32. Game Birds
33. Game Birds
34. Rails and Crakes
35. Moorhen, Coots, Purple Gallinule
36. Bustards, Sandgrouse, Stone Curlew
37. Plovers
38. Ringed Plovers, Pratincoles
39. Large Plovers, Turnstone, Courser
40. Plovers And Turnstone in Flight
41. Phalaropes
42. Large Waders
43. Long-billed Snipe-like Waders and Knot
44. Large Sandpipers
45. Smaller Sandpipers
46. Ruffs and North American Sandpipers

47. **Sandpipers**
48. **Stints and Purple Sandpiper**
49. **Small Sandpipers from North America**
50. **Large Waders in Flight**
51. **Medium-sized Waders in Flight**
52. **Waders in Flight**
53. **Skuas**
54. **Adult Gulls**
55. **Immature Gulls**
56. **Rare or Vagrant Gulls**
57. **Terns**
58. **Terns**
59. **Heads of Terns**
60. **Vagrant Terns**
61. **Auks**
62. **Auks**
63. **Pigeons and Doves**
64. **Owls**
65. **Owls**
66. **Hoopoe, Roller, Bee-eaters, Kingfishers**
67. **Cuckoos**
68. **Nightjars**
69. **Woodpeckers and Wrynecks**
70. **Larks**
71. **Swifts, Martins and Swallows**
72. **Pipits**
73. **Wagtails**
74. **Heads of Wagtails**
75. **Wheatears**
76. **Robins, Chats, Nightingales**
77. **Redstarts, Bluetail, Rock Thrushes**
78. **Thrushes**
79. **Swamp Warblers**
80. **Scrub Warblers, Etc.**
81. **Leaf Warblers and Tree Warblers**
82. **Rare Warblers**
83. **Goldcrests, Dipper, Wren, Creepers and Nuthatches**
84. **Flycatchers and Waxwing**
85. **Shrikes**
86. **Tits**
87. **Smaller Crows, Jays, Oriole and Starlings**
88. **Crows**
89. **Finches**
90. **Finches**
91. **Sparrows, Accentors and Buntings**
92. **Buntings**
93. **Vagrant Wood Warblers from North America**
94. **Vagrant Songbirds from North America**
95. **Some Introduced Birds**
96. **More Introduced Birds**

Preface to the Fifth Revised Edition

In the thirty-nine years since this book first appeared, more than one million copies in twelve different languages have been sold. It has been revised four times and the English editions reprinted twenty-four times. It was the first of its kind and has since 1954 had half a dozen competitors, with similar or even identical titles. A fifth and much more fully revised edition is now issued. The entire text has been rewritten, not only to bring it up to date but also to improve the diagnostic descriptions of the species. The introductory texts to bird Families have been amplified in order to help the beginner and the less expert bird-watchers. To cater for the rapidly increasing expertise of field ornithologists who are now armed with high-magnification telescopes and demand much more detailed information, notes are included concerning the recognisable geographical races of species which occur within our region. Introduced species now breeding in a feral state within this area are also included. Notes are given on identification of the bird in flight and its attitudes and behaviour when perched. In the case of "confusion species" such as some of the waders, raptors and warblers, additional notes draw attention to their distinction from those with which they are most likely to be confused.

The authors determined that the new Field Guide would offer more chances of trustworthy identification of a bird than any other competing book. To meet this aim, they enlisted D.I.M. Wallace to help with the text revision and are extremely grateful for the thoroughness with which he tackled his task. His editorship of the field character sections of the *The Birds of the Western Palearctic* and his continuing expertise in field identification enabled him to advise us on the latest criteria for all European species, particularly the more difficult ones.

The illustrations have been re-painted and 19 new plates added, to provide for new species now admitted to the European list. A considerable number of additional pictures of female and immature plumages have ben included. Some previously crowded plates have been divided into two, enabling the birds to be portrayed larger and in more detail. The total number of species portrayed has risen to 548.

The Accidental section has also been enlarged to include 171 species of vagrants which have been recorded within the area of the book. A few previously included have now been invalidated and have therefore been dropped. Others have now occured more than about twenty times within the area and have therefore been given full treatment in the main text. The total number of species described in the Field Guide is therefore increased to 698. A number of countries have now created panels of experts similar to those of the British Birds Records Committee, to decide on the validity of records of vagrant species. Unfortunately their deliberations sometimes take a year or more before a decision is taken. Even then it is not immune from reconsideration. We have felt it better to describe one or two species too many than to omit information which may be of value. Accordingly, where such vagrants have been reported by responsible observers and appear to warrant serious consideration, we have included them so that their diagnostic features can be described for our readers even if they do not yet appear on an official national list. The next likely-looking Cape Gannet seen in European waters will stand a better chance of being correctly identified to the satisfaction of a rarities committee if the observer has been previously alerted about the features to be looked for or eliminated.

We have retained the English names of birds which are most familiar throughout Great Britain, but have accepted the now 'official' new American names for the small number of North American vagrants involved.

As the geographical distribution of birds is constantly changing and the compiling of "bird atlases" is now widespread in Europe, many of the distribution maps at the back of the Field Guide have been re-drawn. In this connection, we acknowledge the valuable help of the extensive library of the Royal Society for the Protection of Birds. We are also particularly indebted to the reports of *British Birds* magazine on many aspects of vagrancy, records of rare species in the British Isles and changes in breeding ranges. We express our gratitude to the Editors of *The Birds of the Western Palearctic* for giving us access to material awaiting publication in forthcoming volumes in this invaluable series.

Many ornithologists at home and abroad have contributed their expertise to enable us to perfect this Field Guide. We thank them all and only regret that they are too numerous to mention individually.

R.T.P.
G.R.M.
P.A.D.H.

The Geographical Area Embraced by the Field Guide

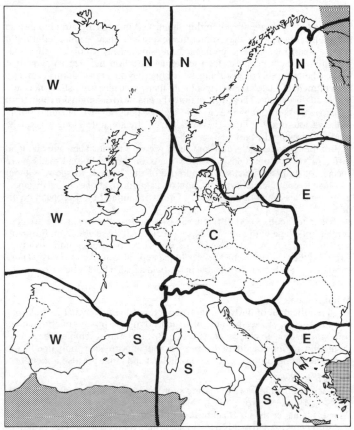

The birds described are those resident or occurring within the unshaded portion of the map, that is to say in the British Isles and Eire, Iceland and continental Europe, eastwards to the 30° line of longitude. The Islands of the Mediterranean basin are included, but Turkey and North Africa are excluded. Species are stated in the text as occurring in N., S., E., W. and C. (central) Europe (but some regions overlap - see map). The regions concerned are:

NORTH Iceland, Faeroes, Norway, Sweden, Finland.

SOUTH Portugal, Spain, Mediterranean France, Italy, Yugoslavia, Albania, Greece, Bulgaria.

EAST Finland, Baltic States, Romania, Bulgaria, Greece.

WEST Iceland, Faeroes, Britain, Ireland, France, Spain, Portugal.

CENTRAL Belguim, Holland, Denmark, West and East Germany, Poland, Czechoslovakia, Hungary, Austria, Switzerland.

How to Identify Birds

Many people who are already mildly interested in birds are afraid to pursue the subject because, as they sometimes express it, they 'cannot tell a robin from a sparrow'. Others, perhaps, have shied away from an unfamiliar terminology. Such people do themselves needless injustice. The enjoyment of birds, whether casual or absorbing, which man has developed during centuries of sentimental attatchment, depends neither upon intensive study nor academic qualifications. Those who claim to be unable to distinguish a robin from a sparrow certainly recognise an eagle, a gull, a duck, an owl, and many others of the various bird families. They are, in fact, already quite a long way on the road to 'knowing the birds'.

But the terms 'eagle', 'gull' or 'duck' are very broad. There are about 50 different species of eagles in various parts of the world, and many more species of gulls and ducks. The purpose of this book is to show, without recourse to complicated symbols, how to distinguish, at reasonable distance, all the species inhabiting or visiting Great Britain and the European continent.

There are about 8,600 different kinds of birds in the world. We are concerned in Europe with only 526 basic species. All these are given full treatment in this book. An additional 171 species have occured in Europe only as vagrants: these are described briefly in the appendix of 'Accidentals'. Those subspecies which are recognisable in the field are also briefly described in the main text.

What to Look For
The identification of birds is largely a matter of knowing what to look for - the 'field marks'. Exact diagnosis then depends upon a process of elimination, by comparison with other species which the birds may resemble. The arrows on the illustrations facilitate this process. But appearance is only one factor. Call-notes, song, attitudes, behaviour, habitat and range are also important.

What is its Size?
First acquire the habit of comparing strange birds with some familiar 'yardstick' - a House Sparrow, a Blackbird, a Pigeon, etc., so that you can say to yourself 'smaller than a Blackbird, a little larger than a sparrow', etc. The measurements quoted in this book indicate the average length of the bird from bill-tip to tail-tip and are given in both inches and centimetres.

What is its shape?
Is it plump, like a Robin (left); or slender, like a Wagtail (right)?

What shape are its wings? Are they sharply pointed, like a Swallow's (left); or short and rounded, like a Warbler's (right)?

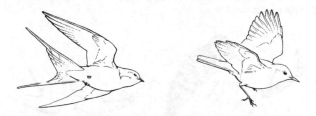

What shape is its bill? Is it small and fine, like a Warbler's (1); stout and short, like a seed-cracking Sparrow's (2); dagger-shaped, like a tern's (3); or hook-tipped, like a Kestrel's (4)?

Is its tail deeply forked, like a Swallow's (a); short and square-ended, like a Starling's (b);deeply notched, like a Linnet's (c); rounded, like a Cuckoo's (d); or wedge-shaped, like a Raven's (e)?

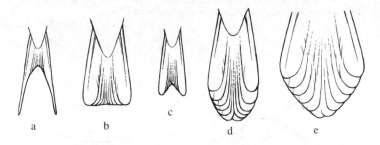

How does it Behave?
Some birds have very characteristic habits. Does it constantly wag its tail, like a Wagtail; quiver its tail, like a Redstart; cock its tail vertically, like a Wren; or sit bolt upright, with its tail downwards, like a Spotted Flycatcher?

Does it climb trees? If so, does it climb upwards in spirals, like a Tree-creeper (1); in short jerks, braced on its stiff tail, like a woodpecker (2); or does it climb, without using its tail as a prop, as readily downwards as upwards, like a Nuthatch (3)?

If it feeds on the ground, does it walk, like a Jackdaw; hop, like a House Sparrow; run spasmodically, like a wagtail; or shuffle along, close to the ground, like a Dunnock?

If it swims, does it sit high in the water, like a Moorhen (a); or low, with its back almost awash, like a diver (b)? Does it dive, like a Coot (c); or merely 'up-end', like a Mallard (d)?

Does it take off from the water gradually, by splashing along the surface, like a Moorhen; or spring clear in one jump, like a Teal?

Does it hover over the water and dive headlong, like a tern, or a Kingfisher; or plunge after fish feet-first, like an Osprey; or walk deliberately beneath the water, like a Dipper?

Does it wade? If so, does it stand motionless in the shallows for long periods, like a heron; or run quickly along the margins, like a sandpiper; or chase the receding waves, like a Sanderling?

How does it fly?
Is its flight deeply undulating, like a woodpecker's (1); or straight and fast, like a Starling's (2)?

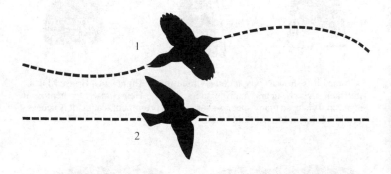

Does it beat its wings slowly, like a heron; or rapidly, like a Mallard; or with alternate periods of wing-beats and 'shooting', like a Fieldfare, or does it soar on motionless wings, like a Buzzard?

What are its Field Marks?
A few birds can be instantly identified by colour alone. There is no mistaking the brilliant yellow and black of a male Golden Oriole, for example. But we need also to look for certain field marks to distinguish most species. These take various forms. They are indicated by pointers on the illustrations in the Field Guide, and correspond to the italicized portions of the accompanying descriptive texts. Obscure field marks are included only when the problem of identification demands completeness.

Many birds are more or less spotted or streaked below. Are these marks over nearly all the under-parts, as in the Song Thrush (a); only on the upper breast, as in the Skylark (b); or only on the flanks, as in the Redpoll (c)?

Does the tail have a distinctive pattern? Has it a white tip, as in the Hawfinch (1); white outer feathers, as in the Chaffinch (2); or white side patches, as in the Whinchat (3)?

1
2
3

Some birds show a conspicuous white rump in flight - Jay, House Martin, Bullfinch, the wheatears, many waders, and the Hen Harrier, to mention a selection. Where so many species share such a prominent feature, it is necessary to look for additional field marks.

Northern Wheatear   House Martin

Wing-bars are very important in such families as the warblers; some are conspicuous, some obscure, some single, some double, some long, some short.

Eye-stripes are equally important in many small passerines (perching birds). Does the bird have a stripe above, through, or below the eye - or a combination of two, or three, of these stripes? Some warblers have distinctively coloured eyes, or eye- rims, or 'moustachial' stripes. These details are useful only when the the bird permits close examination, of course.

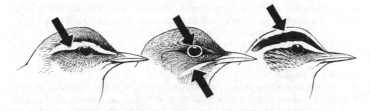

Wing patterns should always be noted, particularly with ducks and waders. Wings may be all-dark, or all-white, or half-and-half, or show conspicuous patches of white or colour. The exact location of such marks on wings, above or below, is important.

Unpatterned wing

Wing-stripe

Wing-patch

Call-notes and Song

Expert ornithologists often rely on their ears as much as on their eyes, to identify birds. It is difficult to portray bird voices in writing, because birds rarely make 'human' sounds, and our interpretations vary: one person hears a call-note as *teu*, another as *chew* or *sioo*. It must be remembered, also that birds, like humans, often develop dialectic variations in their 'speech'. In the Field Guide an attempt has been made to portray the chief call-notes and song phrases by simplified phonetics and similes; but the best way to learn voice identification is to go out with someone who knows the birds. Or get the fine set of recordings called *A Field Guide to the Birds Songs of Britain and Europe* by Sturâ Palmer and Jeffery Boswall, which are produced in collaboration with the authors of this book. The 15 LPs (or 16 tape cassettes) produced by the Swedish Broadcasting Corporation include the voices of nearly 600 bird species. They are available from record shops or from Sveriges Riksradio A. B., Stockholm 105 10, Sweden.

Where is it Found?

Birds, which beginners may have difficulty in identifying by appearance alone, can often be placed by knowledge of the typical habitats. The Long-tailed Duck is likely to be seen only on salt water, but the Pintail, a duck which also has a longish, pointed tail, frequents fresh water. Wood Warblers are birds of the upper leaf canopy of the beech and oak woods, and do not occur in the low, bushy scrub where one would seek the Grasshopper Warbler. Birds have quite strict limits of geography, habitat, and vegetation, except during migration, when they may occur in very unlikely places. The range maps and notes on habitat and distribution, which are included in the Field Guide, should always be consulted in cases of doubtful identification.

When it is Found

It is always interesting to learn the seasons during which different migratory species may occur in one's area. In a few years it becomes possible to forecast with some accuracy when the first Chiffchaff or Swift or Redwing, should appear. These dates may be pencilled in the margins of the Field Guide - for it is intended, not as an ornament to the bookshelf, but as a working companion.

Caution!

Where rarities are concerned, great caution should always be exercised. Detailed written notes and sketches should be made of any suspected rarity on the spot. If possible, an experienced member of the local ornithological society should be invited by telephone to coroborate the discovery. They will also give advice on how to submit rarity records to the *British Birds* Rarity Committee, which maintains a national discipline.

The Ornithological Societies

The principal British societies are listed below. They do not compete but, between them, cater for most ornithological interests.

The senior society is the **British Ornithologists' Union** (BOU) founded in 1859, for the advancement of the science of ornithology Its interests are not restricted to Britain, but are world-wide. The BOU issues an important quarterly journal, *The Ibis*, in which authoritative papers on such subjects as ecology, behaviour, taxonomy and reviews of the British and foreign ornithological literature. Scientific meetings are arranged and in all international ornithological affairs the BOU takes the leading part. Address: *c/o British Museum (Natural History), Sub-department of Ornithology, Tring, Herts, HP23 6AP.*

The **British Ornithologists's Club** (BOC) recruits its members from the BOU. The club meets periodically in London at a dinner, which is followed by short communications, films and lectures. The Club Bulletin contains articles relating to the subjects discussed, and descriptions of new species and races. Address: *c/o British Museum (Natural History), Sub-department of Ornithology, Tring, Herts, HP23 6AP.*

The **British Trust for Ornithology** (BTO) is the focal point for organized field work. Its aim is the encouragement of individual and group research Members take part in bird-ringing and nest- recording schemes and population studies. Many meetings are held with local societies. Bulletins, reports, the quarterly Bird Study and identification guides are published. Address: *The National Centre for Ornithology, The Nunnery, Thetford, Norfolk, IP24 2PU.*

The **Royal Society for the Protection of Birds** (RSPB) is concerned with the scientific application of conservation and strives to improve and enforce the Protection of Birds Acts. It educates the public and finances and manages a large number of bird reserves. The Society produces an Illustrated magazine Birds, and many other publications. It also has a junior section, the Young Ornithologists' Club. Address *The Lodge, Sandy, Beds, SG19 2DL.*

The **Wildfowl and Wetlands Trust** has a unique collection of ducks, geese and swans from all parts of the world. Its reserves offer ideal conditions for studying every species occurring in Britain. The Trust publishes an illustrated magazine and periodic bulletins and journals. Address: *Slimbridge, Glos, GL2 7BT.*

The **Irish Wildbird Conservancy** deals with all aspects of ornithology and bird conservation in Ireland. Address: *Ruttledge House, 8 Longford Place, Monkstown, Co. Dublin, Eire.*

European Check-list

Accidental species (A) are included. Use this list to record the species you have seen.

... Red-throated Diver
... Black-throated Diver
... Great Northern Diver
... White-billed Diver
... Pied-billed Grebe
... Little Grebe
... Great Crested Grebe
... Red-necked Grebe
... Slavonian Grebe
... Black-necked Grebe
... Black-browed Albatross
... Wandering Albatross (A)
... Southern Giant Petrel (A)
... Fulmar
... Soft-plumaged Petrel (A)
... Black-capped Petrel (A)
... Bulwer's Petrel (A)
... Cory's Shearwater
... Great Shearwater
... Sooty Shearwater
... Manx Shearwater
... Mediterranean Shearwater
... Little Shearwater
... Wilson's Petrel
... White-faced Storm Petrel (A)
... Storm Petrel
... Leach's Petrel
... Swinhoe's Petrel
... Madeiran Petrel
... Red-billed Tropicbird (A)
... Red-footed Booby (A)
... Masked Booby (A)
... Brown Booby (A)
... Northern Gannet
... Cormorant
... Double-crested Cormorant (A)
... Shag
... Pygmy Cormorant

... White Pelican
... Dalmatian Pelican
... Magnificent Frigatebird (A)
... Bittern
... American Bittern
... Least Bittern (A)
... Little Bittern
... Schrenck's Little Bittern (A)
... Night Heron
... Green-backed Heron (A)
... Squacco Heron
... Chinese Pond Heron (A)
... Cattle Egret
... Snowy Egret (A)
... Western Reef Heron (A)
... Little Egret
... Great White Egret
... Grey Heron
... Great Blue Heron (A)
... Purple Heron
... Black Stork
... White Stork
... Glossy Ibis
... Bald Ibis (A)
... Spoonbill
... African Spoonbill (A)
... Greater Flamingo
... Lesser Flamingo (A)
... Fulvous Whistling Duck (A)
... Mute Swan
... Bewick's Swan
... Whooper Swan
... Bean Goose
... Pink-footed Goose
... White-fronted Goose
... Lesser White-fronted Goose
... Greylag Goose
... Bar-headed Goose

... Snow Goose
... Canada Goose
... Barnacle Goose
... Brent Goose
... Red-breasted Goose
... Egyptian Goose
... Ruddy Shelduck
... Shelduck
... Mandarin
... Wigeon
... American Wigeon
... Falcated Duck (A)
... Gadwall
... Baikal Teal
... Teal
... Mallard
... Black Duck
... Pintail
... Garganey
... Blue-winged Teal
... Shoveler
... Marbled Duck
... Red-crested Pochard
... Pochard
... Canvasback (A)
... Ring-necked Duck
... Ferruginous Duck
... Tufted Duck
... Scaup
... Lesser Scaup (A)
... Eider
... King Eider
... Spectacled Eider (A)
... Steller's Eider
... Harlequin
... Long-tailed Duck
... Common Scoter
... Surf Scoter
... Velvet Scoter
... Bufflehead (A)
... Barrow's Goldeneye
... Goldeneye
... Hooded Merganser (A)
... Smew
... Red-breasted Merganser

... Goosander
... Ruddy Duck
... White-headed Duck
... Honey Buzzard
... Black-shouldered Kite
... Black Kite
... Red Kite
... Pallas's Fish Eagle (A)
... White-tailed Eagle
... Lammergeier
... Egyptian Vulture
... Griffon Vulture
... Lappet-faced Vulture (A)
... Black Vulture
... Short-toed Eagle
... Marsh Harrier
... Hen Harrier
... Pallid Harrier
... Montagu's Harrier
... Dark Chanting Goshawk (A)
... Goshawk
... Sparrowhawk
... Levant Sparrowhawk
... Swainson's Hawk (A)
... Buzzard
... Long-legged Buzzard
... Rough-legged Buzzard
... Lesser Spotted Eagle
... Spotted Eagle
... Tawny Eagle (A)
... Steppe Eagle
... Imperial Eagle
... Golden Eagle
... Booted Eagle
... Bonelli's Eagle
... Osprey
... Lesser Kestrel
... Kestrel
... American Kestrel (A)
... Red-footed Falcon
... Merlin
... Hobby
... Eleonora's Falcon
... Sooty Falcon (A)
... Lanner

... Saker
... Gyrfalcon
... Peregrine
... Barbary Falcon (A)
... Hazel Grouse
... Red/Willow Grouse
... Ptarmigan
... Black Grouse
... Capercaillie
... Chukar
... Rock Partridge
... Red-legged Partridge
... Barbary Partridge
... Black Francolin
... Grey Partridge
... Quail
... Pheasant
... Golden Pheasant
... Lady Amherst's Pheasant
... Andalusian Hemipode
... Water Rail
... Spotted Crake
... Sora (A)
... Little Crake
... Ballion's Crake
... Corncrake
... Moorhen
... Allen's Gallinule (A)
... American Purple Gallinule (A)
... Purple Gallinule
... Coot
... American Coot (A)
... Crested Coot
... Crane
... Sandhill Crane (A)
... Demoiselle Crane
... Little Bustard
... Houbara Bustard
... Great Bustard
... Oystercatcher
... Black-winged Stilt
... Avocet
... Stone Curlew
... Cream-coloured Courser
... Collared Pratincole

... Oriental Pratincole (A)
... Black-winged Pratincole
... Little Ringed Plover
... Ringed Plover
... Semipalmated Plover (A)
... Killdeer
... Kentish Plover
... Lesser Sand Plover (A)
... Greater Sand Plover
... Caspian Plover (A)
... Dotterel
... Pacific Golden Plover
... American Golden Plover
... Golden Plover
... Grey Plover
... Spur-winged Plover
... Sociable Plover
... White-tailed Plover
... Lapwing
... Great Knot (A)
... Knot
... Sanderling
... Semipalmated Sandpiper
... Western Sandpiper (A)
... Red-necked Stint (A)
... Little Stint
... Temminck's Stint
... Long-toed Stint (A)
... Least Sandpiper
... White-rumped Sandpiper
... Baird's Sandpiper
... Pectoral Sandpiper
... Sharp-tailed Sandpiper
... Curlew Sandpiper
... Purple Sandpiper
... Dunlin
... Broad-billed Sandpiper
... Stilt Sandpiper
... Buff-breasted Sandpiper
... Ruff
... Jack Snipe
... Snipe
... Great Snipe
... Short-billed Dowitcher (A)
... Long-billed Dowitcher

... Asiatic Dowitcher (A)
... Woodcock
... Black-tailed Godwit
... Hudsonian Godwit (A)
... Bar-tailed Godwit
... Little Whimbrel (A)
... Eskimo Curlew (A)
... Whimbrel
... Slender-billed Curlew
... Curlew
... Upland Sandpiper
... Spotted Redshank
... Redshank
... Marsh Sandpiper
... Greenshank
... Greater Yellowlegs
... Lesser Yellowlegs
... Solitary Sandpiper
... Green Sandpiper
... Wood Sandpiper
... Terek Sandpiper
... Common Sandpiper
... Spotted Sandpiper
... Grey-tailed Tattler (A)
... Willet (A)
... Turnstone
... Wilson's Phalarope
... Red-necked Phalarope
... Grey Phalarope
... Pomarine Skua
... Arctic Skua
... Long-tailed Skua
... Great Skua
... White-eyed Gull (A)
... Great Black-headed Gull
... Mediterranean Gull
... Laughing Gull
... Franklin's Gull
... Little Gull
... Sabine's Gull
... Bonaparte's Gull
... Black-headed Gull
... Grey-headed Gull (A)
... Slender-billed Gull
... Audouin's Gull

... Ring-billed Gull
... Common Gull
... Lesser Black-backed Gull
... Herring Gull
... Iceland Gull
... Glaucous Gull
... Great Black-backed Gull
... Ross's Gull
... Kittiwake
... Ivory Gull
... Gull-billed Tern
... Caspian Tern
... Royal Tern (A)
... Elegant Tern (A)
... Lesser Crested Tern
... Sandwich Tern
... Roseate Tern
... Common Tern
... Arctic Tern
... Aleutian Tern (A)
... Forster's Tern
... White-cheeked Tern (A)
... Bridled Tern (A)
... Sooty Tern
... Little Tern
... Least Tern (A)
... Whiskered Tern
... Black Tern
... White-winged Black Tern
... Brown Noddy (A)
... Guillemot
... Brünnich's Guillemot
... Razorbill
... Black Guillemot
... Little Auk
... Ancient Murrelet (A)
... Crested Auklet (A)
... Parakeet Auklet (A)
... Puffin
... Spotted Sandgrouse (A)
... Black-bellied Sandgrouse
... Pin-tailed Sandgrouse
... Pallas's Sandgrouse
... Rock Dove and Feral Pigeon
... Stock Dove

... Woodpigeon
... Collared Dove
... Turtle Dove
... Rufous Turtle Dove
... Laughing Dove
... Mourning Dove (A)
... Rose-ringed Parakeet
... Great Spotted Cuckoo
... Cuckoo
... Black-billed Cuckoo
... Yellow-billed Cuckoo
... Barn Owl
... Scops Owl
... Eagle Owl
... Snowy Owl
... Hawk Owl
... Pygmy Owl
... Little Owl
... Tawny Owl
... Ural Owl
... Great Grey Owl
... Long-eared Owl
... Short-eared Owl
... African Marsh Owl (A)
... Tengmalm's Owl
... Nightjar
... Red-necked Nightjar
... Egyptian Nightjar
... Common Nighthawk (A)
... Needle-tailed Swift (A)
... Chimney Swift (A)
... Swift
... Pallid Swift
... Pacific Swift (A)
... Alpine Swift
... White-rumped Swift
... Little Swift
... Smyrna Kingfisher (A)
... Kingfisher
... Pied Kingfisher (A)
... Belted Kingfisher (A)
... Blue-cheeked Bee-eater
... Bee-eater
... Roller
... Hoopoe

... Wryneck
... Northern Flicker (A)
... Grey-headed Woodpecker
... Green Woodpecker
... Black Woodpecker
... Yellow-bellied Sapsucker (A)
... Great Spotted Woodpecker
... Syrian Woodpecker
... Middle Spotted Woodpecker
... White-backed Woodpecker
... Lesser Spotted Woodpecker
... Three-toed Woodpecker
... Eastern Phoebe (A)
... Acadian Flycatcher (A)
... Bar-tailed Desert Lark (A)
... Hoopoe Lark (A)
... Dupont's Lark
... Calandra Lark
... Bimaculated Lark (A)
... White-winged Lark
... Black Lark
... Short-toed Lark
... Lesser Short-toed Lark
... Crested Lark
... Thekla Lark
... Woodlark
... Skylark
... Shore Lark
... Temminck's Horned Lark (A)
... Sand Martin
... Tree Swallow (A)
... Crag Martin
... Swallow
... Red-rumped Swallow
... Cliff Swallow (A)
... House Martin
... Richard's Pipit
... Blyth's Pipit (A)
... Tawny Pipit
... Olive-backed Pipit
... Tree Pipit
... Pechora Pipit
... Meadow Pipit
... Red-throated Pipit
... Rock Pipit

... Water Pipit
... Buff-bellied Pipit (A)
... Yellow/Blue-headed Wagtail
... Citrine Wagtail
... Grey Wagtail
... Pied/White Wagtail
... Waxwing
... Cedar Waxwing (A)
... Dipper
... Wren
... Northern Mockingbird (A)
... Brown Thrasher (A)
... Grey Catbird (A)
... Dunnock
... Siberian Accentor (A)
... Black-throated Accentor (A)
... Alpine Accentor
... Rufous Bush Robin
... Robin
... Thrush Nightingale
... Nightingale
... Siberian Rubythroat (A)
... Bluethroat
... Siberian Blue Robin (A)
... Red-flanked Bluetail
... White-throated Robin (A)
... Black Redstart
... Daurian Redstart (A)
... Redstart
... Moussier's Redstart (A)
... Güldenstädt's Redstart (A)
... Whinchat
... Stonechat
... Isabelline Wheatear
... Northern Wheatear
... Pied Wheatear
... Black-eared Wheatear
... Desert Wheatear
... White-crowned Black
        Wheatear (A)
... Black Wheatear
... Rock Thrush
... Blue Rock Thrush
... White's Thrush
... Siberian Thrush

... Varied Thrush (A)
... Wood Thrush (A)
... Hermit Thrush (A)
... Swainson's Thrush
... Grey-cheeked Thrush
... Veery (A)
... Tickell's Thrush (A)
... Ring Ouzel
... Blackbird
... Pale Thrush (A)
... Eye-browed Thrush
... Dusky/Naumann's Thrush
... Black-/Red-throated Thrush
... Fieldfare
... Song Thrush
... Redwing
... Mistle Thrush
... American Robin
... Cetti's Warbler
... Fan-tailed Warbler
... Pallas's Grasshopper Warbler
... Lanceolated Warbler
... Grasshopper Warbler
... River Warbler
... Savi's Warbler
... Gray's Grasshopper
        Warbler (A)
... Moustached Warbler
... Aquatic Warbler
... Sedge Warbler
... Paddyfield Warbler
... Blyth's Reed Warbler
... Marsh Warbler
... Reed Warbler
... Great Reed Warbler
... Thick-billed Warbler (A)
... Olivaceous Warbler
... Booted Warbler
... Olive-tree Warbler
... Icterine Warbler
... Melodious Warbler
... Marmora's Warbler
... Dartford Warbler
... Tristram's Warbler (A)
... Spectacled Warbler

... Subalpine Warbler
... Ménétries's Warbler (A)
... Sardinian Warbler
... Rüppell's Warbler
... Desert Warbler
... Orphean Warbler
... Barred Warbler
... Lesser Whitethroat
... Whitethroat
... Garden Warbler
... Blackcap
... Eastern Crowned Warbler (A)
... Green Warbler (A)
... Greenish Warbler
... Arctic Warbler
... Pallas's Warbler
... Yellow-browed Warbler
... Radde's Warbler
... Dusky Warbler
... Bonelli's Warbler
... Wood Warbler
... Chiffchaff
... Willow Warbler
... Ruby-crowned Kinglet (A)
... Goldcrest
... Firecrest
... Brown Flycatcher (A)
... Spotted Flycatcher
... Red-breasted Flycatcher
... Mugimaki Flycatcher (A)
... Semi-collared Flycatcher
... Collared Flycatcher
... Pied Flycatcher
... Bearded Tit
... Long-tailed Tit
... Marsh Tit
... Sombre Tit
... Willow Tit
... Siberian Tit
... Crested Tit
... Coal Tit
... Blue Tit
... Azure Tit
... Great Tit
... Krüper's Nuthatch

... Corsican Nuthatch
... Red-breasted Nuthatch (A)
... Nuthatch
... Rock Nuthatch
... Wallcreeper
... Treecreeper
... Short-toed Treecreeper
... Penduline Tit
... Golden Oriole
... Brown Shrike (A)
... Isabelline Shrike
... Red-backed Shrike
... Rufous-backed Shrike (A)
... Lesser Grey Shrike
... Great Grey Shrike
... Woodchat Shrike
... Masked Shrike
... Jay
... Siberian Jay
... Azure-winged Magpie
... Magpie
... Nutcracker
... Alpine Chough
... Chough
... Jackdaw
... Daurian Jackdaw (A)
... Rook
... Carrion/Hooded Crow
... Raven
... Daurian Starling (A)
... Starling
... Spotless Starling
... Rose-coloured Starling
... House Sparrow
... Spanish Sparrow
... Dead Sea Sparrow (A)
... Tree Sparrow
... Rock Sparrow
... Snowfinch
... Common Waxbill
... Avadavat
... Yellow-throated Vireo (A)
... Philadelphia Vireo (A)
... Red-eyed Vireo
... Chaffinch

... Brambling
... Red-fronted Serin (A)
... Serin
... Citril Finch
... Greenfinch
... Goldfinch
... Siskin
... Linnet
... Twite
... Redpoll
... Arctic Redpoll
... Two-barred Crossbill
... Crossbill
... Scottish Crossbill
... Parrot Crossbill
... Trumpeter Finch
... Scarlet Rosefinch
... Pallas's Rosefinch (A)
... Pine Grosbeak
... Long-tailed Rosefinch (A)
... Bullfinch
... Hawfinch
... Evening Grosbeak (A)
... Black-and-White Warbler (A)
... Golden-winged Warbler (A)
... Tennessee Warbler (A)
... Northern Parula
... Yellow Warbler (A)
... Chestnut-sided Warbler (A)
... Black-throated Blue
    Warbler (A)
... Black-throated Green
    Warbler (A)
... Blackburnian Warbler (A)
... Cape May Warbler (A)
... Magnolia Warbler (A)
... Yellow-rumped Warbler
... Blackpoll Warbler
... American Redstart (A)
... Ovenbird (A)
... Northern Waterthrush (A)
... Common Yellowthroat (A)
... Hooded Warbler (A)

... Wilson's Warbler (A)
... Canada Warbler (A)
... Summer Tanager (A)
... Scarlet Tanager (A)
... Rufous-sided Towhee (A)
... Lark Sparrow (A)
... Savannah Sparrow (A)
... Fox Sparrow (A)
... Song Sparrow (A)
... White-crowned Sparrow (A)
... White-throated Sparrow
... Dark-eyed Junco (A)
... Lapland Bunting
... Snow Bunting
... Black-faced Bunting (A)
... Pine Bunting
... Yellowhammer
... Cirl Bunting
... Rock Bunting
... Meadow Bunting (A)
... Cinereous Bunting
... Ortolan Bunting
... Cretzschmar's Bunting
... Yellow-browed Bunting (A)
... Rustic Bunting
... Little Bunting
... Chestnut Bunting (A)
... Yellow-breasted Bunting
... Reed Bunting
... Pallas's Reed Bunting (A)
... Red-headed Bunting (A)
... Black-headed Bunting
... Corn Bunting
... Dickcissel (A)
... Rose-breasted Grosbeak
... Blue Grosbeak (A)
... Indigo Bunting (A)
... Lazuli Bunting (A)
... Bobolink (A)
... Brown-headed Cowbird (A)
... Common Grackle (A)
... Yellow-headed Blackbird (A)
... Northern Oriole

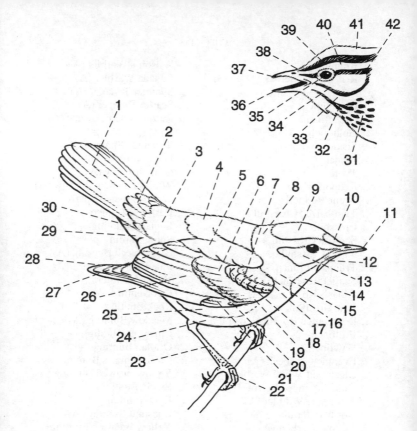

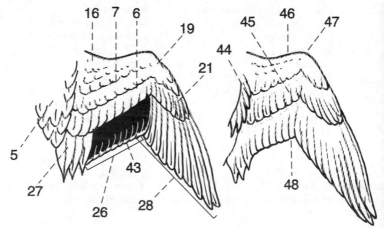

Topography of a Bird

Key showing terms used in this volume

1	Tail (outer tail feathers forming edges)	25	Flanks
2	Upper tail-coverts	26	Secondaries
3	Rump	27	Tertials
4	Back (containing mantle, behind nape)	28	Primaries
5	Scapulars	29	Vent
6	Greater wing-coverts	30	Under tail-coverts
7	Median wing-coverts	31	Gorget
8	Nape	32	Malar stripe
9	Crown	33	Sub-moustachial stripe
10	Forehead	34	Moustachial stripe
11	Bill	35	Eye ring (when incomplete: eye crescent)
12	Chin	36	Lower mandible
13	Ear-coverts (containing cheeks)	37	Upper mandible (top ridge forming culmen)
14	Throat (with chin, bib)	38	Lores (containing loral streak; with fore-cheeks, forming face)
15	Chest and below breast		
16	Lesser wing-coverts	39	Lateral crown stripe
17	Bend of wing (also kown as shoulder but is actually carpal joint)	40	Supercilium
		41	Central crown stripe
		42	Eyestripe
18	Upper wing-bar (on tips of median coverts)	43	Speculum (in ducks)
		44	Axillarie (in wing-pit)
19	Alula	45	Wing-lining (usually including most under wing-coverts)
20	Lower wing-bar (on tips of greater coverts)		
21	Primary coverts	46	Leading (fore) edge of wing
22	Feet (with toes and claws)	47	Carpal (wrist)
23	Leg (tarsus)	48	Trailing (rear) edge of wing
24	Belly		

DIVERS: Gaviidae

Large swimming, ground-nesting birds of taiga and tundra waters, spending most of year in coastal seas. Larger, thicker-necked and longer-bodied than grebes. Dive expertly for fish; able to submerge partly or wholly in alarm. Outline in flight – often surprisingly high over sea – hunch-backed, with slight downward sweep to extended neck, relatively small, narrow and pointed wings and large feet trailing behind rudimentary tails. Marked seasonal change in head, neck and upper-part patterns; sexes similar; immature close to winter adults. Voices haunting.

RED-THROATED DIVER *Gavia stellata*   Plate 1
Du – Roodkeelduiker   Fr – Plongeon catmarin
Ge – Sterntaucher   Sw – Smålom
N. Am. – Red-throated Loon

Identification: 21-23" (53-58cm). The smallest, slightest diver, with smaller head than Black-throated and *quickest, deepest wing-beats of family*. Even at distance, *slender upturned bill on usually uptilted head* of swimming bird distinctive. Breeding adult has smoky-grey head and *red throat-patch* (can look black in shade or at distance) and dull, *unpatterned grey-brown upper-parts*. Winter adult very different, *white face* and fore-neck contrasting with white-speckled grey crown, narrow hind-neck and upper-parts. Darker immature often suggests Black-throated but shows characteristic bill and head angle. Flight form lightest of family, with thinnest head and neck. Sociable, migrating in parties and wintering in assemblies off coasts.

Confusion species: Black-throated little larger, but bill straight and held level, shows bold white rear flank patch above water line in winter; Great Northern and White-billed much larger but beware latter's similar bill and head carriage.

Voice: Flight-call repeated *kwuck*, quacking or cackling in tone. Breeding birds wail and cackle like geese, growling in display.

Habitat: Nests on islands or margins of small lochs and coastal lagoons, going out to feed at sea where it spends rest of year. Map 1.

BLACK-THROATED DIVER *Gavia arctica*   Plate 1
Du – Parelduiker   Fr – Plongeon arctique
Ge – Prachttaucher   Sw – Storlom

Identification: 23-27" (58-68cm). Size between Red-throated and Great Northern, with more swollen head and slower, shallower wingbeats than former. Bill fairly slender, usually held level as is head; may seem to droop at tip. Breeding adult has *blackish face,* grey rear head and hind-neck; black throat patch and *white chequered scapular panels* obvious on black upper-parts. Winter adult shows strong contrast between black upper-parts and white under-parts, with bluish bill, black crown, often greyer nape and white lower head suggesting Guillemot. Bulging rear flanks often present striking *white waterline patch*. Immature faintly scaled above. Flight form less attenuated than Red-throated with swollen head obvious when overhead. Migrates singly or in small groups; solitary in winter.

Confusion species: Immature Red-throated can look as dark but lacks flank

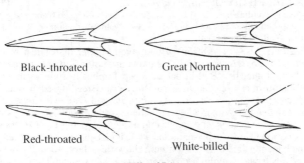

Black-throated   Great Northern

Red-throated   White-billed

Bills of Divers

patch and usually shows uptilted bill and head; small adult Great Northern excluded by differences in bill size and head pattern.

Voice: Flight call a barking *kwow*, deeper than Red-throated. Breeding birds utter shrill rising wail.

Habitat: Nests on islands or margins of inland waters, larger than those used by Red-throated. In winter, mainly on coastal sea. Map 2.

GREAT NORTHERN DIVER *Gavia immer*   **Plate 1**

Du – IJsduiker   Fr – Plongeon imbrin
Ge – Eistaucher   Sw – Islom
N. Am. – Common Loon

Identification: 27-32" (68-81cm). Size of goose but body less deep, wings proportionately smaller and feet larger, trailing obviously in flight. Much bulkier than preceding species, with *deep dagger-like bill held level before steep forehead*. Breeding adult has black bill, head and fore-neck, with broken, white-chequered collar and *evenly white-chequered and spotted upper-parts and flanks*; white chest visible at long range. Winter adult recalls Black-throated but upperparts less black, while uneven edge to crown and hind neck, partial neck collar and dull rear flanks give less contrasting pattern. Bill is sometimes pale but at close range *always shows dark ridge to culmen*. Immature as winter adult but with paler scales on scapulars. Flight action noticeably slow, with shallow but powerful wing-beats; crash-lands on breast with great splash; thrashes on take-off. Scarce, migrating singly or in small groups; forms only loose assemblies in winter.

Confusion species: Beware large Black-throateds which can present similar outline and winter pattern; White-billed even bulkier with usually different outline but similar pattern, at close range shows wholly pale bill. Cormorant and Shag in pale, immature dress present similar pattern, but forms differ, particularly in hooked bills.

Voice: Flight call short barking *kwuk*. Breeding birds wail, laugh and trill in remarkably loud and sustained symphony.

Habitat: Nests on islands and promontories of taiga and tundra lakes. Winters mainly on coastal seas but not unusual inland. Map 3.

WHITE-BILLED DIVER *Gavia adamsii*   **Plate 1**
Du – Geelsnavelduiker   Fr – Plongeon à bec blanc
Ge – Gelbschnäbliger Eistaucher   Sw – Vitnäbbad islom
N. Am. – Yellow-billed Loon

Identification: 33-34" (84-86cm). Huge, even bulkier than Great Northern with *uptilted, deep, scissor-like bill* (see drawing); uptilt further emphasized by similar head angle, like Red-throated. Steep forehead produces more pronounced bump over eye than in Great Northern. Breeding adult like Great Northern except for *yellowish- or ivory-white bill* and *even more boldly white-chequered scapulars*. Winter adult like Great Northern but bill always paler, *lacking dark ridge to culmen*; dark eye emphasized by pale ring, and less sharp boundary between dusky upper-parts and white under-parts. Immature lacks full bill shape but compared to Great Northern shows less dark crown, fainter neck marks and much paler scalloping on upper-parts. Flight form and action heaviest of family, with huge feet bunched behind body; in good light, pale bill and relatively less dark upper-parts visible on flying bird. Indistinguishable from Great Northern when bill and head carriage or colour obscured.
Voice: Similar to Great Northern.
Habitat: Vagrants from N. America and western Arctic most frequent among northern isles and along rocky coasts. May be more pelagic than other divers. Reaches coasts of Norway, Sweden, Finland in winter from eastern Arctic. Vagrant to W. (including Britain), C. and S. Europe.

GREBES: Podicipedidae

Small to quite large raft-nesting birds of still or slow-moving lowland waters, wintering on lakes, reservoirs and estuaries or coastal seas. Larger species share long pointed bills with divers but all present deep-flanked, tailless form, even puffed-up in smaller species. Swim well and dive with gusto, kicking with lobed toes; escape behaviour like divers. Outline in flight (usually just above water surface) shows straight head and neck ahead of cylindrical body and trailing feet; wings whirr or flap, appearing insubstantial due to disruptive pattern on most species. Marked seasonal change in head and neck patterns but sexes similar; juveniles close to winter adults but show distinctive facial patterns. Voices include long trills, barks, croons and wails.

PIED-BILLED GREBE *Podilymbus podiceps*   **Plate 2**
Du – Dikbekuut   Fr – Grèbe à bec cerclé
Ge – Bindentaucher   Sw – Tjocknäbbad dopping

Identification: 12" (31cm). Small, stocky grebe, with *heavy, chicken-like bill*, large head and *very blunt stern*. Plumage dusky-brown, with ivory bill and bright white stern. Breeding adult shows *black vertical band on bill*, black bib under greyish cheeks; winter adult loses black marks but shows white chin and throat, contrasting with reddish neck. Flight outline less compact than Little Grebe, action similar.
Voice: Usually silent in winter but vagrants in spring have uttered loud, slurred, gulping song.

Habitat and Range: Prefers fresh water at all seasons, particularly reservoirs and lakes. Vagrant from N. America to Britain and Ireland.

LITTLE GREBE *Tachybaptus ruficollis* **Plate 2**
Du – Dodaars Fr – Grèbe castagneux
Ge – Zwergtaucher Sw – Smådopping
Identification: 10" (26cm). Smallest, most skulking grebe, with proportionately quite stout bill, round head, short neck and most puffed-up, blunt-ended body. Breeding adult dark brown above, paler rufous below, with distinctive *pale yellowish-green bill-spot* and *chestnut cheeks and throat*; a trace of white on secondaries in flight. In winter, much paler with buff neck and whitish throat and end to body. Juvenile boldly streaked white across face. Flies with rapid whirring action low over water. Rare Pied-billed Grebe larger, with much deeper bill.
Voice: Loud, high trill, often prolonged, sometimes rising and falling; also short *whit, whit.*
Habitat: Widespsread in lowlands, breeding on ponds, lakes, bays of reservoirs, etc. Congregates in winter on large inland and sheltered coastal waters. Map 4.

GREAT CRESTED GREBE *Podiceps cristatus* **Plate 2**
Du – Fuut Fr – Grèbe huppé
Ge – Haubentaucher Sw – Skäggdopping
Identification: 19" (48cm). Largest, longest-billed and -necked but still 'tailless' grebe with warm pink bill, grey-brown upper-parts and satin-white under-parts, gleaming on chest but shaded on flanks. Breeding adult easily distinguished by *blackish eartufts and prominent chestnut and black frills on face.* In winter, loses frills and becomes white-faced, with fore-supercilium and high cheeks contrasting with narrow black crown. In flight, shows conspicuous white patches on shoulders and on secondaries. Juvenile striped black and white on untufted head and neck. Flight outline noticeably attenuated, with head and neck stretched out and low-hung; action whirring. Aquatic courtshup display elaborate. See also Red-necked Grebe.
Voice: Barking *kar-arr;* shrill *er-wick;* other trumpeting, ticking, moaning and chirring notes.
Habitat: Needs larger waters than other grebes; nests where aquatic vegetation allows anchorage, on lakes, reservoirs, gravel-pits, etc. Many move to coasts in winter. Map 5.

RED-NECKED GREBE *Podiceps grisegena* **Plate 2**
Du – Roodhalsfuut Fr – Grèbe jougris
Ge – Rothalstaucher Sw – Gråhakedopping
Identification: 17" (43cm). Quite large but thickset grebe, with *dark-tipped, yellow-based bill* on bulbous head. Breeding adult has contrasting *pale grey cheeks,* slightly tufted black crown, *rich chestnut neck and breast,* dark grey-brown back and dusky flanks. In winter, retains faint but similar pattern but cheeks whiter, neck dusky, breast white and upper flanks paler. Juvenile shows black-striped face and ruddy neck. Flight pattern as Great Crested but white shoulder patch restricted to leading edge; flight action similar but outline less attenuated, thicker-necked.

Confusion species: Can be confused with Great Crested in winter but Red-necked usually appears smaller, more compact and dingier, with yellow (not pink) bill and dark crown enveloping eye (without white supercilium).

Voice: Abrupt *cherk*; also growls, barks, crows and wails.

Habitat: Prefers smaller, shallow waters; nest hidden in dense aquatic vegetation of ponds, lakes, etc. Winters mainly on coasts, rarely inland. Map 6.

SLAVONIAN GREBE *Podiceps auritus*   Plate 2

Du – Kuifduiker	Fr – Grèbe esclavon
Ge – Ohrentaucher	Sw – Svarthakedopping
N. Am. – Horned Grebe	

Identification: 13" (33cm). Medium-sized grebe, with *straight, quite stubby bill*, quite large head with *high rear peak* and solid but not puffed-up body. Breeding adult has *glossy black head*, with *orange stripes rising from eye* to form short horns, *dark chestnut neck and flanks*, dark brown back and silky white under-body. Small white shoulder mark and white secondaries conspicuous in flight. In winter and juvenile plumage, looks very dark above, white below; distinguished by pale tip to dark bill, rather flat *black crown sharply demarcated at eye level*, pure white cheeks almost meeting at rear, high on nape, and clean throat. Flight outline compact but action freer than Little Grebe. See also Black-necked Grebe.

Voice: Chief note a long, squealing trill, falling at end.

Habitat: As Red-necked Grebe but also nests on small hill waters. Winters on sheltered coastal waters, rarely inland. Map 7.

BLACK-NECKED GREBE *Podiceps nigricollis*   Plate 2

Du – Geoorde fuut	Fr – Grèbe à cou noir
Ge – Schwarzhalstaucher	Sw – Svarthalsad dopping
N. Am. – Eared Grebe	

Identification: 12" (30cm). Second smallest grebe, with rounded, puffed-up shape like Little Grebe but with fine, *slightly uptilted bill, steep forehead* and more sinuous neck. Breeding adult black to dark brown above, with *glossy black head and neck* relieved by *brilliant golden, drooping spray of fine plumes* behind eye, chestnut flanks and silky-white under-body. In winter and juvenile plumage, resembles Slavonian Grebe but distinguished by wholly dusky, differently shaped bill, high level or rounded crown, with *dark feathers enveloping eye*, dirty cheeks extending up behind eye, dusky throat and upper neck and, by contrast, white chest. Flight pattern lacks pale shoulder mark of Slavonian Grebe but action similar. Beware also female or young Smew and Ruddy Duck which at distance show similar plumage pattern.

Voice: Quiet *poo-eep*, also harsh, rasping or crooning notes.

Habitat: Prefers small, densely vegetated, food-rich waters. Nests colonially in shallows but apt to shift localities opportunistically in dry seasons. Winters on sheltered coasts and shallow inland waters. Map 8.

ALBATROSSES: Diomedeidae

BLACK-BROWED ALBATROSS *Diomedea melanophris*   **Plate 5**
Du – Wenlbrauwalbatros   Fr – Albatros à sourcils noire
Ge – Mollymauk   Sw – Svartbrynad albatross
Identification: 36–38" (91-96cm). Albatrosses easily recognised by *huge wing-span* 7ft or 2 m and more (50% greater than Great Black-backed Gull), gliding flight above waves and Fulmar-like form, except for *long, drooping bill*. Black-browed recalls Black-backed gull but differs in *pinkish-yellow bill*, uniform sooty wings and mantle, *dark greyish tail* and *white under-wings boldly margined black*, broadly on leading edge but narrowly on trailing. Close-to, shows black 'brow' through and just behind eye. Immature has dusky bill (retaining dark tip until fully adult), greyish head, dusky neck, and less clearly patterned under-wing, with only narrow white centre. Flight majestic, gliding, side-slipping and banking at will; long, narrow wings usually held straight out but bowed down from carpal joints and rarely beaten; in higher wind speeds, wings angled closer to body. Follows ships. Silent at sea.
Confusion species: Wandering Albatross even larger, with different plumages at all ages (see Accidentals). Grey-headed Albatross *D. chrysostoma* and Yellow-nosed Albatross *D. chlororhynchos* both smaller and grey-headed; former differs in black bill with red-yellow upper and lower ridges (held down at 45° or more) and broader white under-wing tract; latter has slenderer neck and tail, proportionately long black bill with yellow upper ridge and almost wholly white under-wing with very narrow black margins. Separation of juveniles untrustworthy.
Habitat and Range: Pelagic, occasionally passing headlands or along coasts. Individuals have twice joined Northern Gannet populations, summering at their Faeroese and (currently) Shetland colonies, but normally rare vagrant from southern oceans, reaching as far north as Iceland.

LARGE PETRELS AND SHEARWATERS: Procellariidae

Medium-sized to large burrow- or ledge-nesting birds of northern and southern oceans, spending most of year well offshore but occasionally concentrating off coasts in adverse weather. Swim well, riding high with tails clear of water; dive expertly. Share with storm petrels tube-like nostrils. Outline in flight – just above to high over sea, with characteristic careening – noticeably cross-like when wings stiffly extended but more angled when manoeuvring, when legs and feet may drop to assist steering. Voices raucous and crooning. Identification at times impossible due to distance and poor light. Commonest two species, Fulmar and Manx Shearwater, are keys to learning larger and smaller relatives. Note that only Fulmar has adult gull-like plumage; all others rather resemble immature gull or auk in winter plumage.

FULMAR *Fulmarus glacialis*   **Plate 3**
Du – Noordse stormvogel   Fr – Pétrel fulmar
Ge – Eissturmvogel   Sw – Stormfågel
Identification: 18" (46cm). Most gull-like of tube-noses, with stubby bill, *bull*

head and neck, stiff narrow wings on barrel body and broad rump and tail. Distinguished from gulls by *thick, ridged yellow bill* with tubed nostrils, *lack of black wing tips* and bluish legs. Southern light phase has head, neck and underparts white; back, wings and tail grey; shows characteristic *pale basal patch on primaries*. Northern darker phases – so-called 'Blue' Fulmars – vary from almost uniform cream-buff to dusky-grey, with increasingly dark under-wing. Flight distinctive, gliding and banking, only occasionally flapping extended wings; usually close to waves; follows ships, flocking round trawlers. Swims buoyantly, pattering on take-off. On land shuffles on tarsi, rarely standing.
Voice: Hoarse cackling or grunting *ag-ag-ag-arr*.
Habitat: Pelagic but some remain near breeding stations. Nests colonially on cliffs and islands, locally inland on cliffs and grass slopes. Abundant in northern fishing grounds. Map 9.

CORY'S SHEARWATER Calonectris diomedea   Plate 3

Du – Cory's pijlstormvogel   Fr – Puffin cendré
Ge – Gelbschnabel Sturmtaucher   Sw – Gulnäbbad lira

Identification: 18" (46cm). Large shearwater, heavier built and broader- and looser-winged than Great. Further distinguished by thick yellow bill, *grey-brown hood* merging gradually into mottled neck sides and white throat, only occasional white 'horseshoe' rump-patch between grey-brown upper-parts and tail, and *pure white under-parts and wing-lining*. Flight recalls gull and Fulmar, typically 5-8 lazy flaps followed by long glide or bank on bowed wings with flexing tips. Swimming and gait as Fulmar.
Confusion species: Northern Gannet, Fulmar and Great Shearwater, which see.
Voice: Long wail and gull-like *ia-gowa-gow*.
Habitat: Pelagic, occasionally offshore. Nests in groups in rock crevices of islands. Mediterranean birds mainly resident but other populations wander N, as far as Faeroes. Map 10.

GREAT SHEARWATER *Puffinus gravis*   Plate 3

Du – Grote pijlstormvogel   Fr – Puffin majeur
Ge – Grosser Sturmtaucher   Sw – Större lira

Identification: 18" (46cm). Large shearwater, with shape much as Manx but 25% more bulk and much more powerful flight. Distinguished by rather narrow black bill, *dark blackish cap* contrasting with pure white throat (head looks narrow), almost complete *white collar*, dark brown upper-parts with white *'horseshoe' mark above tail*, and white under-parts and wing lining, with *smudges on larger coverts and down belly* and on vent. May show irregular white line on upper-wing during moult. Flight action recalls Manx Shearwater but wingbeats slower and heavier, while glides more prolonged and banking becomes majestic careening in high winds.
Confusion species: Northern Gannet, Cory's Shearwater and Black-capped Petrel, which see.
Voice: Feeding birds bark raucously like gulls.
Habitat and Range: Pelagic, occasionally offshore. Breeds on Tristan da Cunha, but in summer and autumn all leave for NE. Atlantic (Iceland to North Sea and Portugal) and less regularly N. Mediterranean.

SOOTY SHEARWATER *Puffinus griseus* Plate 3
Du – Grauwe pijlstormvogel   Fr – Puffin fuligineux
Ge – Dunkler Sturmtaucher   Sw – Grålira

Identification: 16" (40cm). Proportionately small-headed, medium-sized shearwater, *all-black at distance*, with oddly mechanical fast flight allowing direct progress. Distinguished from all other shearwaters in region except darkest morphs of Mediterranean Shearwater *P. y. mauretanicus* by uniform sooty-brown plumage, relieved only by *pale, in sunlight almost shining, panel along under-wing*. Flight usually low over sea, with fast beats of long stiff or flexed wings alternated with glides and banks. Swims well, often resting on sea. Silent at sea.

Confusion species: Separation of smaller Mediterranean Shearwater difficult at long range but with experience, confusion with large shearwater, 'Blue' Fulmar, immature Northern Gannet and dark phase skuas can be overcome.

Habitat and Range: Pelagic but more regularly offshore than large shearwaters; hundreds may pass headlands in some years. Breeds on southern oceanic islands, migrating N. to same northern waters as Great. Vagrant to Baltic.

MANX SHEARWATER *Puffinus puffinus* Plate 3
Du – Noorde pijlstormvogel   Fr – Puffin des Anglais
Ge – Schwarzschnabel Sturmtaucher   Sw – Mindre lira

Identification: 14" (35cm). Second smallest shearwater, commoner than any other except occasionally Sooty, with noticeably cross-like silhouette and gliding and banking flight. *Black upper-parts* contrast sharply with *white under-parts*; close-to, slender black bill, *dark upper cheeks*, neck smudge and dark rim to clean under-wing also show. Often seen in scattered flocks, moving into wind, with glides and banks sustained by *markedly irregular bursts of wingbeats*; veers from wave crest to trough and back again, rarely careening high. Does not follow ships. Swims well but less buoyantly than large shearwaters; flocks gather off breeding colonies at dusk, often swarming on sea. Shuffles on land, using wings to climb.

Confusion species: Atlantic race larger and darker-headed than Little Shearwater, which also has distinctive fluttering flight; Mediterranean races may suggest larger shearwaters, which see.

Voice: Breeding colonies produce loud chorus of wild crows and croons.

Habitat: Offshore waters, rarely in mid-ocean. Nests in dense colonies, burrowing in grass or among rocks. Map 11.

MEDITERRANEAN SHEARWATER *Puffinus yelkouan* Plate 3
Du - Vale pijlstormvogel   Fr – Puffin yelkouan
Sw – Medelhavslira

Identification: 15" (38cm) Closely related to Manx Shearwater, occurring in two poorly differentiated races. W. Mediterranean (so-called Balearic) *P. y. mauretanicus* slightly tubbier and longer-winged than Manx with at times noticeably slower flight; lacks black and white appearance, looking *dark brown above* and *blotched brown and white below*, with broad dark rim to under-wing, particularly on leading edge. E. Mediterranean (so-called Yelkouan) *P. y. yelkouan* smaller on average than Manx; palest birds quite contrastingly brown-black above and dusky-white below, but many more variable in appearance,

overlapping with paler Balearic. Both races lack sharp white surround to cheeks and clean under-wing shown by Manx. Behaviour and voice resemble Manx.
Confusion species: Separation of E. Mediterranean race from dull Manx requires close view of head, neck and under-wing pattern; darkest birds of W. Mediterranean race frequently suggest Sooty Shearwater but latter 25% larger, with less erratic, more powerful flight on looser or more flexed, proportionately narrower wings and uniformly dark underbody.
Habitat: Offshore waters of Mediterranean, with western race regularly passing through Straits of Gibraltar. Nests in colonies, burrowing in grass or among rocks on islands. Map 12.

LITTLE SHEARWATER *Puffinus assimilis*   Plate 3

Du – Kleine pijlstormvogel   Fr – Petit puffin
Ge – Kleine Sturmtaucher   Sw – Dvärglira

Identification: 10" (25cm). Smallest most auk-like shearwater, with paddle-shaped wings and *low, direct, fluttering flight*. Plumage like Manx but *black crown does not extend below eye* (latter sometimes showing at close range, never so in Manx); neck sides greyer and *white wing-lining sharper rimmed* and extending more onto primaries. Occurs in 2 races: more frequent Madeiran *P. a. baroli* has white under tail-coverts; rare Cape Verde *P. a. boydi* has darker face and black under tail-coverts.
Confusion species: Beware runt Manx Shearwater; Audubon's Shearwater *P. lherminieri* may occur but distinction from Cape Verde race unstudied, considered same species by some authors.
Habitat and Range: Annual off Britain and Ireland, twice ashore in Wales; vagrant to N. Atlantic and across Europe to Switzerland.

STORM PETRELS: Hydrobatidae

Rather small to medium-sized burrow-nesting birds of northern and southern oceans, spending most of year well offshore but occasionally driven onshore by gales. Tubed nostrils rarely visible. Outline and action in flight – usually near sea surface – often reminiscent of hirundine or bat, except for raised head and frequently trailed legs. Voices purring and squeaking but silent at sea. Identification at sea or off coast never easy. Important to note that Leach's strays most frequently and has largest, loosest form and most angled wingbeats, while Storm is smallest with most flitting flight.

WILSON'S PETREL *Oceanites oceanicus*   Plate 3

Du – Wilson's stormvogeltje   Fr – Pétrel océanite
Ge – Buntfüssige Sturmschwalbe   Sw – Havslöpare

Identification: 7" (17.5cm). Only slightly larger than Storm Petrel, with similar form but more purposeful flight; flutters and glides like tern or swallow; when feeding, 'walks' on sea with *long legs and feet trailing* and *wings held up like butterfly*. Wings relatively short and broad, held straight particularly along trailing edge; rounded at tips; tail square. Plumage sooty, with *wide white rump* (more 'wrapped' around rear body than Storm), more obvious pale band on greater coverts but only faint pale stripe in wing-pit. Yellow webs of feet rarely visible. Follows ships. Silent at sea.

Confusion species: Storm Petrel, which see.
Habitat and Range: Not strictly pelagic, congregating over shallow shelf waters. Regular in Bay of Biscay, occasionally approaching SW. and W. coasts of Britain and Europe and rarely wandering to C. Europe and Mediterranean; not subject to 'wrecks'.

STORM PETREL *Hydrobates pelagicus*   Plate 3

Du – Stormvogeltje   Fr – Pétrel tempête
Ge – Sturmschwalbe   Sw – Stormsvala

Identification: 6" (15cm). Smallest European seabird, rarely seen from land except near breeding stations; follows ships with seemingly weak, *flitting, bat-like flight*, interrupted by gliding and pattering on sea surface. Wings relatively short, held straight; tail square. Plumage *almost black*, with conspicious *square white rump 'wrapped' around rear body,* irregular but often striking *white stripe in wing-pit* and indistinct narrow whitish bar along greater coverts. Silent at sea.
Voice: At nest, gives long rising and falling purr, with characteristic terminal *hiccough*, also squeaks and croons.
Habitat: Pelagic except when breeding. Nests colonially in scree, boulder beaches, stone walls on islands; not subject to 'wrecks'. Map 13.

LEACH'S PETREL *Oceanodroma leucorhoa*   Plate 3

Du – Vaal stormvogeltje   Fr – Pétrel culblanc
Ge – Wellenläufer   Sw – Klykstjärtad stormsvala

Identification: 8" (20cm). Longest, most attenuated European storm petrel, often seen from land during passage: has *distinctive erratic but bounding flight*, at times dashing, at others wavering; beats wings less often than smaller storm petrels. Relatively long and narrow *wings often angled at carpal joints*; quite long *tail forked* but often held closed. Plumage grey-brown, with *U-shaped white rump* often interrupted by central grey line, *broad pale diagonal band on greater coverts* but no pale mark in wing-pit. Docs not follow ships. Silent at sea.
Confusion species: Madeiran Petrel, which see. In recent years, black-rumped petrels have been trapped on North Sea coasts of England; these recently assigned to closely related **Swinhoe's Petrel** *O. monorhis* (see Pl. 3).
Voice: Over breeding station, emphatic *wicka, wicka*, also interspersed into rhythmic purr *wirra, wirra* and sustained croon given by birds in nest burrows.
Habitat: As Storm Petrel but usually excavates burrow in soft ground. Often blown onshore in 'wrecks'. Map 14.

MADEIRAN PETREL *Oceanodroma castro*

Du – Madeirastormvogeltje   Fr – Pétrel de Castro
Ge – Madeira-Wellenläufer   Sw – Oceanlöpare

Identification: 8" (20cm). Looks smaller than Leach's due to much less forked tail and shorter outer wing. Sooty-brown, with indistinct narrow brown panel on greater coverts but *well demarcated square white rump* 'wrapped' round rear body, unlike Leach's. Distinguished from Wilson's Petrel by lack of projecting toes and narrower brown panel on greater coverts. Flight distinctive, with quick wing-beats between *shearwater-like glides and zig-zags* on flat or bowed but usually angled wings (see Pl. 3).
Habitat and Range: Recently discovered breeding on two island groups off

Portugal; previously thought to be confined to Madeira and other central Atlantic islands. Pelagic when not breeding, straying north to W. Europe (including Britain).

GANNETS: Sulidae

NORTHERN GANNET *Morus bassanus* Plate 5

Du – Jan van Gent   Fr – Fou de Bassan
Ge – Basstöpel   Sw – Havssula

Identification: 36" (91cm). Majestic, goose-sized, cigar-shaped sea-bird, with long pointed bill, *long narrow wings* and *pointed tail*; twice as large as Herring Gull. Adult white, with greyish bill, *yellow hood* and *black outer wings*. Juvenile dusky-brown, closely speckled white; immature increasingly invaded by white over 4-5 years. Flight alternates deep flaps with long glides, with birds passing in characteristic lines astern; when fishing, soars and wheels, then *plunges headlong after fish,* sometimes from 30m. or more and with wings retracted.
Confusion species: Full adult unmistakable; similarly aged Cape Gannet *M. capensis,* reported from Iberia, differs in black secondaries and tail and longer black gular stripe. Immature may suggest frigatebird, booby, albatross and other large tubenoses, constituting serious pitfall for unwary observer.
Voice: Barking *arrah,* growls and gobbling notes.
Habitat: Offshore, sometimes pelagic. Breeds in dense colonies on island tops and cliff ledges. Map 15.

CORMORANTS: Phalacrocoracidae

Medium-sized to very large birds, mound-nesting in marshes, trees and rocky cliffs, spending winter on open waters or coastal seas. Swim and dive expertly, submerging in alarm like divers but presenting hooked bills and bare lower faces and sinuous necks. Perch freely, often with wings held open. Outline, action and formation in flight – at or well above sea surface, even higher over land – recall those of geese but beats of broad-ended wings shallower, while kinked necks held above body line. Seasonal change in adult marks and sheen; immatures lack sheen and may be pale below. Voices guttural.

CORMORANT *Phalacrocorax carbo* Plate 4

Du – Aalscholver   Fr – Grand cormoran
Ge – Kormoran   Sw – Storskarv

Identification: 36" (91cm). Goose-sized reptilian water- bird, with *long, deep, hooked bill* and long head with steep nape held slightly raised in most postures. Plumage *bronze*-black, contrasting with yellow bill and gape and *white chin and cheeks*; when breeding, also shows *round white thigh patch* and, in most European and some British birds, whitish head-ruff and neck. Juvenile dull oily-brown above, dirty white below. Swims low in water like diver but thick neck more erect or kinked. Flight powerful, goose-like but with shallower, jerkier wing-beats; neck extended slightly above body line; flies in lines or V formations, often at some height. Perches upright, often with wings held out. Sociable.
Voice: Low guttural *r-rah.*

Habitat: Coasts, estuaries and increasingly inland waters. Nests colonially on rock ledges, also on trees. Map 16.

SHAG *Phalacrocorax aristotelis* **Plate 4**
Du – Kuifaalscholver Fr – Cormoran huppé
Ge – Krähenscharbe Sw – Toppskarv
Identification: 30" (75cm). Reptilian sea-bird, 20% smaller than Cormorant with proportionately *shorter, slenderer bill*, smaller, high-crowned head and thinner neck; wears *short upright crest* when breeding. Plumage *greenish*-black, relieved only by yellow gape and pale blue-green eyes. Juvenile dark oily-brown, with variable white lower face and foreneck; under-parts usually dull brown below breast but a few British and all Mediterranean birds show some white on centre of under-body; bill finer than adult. Flight weaker than Cormorant, with faster wingbeats of proportionately broader wings; flies in lines or loose flocks, usually close to sea; other behaviour similar. Can be confused with Cormorant when distance obscures size.
Voice: Loud rasping croak; at nest, grunts and hisses loudly.
Habitat: Maritime, frequenting rocky coasts and islands with steep cliffs and sea caves; in winter occasionally inland. Breeds colonially (sometimes singly) on rocky ledges and among boulders. Map 17.

PYGMY CORMORANT *Phalacrocorax pygmeus* **Plate 4**
Du – Dwergaalscholver Fr – Cormoran pygmée
Ge – Zwergscharbe Sw – Dvärgskarv
Identification: 19" (48cm). Smallest, most compact cormorant, only half size of Cormorant with *proportionately shorter bill*, rather small *round head*, shorter neck but *long tail*. Breeding plumage greenish-black, with dusky bill, *dark red-brown head and white spotting* except on dark grey 'saddle' across back and inner wings. In winter, lacks white spots but throat white. Juvenile brown, with yellowish bill, white chin, brown throat and breast and dirty-white under-body. Flight more agile than Cormorant, recalling Coot; other behaviour typical of family.
Voice: Short harsh bark.
Habitat: Prefers inland waters, including rivers and marshes, to sea coast. Breeds colonially, building untidy nest on bushes in marsh. Map 18.

PELICANS: Pelecanidae

Huge, mound-nesting birds of fresh or brackish waters, rarely on sea. Long, pouched bill is retracted with head into shoulders in flight, which is often at great height, when outline suggests stork but lacks trailing legs. Swim well, lunging for fish, often in unison. Flight action consists of long glides interrupted by leisurely wing-beats; formations usually linear, not bunched or in V. Voices low and guttural.

WHITE PELICAN *Pelecanus onocrotalus* **Plate 5**
Du – Gewone pelikaan Fr – Pélican blanc
Ge – Rosapelikan Sw – Pelikan
Identification: 55-70" (139-177cm). Long- and pouch-billed, long-necked,

flat-footed water-bird, at ease on water or in air but awkward on land; huge wing-span. Plumage white, relieved by yellowish bill and throat, red eye, yellow patch at base of neck and *flesh-pink feet*. Flight feathers blackish, looking *wholly dark from below but black-ended from above*. When breeding, grows short ragged crest and plumage has *rosy tint*. Juvenile dirty brown; immature dingy white, speckled brown. Flight powerful but action leisurely, alternately flapping (below bodyline) and gliding, with head retracted; flies in line astern, often at great height.

Voice: Low grunts and growls.

Habitat and Range: Mainly summer visitor to large inland wetlands and coastal lagoons, nesting colonially in reeds. Breeds S.E. Europe, wandering W., C. and N.

DALMATIAN PELICAN *Pelecanus crispus*   Plate 5

Du – Kroeskoppelikaan   Fr – Pélican frisé
Ge – Krauskopfpelikan   Sw – Krushuvad pelikan

Identification: 63-70" (160-177cm). Averages slightly larger than White Pelican. Plumage dingy, even greyish below, looking dirtier than White and showing pale eye, curly fringe to back of head and neck, yellow, not tufted, crop patch and *dark grey feet*. Variegated flight feathers look pale in flight, except for *dusky wing-rim and fingers from below* and almost black ends from above. When breeding, fringe becomes short crest and plumage takes on *silver hue* above, bluish-grey tone below. Juvenile greyer than White. Close-to, adult shows abrupt end to forehead feathers (not extending into a point above upper mandible as in White). Flight and behaviour as White. At distance on water, can be indistinguishable from White.

Voice: Short rasping bark, higher-pitched than White.

Habitat and Range: Much as White but less migratory, wandering in winter within S.E. Europe. Map 19.

HERONS AND BITTERNS: Ardeidae

Medium-sized to very large reed- and tree-nesting birds mainly of wetlands but also coasts; some colonial when breeding; wander or migrate south in winter. All have spear-like bills, long necks and long legs; wade but swim badly. Outline in flight – often at considerable height – characterised by retraction of head and neck, spread of large wings, trailing legs and bulky feet. Seasonal change in adult plumage mainly restricted to differences in bare-part colours and growth of plumes on head, neck and scapulars. Sexes similar except in Little Bittern. Voices barking, crowing in herons; pumped or booming in bitterns.

BITTERN *Botaurus stellaris*   Plate 6

Du – Roerdomp   Fr – Butor étoilé
Ge – Grosse Rohrdommel   Sw – Rördrom

Identification: 30" (75cm). Large, heron-like marsh bird, with *buff-brown plumage, richly mottled and barred*, rather short but large green legs and feet and *distinctive voice*. Flight reluctant and slow, with deep beats of broad rounded wings, heavily barred black on brown. Walks with shoulders hunched, head lowered. Solitary and usually crepuscular, skulking in reeds by day and,

when discovered, adopting characteristic cryptic, upwards-elongated pose with bill pointed vertically. See also American Bittern; immature Night Heron much smaller and spotted.
Voice: More often heard than seen. Song 2-3 quiet grunts, then audible intake of breath followed by deep boom *woomp*; curiously muted like distant fog-horn but carrying up a mile at times. Harsh *aark* when disturbed.
Habitat: Dense reed-beds, marshes, backwaters, lake shores. Nests among reeds. On Continent, sometimes nests around small ponds in cultivated regions. Map 20.

AMERICAN BITTERN *Botaurus lentiginosus*   **Plate 6**
   Du – Amerikaanse roerdomp   Fr – Butor d'Amérique
   Ge – Amerikanische Rohrdommel   Sw – Amerikansk rördrom
Identification: 26" (65cm). Smaller and more rakish than Bittern, with chestnut crown, *long black streak down neck side*, finely freckled (not strongly mottled) upper-parts, narrower, duller, *black-quilled wings*, with buff trailing edge, and yellowish legs and feet. Behaviour like Bittern but less skulking; flight more agile.
Confusion species: Immature Night Heron is close in size but greyer, with pale spots.
Voice: Rapid, throaty *kok-kok-kok* when flushed.
Habitat and Range: Like Bittern but often in open marshes and meadows. Wanders from N. America to W. and N. Europe (including Britain).

LITTLE BITTERN *Ixobrychus minutus*   **Plate 6**
   Du – Wouwaapje   Fr – Blongios nain
   Ge – Zwergrohrdommel   Sw – Dvärgrördrom
Identification: 14" (35cm). Tiny, fast-flying heron, with dark crown and back, *obvious buffish-white wing-coverts contrasting with dark flight feathers* (particularly in flight) and pale buff under-parts. Male's crown and back greenish-black. Female streaked dark brown above, streaked brown and buff below, with less striking buff wing-coverts. Bill yellowish, male's red at base when breeding; legs green. Juvenile more heavily streaked, with dusky bare parts. Flight rarely much above reed tops, with more rapid wing-beats and glides than other small herons. Crepuscular out of breeding season.
Voice: Song deep bark, repeated at 2-4 second interval, sometimes for hours, often at night.
Habitat: Reed beds with pools, wooded swamps, quiet backwaters, overgrown river banks and ditches. Nests near water, occasionally in small loose groups. Map 21.

NIGHT HERON *Nycticorax nycticorax*   **Plate 6**
   Du – Kwak   Fr – Héron bihoreau
   Ge – Nachtreiher   Sw – Natthäger
Identification: 24" (60cm). Stocky, rather short-legged heron, usually inactive during day, hiding hunched in trees, but active at dusk, flying to feeding areas. Adult *black-capped and -backed,* grey-winged and -tailed, *white-faced and -bodied,* with red eye and white head plume. Bill stout, dark grey; legs yellowish, redder when breeding. Juvenile brown above and dull white below, with *pale*

buff spots all over back and wings and brown streaks from throat to vent; immature greyer, less spotted and streaked. Flight outline stumpy, action flapping and gliding.

Voice: Hoarse *quark* or *quok*, usually at dusk.

Habitat: Marshes with trees, tangled swamps, feeding at dusk and into night in open areas, pools and ditches. Nests colonially, often with other herons, in tree thickets, bushes and locally in reeds. Map 22.

SQUACCO HERON *Ardeola ralloides* **Plate 7**

Du – Ralreiger	Fr – Héron crabier
Ge – Rallenreiher	Sw – Rallhäger

Identification: 18" (45cm). Small, quite long-billed but thick-necked, *crested and cloaked* heron. *Pale buff-brown* plumage, relieved by *white wings* concealed on ground but suddenly revealed in flight, with white rump and tail, to produce almost all-white impression. Crest lined blackish; bill dark-tipped greenish, black and blue when breeding; legs greenish, pink in full breeding condition. Juvenile streaked dark on throat and chest, browner on head and back.

Confusion species: Cattle Egret always much whiter, preferring different, drier habitats; beware other members of tribe from E. Asia, reported but not confirmed in Europe and often imported as cage birds. Chinese Pond Heron very similar (see Accidentals).

Voice: Harsh, crow-like *karr*, usually at dusk.

Habitat: As Little Egret but usually skulks in cover. Nests singly or in scattered groups with other herons in trees, bushes and reeds. Map 23.

CATTLE EGRET *Bubulcus ibis* **Plate 7**

Du – Koereiger	Fr – Héron garde-boeufs
Ge – Kuhreiher	Sw – Kohäger

Identification: 20" (50cm). Rather small, quite thick-necked and compact heron with *distinct jowl*. Looks all white at distance but close-to shows *long pale buff tufts on crown, chest and mantle*, particularly in breeding season. Spear-like bill yellowish, with red base when breeding; legs dusky, redder when breeding. Juvenile lacks buff tufts; bill yellow, legs greenish-brown. Flight outline less attenuated than Little Egret, action faster, allowing greater agility. Sociable; *often feeds among livestock* and perch on their backs.

Confusion species: Little Egret larger, with much thinner neck, less stocky body and differently coloured bare parts; Squacco Heron always darker on head, neck and saddle.

Voice: Croaks and bubbles deeply when breeding.

Habitat: Markedly less aquatic than other herons, as often in farmland and open country as in marshes. Nests colonially often with other herons in reeds, trees and bushes, not always near water. Map 24.

LITTLE EGRET *Egretta garzetta* **Plate 7**

Du – Kleine zilverreiger	Fr – Aigrette garzette
Ge – Seidenreiher	Sw – Silkeshäger

Identification: 22" (56cm). Medium-sized, relatively slender heron, with *sword-like bill* and long legs. Plumage typically *snow-white*; breeding adult wears long drooping crest and hazy scapular cloak. Bill black; legs black, ending in *startling yellow toes*, redder when breeding. Rare melanistic morph dusky or black. Flight more graceful than larger herons; gait more delicate. Feeds openly in shallows.

Confusion species: Cattle Egret and Squacco Heron, which see; typical Western Reef Heron similar to melanistic Little Egret; pale Western Reef Heron like dingy Little, both phases best distinguished by duller, longer, thicker bill and duller legs (see Accidentals).

Voice: Croaking *kark*, bubbling *wulla-wulla-wulla*.

Habitat: Marshes, lagoons, swamps. Nests in colonies, often with other herons, in bushes or trees, in wet marsh, swamps, dry open country, sea cliffs and woods. Map 25.

GREAT WHITE EGRET *Egretta alba*   **Plate 7**

Du – Grote zilverreiger   Fr – Grande aigrette
Ge – Silberreiher   Sw – Ägretthäger
N. Am. – American Egret

Identification: 35" (89cm). Largest egret, close in size to Grey Heron; form like much smaller Little Egret but *bill proportionately shorter* and neck even longer, more kinked . Plumage always white; breeding adult wears hazy scapular cloak extending below tail. Bill yellow-green, with variable black tip; gape extends behind eye; *legs and feet wholly greenish-black*, upper legs pink-orange when breeding. Flight outline more graceful than other large herons; action also lighter. Albino Grey Heron retains its own general character, particularly less sinuous head and neck.

Voice: Croaking *kraak*.

Habitat: Reed beds, swamps, lagoons, lake and river banks. Nests in reeds, rarely in trees or bushes, usually in scattered groups. Map 26.

GREY HERON *Ardea cinerea*   **Plate 6**

Du – Blauwe reiger   Fr – Héron cendré
Ge – Fischreiher   Sw – Grå häger

Identification: 36" (91cm). Largest, most ubiquitous heron in W. and C. Europe. Adult has long, yellow dagger-bill, redder in early spring, *black eye-band ending in drooping plumes* on almost white head, *grey upper-parts and tail* contrasting with blackish flight feathers and shoulder patch and greyish-white neck and under-parts, narrowly lined black on fore-neck. Juvenile duller, with dusky crown and duskier upper-parts; occasionally shows buff tones. Flight outline reminiscent of large raptor, with *head and neck retracted onto shoulders*, action slow, with regular deep wing-beats and bowed-wing glides, trailing 'bunch' of feet. Stands or perches motionless for long periods; fishes with great visual attention, lunging from motionless posture or slow careful walk. Solitary except when breeding.

Confusion species: Rare albino tricky (see Great White Egret above); rare buffish juvenile may suggest Purple Heron, which see.

Voice: Harsh, deep *frarnk*; also croaks, retches and snaps bill.

Habitat: Water-meadows, rivers, lakes, sea-shores. Nests in colonies, usually in tall trees. Map 27.

PURPLE HERON *Ardea purpurea* **Plate 6**
Du – Purperreiger Fr – Héron pourpré
Ge – Purpurreiher Sw – Purpurhäger
Identification: 31" (78cm). Large but slender, sinuous heron, with thin head and *noticeably long toes* and furtive behaviour. Plumage dark and rich in tone: adult has yellow bill, *red-buff head and neck*, decorated with black crown and plumes, facial stripe and line down neck adding to serpentine appearance, slate upper-parts with elongated pale chestnut scapulars when breeding, black flight feathers, grey rump and tail; *dark, vinaceous underbody*. Brown legs and feet. Immature sandier, with unlined head and paler under-wing coverts. Flight outline distinctive, narrow-bodied when head-on and with *drooping neck bulge* and long 'bunch' of feet when seen sideways; action characterised by easier beats of narrower wings than Grey. Beware occasional pale buff juvenile Grey.
Voice: Harsh *rrank*, higher pitched than Grey Heron.
Habitat: Swamps, overgrown ditches, dense reed-beds, etc. Breeds in colonies, sometimes with other species, in reed-beds, occasionally in bushes, seldom in trees. Map 28.

STORKS: *Ciconiidae*

Large, with long legs, long necks and long, straight bills. Flight slow and deliberate, with neck extended but slightly drooped. Gait a sedate walk. Sexes similar. Tree or roof nesting.

BLACK STORK *Ciconia nigra* **Plate 7**
Du – Zwarte ooievaar Fr – Cigogne noire
Ge – Schwarzstorch Sw – Svart stork
Identification: 38" (96cm). Shy, solitary stork, slightly smaller than White. Plumage *glossy black, with white wing-pits and under-parts* below breast; bill and legs red. Juvenile duller, with brownish breast. Flight less laboured than White Stork, not dependent on thermals.
Voice: Quite noisy, with bill-clappering and hoarse gasping, 'saw-sharpening' and quite musical notes.
Habitat: Wild marshy tracts or meadows among coniferous or mixed forests. Nests at considerable height in forest trees. Map 29.

WHITE STORK *Ciconia ciconia* **Plate 7**
Du – Ooievaar Fr – Cigogne blanche
Ge – Weissstorch Sw – Vit stork
Identification: 40" (100cm). Very large, long-billed and -legged, stately bird; unlike heron, pelican and vulture, *keeps head and neck extended in flight*. Plumage *white except for jet-black flight-feathers*, red bill and legs. Flight slow, somewhat laboured, with slow wing-beats and glides; soars and sails on thermals. Walks deliberately, lunging at prey; perches on trees and buildings, often on one leg. Sociable; migrates in irregularly shaped flocks, usually at great height.
Voice: Loud, rhythmic bill-clappering in display; also hisses and coughs.
Habitat: Marshes, water-meadows and grassy plains; in breeding season usually near houses. Nests on buildings, haystacks, or stork-poles, also in trees. Map 30

IBISES AND SPOONBILLS: Threskiornithidae

Resemble small herons or storks in general form, but with long and decurved or flattened and spatulate bills. Necks extended in flight. Sexes similar. Reed, bush or tree nesting.

GLOSSY IBIS *Plegadis falcinellus*   Plate 7
Du – Ibis   Fr – Ibis falcinelle
Ge – Brauner Sichler   Sw – Svart ibis

Identification: 22" (55cm). Rather sinuous, prehistoric-looking marsh bird, with Curlew-like form and almost uniform *very dark plumage*. Close-to, adult intensely glossed with purple, bronze and green; immature dull dark brown. Flight outline distinctive, with *long, decurved bill* drooping from extended head and neck low-hung on narrow body, long round-tipped wings and trailing legs; action rather mechanical, with shallow, rapid wing-beats and short glides. Perches on trees. Flight action can recall Cormorant but outline differs in curved bill and trailing legs.
Voice: Infrequent long croak.
Habitat: Marshes, mud-flats. Breeds in colonies, frequently with herons or egrets, in large reed-beds in shallow water, occasionally in bushes or trees. Map 31.

SPOONBILL *Platalea leucorodia*   Plate 7
Du – Lepelaar   Fr – Spatule blanche
Ge – Löffler   Sw – Skedstork

Identification: 34" (85cm). Large, egret-like marsh bird, with *long, spatulate bill*. Adult *snow-white*, with ochre wash at base of neck and, when breeding, 'horse-tail' crest; legs and bill black, latter with yellow tip. Immature has black-tipped primaries, greyish-pink bill and yellowish to greyish legs; lacks ochre on neck. Flight outline differs from all white herons by extended, slightly sagging neck and lengthy bill.
Voice: Claps bill when excited; occasional grunt.
Habitat: Shallow, open water, reedy marshes, estuaries. Breeds in colonies in large reed-beds, on small bare islands, locally in trees or bushes. Map 32.

FLAMINGOS: *Phoenicopteridae*

GREATER FLAMINGO *Phoenicopterus ruber*   Plate 7
Du – Flamingo   Fr – Flamant rose
Ge – Flamingo   Sw – Flamingo

Identification: 50" (127cm). Grotesque, *extremely long-necked,* goose-bodied, *abnormally long-legged* wading bird, with seemingly 'broken', decurved bill. Adult white and rose-pink, showing crimson coverts and black quills of wings mainly in flight; bill whitish-pink, with narrow black line on bent tip; legs fully pink. Immature dingy grey-brown, with duller wings and bare parts. Flight outline extraordinary, with head and neck and legs fully extended and slightly drooped; action somewhat goose-like but less agile. Walks sedately, dipping bill (and head) into water to feed. Gregarious.

Confusion species: Taller and paler than Lesser Flamingo (see Accidentals); beware escaped Chilean race *P. r. chilensis* (adult all pink; shows pink 'knees' at all ages).
Voice: Trumpeting *ar-honk*, particularly in flight; flock chorus gabbling, like geese.
Habitat and Range: Shallow coastal lagoons, or floodwaters, lakes, mud-flats, etc. Breeds, colonially on mud-banks, or in shallow water, building mud-heap nest a few inches above water. Breeds, not always annually, S. France, S. Spain; partial migrant. Irregular visitor to Portugal, Holland. Vagrant elsewhere in Europe.

SWANS, GEESE AND DUCKS: Anatidae

Swans: Large, white, with very long necks extended in flight. Feed by grazing or up-ending. Flight majestic, in lines or V's. Sexes similar; juveniles dusky; voices grunting and bugling.
Geese: Medium-sized to large, mostly grey or blackish with long necks. Feed mainly by grazing. Flight powerful, with less 'necky' silhouettes than swans, but in similar formations; sexes similar; juveniles dingier; voices honking and gabbling.
Shelducks: Quite large, variegated, with goose-like form and flight, but hole-nesting; feed by grazing or up-ending; juveniles less patterned; sexes similar; voices barking.
Surface-feeding ducks: Small to medium-sized; highly variable male plumages but constant wing patterns; flight action rapid and agile, following spring from water. Feed mainly by dabbling and up-ending but also by grazing. Sexes dissimilar; males in eclipse and juveniles resemble females; voices quacking, croaking and whistling.
Diving Ducks: Small to fairly large; variable male plumages but constant wing patterns; flight outline compact, action less agile than most surface-feeding ducks, pattering on take-off. Partly hole-nesting. Feed mainly by diving. Sexes dissimilar; males in eclipse and juveniles resemble females; voices variable, including growling and crooning. Hybrids confusing.
Saw-billed ducks: Small to medium-sized, with slender, toothed bills, crested heads in males and cylindrical bodies; flight outline attenuated, with level head,

Postures of Ducks on Land

Marsh and Pond Ducks (Surface-feeders)	Estuary and Sea-ducks (Divers)	Saw-bills Divers	Stiff-tails (Divers)	Shelducks (Surface-feeders)

body and tail recalling diver. Ground- or hole-nesting. Sexes dissimilar; males in eclipse and juveniles resemble red-headed females; voices harsh.

Stiff-tailed ducks: Small, compact, with bold heads and stiff, straight tails raised in display; variable plumages but specific face patterns; distinctive flight outline with fat head and body, short wings and grebe-like action. Reed-nesting; feed by diving. Sexes dissimilar; voice chucking or ticking in display.

MUTE SWAN *Cygnus olor*   Plate 8, 9

Du – Knobbelzwaan   Fr – Cygne tuberculé
Ge – Höckershwan   Sw – Knölsvan

Identification: 60" (152cm). Large swan, long semi-domesticated and mainly resident. Adult distinguished by *orange bill with black knob* and base (knob enlarged in breeding male) and, when swimming, *gracefully curved neck,* downward pointing bill, rather long pointed tail; readily assumes aggressive posture with wings arched over back. Juvenile dusky brown, with knobless, greyish-pink bill and grey legs. Flight powerful and direct, after laboured take-off; head and neck out-stretched, slightly wobbling; wing-beats make *distinctive throbbing, singing sound.* Sociable, locally in very large herds, breeding birds dispersing in spring.

Voice: Not mute but lacks bugling call, merely honking, grunting and hissing on occasion.

Habitat: Domesticated birds widespread on rivers and still waters, even small ponds; wild birds frequent remote marshes and lakes; in winter, occasionally on sheltered sea coasts. Map 33.

BEWICK'S SWAN *Cygnus columbianus*   Plate 8, 9

Du – Kleine zwaan   Fr – Cygne de Bewick
Ge – Zwergschwan   Sw – Mindre sångsvan

Identification: 48" (122cm). Smallest, *most goose-like* swan, close in form to Whooper but with *gentler expression* due to shorter bill and more *rounded head,* and relatively shorter, proportionately thicker neck. Adult's bill pattern shows only *small, usually square or rounded patch of yellow* (rarely orange) at base; head rarely stained; bill of rare Nearctic race *C. c. columbianus* all black, often with tiny yellow specks at base. Immature as Whooper but noticeably smaller. Flight lightest and most agile of swans, with easiest take-off; wing-beats silent; flight formations usually irregular. Walks more freely than Mute and Whooper; does not arch wings. Sociable, locally in large herds.

Voice: Distinctive, bugling but quiet, sounding like gentle babble from distance, hollow *oop-oop* close-to.

Habitat: Flooded grassland, lakes, reservoirs. Map 34.

WHOOPER SWAN *Cygnus cygnus*   Plate 8, 9

Du – Wilde zwaan   Fr – Cygne sauvage
Ge – Singschwan   Sw – Sångsvan

Identification: 60" (152cm). Large swan, close in size to Mute but always wild, with *rather long bill, flat head,* usually stiff, erect neck, bulging chest and *loud, bugling calls.* Adult's bill pattern shows *large lemon-yellow patch at base, tapering forward to a point*; head often stained rusty or ochre. Immature dusky, greyer-toned than Mute; bill pinkish with dusky tip. Flight as Mute but outline

differs in markedly long and straighter neck; wing-beats silent; flight formations wavering oblique line or chevron. Walks more freely than Mute; kinks neck when grazing. Sociable but rarely in large herds; disperses in breeding season.
Voice: Noisiest of swans; flight-call loud trumpeting or whooping *hoop-hoop-hoop*, bugling in chorus.
Habitat: Widely dispersed on lakes, large rivers, quiet waters and flooded grassland, also tidal waters and sea coasts. Nests on islets in swamps or lakes, moorland bogs, Arctic tundra. Map 35.

BEAN GOOSE *Anser fabalis*   Plate 10, 11
Du – Rietgans   Fr – Oie des moissons
Ge – Saatgans   Sw – Sädgås

Identification: 28-35" (70-88cm). Second largest grey goose, with usually long *wedge-shaped bill and head*, long neck and body. Plumage *brownest* of tribe, with pale margins of rear upper-parts obvious; diagnosis comes from combination of usually *dark bill,* more or less banded orange behind nail, dark head and upper neck, and *orange legs*; beware shorter bill and neck of smaller tundra race *A. f. rossicus*. Flight outline noticeably long-necked, ending in dark head; flight pattern lacks obvious character, but *fore-wing dull brown*; action powerful. Walk waddling, with stern moving from side to side as in all geese. Flight formations variable, usually loose chevron.
Confusion species: Greylag bulkier, with heavier bill and head, paler head and neck and pink legs; Pink-footed closely related but smaller, dumpier, yet daintier, with pink bill and legs; both show pale fore-wings.
Voice: Least vocal of tribe; rich, baritone *ung-unk*, low and reedy in tone.
Habitat: Winters inland, on grasslands near fresh water. Breeds in the Arctic among forest trees near rivers and lakes. Map 36.

PINK-FOOTED GOOSE *Anser brachyrhynchus*   Plate 10, 11
Du – Kleine rietgans   Fr – Oie à bec court
Ge – Kurzschnabelgans   Sw – Spetsbergsgås

Identification: 24-30" (60-75cm). Second smallest grey goose, with *short, triangular bill, rounded head*, short, rather thick neck, *dumpy body* and relatively short legs. Plumage *bluest*-grey of tribe, with almost pink chest on adult; diagnosis by combination of *black, pink-banded bill,* very dark head and neck, latter sharply contrasting with breast, *blue-grey fore-wing* and *pink legs*. Beware juvenile with ochre legs and paler neck. Flight outline compact, with neat head and rather short neck; flight pattern striking, with dark head and neck and pale fore-wing catching eye; action powerful but quite light. Flight formation usually chevron. Bean closely related but larger, longer-necked and -bodied, with dull fore-wing and orange bare parts.
Voice: Merry *wink-wink-wink* or *king-wink* characteristic; musical *ang-ank* multiplies into high-pitched chorus.
Habitat: As Greylag, but more frequently in arable fields. Breeds colonially among rocky outcrops on hillsides and river gorges, also on open tundra. Map 37.

WHITE-FRONTED GOOSE *Anser albifrons* **Plate 10, 11**
Du – Kolgans Fr – Oie rieuse
Ge – Blässgans Sw – Bläsgås
Identification: 26-30" (66-76cm). Medium-sized grey goose, with quite long bill, quite abrupt forehead and rather deep chest. Plumage *olive-toned*, upperparts darkest of tribe; diagnosis of adult by combination of *white fore-face,* almost wholly pale *pink bill,* dull fore-wing, *black-barred belly* and *orange legs.* Adult of Greenland race *A. a. flavirostris* distinguished by dark, even more olive plumage, particularly on head and neck, heavier belly bars and *orange bill.* Juvenile lacks white fore-face and belly bars but shows adult's bare part colours. Flight outline like Pink-footed but neck longer; flight pattern *lacks pale forewing* but breast often catches light; action powerful with more rapid 'jumped' take-off than in other grey species. Flight formation usually chevron over distance, loose-packed on short flights.
Confusion species: Well seen, adult unmistakeable but juvenile confusing, suggesting runt Greylag and best distinguished by size and structure. See also Lesser White-fronted.
Voice: Generally higher-pitched and quicker-phrased than preceding species; cackling *kow-lyow* or *lyo-lyok* characteristic, multiplies into laughing chorus.
Habitat: As Greylag, but seldom in stubble or potato fields. Usually breeds sociably in treeless tundra, open marshes, islets in rivers, etc. Greenland race winters mainly W. Scotland and Ireland. Map 38.

LESSER WHITE-FRONTED GOOSE *Anser erythropus* **Plate 10**
Du – Dwerggans Fr – Oie naine
Ge – Zwerggans Sw – Fjällgås
Identification: 21-26" (53-66cm). Smallest grey goose, with *small triangular bill,* rounded head, dainty build and proportionately long *wing-tips usually extending beyond tail.* Plumage most immaculate of tribe, darker above and below than White-fronted; diagnosis by *wholly pink bill, white fore-face extending onto fore-crown, swollen yellow eye-ring* – beware faint indication of this on some White-fronts – and fewer black bars on belly. Juvenile lacks white on head and belly bars but already shows yellow eye-ring. Flight outline more compact, shorter-necked than White-fronted; action lighter, with quicker wing-beats allowing even more rapid take-off; formations similar. Feeding action faster than White-fronted. White-fronted larger and far less dainty, usually with wing-tips extending only to end of tail; lacks bright eye-ring.
Voice: Squeaky *kyu-yu* or *kyu-yu-yu* from gander, *kow-yow* from goose; higher pitch discernible among chorus of White-fronted.
Habitat: Much as White-fronted, but is a low-Arctic species and breeds at high altitudes only where range extends south, in dwarf birch and willow, around mountain lakes. In extreme north of Norway breeds at sea level. Map 39.

GREYLAG GOOSE *Anser anser* **Plate 10, 11**
Du – Grauwe gans Fr – Oie cendrée
Ge – Graugans Sw – Grågäs
Identification: 30-35" (76-88cm). Largest grey goose, with *deep triangular bill,* rather square head, thick neck, *heavy body* and strong legs. Plumage *greyest* of tribe; diagnosis by combination of wholly *pale orange bill,* rather pale head

and neck (no darker than body), *whitish-grey fore-wing*, unbarred but black-spotted belly and *pink legs*; E. European race *A. a. rubirostris* distinguished by *pale pink bill* and paler-toned plumage, in particular *white margins to rear upper-parts*. Juvenile has dull, greyish-pink legs. Flight outline bulkiest of tribe, with broadest wings; action powerful but wing-beats quite slow, laboured at times; formations usually chevrons or oblique lines. Walk lumbering, with twisting body. With scattered feral groups breeding S. of normal range, Greylag usually first of tribe to confront inexperienced observer; important to remember its bulk and very pale fore-wing, which is lacking in all other grey geese.

Voice: Loud, challenging *aahng-ung-ung* and other nasal and reedy gabbling notes, identical to those of domesticated progeny. Flock chorus may suggest baaing sheep.

Habitat: In winter on grasslands, arable fields near coasts, marshes, estuaries. Breeds sociably on moors, marshes, reed-beds, boggy thickets, islets. Map 40.

SNOW GOOSE *Anser caerulescens*   Plate 8, 9

Du – Skneeuwgans   Fr – Oie des neiges
Ge – Schneegans   Sw – Snögås

Identification: 25-30" (63-76cm). Medium-sized goose, with stout bill, oval head and upright carriage. Adult always *white-headed* but other plumage aberrant, with two colour phases across two races; in smaller western form or Lesser Snow *A. c. caerulescens*, dark phase – so-called Blue Snow – is common but in larger eastern race or Greater Snow *A. c. atlanticus,* dark birds are rare. White birds wholly so except for pink bill (with dark gape line), pink legs and black primaries. Blue birds typically white only on head and upper-neck and dusky blue-grey elsewhere (but occasionally show white on breast, belly and stern). Juvenile of white phase dusky on crown and upper-parts, of blue phase uniformly dark. Flight and behaviour much as Pink-footed but gait nimbler.

Confusion species: Escaped Ross's Goose *A. rossii* 40% smaller and much daintier, with tiny, triangular blue-based bill; adult Northern Gannet has similar plumage pattern but very different structure and almost exclusively maritime range.

Voice: Distinctive, with hard, clarion tone; abrupt harsh *kaank*, high-pitched *kow* and *whonk*, deep *zung-ung-ung*. Flock chorus less uniform than Pink-footed, with individually sharper notes clearly audible.

Habitat and Range: Winter requirements as other grey geese. Occurrences bedevilled by frequent escapes of both phases; wild N. American vagrants appear most often with Greenland White-fronted Geese in NW. Europe.

BAR-HEADED GOOSE *Anser indicus*   Plate 96

Du – Indische gans   Fr – Oie à tete barré
Ge – Streifengans   Sw – Stripgås

Identification: 30" (76cm). Larger than Pink-footed Goose, with rather pale, grey plumage; easily distinguished by yellow bill, white head with double *black bar* (around rear crown and nape), *white line down neck side*, dark rear flanks and orange legs. Juvenile lacks head bars.

Habitat: Escapes from collections join flocks of feral and wild geese. Feral population established in Sweden.

CANADA GOOSE *Branta canadensis*   **Plate 8, 9**
  Du – Canadese gans   Fr – Bernache du Canada
  Ge – Kanadagans   Sw – Kanadagås

Identification: 22-40" (55-100cm). Introduced race *B. c. canadensis* is *largest and longest-necked goose* occurring in Europe; other introduced, escaped and truly vagrant races large to noticeably small, the smallest also much more compact. Although member of black geese, plumage *mainly dark brown*; distinguished by black bill, *white throat and cheek-band* on black head, *black neck contrasting with paler chest* and black legs. Commonest race palest below, with whitish breast, others increasingly darker but retaining same basic pattern. Flight outline most swan-like of all geese; action powerful; formations looser than grey geese, often in lines. Walk quite free, with neck noticeably bent when grazing.
Voice: Resonant, nasal *aa-honk*, with accent on rising second syllable; flock chorus harsher than grey geese.
Habitat and Range: Fields and open marshes near fresh water; sometimes among trees and along sea-shores. Introduced into Europe and occurs frequently in parks. Breeds singly or in small groups on bushy islets in lakes. Feral breeder in Britain, Ireland, Norway, Sweden, Finland; partial migrant to Germany, Holland. Feral birds wander elsewhere in Europe. A few wild birds cross Atlantic to W. Scotland and Ireland, in company with Greenland White-fronted Geese. Map 41.

BARNACLE GOOSE *Branta leucopsis*   **Plate 8, 9**
  Du – Brandgans   Fr – Bernache nonnette
  Ge – Weisswangengans   Sw – Vitkindad gås

Identification: 23-27" (58-68cm). Medium-sized black goose, with small triangular bill but otherwise typical build of tribe. Plumage predominantly black and white, with *obvious cream or white forehead and face*, black crown, neck and deep breast; blackish to *lavender-grey upper-parts*, increasingly barred with black-and-white-edged feathers to rear, black flight feathers, white rump, black tail and *clean whitish-grey under-parts*; bare parts black. Flight outline like medium-sized grey goose but wings look broad; action powerful; formations close-packed but ragged. Walk quite nimble.
Voice: Rapidly barked *gnuk-gnuk*; flock chorus suggests pack of yapping lapdogs.
Habitat: Seldom far inland, preferring salt-marshes, grass fields near estuaries, tidal mud-flats, or small grass-topped islands, but more terrestrial than Brent Goose. Individuals occasionally join grey geese. Breeds colonially, usually on ledges of steep Arctic cliffs, rocky river gorges and hillsides, sometimes open tundra. Map 42.

BRENT GOOSE *Branta bernicla*   **Plate 8, 9**
  Du – Rotgans   Fr – Bernache cravant
  Ge – Ringelgans   Sw – Prutgås

Identification: 22-24" (55-60cm). Second smallest, most duck-like of black geese, with rather flat bill, *proportionately short neck*, longish oval body and *rather short legs*. Plumage predominantly *dull black and dusky*, with *brilliant white stern*; small white neck mark shows close-to. Commonest N. Russian race *B. b. bernicla* – so-called Dark-bellied – can look *as dark below as above*, since

belly dusky and only faintly pale-barred on upper rear flanks; Arctic race *B. b. hrota* – so-called Pale-bellied – much paler below, with *deep whitish-grey flanks* contrasting with black breast (recalling Barnacle). Vagrant N. American race *B. b. nigricans* – so-called Black Brant – like Dark-bellied but *larger white neck mark forms half-collar*, pale barring deeper on flanks, and plumage toned sooty-brown. Juvenile shows pale bars on larger wing-coverts and much darker underparts (in all races). *Much more aquatic than all other geese*, swimming readily on sea, up-ending freely. Flight outline most compact of geese, with least head and neck extension but proportionately longer stern; action free, allowing fast progress; formations usually irregular, changing shape when large, but migrates in lines. Walks easily but looks low-slung.
Voice: Soft, throaty *rronk* or *rruk*; flight or flock chorus growling, roaring in alarm.
Habitat: Maritime outside breeding season, frequenting coasts and estuaries where *Zostera* weed abounds. Breeds sociably on high rocky tundra and islets off Arctic coasts. Map 43.

RED-BREASTED GOOSE *Branta ruficollis*   **Plate 8, 11**
Du – Roodhalsgans   Fr – Bernache à cou roux
Ge – Rothalsgans   Sw – Rödhalsad gås
Identification: 21-22" (53-55cm). Smallest, by far *daintiest of all geese, with tiny bill*, somewhat maned head and neck, rather long wings and legs. Plumage combines *black and red-chestnut*, with beautiful white decoration; even at distance, uniquely *broad white flank stripe diagnostic*. Close-to, white loral patch, white surround to red cheeks, continuing as line down neck and around chest, double white bar on largest wing-coverts, white rump and rear belly all obvious. Juvenile less immaculate, with wider white marks on head. Flight outline has thick-necked look; action agile, allowing easy take-off and considerable speed; formations usually irregular. Walk nimble.
Voice: Shrill, staccato *kee-kwa* or *kik-wik* distinctive, other rather squeaky notes.
Habitat and Range: Normally winters on grassy steppes, being less aquatic than other geese. Vagrant to west Europe (including Britain), associating with White-fronted and (recently) Brent Geese.

EGYPTIAN GOOSE *Alopochen aegyptiacus*   **Plate 96**
Du – Nilgans   Fr – Oie d'Egypte
Ge – Nilgans   Sw – Nilgås
Identification: 27" (68cm). Large, rather long-legged, quarrelsome, aberrant shelduck. Plumage *greyish-buff*, with brown upper-parts and striking *green-black wings with white coverts*; distinctive marks are *dark chestnut eye-patch*, red eye, chestnut rear neck and chestnut belly centre; bill and legs pale pink. Juvenile lacks head marks. Flight outline and action like shelduck's but wings noticeably broad.
Voice: Deep *kek, kek* and other husky, bleating and gabbling calls. Noisy on territory.
Habitat and Range: Freshwater swamps and marshes in home range. Birds introduced to estate waters now feral in E. England; vagrant from Africa to S. Europe.

RUDDY SHELDUCK *Tadorna ferruginea*   **Plate 16, 19, 21**

Du – Casarca   Fr – Tadorne casarca
Ge – Rostgans   Sw – Rostand

Identification: 25" (63cm). Large, rather small-billed, goose-like duck. Plumage *uniform orange-chestnut*, with black bill, *pale head*, green-black flight feathers contrasting with *white fore-wing* (conspicuous in flight), black tail and legs. Male has narrow black collar; female lacks collar and has almost white head. Juvenile like female. Flight and behaviour much as Shelduck but less gregarious. Walks easily.

Confusion species: Beware escaped Cape Shelduck *T. cana*, with grey head but otherwise similar plumage, and Egyptian Goose, which see.

Voice: Loud, nasal *ah-onk*, musical *roo-roo-roo*, also rattles.

Habitat: Much more terrestrial than Shelduck. In winter frequents sandy lake shores, river banks, fields and even arid steppes. Breeds in holes in dunes, cliffs, old trees and walls. Map 44.

SHELDUCK *Tadorna tadorna*   **Plate 16, 19, 21**

Du – Bergeend   Fr – Tadorne de Belon
Ge – Brandente   Sw – Gravand

Identification: 24" (60cm). Large, knob-billed, long-bodied goose-like duck. At distance, looks white and black but close-to, shows red bill (male with prominent knob), *green-black head* and upper-neck, *broad chestnut band around chest* and upper mantle, *black scapulars*, white fore-wing contrasting with black flight feathers, *black line down belly centre*, chestnut-buff under tail, black tail and pink legs. Juvenile shows pink bill, whitish face, ashy-brown back, no chest band and greyish legs. Flight outline and action goose-like, with slower wingbeats than most ducks; flight formation usually linear. Swims well, high on water; walks easily.

Voice: Noisy when breeding, quiet at other times. Quick, nasal, laughing *ak-ak-ak*, deeper, louder *ark, ark*; female calls young with soft twanging note.

Habitat: Sandy and muddy coasts, occasionally inland. Breeds in rabbit burrows, etc., in sand-dunes and on bushy commons. Map 45.

MANDARIN *Aix galericulata*   **Plate 12**

Du – Mandarijneend   Fr – Canard mandarin
Ge – Mandarinente   Sw – Mandarinand

Identification: 17" (43cm). Rather small, large-eyed, long-tailed duck, with *high forehead and maned nape* giving distinctive head shape. Plumage noticeably decorative in both sexes. Male most beautiful of all ducks, with wine-pink bill, glossy bronze-purple-green crown and mane contrasting with *deep orange-white supercilium,* spray of *buff-tipped chestnut feathers below and behind eye*, two white bars around base of dark purple chest, deep vermiculated buff flanks, *orange 'sails' raised high over rear flanks*, white-edged primaries and blackish rump and tail. Contrasting white belly and under-tail obvious in flight. Female mainly olive-grey above and dusky below with blackish bill, *narrow white 'spectacles',* white band down side of bill base joined to white throat and pale-lined and -dappled breast and flanks. Juvenile like female. Flight outline recalls Goldeneye but action lighter. Waddles with low-slung body.

Confusion species: Female and immature easily confused with escaped Wood

Duck *Aix sponsa* (periodically feral in Britain, see plate 96) which has green on rear crown, wider white 'spectacle' and *complete white line round deeper base of bill*. Male Wood Duck has back and body plumage like Mandarin but lacks 'sails'; head pattern different with two white lines along mane and *white cheek-bar and throat interrupting dark green crown and face*.

Voice: Fairly loud, high *tweek*, not unlike Coot; short *hwick* in flight.

Habitat: Usually on wooded inland waters and ornamental ponds. Artificially introduced and now breeding in feral state (in trees) in some parts of England (mainly in SE.), also Scotland, Germany, Denmark, Holland. Feral or escaped vagrant to other parts of Europe.

WIGEON *Anas penelope*   **Plate 12, 19, 21**

Du – Smient   Fr – Canard siffleur
Ge – Pfeifente   Sw – Bläsand

Identification: 18" (45cm). Rather small, *short-billed*, round-headed, compact, low-slung duck, with rather narrow wing-points and pointed tail. Male has broad *yellow crown stripe on bright chestnut head*, pinkish breast, *grey body,* white belly and *black stern;* in flight, *large white panels on wing-coverts* catch eye; in eclipse, like female but more rufous, retaining white on wings. Female and juvenile demure, with grey or rufous ground to plumage, warmest-toned on face and flanks; lack white wing-panels and white-black stern. Bill bluish-grey. Flight outline well-balanced, with rather short, pinched neck, and wings set mid-way; action free, allowing rapid and agile manoeuvres; walk waddling, feeding flocks 'creeping' over sward. Highly gregarious in winter.

Confusion species: Beware escaped Chiloe Wigeon *A. sibitatrix* with green-patched head, and vagrant American Wigeon, which see.

Voice: Characteristic high whistle *whee-oo* given by male; low growl from female.

Habitat: Many maritime in winter, numbers also seen on fresh-water. Breeds on moors, lake islands, marshes. Map 46.

AMERICAN WIGEON *Anas americana*   **Plate 18**

Du – Amerikaanse smient   Fr – Canard siffleur d'Amérique
Ge – Nordamerikanische Pfeifente   Sw – Amerikansk bläsand

Identification: 18-20" (45-50cm). Slightly larger-headed, broader-beamed and longer-tailed than Wigeon. Male has similar plumage plattern to Wigeon but easily distinguished by *white crown stripe,* dark *green panel from eye to nape*, grey-speckled lower head and upper neck, *pinkish-brown back, breast and flanks*. Close-to, shows dark line down base of upper mandible and, in flight, white central wing-coverts and axillaries (latter grey in Wigeon). Female and immature recall Wigeon but as well as dark bill line and white wing lining, have *paler, greyish-white head, coarsely speckled black*, often with dark patch round eye; rather paler, more fulvous or orange body, more coarsely mottled on breast; paler-margined scapulars, tertials and rump; whitish-mottled wing-coverts. Shorter wing-tips do not extend beyond upper tail-coverts. Flight and behaviour as Wigeon.

Confusion species: Variant Wigeon and hybrids between Wigeon and Chiloe Wigeon can closely resemble this species; detailed observation required for certain identification.

Voice: Less incisive than Wigeon, weak *wee, whee-oo.*
Habitat and Range: Habitat preferences as Wigeon. N. American vagrant to W., N. and C. Europe (including Britain).

GADWALL *Anas strepera*   **Plate 12, 19, 21**
Du – Krakeend   Fr – Canard chipeau
Ge – Schnatterente   Sw – Snatterand

Identification: 20" (50cm). Medium-sized, slight but quite compact duck, with rather narrow bill, steep forehead on rather square head, rather short neck and flat or forward sloping back. Both sexes show white belly and *black outer and white inner speculum* but this restricted, even lacking on some females or immatures. Male dusky, with dark grey bill, close-speckled slightly browner head and whitish lower face, densely *black-marbled chest* and *fully black stern*; in eclipse, resembles female but retains chestnut wing-coverts. Female like female Mallard but colder and greyer, especially on plainer head; *orange edges of upper mandible* distinctive (rare on Mallard). Juvenile like female but face more striped and *breast neatly streaked black on orange-buff*; lacks white belly. Flight outline more compact than Mallard but wings more pointed; action freer and escape flight longer. Shy.
Voice: Male utters nasal *argh* or *rrep* call suggesting Corncrake, and wheezy whistle; female's quack higher-pitched than Mallard, with falling diminuendo: *kaaak-kaaak-kak-kak-kak.*
Habitat: Needs shallow fresh-water with dense vegetation for breeding; less cosmopolitan than Mallard, seldom on sea. Map 47.

BAIKAL TEAL *Anas formosa*   **Plate 18**
Du – Siberische taling   Fr – Sarcelle élégante
Ge – Gluckente   Sw – Gulkindad kricka

Identification: 16" (40cm). Largest teal occurring in region, with distinctly *longer wings and body than Teal* most obvious in flight. Male has unmistakable green-black cap and hind-neck contrasting with *creamy face strikingly lined with black from eye to chin*, narrow curving white rear supercilium and neck collar; *long, drooping rufous-black-cream scapulars*; spotted pinkish breast and grey flanks with *white vertical lines 'fore and aft'*; black stern. In flight, upperwing shows buff bar above green, pale-tipped speculum. Female and immature recall Garganey more than Teal, having *bold whitish spot* at base of bill, *pale supercilium* interrupted at eye (emphasizing both dark crown and eye-stripe) and usually shadow of male's vertical cheek line; upper-wing as male but bar above speculum whitish in immature. In flight, under-wing shows *noticeable dark leading edge* and pale belly stands out as in Wigeon. Behaviour Teal-like but flight less swift or erratic.
Voice: Male utters curious deep chuckling *wot-wot* or *proop*, female jerky, wavering quack.
Habitat and Range: Normally in fresh waters of tundra and riverine taiga; occasionally on sea. Vagrant from E. Asia to Europe (including Britain).

TEAL *Anas crecca* **Plate 12, 19, 21**
Du – Wintertaling Fr – Sarcelle d'hiver
Ge – Krickente Sw – Kricka
Identification: 14" (35cm). Smallest, most compact European duck, with relatively large head and fast, almost wader-like flight. At distance, looks small and grey-brown; close-to, duck and immature remain remarkably featureless, lacking distinct face pattern but displaying *broad white bar on greater coverts* above bright green-black speculum in flight and *whitish streak along tail base* at rest. Close-to, male shows *chestnut head* with cream-edged, curving *green eye-patch*, spotted cream-pink breast, conspicuous *horizontal white line along scapulars* and bright cream-buff patches either side of black stern. Male of N. American race *A. c. carolinensis* – so-called Green-winged Teal – has *vertical white line* before grey vermiculated flanks instead of scapular blaze. Flocks pack tight, even in often erratic flight. Dabbles in shallows and water-edge plants.
Voice: Very vocal; male utters low musical *krrit*, female high, harsh quack; feeding flock makes pleasing chuckling chorus of short nasal notes, recalling child's toy squeaker.
Habitat: Reedy pools and streams. In winter, frequents marshes, occasionally estuaries and sea coasts. Breeds on moors, marshes, among bracken in woods often far from open water. Map 48.

MALLARD *Anas platyrhynchos* **Plate 12, 19, 21**
Du – Wilde eend Fr – Canard colvert
Ge – Stockente Sw – Gräsand
Identification: 23" (58cm). Commonest, most widespread surface-feeding duck of region, in many areas producing hybrids with domestic relatives and albinistic individuals. Male unmistakable, with greenish-yellow bill, *glossy dark green head and neck,* white collar, *purplish breast*, pale buff-grey body, black stern with *two curled feathers* over whitish tail; shares with female broad white-edged, *purple speculum* and orange legs. Female and immature mottled brown, with indistinct face pattern and brownish, usually mottled orange bill. Male in eclipse like dark female but retains ruddier chest and darker crown. White under-wing obvious in flight. Flight agile, with quite shallow wing-beats. Female and immature need care to be separated from Gadwall and Pintail, which see.
Voice: Male utters quiet *yeeb*, female loud, far-carrying quack.
Habitat: Almost any water; in winter, also on sea coasts and estuaries. Freely introduced for sport. Nests beneath undergrowth near water, occasionally in holes. Map 49.

BLACK DUCK *Anas rubripes* **Plate 18, 19**
Du – Zwarte eend Fr – Canard obscur
Ge – Dunkelente Sw – Svartand
Identification: 23" (58cm). Size, shape and behaviour as Mallard. Adult plumage basically blackish-brown, with narrow buff 'scalloped' fringes to feathers visible close-to. Male has yellow bill, streaked *greyish supercilium, face and fore-neck*, black-bordered *purple speculum with only thin white trailing edge,* dark tail and orange legs. Female distinguished by duller blackish-olive bill and yellower legs. In flight, displays *most contrasting white wing-lining* of all sur-

face-feeding ducks. Juvenile paler brown and more streaked but still with paler supercilium and face, while lacking ruddy breast, pale, spotted vent and pale-sided tail of young Mallard.

Confusion species: Beware dark variants of Mallard and hybrids between Black Duck and with Mallard, latter frequent in N. America and produced by vagrants to Britain; certain identification depends on full observation of speculum and tail colours.

Voice: As Mallard.

Habitat and Range: Close relative of Mallard from N. America, wandering across Atlantic to N., C. and W. Europe (including Britain).

PINTAIL *Anas acuta*   **Plate 12, 19, 21**
   Du – Pijlstaart   Fr – Canard pilet
   Ge – Spiessente   Sw – Stjärtand

Identification: 22-26" (55-65cm). Body size as Wigeon but lengthy neck and tail produce elegant attenuated shape unique to species, with male's tail ending in needle-point. Male has *dark chocolate-brown head and throat*, interrupted near hind neck by white streak which leads into *conspicuous white fore-neck, breast* and belly; vermiculated grey body, with long black and white scapulars, white, then black stern and white-edged tail. Like female, has narrow green-black speculum, broadly edged white, and fawn under-wing with dark leading edge. Female and immature less striking, with speckled, spotted and scalloped *dun-brown plumage*, looking more evenly coloured on head than other ducks but, close-to, show pale eye-ring and throat. Usually distinguishable from other female ducks by thinner, more coiled or extended neck and elongated tail, also by grey bill (unlike Mallard and Gadwall), *pale wing-bars* with broad lower one compressing dull speculum (unlike Wigeon) and paler primaries. Long-tailed Duck also has long pin-tail but is maritime diving species, with white patched head and all-dark wings.

Voice: Seldom vocal: male utters low whistle recalling male Teal, female low quack and growl.

Habitat: Common in northern Europe, elsewhere chiefly coastal or on flooded washes in winter. As Wigeon in breeding season, but also nests in sand-dunes. Map 50.

GARGANEY *Anas querquedula*   **Plate 12, 19, 21**
   Du – Zomertaling   Fr – Sarcelle d'été
   Ge – Knäkente   Sw – Årta

Identification: 15" (38cm). Little larger than Teal but shape differs in *straighter bill*, steeper forehead, *flatter crown* and slimmer, longer neck; looks less compact in flight and carries tail higher on water. Flying male shows distinctive *pale lavender-grey fore-wing* and dark brown head and breast contrasting with white belly. At rest, male easily identified by conspicuous *white band curving from eye to nape* and long black and white scapulars drooping over grey flanks and *spotted stern*; retains pale fore-wing in otherwise female-like eclipse plumage. Female and immature have distinctly lined head, with obvious *dusky cheek bar*, in addition to dark crown and eye-stripe; fore-wing duller than male but has *indistinct speculum bordered white*, particularly on trailing edge; primaries look pale (like Pintail, not Teal). In flight, leading edge of under-wing

darker than Teal. Flight rapid and agile, with longer-necked outline than Teal.
Behaviour and feeding habits closer to Shoveler than Teal. Female and immature can suggest Baikal Teal, which see.
Voice: Male utters peculiar dry rattle or grating croak, female rather short
quack.
Habitat: Much as Teal, but seldom on salt water. Breeds in long grass or rank
vegetation near water. Map 51.

BLUE-WINGED TEAL *Anas discors*   Plate 18
Du – Blauwvleugeltaling   Fr – Sarcelle soucrourou
Ge – Blauflügelente   Sw – Amerikansk årta

Identification: 15" (38cm). Size as Garganey but shape closer to Teal, though
bill longer and straighter. At distance, looks even darker than Teal but *fully blue
fore-wing* shows well in flight. Close-to, male distinguished by *dusky head with
striking white crescent* around front, evenly spotted brownish chest and flanks
and bold white, then black stern. Female and immature suggest Teal before Garganey, separated by combination of *whitish spot at base of bill*, more defined
pale supercilium, *broken white eye-ring;* narrow dark eye-stripe, more evenly
spotted fore under-parts, *uniformly dark speculum* (lacking pale trailing bar),
and *yellowish legs* (grey in Teal and Garganey). Flight and behaviour as Teal.
Likes small quiet waters.
Confusion species: Beware escaped Cinnamon Teal *A. cyanoptera* with similar fore-wing colour: adult noticeably cinnamon and plain-faced but immature
confusingly darker, best distinguished by longer, even straighter, more spatulate
bill, finer marks on breast and solid, darker centres to rear flanks.
Voice: Male has short squeaking note; female quacks faintly.
Habitat and Range: In winter frequents large marshes, rice fields, small
ponds. Breeds around fresh-water ponds. Vagrant from N. America to W. (including Britain), N. C. and S. Europe.

SHOVELER *Anas clypeata*   Plate 12, 19, 21
Du – Slobeend   Fr – Canard souchet
Ge – Löffelente   Sw – Skedand

Identification: 20" (50cm). Dumpy, neckless surface-feeding duck with *disproportionately long and spatulate bill* pulling head down; often raised wing-
points add to front-heavy appearance. In flight, *pale blue fore-wing* is
emphasized by broad white bar on greater coverts but green-black speculum
lacks pale trailing edge. At distance, male has unique pattern: *dark-white-dark-
white-dark;* close-to, pattern consists of *blackish bill, dark green head* and fore-
neck, white shoulders and chest, *chestnut body*, and white, then black stern, with
pale tail and *bright orange legs.* Female and immature patterned and coloured
like bright Mallard but long bill has characteristic orange sides. Male has staring
yellow eye. Flight outline distinctive, with disproportionately long bill and head
and rather short, pointed wings appearing set far back; action fast and agile.
Voice: Breeding male utters gruff, nasal *sluck-uck* or *took, took*; female answer-
s with disyllabic quack *pe-eff*, also calls *tuk, tuk* in flight.
Habitat: Usually in marshes and overgrown ponds; rarely on sea. Breeds in
water-meadows, marshes, wet bushy commons. Map 52.

MARBLED DUCK *Marmaronetta angustirostris*   **Plate 12**
Du – Marmereend   Fr – Sarcelle marbrée
Ge – Marmelente   Sw – Marmorand
Identification: 17" (43cm). Size close to Garganey but with longer bill, head and particularly neck. Sluggish, retiring duck; mainly pale dun-brown, *spotted and dappled off-white;* close-to, shows white lower face, *dusky eye-patch,* and white-ended tail. Male slightly maned on nape. Juvenile creamier below and much less dappled. In flight, dun-white secondaries catch eye. Flight outline differs from Teal in *long neck*; action slower, with less springing take-off.
Voice: Male has low wheezing croak; female feeble quack.
Habitat and Range: Fresh-water species, preferring overgrown to open water. Nests near water, along stream banks, etc. Summer visitor S. Spain, has occasionally bred elsewhere in S. Europe, otherwise vagrant to S., C. and E. Europe.

RED-CRESTED POCHARD *Netta rufina*   **Plate 13, 20, 22**
Du – Krooneend   Fr – Nette rousse
Ge – Kolbenente   Sw – Rödhuvad dykand
Identification: 22" (55cm). Large, round-headed, quite long-necked duck, with habits mixing those of surface-feeding and diving ducks. Male has crested *'flaming' orange-brown head*, black neck, under-body and stern, brown back and *white flanks*, with unique combination of long, *slightly upturned red bill and red legs*. In flight, long *broad white wing-bar* more obvious than in any other duck. Female rather uniform dull brown except for pink-banded, grey bill, *whitish lower head and throat*, white vent and reddish legs; recalls female Common Scoter but latter has no wing-bar. Flight outline less compact than other diving ducks, with bull head and longer neck; action less whirring. Rides high on water.
Voice: Male utters hard wheezing note; female harsh *kurr*.
Habitat: Large reedy fresh-water lakes or brackish lagoons, seldom on sea. Breeds among vegetation on islands in lagoons. Frequently excapes from collections in W. Europe. Map 53.

POCHARD *Aythya ferina*   **Plate 13, 22**
Du – Tafeleend   Fr – Fuligule milouin
Ge – Tafelente   Sw – Brunand
Identification: 18" (45cm). Medium-sized diving duck, second commonest of tribe in Europe, with high crown and *sloping profile ending in scoop-like bill* and characteristic dull wings with *pale grey, not white bar*. Male distinguished by *bright chestnut head*, black breast, *uniform pale grey back and body* and black stern. Pattern of bill with large *pale blue-grey patch* between black tip and dusky base important, as lacking in frequent Pochard-like hybrids. In eclipse, male like female but greyer above. Female basically brown-headed and -breasted, with body paler and greyer in winter, but almost uniform in summer, relieved by generally dappled look, paler chin and *whitish spectacle*. Flight outline lengthier than Tufted but action similar. Relatively inactive during day, resting on water, rarely on shore; feeds at dawn and dusk.
Confusion species: Canvasback similarly coloured but larger (see Accidentals); Redhead *A. americana* is another potential vagrant to Europe from N. America but male has darker back with yellow eye; lacks Pochard's patched bill.

Voice: Usually silent. Male utters hoarse wheezing *bhee-bhee* when courting and nasal whistle; female harsh growling *krrah, krrah.*
Habitat: Seldom on sea. Frequents large and small lakes, backwaters, etc. Breeds in dense reeds. Map 54.

RING-NECKED DUCK   *Aythya collaris*   Plate 18

Du – Amerikaanse kuifeend   Fr – Fuligule à bec cerclé
Ge – Halsringente   Sw – Ringand

Identification: 17" (43cm). Size as Tufted but shape differs in Pochard-like bill, *very high rear crown with short crest 'bump'* and deep flanks with remarkable 'S' shaped outline. Male recalls Tufted but *flanks pale grey with white peak and line at breast*; striking pattern of bill important as combination of narrow white surround of grey base, white subterminal and black terminal bands is diffused in hybrids. In flight, *grey wing-bar* not as striking as Tufted. Female Pochard-like, with similar seasonal change in plumage tone; distinguished by more obvious pale surround to bill, rather pale cheeks, *white eye-ring,* darker breast and under tail coverts. Flight and behaviour as Tufted.
Voice: Male has low, wheezy whistle; female growls.
Habitat and Range: Marshes, estuaries, sheltered bays. Vagrant from N. America to W. (including Britain), N. and C. Europe.

FERRUGINOUS DUCK   *Aythya nyroca*   Plate 13, 20, 22

Du – Witoogeend   Fr – Fuligule nyroca
Ge – Moorente   Sw – Vitögd dykand

Identification: 16" (41cm). Rather small diving duck with longish bill and high rear crown giving longer, *less rounded head* than Tufted Duck. Both sexes look neat and dark, with *pure white under tail-coverts* and *broad, curved white wing bar.* Male has copper-glossed, *mahogany head and chest*, with *prominent white eye.* Eclipse male and female lack copper gloss and white eye but share almost black back and rufous flanks. Juvenile like female but chest mottled. Rides higher on water than Tufted Duck, often with tail slightly cocked. Wing-bar and white belly obvious in flight.
Confusion species: Beware female or juvenile Tufted Ducks with partly or wholly white under tail-coverts and hybrids between them and Pochard.
Voice: Quiet *tuk-tuk-tuk* and low growling notes.
Habitat: Similar to Pochard. Map 55.

TUFTED DUCK   *Aythya fuligula*   Plate 13, 20, 22

Du – Kuifeend   Fr – Fuligule morillon
Ge – Reiherente   Sw – Vigg

Identification: 17" (43cm). Commonest fresh-water diving duck; small, compact, with rather short bill, *markedly round head with thin 'pigtail'* (long and drooping in male; shorter, more crest-like in female), and long white wing-bar. Male *black with bold white flanks*; eclipse male and female dusky-brown, with slightly paler flanks; when worn, female has whitish Scaup-like patch at bill base. Juvenile browner than female. Packs densely; flies in close formation.
Confusion species: Pochard and Ring-necked Duck separated by bill and head shape and plumage colours, Scaup by broader bill and head, larger size and paler back, Ferruginous Duck by bill and head shape and pure white under tail coverts.

Voice: Male babbles softly in courtship; female growls like female Pochard.
Habitat: Seldom on sea. Frequents large and small lakes, often joining tame ducks in parks. Breeds, often sociably, on lakes and ponds. Map 56.

SCAUP *Aythya marila*   **Plate 13, 20**
   Du – Toppereend   Fr – Fuligule milouinan
   Ge – Bergente   Sw – Bergand
Identification: 19" (48cm). Marine diving duck; quite large, *broad-beamed*, heavy-looking, with broad bill, ball-like head and bold white wing bar. Distant male *black at both ends, white in the middle*; close-to, back pale grey and bill pale blue-grey. Eclipse male and female recall Tufted Duck but male paler-backed, while female always has *large white patch at base of bill*. Juvenile best told by size and structure. Lesser Scaup noticeably smaller (see Accidentals). Rides rough water well, diving expertly. Flies in close irregular packs or lines.
Voice: Seldom vocal. Male has soft crooning courtship notes. Female has low harsh *karr-karr*.
Habitat: Maritime except when breeding; usually in bays and estuaries. Breeds sociably on lake islands. Map 57.

EIDER *Somateria mollissima*   **Plate 15, 20, 22**
   Du – Eidereend   Fr – Eider à duvet
   Ge – Eiderente   Sw – Ejder
Identification: 23" (58cm). Largest sea-duck, commonest of tribe, with greater body bulk than any other relative, *long sloping bill and head profile* (see diagram Pl. 15) and distinctive flight. Male only duck with *white back and fore-wing over black belly*, latter also contrasting with pinkish-white breast; greyish bill runs into white face and *black fore-crown*; rear cheeks and *nape patched pale green;* black stern decorated with large white spot. Immature and eclipse male show bewildering range of patchy plumages; at first, resemble female which is shaped like male but has brown plumage, closely barred dark brown and black. Lacks true speculum but female has white central and buff trailing wing-bars. Male of vagrant arctic race *S. m. borealis* has orange-yellow bill. Head shape and bulk prevent confusion with scoters but female eiders difficult to separate (see following species). Flight outline distinctive, with bill and head held out rather low; action rather slow, with regular padding wing-beats; formation usually linear. Stands up; waddles. Gregarious.
Voice: Vocal but not noisy; male gives low soft pleasing croon *coo-roo-uh*, second syllable rising and stressed, female growls with grating *cor-r-r*.
Habitat: Strongly maritime, including rocky coasts. Breeds along coasts; locally inland around lakes, or on river islands. Map 58.

KING EIDER *Somateria spectabilis*   **Plate 15, 20, 22**
   Du – Koningseidereend   Fr – Eider à tête grise
   Ge – Prachteiderente   Sw – Praktejder
Identification: 22" (55cm). Large, rather round-headed eider, more compact and slightly shorter-billed than Eider. Distant male shows white fore-parts on almost wholly *black body*, lacking Eider's white back; close-to, short orange bill swells upwards into *large orange shield* ahead of *pearl-grey crown and pendant nape* and greenish face; large white fore-wing panel shows as horizontal line

over flanks; round white spot on stern. Eclipse and immature male plumages vary as Eider. Distant female more rufous than most Eiders but safely identified only by shorter bill and forehead profile, giving softer outline; close-to, shows diagnostic *forward extension of feathering onto culmen* (see diagram Pl. 15), pale eye-ring (not dull supercilium of Eider), pendant nape, pale throat and more delicate body markings, with *more crescentic bars on breast and flanks*, bolder spots on scapulars and pale drooping tertials. Flight outline slightly more compact and action somewhat quicker than Eider.

Voice: Male's croon more vibrant than Eider; female utters grunting croak, recalling surface-feeding duck; also rapid gabble.

Habitat and Range: As Eider but usually breeds fairly sociably by fresh-water ponds on tundra. In summer, non-breeding N. Norway, Iceland. Winters on N. Norwegian coast south to Arctic Circle, Faeroes, Iceland. Vagrant elsewhere in N., W. (including Britain), C. and S. Europe.

STELLER'S EIDER *Polysticta stelleri*   **Plate 15**

Du – Steller's eidereend   Fr – Eider de Steller
Ge – Scheckente   Sw – Alförrädare

Identification: 18" (45cm). Compact seaduck, in size close to Goldeneye with *small, thick, slightly drooping bill* (see diagram Pl. 15), rather square head and noticeably long tertials and tail, last usually held clear of water. Male unmistakable, with *white head* spotted green and black at eye and on nape, black chin and throat, *black necklace* joined to hind neck, black back centre, *black and white drooping scapulars and tertials* and black stern, contrasting with *rufous breast and body,* with *black spot below shoulder.* Eclipse male almost uniform sooty, except for *white inner-wing with deep purple-blue speculum.* Female and immature dusky buff-brown, streaked above and barred below, with pale eye-ring, white-bordered speculum and *striking white under-wing.* Flight outline and action unlike Eider, most recalling Scoter; wing-beats produce whistling sound.

Voice: Rather silent, particularly in male; female growls and barks.

Habitat and Range: Winters along rocky northern coasts. Breeds on tundra. In winter N. Norway (may have bred) and Baltic. Vagrant elsewhere in N., C. and W. Europe (including Britain).

HARLEQUIN *Histrionicus histrionicus*   **Plate 16, 22**

Du – Harlekijneend   Fr – Garrot arlequin
Ge – Kragenente   Sw – Strömand

Identification: 17" (43cm). Small, buoyant, short-billed and -necked sea-duck, with pointed tail. Male has dark blue-grey plumage (looks black at distance) with chestnut flanks and *bizarre pattern of white spots and streaks* on head, neck and breast. Has same flight-silhouette as Goldeneye, but is *uniformly dark below.* In eclipse, male distinguished from female by dark slate-grey upper-parts and lack of white on breast. Female uniformly dark brown with mottled brown and whitish breast; pattern of *two indistinct white spots in front of eye, one bright white spot behind eye* distinctive. Flight action fast, almost Teal-like. Swims buoyantly, jerking head constantly, often cocking tail. Likes to dive in rough surf.

Confusion species: Distinguished from female Velvet and Surf Scoters by small size, small bill; female and immature easily confused with young Long-tailed which, however, is much whiter on belly.

Voice: Usually silent, but male has short quiet whistle. Female croaks harshly.
Habitat: Winters along steep coasts with plenty of submerged rocks. Breeds socially on islands in swift rivers, usually near rough water or waterfalls. Resident Iceland. Vagrant elsewhere in N., W. (including Britain), C. and S. Europe.

LONG-TAILED DUCK *Clangula hyemalis*   Plate 16, 20, 22

Du – IJseend   Fr – Harelde de Miquelon
Ge – Eisente   Sw – Alfågel
N. Am. – Old Squaw

Identification: 16" (40cm), but adult male with long tail streamers 21" (53cm). Small-billed, round-headed, quite delicate sea-duck, with *uniformly dark wings* and *long pointed tail*. Breeding male blackish-brown, with bold *grey- white eye-patch*, grey-edged scapulars and *striking white under- body* and tail side; winter male becomes *white on head and neck*, leaving only greyish eye patch joined to *dark brown lower cheek*, and wholly white on scapulars. Female and immature far less striking and more variably patterned than male, with dark crown, *pale face and neck with dark cheek patch*, dusky breast, brown upper-parts and mottled buff-white body. Breeding female may be almost as dark as male; but pointed tail lacks streamers. Flight outline rather pheasant-like though wings have characteristic triangular shape; action free but beats of down-curved wings, restricted, being mostly below line of back and producing characteristic *swinging, side-to side progress* in which first dark upper-, then white under-surface shows. Swims buoyantly, diving bravely into rough seas. Pintail also long-tailed but rarely at sea; has much longer neck and shows prominent wing-bars.
Voice: Noisy. Male has lively call of about four loud yodelling notes, giving musical goose-like effect from distant flock. Female has low barking note.
Habitat: Mainly maritime except in breeding season. Nests on lake islands, in tundra, or among arctic scrub. Map 59.

COMMON SCOTER *Melanitta nigra*   Plate 14, 20, 22

Du – Zwarte zeeeend   Fr – Macreuse noire
Ge – Trauerente   Sw – Sjöorre

Identification: 19" (48cm). Squat sea duck, commonest of tribe, with shortish bill, thick neck and rather long, pointed tail often raised. Male only *entirely black* duck, relieved only by bright orange-yellow patch before black bill knob and *'shining' silvery grey under-surface to flight feathers*. Vagrant N. American race *M. n. americana* has smaller knob and whole of bill base orange-yellow. Female and immature dark brown, with scalloped flanks, whitish belly and *pale greyish face and throat contrasting with blackish crown*, quite unlike face pattern of other scoters. Legs grey. Flight outline compact, with round head on rather narrow neck and tubby body; action strong and rapid, allowing direct progress even into gale; formation wavering line or close pack. Swims buoyantly. Gregarious.
Voice: Male has variety of melodious, cooing notes and a rapid tittering cry. Female growls harshly.
Habitat: Chiefly maritime except in breeding season, but prefers quieter water than Velvet Scoter. Breeds around lakes on high moors or tundra. Map 60.

SURF SCOTER *Melanitta perspicillata*   **Plate 14, 20, 22**
Du – Brilzeeeend   Fr – Macreuse à lunettes
Ge – Brillenente   Sw – Vitnackad svärta
Identification: 21" (53cm). Size between Common and Velvet but with more Eider-like bill and head profile and even tubbier body. Male black except for *white patches on forehead and nape* and *striking yellow and white bill*, with black spot and red border at base. In flight, under surfaces of flight feathers paler than coverts but do not 'shine' like Common. Female and immature duskybrown, with variable pale spots before eye and on rear cheeks (and greyish nape in some females); recall Velvet but lack white secondaries. Legs orange, unlike Common. Flight and behaviour as Common.
Voice: Seldom vocal: male gurgles, female crows.
Habitat and Range: Maritime outside breeding season. Vagrant from N. America to W. (including Britain annually), N. and C. Europe.

VELVET SCOTER *Melanitta fusca*   **Plate 14, 20, 22**
Du – Grote zeeeend   Fr – Macreuse brune
Ge – Samtente   Sw – Svärta
Identification: 23" (58cm). Largest scoter, with *long, pointed bill* (swollen in male), lengthy head but rather short tail; *diagnostic white secondaries* conspicuous in flight but sometimes hidden on sea. Male otherwise black except for yellow sides to bill, *white streak at eye* and reddish-orange legs. Female and immature otherwise dusky, with variable pale spots before eye and on rear cheeks and mottled underbody. Flight is more powerful, yet looks slower than Common. Usually seen in singles or small parties; often mixes with Eiders.
Voice: Much less vocal than Common Scoter. Male's usual note whistled *whur-er*; female growls harshly.
Habitat: As Common Scoter, but often seen in rougher water. Breeding places vary from offshore islands and open tundra to undergrowth in northern forests. Map 61.

BARROW'S GOLDENEYE *Bucephala islandica*   **Plate 13**
Du – Ijslandse brilduiker   Fr – Garrot d'Islande
Ge – Spatelente   Sw – Islandsknipa
Identification: 21" (53cm). Larger, heavier-built than Goldeneye, with deeper stubbier bill, steeper forehead and more pendant or ragged mane. Plumage pattern and colours similar to Goldeneye but breeding male has *purple-glossed head with white crescent* (not spot) by bill, *white scapular spots* (not lines) and extension of black back downwards past shoulder; female has darker head and yellower, sometimes all-yellow bill. In flight, male's inner wing shows thicker black leading edge than Goldeneye and *black bar above secondaries* lacking in Goldeneye. Flight action and behaviour as Goldeneye; wing-beats produce quieter whistling sound.
Voice: Male utters grunting *ka-kaa* and click in courtship; female croaking growl *grr-gärr*.
Habitat and Range: N. American species with outpost of primarily resident birds in Iceland, breeding on fresh waters. Vagrant to N., W. and C. Europe.

GOLDENEYE *Bucephala clangula*   **Plate 13, 20, 22**
Du – Brilduiker   Fr – Garrot à oeil d'or
Ge   Schellente   Sw – Knipa

Identification: 18" (45cm). Medium-sized, rather short-billed, *triangular-headed* duck, with rear body sloping into water; in flight shows large *square, white wing-patches on inner wing*. Breeding male has black *green-glossed head with bold white spot* before yellow eye, black back and stern, *white-lined scapulars* combining with white neck, breast and body to give impression of high flanks. Eclipse male retains blacker head and whiter chest than female, which has yellow-tipped, black bill, *rich chocolate-brown head, white collar*, rather uniform dusky-grey back and body, pale mottled on flanks and usually showing white secondaries over rear flanks. Immature browner than female, without pale collar. Flight outline dominated by large head on short neck; action rapid, with wing-beats particularly of male producing loud whistling or singing sound. Gregarious. Often with Scaup; see also Barrow's Goldeneye.
Voice: Usually silent except in display when male utters harsh nasal disyllable and female answers with *Aythya*-like note.
Habitat: Coastal waters, also now regularly on inland waters and rivers. Breeds in holes in trees, rabbit burrows, etc., along river banks and around wooded lakes. Map 62.

SMEW *Mergus albellus*   **Plate 17, 19, 21**
Du – Nonnetje   Fr – Harle piette
Ge – Zwergsäger   Sw – Salskrake

Identification: 16" (41cm). Small 'saw billed' duck, recalling Goldeneye as much as relatives but with distinctive plumage and short crest on rear crown; bill shortest and deepest of tribe. Male beautiful; at distance looks *snow-white with black eye* but close-to shows also black base to crest, black back, narrow black tracings above flanks and towards centre and lower edge of breast, fine grey vermiculations on flanks and grey stern. In flight, shows white scapulars and panel across fore-wing and narrow white bars above and on tips of *dark secondaries*. Female and immature have *red-chestnut crown* and nape, with blackish fore-face contrasting with *white cheeks and throat*, dusky back and stern and grey breast and flanks. Beware occasional hybrid with Goldeneye. Flight outline much more compact than other 'saw-bills'; action faster, with rapid wing-beats producing swinging side-to-side progress. Sociable.
Voice: Usually silent, except for low, grating *uk-uk-uk*. Male also has weak whistling note. Female notes as female Goosander.
Habitat: Lakes, reservoirs and rivers, occasionally in estuaries and along coasts. Nests in hollow trees near water. Map 63.

RED-BREASTED MERGANSER *Mergus serrator*   **Plate 17, 19, 21**
Du – Middelste zaagbek   Fr – Harle huppé
Ge – Mittelsäger   Sw – Småskrake

Identification: 23" (58cm). Very narrow-billed, *ragged- headed*, long-bodied, fish-eating duck, equally at home on fast rivers or coastal waters. Breeding male colourful, with red bill, red eye on *green-black head,* white neck-collar, *streaked chestnut breast*, black back with *white-chequered feathers at shoulder*, white scapulars, and long grey flanks. In flight, shows white greater coverts and secondaries divided by black bar. Female and immature have *orange-brown head* with faint black and whitish loral streaks and indistinctly paler chin, merging into dusky upper-parts; lack cleanliness of Goosander's plumage pattern. Flight outline skinny, with straight bill, head and neck extended from long slim body; action fast and even, with strong wing-beats. Swims low in water and dives expertly. Gregarious.

Voice: Usually silent: male utters rasping disyllable in courtship; female barks *prrak, prrak*.

Habitat: Chiefly maritime outside breeding season. Breeds in heather, vegetation among rocks, etc., by wooded lakes or rivers, on islands in sea lochs and in tundra. Map 64.

GOOSANDER *Mergus merganser*   **Plate 17, 19, 21**

Du – Grote zaagbek   Fr – Harle bièvre
Ge – Gänsesäger   Sw – Storskrake

Identification: 26" (66cm). Shape close to Red-breasted Merganser but noticeably longer- and broader-bodied, with *maned*, not ragged head. Breeding male has red bill, *large glossy green-black head*, black mantle, white neck, scapulars and body, with pale *salmon-pink flush from breast to flanks*, and grey stern. In flight, shows fully white greater coverts and secondaries. Female and immature differ from Red-breasted Merganser in *chestnut head* contrasting strongly with *white throat* and pale grey neck and white breast, almost uniform grey back, flanks and stern. Flight outline lengthy but not skinny; action quite fast and even, with strong wing-beats; less agile in air than Red-breasted Merganser. Swims higher in water than Red-breasted Merganser. Sociable.

Voice: Usually silent. Male has double croaking note; female guttural *karr*.

Habitat: Winters on large rivers, lakes, reservoirs. Breeds in hollow trees, holes in peat banks, etc., usually among trees near water, also beyond tree limit in north. Map 65.

RUDDY DUCK *Oxyura jamaicensis*   **Plate 17, 18**

Du – Zwartkopeend   Fr – Erismature à tête noire
Ge – Schwarzkopf-Ruderente   Sw – Amerikansk kopparand

Identification: 16" (40cm). Smaller than White-headed, with less swollen bill, relatively larger head and much shorter 'stiff-tail'. Male easily distinguished by blue bill, *full black cap down to eye level*, bright white cheeks and throat, blackish breast, *ruddy back and body* and black tail. In flight, small wings unpatterned dusky. Female and immature dusky brown, mottled on breast and on greyish or buff face, with *indistinct brown bar across cheeks* Flight outline short, with blunt head, short wings and narrow stern; action whirring. Gregarious in winter. Beware hybrids with White-headed Duck in Spain.

Voice: Usually silent. Displaying male makes low chuckling *chuck-uck-uck-ur-r-r*.

Habitat: Fresh-water ponds, marshes. In winter also on large reservoirs. Escaped birds of N. American species feral in Britain and becoming so in Netherlands, France and Spain. Vagrant elsewhere in W., N., S. and C. Europe.

WHITE-HEADED DUCK *Oxyura leucocephala*   **Plate 17**
  Du – Witkopeend   Fr – Erismature à tête blanche
  Ge – Ruderente   Sw – Kopparand
Identification: 18" (45cm). Only native 'stiff-tail' duck of Europe, with *extraordinary shape* most obvious in swollen bill, deep head, round plump body, short triangular wings and *remarkable long, pointed tail,* often vertically cocked. Male has blue bill, *white head with black crown centre* and hind-neck, ruddy breast and upper tail-coverts, *faintly orange-brown, vermiculated back and body* and blackish tail. Female and immature duller, with fully black head cap, *distinct dark band across off-white face* broadest under eye, and stronger vermiculation. Wings uniformly dusky. Flight outline as Ruddy but longer, with thinner tail; action similar but takes to air less frequently. Beware hybrids with Ruddy in Spain.
Voice: Silent except when breeding: male grunts, purrs and pipes; female purrs to young.
Habitat: Reedy inland waters and brackish lagoons. Nests among reeds and aquatic vegetation near water. Map 66.

KITES, VULTURES, HARRIERS, HAWKS, BUZZARDS, EAGLES: Accipitridae

Kites: Long-winged, small-headed and fork-tailed raptors, with buoyant, loose-tailed flight; often at carrion; tree-nesting; sexes similar.
Vultures: Large to huge, long and broad-winged raptors, with naked heads,

Basic Flight Silhouettes of the Accipitridae

Harriers; long wings, long tail

Falcons; pointed wings, narrow tail

Buzzards; broad wing, broad rounded tail

Accipiters; short rounded wings, long tail

short tails and weak feet incapable of killing grip; usually dependent on carrion. Flight effortless, gliding between heavy flaps; cliff and tree-nesting; sexes similar.
Harriers: Medium-sized, slender, long-tailed raptors, with owl-like heads, long wings raised in shallow V during wavering glides. Quarter ground, pouncing on prey; ground or reed nesting; sexes dissimilar.
Hawks: Small to large, round-winged and long-tailed raptors, females noticeably larger than males; flight dashing and agile. Hunt by using cover to surprise mainly bird prey; tree-nesting; sexes dissimilar.
Buzzards: Large, broad-winged and full-tailed raptors, with relatively smaller bills and heads than eagles. Soar in sky, pounce from perch or hover onto prey but chiefly eat carrion; cliff and tree-nesting; sexes similar.
Eagles: Large to very large, long-winged raptors, with prominent bills and heads; cliff and tree-nesting; sexes similar. Soar majestically; hunting varies but usually more aerial and aggressive than buzzard.
Exceptions to above are highly specialised Honey Buzzard, Black-shouldered Kite, Lammergeier, Short-toed Eagle, Booted Eagle and Bonelli's Eagle; see texts.

HONEY BUZZARD *Pernis apivorus*   **Plate 26, 27**

Du – Wespendief   Fr – Bondrée apivore
Ge – Wespenbussard   Sw – Bivråk

Identification: 20-23" (51-59cm). Rather kite-like, with flight outline differing from *Buteo* buzzards in *pigeon-like head* on narrower neck, *narrow-based wings* usually showing protruding carpal joints and rather straight trailing edges, and *longer tail* held closed when gliding and then showing *convex sides*. Soars less than Buzzard except on migration, never hovers; *glides on wings depressed from carpal joints*. Plumage pattern and colours variable but all adults show *strongly cross-barred under wing- coverts* and flight feathers, full *dark rim to wing* formed by dark 'finger-tips' to primaries (short on male, long on female) and dark tips to secondaries and three *dark tail bars, two near base, one at end*. Male has *ash-grey head*, greyish-brown upper-parts and usually heavily barred under-parts; female browner on head and back; both may have dark, rarely white under-parts. Immature also variable but, compared to adult are typically darker brown; all show longer dark 'fingers', *darker secondaries and more evenly barred tail*; some have white or rufous head and ground to streaked under-parts. Far less predatory than *Buteo* buzzards, feeding on wasp and bee larvae, sometimes mice, small birds and eggs. Migrates in large streams but can be inconspicuous when breeding.
Voice: Call clear musical, melancholy *peelu* or *kee-er* unlike Buzzard's mew; also rapid *kikiki*.
Habitat: Open glades or outskirts of woods. Usually builds on old nest of crow. Map 67.

BLACK-SHOULDERED KITE *Elanus caeruleus*   **Plate 24**

Du – Grijze wouw   Fr – Elanion blanc
Ge – Gleitaar   Sw – Svartvingad glada

Identification: 13" (33cm). Size close to Kestrel but has large, rather harrier-like head, long but broad-based wings and *short, notched tail*. Plumage distinctive with *white head* relieved by red eye in dark 'pit', pale grey upper-parts and wings, *black 'shoulders' and under-surface to primaries* and white under-body, wing lining and tail. Immature less immaculate, with pale-scaled, grey-brown upper-parts and lightly streaked, rufous-tinged under-parts. Behaviour not at all kite-like, combining swift, owl-like wing-beats, *harrier-like glides* on raised wings and rather *ponderous hovering*. Feeds mainly on small rodents and large insects. Often crepuscular.

Voice: Weak, whistling *gree-er*.

Habitat and Range: Cultivated areas with scattered trees, or woodland glades, forest edges, etc. Nests fairly low in trees. Resident Portugal and Spain. Vagrant elsewhere in S., W., C. and E. Europe.

BLACK KITE *Milvus migrans*   **Plate 24, 25**
Du – Zwarte wouw   Fr – Milan noir
Ge – Schwarzer Milan   Sw – Brunglada

Identification: 22" (56cm). Commonest of Europe's kites, shorter and scruffier than Red Kite, often suggesting dark Marsh Harrier. Well seen, quickly distinguished from Red Kite by *much less forked tail*, which when spread is virtually straight-ended; also by slightly shorter, relatively broader wings and *much darker, duller plumage*, relieved above only by paler panel across leading inner wing-coverts and below, particularly in immature, by paler inner primaries, vent and under-tail. Flight and feeding habits like Red Kite but also takes dead fish from water. Where numerous, flocks quickly gather at carrion.

Confusion species: Distinguished from typical female or immature Marsh Harrier by *lack of cream head and 'shoulders'* and level, not shallow V wing attitude when gliding.

Voice: Very noisy in breeding season; a thin, quavering, gull-like squeal, sometimes followed by chatter.

Habitat: In western range usually near lakes or rivers, in areas with woods or scattered trees. In south and east of range more frequently in drier localities and villages. Nests, often sociably, in trees, occasionally on old nest of crow. Map 68.

RED KITE *Milvus milvus*   **Plate 24, 25**
Du – Rode wouw   Fr – Milan royal
Ge – Roter Milan   Sw – Glada

Identification: 24" (60cm). Elegant, long-winged and deeply fork-tailed, with buoyant and agile flight on angled wings sustained by deep wing-beats and effortless soaring; droops head and continually *twists tail* in flight. In good light, adult shows *streaked whitish head*, red-brown upper-parts, *dark-streaked rufous under-parts*, tri-coloured wings with rufous leading coverts, *brilliant white bases to primaries* contrasting with long black 'fingers' and dusky greater coverts and secondaries. Tail *pale orange-chestnut*, faintly barred and dark-tipped on fork ends. Immature duller, with brownish head and stronger barring on flight-feathers. Partial to carrion but also preys on rabbits and small birds. Easily distinguished from Black Kite by more colourful and contrasting plumage and more attenuated silhouette, particularly always clearly forked tail.

Voice: Call drawn-out, piping whistle, rising and falling *hi-hi-heea* or *pee-oo-ee-oo-ee-oo*.

Habitat: Usually in wooded hills, but also locally in lowlands and open country with scattered trees. Nests in trees, occasionally on old nest of crow. Map 69.

WHITE-TAILED EAGLE *Haliaeetus albicilla*   **Plate 28, 29**
Du – Zeearend   Fr – Pygargue à queue blanche
Ge – Seeadler   Sw – Havsörn
Identification: 32-38" (80-95cm). Largest, most vulture-like of European
eagles, with long, deep bill on heavy, projecting head and neck, *broad rectangular wings* and *short wedge-shaped tail*. Soars on *level wings*, travels by *slow, shallow wing-beats*, interspersed by glides on slightly arched wings; flight much more active when fishing, usually takes fish from just below surface but occasionally plunges for them. Also preys on mammals as large as Roe Deer and birds as large as Eider and eats carrion. Plumage essentially dark grey-brown, with *yellow bill, whitish head and neck* and fully *white tail in adult*; dark bill and pale-mottled blacker body and tail in immature. Tarsi unfeathered. Readily distinguished from Golden Eagle by differences in outline and flight action and lack of white or pale-barred bases to outer flight-feathers.
Voice: Calls include creaking or singing *kri, kri, kri* or *klee, klee, klee* and lower-pitched, barking *kra*.
Habitat: Rocky coasts, or remote inland waters. Nests on cliff-face, or on top of rocky pinnacle, in large trees, occasionally on ground. Map 70.

LAMMERGEIER (BEARDED VULTURE) *Gypaëtus barbatus*   **Plate 23**
Du – Lammergier   Fr – Gypaète barbu
Ge – Bartgeier   Sw – Lammgam
Identification: 40-45" (100-114cm). Huge, majestic, with long, quite narrow angled wings and *long diamond-shaped tail*. Less sluggish than other vultures, patrolling mountain sides with effortless soaring. Adult has rather short, narrow bill, cream-white head with black eye-patch and projecting black whiskers; *yellow-orange neck and under-parts* contrast with greyish-black upper-parts, wings and tail. Immature has dark blackish head and neck and pale-patched under-body. Normally solitary. Usually at fresh carrion but also drops and breaks bones in order to eat marrow; occasionally attacks mammals.
Voice: Calls include thin querulous *quee-er* and loud whistle at nest.
Habitat: Remote mountain ranges. Nests in caves on precipices. Map 71.

EGYPTIAN VULTURE *Neophron percnopterus*   **Plate 23**
Du – Aasgier   Fr – Percnoptère d'Egypte
Ge – Schmutzgeier   Sw – Smutsgam
Identification: 23-26" (58-66cm). Smallest European vulture, with *long slim bill*, bare face, shaggy ruff, long straight-edged wings and *diamond-shaped tail*. Flight consists mostly of effortless soaring, interspersed by quite quick wing-beats; take-off more rapid than larger relatives. Adult has pale orange-yellow bill-base and face and *dingy white* plumage relieved by *black flight-feathers* and brownish patch and black bar on greater coverts. Immature initially all dark brown, becoming increasingly whitish over four years. Less sociable than Griffon but small numbers gather at carrion or offal. Beware confusion with high-flying White Stork and White Pelican which show similar flight pattern. Usually silent.
Habitat: Most widespread of tribe, preferring mountainous areas with livestock but also in lowlands; regularly joins Black Kites at rubbish dumps. Nests in cliff crevice or cave. Map 72

GRIFFON VULTURE *Gyps fulvus* **Plate 23**

Du – Vale gier Fr – Vautour fauve
Ge – Gänsegeier Sw – Gåsgam

Identification: 38-41" (96-104cm). Commonest large vulture, with deep bill but relatively *small round head* (drooping in flight), long neck (retracted at rest and in flight), *very long and broad, at times triangular-looking wings* ending in widely spread 'fingers' and *very short, square tail.* Flight consists of effortless soaring and gliding on *slightly raised wings,* interspersed with slow but powerful beats. Adult has whitish down on head and neck, pale buff ruff, *sandy or greyish upper-parts and wing-linings,* relieved by *whitish lines across under wing-coverts* and blackish brown flight-feathers and tail. Immature has duller plumage, with brown ruff. Sociable when feeding at carrion and at roosts.
Voice: Croaking and whistling notes when breeding, roosting or at carcasses.
Habitat: Ranges over all types of country, but normal habitat is mountainous. Breeds sociably in caves, or on ledges. Map 73.

BLACK VULTURE *Aegypius monachus* **Plate 23**

Du – Monniksgier Fr – Vautour moine
Ge – Mönchsgeier Sw – Grågam

Identification: 39-42" (99-106cm). Size and flight-outline similar to Griffon but has much deeper, more massive bill, more angular head sloping up to rear crown, and (when unworn) *longer, slightly more wedge-shaped tail.* Adult appears greyish on head and upper-ruff, with dark eye-pit, but uniform sooty-brown elsewhere, looking *all black at distance.* Immature has dark brown head and ruff. Glides on *level or very slightly bowed wings.* Behaviour and voice as Griffon but usually far more solitary.
Habitat: Remote mountains and plains. Nests in trees, very occasionally on ledge on cliff-face. Map 74.

SHORT-TOED EAGLE *Circaetus gallicus* **Plate 27**

Du – Slangenarend Fr – Circaète Jean-le-Blanc
Ge – Schlangenadler Sw – Ormörn

Identification: 25-27" (63-68cm). Large-headed, long-winged and rather long-tailed serpent eagle, with *small bill,* rather owl-like face and *long bare tarsi.* Although little more than buzzard-sized, active flight majestic with *powerful wing-beats*; glides on arched wings, with carpal joints pushed forward and outer halves drooped with 'fingers' raised; soars on level wings and *hovers regularly,* dangling legs as it looks for snakes, lizards and amphibians. Plumage pattern recalls Osprey with usually *brownish-buff hood over head and upper breast,* grey-brown upper-parts with blackish flight feathers and tail. From below at distance, under-parts look *nearly uniform white* except for *dark breast*; close-to, show lines of dark spots across wing-coverts and secondaries, never strongly enough to create dark carpal areas; tail shows 3 (sometimes 4) distinct bars. Juvenile browner with darker spots and bars below. Beware confusion with Osprey and pale Honey Buzzard, both of which show dark carpal patches.
Voice: Rather noisy, uttering harsh plaintive *jee,* rather weak *ok, ok, ok* or *mew-ok* and melancholy *peek-o.*
Habitat: Mountain slopes and gorges, secluded woodlands, plantations, marshy plains, coastal dunes. Nests in tree. Map 75.

MARSH HARRIER *Circus aeruginosus*   **Plate 24, 25**
Du – Bruine kuikendief   Fr – Busard des roseaux
Ge – Rohrweihe   Sw – Brun kärrhök
Identification: 19-22" (48-55cm). Distinguished from other harriers by larger size, heavier build, *broader wings* and *absence of white on rump*. Has *low, quartering flight*, with occasional wing-beats and long, wavering glides, with wings held in shallow V. Plumage variable. Adult male distinguished from other harriers by *dark mantle and secondary wing-coverts,* contrasting with grey tail and secondaries; streaked buffish head, nape and breast and rich brown under-parts. Female and immature male usually lack grey and are fairly uniform dark chocolate brown with *pale heads and shoulders*; female sometimes all-dark, suggesting Black Kite. First-winter birds are dark chocolate-brown with *bright creamy crown and throat*. Hunts by pouncing from low altitude into reeds, etc.
Voice: High, Lapwing-like *quee-a* in display and chattering alarm.
Habitat: Almost invariably fens, swamps and marshes, with large areas of dense reeds. Builds large nest in reed-bed usually surrounded by water. Map 76.

HEN HARRIER *Circus cyaneus*   **Plate 24, 25**
Du – Blauwe kuikendief   Fr – Busard Saint-Martin
Ge – Kornweihe   Sw – Blå kärrhök
N. Am. – Marsh Hawk (Northern Harrier)
Identification: 19-22" (48-55cm). Largest of three 'ring-tailed' and pale-rumped species in Europe, with small bill, owl-like face and long bare tarsi typical of tribe but with *heavier body* and relatively broader and *rounder-ended wings* than Pallid and Montagu's, with 4 spread 'fingers' at end. Adult male ash-grey on hood and upper-parts, with black outer primaries, *large white rump, blackish trailing edge to under-surface of secondaries* and off-white, unstreaked under-wing, body and thighs. Female dull brown above, brownish-white below, relieved by indistinct facial pattern, strong streaks around neck, on breast and flanks, *bold white rump larger than in Pallid and Montagu's* and bold dark barring across under-wing and tail. Juvenile resembles female but warmer-toned, with paler upper wing-coverts and orange wash below; a few show wholly rufous unstreaked under-body, like N. American race *C. c. hudsonius*, of which vagrancy to Europe not yet proved. Flight outline characterised by lengthy body and tail crossed by rather broad wings, held in shallow V when gliding; 5-10 strong wing-beats are steadier and less elastic than other 'ring-tailed' harriers.
Voice: Chatters with high *ke-ke-ke*, also utters long wailing *pee-e*.
Habitat: Most northerly-ranging of tribe, using more varied open ground than Pallid or Montagu's. Nests on ground on moors, in swamps, thickets, or crops. Map 77.

PALLID HARRIER *Circus macrourus*   **Plate 24**
Du – Steppenkuikendief   Fr – Busard pâle
Ge – Steppenweihe   Sw – Stäpphök
Identification: 17-19" (43-48cm). Near size of Hen but with outline and flight action similar to Montagu's, except for slightly broader base to wing, shorter outer wing and quicker, stiffer wing-beats. Male *greyish-white on head and breast*, otherwise white below, and pale blue-grey above, with indistinct, off-

white rump and *small black 'wedge' on primaries*; wing lacks dark trailing edge of Hen. Female similar to Montagu's but distinguished by inner wing-pattern, with *secondaries unbarred above* and together with larger coverts *strikingly dark below* (see diagram Pl. 25). Immature very like Montagu's but less rufous, and unstreaked below, with pale collar enhanced by *dark 'boa'-like marks on neck* and similar wing-pattern to female.

Voice: Female utters distinctive *preee-pri-pri-pri*.

Habitat: As Hen Harrier, but also in dry steppes, open plains and hill country with sparse trees. Map 78.

MONTAGU'S HARRIER *Circus pygargus*   Plate 24, 25

Du – Grauwe kuikendief	Fr – Busard cendré
Ge – Wiesenweihe	Sw – Ängshök

Identification: 16-18" (41-46cm). Smallest and most elegant of European harriers, with *long, pointed wings* ending in 3 spread 'fingers' giving buoyant, tern-like flight. Male has *duskier* grey plumage than Hen and Pallid, with indistinct pale rump, *one black bar above and two below on secondaries* and *chestnut streaks on belly and thighs*. Female like Hen but white rump smaller and V-shaped; under-wing shows *broad pale bar across secondaries to base* and less heavily marked greater coverts (see diagram Pl. 25), this pattern also distinguishing it from Pallid, as does large white patch behind eye. Immature like Pallid but always *intensely rufous-chestnut below*, lacking obvious neck collar and 'boa' marks.

Voice: Querulous *kek-kek-kek*, more shrill than Hen Harrier's chatter.

Habitat: Marshes, fens, moors with clumps of trees, or agricultural land. Nests in wet vegetation, or on dry heaths, occasionally in cornfields. Map 79.

GOSHAWK *Accipiter gentilis*   Plate 26, 31

Du – Havik	Fr – Autour des palombes
Ge – Habicht	Sw – Duvhök

Identification: 20-25" (50-63cm). Largest round-winged hawk of Europe. Female much larger than male and although shorter-winged than Buzzard, longer-tailed and more robust in appearance. Male near size of largest female Sparrowhawk but has proportionately smaller head, *deeper chest, bushier vent*, broader inner wing but relatively *shorter, more pointed primaries* and shorter tail. Plumage of both sexes recalls female Sparrowhawk, though upper-parts greyer and under-parts more closely barred, with *markedly white vent*; close-to, *whitish supercilium* and *dusky cheek patch* catch eye. Juvenile dappled pale above and *distinctly buff below*, with diagnostic *dark brown, drop-shaped streaks*. Legs and feet sturdy. Northern Russian race *A. g. buteoides* paler bluish-grey above and noticeably white below in adult and paler with noticeably mottled upper-wing in juvenile. British birds include inter-racial hybrids. Flight more powerful than Sparrowhawk; dramatically agile among trees, causing panic in Wood Pigeons and other birds. Often soars higher than Sparrowhawk. Size comparison important to distinction from Sparrowhawk; usefully, often mobbed by Crows whose size is between female Sparrowhawk and male Goshawk.

Voice: Short melancholy *peee-leh* and loud chattering *gek-gek-gek* or *kye-kye-kye*.

Habitat: Woods (especially coniferous), often near open country. Builds large nest, or adopts old nests of other birds, in secluded wood. Map 80.

SPARROWHAWK *Accipiter nisus* — Plate 26, 31
Du – Sperwer   Fr – Epervier d'Europe
Ge – Sperber   Sw – Sparvhök

Identification: 11 -16" (27-41cm). Female much larger than male, which is smaller than Kestrel but both sexes show *rather short, broad, rounded wings*, slim body and *long, narrow- based tail*. At all ages, shows *barred under-parts* and long thin legs and feet. Male dark slate-grey above, with rufous cheeks, and *fine red-brown barring below*; in dashing flight, can suggest Merlin. Female dusky above with whitish supercilium behind eye, and *grey-brown barring below*; largest birds can recall Goshawk, which see. Juvenile browner than female and more irregularly barred below; *never streaked like young Goshawk*. Flight outline deceptive: when round wing-tip obscured, can look like small falcon. Flight action alternates rapid, clipped wing-beats with long glides along edge of or within cover. Soars quite frequently. See also Levant Sparrowhawk.
Voice: Has large vocabulary in breeding season: loud, rapid *kek-kek-kek, keeow, kew*, etc.
Habitat: Chiefly woodlands and farmlands, with coppices, plantations, etc. Nests in spruce or other conifer in mixed woods, occasionally in tall bushes, thickets, etc. Map 81.

LEVANT SPARROWHAWK *Accipiter brevipes* — Plate 26
Du – Balkansperwer   Fr – Epervier à pieds courts
Ge – Kurzfangsperber   Sw – Balkanhök

Identification: 13-15 (33-38cm). Size varies between sexes less than in Sparrowhawk; relatively *longer, more pointed wings* and somewhat shorter tail produce more falcon-like outline. Adult shows *red-brown, not yellow, eyes* (hence gentler expression than Sparrowhawk) and much paler, *almost white under-wings* ending in contrasting, *sooty 'finger-tips'*. Male larger than male Sparrowhawk, with distinctly *bluer and paler upper-parts* including cheeks and more faintly barred under-parts which can appear uniformly *pink-buff on breast*, heightening pigeon-like appearance. Female greyer above than Sparrowhawk and spotted brown on throat. Juvenile distinctive, with *large brown spots on very pale under-parts* recalling young Goshawk. Toes shorter than Sparrowhawk's. Gregarious on migration, forming flocks even of hundreds and soaring in thermals.
Voice: Shrill *keeveck-veck-veck*, suggesting Tawny Owl and quite unlike Sparrowhawk.
Habitat: Favours drier, more open country than Sparrowhawk, feeding largely by pouncing on lizards, grasshoppers, etc. Map 82.

BUZZARD *Buteo buteo* — Plate 26, 27
Du – Buizerd   Fr – Buse variable
Ge – Mäusebussard   Sw – Ormvråk

Identification: 18-21" (45-53cm). Large, blunt-headed, short-necked and broad-winged, with ample, rounded tail when spread; commonest and most widespread of tribe. Often perches on lookout, flying off with quite fast, stiff and usually shallow wing-beats leading into flat-winged glides; *soars on slightly raised wings*; hovers awkwardly. Variable plumage pattern often suggests other buzzards and small eagles. Most distinctive characters of commonest dark phase are brown head and breast, contrasting with *whitish band across lower breast*, cross-barred wing-coverts and flight feathers and *closely barred grey tail*. Hunts by pouncing from low height onto small animals, insects, rarely birds; may feed on ground, especially at carrion. Sociable, often in small groups; forms large flocks on migration.

Confusion species: In eastern race *B. b. vulpinus*, plumage more rusty, particularly on tail suggests Long-legged Buzzard. Particularly uncommon pale phase very confusing, often with white head, under-body and wing linings but shows dark carpal patches; see also Booted and Short-toed Eagles, Osprey and Rough-legged Buzzard.

Voice: High, plaintive mew *peeoo*, often drawn out into *pee-ee-oo*; also short croak.

Habitat: Secluded rocky coasts, moors, plains, mountain slopes, cultivated and wooded regions. Nests on rock ledges, in trees and on broken ground. Map 83.

LONG-LEGGED BUZZARD *Buteo rufinus*   **Plate 26, 27**
  Du – Arendbuizerd   Fr – Buse féroce
  Ge – Adlerbussard   Sw – Örnvråk

Identification: 23-26" (59-66cm). Largest of tribe, with relatively longer wings than Buzzard and somewhat aquiline flight, including glide on slightly raised wings with protruding carpal joints. Plumage pattern variable, overlapping particularly with eastern race of Buzzard. Most distinctive characters of commonest rufous phase are *pale cream-buff head and breast*, contrasting with *dark belly, and orange-rufous under wing-coverts* ending in black carpal patches; flight feathers dusky but only faintly cross-barred; *tail pale, unbarred rufous-white*. Variants include melanistic birds. Immature usually inseparable from Buzzard.

Voice: Buzzard-like, but less querulous.

Habitat and Range: Dry, open plains and steppes; locally in mountains. Nests on cliffs or in isolated tree, occasionally on ground. A few breed in Greece. Vagrant elsewhere in S., C., N. and W. Europe.

ROUGH-LEGGED BUZZARD *Buteo lagopus*   **Plate 26, 27**
  Du – Ruigpootbuizerd   Fr – Buse pattue
  Ge – Rauhfussbussard   Sw – Fjällvråk
  N. Am. – Rough-legged Hawk

Identification: 21-25" (53-63cm). Size between Buzzard and Long-legged but shape differs in *rather long and narrow wings* and *lengthy tail*, sometimes suggesting eagle, at others harrier. Flight action differs from Buzzard in *slower, looser wing-beats* and more frequent, *skilful hover*; while gliding head-on, shows distinctive kink at carpal joint. Legs feathered, unlike nearly all Buzzards. Adult plumage less variable than other buzzards, with distinctive combination of *pale head*, dark throat, *sooty thighs or belly*, black carpal patches contrasting particularly with *strikingly white bases to black-tipped primaries* and *white base to conspicuously black-ended tail*. Immature has white areas tinged cream. Beware adult males with paler bellies and partly barred tails which closely re-

semble some pale phase Buzzards. Resemblance to harrier enhanced by habit of hunting low over ground, feeding chiefly on rabbits and rodents.
Voice: Fairly loud, cat-like *mee-oo*, more mournful than Buzzard.
Habitat: Usually barren open country and mountain slopes, also marshes and sand dunes. Nests on cliff ledges, trees or on ground in high tundra. Map 84.

LESSER SPOTTED EAGLE *Aquila pomarina*   Plate 28
Du – Schreeuwarend	Fr – Aigle pomarin
Ge – Schreiadler	Sw – Mindre skrikörn

Identification: 24-26" (61-66cm). Smallest of tribe in Europe; slighter and *narrower-winged than Spotted* so that head and tail appear more protruding. Flight action includes rather quick wing-beats; soars on flat wings or with slightly drooping primaries and glides on slightly arched wings with noticeably drooping primaries. When fully spread, wings held slightly forward, showing *six 'fingers'*. Face rather flat, with eyes looking forward; lacks baggy 'trousers'. Adult brown, with greyish head, *paler, greyish- or sandy-toned forewing-coverts always contrasting with blacker flight feathers* on both wing surfaces, and pale patches at base of primaries and above tail. Immature slightly darker, further relieved by *narrow pale bar along dark greater coverts* of under-wing and pale rim to tail. May show pale rusty patch on nape. Juvenile shows whitish spots only on tips of tertials, secondaries and greater coverts.
Voice: Call thin *kyeep, kyeep*, less vibrant than Spotted.
Habitat: Often found near water, though to lesser extent than Spotted. Frequents remote wooded country, with open ground accessible for hunting. Nests in tree. Map 85.

SPOTTED EAGLE *Aquila clanga*   Plate 28, 29
Du – Bastaardarend	Fr – Aigle criard
Ge – Schelladler	Sw – Större skrikörn

Identification: 25-29" (63-74cm). Size larger on average than Lesser Spotted; shape differs in *broader, more square-cut wings* and *rather short tail*, recalling White-tailed Eagle. Flight action includes quick, Buzzard-like wing-beats; soars and glides with always drooping primaries. When fully spread, wings held straight showing *seven 'fingers'*. Adult dark purplish- brown, with similar pale patches at base of primaries and above tail as Lesser Spotted. Immature almost black, *widely spotted white on rear scapulars, on tips of median and greater coverts* (showing as two long bars in flight) and on tips of upper tail-coverts (often showing as 'V' mark); paler brown inner primaries have buff tips which extend along bulging secondaries. Pale morph very confusing with honey-coloured head, body and wing-coverts; paler than Steppe and Imperial Eagles, which see. When perched, hunched body recalls much larger White-tailed Eagle. Behaviour sluggish.
Voice: Trisyllabic bark *kyak, kyak, kyak*, like yap of small dog, less shrill than Lesser Spotted.
Habitat: A tree-loving species; usually near inland lakes, rivers, marshes. Nests in forest tree or bush. Map 86.

STEPPE EAGLE *Aquila nipalensis*   **Plate 28**
Du – Steppenarend   Fr – Aigle des steppes
Ge – Steppenadler   Sw – Stäppörn
Identification: 26-32" (66-81cm) Size between Spotted and Golden or Imperial, shape and flight closest to Imperial but shows characteristic indentation of outer wing due to *rather short inner primaries*. Soars on straight and level wings with very slightly depressed primaries; glides on angled wings with primaries crooked back. Wide moult or wear variations in drab, dark brown plumage, relieved by yellowish nape, pale mottling on larger under wing-coverts, *fully grey-barred flight feathers with dark trailing edge* and indistinctly barred tail. Close-to, shows pale yellow gape extending to rear of eye (not just to front as in Tawny). Juvenile and immature suggest larger Imperial and smaller Lesser Spotted, having very similar wing patterns except for *broad, almost white band along edge of primary and greater coverts* on under-wing which immediately distinguishes Steppe. Behaviour less majestic than relatives, spending much time perched or hunting small prey on ground, waiting for carrion; surprisingly, determined pirate. See also Tawny Eagle (Accidentals).
Voice: Commonest call rather crow-like bark, high *kow, kow, kow*.
Habitat: Eagle of arid habitats, preferring bushy plains or steppes to mountains. Usually nests on low eminence of plain. Vagrant from Asia; occasionally winters in Greece, rare in rest of Europe.

IMPERIAL EAGLE *Aquila heliaca*   **Plate 28**
Du – Keizerarend   Fr – Aigle impérial
Ge – Kaiseradler   Sw – Kejsarörn
Identification: 29-34" (74-86cm). Second largest of tribe in Europe, with heaviest bill, fiercest expression; in flight, has noticeably protruding head, long parallel-edged wings and relatively shorter tail than Golden. Soars on level wings, glides with slightly lowered primaries, beats wings with heavy, flopping action. Adult black-brown, relieved by *pale golden crown and nape*, grey base to tail and *conspicuous white 'braces'* on scapulars, extending in Spanish race *A. h. adalberti* onto shoulders and along leading edge of inner wing. Juvenile and immature paler and more variegated than adult, yellow-brown with rump, wing and tail pattern suggesting Lesser Spotted, pale Spotted, Tawny and Steppe; best distinguished by bolder streaks on under-wings and body, lack of pale band along under wing-coverts and more majestic and larger build. Behaviour sluggish for long periods but high flight remarkably fast. Solitary, even on migration.
Voice: Call quick, barking *owk-owk-owk*.
Habitat: Plains, steppes and marshes. Builds huge conspicuous nest in isolated tall tree. Map 87.

GOLDEN EAGLE *Aquila chrysaetos*   **Plate 28, 29**
Du – Steenarend   Fr – Aigle royal
Ge – Steinadler   Sw – Kungsörn
Identification: 31-36". Largest and most majestic of tribe, overlapping in size with White-tailed Eagle but showing comparatively shorter bill, broader neck, proportionately *longer wings noticeably narrowing at base*, and *longer, ample tail*. Unlike all other *Aquila* eagles, *soars with wings raised in shallow V* and beats wings with deep, powerful strokes. Adult dark brown, with *golden crown,*

shawl and middle coverts of upper-wing (last mark lacking on Imperial) and broadly black-banded tail; bases of flight feathers and tail faintly barred. Juvenile darker than adult, with more rufous crown and shawl, uniform upper wing-coverts, *bold white panels* on upper wing at base of inner primaries and on under wing from base of primaries along edge of greater coverts to near body, and *broad white base to tail*. Immature shows reducing white on wings and tail. Hunts by quartering mountainsides and nearby plains, pouncing on prey from long dive. Solitary.

Voice: Has very occasional yelping *kya* and whistling notes.

Habitat: Barren mountainsides, locally also mountain forests, sea cliffs and plains. Nests on rocky ledge, sometimes in tree. Map 88.

BOOTED EAGLE *Hieraaetus pennatus*   Plate 27

Du – Dwergarend   Fr – Aigle botté
Ge – Zwergadler   Sw – Dvärgörn

Identification: 18-21" (45-53cm). Smallest European eagle, size as Buzzard but with longer wings with six obvious 'fingers' and longer and looser tail. Flight action includes soaring on level wings held slightly forward, skilful *hanging on the wind* (but not hovering) and steep fast diving and weaving among trees. Dimorphic, with pale birds about twice as common as dark, showing dark buffish-brown upper-parts with *dark hood* and *pale band across inner-wing* (like Red Kite), *dull white under-body and under-wing coverts* contrasting with *almost black flight feathers*, and *pale grey to buff tail*. Dark morph is *black-brown below*, with pale 'wedge' on inner primaries more emphasized, and apparently paler tail; intermediates occur. Beware confusion with Marsh Harrier, Black Kite and buzzards, which see. Solitary; often high in sky.

Voice: Commonest call thin, high *keee*, with downward inflection.

Habitat: Deciduous and pine forests, near clearings for hunting. Seldom far from trees. Map 89.

BONELLI'S EAGLE *Hieraaetus fasciatus*   Plate 27

Du – Havikarend   Fr – Aigle de Bonelli
Ge – Habichtsadler   Sw – Hökörn

Identification: 26-29" (65-73cm). Only hawk-eagle in Europe. Size approaches *Aquila* eagle but outline differs distinctly in *protruding head*, long, broad but *'short-fingered' wings* (with often crooked shape due to prominent carpal joints) and *long tail* – all recalling Honey Buzzard. Flight noticeably active, with shallow quick wing-beats interspersed with glides on flat wings but little soaring – suggesting huge falcon, particularly when stooping on prey. Adult plumage distinctive, with *white patch high on back* contrasting with otherwise dark brown upper-parts, dark-hooded head, *whitish under-body* and lesser under wing-coverts contrasting with *black band along primary and larger coverts* and dark grey-black flight feathers, and greyish-brown, *broadly dark-ended tail*. Juvenile very different from adult, with rufous buff under-body and under-wing coverts, only a trace of black along edge of primary and greater coverts; pale, cross-barred flight and tail feathers sharply relieved by black 'fingers'. Immature shows increasing black band in centre of under-wing. Hunts aggressively for rabbits, ducks and other birds. Often seen in pairs.

Voice: Often noisy when breeding; utters chattering *kie, kie, kikiki* recalling Goshawk.

Habitat: Rocky mountainous country, but seldom at great altitudes; descends to plains, wetlands and deserts in winter. Nests on precipitous rock-face, occasionally in tree. Map 90.

OSPREYS: Pandionidae

OSPREY *Pandion haliaetus*　　　　　　　　　　　　　　**Plate 29**
Du – Visarend　　　　　　　　　　Fr – Balbuzard pêcheur
Ge – Fischadler　　　　　　　　　　Sw – Fiskgjuse

Identification: 20-23" (50-58cm). Buzzard-sized, fish-eating raptor, with *long, narrow, often crooked wings* and strong bare, scaly legs and feet. No other similar bird of prey except Short-toed Eagle or pale phase Buzzard has *dark brown upper-parts contrasting with snow-white under-parts*; close-to, shows *broad blackish patch through eye*, slight crest, *dusky breast-band*, small black carpal patches and spotted or barred flight-feathers and tail. Flight outline looser than buzzard or eagle, with deep wing-beats of long angled wings as evocative of large gull as is its distant plumage pattern; hovers heavily before *plunging feet-first for fish*. Often perches on dead tree or rock near water.

Voice: Short, whistling *pew-pew*, sometimes slightly declining.

Habitat: Invariably near water; lakes, large rivers, or sea coasts. Nests on small remote islands, rocky cliffs, trees, ruins, occasionally on sandy or rocky ground. Breeds in scattered groups in some localities. Map 91.

FALCONS: Falconidae

Large family of small to quite large raptors, all capable of chasing or diving flight after prey on closed, pointed wings; several species hover; relatively large-headed and long-tailed; tree, cliff and ground nesting; voices chattering, plaintive or menacing.

LESSER KESTREL *Falco naumanni*　　　　　　　　　**Plate 30, 31**
Du – Kleine torenvalk　　　　　　　Fr – Faucon créccrellette
Ge – Rötelfalke　　　　　　　　　　Sw – Rödfalk

Identification: 12-14" (30-35cm). Small, rather delicate kestrel, with slender form, faster wing-beats, less hovering but more gliding and noisier behaviour than Kestrel; form differs in slight extension of central tail feathers. Adult male more colourful than Kestrel, with bluer head *without dark 'moustache'*, bright chestnut-red upper-parts *without spots,* diagnostic *pale blue patch on greater wing-coverts*, cleaner under-parts with fewer spots and bluer tail. Female and immature hardly separable except by size, flight and, if visible, diagnostic pale whitish claws. Gregarious, flocks hunting chiefly flying insects.

Voice: Noisy at breeding sites, uttering diagnostic rasping *chay-chay-chay*, more rapid chatter than Kestrel and plaintive, rising *whee*.

Habitat: Frequents old buildings, rocky gorges, etc., but usually hunts over open country. Breeds in colonies in holes in high walls, roofs, crevices in cliffs, often among colonies of pigeons or sparrows. Map 92.

KESTREL *Falco tinnunculus*   **Plate 30, 31**
   Du – Torenvalk   Fr – Faucon crécerelle
   Ge – Turmfalke   Sw – Tornfalk

Identification: 13-15" (33-39cm). Commonest and most widespread falcon in Europe; frequently seen *hovering with winnowing wings and depressed, spread tail*, often over motorway verges. Adult male has *dusky 'moustache' on greyish head, fully spotted pale chestnut upper-parts and wing-coverts*, dusky outer wing, *grey rump and tail, last ending in black, white-tipped band*, and spotted buff under-body. Female has rusty-brown upper-parts and inner wings, duskier outer wings, rusty tail and buff-white under-parts, strongly barred above and boldly spotted in lines below except on vent. Immature brighter than female, with paler ground to plumage; both show dark subterminal tail band. Claws black. Flight outline consists of short head, quite long body and long tail, with long, fairly narrow wings. Flight action combines both shallow and deep wing-beats with glides and hover; can soar and wheel, then more easily confused with other small raptors, which see. Hunts chiefly insects and small rodents on ground, rarely pursuing birds. Sociable only on migration.

Voice: Shrill repeated *kee, kee, kee*, and more musical double note *kee-lee*. Usually silent outside breeding season.

Habitat: Moors, coasts, farmlands, open woodlands, locally cities. Breeds in old nests of crows, Magpie, etc., and on cliffs, buildings, occasionally in split trees. Map 93.

RED-FOOTED FALCON *Falco vespertinus*   **Plate 30, 31**
   Du – Roodpootvalk   Fr – Faucon kobez
   Ge – Rotfussfalke   Sw – Aftonfalk

Identification: 12-14" (30-35cm). Small, rather large-headed and relatively long-winged falcon, recalling Hobby in full flight and aerial insect-hunting, and Kestrel in hovering and prominent perching. Adult male unmistakable, *slate-grey with silvery flight-feathers* catching light, and *rusty thighs and vent*. Adult female equally distinctive, with *rufous crown*, dark eye-patch and 'moustache', whitish throat, *sandy rufous under-body, and black and grey-barred back*, inner wings and tail. Base of bill and legs red. Immature confusing, with plumage pattern suggesting Hobby but close-to, shows *pale forehead and brown crown*, closer-barred brownish upper-parts, less boldy streaked under-parts and proportionately longer, fully barred tail. During hover, holds body at steeper angle than Kestrel. Gregarious.

Voice: Shrill *kikikiki*, higher than Kestrel's cry.

Habitat: Open plains dotted with scrub and coppices, edges of woods, and around farmsteads. Breeds colonially in old nests of Rook, Magpie, etc. Map 94.

MERLIN *Falco columbarius*   **Plate 30, 31**
   Du – Smelleken   Fr – Faucon émerillon
   Ge – Merlin   Sw – Stenfalk

Identification: 10-12 (26-31cm). Male smallest of European raptors; female near size of male Kestrel. Dashes after birds at low height, using *rapid, stiff, often swept-back wing-beats*, short, fast glides and final fluttering bind onto prey. Flight outline distinctive, with *short, pointed wings but relatively long tail*. Male slate-blue above, *striped rufous below*, with barred tail ending in *broad* *black terminal band.* Female dark brown above, *heavily streaked blackish-brown below*, with *boldy chequered brown and cream tail.* Immature faintly scaled buff above; like female, has indistinct facial pattern lacking obvious 'moustache'.

Confusion species: Beware confusing male with male Sparrowhawk, latter shorter and rounder-winged, and female with female Kestrel, latter paler brown and never heavily streaked below and without chequered tail.

Voice: Male has quick high chatter *ki-ki-ki-ki*. Female has slow, plaintive *eep-eep*.

Habitat: Open, hilly and marshy moors, sea cliffs and sand-dunes. Breeds on open ground among heather, coarse grass, or on sand, or in trees in old nest of crow. Map 95.

HOBBY *Falco subbuteo* **Plate 30, 31**
   Du – Boomvalk   Fr – Faucon hobereau
   Ge – Baumfalke   Sw – Lärkfalk

Identification: 13-15" (33-38cm). Most aerial of common falcons, slightly larger than Kestrel but with relatively longer, sickle-shaped wings and shorter tail producing *Swift-like outline.* Flight dashing, with *rapid, clipped wing-beats* producing chase fast enough to catch even Swift; when patrolling, action slower, more rowing, recalling Peregrine; never hovers. Adult distinctly patterned, with dark slate 'moustache', head cap and upper-parts contrasting with *bright cream throat, heavily streaked under-body, chestnut thighs and vent* and darkly barred under-wing. Juvenile lacks chestnut areas, may show pale forehead like smaller Red-footed Falcon but is still basically slaty above. Predator of hirundines and flying insects, particularly active at dusk.

Voice: Clear, repeated *kew or ket*; when excited, gives rapid frenetic scream *kikiki....*

Habitat: Open lowlands, with scattered woods and preferably some damp areas. Breeds in trees, in old nests, particularly of crow family. Map 96.

ELEONORA'S FALCON *Falco eleonorae* **Plate 30, 31**
   Du – Eleonora's valk   Fr – Faucon d'Eléonore
   Ge – Eleonorenfalke   Sw – Eleonorafalk

Identification: 15-17" (38-44cm). Length overlaps with Peregrine but flight outline suggests long-winged, long-tailed Hobby, as does energetic action except for *remarkably slow patrol* with slow skua-like wing-beats. Dimorphic; 25% dark, 75% light phase. Dark phase uniform slaty-brown, occasionally streaked on breast; may suggest male Red-footed but much larger, *lacking chestnut thighs and vent.* Light phase recalls Hobby and immature Peregrine, but under-wing shows *dark under-wing coverts* contrasting with pale bases of flight feathers. Increasingly *rusty-brown from belly to vent,* latter not sharply demarcated as in Hobby. Juvenile less distinctive, with paler, barred under wing-coverts but obvious dark trailing edge to flight feathers and paler belly. Hunting tactics include hover, insect-hawking and headlong stoop upon migrant passerines. Colonial.

Voice: Harsh *keya,* extended to *kje-kje-kje-kjah.*

Habitat and Range: Rocky Mediterranean islands and sea cliffs. Migratory, breeding mainly in late summer on Greek islands, Sardinia, Balearics. Vagrant elsewhere in S., W. (including Britain) and C. Europe.

LANNER *Falco biarmicus*   **Plate 30**
  Du – Lanner valk   Fr – Faucon lanier
  Ge – Feldeggsfalke   Sw – Slagfalk
Identification: 18-21" (45-54cm). Lengthier than Peregrine but less compact
and powerful, looking slender on the wing. Adult of S.E. European race *F. b.
feldeggi* suggests Saker as much as Peregrine, with bluish-brown upper-parts,
cream-white spotted under-body and *noticeably pale under wing-coverts*; close-
to, shows *pale rufous crown and nape, emphasized by blackish forehead band,*
line through eye and narrow 'moustache'. Immature even more like Saker but
smaller, *lacking pale translucent bases to flight feathers.* Flight outline presents
distinctive long but blunt-ended wings; action rather loose, with outline hinting
at Eleonora's as much as Peregrine and not evoking Saker. Takes smaller prey
than Peregrine. Beware taking escaped falconer's bird for wild one; look for
jesses.
Voice: Shrill *kri, kri, kri* and various wailing cries during breeding season.
Habitat: Cliffs, ruins, rocky mountain slopes, extending to stony plains and
semi-desert. Nests among rocks, sometimes in trees. Map 97.

SAKER *Falco cherrug*   **Plate 30**
  Du – Saker valk   Fr – Faucon sacre
  Ge – Würgfalke   Sw – Tatarfalk
Identification: 19-23" (49-58cm). Second largest falcon of Europe but unlikely
to overlap geographically with Gyrfalcon, needing careful separation from large
immature Lanner and brownest Peregrines. Flight outline more massive and less
compact than Peregrine and particularly Lanner, with broader wings and longer
or more ample tail; action noticeably slow and loose, even in usually low pur-
suits of prey. Upper-parts *sepia-brown with rufous tinge in good light*, with
contrasting almost black flight feathers and diagnostic *oval white spots on outer
tail feathers*; under-parts dull white, with increasingly heavy splashes of dark
brown from breast to thighs and *dark bar across larger under wing-coverts.*
Close-to, shows *whitish head and nape*, streaked brown but with only *indistinct
moustache.* Immature has more streaked crown and even darker under-parts.
Bold and ferocious. Beware escaped falconer's birds, as noted in Lanner.
Voice: Duller than Peregrine; includes harsh, high-pitched *i-jack.*
Habitat: Open plains, semi-deserts. Usually nests high in large tree, occasion-
ally among rocks. Map 98.

GYRFALCON *Falco rusticolus*   **Plate 31**
  Du – Giervalk   Fr – Faucon gerfaut
  Ge – Gerfalke   Sw – Jaktfalk
Identification: 22-25" (55-64cm). Largest falcon of Europe, over-lapping in
bulk with buzzards and female Goshawk. Distinguished from Peregrine by 25%
greater size, *relatively broader-based and rounder-tipped wings* and broader
and longer tail. Flight action *slow and majestic*, with distinctive shallow beat of
outer wing on patrol and dramatically increased power during level pursuit of
prey. Plumage variable, from almost pure white through grey and brown to uniform dusky; pattern of darker birds may suggest Peregrine but *moustache less
demarcated due to dirty cheeks*; white birds barred grey above, with dusky primaries, may briefly recall Snowy Owl. Thickset and upright on perch.

Voice: Usually silent. Occasional wailing *aaahi* and high, yapping chatter are slightly lower-pitched than similar notes of Peregrine.
Habitat: Wild rocky open country, sea coasts and islands. Locally also around edges of coniferous forests. Breeds on rocky cliff-faces. Map 99.

PEREGRINE *Falco peregrinus*   **Plate 30, 31**
  Du – Slechtvalk   Fr – Faucon pélerin
  Ge – Wanderfalke   Sw – Pilgrimsfalk
  N. Am – Duck Hawk
Identification: 16-21" (41-54cm). Most widespread large falcon of Europe but now rare except in Britain and Ireland. Flight outline shows *bull-head*, quite *broad-based but pointed wings,* broad-rumped body and relatively *short but ample tail*; action variable, slow and steady on often high patrol, but swift, agile and powerful in pursuit of or during *dramatically steep stoop upon prey*; at other times, suggests crow-sized pigeon. Plumage distinctive with *very black crown and broad moustache* relieved by *bright white cheeks, throat and breast*, slaty upper-parts, paler grey rump, dusky barred tail and *buff-white, close-barred under-body and wing-lining*, looking pale grey at distance. Female distinctly larger and often darker than male. Immature dark brown above, some with confusing pale supercilium, heavily streaked below; tail shows pale rim. Like Gyrfalcon, feeds chiefly on birds up to size of grouse.
Voice: Has wide range of notes during breeding season: repeated *we-chew*, loud, menacing *kek-kek-kek*, short *klack*, thin squeal, etc.
Habitat: Open wild country, cliffs, mountains, moors; in winter, also marshes, locally high spires and towers. Breeds on steep cliffs, mountain crags, etc., sometimes on buildings and on ground in Arctic. Map 100.

GROUSE: Tetraonidae

Small to large, plump chicken like gamebirds, lacking long tails of pheasants but with feathered legs; usually restricted to woods and moors; ground nesting; walk and run, flying in sudden escape low over ground, with broad wings alternately whirred and depressed. Plumages cryptic, changing seasonally in two species; sexes dissimilar; juveniles duller; voices crowing, barking, rattling, cooing.

HAZEL GROUSE *Bonasa bonasia*   **Plate 32**
  Du – Hazelhoen   Fr – Gélinotte des bois
  Ge – Haselhuhn   Sw – Järpe
Identification: 14" (35cm). Rather small, slightly crested, rather long-tailed taiga grouse, perching freely in trees. In flight, shows conspicuously *pale grey lower back and tail,* latter with subterminal black band. Plumage variable: predominantly grey in north of range but more rufous in south (and female); richly spotted and barred black and rufous-brown, with *white bands on sides of neck and along scapulars*. Male has *jet-black throat, etched white*, and small red comb over eye. Flight light for grouse. Usually in pairs, difficult to find but not shy. Briefly raises crest when nervous.
Voice: Male advertises with high, thin whistling *tsissi- tseri-tsi, tsi,tsi* or *tseeuu-eee tatititi*, recalling phrasing of Goldcrest song. Twitters in alarm.

Habitat: Coniferous forest, particularly spruce with birch and alder-lined streams, in both hills and plains. Map 101.

WILLOW GROUSE and RED GROUSE *Lagopus lagopus*   **Plate 33**

Du – Moerassneeuwhoen   Fr – Lagopède des saules
Ge – Moorschneehuhn   Sw – Dalripa
N. Am. – Willow Ptarmigan

Identification: 16-17" (40-43cm). Commonest grouse of N.W. Europe. Stout and relatively broad-winged, with alternately whirring and gliding flight on markedly bowed wings. Takes off explosively, characteristically looking back over shoulder. Apart from black tail, plumage is variable. Continental races of Willow Grouse always show wholly *white wings* and become all-white in winter. British and Irish races of Red Grouse are always tawny to rufous-brown and purplish-black except for *white under-wing coverts*; most females and Irish birds show paler yellowish tones. Many Scottish birds have white bars or patches on under-parts in winter, showing link with Willow Grouse through even patchier Norwegian birds. Distinction between Willow and Ptarmigan is often impossible at distance but former usually found at lower altitudes and within damp birch and willow where Ptarmigan occurs only in winter. Close-to, Willow shows stouter bill, darker, more rufous breeding plumage, in autumn becoming patched but *never grey* and in winter never showing black lores of male Ptarmigan (see diagram Pl. 33).
Voice: Basically similar in all races, with crowing *kowk,ok,ok,ok*, often preceded by quiet *ow...ow...*, and strident *go-bak, go-bak, bak-bak-bak*.
Habitat: Willow inhabits moors, heather, with willow, birch and juniper scrub, at lower altitudes than Ptarmigan; nests in scrub. Red prefers moors and peat-bogs with crowberry and cranberry, descending in autumn to lower levels and stubble fields; nests among heather and rough grass. Map 102.

PTARMIGAN *Lagopus mutus*   **Plate 33**

Du – Sneeuwhoen   Fr – Lagopède des Alpes
Ge – Alpenschneehuhn   Sw – Fjällripa
N. Am. – Rock Ptarmigan

Identification: 14" (36cm). Scarce, alpine grouse, of similar form but smaller and slighter than Willow and Red Grouse, with narrower bill and *white wings and white belly at all seasons*. In breeding plumage, male has richly mottled blackish-brown upper-parts, breast and flanks; female is tawnier. In autumn, male's upper-parts, breast and sides are grey, closely marked with black and white, belly mainly white; female is yellowish-grey and looks darker than male. In winter, both sexes are *pure white with exception of black tail* (which is largely hidden at rest by white tail-coverts) but male has *black mark from bill through eye* – a clear distinction from Willow Grouse. Flight outline shows narrower wings than Willow and Red Grouse; action similar but speed even more marked, particularly uphill. Runs up rocks and scree with ease.
Voice: Quieter than Willow and Red Grouse, uttering low harsh, ticking croak, *aar-aar-ka-ka-ka* in flight and a rattling *kar-r-rk* alarm.
Habitat: Barren stony mountain slopes (usually higher than Willow Grouse, except when driven down by weather); breeds at lower levels in Arctic. Nests in shelter of rock or clump of vegetation. Map 103.

BLACK GROUSE *Tetrao tetrix*   **Plate 32**
Du – Korhoen   Fr – Tétras lyre
Ge – Birkhuhn   Sw – Orre

Identification: Male 21" (53cm), female 16" (41cm). Second largest grouse of region, with longer neck and longer, notched or forked tail giving clearly different flight outline from Willow and Red Grouse and much larger Capercaillie. Male (Blackcock) easily distinguished by glossy *blue-black* plumage with *lyre-shaped tail*, conspicuous *white under tail-coverts and white wing-bar*. Female (Greyhen) distinguished from Red Grouse by larger size and *less rufous plumage*; from female Capercaillie by smaller size and *less boldy barred plumage*; from both by narrow, pale wing-bars and forked tail (neither easy to observe). Both sexes have scarlet wattle above eye. Male in autumn eclipse looks dingy, mottled above, with white throat; tail lacks distinctive shape until full grown. Usually flies higher than Red Grouse, with longer glides. Perches freely in trees. Confusing hybrids with Capercaillie, Red Grouse and Pheasant occur occasionally.

Voice: Song at 'lek' (display ground) rapid, protracted, musical chorus of bubbling pigeon-like *roo-koo* notes; male has a deliberate, sneezing *tchu-shwee*.

Habitat: Near trees bordering moors, marshy ground with rushes and scattered trees, peat-mosses, rocky heather-covered hills, plantations, etc. Nests on ground. Map 104.

CAPERCAILLIE *Tetrao urogallus*   **Plate 32**
Du – Auerhoen   Fr – Grand tétras
Ge – Auerhuhn   Sw – Tjäder

Identification: Male 34" (86cm), female 24" (60cm). *Largest grouse* of region, with male recalling turkey particularly when *ample rounded tail* is cocked and fanned in display. Male *slate-grey*, with rich brown wing-coverts, glossy blue-green breast, shaggy 'beard', whitish bill and scarlet skin above eye; under-parts and tail boldy marked with white. White carpal-patch conspicuous during display. Female may be confused with female Black or Red Grouse, but is much larger, with broad tail and *rufous patch on breast* contrasting with paler under-parts. Usually seen on ground in coniferous forest in summer; in trees in winter. Flight usually brief, with alternate spells of quick wing-beats and long glides; bursts out of cover noisily. Hens may hybridize with Blackcock.

Voice: Male's song is quiet, with *tik-up, tik-up, tik-up* accelerating rapidly and ending with *pop* (like withdrawing a cork), followed by short phrase of grating, whispering notes. Female gives Pheasant-like *kok-kok*.

Habitat: Coniferous hilly woodlands. Nests among undergrowth at foot of pine, or in scrub on open high ground. Map 105.

PARTRIDGES, QUAILS AND PHEASANTS Phasianidae

Chicken-like birds, with unfeathered legs and terrestrial habits; ground nesting; often introduced.

Partridges: Usually have strong face patterns and red legs; *Alectoris* species occur in increasingly hybrid groups; flight like grouse, always near ground level; sexes similar, juveniles plainer-headed, voices cackling and whistling.

Rock Partridge   Chukar

Quails: Small and compact, with very short tails; more often heard than seen; flight rather loose, swinging; sexes similar. Very skulking.

Pheasants: Large gamebirds, with long pointed tails which in flight trail behind whirring or bowed wings; sexes dissimilar; voices crowing.

CHUKAR *Alectoris chukar*   Plate 33
Du – Aziatische steenpatrijs   Fr – Perdrix choukar
Ge – Chukarhuhn   Sw – Berghöna

Identification: 14" (35cm). Closely resembles Rock Partridge, hybridising with it within mainland European range. Best distinguished by *clucking or cackling voice*, recalling domestic hen or Red-legged Partridge more than Rock. Close-to, separated by white lores, *narrower black forehead and eyestripe* interrupted by rufous behind eye; cream or buff throat, *blunt point at centre of black collar*, thick black and chestnut flank-bars and *pale blue centres to rufous scapulars*. Flight and behaviour as Rock.

Voice: Nervous, decelerating nasal cackle *tchouk-tchouk- tchoukor-tchoukor* or *kakakaka chuckar-chuckar-chuckar*.

Habitat and Range: Habitat similar to Rock Partridge, but also in more arid regions. Resident E. Greece, E. Bulgaria, Aegean.

ROCK PARTRIDGE *Alectoris graeca*   Plate 33
Du – Steenpatrijs   Fr – Perdrix bartavelle
Ge – Steinhuhn   Sw – Stenhöna

Identification: 14" (35cm). Size and form as Chukar; best distinguished by distinctive *whistling voice*. Close-to, separated by black lores, *broader black frontal band and eyestripe not showing rufous behind eye*, whiter throat, *clean-cut black collar*, about 10 thin flank-bars and greyer upper-parts. Flight and behaviour typical of tribe.

Voice: Song, given in spring and autumn, staccato, grating *tchertsi-ritt-chi*, with many variants. Calls include Nuthatch-like *whit-whit-whit* and, in alarm, explosive *k-k-kwowk* and incisive *pitch-i*.

Habitat: Stony and rocky slopes and lightly wooded high ground, descending to lower altitudes in winter. Nests among rocks. Map 106.

RED-LEGGED PARTRIDGE *Alectoris rufa*   Plate 33
Du – Rode patrijs   Fr – Perdrix rouge
Ge – Rothuhn   Sw – Rödhöna

Identification: 14" (35cm). Rotund, heavy game-bird, noticeably larger-headed and fuller-chested than smaller Grey. Plumage *quite dark*, with distinctive head and throat pattern including grey forecrown, *white supercilium*, black eyestripe interrupted by yellow-buff behind eye, small white throat and *high black necklace breaking up into streaked bib*. Dull olive-brown upper-parts and lavender grey and buff under-parts, with about 8 thin white and wide black and rufous bars on flanks. Bill and legs red. Flight outline and action heavier than Grey. Beware hybrids with Chukar, showing mixed characters, particularly incomplete necklace.

Voice: Usual note of male *chuck, chuck-er*, or slow harsh *tschreck ...tschreck...*, when flushed, calls *kuk-kuk*.

Habitat: Much as Grey Partridge. Although often on marshy ground, normally prefers dry localities, sandy soil, chalk downs, stony wastes. Map 107.

BARBARY PARTRIDGE *Alectoris barbara*   **Plate 33**
Du – Barbarijse patrijs   Fr – Perdrix gambra
Ge – Felsenhuhn   Sw – Klipphöna
Identification: 14" (35cm). Size and form of Red-legged but even at distance looks paler and pinker. Close-to, easily identified by more open head pattern, with *wine-chestnut crown, nape and collar, pale blue-grey supercilium, face and throat*, 'inflamed' pink eye-ring and orange-buff streak behind eye, and reddish, blue-centred scapulars. Under-parts as Red-legged.
Voice: Noisy at dawn and dusk. Typical song loud, slow *kakelik, kakelik*.
Habitat and Range: Scrub-covered hillsides, wadis, semi- deserts with a certain amount of water and cover. Resident Gibraltar, Sardinia.

BLACK FRANCOLIN *Francolinus francolinus*   **Plate 95**
Du – Zwarte Frankolijn   Fr – Francolin noir
Ge – Halsbandfrankolin   Sw – Svart frankolin
Identification: 14" (35cm). Only partridge-like bird with *black head and under-parts*, more intense on male than female. Male also has prominent *white cheek-mark* and *orange-chestnut collar*; female shows *chestnut nape-patch*. Male's brown upper-parts and black flanks are heavily 'scaled' and spotted; female similarly patterned but duller. Rather solitary and reluctant to leave cover. Runs swiftly.
Voice: Displaying male utters harsh rythmic *kok, keek, kee-kek-keh kee-keek*.
Habitat and Range: Usually thick cover on open slopes or plains. Became extinct in W. Mediterranean in 19th century but recently reintroduced to Italy.

GREY PARTRIDGE *Perdix perdix*   **Plate 33**
Du – Patrijs   Fr – Perdrix grise
Ge – Rebhuhn   Sw – Rapphöna
Identification: 12" (31cm). Small-headed, rotund, chicken-like bird, with short rounded wings and short tail spread in flight. Flies rapidly just above ground, alternating burst of whirring wing-beats and slightly unstable glides on deeply bowed wings. At distance or in flight, easily confused with *Alectoris* partridges but somewhat smaller, *less broad-beamed*, with diagnostic *pale orange face*, greyer fore-neck and chest, chestnut bars on flanks, and *white under-wings* (not orange-buff as in *Alectoris*). White under-body marked in male by conspicuous *dark chestnut 'horseshoe'* on lower breast. Flight feathers, upper-parts and flanks all faintly barred and streaked, quite unlike *Alectoris*. Walks freely but in

crouched attitude, squatting in alarm and often running away with head well up (in preference to flight). Much shorter-tailed than young pheasant and larger and less sandy or streaked than Quail.

Voice: A penetrating, grating *kree-arit* and rapid *eck-eck-eck*.

Habitat: Farmlands, pastures, wasteland, moors, sand-dunes, etc. Nests well hidden in hedge bottoms, in growing corn, etc. Map 108.

QUAIL *Coturnix coturnix* Plate 33

Du – Kwartel	Fr – Caille des blés
Ge – Wachtel	Sw – Vaktel

Identification: 7" (18cm). Form as partridges but only half their size; *distinctive voice* heard far more often than bird seen. Flies off with initially rather weak, *crake-like flutter of surprisingly long wings*. Plumage sandy, noticeably *dark- and pale-streaked on head, back and flanks* and faintly barred on flight feathers. Head colours variable, strongest on male: typically dark brown crown with cream divide, cream supercilium, brown eye-stripe, and cream lower face with *dark throat, cheek marks and necklace*, combining into complex pattern; rarely almost wholly chestnut. Female best distinguished by pale buff throat and spotted, not buff, breast. Flushes readily as migrant but very skulking in breeding season.

Voice: Ventriloquial. Characteristic trisyllabic call of male has accent on first syllable: repeated *whic, whic-ic*. Female has wheezing double note *queep...queep*. Heard day and night.

Habitat: Seldom seen in open. Frequents and breeds in rough pastures, crops, grass tussocks, etc. Map 109.

PHEASANT *Phasianus colchicus* Plate 32

Du – Fazant	Fr – Faisan de chasse
Ge – Fasan	Sw – Fasan

Identification: Male 30-35" (75-88cm), female 21-25" (53-63cm). Familiar game-bird with *long, pointed tail*. Male highly coloured, with glossy dark green head, scarlet wattles around eyes and short ear-tufts. Plumage very variable owing to variety of introduced stock, but usually has *white neck-ring*. Female soberly mottled buff and blackish, with shorter but still lengthy tail. Runs swiftly to cover rather than taking wing. Flight strong (take-off noisy), but seldom long sustained or high. Melanistic form resembles occasionally released Green Pheasant *P. versicolor* but lacks its bluish rump.

Voice: Crowing male has strident double note *korrk-kok*, usually followed by brief burst of wing-flapping. Female has thin whistling note on taking off.

Habitat: Woodland borders, parkland, farmland, shrubberies, reeds. Nests on ground, beneath low vegetation and bracken. Map 110.

GOLDEN PHEASANT *Chrysolophus pictus* Plate 95

Du – Goudfazant	Fr – Faisan doré
Ge – Goldfasan	Sw – Guldfasan

Identification: Male 33-38" (83-96cm), female 26-32" (66-81cm). Lighter-bodied than Pheasant, with domed crown and long curved, drooping tail. Male unmistakable, with *scarlet under-parts*, fan-shaped, *black-barred gold hood*, red, green and blue wings, *golden rump* and marbled tail. Female like golden-

brown Pheasant but *slightly decurved tail feathers more boldly barred*. Shy, keeping to dense cover. Interbreeds with Lady Amherst's.
Voice: Rasping crow of male higher-pitched than Pheasant.
Habitat and Range: Now breeds ferally in parkland shrubberies in several parts of Britain.

LADY AMHERST'S PHEASANT *Chrysolophus amherstiae*   Plate 95
Du – Lady Amherst-fazant   Fr – Faisan de Lady Amherst
Ge – Diamantfasan   Sw – Diamantfasan
Identification: Male 35-43" (88-109cm), female 27-35" (68-88cm). Slightly larger and even longer-tailed than Golden. Male unmistakable, with *dark green head, breast and back*, red mane, *black-barred, white hood*, blue wings, yellow rump and *black-barred, marbled white tail*. Female browner than Golden, with *rufous forehead and crown* and paler, more strongly barred tail. Voice as Golden. Breeds ferally in central England.

BUTTON-QUAILS: Turnicidae

ANDALUSIAN HEMIPODE *Turnix sylvatica*   Plate 33
Du – Vechtkwartel   Fr – Turnix d'Andalousie
Ge – Laufhühnchen   Sw – Springhöna
Identification: 6" (15cm). Small, almost tailless terrestrial bird, recalling Quail or small crake. Plumage recalls Quail but combination of *orange-rufous breast and bold black spots on flanks* diagnostic. Flies reluctantly, with rounded wings blurring and making *distinctive whirring noise* in short skimming escape; on landing, *holds wings briefly upright*, then runs off in zig-zag. Solitary and difficult to find.
Voice: Very distinctive *croo*, increasing in intensity, resembling distant fog-horn; heard particularly at dawn and dusk; when calling, often 'blows itself up' like a ball. Also quiet whistling notes.
Habitat and Range: Sandy plains with palmetto scrub, brush-covered wastes, extensive low thickets, stubble and sugar-beet fields. Nests in dense vegetation. Bred very locally in Spain, S. Portugal, now perhaps extinct there.

RAILS, CRAKES AND COOTS: Rallidae

Rails and crakes are compact, skulking marsh birds, more often heard than seen; wings short and rounded; tails short but often cocked; flight usually brief and reluctant, with legs and long toes dangling. Moorhens and coots have stout bodies, small heads and long toes for walking on aquatic vegetation; heads often jerked while swimming. Sexes usually similar. Reed or ground nesting.

WATER RAIL *Rallus aquaticus*   Plate 34
Du – Waterral   Fr – Râle d'eau
Ge – Wasserralle   Sw – Vattenrall
Identification: 11" (28cm). Medium-sized, lithe, narrow-bodied marsh bird, with rather weak flight but nimble, darting gait. Distinguished from all relatives

by *long bill* and *very distinctive voice*. Plumage dark olive-brown above and slate-blue below, with *black-and-white barred flanks* and conspicuous *white under-tail* which 'winks' as bird retreats into cover. *Bill red*; legs pink-brown. Juvenile less distinctive, with shorter, less red bill and mottled grey under-parts. Flight outline distinctive, with drooping bill and head, long wings and dangling legs and feet; action hesitant but bird more often seen on wing between feeding areas than smaller crakes. Tail flicked in alarm.

Voice: Wide vocabulary includes short crake-like calls and diagnostic *piglet-like* squealing *tjuir-r-r* (known as 'sharming') and dry clipped *kek*, often repeated.

Habitat: Dense aquatic vegetation, reed- and osier-beds, sewage-farms, overgrown ponds, ditches, river banks. Nests among reeds or sedges above shallow water. Map 111.

SPOTTED CRAKE *Porzana porzana* Plate 34

Du – Porceleinhoen
Ge – Tüpfelsumpfhuhn
Fr – Marouette ponctuée
Sw – Småfläckig sumphöna

Identification: 9" (23cm). Commonest and most widespread of small crakes; difficult to observe but *calls distinctive*. Shape compact and *noticeably oval*, with tail held up and jerked in suspicion. Plumage soft-toned, with olive-brown upper-parts and wings, *greyish face and fore-neck*, olive-brown breast, black-barred flanks and *pale buff under tail*; from neck to breast, over back and on wings *profusely spotted and marbled white*. In flight, shows white leading edge to wing. Bill yellow, with red base; legs greenish. Flight like Water Rail but more fluttering. Most active at dawn and dusk. Solitary.

Voice: High, whipping *whitt...whitt...whitt*, long repeated on the same note. Male also has monotonous hard ticking note *tchit-a, tchit-a*, recalling Snipe's clock-like note.

Habitat: Rather less aquatic than Baillon's or Little Crakes. Swamps and fens, overgrown ditches, margins of ponds, rivers, etc. Nests in boggy locations. Map 112.

LITTLE CRAKE *Porzana parva* Plate 34

Du – Klein waterhoen
Ge – Kleines Sumpfhuhn
Fr – Marouette poussin
Sw – Mindre sumphöna

Identification: 7" (18cm). Noticeably small crake, shaped as Spotted but with *much longer wing-points,* extending well beyond tertials. Male slate-blue on face, neck and under-body, olive-brown on crown, hind neck and upper-parts and wings, with reliefs restricted to *yellow bill with red base*, thin white flecks on mantle, scapulars and greater coverts and *dull whitish barring only on rear flanks* and under tail. Female has whitish throat and *buff under-parts* with dull bars on rear flanks. Juvenile like female; best distinguished from Baillon's by virtually uniform wing-coverts. Legs green. Flight and behaviour as Spotted.

Voice: Male courts with far-carrying, barking *quek, quek, quek*, or *kuak, kuak*, gradually dropping notes down scale and accelerating into short trill *kwa-wa-a-a-a-a-a*. Other calls include *kueck-kuck-kwarrr* from female and explosive *kir-rook*.

Habitat: As Spotted, but with fondness for high *Phragmites* reeds and lagoons with floating vegetation. Map 113.

BAILLON'S CRAKE *Porzana pusilla*   **Plate 34**
  Du – Kleinst waterhoen   Fr – Marouette de Baillon
  Ge – Zwergsumpfhuhn   Sw – Dvärgsumphöna
Identification: 7" (18cm). Smallest European crake, no larger than Starling. Shape as Little but *wing-point short*, almost cloaked by tertials. Plumage of adult male and female resembles male Little but close-to, easily distinguished by wholly *dull green bill*, strongly *rufous upper-parts and wings, boldly and closely etched with white*, fully *black-and-white barred rear flanks* and dull greyish-pink to olive- brown legs. Juvenile like female or juvenile Little but separated by much more extensive white marks above and more black and white bars below. At all ages, outer wing shows narrow white leading edge. Flight and behaviour as Little but even more secretive.
Voice: Most distinctive call low, dry, jarring trill or rattle *trrr-trrr-trrr* .., recalling Garganey and several frogs before other crakes.
Habitat: Usually prefers lower, denser vegetation and smaller pools than Little Crake, in swamps, fens and overgrown ponds. Map 114.

CORNCRAKE *Crex crex*   **Plate 34**
  Du – Kwartelkoning   Fr – Râle de genets
  Ge – Wachtelkönig   Sw – Kornknarr
Identification: 10" (26cm). Rather large crake, suggesting slim young Grey Partridge at times but with behaviour and actions of true rail; more often heard giving *rasping call* than seen. Plumage softly but richly coloured, with pale grey face, fore-neck and breast, yellowish-buff upper-parts, lined with cream and spotted or streaked blackish-brown, *chestnut wings 'catching fire' in flight*, barred white flanks. Bill and legs dull pink. Flight typical of family, loose-winged and clumsy; usually escapes by running into dense cover. Secretive but male sometimes calls from low perch; investigates call imitation. Makes fluttering leaps in courtship.
Voice: In breeding season, male has penetrating and persistent call, a rasping, disyllabic *rerrp-rerrp* (often written *crex-crex*), usually given at night but often also by day. Also loud, high squealing note.
Habitat: Frequents and nests in meadows, lush vegetation, crops. Map 115.

MOORHEN *Gallinula chloropus*   **Plate 35**
  Du – Waterhoen   Fr – Poule d'eau
  Ge – Teichhuhn   Sw – Rörhöna
  N. Am. – Florida Gallinule
Identification: 13" (33cm). Commonest and most widespread rail, with build of small chicken but longer tail often flirted and long legs and feet. Adult basically blackish-slate, with bright *yellow bill with red base and shield*, bold irregular *white line along top of flanks*, conspicuous *white lateral under tail-coverts* and pale green legs, 'red-gartered' above tarsal joint. Juvenile dark greyish-brown, with whiter belly, more broken flank line and dull greenish bill, shield and legs; under-tail shows white as adult. Swims buoyantly with *nodding head*; flies better than smaller relatives but still with dangling legs. Sociable but does not pack closely like Coot.
Voice: Wide vocabulary includes diagnostic sudden, explosive but bubbled *purrck*, harsh *kr-r-rk* or *kittick* and chattering *kekeke*.

Habitat: Ponds, slow streams, marshes, tarns, sewage-farms and meadows, even farmyards. Nests in reeds and bushes near water, occasionally in trees and old nests of other species. Map 116.

PURPLE GALLINULE *Porphyrio porphyrio*   Plate 35

Du – Puperkoet   Fr – Poule sultane
Ge – Purpurhuhn   Sw – Purpurhöna

Identification: 19" (48cm). Largest rail of Europe; as big as chicken, with deep bill, broad shield, rather long wing-points and long 'thick-kneed' legs and huge feet. Adult *dark blue*, with violet tone above and blacker under-body, relieved by *red bare parts* and white under-tail. Juvenile duller, with greyish bill and shield and dusky under-parts. Flight outline and action suggest huge Moorhen. Gait heron-like, due to long toes. Beware escaped birds of African race *P.p.madagascariensis,* which have *green back.*

Voice: Weird hooting and shrieking noises.

Habitat and Range: Swamps with extensive reed-beds, borders of lakes fringed with dense cover. Nests in reeds, cane-brakes, etc. Breeds in S. Spain, Sardinia, Portugal. Vagrant elsewhere in W. and C. Europe.

COOT *Fulica atra*   Plate 35

Du – Meerkoet   Fr – Foulque macroule
Ge – Blässhuhn   Sw – Sothöna

Identification: 15" (38cm). Very round-headed and -backed rail, noticeably larger and shorter-tailed than Moorhen, with conspicuous *white bill and large frontal shield*, black head but slightly paler, black-slate body, wings and tail. In flight, shows slightly paler flight feathers with *narrow white trailing edge to secondaries* and trails greenish legs and lobed toes. Juvenile paler than adult, with whitish face, throat and under-body; immature retains whitish chin and mottled dusky flanks in first winter. Flight initially laboured, with pattering take-off, but becomes more powerful, even duck-like over distance; alights with big splash. Swims buoyantly, often in large flocks which also graze nearby grass; 'plop-dives' for food, submerging for up to half a minute. Does not enter farmland like Moorhen, needing open water for escape.

Voice: A loud, short *twek*, also various disyllabic calls *kt-kowk*, etc., and a hard, explosive *skik*.

Habitat: Usually prefers larger areas of open water than Moorhen. Packs occur on reservoirs and salt water in winter. Nests among reeds and other aquatic vegetation. Map 117.

CRESTED COOT *Fulica cristata*   Plate 35

Du – Knobbelmeerkoet   Fr – Foulque à créte
Ge – Kammblässhuhn   Sw – Kamsothöna

Identification: 16" (41cm). Larger than Coot, with similar plumage but *distinctive voice*. Adult differs in bluish bill, *red knobs on top of shield* (reduced in winter), *all-black wings* and bluish-grey legs and toes. Juvenile paler than Coot, with less contrast between brownish upper-parts and greyish-white lower face and under-body. Flight, behaviour and habitat as Coot but shyer, not straying far from cover.

Voice: Usual note a loud, almost human *hoo-hoo*, and loud clucking notes.

Range: Rare S. Spain, apparently resident. Vagrant elsewhere in S. Europe.

CRANES: Gruidae

Large, stately, terrestrial birds, superficially resembling storks. Inner second-aries much elongated, drooping over the tail. Long neck and legs extended in flight. Usually migrate in V or line formation. Voices trumpet-like. Sexes similar. Ground nesting.

CRANE *Grus grus*   **Plate 6**
  Du – Kraanvoge   Fr – Grue cendrée
  Ge – Kranich   Sw – Trana
Identification: 45" (113cm). Long-necked, long-legged, stately, stork-like bird. Much elongated inner flight feathers form *drooping, bushy, 'cloak'* over tail; shorter bill than stork or heron. Adult dusky grey, with distinctive *white stripe curving from eye down upper neck* (emphasized by black on face, long nape and even longer throat), dusky under-body and blackish 'cloak'; close-to, *red central crown* and eye show. In flight, dusky to black flight feathers with deeply 'fingered' primaries contrast with coverts and body. Juvenile lacks adult's head pattern, being sandy-buff on head, neck and body and having only half-grown 'cloak'. Flight outline distinctive, with *head and neck and legs drooping below body line*, and long, square-cut wings; action also distinctive, with powerful wing-beats quicker on upstroke, leading into long glides and soaring on migration. Migrates in goose-like formations, unlike storks. Walks slowly but gracefully, stretching upright in alarm; crouches in distraction run; 'dances' during courtship. Usually shy. Gregarious on migration and in winter.
Voice: Strident, trumpeting *kr-rooh* and quieter guttural *kror-r-r,* various grating and hissing notes.
Habitat: In winter, avoids wooded regions, occurring on river banks, lagoons, fields and steppes. Breeds on ground in wet bogs, lightly wooded swamps, reed-beds, etc. Map 118.

DEMOISELLE CRANE *Anthropoides virgo*   **Plate 6**
  Du – Jufferkraan   Fr – Demoiselle de Numidie
  Ge – Jungfernkranich   Sw – Jungfrutrana
Identification: 38" (95cm). Smaller and more delicately built than Crane, with *looser plumage and long plumes* on nape, drooping from neck, and much longer, straighter, less bushy 'cloak'. Adult clean bluish-grey, with dark slate head, neck and breast, relieved by *white spray behind eye*, and almost black flight-feathers. Juvenile duller, buffy-grey; lacks adult's head and neck pattern. Bill orange-tipped. Flight outline as Crane but action lighter, as is gait.
Voice: Harsh, grating *kar-r-r* and loud, musical trumpeting, noticeably higher-pitched than Crane's.
Habitat and Range: Open plains and high plateaux, visiting fresh water regularly in hot weather. Nests on dry ground. Formerly bred Romania. Vagrant to S., E., C., N. and W. Europe.

BUSTARDS: Otididae

Chiefly terrestrial, frequenting grassy steppes and extensive cultivated fields. Gait a stately walk. Behaviour very shy, crouching or running swiftly at first sign of danger. Flight is powerful; wings broad, bodies stout. Sexes dissimilar. Ground nesting.

LITTLE BUSTARD *Tetrax tetrax*   **Plate 36**

Du – Kleine trap   Fr – Outarde canepetière
Ge – Zwergtrappe   Sw – Småtrapp

Identification: 17" (43cm). Sturdy ground bird, with small head on long straight neck and rather long legs; less than half size of Great. Breeding male shows grey face, *black neck* decorated with *white V below throat* and *white band on upper breast,* and vermiculated sandy-buff crown and upper-parts. In flight, *wings look mainly white* with black outer primary coverts, black 'fingers' and rim to primaries and outer secondaries. Winter male, female and immature lack striking marks on head and neck, which appear uniform with upper-parts, more barred black in female and immature (which also show black bars on secondaries in flight). Flight outline shows straight neck and broad wings, with male's short 7th primary producing whistling noise; action and speed recall grouse or duck. Sociable, often in small or large groups in autumn.

Voice: Short *dahg* or *kiak,* and snorting *ptrrr* or *prett* which carries considerable distance.

Habitat: Grassy or stony plains, large fields of corn, clover and other crops. Map 119.

HOUBARA BUSTARD *Chlamydotis undulata*   **Plate 36**

Du – Kraagtrap   Fr – Outarde houbara
Ge – Kragentrappe   Sw – Kragtrapp

Identification: 25" (63cm). Size between Little and Great but shape recalls female turkey, with noticeably long neck and tail and *long and relatively narrow wings.* Close-to, distinguished by conspicuous *black and white feathers drooping from short crest, mane and sides of neck* which are conspicuously displayed in courtship or aggression. Adult otherwise sandy-buff, heavily blotched on head, back and leading wing-coverts, whitish-grey from throat to breast, white on under-body, and rufous banded pale grey on tail. In flight, shows *mainly black flight feathers* with long white patch on five outer primaries and greyish patches and band on inner primary and greater coverts; wings thus much darker than other bustards. Juvenile lacks greyish throat. Compared to other bustards, flight outline more attenuated, with longer wings and tail; action slower with strangely 'plucked' wing-beat. Usually escapes by creeping away.

Voice: Low grunting bark, rarely heard.

Habitat and Range: Bare stony or sandy steppes, or semi-desert. Also occurs in corn and other crops. Vagrant from Africa and Asia to most of Europe (including Britain).

GREAT BUSTARD *Otis tarda*   **Plate 36**
Du – Grote trap   Fr – Outarde barbue
Ge – Grosstrappe   Sw – Stortrapp
Identification: Male 40" (100cm), female 30" (75cm). Male heaviest bird in
Europe, as large and stout as Canada Goose but standing taller due to long thick
neck and long sturdy legs; female smaller and slimmer. Sexes alike in *pale grey
head and upper neck,* black-blotched and-waved rufous upper-parts, white
under-body, *pale greyish-white wings* with dark 'fingers' and long black tips to
inner primaries and secondaries, and rufous, white-sided tail. Breeding male
distinguished by *orange-chestnut sides of lower neck and breast* and spray of
whitish whiskers on lower face. Juvenile duller, lacking obvious pale eye-ring of
adult but having buffier neck. Male in display inverts plumage; looks all white
and shaggy, conspicuous at long range. Flight outline somewhat goose-like but
head carried higher, wings rectangular; action slow and powerful. Walks sedately with head erect and held slightly back. Usually in small flocks, females
predominating except when incubating.
Voice: In breeding season an occasional deep bark, more rarely a squeal.
Habitat: Frequents and breeds on open treeless plains, grassy steppes, extensive fields of corn, maize, etc. Map 120.

OYSTERCATCHERS: *Haematopodidae*

OYSTERCATCHER *Haematopus ostralegus*   **Plate 42, 50**
Du – Scholekster   Fr – Huitrier pie
Ge – Austernfischer   Sw – Strandskata
Identification: 17" (43cm). Large, stocky, noisy shore-bird with long strong
bill and stout legs. *Plumage pied,* with black head, breast and upper-parts contrasting with white wing-bar, rump, tail-base and under-parts; non-breeding bird
banded white on throat. *Bill red-orange,* flattened laterally; *legs pink.* Flight
outline quite compact; action powerful, with shallow wing-beats; flock shape
irregular.
Voice: Song long piping trill, accelerating, varying in volume. Loud *pic, pic,
pic;* in alarm, strident *kleep, kleep.*
Habitat: Sea-shores, islands, estuaries, feeding on rocks, mussel beds and flats,
roosting on islets and sand bars at high tide; locally inland on upland fields and
moors. Breeds in same areas; increasingly, far from large waters. Map 121.

STILTS AND AVOCETS: Recurvirostridae

BLACK-WINGED STILT *Himantopus himantopus*   **Plate 42, 50**
Du – Steltkluut   Fr – Echasse blanche
Ge – Stelzenläufer   Sw – Styltöpare
Identification: 15" (38cm). Astonishingly attenuated wader, with *incredibly
long legs.* Black back and *black upper and under-wings* contrast with gleaming
white head and under-parts. Needle-like bill black, legs pink. Breeding male

may be patched black on crown or nape; female usually no more than mottled dusky there, with browner back. Juvenile like winter adult, with muddy upper-head, hind-neck and even browner back. Flight outline unmistakable, with sharply pointed, *'triangular' wings* and *legs trailing 7" (18cm) behind tail*; action free, with loose wing-beats. Walk long-paced, deliberate; wades deeply. Nervous, noisy.

Voice: Shrill, yelping *kyik, kyik, kyik*, Coot-like *kek* and a tern-like *kee-arr*.

Habitat: Lagoons, marshes, flooded meadows. Often breeds colonially, building nest on tussock or mud pile in shallow water. Map 122.

AVOCET *Recurvirostra avosetta*   **Plate 42, 50**

Du – Kluut   Fr – Avocette
Ge – Säbelschnäbler   Sw – Skärfläcka

Identification: 17" (43cm). Elegant, dashing wader, with *long, slender, up-curved bill* and long legs. Plumage *predominantly white*, decorated with *black crown and hind-neck*, black back stripes and *black-banded and -ended wings*; bill black, *legs distinctly lead-blue*. Juvenile mottled brownish on upper-parts. Flight outline well-balanced, with wings seemingly short but feet trailing behind tail; action free, allowing both speed and agility. Walk graceful, often accelerated into lunge; feeds with side-to-side sifting movement of bill; often enters deep water, even swimming and 'up-ending' like duck.

Voice: Far-carrying, fluted *kloo-it* or *kleep*; yelping *kyik* or *kew*.

Habitat: Exposed mud-flats, estuaries and sandbanks. Breeds colonially among scrub and tussocks near shallow water, on sandbanks, low islands in river deltas and in brackish lagoons. Map 123.

THICK-KNEES: Burhinidae

STONE CURLEW *Burhinus oedicnemus*   **Plate 36, 52**

Du – Griel   Fr – Oedicnème criard
Ge – Triel   Sw – Tjockfot

Identification: 16 (41cm). Large, long-tailed, rather ungainly wader, with *stout bill, large eyes* and *thick 'knees'* on sturdy legs. Plumage streaked sandy-brown above, white below breast, with black-tipped yellow bill, *yellow eye* in lined face, narrow *black-edged, whitish wing bar* (with pale band deeper in male than female), black-edged greyish panel on greater coverts and pale yellow legs. In flight, black flight feathers contrast with pale band on coverts and are patched white on inner and outer primaries. Flight outline long-tailed; flight usually low, with deliberate, depressed wing-beats and glides. *Run and walk furtive*, often with head sunk into shoulders and body hunched. Rests on horizontal tarsi, depressing body and head to ground when hiding.

Voice: Most vocal at or after dusk; wailing, Curlew-like *coo-ree* and shrill *kee-rrr-eee*, lower pitched on second syllable.

Habitat: Frequents and breeds on stony, sandy and chalky open ground, bare downs, heaths, etc. with scant vegetation, occasionally among scattered pines, marshes, etc., slightly in cultivation. May occur in winter on sea coasts. Map 124.

COURSERS AND PRATINCOLES: Glareolidae

CREAM-COLOURED COURSER *Cursorius cursor*   **Plate 39**
Du – Renvogel   Fr – Courvite isabelle
Ge – Rennvogel   Sw – Ökenlöpare
Identification: 9" (23cm). Slim, elegant, tall plover-like bird, with shortish, sharply-pointed decurved bill and long legs. Plumage *pale sandy*, on ground relieved only by rufous to blue-grey crown, prominent *white supercilium contrasting with black rear eye-stripe* (both meeting on nape) and white under tail, but in flight suddenly showing broad, almost wholly *black outer wing and wing lining*. Juvenile has weak head pattern and scaled back. Flight outline bulky, with trailing feet; action reminiscent of Lapwing but wing-beats more regular in low skim over desert. Walk and run interrupted by erect pause or crouch to feed or escape detection.
Voice: Deep bark *praak-praak*, quieter *tuk-tuk*.
Habitat and Range: Steppes and sub-deserts, with sand and pebbles. Vagrant to sandy or light soil areas of most European countries, west to Britain, north to Scandinavia.

COLLARED PRATINCOLE *Glareola pratincola*   **Plate 38**
Du – Vorkstaartplevier   Fr – Glaréole à collier
Ge – Brachschwalbe   Sw – Vadaresvala
Identification: 10" (25cm). Strange, tern-like marsh bird, with short, stubby decurved bill and *long, deeply forked tail*. Plumage slightly sandy olive-brown above, with *white-tipped dusky secondaries* and *black tail*, buff breast and fore-flanks and white rear under-parts contrasting in flight with dark under-wing – often looking black, but in good light showing *rufous-chestnut on all but lesser coverts*. Close-to, head decorated by black-tipped, red bill with *gape-line running back to below eye*, black lores and necklace, enclosing orange-cream throat-patch. Juvenile pale-margined above; lacks head decorations and has breast-band streaked dark brown. Flight outline and action recall tern or large rakish hirundine; hawks for insects in large noisy flocks. Often crepuscular.
Confusion species: At distance, easily confused with darker Black-winged and Oriental Pratincoles, particularly latter which has similar under-wing pattern but can be distinguished by shorter, less forked tail.
Voice: Hard, rather tern-like *kyik*, chattering *kitti-kirrik-kitik-tik*.
Habitat: Sun-baked mud-flats, with low vegetation, marshes, plains, often near water. Breeds colonially. Map 125.

BLACK-WINGED PRATINCOLE *Glareola nordmanni*   **Plate 38**
Du – Steppenvorkstaartplevier   Fr – Glaréole à ailes noires
Ge – Schwarzflügelige Brachschwalbe   Sw – Svartvingad vadaresvala
Identification: 10" (25cm). Form and behaviour as Collared Pratincole. Plumage pattern similar to Collared but close-to, shows darker upper-parts and particularly *wholly black flight feathers and wing-lining*, with no trace of Collared's white trailing edge and chestnut under-wing coverts, and shorter black tail,

falling well short of, not under, wing tips on ground. Face lacks long gape line but has deeper black lores. Beware rare hybrid with Collared.
Voice: Lower-pitched, more strident than Collared; falcon-like *pwik-kik-kik* distinctive.
Habitat and Range: Similar to Collared, breeds in Danube delta. Vagrants from Asian steppes reach W., N. and C. Europe.

PLOVERS: Charadriidae

Wading birds, more compactly built, thicker-necked and more boldly patterned than sandpipers; bills are shorter and stouter, eyes larger. Distinctive tilting action when feeding. Plumage patterns in flight, and call-notes, are important in identification. Immatures of many species summer on coasts south of breeding range. Sexes usually similar. Ground nesting.

LITTLE RINGED PLOVER *Charadrius dubius*   Plate 38, 40
Du – Kleine plevier   Fr – Petit gravelot
Ge – Flussregenpfeifer   Sw – Mindre strandpipare
Identification: 6 ¾" (17cm). Smaller than Ringed, with proportionately shorter, more rounded head, *shorter, broader wings lacking wing-bar*, and *distinctive voice*. Adult differs from Ringed in bright *yellow eye-ring*, white supercilium continuing over crown behind black forehead-band and *dull flesh or yellowish legs*. Juvenile has indistinct eye-ring but has *yellowish-brown forehead*, no supercilium and often incomplete gorget. Flight outline more compact than Ringed, with shorter tail and *more jerkily beaten wings* giving action recalling Common Sandpiper. Cautious but quite tame.
Voice: Rather loud and ringing, with commonest call *tee-u* and trilling song *tree-a, tree-a* and *tree, tree, tree*.
Habitat: Fresh-water localities, particularly flooded gravel-pits and gravelly river islands; on coasts in winter. Breeds on gravel or sand shores of inland waters, locally on coasts. Map 126.

RINGED PLOVER *Charadrius hiaticula*   Plate 38, 40
Du – Bontbekplevier   Fr – Grand gravelot
Ge – Sandregenpfeifer   Sw – Större strandpipare
Identification: 7" (18cm). Plump, lively shore-bird, running rapidly and then tilting forward to pick up food. Adult distinguished by *short black-tipped orange bill*, bold white forehead, black bands over forehead and through eye, complete white collar contrasting with *broad black 'ring' round upper breast*, hair-brown upper-parts, white under-body and rather short *orange legs*. Juvenile has dark bill, white forehead but no black on head, blackish-brown breast-band (often broken in centre), pale scales on upper-parts and dull legs. At all ages, *long white wing bar* and *long rufous-centred and white-edged tail* catch eye in flight. Flight outline lengthy, with noticeably extended tail; action loose with either rapid or, in display, slow 'butterfly' wing-beats. Quite bold; gregarious.
Voice: Call melodious *too-li*, or *coo-eep*. Flight song begins slowly, becoming a trilling repetition of the phrase *quitu-weeoo*.
Habitat: Sandy and muddy shores, visiting inland waters, etc., on migration.

Breeds on beaches, among dunes, salt-marshes, locally inland on tundra, sandy ground and dry stream-beds. Map 127.

KILLDEER *Charadrius vociferus* **Plate 38**
Du – Killdeerplevier Fr – Gravelot à double collier
Ge – Keilschwanzregenpfeifer Sw – Skrikstrandpipare
Identification: 10" (26cm). Larger and much more attenuated than Ringed, with proportionately longer, fine bill and *much longer, wedge-shaped tail*. Distinguished by diagnostic *double black breast band*, long *orange-rufous rump* and tail centre, *black subterminal and white terminal bands round tail* and bold white wing-bar. *Bill black*; legs pale flesh. Flight outline dominated by trailing tail; action loose but powerful.
Voice: Usually noisy; a loud, insistent and repeated *kill-dee* or *kill- deea*; also plaintive *dee-ee*, with rising inflection.
Habitat and Range: In N. America, counterpart of Lapwing, breeding on ploughed fields and pasture. In winter, occurs both inland and on coasts. Vagrant to N.,C. and W. Europe (including Britain).

KENTISH PLOVER *Charadrius alexandrinus* **Plate 38, 40**
Du – Strandplevier Fr – Gravelot à collier interrompu
Ge – Seeregenpfeifer Sw – Svartbent strandpipare
N. Am – Snowy Plover
Identification: 6 ¾" (17cm). Plumper and relatively longer-legged than Ringed, with *fine bill* and remarkable 'twinkling' gait. Distinguished from Ringed and Little Ringed by paler upper-parts, *always black bill*, usually dark legs and '*in*complete' head and breast marks. Breeding male shows only small black patch before *orange-rufous crown*, black eye-stripe and *narrow black patch on sides of breast*. Female and immature have off-white forehead and supercilium and only *dusky eye patch and sides to breast*. Wing-bar narrower than Ringed but tail even more conspicuously white-edged. Beware rare adult and frequent juveniles with yellowish or flesh coloured legs. Best separated from Ringed by voice. Flight outline more compact than Ringed; action more rapid, often skimming low over sand.
Voice: Soft *wit-tit-tit*, fluty *pòo-eet*, or *po-it* calls. Alarm, *kittup*. Song, a long trill, beginning slowly and accelerating.
Habitat: Mainly coastal. Frequents and nests on shingle, or mixed sand and mud beaches, dry mud-flats. Map 128.

GREATER SAND PLOVER *Charadrius leschenaultii* **Plate 38**
Du – Woestijnplevier Fr – Gravelot mongol
Ge – Wüstenregenpfeifer Sw – Ökenpipare
Identification: 9" (23cm). Lengthy and tall plover, with heavy *tern-like, bulbous bill*, large, rather square head and *long legs*, all proportionately more striking than on Lesser Sand (see Accidentals). Plumage pattern and colours similar to female Kentish but breeding male has distinctive *black mask* with only small white forehead patch, *rufous sides to neck and deep breast-band*. At all ages and particularly on juvenile, pale edges to scapulars and wing-coverts more distinct than on Lesser Sand. Bill black; *legs greenish-grey*. Flight outline and action

recall Golden Plover, with less tail extension than Ringed but *trailing feet*, unlike Lesser Sand.

Voice: Quiet for plover. Calls include musical, whistling *peeph* and soft, rolling *trrr*, latter suggesting Turnstone.

Habitat and Range: Normally inhabits saline waters of desert and steppe but in winter frequents coastal sands and mud-flats. Vagrant from W. and C. Asia to S., W., C., N. and E. Europe (including Britain).

DOTTEREL *Charadrius morinellus*   Plate 38, 40

Du – Morinelplevier   Fr – Pluvier guignard
Ge – Mornellregenpfeifer   Sw – Fjällpipare

Identification: 8-10" (21-25cm). Smaller than any *Pluvialis* plover, though with similar but somewhat tubbier shape on ground and shorter-tailed outline in flight; female rather brighter-marked and larger than male. Breeding plumage recalls *Alectoris* partridge with *broad white rear supercilium joining in 'V'* at rear of almost black crown, whitish face, black-streaked throat, grey (female) or brown (male) breast ending in black-edged white band, *orange-chestnut underbody with large black belly* and long buff scales on brown scapulars and wingcoverts. In flight, *wings uniform with back* but white shaft of outer primary and white rim to terminal black tail-band often catch eye. Winter adult and juvenile less colourful, with ashy breast and pale buff under-parts, but combination of buff-white rear supercilium and *whitish breast-band* diagnostic, eliminating immature *Pluvialis* plover. Fearless at nest, often tame on passage.

Voice: Repeated, soft *titi-ri-titi-ri*, becoming rapid trill.

Habitat: Stony heights and tundra; on migration on lowland heaths, coastal fields. Breeds on bare high ground. Map 129.

PACIFIC GOLDEN PLOVER *Pluvialis fulva*   Plate 37

Du – Aziatische Goudplevier   Fr – Pluvier fauve asiàtique
Ge – Sibirischer Goldregenpfeifer   Sw – Sibirisk tundrapipare

Identification: 10" (25cm). Rather smaller than American Golden, with proportionately shorter *wings almost cloaked by tertials at rest* but longer bill and legs. *Dusky under-wing* similar to American Golden but breeding adult distinguished by *mostly white flanks and under-tail coverts*, while immature has distinctly *more golden appearance* and less pale forehead and supercilium recalling Golden. Flight and behaviour like American Golden. See also Golden.

Voice: Most distinctive call plaintive *dlu-eep*, reminiscent of Spotted Redshank.

Habitat and Range: N. Asian counterpart of American Golden. Vagrant to most of Europe (including Britain).

AMERICAN GOLDEN PLOVER *Pluvialis dominica*   Plate 37

Du – Kleine goudplevier   Fr – Pluvier fauve d'Amérique
Ge – Amerikanischer Goldregenpfeifer   Sw – Nordamerikansk tundrapipare

Identification: 11" (28cm). Size between Golden and Pacific Golden with proportionately larger bill and *longest, narrowest wings of tribe*, with points extending well beyond tail; relatively squarer head and *longer, thinner legs than Golden*. In flight, instantly separated from Golden by *brownish-grey under-wing* and, except when breeding, generally *duller, greyer plumage*, with pale yellowish spots often appearing whitish in field. Breeding plumage darker than Golden and Pacific Golden, with more black in gold-flecked upper-parts, *wide white blaze* down neck to shoulder, and *all black under-body and vent*. Immature plumage recalls Grey Plover, with *whiter supercilium*, darker ear-spot, more mottled breast and *more softly barred flanks and belly than Golden*. Flight and gait like Golden but always looks long-winged and spindly-shanked. See also Golden.

Voice: Most distinctive calls Lapwing-like *pee-wit* and *klee-e-eet*; also quiet *pu*,

Habitat and Range: Normally inhabits tundra, wintering on pampas. In Europe, joins Golden in various habitats. Vagrant from N. America to N., C., E. and W. Europe (including Britain).

GOLDEN PLOVER *Pluvialis apricaria*   **Plate 37, 40**
    Du – Goudplevier   Fr – Pluvier doré
    Ge – Goldregenpfeifer   Sw – Ljungpipare

Identification: 11" (28cm). Commonest and most widespread of golden plovers, easily distinguished from smaller, slighter American and Pacific Golden by *white wing linings* and always golden-spotted upper-parts, with rather *uniform, large-eyed face* in winter plumage. Slightly smaller and shorter-winged than Grey Plover, lacking its black axillary patch. Breeding plumage variable; so-called Northern form from Iceland and arctic Europe *fully black on face, neck and under-body* as far as vent, with well-defined clean white divide from upper-parts. Southern form from Britain and S. Fenno-Scandia less completely black below, often with *patchy face and neck* and wider, black and gold splashed divide; looks far less clean-cut than Northern. Winter adult and juvenile assume golden face and breast, latter spotted and streaked dusky; adult has *cleaner, whiter belly* than juvenile and American and Pacific Golden. Most birds show quite obvious whitish panel across primaries, unlike American and Pacific Golden, but mark never as striking as long bar of Grey. Flight outline quite compact, with bull head and pointed wing tips; action rapid, allowing remarkable acceleration; often indulges in long glides and spectacular tumbling descents to roosts. Flock formation tight, unlike frequent companion but always straggling Lapwing.

Voice: Call-note (usually in flight) clear liquid *tlui*; in alarm, melancholy *tlu-i*. Song, in display flight, varied rippling trill, embodying repeated phrases *toori*, *tirr-peeoo*, etc.

Habitat: Hilly and lowland moors, and, in winter, also fields, sea-shores and estuaries. Nests among heather. Map 130.

GREY PLOVER *Pluvialis squatarola*   **Plate 37, 40**
    Du – Zilverplevier   Fr – Pluvier argenté
    Ge – Kiebitzregenpfeifer   Sw – Kustpipare
    N. Am – Black-bellied Plover

Identification: 12" (30cm). Noticeably bulkier than Golden, with deeper, slightly bulbous bill, rather larger head, hunched back, fuller chest and longer outer wing. Easily distinguished in all plumages by *conspicuous black axillaries, white wing-bar*, whitish rump, white-barred tail and *distinctive call*. Breeding plumage very striking, with *silver, white and black chequered upper-*

parts, white divide and fully *black face and under-body.* Winter adult and immature much duller grey, patterned as Golden but with restricted pale belly. Beware confusing juvenile, closely spotted with yellow on mantle and wing-coverts, with duller individuals of Golden and American Golden. Flight outline and action noticeably looser than Golden. Looks dejected when feeding, with *slower gait* than Golden.

Voice: Call plaintive, *trisyllabic,* slurred whistle *tlee-u-ee.*

Habitat: Chiefly coastal mud-flats, sandy beaches and shores. Breeds on arctic tundra. Map 131.

SPUR-WINGED PLOVER *Hoplopterus spinosus*   Plate 39

Du – Sporenkievit   Fr – Vanneau éperonné
Ge – Spornkiebitz   Sw – Sporrvipa

Identification: 11" (28cm). Slightly smaller than Lapwing, with blunt but not round-ended wings and only slight crest. Dun-brown upper-parts with drooping dark-edged scapulars contrast with striking *black and white head and neck, black throat and under-body,* white vent and rump, mostly black tail. In flight shows white greater coverts and wing linings, relieved by dun-brown leading coverts above and *wholly black flight feathers above and below.* Flight and behaviour recall Lapwing, feeding with hunched posture. Spur on carpal joint rarely visible. Eye red.

Voice: Calls include harsh but sonorous *charadee-deeoo* in display and loud *zac-zac-zac* or *tick-tick* in alarm.

Habitat and Range: Open ground and marshes, often saline. A N. African and Asiatic species, breeding in N.E. Greece and on Black Sea coast. Vagrant S. and C. Europe.

SOCIABLE PLOVER *Chettusia gregaria*   Plate 39

Du – Steppenkievit   Fr – Pluvier sociable
Ge – Steppenkiebitz   Sw – Stäppvipa

Identification: 12" (31cm). Rather large plover, close in size to Lapwing but with form differing in narrower, less rounded wings and noticeably longer legs. At distance, looks grey-brown on ground but close-to, breeding adult shows Dotterel-like *black crown contrasting with white forehead and long supercilia* joining at nape and *dark chestnut belly,* but rest of plumage far more uniform, with almost orange cheeks below dark eye-stripe, buff breast and flanks and pinkish-grey upper-parts. In flight, shows strong contrast between *mainly black outer wings and tail* and *white rump, secondaries and under-wing coverts.* Winter adult and immature lack dark belly and have subdued head pattern, while upper-parts show thin pale scales; juvenile shows heavily spotted breast. Flight action includes *faster wing-beats than Lapwing* noticeable at long range; gait higher-stepping than Lapwing.

Voice: In winter shrill, short whistle and harsh rasping *etch-etch-etch,* sometimes becoming long chatter.

Habitat and Range: Open sandy or grassy plains, wastelands near upland cultivation; also occurs near coasts. Breeds in steppe. Vagrant from Asia to E., C., N., S., amd W. Europe (including Britain).

WHITE-TAILED PLOVER *Chettusia leucura*   **Plate 39**
   Du – Witstaartkievit   Fr – Vanneau à queue blanche
   Ge – Weisschwanzsteppenkiebitz   Sw – Sumpvipa

Identification: 11" (28cm). Smaller than Lapwing, with proportionately longer bill, *much longer legs* and shorter tail. Adult distinguished by *pale-faced, greyish head,* deep *grey lower breast, fully white tail* and *yellow legs*; close-to, bronze-brown upper-parts and rosy rear flanks also catch eye. Wing pattern like Sociable but outer secondaries black-tipped and inner primary coverts partly white. Wing shape and flight as Lapwing but *legs and feet trail noticeably.*
Voice: Usual call shrill *kit-kit.*
Habitat and Range: Fresh-water marshes and lagoons. Vagrant from W.Asia to E., S. and W. Europe (including Britain).

LAPWING *Vanellus vanellus*   **Plate 39, 40**
   Du – Kievit   Fr – Vanneau huppé
   Ge – Kiebitz   Sw – Tofsvipa

Identification: 12" (31cm). Commonest and most widespread, round-winged plover of Europe, with unique *long wispy crest,* almost wholly *greenish-black and white plumage* and rather short legs. In flight, has distinctive *pied, 'twinkling'* appearance; extraordinarily *broad and rounded ends to wings* catch eye. Close-to, shows orange-chestnut under tail-coverts. Juvenile has buff scales on back. Breeding male has cleaner head pattern and longer crest than female. Flight outline distinctive, with much flapping wing more visible at distance than body; action usually slow and loose, seemingly weak on migration but fast and strong during astonishing aerobatic display in spring. Gregarious, often in huge straggling flocks in winter.
Voice: Loud, nasal *peeze-weet,* or longer *pee-r-weet,* with variants.
Habitat: Farmlands, sewage-farms, marshes and mud-flats. Breeds on arable land, moors, marshes, etc. Map 132.

SANDPIPERS, STINTS, GODWITS, CURLEWS, SNIPE, PHALAROPES: Scolopacidae

Wading birds, less compactly built, mostly longer-necked and -legged and more intricately patterned than plovers; wings usually pointed and angular; bills usually long and slender. Plumages often differ in summer, winter and first autumn; wing-bars, rump and tail patterns important diagnostically. Many species summer on coasts south of breeding range, sometimes in large flocks. Sexes mostly similar. Usually ground nesting. For convenience, may be divided into:
Shore Sandpipers: Relatively large members of *Calidris*; key species Knot and Dunlin.
Stints: Relatively small, even tiny members of *Calidris*; key species Little Stint.
Snipe: Skulking, cryptically plumaged members of *Limnocryptes* and *Gallinago,* flushing at close range; key species Snipe.
Dowitchers: Snipe-like members of *Limnodromus*, with some behaviour and plumage also recalling shank.

Godwits: Long- and straight-billed members of *Limosa*, approaching Curlew in size.
Curlews: Mostly long-and curved-billed members of *Numenius*, with rather uniform plumages except for pale rumps, and loud calls; key species Curlew.
Shanks and Shank-like Sandpipers: Small to quite large, usually straight-billed members of *Tringa*, with calls, colours of legs and wing and rump patterns particularly important to diagnosis; key species Redshank and Green Sandpiper.
Phalaropes: Rather small, swimming members of *Phalaropus*, somewhat re-calling *Calidris* but going out to sea after breeding; key species Grey Phalarope.

The family also includes several other single or pairs of specialised waders; see texts.

KNOT *Calidris canutus*   **Plate 43, 52**
     Du – Kanoetstrandloper   Fr – Bécasseau maubèche
     Ge – Knutt   Sw – Kustsnäppa
Identification: 10" (26cm). Largest common member of tribe in Europe; half as large again as Dunlin but with relatively shorter bill and legs and longer wings. Breeding adult *russet-red on face, under-body and sides of back*, boldly marked black on crown and back, with grey wing-coverts. Winter adult *nonde-script 'scaly' ash-grey above* and on breast, and whitish below; fine streaking or bars on head, breast and flanks visible close-to. Juvenile like winter adult but shows *warm pinkish-buff hue on breast and flanks*. In flight, shows white wing-bar and barred, at any distance *dull, white rump*. Flight outline shows long deep body and long pointed wings; often in densely packed 'carpets' on mud; per-forms mass evolutions when moving along tides. Great Knot recently recorded in Europe (see Accidentals).
Voice: Low *nut*, flight call whistling *twit-wit*.
Habitat: Frequents sandy and muddy sea-shores, occasionally on inland waters. Breeds on high arctic barrens. Map 133.

SANDERLING *Calidris alba*   **Plate 47, 52**
     Du – Drieteenstrandloper   Fr – Bécasseau sanderling
     Ge – Sanderling   Sw – Sandlöpare
Identification: 7" (18cm). Extremely active, plump shoreline wader which *races after retracting waves* like clockwork toy. In all plumages, *pure white under-body* and *long, broad white wing-bar* contrasting with black-edged wings distinctive. Breeding adult has head, breast, upper flanks and upper-parts *chest-nut, spangled black and white* on back and spotted black on breast. Winter adult *white-faced and -breasted* with *pearl-grey upper-parts*; by far whitest of tribe, lacking dark eye-patch and crown of phalarope but showing distinct patch of *dusky lesser wing-coverts* at shoulder. Juvenile like winter adult but *heavily che-quered black and white above*, with initially pinkish-buff on head and breast. Flight outline like Dunlin but tubbier.
Confusion species: Often confused with Dunlin but larger size, shorter bill and bolder wing-bar soon learnt; beware also confusion with much smaller stints particularly Red-necked and Baird's Sandpiper, which see.
Voice: Short *twick* or *quit*.
Habitat: Winters on sandy beaches; a few occur inland on passage. Breeds on stony arctic tundra. Map 134.

SEMIPALMATED SANDPIPER *Calidris pusilla*   **Plate 49**
Du – Kleine grijze strandloper   Fr – Bécasseau semi-palmé
Ge – Sandstrandläufer   Sw – Sandsnäppa
Identification: 6" (15cm). Rare N. American stint, with rather thick-tipped bill, rotund body and deliberate plover-like gait when feeding. Small webs between toes occasionally visible, particularly when viewed from behind. All plumage colours and patterns rather dull, legs black, *best distinguished by call*. Breeding adult ochre-brown above; breast streaks extend along flanks. Winter adult ochre-grey above, with *noticeable patch of dark centres on rear scapulars*. Juvenile drabber than breeding adult, lacking obvious 'V' on mantle but showing pale-edged, dark scapulars; head strongly patterned, with *fully streaked crown*, prominent *white supercilium and half-collar*. Whitish wing-bar extends into primaries.
Confusion species: Call crucial to distinction from Red-necked Stint, Little Stint and Western Sandpiper in winter and juvenile plumage. Beware particularly long-billed Semi-palmated from E. Canada, resembling last-named species.
Voice: Call short, flat, husky *chirrup*, recalling Dunlin and Pectoral Sandpiper.
Habitat and Range: In Europe, as Little Stint. Vagrant from N. America to W. and N. Europe (including Britain).

LITTLE STINT *Calidris minuta*   **Plate 48, 52**
Du – Kleine strandloper   Fr – Bécasseau minute
Ge – Zwergstrandläufer   Sw – Småsnäppa
Identification: 5" (13cm). Commonest stint, with short, straight bill, neat build and 'twinkling' legs. Breeding adult foxy on crown, cheeks and upper-parts, last spotted and marked brown-black; rufous-buff on breast, streaked dusky; pure white on under-body. Close-to, buff-white supercilium, yellowish fringes to mantle edges, *rufous-edged inner wing-coverts and tertials*, grey outer tail feathers and *black legs* diagnostic in combination. Winter adult mouse-grey above, whiter below; scapulars retain dusky centres. Juvenile like breeding adult but differs in whiter forehead, *split supercilium*, paler breast, *obvious white V on mantle* and white scaling of scapulars. Due to considerable variation in plumage tones, can be confused with all other stints, which see; runt Dunlin has decurved bill-tip. Flight more agile than larger *Calidris*, with distinctive flutter.
Voice: Song long undulating trill. Call sharp *tit* or *tirri-tit-tit*.
Habitat: Breeds on coastal swards and tundra. Migrants prefer soft mud along estuary edges. Map 135.

TEMMINCK'S STINT *Calidris temminckii*   **Plate 48, 52**
Du – Temminck's strandloper   Fr – Bécasseau de Temminck
Ge – Temminckstrandläufer   Sw – Mosnäppa
Identification: 5" (13cm). Secretive stint, with fine bill, lengthy silhouette and rather short legs; *'towers' when flushed*. White outer tail feathers and rump sides form *long white panels on sides of blackish rump and tail*; whitish wing-bar restricted to inner wing; *legs greenish-yellow*. All plumage colours and patterns rather dull and uniform; *sides of chest always clouded*. Breeding adult brown-grey above, irregularly patched dark; has indistinct fore-supercilium; winter adult drabber. Juvenile almost uniform olive-brown above, with narrow *black*

subterminal band on larger feathers unique within stints. Mouse-like on ground. In flight, wings and tail look lengthy. Solitary on passage. Brightest breeding birds may suggest pale Little Stint.

Voice: Short trill *tirrr* and buzzy, prolonged tittering, in display-flight and from ground.

Habitat: Seldom on sea-shore. On passage frequents wet marshes, lakes with vegetation, occasionally saltings and estuaries. Breeds among low vegetation on tundra, shores and islets. Map 136.

LEAST SANDPIPER *Calidris minutilla*　　　　　　　　　**Plate 49**
　　Du – Amerikaanse kleinste strandloper　　Fr – Bécasseau minuscule
　　Ge – Wiesenstrandläufer　　　　　　　　　Sw – Dvärgsnäppa
Identification: 4½" (12cm). Rare N. American stint, smallest of tribe, with *needle bill*, rather square head, rather short body and wings but rather long toes. All plumage colours rather dark, due to large feather centres; *streaked breast obvious at all times*. Breeding adult rich dark brown above, with indistinct supercilium; in contrast, very white below. Winter adult dusky-brown above. Juvenile *black-brown above*, with head, mantle and scapular pattern like Little Stint. Bill pale-based, *legs and toes usually pale, olive-yellow*. Whitish wing-bar narrow, indistinct. Flight action very rapid; gait 'twinkling'. Rears up in alarm.
Confusion species: Small dark Little Stint has dark legs (exceptional in Least); real bogey is Long-toed Stint but it lacks such sharp call (see Accidentals).
Voice: Calls high, drawn-out *kreet*; variations of *trrip-trip* and *quee*.
Habitat and Range: Tidal flats, shores, marshes. Vagrant from N. America to W. (including Britain), N. and C. Europe.

WHITE-RUMPED SANDPIPER *Calidris fuscicollis*　　　　**Plate 49**
　　Du – Bonaparte's strandloper　　　　Fr – Bécasseau de Bonaparte
　　Ge – Weissbürzelstrandläufer　　　　Sw – Vitgumpsnäppa
Identification: 7" (17.5cm). Size between stint and Dunlin but form more attenuated than both, with wing-tips extending well past tail and relatively short legs. In flight, *small white rump* – placed low over tail – suggests Curlew Sandpiper, but *white wing-bar thin and restricted to secondaries.* Breeding adult noticeably streaked, with rufous crown, whitish supercilium, *fully lined gorget* and *blackish chevrons on flanks*. Winter adult retains clean supercilium and streaked breast, but upper-parts become dull dun-grey. Juvenile more colourful than adult, with *rufous crown and back*, last decorated with *thin white lines and delicate white scales* continuing onto wing-coverts. Short bill droops at tip. Flight outline suggests long-winged stint; action typical of small *Calidris*.
Voice: Thin, mouse-like *jeet* or *tzeet*.
Habitat and Range: Wanderers join other *Calidris* on coasts and other muddy localities including sewage farms. Vagrant from N. America to N., C., E. and W. Europe (including Britain).

BAIRD'S SANDPIPER *Calidris bairdii*　　　　　　　　　**Plate 49**
　　Du – Baird's strandloper　　　　　Fr – Bécasseau de Baird
　　Ge – Baird-Strandläufer　　　　　Sw – Gulbröstad snäppa
Identification: 7" (17.5cm). Size as White-rumped, but shape even slimmer with deep chest contributing to horizontal stance, *long wing-tips extending well*

past tail, and narrow, fine-tipped bill. In flight, *lower back, rump and tail-centre black, looking broader than in stints* but white wing-bar thin and faint. Breeding adult and juvenile plumage buffish-brown, with *pale grey and almost white fringes on back and scapulars and tertials forming obvious scales* and full, softly streaked gorget. Winter adult more uniform above, brown to dun-grey. At all ages, under-body white, unmarked on flanks. Flight outline and action like White-rumped.
Voice: Call rolled *churrut* or *krreep*.
Habitat and Range: As White-rumped. Vagrant from N. America to N., C., E. and W. Europe (including Britain).

PECTORAL SANDPIPER *Calidris melanotos*   **Plate 46, 52**
Du – Gestreepte strandloper   Fr – Bécasseau tacheté
Ge – Graubruststrandläufer   Sw – Tuvsnäppa
Identification: 8¾" (22cm). Larger than Dunlin but with proportionately shorter, straighter bill, smaller head and longer neck in alarm posture. *Pectoral band distinctive*, being fully streaked and ending abruptly on lower breast in all plumages and heavily mottled blackish-brown in breeding male. Upper-parts patterned like young Ruff, with *intricate buff and white scales and stripes* on rufous and blackish ground; relieved by shallow, dark head-cap, whitish supercilium (brightest in juvenile) and white under-body. Winter adult duller, greyer above, with broader scaling. In flight, wings look dark with only thin faint whitish wing-bar, but *black centre to lower back, rump and tail contrasts with extensive white lateral tail-coverts*, as in Ruff. *Legs ochre*. Flight outline looser than Dunlin; erratic flight when flushed may recall Snipe.
Voice: Rather hoarse *krrik* or *tchree-eep*.
Habitat and Range: Occurs on passage on grassy mud-flats and marshes, occasionally on sea-shores. Autumn visitor from N. America to Britain, Ireland. Vagrant elsewhere in W., N., C. and E. Europe.

SHARP-TAILED SANDPIPER *Calidris acuminata*   **Plate 46**
Du – Siberische gestreepte strandloper   Fr – Bécasseau à queue pointue
Ge – Spitzschwanzstrandläufer   Sw – Spetsstjärtad snäppa
Identification: 8" (20cm). Size, shape and behaviour close to Pectoral but slightly shorter-billed and noticeably shorter-legged. Breeding adult instantly distinguished from Pectoral by *dark chevrons over most of under-body*, more rufous crown and upper-parts and usually greenish-grey legs. Winter adult less distinctive but shows sharper scales above and often flecked flanks in addition to structural differences. Juvenile very distinctive, with dark-lined, *rufous crown cap contrasting with long cream supercilium* and *orange-buff breast* only streaked at sides; upper-parts with more rufous fringes than Pectoral. Thin white wing-bar more obvious than on Pectoral.
Voice: Rather rasping *trrit-trrit*, or more Swallow-like *chree-creep*, less harsh than Pectoral's call.
Habitat and Range: Sea-shores and grassy edges of salt-marshes. Vagrant from Siberia to W. (including Britain), N. and C. Europe.

CURLEW SANDPIPER *Calidris ferruginea* **Plate 52**
Du – Krombekstrandloper Fr – Bécasseau corcorli
Ge – Sichelstrandläufer Sw – Spovsnäppa

Identification: 8" (20cm). Head and body size as Dunlin but with *long, slender, evenly decurved bill*, long wing-points and legs all contributing to more elegant form. In flight, shows unique combination in small waders of *pure white rump and long white wing-bar*. Breeding adult *russet-red on head, neck and under-body*, with black spangles on scapulars and pale greyish wing-coverts; close-to, white chin shows. Winter adult rather plain grey-brown above, looking cleaner than Dunlin with *long white supercilium* and virtually unmarked underparts. Juvenile distinctive, with dark brown upper-parts *delicately scaled buff and white*, obvious white supercilium and pale rosy-buff wash on foreneck and breast. Flight outline looser than Dunlin, with greater wing-span; action less fast, more fluent over distance. Habitually feeds while wading.

Voice: Liquid, trilling, not far-carrying *chirrip*.

Habitat and Range: On passage, as Dunlin. Breeds in E. arctic Asia. On passage throughout Europe; in winter occasionally north to British Isles.

PURPLE SANDPIPER *Calidris maritima* **Plate 48, 52**
Du – Paarse strandloper Fr – Bécasseau violet
Ge – Meerstrandläufer Sw – Skärsnäppa

Identification: 8" (20cm). Larger than Dunlin with long bill but otherwise dumpiest of all *Calidris*, with short legs. Winter plumage *darkest of small waders*, appearing almost wholly dusky except for bold *white lateral coverts emphasizing blackish tail* and rump centre, white wing-bar, white belly and inner under-wing; *base of bill and legs yellowish*. Breeding adult and juvenile much brighter, with *rufous fringes on back* and pale supercilium and chin, streaks on lower breast. Flight outline tubby, rump and tail looking broad behind flickering wings. Tame.

Voice: When flushed, high-pitched trilling *tritt, tritt* or piping *weet-wit*.

Habitat: Breeds on mountain tops and in Arctic on coastal tundra. Winters in inter-tidal zone of offshore isles and rocky coasts. Map 137.

DUNLIN *Calidris alpina* **Plate 47, 52**
Du – Bonte strandloper Fr – Bécasseau variable
Ge – Alpenstrandläufer Sw – Kärrsnäppa
N. Am – Red-backed Sandpiper

Identification: 7" (18cm). Commonest and most widespread of tribe; larger than any stint, with quite long bill with decurved tip. Breeding adult distinctive, with *rufous crown and back*, black and white streaked face, neck and upper breast and *conspicuous black patch on lower breast and fore-belly*. Northern tundra race *C. a. alpina* larger, longer-billed and brighter than southern moorland race *C. a. schinzii*. Winter adult dull grey-brown above, with dull face *lacking clear supercilium*, and white below, except for clouded sides to breast. Juvenile buff-brown, with rufous crown and back not as neatly scaled as stint and *streaks on breast enlarging on flanks to become dusky blotches*. In flight, shows conspicuous black rump centre. Flight outline bulkier than stint but action similar. Gregarious except when breeding. Feeds in distinctive hunched posture.

Beware confusing cleaner birds with Curlew Sandpiper and smallest, shortest-billed birds with Baird's Sandpiper and stints.
Voice: Song, purring trill. In flight short, high, nasal *dzee* or *schree*.
Habitat; Sea-shores, estuaries, also inland waters, sewage-farms, etc. Breeds near water on high moors, bogs, salt-marshes. Map 138.

BROAD-BILLED SANDPIPER *Limicola falcinellus* **Plate 48**
  Du – Breedbekstrandloper   Fr – Bécasseau falcinelle
  Ge – Sumpfläufer   Sw – Myrsnäppa
Identification: 7" (18cm). Looks smaller than Dunlin, with rather short legs and disproportionately *long bill with heavy base and kinked tip*. Distinguished in breeding plumage by very dark upper-parts, with bold Jack Snipe-like *creamy streaks on back*, bold double *white supercilium forking before eye*, giving head distinctive striped appearance, and breast streaks extending along flanks over white belly. In flight, looks very dark, with tail and rump as Dunlin but wing has blackish leading edge and only faint wing-bar. Winter adult pearl-grey above, with delicate *white scales on scapulars and wings* and less contrasting head stripes. Juvenile like breeding adult but central wing-coverts fringed paler and flanks unmarked. Flight outline and action suggest large stint. Unobtrusive and often less active than most shore-birds.
Voice: Deep, trilling *chr-r-eek* or *brrreit*, suggesting Sand Martin, and short *tett* in flight.
Habitat: On passage, usually in salt-marshes, mud-flats, sewage-farms, less often on sea-shore. Nests in tussocks in wet bogs and morasses. Map 139.

STILT SANDPIPER *Micropalama himantopus* **Plate 45**
  Du – Steltstrandloper   Fr – Bécasseau à échasses
  Ge – Bindenstrandläufer   Sw – Styltsnäppa
Identification: 8" (20cm). Body-size near Pectoral but with noticeably longer bill kinked downwards, long neck and *long, spindly legs*. Breeding adult unmistakable with *strongly barred under-parts* and *rusty cheek-patch under white supercilium*. Winter adult brownish-grey above, closely streaked from face to flanks. Juvenile browner and pale-scaled on back, with buffish neck and clean white flanks and under-body. In flight, shows *long white rump and upper tail-coverts*, partly barred when breeding, and *trailing greenish legs*; lacks white wing-bar of Curlew Sandpiper but may be confused with Lesser Yellowlegs and Wilson's Phalarope, which see. *Feeds like dowitcher*.
Voice: Call quiet rattled *kirrr* or *grrrt*.
Habitat and Range: As *Calidris*. Vagrant from N. America to N., C., and W. Europe (including Britain).

BUFF-BREASTED SANDPIPER *Tryngites subruficollis* **Plate 46**
  Du – Blonde strandloper   Fr – Bécasseau roussâtre
  Ge – Grasläufer   Sw – Prärielöpare
Identification: 7-8" (18-20cm). Distinctive, medium-sized wader combining rather plover-like shape with plumage pattern of juvenile Ruff; male larger than female. Shows *short, straight bill, round head*, stretched neck in alarm and *shortish, high-stepping legs*. Face and under-parts *clear orange-buff*, fading to white on belly or vent; close-to, dark eye emphasized by whitish eye-ring.

Under-wing white, with dusky rim and carpal marks, *legs pale orange*. Flight free and graceful, recalling shank. Often tame.
Voice: Low, trilled *pr-r-r-reet* and clicking *tik*.
Habitat and Range: Dry fields with very short grass, in preference to shores. Vagrant from N. America. Recorded chiefly in British Isles, particularly at S.W. airports; also elsewhere in W., C., N. and E. Europe.

RUFF *Philomachus pugnax*   **Plate 46, 52**
   Du – Kemphaan   Fr – Chevalier combattant
   Ge – Kampfläufer   Sw – Brushane
Identification: Male (Ruff) 11" (28cm), female (Reeve) 9" (23cm). Marked size variation produces confusion with both sandpipers and shanks but has distinctive lumbering gait and hunch-backed, *loose-winged*, gliding flight. In all seasons, shows characteristic *dark tail with conspicuous white lateral coverts on each side of rump*, occasionally joining in pale 'horseshoe'; dark wings with only faint wing-bar, and *boldly scaled or barred upper-parts*. Juvenile puzzling, with *pinkish-buff breast* suggesting Buff-breasted Sandpiper. Winter adult dull grey-brown above, with *pale scales*, white below and occasionally on face (male), with clouded breast; can suggest Redshank especially when legs pink or orange though these normally greyish. Male and female in early breeding season become much darker, with *strong dark mottling or barring on breast*. Male in full breeding dress wears astonishing, *enormous erectile ruff and ear-tufts* in various combinations of black, white, purple, chestnut and buff, with pale colours also often barred. Often stands upright, with slightly decurved bill and small angular head looking small on long neck.
Voice: Low *chut-ut*; has occasional deep guttural gobbling note, at display mounds, where sexually promiscuous.
Habitat: In winter and on passage on inland marshes, lake shores, occasionally estuaries. Breeds on northern tundra: in southern range in water-meadows and marshes. Map 140.

JACK SNIPE *Lymnocryptes minimus*   **Plate 43, 51**
   Du -Bokje   Fr – Bécassine sourde
   Ge – Zwergschnepfe   Sw – Dvärgbeckasin
Identification: 8" (20cm). Smallest snipe, with proportionately short bill on large head, narrow inner wings and *short, wedge-shaped tail*. Sits very tight, *flushing late in fluttering but slow, usually short and direct flight* with head held up and rarely calling. Close-to, shows four *long, straight golden lines down dark purplish back*, dark central crown stripe unlike all other snipe, streaked, not barred flanks and dark tail.
Voice: High rattling, somewhat muffed *kollorap-kollorap*, like sound of galloping horse, given in steep dive during high undulating display flight. Call quiet *catch*.
Habitat: As Snipe. Breeds in wet swamps and bogs. Map 141.

SNIPE *Gallinago gallinago* **Plate 43, 51**
  Du – Watersnip Fr – Bécassine des marais
  Ge – Bekassine Sw – Enkelbeckasin
  N. Am – Wilson's Snipe

Identification: 10" (26cm). Secretive wader of marshes with *long straight bill*, relatively small head, *chesty body* and rather short legs. Sits tight, flushing in *sudden zig-zag, then 'towering', long escape flight, almost invariably calling.* Much larger than Jack, smaller and distinctly less bulky than Great and much smaller than Woodcock. Plumage intensely black and chestnut-buff, intricately patterned but showing particularly dark lines along head, golden lines down back, *white trailing edge to inner wing*, small white corners to tail, *white-lined under-wing* and *strong flank barring contrasting with large white belly.* Flight outline shows longest bill and fastest wing-beats of tribe. Sociable in winter, flying in small parties or 'wisps'.
Voice: Song, rhythmic monotonously repeated *chic-ka*. In oblique dives during display-flight, a vibrating sound (so-called 'drumming') is produced by the widely spread outer tail feathers, like rapidly repeated *huhuhuhuhu*. When flushed, dry, rasping *schaap.*
Habitat: Marshes, water-meadows, sewage-farms, boggy moors, etc. Nests in coarse grass or rushes, occasionally in heather. Map 142.

GREAT SNIPE *Gallinago media* **Plate 43, 51**
  Du – Poelsnip Fr – Bécassine double
  Ge – Doppelschnepfe Sw – Dubbelbeckasin

Identification: 12" (30cm). Medium-sized, bulky snipe, with relatively short bill and deep-chested *round body*; size between Snipe and Woodcock. Sits tight, flushing in usually *direct, slow, padding escape flight, dropping soon*; rarely calls but wings make throbbing sound in still air; on landing, *runs away*. Plumage recalls Snipe but close-to, distinguished by more 'oatmeal' pattern on face and neck, *wholly barred under-body*, more white on tail corners and sides (particularly on adult), *fully barred grey under-wing* and long, central, *white-bordered black panel on upper-wing*, more eye-catching than dull trailing edge. Solitary.
Voice: Occasional brief croak *etch*, sometimes repeated. Males at display grounds in spring indulge in remarkable bubbling, popping, croaking chorus-singing.
Habitat: Except in breeding season often frequents drier localities than Snipe – stubble fields, bracken-covered heaths, etc. In breeding season usually in marshy country, banks of rivers, etc. Map 143.

LONG-BILLED DOWITCHER *Limnodromus scolopaceus* **Plate 43**
  Du – Noordelijke grizze snip Fr – Bécasseau à long bec
  Ge – Langschnabel-Schlamläufer Sw – Större beckasinsnäppa

Identification: 12" (31cm). Quite bulky and Snipe-like, except for rather long legs; most somewhat larger and distinctly longer-billed than rare Short-billed (see Accidentals). In flight, pattern of rather dark uniform wings enclosing *narrow, oval white panel* on lower back recalls Spotted Redshank but best clue is *mono-or multi-syllabic sharp* call *keek*, recalling piping call of Oystercatcher and unlike commonest call of Short-billed. Breeding adult has *dull rufous on* *face, neck and all of under-body*, chestnut, black and white upper-parts, greyer wing-coverts and strongly barred rump, upper tail coverts and tail, last with *black bars wider than white ones*. Winter adult distinctly grey on head and breast, dusky on back and wings, with *narrow whitish fringes* (not ochre or buff as in Short-billed). Juvenile initially grey-headed and buff-breasted and -bodied, with brown back and tertials with rufous fringes but *lacking notches and pale internal marks on scapulars and tertials* of Short-billed. Moults quickly to winter plumage. Flight outline rather front-heavy, with short-tailed look particularly when legs retracted forward; action suggests shank more than snipe. *Feeds with 'sewing machine' motion*, rapidly jabbing bill perpendicularly into mud.

Voice: In addition to diagnostic call (see above), utters short notes recalling Sanderling or stint and may even give snatch of fast song *pee-ter-wee-too*.

Habitat and Range: In N. America, Long-billed prefers fresh or brackish pools to open, often tidal mud liked by Short-billed, but such predilections often lost on passage. Vagrant from N. America to N., C., S., E. and W. Europe (including Britain).

WOODCOCK *Scolopax rusticola* — Plate 43, 51

Du – Houtsnip   Fr – Bécasse des bois
Ge – Waldschnepfe   Sw – Morkulla

Identification: 15" (38cm). Rather large, round-bodied Snipe-like wader of woods, with rather thick bill, *eye set remarkably high on head*, broad rounded wings and rounded tail. Sits tight, *exploding from ground with burst of swishing wing-beats* and jinking away through trees; on migration, flight action more regular with deep, rather owl-like beats and characteristic swinging progress. Close-to, shows diagnostic *thick dark bands over rear crown*, astonishing *'dead leaves' pattern* on red-brown upper-parts and wholly grey-barred, buffish underbody; in flight, tail shows *rim of grey-white spots*. Solitary and crepuscular except in hard weather or on coast after immigration.

Voice: During slow display-flight (known as 'roding') above trees, at dawn and dusk, male has soft, croaking *orrrt-orrrt*, followed by louder, high sneezing *tsiwick*.

Habitat: Wooded regions particularly with wet, overgrown rides and patches of evergreen. Usually nests at foot of tree. Map 144.

BLACK-TAILED GODWIT *Limosa limosa* — Plate 42, 50

Du – Grutto   Fr – Barge à queue noire
Ge – Uferschnepfe   Sw – Rödspov

Identification: 16" (42cm). *Tall, upstanding* wader, with long, *straight bill,* relatively small head and long legs trailing behind tail in flight. Easily distinguished from Bar-tailed by *broad white wing-bar*, black outline to white underwing and *wide white rump over wholly black tail*. Breeding adult reddish-chestnut, with black and white chequered back, grey-brown wing-coverts, and *black-barred belly*, last patched chestnut in N. Atlantic race *L. c. islandica* but hardly so in European race *L. c. limosa*. Winter adult *almost uniform grey*, with prominent *whitish supercilium* and belly. Juvenile cinnamon-buff, with dark scaled upper-parts and unbarred belly. Basal half of bill pink. Flight outline noticeably cross-like; action fast and energetic. Habitually feeds in shallows.

Voice: Song clear repeated *wheddy-whit-o*. Flight-call clear *reeka-reeka-reeka*; notes on breeding ground include nasal *quee-yit*, recalling Lapwing.
Habitat: In winter, estuaries, marshes; on passage, inland lakes and sewage-farms. Nests in water-meadows, moors and dunes. Map 145.

BAR-TAILED GODWIT *Limosa lapponica*   Plate 42, 50

Du – Rosse grutto   Fr – Barge rousse
Ge – Pfuhlschnepfe   Sw – Myrspov

Identification: 15" (38cm). Slightly smaller and less attenuated than Black-tailed, with shorter, *slightly upturned bill*, dumpier body and *shorter legs* barely projecting behind tail. Easily distinguished from Black-tailed by *lack of wing-bar*, white under-wing, *white rump extending up back* and *barred tail*. Breeding male uniform *chestnut from head and mantle to vent*, lacking belly bars of Black-tailed. Females and winter adult greyish-brown, *pale-scaled above* and narrowly streaked from face to breast, with narrow whitish supercilium and white belly. Juvenile warmer, buffier than winter adult. No more than basal third of bill pinkish. Flight outline more compact than Black-tailed but action similar.
Voice: Song higher-pitched and faster than Black-tailed's. Usually silent outside breeding season. Flight-note harsh *kirrik*, alarm shrill *krick*.
Habitat: Usually coastal. Often seen in winter in dense packs at water's edge. Breeds on swampy peat-moss, in marshes near or beyond tree limits. Map 146.

WHIMBREL *Numenius phaeopus*   Plate 42, 50

Du – Regenwulp   Fr – Courlis corlieu
Ge – Regenbrachvogel   Sw – Småspov

Identification: 16" (42cm). Noticeably smaller than Curlew, with *shorter bill more kinked than decurved*, more compact outline with less neck and *distinctive flight call*. Plumage essentially dusky-brown, notched and barred above, streaked on neck and breast and *barred on flanks*, under-wing and inner flight-feathers; relieved by bold *dark crown stripes* over whitish supercilium, *dark eye-stripe* and pale face. Lower back and rump white in European race *N. p. phaeopus*, forming obvious narrow divide between wings, but far less so in Asian race *N. p. variegatus* and *wholly brown* in N. American race *N. p. hud-sonicus*. Flight action quicker than Curlew, with godwit-like, not gull-like, wing-beats.
Voice: Unmistakable flight call about seven whistling notes in *even titter*. Song opens with melancholy soft notes but ends in fluty, bubbling, Curlew-like trill.
Habitat: As Curlew. In breeding season frequents boggy moors; nests among heather and rough grass. Map 147.

SLENDER-BILLED CURLEW *Numenius tenuirostris*   Plate 42

Du – Dunbekwulp   Fr – Courlis à bec gréle
Ge – Dünnschnabel-Brachvogel   Sw – Smalnäbbad spov

Identification: 16" (42cm). Size as Whimbrel but form as Curlew; slighter built than both, with *slender, decurved bill* and thinner legs. Plumage pattern like Curlew but close-to, shows *buffier upper-parts* with slightly darker cap and more distinct pale supercilium, paler throat, *less clouded chest* and, on adult, much whiter under-parts with *heart and arrow shaped black spots on lower chest and flanks*. In flight, almost black outer primaries contrast with white-spotted inner flight feathers and white-fringed greater coverts, while *pure white lower back and rump and largely white under-wing* look much cleaner than on Curlew. Flight like Whimbrel. Now very rare. Beware small, pale Curlew in first winter plumage.

Voice: Resembles Curlew's *cour-lee*, but shorter and less deep in alarm, sharp *kew-ee*.

Habitat and Range: In winter as Curlew. Breeds in marshy steppes. Occurs rarely on passage in Balkans and Italy. Vagrant to S., C. and W. Europe.

CURLEW *Numenius arquata*   **Plate 42, 50**
Du – Wulp   Fr – Courlis cendré
Ge – Grosser Brachvogel   Sw – Storspov

Identification: 21-23" (53-58cm). Largest European wader, with very *long, deep-based and decurved bill*, rather hunched posture, strong legs and *distinctive voice*. Plumage greyish or buffish-brown, closely streaked; *whitish rump extends to lower back*. Flight strong and rather gull-like, with measured beat; flocks usually fly high, in lines or chevrons. Whimbrel is smaller, with shorter kinked bill, striped crown and barred flanks. See also Slender-billed Curlew.

Voice: Commonest calls pure, ringing *cour-li* and fuller, pronounced *whaup*. Song is heard almost all year: loud, slowly delivered and remarkably liquid, embodying long bubbling trill. Rarely titters like Whimbrel.

Habitat: Mud-flats and estuaries. Occurs inland during migration. Nests on moors, marshes, meadows, sand-dunes. Map 148.

UPLAND SANDPIPER *Bartramia longicauda*   **Plate 46**
Du – Bartram's strandloper   Fr – Bartramie à longue queue
Ge – Bartrams Uferläufer   Sw – Höglandssnäppa

Identification: 11-12" (28-30cm). Size as Ruff but shape highly distinctive, with fine bill, *small angular head*, thin neck, plover-like body, rather long tail and relatively short legs. Plumage pattern recalls Curlew but close-to, shows intricate feather marks consisting mainly of *buff scales on brown upper-parts and cream-buff notches on tertials and larger wing-coverts* and barred flanks and tail. In flight, shows blackish primaries with narrow white leading edge, virtually *black lower back and rump contrasting with yellow-buff ground* to outer tail-feathers, and wholly close-barred under-wing. Lower mandible and *legs yellow*. Flight outline shows *head retracted in front of long wings* and *long tail cloaking legs*; action mixes flutter and glide on bowed wings with loose wing-beats recalling Ruff; skims close to ground to land with tremble of outstretched wings. Gait and feeding habits recall *Pluvialis* plover. Perches freely, holding wings erect before folding.

Voice: Mellow whistle in flight, *kip-ip-ip-ip*.

Habitat and Range: Extensive fields, burnt ground, etc. (not sea-shores). Vagrant from N. America. Has been recorded chiefly in British Isles; also C. and S. Europe.

SPOTTED REDSHANK *Tringa erythropus*   **Plate 44, 51**
Du – Zwarte ruiter   Fr – Chevalier arlequin
Ge – Dunkler Wasserläufer   Sw – Svartsnäppa

Identification: 12" (30cm). Elegant wader with distinctly longer bill, neck and

legs than Redshank, and *distinctive call*. Breeding plumage *uniquely sooty-black* relieved by white speckles and striking, *narrow white wedge in centre of back and white underwing*. Winter adult more like Redshank but *cleaner grey above, with distinct whitish supercilium*. Juvenile much darker than winter adult with sepia-brown head, breast and upper-parts heavily spotted and chequered with white; *buff-grey under-parts* irregularly barred, particularly on flanks. Base of thin bill and *legs dark red*. Flight outline more rakish than Redshank, with *trailing feet*; action very fast. Feeds in deeper water than Redshank, lunging after prey, sweeping bill from side to side. Gait delicate.
Voice: Loud, distinctive *tchuit*, and quiet contact-note *gek, gek*.
Habitat: As Redshank. Breeds in open areas in northern forests. Map 149.

REDSHANK *Tringa totanus* **Plate 44, 51**
Du – Tureluur Fr – Chevalier gambette
Ge – Rotschenkel Sw – Rödbena
Identification: 11" (27cm). Commonest and most widespread of larger sandpipers, with quite long bill and legs and *distinctive, at times hysterical voice*. In flight, shows dark outer primaries contrasting with *white inner primary tips and secondaries*, which form conspicuous trailing panel to wing, and *white wedge up lower back*. On ground, olive-brown above, with only short pale supercilium and eye-ring and streaked clouded breast catching eye; white below, with barred tail. Base of bill and *legs red*. Breeding adult liberally speckled and notched black; juvenile buffier, with *orange legs* inviting confusion with Lesser Yellowlegs, which see. Flight outline quite compact though long bill and trailing feet show; action strong but often erratic, ever tilting from side to side during glide. Gait free but not graceful. Perches freely, bobbing in alarm; inspects and mobs predators fearlessly.
Voice: Song has various repeated musical phrases, notably *taweeo*. When flushed, volley of loud, high-pitched notes. Usual call musical, down-slurred *tleu-hu-hu*. In alarm, incessant yelping *teuk*.
Habitat: Marshes, moors, saltings, water-meadows, sewage-farms. Winters on estuaries and mud-flats. Nests in tussock. Map 150.

MARSH SANDPIPER *Tringa stagnatilis* **Plate 45**
Du – Poelruiter Fr – Chevalier stagnatile
Ge – Teichwasserläufer Sw – Dammsnäppa
Identification: 9" (23cm). Hardly bigger than Wood Sandpiper but with most attenuated form of tribe, with *long, very fine, straight bill,* thin neck and *very long, spindly legs*. Plumage pattern and colours including white rump and wedge up back recall Greenshank, but in breeding dress *upper-parts buff liberally spotted blackish-brown*, with more obvious whitish forehead and supercilium; in winter and juvenile plumage, *face whiter,* neck paler and upper-parts plainer. White wing-lining shows dark bar on primary coverts. Legs usually olive-green, yellower when breeding. Flight outline slender, with *feet projecting far beyond tail*; action light and graceful, as is gait.
Voice: Usual notes (none very loud) *tew, teea, chik, chick-cleuit*, etc., and twittering trill.
Habitat: Seldom on sea-shore. Winters around inland waters and marshes.

Breeds (occasionally in small groups) on grassy borders of lakes and on marshy steppes. Map 151.

GREENSHANK *Tringa nebularia*   Plate 44, 51
Du – Groenpootruiter   Fr – Chevalier aboyeur
Ge – Grüschenkel   Sw – Gluttsnäppa

Identification: 13" (33cm). Large, quite stout but still rather elegant wader, with deep, *slightly up-turned bill* and quite long legs; noticeably larger than Redshank, with *distinctive, ringing voice* carrying far. Plumage essentially grey above, with dark wings and tertials divided by *long white rump and wedge up back*, and white below, with grey streaks on rear head and neck but clean white centre of breast. Breeding adult heavily streaked on head, breast and fore-flanks and patched black on scapulars. Bill grey; *legs yellowish- to greyish-green*. Flight outline and action looser than Redshank, with deeper, slower wing-beats.

Voice: Song mellow, repeated *tew-i*. Commonest call loud, ringing *tchew-tchew-tchew*, to imitation of which bird comes readily; also repeated scolding *tyip*.

Habitat: As Redshank. Breeds on moors or in patches of grass or heath in forest, usually not far from water. Map 152.

GREATER YELLOWLEGS *Tringa melanoleuca*   Plate 44
Du – Grote geelpootruiter   Fr – Grand chevalier à pattes jaunes
Ge – Grosser Gelbschenkel   Sw – Större gulbena

Identification: 14" (36cm). Largest sandpiper to reach Europe, *about one-third larger than otherwise similar Lesser Yellowlegs* with stouter legs. Upper-parts slightly darker, more uniform grey than Greenshank without dark 'shoulders' but with liberal white spotting and *only small, square white rump*; under-parts less white, with *uniformly streaked face, neck, breast and fore-flanks*. Breeding adult heavily patched black on back and from sides of breast along flanks. *Legs rich yellow*. Flight outline shows long, rather broad wings and trailing feet.

Voice: 3-4 syllable *heu-heu-heu*, very like Greenshank, but louder, higher and more ringing than Lesser Yellowlegs.

Habitat and Range: Outside breeding season usually on grassy marshes, around pools and on coastal mud-flats. Vagrant from N. America to W. (including Britain) and N. Europe.

LESSER YELLOWLEGS *Tringa flavipes*   Plate 44
Du – Kleine geelpootruiter   Fr – Petit chevalier à pattes jaunes
Ge – Gelbschenkel   Sw – Mindre gulbena

Identification: 10" (25cm). Larger than Green Sandpiper, with proportionately more slender bill and *much longer legs*, but much smaller than Greater Yellowlegs though with proportionately longer tail. Plumage pattern and colours as Greater Yellowlegs, with similar *square white rump*. In winter, back and smaller wing-coverts plain dusky-grey, with white spots restricted to greater coverts and tertials. Close-to, shows *white supercilia joining over bill*. Flight outline like Wood Sandpiper, with trailing feet; action noticeably fluent.

Voice: Soft whistle of one, two or occasionally three notes, *cu* or *cu-cu*.

Habitat and Range: Frequents mud-flats, marshes. Vagrant from N. America, chiefly to British Isles; recorded C. and N. Europe.

SOLITARY SANDPIPER *Tringa solitaria*   **Plate 45**
Du – Amerikaanse bosruiter   Fr – Chevalier solitaire
Ge – Einsiedelwasserläufer   Sw – Amerikansk skogssnäppa
Identification: 8 ¾" (22cm). Close in size, form and plumage to Green Sand-piper but with relatively narrower wings extending past tail tip and slightly shorter legs. Instantly distinguished in flight by *dark rump and dark-centred, wholly barred tail*; close-to, shows white 'spectacle' round eye and on fore-supercilium like Green, but *less clouded breast*. Flight outline and action recall Wood.
Voice: Usual call quieter than Green; high *peet-weet* amd sharp *tew*.
Habitat and Range: Fresh-water marshes, ponds, stream-sides. Vagrant from N. America to W. (including Britain) and N. Europe.

GREEN SANDPIPER *Tringa ochropus*   **Plate 45, 51**
Du – Witgatje   Fr – Chevalier culblanc
Ge – Waldwasserläufer   Sw – Skogssnäppa
Identification: 9" (23cm). Slightly larger and lengthier than Wood Sandpiper, with proportionately shorter legs. Easily distinguished in flight by *dark blackish upper- and under-wings* and upper-parts, contrasting with *brilliant white rump*; boldly barred tail and *white under-body*. Close-to, head, breast and upper-parts dark olive-brown, relieved only by short, *white fore-supercilium and narrow eye-ring*; breeding adult shows sparse white spots, juvenile has dull buff ones (many fewer than on Wood). Legs greenish. Flight outline characterised by *rather broad wings* and rather short tail, behind which toes rarely show; action snipe-like, with fast clipped wing-beats and remarkable looping descent from towering escape. 'Bobs' head and tail. Solitary.
Voice: Song medley of fluted, trilling *titti-looi*, *titti-looi*, etc. When flushed, utters ringing *weet-tluitt, weet-weet*.
Habitat: Outside breeding season on marshes, sewage-farms, lakes and streams, seldom on sea-shore. Breeds in swampy forest regions, often in old nests in trees. Map 153.

WOOD SANDPIPER *Tringa glareola*   **Plate 45, 51**
Du – Bosruiter   Fr – Chevalier sylvain
Ge – Bruchwasserläufer   Sw – Grönbena
Identification: 9" (23cm). Size between Common and Green with distinctive *delicate build* and rather long legs. Upper-parts less olive, browner than Green, with *liberal buff-white speckles and spots* except in winter; close-to, shows *full length whitish supercilium*, streaked, not clouded breast and *yellow to yellowish-green legs*. In flight, shows white rump and under-body but these contrast less with close-barred tail and pale dusky-buff wing-lining than in Green. Flight outline and action also delicate, with trailing feet, fluttering wing-beats and almost stint-like agility. Often circles high in alarm. Gregarious on passage and in winter.
Voice: Habitually noisy, parties making high liquid trilling. Song embodies musical *tleea-tleea-tleea*, in high flight. When flushed, shrill, rapid *chiff-chiff-chiff*. Also rising, liquid *tlui*.
Habitat: On passage frequents marshes, sewage-farms, lake shores, etc. Breeds in fairly open ground near water in northern forest regions and on tundra. Map 154.

TEREK SANDPIPER *Xenus cinereus*   **Plate 51**
Du – Terek strandloper   Fr – Bargette de Térek
Ge – Terekwasserläufer   Sw – Tereksnäppa
Identification: 9" (23cm). Size close to Green Sandpiper but form and behaviour recall Common. Easily distinguished by *long, dark, noticeably up-curved bill*, dashing, forward-leaning, *erratic gait* and rather short, *orange legs*. Breeding adult noticeably grey above, with whitish fore-supercilium, *dark eye stripe*, lightly streaked breast and *broad black stripes on scapulars*; winter adult and juvenile browner above, lacking dark scapular marks. In flight, shows conspicuous *broad white trailing edge to secondaries* and white edges to grey rump and tail. Flight outline somewhat front-heavy; action recalls both Knot and Common Sandpiper. 'Bobs' like Common.
Voice: Rather noisy: fluty *dudududu*, or piping *twita-wit-wit-wit*. In breeding season, *too-lee* and other melodious notes, some recalling Whimbrel.
Habitat and Range: Occurs along shores of large rivers, saltings, coastal flats. Breeds in marshes among willow scrub. Breeds Finland, Latvia (? regularly). Vagrant elsewhere in Europe (including Britain).

COMMON SANDPIPER *Actitis hypoleucos*   **Plate 47, 52**
Du – Oeverloper   Fr – Chevalier guignette
Ge – Flussuferläufer   Sw – Drillsnäppa
Identification: 8" (20cm). Rather small, short-legged, long-tailed sandpiper, with distinctive tribal character which includes constant bobbing of head, *teetering of rear body*, winnowing flight with *rapid, shallow beats of and glides on decurved wings*, and merry ringing song. Olive-brown above with dark rump and full *dull streaked gorget* and transverse buff bars on wing coverts; white below, with *greenish-grey legs*. Close-to, shows *bright white eye-ring* in dull supercilium. In flight, *white wing-bar* and *white, widely barred sides to long tail* striking, while black and white-striped under-wing may show; head on, shows white 'head light' at carpal joint.
Voice: Song high, rapid *titti-weeti, titti-weeti*. When flushed, shrill piping *twee-see-see*.
Habitat: Clear, running rivers, hill streams and lakes; on passage at sewage-farms, estuaries, etc. Breeds on banks of streams and lakes, river shingle-bars, etc. Map 155.

SPOTTED SANDPIPER *Actitis macularia*   **Plate 47**
Du – Amerikaanse oeverloper   Fr – Chevalier grivelé
Ge – Drosseluferläufer   Sw – Fläck drillsnäppa
Identification: 7¾" (19.5cm). Distinctly *shorter-tailed than Common*, with wing-tips approaching tail-end, not falling well short, and diagnostic calls. Breeding adult unmistakable, with fully *spotted lower face, neck and underbody*, pinkish-red base to bill and *pinkish legs*. Winter adult and juvenile resemble Common but close-to, distinguished by usually pale base to bill, *whiter supercilium*, colder, less barred back and tertials (latter fully notched pale in Common), more distinct, *whiter transverse barring on wing-coverts*, and usually *yellowish legs*. In flight, shows shorter, less strong wing-bar, complete thin white trailing edge to secondaries (just patched white near body in Com-

mon), and more closely barred outer tail feathers. Flight and behaviour as Common.

Voice: Quickest clue to identity, with sharp *peet* and more piped, less ringing *peet-weet-weet*, recalling Green Sandpiper.

Habitat and Range: In N. America, much as Common but vagrants as much at home on coasts and islands as inland waters. Has bred Scotland. Wanders from N. America to S., C., N. and W. Europe (including Britain).

TURNSTONE *Arenaria interpres*   **Plate 39, 40**
Du – Steenloper   Fr – Tournepierre à collier
Ge – Steinwälzer   Sw – Roskarl

Identification: 9" (23cm). Robust, busy, noisy shore-bird with *'tortoiseshell' plumage*, stout but pointed black bill used to turn over stones and shells, and *short orange legs*. Breeding bird has whitish crown, black and white-patched face, *deep black breast* and back and wings beautifully splashed *buff-chestnut and black*. Winter adult loses all chestnut and becomes *'swarthy'*, looking much duller and darker, as does juvenile. At all ages, under-body below breast white. *Lined pattern of wings and rump complex* and diagnostic; see Pl. 39 and 40. In flight, outline short-headed and stocky; action strong, with short wing-beats. Gregarious on rockier shores; more solitary elsewhere.

Voice: Quick, staccato *tuk-a-tuk* and long rapid trill.

Habitat: Winters along rocky or pebbly coasts. Usually breeds on exposed rocky ground on coastal islands, but in Arctic also occasionally on river islands. Map 156.

WILSON'S PHALAROPE *Phalaropus tricolor*   **Plate 41**
Du – Wilson's franjepoot   Fr – Phalarope de Wilson
Ge – Wilsons Wassertreter   Sw – Wilsons simsnäppa

Identification: 8 ¾"-10" (22-65cm). Largest of phalaropes, least likely to be seen at sea in Europe; female noticeably larger than male. In flight, easily distinguished from other phalaropes by white rump and trailing yellowish feet and lack of wing-bar; on land, shows relatively long bill and neck and *lurching gait*. Breeding female colourful, with *wine-chestnut bands over grey wings*, white face and pink-buff fore-neck divided by *black eye stripe and band down neck*; male duller, with dark, not grey, crown and hind-neck. Winter adult grey above but retaining dark wings; *lacks discrete black eye-patch of other phalaropes*. Juvenile dark brown above, with *delicate buff scales*. Beware confusion with Lesser Yellowlegs and Stilt Sandpiper in non-breeding plumage, which see. Flight recalls sandpiper more than other phalaropes.

Voice: Nasal, grunting *aangh* and Yellowlegs-like *chu* in flight.

Habitat and Range: Less aquatic than other phalaropes, usually seen on muddy shores or in shallows. Vagrant from N. America to W. (including Britain), N. and C. Europe.

RED-NECKED PHALAROPE *Phalaropus lobatus*   **Plate 41, 52**
Du – Grauwe franjepoot   Fr – Phalarope à bec étroit
Ge – Odinshühnchen   Sw – Smalnäbbad simsnäppa

Identification: 6" 15cm). Smallest and most widespread of tribe in N. and arctic Europe, with lobed feet characteristic of tribe but distinctive *needle-like bill*.

Red-necked Phalarope Swimming

Breeding plumage basically dark grey, with *orange-red blaze from nape down neck, white throat* and orange-buff stripes and scales on sides of back; male much duller than female. Winter adult has grey-white head, with *long, drooping black eye panel* and dark grey upper-parts over white body. Juvenile has *black and buff-lined face*, buff neck and breast, and upper-parts more striped and scaled than breeding adult. In flight, upper-parts *darkest of phalaropes* with bold white wing-bar recalling Sanderling and long white lateral rump-coverts contrasting with dark tail. Flight outline tubby but action whirring and dashing. Swims buoyantly, with tail held up; 'spins' on water.
Voice: Similar to Grey, but lower-pitched.
Habitat: As Grey Phalarope. Breeds in small scattered groups in wet marshes, lake shores and river islands. Map 157.

GREY PHALAROPE *Phalaropus fulicarius*   Plate 41, 52
Du – Rosse franjepoot   Fr – Phalarope à bec large
Ge – Thorshühnchen   Sw – Brednäbbad simsnäppa
Identification: 8" (20cm). Slightly larger than Red-necked, with *thicker and broader bill* and broader beam; occurs more commonly and widely through Atlantic Europe than Red-necked. Breeding plumage unmistakable, with *white face-blaze* and *deep chestnut under-parts*; male less immaculate than female. Winter adult whitest and palest grey of tribe, with only *short black eye-panel*, not drooping at end as in Red-necked, and shorter black crown. Juvenile resembles Red-necked but *lacks obvious dark eye-line*; immature with grey and black patched upper-parts confusingly like Red-necked, best separated by bill. In flight, shows similar wing-bar but less white on sides of rump. Beware confusion with winter Sanderling, which see. Flies and swims like Red-necked but appearance always more robust.
Voice: Courting female makes trilling mixture of musical and grating notes. Shrill *whit*, or *prip*, recalling Sanderling, and quiet *eeee*.
Habitat: Pelagic outside breeding season, but occurs occasionally on passage on coasts and inland waters. Breeds on tundra around pools or coastal lagoons. Map 158.

SKUAS: Stercorariidae

Large, rather hawk-like sea-birds with dark plumage and angled wings. Centre tail-feathers usually elongated in adults. Plumage very variable and confusing, occurring in light, intermediate and dark phases; all but adult Long-tailed show flash of white on the wing created by white wing-quills and bases to primaries. Behaviour piratical, chasing other birds until they disgorge. Settle freely on water. Sexes similar. Ground nesting.

POMARINE SKUA *Stercorarius pomarinus*   Plate 53
Du – Middelste jager   Fr – Labbe pomarin
Ge – Mittlere Raubmöwe   Sw – Bredstjärtad labb
N. Am – Pomarine Jaeger

Identification: 21" (53cm), including 3" (8cm) tail projection. Large skua, with size between Great and Arctic, heavy bill, *deep chest* on barrel body, *broad-based wings* and ample tail with *broad twisted streamers or 'spoons' in adult.* On passage, looks heavy and gull-like due to deep regular wing-beats and ponderous glides and banks. Common light phase shows blackish face and cap, cream cheeks and collar, white under-parts with *shaggy dark breast-band and heavily barred flanks*; white bases to primaries form pale patches almost as striking as Great. Uncommon dark phase has almost uniform dusky-brown body. Juvenile and immature variably mottled buffish and dark brown, showing *stronger barring under wing and around rump* than smaller skuas.
Voice: Harsh, barking *gek-gek* and squealing *yee-e-e.*
Habitat and Range: Chiefly offshore, but also pelagic. Breeds in small widely scattered colonies on Russian tundra. On passage W. European coasts (including Britain) and Baltic. Vagrant to C. Europe and Mediterranean.

ARCTIC SKUA *Stercorarius parasiticus*   Plate 53
Du – Kleine jager   Fr – Labbe parasite
Ge – Schmarotzerraubmöwe   Sw – Labb
N. Am – Parasitic Jaeger

Identification: 19" (48cm), including 3" (8cm) tail projection. Commonest of tribe in N. Europe; size and form intermediate between Pomarine and Long-tailed, with *dashing, somewhat falcon-like appearance*, less deep body and narrower wings than Pomarine and *short pointed streamers in adult.* In flight, looks rather light but nevertheless powerful, with beats of angled wings noticeably accelerated in *piratical, aerobatic chase* of gulls and terns. Light phase commonest in north, dark commonest in south, with many intermediates. Plumage differs from Pomarine in softer contrasts between light and dark areas, *under-parts lacking bars*, and pale bases to primaries forming more striking patch below than above. Juvenile and immature generally dark but with variable head and belly colour, usually *not as strongly barred around rump* as Pomarine and Long-tailed.
Voice: Higher-pitched than Great Skua's, also nasal, wailing *eee-air*; in alarm, *ya-wow* repeated.
Habitat: Offshore and pelagic waters, occurring occasionally in large numbers on coasts on migration. Breeds colonially on tundra and moors. Map 159.

LONG-TAILED SKUA *Stercorarius longicaudus* **Plate 53**
Du – Keleinste jager Fr – Labbe à longue queue
Ge – Kleine Raubmöwe Sw – Fjällabb
N. Am – Long-tailed Jaeger

Identification: 20-22" (50-55cm), including 5-8" (12-20cm) tail projection. Scarcest and smallest of tribe, exhibiting piratical behaviour rarely on passage and not on breeding grounds where predator on small mammals. Slim body and narrow wings *no larger than Kittiwake's* (whereas Arctic as large as Common Gull and Pomarine near size of Herring Gull); in adult, *tail streamers very long, 'whipping' in flight*. In flight, can recall both shearwater when planing into wind and tern when dip-feeding from sea, having most buoyant and graceful action of tribe. Dark phase now unknown in adult; so all resemble pale Arctic though in good light distinguished by *sharper-cut head-cap*, yellower cheeks, *greyer upper-parts*; lacks pale wing patches and has no breast-band on *white, shading to dusky under-body*. Juvenile and immature extremely variable but most buffy-grey, with bright wing patches and obvious barring around tail. Swims with head and long tail held up.
Voice: Seldom vocal. At breeding grounds, shrill *kreee*, or *kree-ep*.
Habitat: More pelagic than Arctic Skua, but regular off west-facing coasts in spring and in North Sea in autumn. Breeds in widely scattered colonies on high tundra and stony fells. Map 160.

GREAT SKUA *Stercorarius skua* **Plate 53**
Du – Grote jager Fr – Grand labbe
Ge – Grosse Raubmöwe Sw – Storlabb
N. Am – Skua

Identification: 24" (61cm). Largest skua, exceeding size of Herring Gull and chasing sea-birds as large as Gannet. Form shows proportionately *broader and rounder-tipped wings*, much tubbier body and *shorter, rounder tail* than other skuas. Tail lacks any projection. Bill noticeably stout and hooked. Passing flight heavy and padding, suggesting large gull or even raptor at times, but chase is fast, powerful and surprisingly agile. Plumage more variable than most books imply, with adult usually pale-mottled brown above, more rufous-grey below, with striking *huge white patches at base of primaries* 'flashing' with every wing-beat. Immature warmer overall, with *almost orange-buff under-body* when sunlit, and reduced wing patches. Rides high on sea; drowns small gulls. Less gregarious than other skuas.
Confusion species: Retention of paler plumage during immaturity may cause dark head-cap to contrast with pale neck, suggesting South Polar Skua *S.maccormicki* reported but not yet accepted in W. Europe.
Voice: When attacking, guttural *tuk-tuk*, also harsh, nasal *skeerrr* amd deep barking *uk-uk-uk*.
Habitat and Range: Pelagic and coastal waters. Breeds in scattered colonies on moors near sea, Iceland, Faeroes, Shetland, Orkney, Outer Hebrides, N. Scotland and N. Norway. Mainly migrant, in winter extending south over Atlantic and western North Sea to S. Spain (and beyond). Vagrant elsewhere in N., C. and S. Europe.

GULLS: Laridae

Gulls are long-winged sea-birds; some are seen regularly over land. Mostly white, with grey or black backs and wings. More robust, wider-winged and longer-legged than terns, walking readily. White-headed species often have dusky marks on heads in winter; dark-hooded species have mainly white heads in winter, more or less marked with black. Sexes similar. Ground or cliff nesting.

GREAT BLACK-HEADED GULL *Larus ichthyaetus*   Plate 56
Du – Reuzenzwartkopmeeuw   Fr – Goéland à tête noire
Ge – Fischmöwe   Sw – Svarthuvad trut

Identification: 26" (66cm). Size as Glaucous, shape also similar except for rather longer bill with conspicuous frontal feathering producing sloping, angular head, even broader, yet longer wings with *folded tertials bulging over primaries*. Flight outline suggests Great Black-backed but *action almost Heron-like*, with very arched wings beating powerfully. Breeding adult unmistakable, with *yellow bill banded black, then red at tip*, black head with *broken white eye-ring*, dusky-grey upper-parts and black transverse band across wing end; in winter, retains *large black eye-patch*. Juvenile like other large gulls except for structure and noticeably white under-parts except for mottled chest. Immature adopts adult plumage over three years; in first year, resembles Herring except for structure, *black-tipped, greyish-yellow bill*, white eye-lids, blackish marks behind eye, paler upper wing-coverts, *broad black band on white tail* and black and white wing pattern. Legs yellowish-green when adult.

Voice: Harsh *kraaka*. Various yapping and laughing notes at nest.

Habitat and Range: Normally coastal, occurring inland on passage. Vagrant from Russia, Asia to Europe (including Britain).

MEDITERRANEAN GULL *Larus melanocephalus*   Plate 54
Du – Zwartkopmeeuw   Fr – Mouette mélanocéphale
Ge – Schwarzkopfmöwe   Sw – Svarthuvad mås

Identification: 15" (38cm). Slightly larger and noticeably stockier than Black-headed, with *drooping, deeper bill*, deeper chest, longer legs and *broader, less pointed wings* obvious in *steadier, buoyant, often gliding flight*. Breeding adult distinguished by *yellow and black tip* to red bill, fully *black head* with broken white eye-ring, paler grey mantle, and *pure white primaries*; in winter, can be briefly confused with other larger white-winged gulls but head retains black patch behind eye and flecked nape. Juvenile and immature recall pale Common Gull but have relatively heavier bill, *paler grey back*, more variegated wings with dusky leading edge, *blackish primaries* and inner secondaries, containing *greyish-white band across larger coverts, extending as spots onto inner primaries*, and narrower black tail-band. Sub-adult shows black marks behind primary tips. Behaviour as Black-headed.

Voice: Deeper and more wailing than Black-headed. Nasal *ayeea* and guttural *kwow*.

Habitat: As Black-headed, but less often seen inland. Breeds on islets in lagoons and lakes. Map 161.

LAUGHING GULL *Larus atricilla* **Plate 56**
Du – Lachmeeuw Fr – Goéland atricille
Ge – Aztekenmöwe Sw – Sotvingad mås

Identification: 16" (40cm). Medium-sized gull, with *long, drooping bill* extending from sloping forehead, long neck and body, *long-pointed wings* producing marked taper beyond tertials at rest and rakish appearance on the wing. Breeding adult has black bill and hood with broken white eye-ring, *decidedly dusky mantle and wings*, latter with white trailing edge and wedge-shaped black ends, and *blackish legs*; in winter, head white except for black 'eye-pit' and dusky smudges on rear cheeks. First winter grey and sooty-brown above, dusky on breast and head except for white face and eye-ring; wings dark, with *blackish outer-wing and secondaries*, relieved above by dusky-brown coverts and narrow white trailing edge; *dusky lining* shows blackish edges to lesser coverts and axillaries; rump white, contrasting with *grey-based, black-banded tail*. Flight action noticeably leisurely, with deep wing-beats and skilled soaring and gliding.
Voice: Strident, laughing *ha-ha-ha-ha-haah-haah-haah* and *ka-ha, ka-ha*.
Habitat and Range: Coastal, beaches, salt-marshes. Vagrant from N. America to W., C., S. and N. Europe (including Britain).

FRANKLIN'S GULL *Larus pipixcan* **Plate 56**
Du – Franklins Meeuw Fr – Mouette de Franklin
Ge – Franklinmöwe Sw – Prariemås

Identification: 14" (36cm). Smaller and rounder-winged than Laughing, with paler back. *Wings banded translucent white above black and white ends to primaries* and broadly tipped white on trailing edge; *tail-centre greyish*. Immature also cleaner than Laughing, with *blacker partial hood*, whiter under-parts and under-wing, and *white edges to grey-centred and black-banded tail*. Bill heavy but short. Often fly-catches, like Black-headed.
Voice: Calls include shrill *kuk-kuk-kuk* and high nasal *kaar, kaar*.
Habitat and Range: Mainly on prairie marshes in N. America. Vagrant to N. and W. Europe (including Britain).

LITTLE GULL *Larus minutus* **Plate 54, 55**
Du – Dwergmeeuw Fr – Mouette pygmée
Ge – Zwergmöwe Sw – Dvägmås

Identification: 11" (28cm). World's smallest gull, with paddle-shaped wings 20% shorter than Black-headed, virtually square tail and alternatively direct padding and then *agile, dipping flight recalling marsh tern*. Breeding adult has *small black bill*, black hood, pale grey mantle and wings, last with striking *white trailing edge and tip* and diagnostic *dusky-black lining*. In winter, hood reduced to blackish cap and smudge behind eye. Legs red. Juvenile distinctive, with more pointed wings and back patterned with *black-brown cap and eye-patch*, bold *black zig zag* on back and wings, and black tail-band; under-wing pale. First winter birds grey-backed, but often retain dark patch on mantle; always show full zig-zag across lower back and wings, thus closely resembling much larger, young Kittiwake and also young Ross's, which see.
Voice: Rather low *kek-kek-kek* and repeated *kay-ee*.

Habitat: As Black-headed. Nests in small scattered colonies, often with terns or other gulls, usually around inland marshes. Map 162.

SABINE'S GULL *Larus sabini*   **Plate 54, 55**

Du – Vorkstaartmeeuw   Fr – Mouette de Sabine
Ge – Schwalbenmöwe   Sw – Tärnmås

Identification: 14" (35cm). Size between Little and Kittiwake, with slight, somewhat tern-like form including most distinctly *forked tail* of European gulls; deep beats of rather long, pointed wings give light, rather wavering flight. At all ages, wings tri-coloured in triangular pattern, with dusky-grey (adult) or mottled brown (juvenile) wing-coverts contrasting with *white inner primaries and secondaries* and *black (adult) or blackish-brown (juvenile) outer primary coverts and primaries*. Breeding adult has yellow-tipped, black bill and *slate, black-rimmed hood*; in winter, retains dusky collar on nape. Juvenile shows white face under *mottled brown head cap*, pale-scaled *brown shawl* and back, *striking dusky band on greater coverts of under-wing*, and black band emphasizing tail fork. Dives like clumsy tern and spins like phalarope.
Confusion species: Beware apparently similar wing pattern shown by distant young Kittiwake and Little; check structure and flight action carefully.
Voice: Call grating, recalling tern.
Habitat and Range: Coastal waters of Greenland and N. America, in breeding season on tundra and level shores. Storm-blown annually to Ireland and Britain, occasionally to Iceland, Faeroes and coasts of W. Europe, rarely to N. and C. Europe.

BONAPARTE'S GULL *Larus philadelphia*   **Plate 56**

Du – Kleine Kokmeeuw   Fr – Mouette de Bonaparte
Ge – Bonaparte-Möwe   Sw – Svartnäbbad skrattmås

Identification: 12" (31cm). Distinctly smaller and more elegant than Black-headed, with short, fine bill, more compact form, and noticeably *buoyant flight* recalling Little Gull and tern. At all ages, under-wing greyish on coverts but *almost white on primaries except for sharp black tips*; upper surface of outer wing shows similar white panel on outer primaries to Black-headed. Breeding adult has *black bill*, sooty-black hood reduced to crown smudge and black 'ear spot' in winter, grey upper-parts and bright red legs. Juvenile and first winter closely resemble Black-headed, but, well seen, show small dark bill, darker bar across leading wing-coverts, *clean inner but dark-tipped outer primary coverts* and narrower black trailing bar on inner primaries.
Voice: Rather quiet for gull; gives nasal rasping *cheeer* and low cackle, recalling Coot.
Habitat and Range: Habitat much as Black-headed. Nests near coasts in spruce forest belt. Vagrant from N. America to W. (including Britain) and C. Europe.

BLACK-HEADED GULL *Larus ridibundus*   **Plate 54, 55**

Du – Kokmeeuw   Fr – Mouette rieuse
Ge – Lachmöwe   Sw – Skrattmås

Identification: 15¾" (39cm). Commonest and most widespread of small hooded gulls, with quite long pointed bill, long pointed wings giving marked taper to body on ground, and square tail. Flight light and graceful, *more agile than larger gulls* and recalling tern at times. At all ages, outer wing shows *broad white leading panel* and diagnostic *dusky under-surface to inner primaries*. Breeding adult has dark crimson bill and legs, *dark chocolate-brown head* with white eye-ring, pale grey upper-parts and black rim to outer primaries; in winter, head white with one or two smudges behind eye. Juvenile has distinctive dark-tipped, yellowish-brown bill, *gingery shawl and upper-parts*, becoming grey on mantle in first winter; upper-wing shows dark brown bar across leading coverts, *dark-tipped inner primary coverts* and full blackish trailing edge to primaries and secondaries. Now totally adapted to exploiting almost any marine or terre-strial food source, freely entering cities; habitually follows ploughs and hawks for insects.

Voice: Noisy in breeding season. Usual notes, harsh *kwarr*, short *kwup*, etc.

Habitat: Common inland and on coast, rarely far from land. Frequents lakes, sewage-farms, harbours, farmlands. Breeds colonially on marshes, moors, shingle-banks, lake islands. Map 163.

SLENDER-BILLED GULL *Larus genei*   Plate 54

Du – Dunbekmeeuw   Fr – Goéland railleur
Ge – Dünnschnäblige Möwe   Sw – Langnäbbad mås

Identification: 16" (41cm). Slightly larger than Black-headed, with propor-tionately *longer, slightly drooping bill*, more extensive frontal feathering pro-ducing shallow forehead angle; has longer neck and body and more rounded tail than Black-headed. In flight, combination of longer bill, head, and neck, longer inner wing and *slower, more powerful wing-beats* produces distinctive *hump-backed profile*. At all ages, wing pattern like Black-headed, but leading white edge broader, while marks of immaturity are paler. Adult has dark red bill, look-ing black at distance, *white head* with faint dusky ear-spot in winter and *rosy under-parts*. *White eye looks 'blind'* at close range. Immature less distinctive than Black-headed, with grey ear-spot, brown covert bar and secondaries and bold black tail-band; bill as Black-headed but legs usually paler yellowish.

Voice: Nasal *yep, yep* and high chattering notes.

Habitat: Coastal waters and estuaries. Nests in small groups or colonies, some-times among terns, on dry mud-banks, islands in lagoons, in marshes, along river banks. Map 164.

AUDOUIN'S GULL *Larus audouinii*   Plate 54

Du – Audouin's meeuw   Fr – Goéland d'Audouin
Ge – Korallenmöwe   Sw – Rödnäbbad trut

Identification: 20" (50cm). Distinctly smaller than Mediterranean race of Her-ring Gull *L. argentatus michahellis*, with *deep, drooping bill*, elongated fore-head, *rather narrow wings and tail* and long legs. More elegant on the wing than Herring, with deeper wing-beats and greater agility. Adult resembles Herring but close-to, shows *deep red bill with black and yellow tip* (looking black at any distance), *dark eye* (hence gentle expression), no sharp division between white neck and grey mantle, prominent *black wedge on outer primaries* (white-tipped but lacking Herring's 'mirror'), and *dark olive-green legs*. Juvenile differs from Herring in paler cheeks, pale-scaled scapulars and tertials, very *dark wings* (like

Lesser Black-backed), white 'horseshoe' on upper tail-coverts and mostly *dark, not just banded, tail*. Carriage and gait graceful.
Voice: More varied than Herring, with hoarse, braying or gaggling quality; includes *gi-ou* or *gi-errk* in alarm.
Habitat: Deep-sea species. Locally around islands, occasionally along rocky mainland coasts. Nests colonially on sloping cliffs or among rocks on small Mediterranean islands. Map 165.

RING-BILLED GULL *Larus delawarensis*   Plate 56
　Du – Ringsnavelmeeuw   Fr – Goéland à bec cerclé
　Ge – Ringschnabelmöwe   Sw – Ringnäbbad mås
Identification: 20" (50cm). Size and form intermediate between Common and Herring, with *quite heavy bill* and fierce expression most suggesting latter. Adult plumage resembles Common but close-to, distinguished by *black-ringed, yellower bill, noticeably paler grey mantle* and wings, smaller white 'mirror' on black primaries and *pale eye*. First winter like Common but shows *heavier spotting on nape and breast-sides*, more variegated back and wings (with pattern like Mediterranean), spotted rump and *less sharply defined tail-band*; when perched, *dark tertials* catch eye. Flight action heavier and more powerful than Common; carriage more upright.
Voice: Shrill *kyow*, various squealing notes and anxious *ka-ka-ka.*
Habitat and Range: Coasts, estuaries, lakes, refuse dumps, breeding on lake islands. Vagrant from N. America to W. (including Britain) and N. Europe.

COMMON GULL *Larus canus*   Plate 54, 55
　Du – Stormmeeuw   Fr – Goéland cendré
　Ge – Sturmmöwe   Sw – Fiskmås
　N. Am – Short-billed Gull
Identification: 17" (43cm). Size and form intermediate between Black-headed and Herring, with relatively smaller bill, rounder head, slimmer body and narrower wings than latter. Plumages recall Herring but adult easily distinguished by *greenish-yellow bill and legs,* dark eyes; *duskier grey mantle and wings,* particularly in rare eastern race *L. c. heini*; more prominent white trailing edge to wing, and larger 'mirror' on black primary wedge. For distinction from Ring-billed and Kittiwake, see those species. Juvenile and first winter more variegated above than Herring, with wing-pattern suggesting Mediterranean and Ring-billed, but distinguished from both by duskier grey ground to back and wings, *lack of partial hood,* as in Mediterranean, and *discrete black tail-band,* unlike broken mark of Ring-billed. Flight outline less bulky than Herring and Ring-billed, closer to Kittiwake but without slightly forked tail; action quite rapid and vigorous but not as light as Kittiwake. Walks with high steps. Locally common but usually outnumbered by Black-headed and Herring.
Voice: Much higher and shriller than Herring Gull's. Squealing *kee-a*, or *hieea.*
Habitat: As Herring Gull, but more often inland. Breeds colonially on moors, hillsides and around lochs. Map 166.

LESSER BLACK-BACKED GULL *Larus fuscus*   **Plate 54, 55**
Du – Kleine mantelmeeuw   Fr – Goéland brun
Ge – Heringsmöwe   Sw – Silltrut

Identification: 21" (53cm). Close in size to Herring, distinctly smaller than Great Black-backed, with seemingly narrower wings than either. Adult shows *bright yellow legs*, black, white-mirrored wing-tips and *dusky band along under-surface of primaries and secondaries*, with colour of mantle and wings varying from *dusky-grey* in British and Irish race *L. f. graellsii* to slate in S.W. Scandinavian race *L. f. intermedius* and *almost black* in Baltic and Russian race *L. f. fuscus* (last provoking confusion with Great Black-backed). Juvenile and first winter birds darker-backed, -winged and tailed than Herring, with outer wing, secondaries and greater coverts uniformly dark, *lacking pale 'mirror' on inner primaries*. Flight and behaviour much as Herring.

Voice: Voice more nasal and deeper-toned than Herring.

Habitat: As Herring Gull, but more frequent inland and out at sea. Nests colonially in inland moors and bogs, grassy sea islands, cliff-tops. Map 167.

HERRING GULL *Larus argentatus*   **Plate 54, 55**
Du – Zilvermeeuw   Fr – Goéland argenté
Ge – Silbermöwe   Sw – Gråtrut

Identification: 22-26" (55-66cm). Commonest coastal gull, larger than all others except Glaucous and Great Black-backed. Adult of British race *L. a. argenteus* pale *grey above*, with *flesh-pink legs* and much black on wing-tips. Adult of Scandinavian forms *bluer* or in eastern population *L. a. argentatus* noticeably *duskier above*, with *pink or yellow legs* and reduced black in wing-tips. Adult of Mediterranean race *L. a. michahellis* (by some assigned to separate species called Yellow-legged Gull *L. cachinnans*) like darkest Scandinavian birds, always with *yellow legs* and *large, squared-off black wing tips*. Juvenile pale uniform brown, mottled overall, with dark outer primaries, dark secondary bar and tail-band; northern races show pale mirror on inner primaries but Mediterranean form does not and also has dark band on outer greater coverts. N. American race *L. a. smithsonianus*, recently reported in British Isles, much darker and browner in immature plumage, with almost wholly black-brown tail. Grey mantle appears from second spring. Flight heavy but less powerful than largest relatives.

Confusion species: Lesser Black-backed Gull shows convergent appearances with darkest races of Herring; immature Great Black-backed Gull much more chequered above; Common Gull much smaller and weaker-billed; beware hybrids between Herring and other large gulls.

Voice: Repeated, strident *kyow*, anxiety-note when breeding: dry *gah-gah-gah*, also varied mewing, barking and laughing notes.

Habitat: Coasts, estuaries, also waters and fields often far inland. Breeds usually colonially, on cliffs, islands, beaches, occasionally in marshes. Map 168.

ICELAND GULL *Larus glaucoides*   **Plate 54**
Du – Kleine burgemeester   Fr – Goéland à ailes blanches
Ge – Polarmöwe   Sw – Vitvingad trut

Identification: 22" (55cm). Near size of Herring Gull but with *rather dove-like appearance* due to shorter, less heavy bill, more domed head, gentler expression

and long wings, cloaking tail. Adult pale grey on inner wing and saddle, white elsewhere; rare arctic American race *L. g. kumlieni* has dusky marks on wing tips; eye-ring red. Juvenile greyer-brown than Glaucous Gull, with neater mottling and *extensively black-tipped bill, lacking contrasting pale base*. Looks narrow-winged in rapid, agile flight.
Confusion species: So-called Thayer's Gull *L. g. thayeri* recently reported; now regarded as a form of arctic American race but has dark eye when adult; Glaucous Gull larger and gawkier, with broader wings. Beware confusing hybrid with Herring Gull for one of rarer races.
Voice: Higher-pitched than Herring's.
Habitat and Range: Coasts, inland waters. Winter visitor from high Arctic to Iceland, Britain, Scandinavia. Vagrant elsewhere in W., C. and S. Europe.

GLAUCOUS GULL *Larus hyperboreus*   Plate 54, 55

Du – Burgemeester   Fr – Goéland bourgmestre
Ge – Eismöwe   Sw – Vittrut

Identification: 25-29" (63-73cm). Larger than Atlantic forms of Herring, approaching Great Black-backed in size, with similar *long, massive bill* but relatively chestier, shorter body and *broad-based but pointed wings*. Compared with Iceland, larger bill, more *angular head* with long sloping profile, broader *wings cloaking but not extending noticeably beyond tail*, and longer legs (giving tall stance) combine into much more powerful, threatening character. Adult pale bluish-grey on mantle and inner wing, wholly white elsewhere except for dappled head and breast in winter; eye-ring yellow, not red as Iceland. Juvenile distinctive, with *buff-ochre 'coffee'* plumage softly mottled and barred even on tail, becoming blotchy and then pale-patched with advancing age; always shows white wing-tip. Immature's bill pattern of *deep blackish tip vertically demarcated from pale pink base* catches eye. Flight action like Great Black-backed, includes distinctive short 'rowing' stroke; less agile on the wing than Iceland.
Voice: Resembles Herring Gull's, but usually shriller.
Habitat: As Great Black-backed. Breeds colonially above and below sea cliffs, on stacks and islands in Arctic. Map 169.

GREAT BLACK-BACKED GULL *Larus marinus*   Plate 54, 55

Du – Mantelmeeuw   Fr – Goéland marin
Ge – Mantelmöwe   Sw – Havstrut

Identification: 27-30" (68-76cm). Largest European gull, widespread on coasts and western lowlands. Deep bill, head and chest and long and broad wings all look massive so that character and flight *by far most powerful of family*. Adult *almost black on mantle and wings*, as dark as north-eastern forms of Lesser Black-backed but distinguished by *bright white wing-tip*, bunched tertials cloaking quite short wing-point, paler head in winter and *pinkish legs*. Juvenile identified by distinctive strong, *chequered pattern of dark brown marks on mantle and especially wings* and broadest, *darkest tail-band of tribe*. Idle at roost but fiercest predator of all gulls.
Voice: Usual note curt, deep *owk*.
Habitat: Offshore waters, coasts and estuaries. Locally inland in winter. Breeds either singly or colonially, sometimes with Lesser Black-backed, on rocky coastal islands, moors, also cliffs and lake islands. Map 170.

ROSS'S GULL *Rhodostethia rosea* **Plate 56**
Du – Rose Meeuw Fr – Mouette de Ross
Ge – Rosenmöwe Sw – Rosenmås
Identification: 12" (31cm). Small dove-like gull, slightly larger than Little, with *longer, more pointed wings* and *wedge-shaped tail*. Flight very buoyant, lacks 'padding' wing-beat of Little and includes Kittiwake-like shearing in high wind and marsh tern-like hover and dip; on sea, sits up and feeds like phalarope. Adult has *white head*, under-parts and tail and mauve-grey mantle and wings, last distinctively patterned with narrow black edge to outermost primary and *long broad white trailing panel* on secondaries and inner primaries contrasting noticeably with *dusky wing lining* (but not as vividly as in adult Little). When breeding, under-parts strongly pink and *neck narrowly ringed black*; in winter, eye 'enlarged' by dusky pit and rear cheek shows dusky mark. Juvenile has striking 'W' pattern across wings in flight; close-to, *darker lower back, striking black tip to tail-wedge* and greater extension of white behind black tips of primaries provide differences from Little and Kittiwake.
Voice: Variable; high-pitched and more melodious than most gulls; typical calls are bubbling *e-wo, e-wo, e-wo*, or *kliaw*.
Habitat and Range: Strays frequent, sea coasts and coastal lagoons. Seen regularly perched on ice-floes and glacier edges, seldom swimming. Breeds in swampy arctic tundra. Vagrant from NE. Siberia to W. (including Britain), N., C. and S. Europe.

KITTIWAKE *Rissa tridactyla* **Plate 54, 55**
Du – Drieteenmeeuw Fr – Mouette tridactyle
Ge – Dreizenmöwe Sw – Tretåig mås
Identification: 16" (40cm). Quite small, graceful gull of open sea and cliffs; size between Black-headed and Common but outline differing in apparently *parallel-edged wings*, slightly forked tail and *short legs*. Flight distinctive, with regular padding wing-beats providing buoyant progress; capable of remarkable shearing into high winds. Adult has grey mantle and inner wings, narrowly white on trailing edge and becoming pale grey, almost white and then deep black on primaries so that *wings appear 'dipped in ink'*; bill yellow, *legs black*. In winter, has variable dusky marks behind eye and around hind neck. Juvenile has striking *black, partial 'W 'pattern across wings* but not over lower back, noticeable *black half-collar round hind neck* and black band on tail; close-to, greyish-white inner primaries and secondaries less clean than on Sabine's but at distance may appear pure white, constituting identification pitfall.
Voice: Noisy only at breeding grounds. Loud *kitti-wa-ak*, or *kaka-week*, with rising inflection.
Habitat: Usually well out at sea, often at northern fishing grounds: rare inland. Breeds in close colonies on steep cliff-faces and in sea caves; locally on buildings. Map 171.

IVORY GULL *Pagophila eburnea* **Plate 54**
Du – Ivoormeeuw Fr – Mouette blanche
Ge – Elfenbeinmöwe Sw – Ismås
Identification: 18" (46cm). Size as Common Gull but shape distinct, with remarkably *pigeon-like outline* including short legs on ground and long, pointed

wings giving light, elegant flight. Adult unmistakable, with *short orange-tipped, greyish bill*, dark eye, *all-white plumage* and *black legs*. Juvenile looks white at distance but close-to shows darker bill, *dirty face* and *sparse dusky-black spots* on head, neck, scapulars, along wing-covert tips and on primary and tail feather tips. Beware albino Common Gull, Kittiwake and Black-headed Gull, checking bare parts carefully; other white-winged gulls are much larger.

Voice: Commonest call *feeoo* recalls drake Wigeon; also tern-like *kee-er*.

Habitat and Range: Arctic species usually seen on fringe of pack-ice, but wanders south occasionally in winter. Breeds colonially on more or less ice-bound rocky cliffs and ground. Regular Iceland in winter. Vagrant elsewhere in N. and W. (including Britain), C. and S. Europe.

TERNS: Sternidae

Terns are slender-bodied compared with gulls, narrower-winged and more graceful in flight; bills also more slender, sharply pointed, often carried downward in flight; tails forked. Most terns are whitish, with black caps; in winter, foreheads are white. Usually hover and plunge for fish. Poor walkers. Sexes similar. Ground or pond nesting.

GULL-BILLED TERN *Gelochelidon nilotica*   **Plate 57, 59**
Du – Lachstern   Fr – Sterne hansel
Ge – Lachseeschwalbe   Sw – Sandtärna

Identification: 16" (41cm). Size close to Sandwich, but with distinctly *shorter, less forked tail*, relatively broader wings, heavier body and *leisurely flight* suggesting large marsh tern. Breeding plumage resembles Sandwich but, well seen, much shorter, '*swollen*', *wholly black bill*, deeper black cap, duskier wedge on outer primaries and *grey tail* are distinctive. In winter, black cap reduced to *dark panel through eye* so that head much whiter than Sandwich. Juvenile has buffish crown with dark eye-patch. Behaviour much as other terns, but habit of *hawking for insects over land* is certain distinction from Sandwich; seldom plunges into water.

Voice: Throaty, rasping *cahac, cahac*, or *za-za-za*, and rapid laughing notes, quite distinct from Sandwich Tern's higher note.

Habitat: Salt-marshes, sandy coasts and inland waters. Breeds colonially on sandy shores and islets in saline lagoons. Map 172.

CASPIAN TERN *Sterna caspia*   **Plate 57, 59**
Du – Reuzenstern   Fr – Sterne caspienne
Ge – Raubseeschwalbe   Sw – Skräntärna

Identification: 22" (56cm). Largest European tern, *almost as big as Herring Gull*, with *large, heavy, bright blood-red bill*, long head and neck projecting forward in powerful, gull-like flight but outline ending in forked tail. Full black cap of breeding plumage extends below eye but becomes greyish with darker eye-panel in winter; *dusky-black under-surface of all but innermost primaries* conspicuous in flight. Juvenile like winter adult but mottled brown above. Wing-beats slow and heavy, producing less buoyant action than smaller terns. Can be confused with Royal Tern, which see.

Voice: Loud, deep, corvine *kraa-uh*, or hoarse *scheeg* and various cackling notes.
Habitat: Chiefly coastal, but occurs also on lakes and large rivers. Breeds singly or colonially on sandy coasts or islands. Map 173.

LESSER CRESTED TERN *Sterna bengalensis* Plate 60

Du – Bengaalse stern   Fr – Sterne voyageuse
Ge – Rüppellseeschwalbe   Sw – Mindre tärna

Identification: 15-17" (38-43cm). Near size of Sandwich but with elegant form and flight recalling Common. Adult distinguished by *slightly drooping, rich orange bill*, pale *blue-grey mantle, rump and tail* and *silvery-white primaries*, narrowly rimmed black below; crest extends further down nape than on Sandwich. In winter, bill paler but upper-parts often darker. Juvenile distinguished from Sandwich by *two dark bars on inner wing* (one across greater coverts and one along secondaries) and *pale, greyish-yellow bill*. Flight outline shows centrally placed wings and almost horizontally held bill; action graceful.
Voice: High-pitched *kreet-kreet* or *krriik, kriik* recalls Sandwich but is less ringing and less disyllabic.
Habitat and Range: Strictly coastal. Vagrant from Africa to S., C. and W. Europe, but recently breeding or hybridisation recorded irregularly in Spain, France, Italy and Britain.

SANDWICH TERN *Sterna sandvicensis* Plate 57, 59

Du – Grote stern   Fr – Sterne caugek
Ge – Brandseeschwalbe   Sw – Kentsk tärna
N. Am – Cabot's Tern

Identification: 16 (41cm). Quite large, long-billed sea tern, with proportionately shorter tail than Common; in flight, often droops head and utters *distinctive call*. Plumage noticeably pale, *looks whiter at distance than all other terns except Roseate* and faded Royal. Distinguished by *narrow black, yellow-tipped bill*, long *shaggy black crown* – erected in excitement – and short black legs; wings when fresh greyish-white with dusky tips to outer primaries, when worn dusky on both surfaces of primaries. In winter, crown white, speckled on crest. Juvenile noticeably smaller, more compact, with shorter, sometimes all-black bill, flecked upper-parts, dark primaries and less forked tail; beware confusion with Gull-billed. Flight outline differs from Common in apparently *more backward set of wings*, like Roseate; action strong and rather stiff, allowing easier progress into wind; dives strongly.
Voice: Noisier than most terns. Strident, rasping *keer-reck*, a sharp *tripp*, or *kirr-kit*.
Habitat: Almost exclusively maritime. Nests in crowded colonies on sandy or shingle beaches, rocky or sandy islands, occasionally on shores of inland waters. Map 174.

ROSEATE TERN *Sterna dougallii* Plate 57, 59

Du – Dougall's stern   Fr – Sterne de Dougall
Ge – Rosenseeschwalbe   Sw – Rosentärna

Identification: 15" (38cm). Size close to Common but shape differs in rather *longer, slightly drooping bill*, relatively *short and narrow wings*, slender body and rather short tail extending into *very long, whipping streamers*. Plumage pale, recalling Sandwich more than Common, with combination of *black, red-based bill*, pearl-grey upper-parts, rose-washed under-parts, *silvery translucent wings*, pure white streamers and rather long red legs distinctive. In winter, forehead white, rosiness almost lost and outer primaries dusky-lined. Juvenile shows blacker cap than Common or Arctic and *fully white trailing edge to wing*. Flight outline recalls Sandwich more than Common; action fast, with flickering wing-beats like Little.

Voice: Long rasping *aaak*, soft, very characteristic *chu-ick* and long angry chattering *kekekekek*, like Common or Arctic.

Habitat and Range: As Common Tern, but exclusively maritime. Nests sociably with Common or Arctic Terns, on islets, occasionally on beaches. Summer visitor, breeding very locally in Britain from Clyde and Tay southwards, also on coasts of Ireland and off Brittany. Vagrant elsewhere in W., N., S. and C. Europe.

COMMON TERN *Sterna hirundo*   **Plate 57, 59**

Du – Visdiefje   Fr – Sterne pierregarin
Ge – Flussseeschwalbe   Sw – Fisktärna

Identification: 14" (36cm). Commonest and most widespread tern of Europe, with elegant form, forked tail and buoyant flight. Close in size to Arctic, but with slightly more prominent bill and head, less slender body and *shorter tail-streamers not extending beyond closed wing-tips* (see Plate 00). Breeding plumage differs from Arctic in *black tip to bill*, longer black crown, *pale 'mirror'* on four innermost primaries, *broader blackish tips to outer primaries* and less grey under-body. In winter, shows white forehead and *dusky leading edge to inner wing* and retains reddish legs, unlike Arctic. Juvenile like winter adult but has dusky primaries and *bar across secondaries*. Gregarious at all times.

Voice: Noisy, with most distinctive calls grating *kee-yah* with downward inflection in alarm, and angry *kek-kek* and *karr*.

Habitat: Coastal and some inland waters, beaches and islands. Breeds colonially on beaches, sand-dunes and islands. Map 175.

ARCTIC TERN *Sterna paradisaea*   **Plate 57, 59**

Du – Noordse stern   Fr – Sterne arctique
Ge – Küstenseeschwalbe   Sw – Silvertärna

Identification: 15" (39cm). Shape differs from Common in proportionately *shorter bill and head*, slenderer body, *narrower wings shorter on inner half* and longer tail-streamers in adult extending a little beyond closed wing-tips (see Plate 00). Breeding plumage differs from Common in wholly *blood-red bill*, deeper, shorter black crown, faintly bluer upper-parts, whiter tail and *almost dusky under-body*, emphasizing white cheek-panel below head-cap. Wings appear uniformly pale above but show *narrow, intensely black rim to outer primaries* below. In winter, shows shorter, deeper head-cap and paler leading edge to wing than Common. Juvenile smaller than adult, size suggesting marsh tern; plumage colder grey and white than Common, with *broad white trailing panel on inner primaries and secondaries* further emphasizing narrow black tips to outer primaries. Flight action differs from Common in somewhat less elastic wing-beats and persistent *hovering at several levels* before dive. Gregarious but often further out to sea than Common.

Voice: Similar to Common but higher-pitched, squeakier, with harsh *kee-arr* in alarm, scolding *kit-it-it-karr* and repeated whistled *kee-kee* or *pee-pee* distinctive.

Habitat: As Common Tern, but more maritime and more frequently on rocky offshore islets. Map 176.

FORSTER'S TERN *Sterna forsteri*   Plate 60

Du – Forster's stern	Fr – Sterne de Forster
Ge – Sumpfseeschwalbe	Sw – Karrtärna

Identification: 15" (38cm). More robust than Common, with proportionately *heavier bill*, larger head and longer legs; perched adult's tail streamers project past wing-tips. Adult's appearance differs in more orange-toned bill, *diagnostic silvery-white inner primaries* (outer wing lacking dark wedge of Common), grey tail with *white outer feathers* (reverse of Common's pattern), white under-parts and dull orange legs. In winter, bill becomes blackish, and head is white except for conspicuous *black face-mask* through eye to rear cheeks. First winter bird *lacks variegated wing pattern of Common*, resembling winter adult except for larger face mask and blackish tips to inner feathers of tail fork. In winter, general character and pale plumage of distant bird may suggest 15%-larger Sandwich. Wing-beats faster and shallower than Common.

Voice: Calls include harsh nasal *za-a-ap*, nasal *kyarr* (both less drawn-out than similar calls of Common) and distinctive metallic *klick*.

Habitat and Range: Breeds in both fresh-water and salt marshes in N. America. Vagrant to W. Europe (including Britain).

SOOTY TERN *Sterna fuscata*   Plate 60

Du – Bonte stern	Fr – Sterne fuligineuse
Ge – Russseeschwalbe	Sw – Sottärna

Identification: 16" (41cm). Quite large, robust sea tern, built like Sandwich, but with deeply forked tail. No other adult tern reaching Europe is *black above*, except for large white forehead and sides of tail, and *white below*. Immature distinctive, almost uniform sooty-brown, flecked white on back. Beware confusing adult with Bridled Tern and immature with Brown Noddy, which see. Flight powerful, with thrusting wing-beats. Does not dive, snatching fish from surface.

Sooty Tern

Voice: Noisy: commonest call nasal *ker-wacky-wack* or *wideawake* (vernacular name).
Habitat and Range: Breeds on islands in warm southern oceans, wandering north to S., C., N. and W. Europe (including Britain).

LITTLE TERN *Sterna albifrons*   Plate 58, 59
Du – Dwergstern   Fr – Sterne naine
Ge – Zwergseeschwalbe   Sw – Småtärna

Identification: 9" (23cm), *Diminutive, noisy, short-tailed* tern, often hovering. Flying at distance, looks *all-white and fairy-like* but close-to, shows *black-tipped yellow bill and white forehead* extending back to eye over black lores; narrow black outer web on leading primary and orange legs. Juvenile has dark bill, dark mottled saddle and variegated wings. Flight outline unusual, with *quite tubby body offset by narrow wings* beaten noticeably quicker than other terns in prolonged *hover before shallow splash-dive.*
Voice: Calls include high rasping *kree-ik*, sharp repeated *kitt* and rapid gibbering *kirri-kirri-kirri.*
Habitat: Sand and shingle beaches, occurring inland on migration. Breeds in small scattered colonies on beaches; on Continent also on shores of lakes and rivers. Map 177.

WHISKERED TERN *Chlidonias hybridus*   Plate 58, 59
Du – Witwangstern   Fr – Guifette moustac
Ge – Weissbartseeschwalbe   Sw – Skäggtärna

Identification: 10" (25cm). Largest of three marsh terns, all with generally dark breeding plumage and distinctively *dipping feeding-flight.* In summer, Whiskered is distinguished from Black Tern and White-winged Black Tern by *white cheeks and sides of neck*, contrasting with black crown and *dark grey under-parts*; in flight, white beneath wings and white under tail-coverts fairly conspicuous. Looks much paler than other truly black marsh terns, with resemblance to Arctic Tern strengthened by forked tail, more direct flight and plunging for food. Winter adult distinguished from Black by paler upper-parts, *absence of dark patches on sides of breast* and *less black on crown*; from White-winged Black by greyish (not white) on nape, longer bill and uniform upper-parts. Immature distinguished from young Black by *variegated 'saddle'* contrasting with pale wings, absence of breast-patches; from young White-winged Black by pale grey (not white) rump and longer bill. Bill dark red in summer, blackish in winter, as long as head and deeper than other marsh terns.
Voice: Commonest call short loud *krsch* or *zeck*, suggesting Corncrake; also *ky-ik* and other raucous notes.
Habitat: Like Black, but prefers deeper waters. Map 178.

BLACK TERN *Chlidonias niger*   Plate 58, 59
Du – Zwarte stern   Fr – Guifette noire
Ge – Trauerseeschwalbe   Sw – Svarttärna

Identification: 9" (23cm). Slimmest marsh tern, with *narrower bill* and *relatively longer wings* and tail than White-winged Black. Only tern with *all-blackish-grey breeding plumage*, except for pale grey under-wing and *conspicuous white under tail-coverts.* During moult looks patchy. In winter has white forehead, neck and under-parts but retains *deep black cheeks* below crown and *small blackish patches on sides of breast*. Immature like winter adult but with darker back. Flies back and forth over water, dipping erratically to pick insects off surface and only plunging when at sea.

Confusion species: See Whiskered and White-winged Black for winter and immature comparisons. Beware occasional immature lacking breast patches.

Voice: Commonest calls quiet *kik-kik* in flight and sharper *teek-teek* or *teeuw* in alarm.

Habitat: Inland waters, also coastal on passage. Breeds in scattered colonies, building floating nest in shallows of marshes and lagoons. Map 179.

WHITE-WINGED BLACK TERN *Chlidonias leucopterus*   **Plate 58**
  Du – Witvleugelstern   Fr – Guifette leucoptère
  Ge – Weissflügelseeschwalbe   Sw – Vitvingad tärna

Identification: 9" (23cm). Rather compact marsh tern. Unmistakable in summer, with startling *black plumage* except for *white upper-wing coverts and tail*; further distinguished from Black by black (not pale grey) under wing-coverts. Adult in winter distinguished from Black by *absence of dark breast patches*, less black on crown, stouter build and steadier flight; from Whiskered by *complete white collar*, paler rump and squarer tail. Immature distinguished from young Black by *dark brown 'saddle'* contrasting with pale grey wings; from young Whiskered by *uniform* dark 'saddle' and clear white rump. Bill red in summer, blackish in winter; shorter and stubbier than Black or Whiskered.

Voice: Rasping *cherr*, or *kerr*.

Habitat: As Black Tern, with which it frequently associates throughout the year. Map 180.

AUKS: Alcidae

Black and white, salt-water, diving birds with short necks, very short, narrow wings, and legs set far back. Flight is whirring, large feet jutting out sideways before alighting. Carriage usually upright when standing. Sexes similar. Cliff or hole nesting.

GUILLEMOT *Uria aalge*   **Plate 61**
  Du – Zeekoet   Fr – Guillemot de Troil
  Ge – Trottellumme   Sw – Sillgrissla
  N. Am – Common Murre

Identification: 16" (41cm). Commonest large auk in NE. Atlantic, with *long, tapering bill and head*, rather thin neck, bottom-heavy outline on land but level back-line on sea. In breeding plumage, head, neck and upper-parts uniformly dark, relieved by white trailing edge to secondaries and, in 'bridled' morph, white spectacle around eye; under-parts white, relieved by dark flight feathers and *streaks on flanks and wing-lining*. In winter, most of face and fore-neck become white but retains *narrow dark line behind eye*. In good light, northern race *U. a. aalge* looks as black as Razorbill except for browner head, while southern race *U. a. albionis* is chocolate-brown, fading greyer. Flight outline shows tubby, quite long but blunt-ended body behind narrow, often uptilted bill and hunched head; action almost constant flap; formations linear. Swims and

dives well, literally *flying under water*. Beware bird carrying fish in partly open bill and showing 'line' like that of Brünnich's Guillemot (see below).
Voice: Long, harsh *arr* or *arra*, combining into noisy chorus at colonies.
Habitat: Coastal and offshore waters, breeding on sea cliffs in colonies, usually with other auks. Map 181.

BRÜNNICH'S GUILLEMOT   *Uria lomvia*   **Plate 61**
Du – Kortsnavelzeekoet   Fr – Guillemot de Brünnich
Ge – Dickschnabellumme   Sw – Spetsbergsgrissla
N. Am – Brünnich's Murre

Identification: 16" (41cm). Size overlaps with Guillemot but form differs in *shorter, blunter bill*, thicker head often with bump on fore-crown and deeper body, more hunch-backed in flight. Plumage similar to dark northern Guillemot but close-to distinguished by *thin pale streak on bill base*, broader white secondary trailing edge (creating small patch on innermost feathers), and *unstreaked wing-lining and flanks*, latter rising higher beside rump. In breeding plumage, dark neck divided by white up to lower throat; in winter, head stays dark down to mid-ear-coverts and so *lacks dark eye-line and white side to nape of Guillemot*, looking capped; throat may be banded dusky. Confusion with young Razorbill more likely than with Guillemot, particularly at distance. Flight, behaviour and voice as Guillemot.
Habitat and Range: As Guillemot, but roams farther out to sea in winter. Breeds Iceland, N. Norway; winters south to Norway, occasionally Faeroes. Vagrant to coasts south to British Isles, N. France, also inland in C. Europe.

RAZORBILL   *Alca torda*   **Plate 61**
Du – Alk   Fr – Petit pingouin
Ge – Tordalk   Sw – Tordmule
N. Am. – Razor-billed Auk

Identification: 16" (41cm). Size approaches Guillemot but form differs in *deep, almost rectangular, laterally compressed bill*, deeper head, thicker neck, smaller wings and *distinctly pointed tail*, usually cocked up on sea. Plumage black above, white below, with similar basic pattern to other large auks, relieved by *conspicuous white line across bill, white streak over lores* and white tips to secondaries forming bar, conspicuous in flight. In winter, *head darker than Guillemot*, with more black on cheeks and ear-coverts; shows extension of white towards nape, unlike Brünnich's. Juvenile far less distinctive than adult, with no streaks on bill and lores, white tips to secondaries ungrown until first moult, and having stubby rounded bill which invites confusion with Brünnich's. Flight outline 'front-heavy', not narrow-headed as Guillemot; action most whirring of large auks, even more lacking in manoeuvrability at cliffs. Other behaviour as Guillemot.
Voice: Protracted querulous growl and tremulous snore.
Habitat: As Guillemot but uses lower level of cliffs, even boulders, for breeding. Map 182.

BLACK GUILLEMOT *Cepphus grylle*   **Plate 62**
Du – Zwarte zeekoet   Fr – Guillemot à miroir
Ge – Gryllteiste   Sw – Tobisgrissla
Identification: 13" (33cm). Medium-sized, compact auk, with rather small,
fine bill and round head. In breeding plumage brown-black, strikingly relieved
by *large oval white patches on both surfaces of wing* and *bright red feet*. In
winter, appearance very different with only wings and tail unchanged, *upper-
parts and flanks strongly mottled white (looking hoary)*, under-body pure white.
Juvenile like winter adult but darker above, with dark lines across wing-patches.
Flight outline shows tubby head and body, with *oval-looking wings*; action fluttering. Behaviour much as Guillemot but far less sociable, usually seen singly or
in pairs and small groups. In winter, may suggest grebe but none shows similar
wing-patch and wing-shape.
Voice: Feeble but distinctive; weak whistle, occasionally runs into trilling twitter when red gape may show.
Habitat: Stays closer to shore than other guillemots, often among rocky, even
well-wooded, islands. Nests singly or in small scattered groups, in holes or
under boulders on rocky shores, cliff ledges, islands. Map 183.

LITTLE AUK *Alle alle*   **Plate 62**
Du – Kleine alk   Fr – Mergule nain
Ge – Krabbentaucher   Sw – Alkekung
N. Am – Dovekie
Identification: 8" (20cm). Smallest auk regular in N.E. Atlantic and North Sea;
little bigger than Starling with 'snub-nosed, neckless' form. In breeding plumage, head, neck, breast and upper-parts brown-black to black, with *white-lined
scapulars* and white trailing edge to secondaries; *under-wing dusky*, unlike all
other common auks. In winter, retains black face but dirty white invades nape,
throat and breast. Flight far less laboured than large auks, with quick take-off
and rather wader-like, free flapping action; formations often bunched. Appears
to enjoy rough water. Beware immature Puffin with apparently dark under-
wings.
Voice: High, shrill chatter; chorus of breeding colony very noisy.
Habitat and Range: Normally offshore, even pelagic but often storm-driven
close to headlands and occasionally 'wrecked' inland. Breeds in vast colonies, in
holes of arctic sea cliffs and mountains (from Iceland north to Spitzbergen).
Ranges in winter south to N.W. Britain and North Sea, wanders down English
Channel and into C. and S. Europe.

PUFFIN *Fratercula arctica*   **Plate 62**
Du – Papegaaiduiker   Fr – Macareux moine
Ge – Papageitaucher   Sw – Lunnefågel
Identification: 12" (30cm). Rather small, compact auk, with rather parrot-like,
leaf-shaped, laterally compressed bill and proportionately large head on stumpy
body. Surround to face, neck and upper-parts black, unmarked; *large round face
almost white*, with decorated eye and *astonishing red-ended and blue-based,
yellow-lined bill*; under-parts white; under-wing dull silver-grey on coverts and
sooty on flight-feathers; *feet bright orange-red*. In winter, bill smaller, less red,
more yellow; fore-face becomes dusky, making bird look 'dejected'. Juvenile

duller than adult, with much smaller *triangular dusky bill* and even darker face. Flight outline dominated by large bill and head and paddle-shaped wings; action whirring, with frequent changes in body angle. Rides high on sea; other behaviour as other auks. Bustles on land.
Voice: Long growl *ow* or *arr* from breeding birds.
Habitat: Coastal and offshore waters. Breeds colonially in rabbit or shearwater burrows, or in holes excavated in turf, on cliffs or grassy islands. Map 184.

SANDGROUSE: Pteroclididae

Plump, pigeon-like terrestrial birds, with very short, feathered legs and toes. Wings and tails long and pointed. Flight very rapid. Gait mincing and dove-like. Habitat usually deserts and arid ground. Noisy. Ground nesting.

BLACK-BELLIED SANDGROUSE *Pterocles orientalis*   Plate 36
Du – Zwartbuikzandhoen   Fr – Ganga unibande
Ge – Sandflughuhn   Sw – Ringflyghöna
Identification: 14" (35cm). Bulkiest of tribe in Europe, with heavy body, relatively short tail and rather broad wings. Appearance rather partridge-like; underwing white, with black primaries and *very narrow black rim to secondaries.* Male has pale grey head and neck with *orange-chestnut, black-based throat and neck patch*, black band over pale buff breast, *fully black flanks and belly* and rufous-buff spotted or splashed grey back and wings. Female less colourful, with black streaks on neck, back and wing-coverts. Flight outline and action heavier than other sandgrouse.
Voice: Usual note explosive, rattling *churr-rur-rur*, sounding over distance like short horse-like snort.
Habitat and Range: Semi-desert, or undulating stony country. Nests on ground. Resident Spain, Portugal. Vagrant elsewhere in S. and C. Europe.

PIN-TAILED SANDGROUSE *Pterocles alchata*   Plate 36
Du – Witbuikzandhoen   Fr – Ganga cata
Ge – Spiessflughuhn   Sw – Långstjärtad flyghöna
Identification: 12 (31cm). Smallest of tribe regular in Europe, with long, needle-pointed central tail-feathers, neckless flight silhouette and distinctive voice. In flight, shows diagnostic *white belly and broad wing-lining* contrasting with narrow black rim to secondaries and primaries. Breeding male has orange head with *black eye-streak and throat*, two narrow black lines above and below chestnut breast-band, *lemon-yellow spots on back and scapulars* and *wine-chestnut, white-lined wing-coverts*; in winter, resembles female but lacks lavender barring. Female has *whitish throat,*, orange neck, close-barred yellowish upperparts, with distinctive *lavender-grey bars on scapulars and tertials*, more numerous white bars on wing-coverts and two or three black bands across lower neck and breast. Flight outline and action recall both pigeon and plover, with deep regular wing-beats producing slight whistle as in all sandgrouse; gregarious, carrying out massed evolutions at water.
Voice: Commonest call far-carrying, nasal, harsh, ringing *catarr, catarr*.
Habitat and Range: Dry, dusty plains, high stony plateaux, sun-baked mud-

flats, and edges of marismas. Nests on ground. Resident S. France, Spain, Portugal. Vagrant elsewhere in S. Europe.

PALLAS'S SANDGROUSE *Syrrhaptes paradoxus*   Plate 36
   Du – Steppenhoen   Fr – Syrrhapte paradoxa
   Ge – Steppenhuhn   Sw – Stäpphöna
Identification: 14-16" (35-40cm). Less bulky than resident European relatives but with *even longer pins on tail* and smaller head, making wings appear to be set further forward on body. Wings pointed, buff above, with chestnut bar and greyish primaries, and *silvery-white with buff coverts below*, with only narrow dusky rim to secondaries; *rear belly conspicuously banded black*. On ground, both sexes strongly recall Grey Partridge, with *orange face and fore-neck surrounded by grey neck and breast*; back sandy, waved black; fore-belly and vent buff-white. Female distinguished by *black half-collar* and copious black spots on wing-coverts. Immature marbled on head and neck; already shows diagnostic under-wing and belly pattern. Flight action similar to *Pterocles* but whistling of wing-beats stronger.
Voice: Commonest calls rather low-pitched, clucking *cu-ruu cu-ruu cu-ou-ruu* or *cho-ho-ho-ho* and more insistent *kirik, kukerik* or *kerkerki.*
Habitat and Range: Sandy semi-desert regions. During periodic irruptions into Europe usually occurs on sandy coasts, stubble fields, etc. Nests on ground. Has occurred sporadically throughout Europe, west to Britain (where it has bred, also in Denmark) and has reached Ireland, Faeroes. Last big invasion 1908.

PIGEONS AND DOVES: Columbidae

Plump, fast-flying birds, with small heads and characteristically deep, crooning voices. The terms 'pigeon' and 'dove' are loosely used and interchangeable, but in a general way 'pigeon' refers to the larger species with ample, squared or rounded tails, 'dove' to the smaller, more slender species with longer, graduated tails. Sexes similar. Tree or hole nesting.

ROCK DOVE and FERAL PIGEON *Columba livia*   Plate 63
   Du – Rotsduif   Fr – Pigeon biset
   Ge – Felsentaube   Sw – Klippduva
Identification: 13" (33cm). Wild bird ancestor of familiar feral pigeon and other racing and decorative breeds. Distinguished from Stock Dove and much larger Woodpigeon by *white lower back,* white wing-lining and *two black bands across rear inner wing*, contrasting with blue-grey body, paler grey back and wings, and grey, white-edged and *broadly black-banded tail*. Large glossy green and lilac neck-patch, dull on juvenile. Feral and racing birds show many blackish, tan and white varieties; interbreed freely with wild birds. Flight outline most streamlined of pigeons, suggesting small falcon at times; action fast, with clipped wing-beats. Walks with bobbing head.
Voice: Muffled croon *druoo-u* or *oo-roo-coo.*
Habitat: Rock Dove usually in small numbers around rocky sea-cliffs and nearby fields but locally abundant around seabird colonies, in Europe also on inland cliffs. Feral pigeon mainly in towns and cities. Nests in crevices or caves. Map 185.

STOCK DOVE *Columba oenas*   **Plate 63**
  Du – Holenduif   Fr – Pigeon colombin
  Ge – Hohltaube   Sw – Skogsduva

Identification: 13" (33cm). Noticeably smaller and shorter-tailed than Wood Pigeon, from which easily distinguished by lack of white on wing and neck and *striking broad, pale grey panel on dusky-rimmed wings*. Plumage rather uniform blue-grey except for wing-panel and paler lower back and rump. Close-to, shows *glossy green patch* on neck and *two short broken black bars on rear inner wing*. Juvenile lacks neck-patch. Flight outline rather chunky, with shortish neck and tail and paddle-shaped wings; action fast but rather fluttering at times, wing-beats whistle. Behaviour like Wood Pigeon but shyer and less gregarious. Beware confusion with grey-rumped feral pigeons.

Voice: Croon distinguished from Wood Pigeon's by more monotonous inter-mittent delivery: *ooo-roo-oo*, etc., the first syllable being usually emphasized.

Habitat: As Wood Pigeon, but prefers more open parkland with old trees, also cliffs, sand-dunes, etc. Nests in holes in old trees, rocks, rabbit burrows, build-ings, etc. Map 186.

WOOD PIGEON *Columba palumbus*   **Plate 63**
  Du – Houtduif   Fr – Pigeon ramier
  Ge – Ringeltaube   Sw – Ringduva

Identification: 16" (40cm). Largest and commonest European pigeon, with small head on long, fat body, ample wings and *longer tail than relatives*. Shows diagnostic *bold transverse white band across centre of wing* – conspicuous in flight – and *white patches below glossy green-purple blaze* on neck, both ob-vious above deep vinous breast. Juvenile lacks neck-marks. Flight outline hea-viest and longest of family; action powerful, with looser wing-beats than smaller relatives; *wings clatter on take-off* and at peak of display flight. Gait rather wad-dling, hugging ground. Gregarious, roaming in huge winter flocks; mixes freely with other pigeons. 'Explodes' from trees when alarmed.

Voice: Croon loud and far carrying though curiously muffled; repeated *coo-cooo-co-co-coo*.

Habitat: Occurs almost anywhere, including town centres, but not often in treeless regions or extreme north. Nests in trees, hedges, old nests, etc. Map 187.

COLLARED DOVE *Streptopelia decaocto*   **Plate 63**
  Du – Turkse tortel   Fr – Tourterelle turque
  Ge – Türkentaube   Sw – Turkduva

Identification: 13" (33cm). Markedly longer and fuller-tailed than Turtle, with *distinctive song*. Plumage most uniform of European doves, generally *pale dusty-brown*, relieved by paler, greyer face, *narrow black half-collar on hind neck*, dusky rim to open wing darkest on primaries and, from below, *white ter-minal half to black tail*. Escaped, slighter Barbary Dove *S. risoria* has paler cream-buff plumage, lacking dark primaries. Flight as Turtle but wing-beats less angled. Gregarious, flocking at grain stores, farmyards.

Voice: Monotonous, endlessly repeated, deep *doo-dooh-do*, with stress on sec-ond syllable and usually given in rhythmic couplet (Barbary usually accents first syllable). Flight-call nasal, harsh *kwarr*.

Habitat: Mainly around and in towns and villages. Usually nests in conifers; locally on buildings. Map 188.

TURTLE DOVE *Streptopelia turtur* Plate 63

Du – Tortelduif	Fr – Tourterelle des bois
Ge – Turteltaube	Sw – Turturduva

Identification: 11" (28cm). Rather small, delicate dove, with *rapid, wing-flicking flight*. Plumage pattern dominated by *dark-spotted, sandy-rufous back and inner wing-coverts*, bluish outer wing-coverts and *well graduated blackish tail with bright white rim*. Close-to, shows greyish head, *black and white-striped patch on neck*, pinkish throat and breast and pale whitish belly contrasting with dusky under-wing. Juvenile duller, without neck-marks. Flight outline insubstantial, with long wings and full tail when spread; action alternates bursts of wing-beats and fast glides. Solitary when breeding but forms flocks in autumn and on migration. Collared and Rufous Turtle are distinctly larger; Laughing is smaller and slighter.

Voice: Croon soft, quieter and 'sleepier' than other relatives; repeated purring *roòr-r-r*.

Habitat: Open bushy country with uncut hedges and small woods. Nests in bushes, thickets, orchards, etc. Map 189.

RUFOUS TURTLE DOVE *Streptopelia orientalis* Plate 63

Du – Oosterse tortelduif	Fr – Tourterelle orientale
Ge – Orient Turteltaube	Sw – Större turturduva

Identification: 13" (33cm). Noticeably *larger and deeper-bodied than Turtle*, with heavier, straighter flight. Plumage pattern recalls Turtle but generally dark. Close-to, adult shows brown on rear head and hind neck (grey on Turtle), rosy eye-ring (red and slightly elongated on Turtle), larger but indistinct neck-patch fringed blue-grey (white on Turtle), *darker brown breast* (mauve-grey on Turtle). Upper-parts show larger but rather ill-defined, almost black centres on inner wing-coverts and whiter edges to dark outer wing-coverts; often shows double whitish wing-bar (lacking in Turtle whose wing-coverts are paler, more orange and pale blue on outer coverts). E. Asian race *S. o. orientalis* has tail narrowly tipped grey but W. Asian *S. o. meena* particularly confusing, showing pale belly and white tail-rim like Turtle. Juvenile paler, without neck-patches but otherwise patterned as adult.

Voice: Silent as vagrant. Song recalls Wood Pigeon.

Habitat and Range: Light open forest in Asia, whence vagrant to S., C., N. and W. Europe (including Britain).

LAUGHING DOVE *Streptopelia senegalensis* Plate 63

Du – Palmtortel	Fr – Tourterelle de Sénégal
Ge – Palmtaube	Sw – Palmduva

Identification: 10" (26cm). Smallest dove reaching Europe, with slim build, proportionately short wings, long tail and fluttering flight. Plumage essentially *red-brown above* and buff-white below, with pinkish head, *deep copper, black-speckled gorget*, pale *blue-grey wing-coverts* shining in flight, blue-grey lower back, and dusky rump and tail, last tipped broadly white. Juvenile lacks gorget. Tame.

Voice: Commonest call quick, rising then falling, laughing multi-syllable *p-ooo pe-poo-oo pup oo*; particularly pleasing in chorus.
Habitat and Range: Widespread in and around towns and villages in parts of Africa and SW. Asia, nesting in thorn bushes, small trees and on buildings. Breeds European Turkey; vagrant S., W. and N. Europe.

PARROTS: Psittacidae

ROSE-RINGED PARAKEET *Psittacula krameri*   Plate 95
Du – Halsbandparakiet   Fr – Perruche à collier
Ge – Halsbandsittiche   Sw – Halsbandsparakit
Identification: 16½" (42cm). Large-headed parrot, with deep hooked pinkish-red bill, *very long tail* and *unmistakable pale emerald-green plumage*, relieved in male by narrow *black and rose-red neck-ring*. Flies fast with characteristically clipped wing-beats. Gregarious.
Voice: Noisy, uttering *loud, rasping screech*.
Habitat and Range: Inhabits mature trees in African and Asian savannah. In W. Europe, escaped, now feral birds exploit old timber in suburbs. Resident in parts of England, Belgium, Holland, Germany, Yugoslavia; also recorded Scotland, Wales.

CUCKOOS: Cuculidae

Rather slim, long-tailed, slender-winged birds, with two toes forward and two behind. Brood-parasitic in nesting. Sexes similar.

GREAT SPOTTED CUCKOO *Clamator glandarius*   Plate 67
Du – Kuifkoekoek   Fɪ – Coucou-geai
Ge Häherkuckuck   Sw – Skatgök
Identification: 15" (38cm). Largest cuckoo of region, with *conspicuous crest*, loosely feathered thighs and proportionately longest graduated tail of tribe. Upper-parts dark brown, relieved by pale grey crown and crest and *copious white spots* on scapulars, inner-wings, above tail and on tips of tail-feathers; under-parts creamy white, *almost yellow on chin and throat*; bright orange eye-ring emphasizes eye. Juvenile lacks grey crown and full crest, but shows large *chestnut patch on primaries*. Flight outline with trailing tail distinctive; action stronger than Cuckoo, allowing more direct, less floating progress. Conspicuous when breeding, adopting Magpie-like postures.
Voice: *Noisy cacophony* includes chattering, tern-like *kittera, kittera, kittera*, followed by gobbling notes; harsh, rising *zhree* (recalling Azure-winged Magpie), crow-like *kark* of alarm, etc.
Habitat and Range: Outskirts and glades of woods, olive groves, bushy plains with occasional trees. Brood-parasitic, eggs usually laid in nests of crow family, particularly Magpie; often lays several eggs in same nest. Summer visitor to Spain, Portugal, S. France, Yugoslavia, perhaps Greece, Bulgaria. Vagrant elsewhere in Europe (including Britain).

CUCKOO *Cuculus canorus* **Plate 67**
  Du – Koekoek   Fr – Coucou gris
  Ge – Kuckuck   Sw – Gök
Identification: 13" (33cm). Quite lengthy, somewhat falcon-like bird, with narrow wing-points, *long, graduated tail* and *unmistakable call*. Head, breast and upper-parts bluish-grey, wings and tail dusky, latter white-spotted on tips; under-body and under-wing whitish, copiously *barred dark grey*. Rare erythristic female and some juveniles red-brown above, copiously barred there as well as below; other juveniles variable, dusky-to-grey-brown above, with faint to obvious barring; all juveniles patched *white on nape*. Flight outline recalls both falcon and round-winged hawk but bill and head often carried above body line, wings set further forward and tail proportionately much longer; action distinctive, with weak, deep wing-beats seemingly below body line. Solitary except when breeding.
Voice: Mellow, penetrating *cuc-coo*, sometimes single or treble notes; also deep *wow-wow-wow*. Female has long, bubbling note.
Habitat: Edges of woodland, bushy commons, etc., also in treeless areas, locally on open high ground. Polyandrous and brood-parasitic; individual birds usually parasitizing only one species, laying single egg in each nest. Map 190.

BLACK-BILLED CUCKOO *Coccyzus erythrophthalmus* **Plate 67**
  Du – Zwartsnavellkoekoek   Fr – Coulicou à bec noir
  Ge – Schwarzschnabel Koekoek   Sw – Svartnäbbad regngok
Identification: 12" (30cm). Size and form as Yellow-billed below but distinguished by *lack of rufous wing-panel*, small, less conspicuous white spots on tail, black bill and narrow red eye-ring.
Voice: Fast, rhythmic *cu-cu-cu-*, *cu-cu-cu*, repeated 3-5 times; also occasionally long series of rapid *cuck* notes (not becoming slower like Yellow-billed). Vagrants silent.
Habitat and Range: Deciduous forest and coppices. Vagrant from N. America to W. Europe (including Britain).

YELLOW-BILLED CUCKOO *Coccyzus americanus* **Plate 67**
  Du – Geelsnavelkoekoek   Fr – Coulicou à bec jaune
  Ge – Gelbschnabelkuckuck   Sw – Gulnäbbad regengök
Identification: 12" (30cm). Smaller, slimmer and more dove-like than Cuckoo; dull brown above and whitish below. Distinctive marks are *yellow lower mandible*, large white spots at tips of dark tail-feathers and *rufous panel on primaries*, conspicuous in flight. See also rarer Black-billed Cuckoo.
Voice: Rapid, throaty *ka-ka-ka-ka-ka-kow-kow-kowp-kowp-kowp* slower towards end. Vagrants silent.
Habitat and Range: Copses, thickets, woodlands. Vagrant from N. America to W. (including Britain), N., C. and S. Europe.

BARN OWLS: Tytonidae

BARN OWL *Tyto alba*   **Plate 64**
Du – Kerkuil   Fr – Chouette effraie
Ge – Schleiereule   Sw – Tornuggla
Identification: 14" (35cm). Medium-sized, very pale owl, with distinctive *heart-shaped face*, tapering lower body and long visible legs. Hunting flight usually low, slow, buoyant but characteristically *wavering*, as bird looks down intently for small rodents. *Upper-parts golden buff*, sullied grey and finely speckled; *face white, with dark eyes*; under-parts mainly white in W. and S. European race *T. a. alba* but wholly buff in C. European *T. a. guttata* (so-called Dark-breasted) which wanders west to Britain. Flight outline shows flat face on large head and dangling legs. Perches upright, with 'knock-kneed' stance. Nocturnal but often hunts by day in winter.
Voice: Long, wild shriek. Hissing, snoring and yapping notes also given.
Habitat: Very partial to human habitation, breeding in farm buildings, church towers, ruins, etc. Also frequents parks with old timber, occasionally cliffs. Map 191.

OWLS: Strigidae

Generally nocturnal birds of prey, with large heads, flattened faces forming 'facial discs', and forward-facing eyes. Half-hidden, hooked bills and powerful claws. Flight noiseless. Some species have conspicuous feather-tuft 'ears'. Most owls have large eyes and closely feathered feet. Sexes usually similar. Nest in holes, old nests, or on ground.

SCOPS OWL *Otus scops*   **Plate 64**
Du – Dwergooruil   Fr – Hibou petit-duc
Ge – Zwergohreule   Sw – Dvärguv
Identification: 7" (18cm). Second smallest owl of region, with relatively large head and quite long wings; *voice distinctive*. Wing-beats more regular than Little, producing much less bounding and undulating progress. Plumage grey to brown, *closely speckled and vermiculated*, with *rather broad ear-tufts* erected in alarm; eyes yellow. Perches upright, with stance as slim as Long-eared when disturbed. Nocturnal. Preys on insects.
Voice: Usual note soft, penetrating, persistently repeated *pew*, closely resembling voice of Midwife Toad, which often causes confusion.
Habitat: Trees near human habitation, plantations, gardens, etc.; also among old buildings. Nests in holes, occasionally in old nests of other birds. Map 192.

EAGLE OWL *Bubo bubo*   **Plate 64**
Du – Oehoe   Fr – Hibou grand-duc
Ge – Uhu   Sw – Berguv
Identification: 26-28" (65-70cm). Largest European owl, *as big as Buzzard*, with *prominent ear-tufts*, broad head, barrel-like body and *distinctive voice*. Flight powerful and fast, with *Buzzard-like wing-beats* arcing mostly above body line and *low, straight glides*; hunts prey as large as Hare and Capercaillie.

Plumage *tawny*-brown, with bold dark mottling above and strong blackish streaks below. *Large orange eyes 'glow'* in dark facial disc. Perches upright. Active at dawn and dusk; roosts in holes.

Voice: Deep, but brief *ooo-hu*, second syllable falling slightly, sometimes followed by a quiet, guttural chuckling. Female has fox-like bark.

Habitat: Rocky promontories in forest, crags, mountainsides and open steppes. Breeds in hollow among rocks and scrub, in hollow trees, or old nests of birds of prey. Map 193.

SNOWY OWL *Nyctea scandiaca*   Plate 64
Du – Sneeuwuil   Fr – Chouette harfang
Ge – Schneeule   Sw – Fjälluggla

Identification: 21-26" (53-66cm). Very large, round-headed, *'cat-faced'* owl, with basically *white plumage* sparsely spotted black in adult male but copiously *barred and spotted dusky in female and especially immature*. Eyes yellow. Flight more active than most owls, with *deep regular beats of relatively long, 'fingered' wings* suggesting Buzzard; capable of both buoyant glides and falcon-like chase of prey as large as Arctic Hare and Eider. Perches upright or half so on low eminence, occasionally crouching down (then very like white cat). Distinguished from Barn Owl by much larger size and grey or white upper-parts, from Gyrfalcon by owl shape and slower flight. Chiefly diurnal; solitary.

Voice: Usually silent. Flight-notes when breeding, repeated loud *krow-ow*, or repeated *rick*.

Habitat: Arctic tundra and barren hills. During periodic irruptions frequents open country, dunes, airfields, marshes, sea and lake shores, etc. Nests on mossy hummocks in tundra. Map 194.

HAWK OWL *Surnia ulula*   Plate 65
Du – Sperweruil   Fr – Chouette épervière
Ge – Sperbereule   Sw – Hökuggla

Identification: 14-16" (35-40cm). Medium-sized owl with distinctly hawk-like form, having proportionately *long tail* and *pointed wings*. Flight outline and action recall Sparrowhawk, with bursts of fast, often clipped wing-beats and glides, ending in characteristic *upward sweep to prominent perch*. Plumage strongly patterned, with *whitish face heavily bordered black*, white blaze and black patch on sides of nape, pale mottled back, barred wings and tail and whitish, barred body. Eyes yellow. Perches upright or at angle; frequently *jerks tail up, then slowly lowers it*. Hunts by day but calls at night. May attack in defence of nest.

Voice: Song sonorous bubbling trill *prullul-lullu*; also screams and chatters with Merlin-like *kikikiki*.

Habitat: Coniferous forest and open birch scrub, irrupting south in years of scarce rodent prey. Breeds in shelter of broken tree-top, in hollow trees, old nests of hawks, etc. Map 195.

PYGMY OWL *Glaucidium passerinum*   Plate 65
Du – Dwerguil   Fr – Chouette chevêchette
Ge – Sperlingskauz   Sw – Sparvuggla

Identification: 6" (15cm). Smallest European owl, with rather small round head on Starling-sized body; quite long *tail frequently waved and flicked up-wards*, even held up like flycatcher. *Flight active, dashing*, with bursts of wing-beats, wing-closures and swift turns in pursuit of small passerines; *markedly bounding over distance*, like woodpecker. Head and upper-parts dark brown, spotted whitish-buff; face lacks obvious disc but *short white eyebrows produce 'frown'*; under-parts off-white, barred at shoulders, streaked elsewhere; wings and tail dark brown, barred white. Partly diurnal. Little Owl much larger, see below.

Voice: Noisy. Male's territorial call softly whistled *hjuuk*, repeated at one sec-ond intervals at dawn and dusk and suggesting Bullfinch; interspersed with stammered hoot *huhuhu* in excitement. Female replies with high *pseeeee* and probably *hyeelk*. In autumn, utters short series of shrill fluted notes.

Habitat: Mature secluded forests, usually coniferous, in mountainous regions. Nests in hollow trees, and woodpecker holes. Map 196.

LITTLE OWL *Athene noctua*   **Plate 65**

   Du – Steenuil   Fr – Chouette cheveche

   Ge – Steinkauz   Sw – Minervauggla

Identification: 9" (23cm). Rather small compact owl, with *broad, flat-crowned head* and rather long, visible legs. Flight alternates bursts of quick, angled wing-beats and closures, producing *low, rapid bounding progress* like large wood-pecker. Upper-parts dark brown, *spotted dull white especially on scapulars* and wing-coverts and barred whitish on wings and tail; under-parts whitish, boldly dappled and streaked dark brown. Face has yellow eyes set in brownish cheeks, *whitish supercilia and broad white throat* contrasting with dark brown ruff-line, all contributing to *glaring expression*. Often perches openly during day, with angled stance. Feeds chiefly on insects and small rodents. Tengmalm's not much larger but is strictly bird of forest.

Voice: Shrill, rather plaintive *kiu*, sharp, barking *werro*, etc.

Habitat: Varied, but usually fairly open farming country and stony wasteland. Nests in holes in trees, especially pollarded willows, and in rocks, buildings, burrows. Map 197.

TAWNY OWL *Strix aluco*   **Plate 65**

   Du – Bosuil   Fr – Chouette hulotte

   Ge – Waldkauz   Sw – Kattuggla

Identification: 15" (38cm). Commonest and most widespread owl of region, only one to enter towns and cities. Quite large, with *round head,* barrel body and *noticeably broad, round wings* beaten rather quickly and strongly or held out in long level glide. Plumage *rather uniform, mottled and barred brown* on grey to rufous ground. *Dark eyes* give kindly expression. Whitish stripes on crown, along edge of scapulars and along greater coverts catch eye. Strictly nocturnal except in extreme hard weather. Uniform appearance and stable flight quickly exclude other similarly-sized owls.

Voice: Song deep musical *hoo-hoo-hoo*, followed at an interval by a long, tre-mulous *oo-oo-oo-oo*. Shrill *ke-wick*.

Habitat: Mature woods, parks, large gardens. Nests in hollow trees, old nests of large birds, occasionally in buildings and rabbit burrows. Map 198.

URAL OWL *Strix uralensis* Plate 65
Du – Oeraluil Fr – Chouette de l'Oural
Ge – Habichtskauz Sw – Slaguggla

Identification: 24" (60cm). Large, round-headed lengthy owl, with pale, underlined face, small dark eyes and rather *long, wedge-shaped tail.* Kindly expression and sustained glides may suggest Tawny but Ural is much larger and paler, recalling Buzzard or Goshawk in flight. Plumage *rather pale ochre-grey,* copiously streaked on back of head, upper- and under-parts and *strongly barred blackish on flight feathers*, with markings on secondaries heaviest of all owls. Beware confusion with even larger Great Grey and narrow-winged Short-eared Owl, which see. Aggressive at nest.

Voice: Courtship call far-carrying, deep *whohoo*, followed 4 seconds later by *whohoo owhoohoo*. Other calls include muffled, rising *poopoopoopoo...* (up to 8 syllables), harsh *kawveck* from female and barking *waff* in alarm.

Habitat: Mixed woods, coppices and forests. Nests in fractures of broken-off trees, occasionally in old nests of birds of prey. Map 199.

GREAT GREY OWL *Strix nebulosa* Plate 65
Du – Laplanduil Fr – Chouette lapone
Ge – Bartkauz Sw – Lappuggla

Identification: 27" (68cm). Size between Ural and Eagle, with *large circular head* with frowning expression, lengthy body, *broad, round wings* and *rather long, wedge-shaped tail.* Flight distinctive, with slow ponderous wing-beats recalling Heron and floating glide. Plumage dusky-grey, with large, *remarkably lined facial discs* containing *tiny yellow eyes*, whitish eyebrows under blackish forehead and pale whiskers over *blackish chin*; mottled upper-parts and softly steaked under-parts. Wings barred, with *pale rufous-yellow primary bases* creating bright chequered patch on outer wing; *tail broadly banded dark at end.* Eagle Owl lacks vertical face profile and has proportionately much longer wings and much more tawny plumage.

Voice: Deep-toned, booming *hu-hu-hu-hoo*, often rising and repeated at regular intervals; also high, shrill *ke-wick*, both calls not unlike Tawny's.

Habitat and Range: Dense, northern coniferous forests. Lays in old nests of large birds of prey. Resident in arctic Norway, Sweden, Finland. In 'invasion' years, extends south over much of Scandinavia, Finland, Estonia, occasionally eastern Germany, Poland.

LONG-EARED OWL *Asio otus* Plate 64
Du – Ransuil Fr – Hibou moyen-duc
Ge – Waldonhreule Sw – Hornuggla

Identification: 14" (36cm). Only medium-sized owl with *long ear-tuffs*. Rather oval face, rather long wings and occasionally wavering flight suggest Short-eared but distinguished by *orange eyes*, contributing when body plumage fluffed out to strong resemblance to Persian tabby cat. Plumage *grey and rufous-buff*, more uniformly streaked below and with more *finely barred under-surface to wing-tip* than Short-eared; lacks pale rim to secondaries. Hunting flight essentially gliding, on level wings. Roosts by day in dark thicket or in attenuated upright posture on branch, close to trunk. Feeds chiefly on small rodents. Forms communal roosts in autumn and winter. Strictly nocturnal, except on passage.

Voice: Rather quiet except in early spring. Male *hoots feebly* with low, sighing *oo* repeated at 2 second intervals. Barks *kwek-kwek* in alarm.
Habitat: Coniferous forests, also small coppices of conifers, locally in deciduous woods. Breeds in old nests, and occasionally on ground in wood, or on moorland. Map 200.

SHORT-EARED OWL *Asio flammeus*   Plate 64

Du – Velduil	Fr – Hibou des marais
Ge – Sumpfohreule	Sw – Jorduggla

Identification: 16" (40cm). Lengthiest of medium-sized owls, with rather squashed face, short ear tufts, proportionately longest and narrowest wings of group and pronounced diurnal behaviour. Flight markedly wavering, with *slow 'rowing' beats with hint of upward jerk* and characteristically *unstable glide* on slightly raised wings. Plumage *pale yellowish above*, whitish below, with heavy dark brown mottles, bars and streaks. Most striking marks are *yellow eyes set in dark eye-patches* giving baleful look; *black-barred wing-tips*, almost black carpal patches, pale buff panel at base of primaries, strongly barred flight feathers with *pale rim to inner primaries and secondaries* obvious on retreating bird, and pale, little-streaked under-body contrasting with dark breast. Perches openly on low eminence or in grass. Forms parties during rodent 'plagues'.
Voice: Song, repeated, deep *boo-boo-boo*, usually during circling display-flight. Wing-clapping also occurs. Female has grating *gweek* call. High sneezing bark.
Habitat: Open marshy country, sand-dunes, moors. Breeds on ground among heather, sedges, clumps of marram grass, etc. Map 201.

TENGMALM'S OWL *Aegolius funereus*   Plate 65

Du – Ruigpootuil	Fr – Chouette de Tengmalm
Ge – Rauhfusskauz	Sw – Pärluggla
N. Am – Boreal Owl	

Identification: 10" (25cm). Slightly larger than Little, with *rounded, deeper facial discs set in square head*, rather longer tail and more erect posture. Flight combines rapid wing-beats and glides on straight wings, suggesting miniature Tawny rather than Little. Upper-parts *chocolate-brown, spotted white*, under-parts white, blotched brown. Wings well-barred below but showing almost uniformly dark primaries above. Face strongly marked, with yellow eyes set in dusky-white discs, bordered black, and with *broad white eyebrows and black corners to fore-crown*. Juvenile almost *uniform mahogany*, with dark facial discs contrasting with white eyebrows. Hunts chiefly small rodents. Strictly nocturnal.
Voice: Fairly rapid phrase of 3-6 similar, high, but musical notes *poo-poo-poo*, etc. the final note often diminishing in emphasis, sometimes accelerating almost to trill. Alarm, *ja-week*.
Habitat: Coniferous forests in mountainous regions, locally in mixed woods. Winters in valleys and lowlands. Nests in woodpecker holes or natural holes in trees. Map 202.

NIGHTJARS: Caprimulgidae

Nocturnal insectivorous birds, with large eyes, huge gapes, tiny bills and feet, long wings and ample tails. Plumage beautifully camouflaged with 'dead leaf' pattern. Usually pass day immobile, on ground or perched lengthways along branch. Sexes similar. Ground nesting.

NIGHTJAR *Caprimulgus europaeus*   Plate 68
    Du – Nachtzwaluw   Fr – Engoulevent d'Europe
    Ge – Ziegenmelker   Sw – Nattskärra

Identification: 11" (28cm). Broad-headed but flat-crowned, *long-winged and tailed*, nocturnal predator of moths, best known for remarkable *churring song*. Plumage grey-brown, *closely speckled and barred* with dark brown and buff; affords perfect ground camouflage. Male distinguished from female by *short white bar across outer primaries* and conspicuous *white corners on tail*. During day, crouches motionless along (occasionally across) branch or on ground but at dusk takes wing, pursuing prey in strangely erratic, floating and silent flight. Close-to, large eye and huge gape may show. Claps wings loudly in breeding display.

Voice: Nocturnal song *loud rapid churring, rising and falling*; sometimes long sustained, sometimes 'running down' with a few clucking notes. Beware similar quieter sound made by Mole Cricket. Calls include soft nasal *goo-ek* and high *quick-quick-quick* in alarm.

Habitat: Moors, commons, open woodland glades with bracken, and sand-dunes. Lays eggs on bare ground. Map 203.

RED-NECKED NIGHTJAR *Caprimulgus ruficollis*   Plate 68
    Du – Moorse nachtzwaluw   Fr – Engoulevent à collier roux
    Ge – Rothalsziegenmelker   Sw – Rödhalsad nattskärra

Identification: 12" (30cm). Noticeably heavier-headed and generally bulkier than Nightjar, with more rufous plumage. Both sexes have more conspicuous *white bars on primaries and tail-corners*. Close-to, shows *almost orange collar and large white throat*. Flight and behaviour as Nightjar but looks heavier and longer-tailed on the wing.

Voice: Far-carrying song consists of double, or sometimes single, incessantly repeated notes, *kutuk-kutuk-kutuk*, etc., like hard rapping on hollow wood, up to 100 notes per minute.

Habitat and Range: Pine woods, bushy semi-desert regions and pine-clad hillsides. Lays eggs on bare ground. Summer visitor Spain and Portugal. Has bred S. France. Vagrant elsewhere in S. and W. Europe (including Britain).

EGYPTIAN NIGHTJAR *Caprimulgus aegyptius*   Plate 68
    Du – Egyptische nachtzwaluw   Fr – Engoulevent d'Egypte
    Ge – Ägyptischer Ziegenmelker Sw – Ökennattskärra

Identification: 10" (25cm). Somewhat slighter in build than Nightjar, with much paler and more uniform *sandy* plumage from which only darker primaries catch eye. Lacks well defined white marks on wings and tail but webs of inner primaries are whitish.

Voice: Utters single hollow-sounding knocking note in long series, *tok, tok, tok,...* or *kroo-kroo-kroo-kroo*. Vagrants silent.
Habitat and Range: Desert water-courses and oases. Occurs casually around Mediterranean coasts, rarely wandering to C. and W. Europe (including Britain).

SWIFTS: Apodidae

Essentially aerial. Slim, with long, scythe-like wings and short tails. Flight extremely rapid. Sexes similar. Hole nesting.

SWIFT *Apus apus*   **Plate 71**
Du – Gierzwaluw	Fr – Martinet noir
Ge – Mauersegler	Sw – Tornseglare

Identification: 6" (16cm). Tiny-billed but broad-gaped, round-headed insectivore, with *long, scythe-shaped wings* and *rather short forked tail*; distinguished from hirundines by more direct flight on stiffly-beaten wings and *almost uniformly dark plumage*. At distance, looks all-black; close-to, sooty-black, with small whitish chin and slightly paler upper surfaces to secondaries occasionally showing. Flight rapid, impelled by quick, seemingly unbending, at times 'twinkling' wing-beats and varied by glides and wide turns; close quarter manoeuvres acheived only with much flapping. Sociable and noisy when breeding, forming chasing, screaming parties. Beware albinistic individuals with white on rump or under-parts which may suggest Pacific or White-rumped, which see.
Voice: Long, piercing screech; rapid chirrup.
Habitat: Most aerial of European birds, wandering widely but concentrated over areas with suitable nest sites and nearby waters. Nests mainly in building roofs or towers, entering under eaves; occasionally in cliff or tree holes. Map 204.

PALLID SWIFT *Apus pallidus*   **Plate 71**
Du – Vale Gierzwaluw	Fr – Martinet pâle
Ge – Fahlsegler	Sw – Blek tornseglare

Identification: 6" (16cm). Form like Swift but wing-tip slightly rounder, *head flatter and broader*, body and rump slightly broader and tail-fork blunter. Plumage essentially brown, can look as dark as Swift's but palest birds in diffuse light can appear almost milky-toned. Close-to, shows greyish forehead, dark eye-pit, *conspicuous white throat* (broader than Swift's), dark saddle, and 'rough' body plumage (due to pale feather margins). Wings catch light more than Swift with *sandy-grey surfaces to all but outermost flight feathers* and (by contrast) very dark under-wing coverts. Flight *deliberate*, lacking 'twinkling' character of Swift. Sociable but much scarcer than Swift. Beware effect of different lights on Swift, particularly juvenile.
Voice: Deeper, less shrill than Swift.
Habitat: As Swift but less frequently nesting in buildings. Map 205.

ALPINE SWIFT *Apus melba*   **Plate 71**
Du – Alpengierzwaluw   Fr – Martinet alpin
Ge – Alpensegler   Sw – Alpseglare
Identification: 8" (21cm), wing-span 21" (53cm). Largest, most impressive swift; thick-set with relatively short but still forked tail. Plumage *umber-brown,* strikingly relieved by *white throat and belly* crossed by *broad brown breast-band.* Flight outline bulky, may even suggest small falcon; action *powerful* (with audible wing-beats close-to) and speed greater than other swifts.
Voice: High-pitched trill, rising and falling, also suggesting distant falcon; often in chorus.
Habitat: Chiefly in high, rocky mountainous regions, locally also along sea cliffs and among old buildings. Builds cup-shaped nest in cleft rocks, natural crevices and beneath rafters. Usually nests in colonies. Map 206.

WHITE-RUMPED SWIFT *Apus caffer*   **Plate 71**
Du – Kaffergierzwaluw   Fr – Martinet cafre
Ge – Kaffernsegler   Sw – Kafferseglare
Identification: 5" (13cm). Rather small, slim swift, with proportionately *longer rear body and more forked tail* than other species. Plumage black-blue (looking jet black), relieved by greyish face, white chin, *silvery under-side of flight feathers* and narrow *white band over upper-rump.* Flight action most 'twinkling' of tribe; greater aerial agility allows entry to low nest-sites. Often associates with Red-rumped Swallows and Little Swifts.
Voice: Rather guttural twitter, recalling bat.
Habitat and Range: Rocky outcrops in farmland; small migrant Spanish population dependent on nests of Red-rumped Swallow. Vagrant N. Europe.

LITTLE SWIFT *Apus affinis*   **Plate 71**
Du – Huisgierzwaluw   Fr – Martinet à dos blanc
Ge – Stubbstjärtseglare   Sw – Stubbstjärtad seglare
Identification: 5" (12cm). Small, noticeably compact swift with slightly paddle-shaped, somewhat translucent wings and *short, square-ended tail.* Plumage sooty, with *pale face* including forehead as well as throat; *square white rump* is 'wrapped' over body, looking larger and wider than in White-rumped. Flight not as graceful as other swifts, with *much rapid fluttering* and sailing.
Voice: Long, high-pitched level trill; also sharp *tick.*
Habitat and Range: Varied, from natural rocky ravines to town buildings. Vagrant from N., W. Africa to S., W. and N. Europe (including Britain).

KINGFISHERS: Alcedinidae

KINGFISHER *Alcedo atthis*   **Plate 66**
Du – IJsvogel   Fr – Martin-pêcheur
Ge – Eisvogel   Sw – Kungsfiskare
Identification: 6" (15cm). Unmistakable, quite small, fish-eater. Looks stumpy when perched but *dart-shaped in flight*, with *dagger bill*, large head, short wings and tail and small feet. Plumage flashing, *iridescent blue and emerald-green above and orange-chestnut below*, with white patches on neck and throat; bill

black, legs bright red. Perches alertly, looking down and 'bobbing' nervously at times, then plunges after small fish and insects, occasionally employing prior hover. Flight over water low, direct, very fast. Solitary.

Voice: High, piping, slightly grated *chee* or *chee-kee*, repeated rapidly in excitement. Infrequent song consists of similar notes in short trill.

Habitat: Streams, rivers, canals, lakes. In winter also sea coast and tidal marshes. Nests in holes bored in stream banks, sometimes far from water. Map 207.

BEE-EATERS: Meropidae

BLUE-CHEEKED BEE-EATER *Merops superciliosus*   **Plate 66**

Du – Groene bijeneter	Fr – Guêpier de Perse
Ge – Blauwangenspint	Sw – Grön biätare

Identification: 12" (30cm). Form as Bee-eater except for longer bill, larger head and *much longer tail-point*; flight and behaviour also similar. Plumage almost uniform, *bright green*, relieved by *yellow-chestnut throat* and *bright copper-chestnut under-wing*. Close-to, shows blue over and under black eyestripe.

Voice: Higher-pitched and huskier than Bee-eater; commonest call less liquid *greep* or *treet*, not as far- carrying.

Habitat and Range: As Bee-eater. Vagrant from Africa, Asia to S., W. (including Britain), C. and N. Europe.

BEE-EATER: *Merops apiaster*   **Plate 66**

Du – Bijenter	Fr – Guepier d'Europe
Ge – Bienenfresser	Sw – Biätare

Identification: 11" (28cm). Unmistakable, long-bodied, long-winged and rectangular-tailed insectivore, with *long curved bill* and projecting tail-point. Flight distinctive, with 'shooting' accelerations, sailing on flat wings, and graceful gliding turns. Plumage vividly coloured, with *chestnut crown, mantle and inner-wings*, contrasting with *yellow scapulars*, blue-green primaries and tail; from below, *pinkish-buff under-wing* and *blue under-body* show better than brilliant yellow throat. Juvenile much duller, lacks tail-point. Gregarious; perches conspicuously, often on wires.

Voice: As distinctive as shape and colours: throaty but liquid, far-carrying, repeated *prruip*.

Habitat: Prefers open bushy country with a few trees, telegraph poles, but also occurs in woodland glades. Breeds colonially in holes bored in cuttings, sandpits, river banks, sometimes level ground. Map 208.

ROLLERS: Coraciidae

ROLLER   *Coracias garrulus*   **Plate 66**

Du – Scharrelaar	Fr – Rollier d'Europe
Ge – Blauracke	Sw – Blåkråka

Identification: 12" (30cm). Heavy, upright-perching bird, with crow-like bill; recalls both Jay and large shrike. Plumage pale *azure-blue*, with bright *chestnut back*, vivid dark blue and black wings ('flashing' in flight) and brown-centred,

greenish-blue tail. Flight outline and action somewhat crow-like, with deep flaps and glides; 'tumbles' in nuptial display. Feeds like shrike, pouncing from open perch on passing insects or small reptiles.
Voice: Loud, deep, corvine *kr-r-r-ak* or *krak-ak*, also harsh chatter.
Habitat: Mature forests and fairly open country with a few trees. Breeds in old hollow trees, holes in banks, ruins, etc. Map 209.

HOOPOES: Upupidae

HOOPOE *Upupa epops*   **Plate 66**
  Du – Hop   Fr – Huppe fasciée
  Ge – Wiedeuhopf   Sw – Härfågel
Identification: 11" (28cm). Unmistakable, broad-winged and long-tailed bird, with *long curved bill* and *long crest*, creating 'fan' over head when erected. Plumage *pale pinkish-brown*, black-tipped on crest feathers and *boldly barred white and black on wings and tail*. Flight outline varies dramatically from 'shut' lengthy form to 'suddenly open' butterfly-like shape; action seemingly weak with slow wing-beats, creating undulations. Often feeds on open ground.
Voice: Low but far-carrying *poo-poo-poo*, also mews and chatters quietly in alarm.
Habitat: Open woodlands, orchards, parklands, etc. Winters in more open bushy country. Nests in hole in old trees, occasionally in ruins. Map 210.

WOODPECKERS: Picidae

Chisel-billed birds, with powerful feet (usually two toes front, two rear), re-markably long tongues, and short, stiff tails which act as props in climbing tree trunks. Flight usually strong, but undulating. Most males have some red on head. Nest in holes excavated in trees.

WRYNECK *Jynx torquilla*   **Plate 69**
  Du – Draaihals   Fr – Torcol fourmilier
  Ge – Wendehals   Sw – Göktyta
Identification: 6" (15cm). Strange, somewhat serpent-like non-passerine, re-calling small long-tailed thrush but differing in strong pointed bill, sometimes crested appearance and undulating flight. Plumage *vermiculated grey-brown*, with paler under-parts; close-to, dark line from eye down neck-side, *brown-black centre to back*, black-splashed scapulars, dark-chequered and -barred wings, *black- and grey-banded tail* and closely waved under-parts create intri-cate pattern. Hops with raised tail; often feeds on ground. Perches across bran-ches but clings to tree trunks.
Voice: Nasal, repeated *kyee kyee*, louder and less shrill than Lesser Spotted Woodpecker's call, resembling distant Hobby.
Habitat: Gardens, orchards, parks, hedgerows with trees. Nests in hole in trees, masonry, nest-boxes, etc. Map 211.

GREY-HEADED WOODPECKER *Picus canus*   **Plate 69**
Du – Grijskopspecht   Fr – Pic cendré
Ge – Grauspecht   Sw – Gråspett
Identification: 10" (25cm). Medium-sized, rather fine-billed woodpecker, similar in form to Green but 20% smaller. Shares green back and inner-wings and yellow rump with Green but close-to, distinguished by *narrow black 'moustache' on dusky-grey head* and greyish neck and under-parts. Male has crimson-patch on fore-crown. Juvenile duller, with diffusely barred flanks. Flight lighter than Green, with faster wing-beats; other behaviour similar. Beware Spanish race *P. v. sharpei* of Green Woodpecker, which has grey cheeks, neck-side and breast.
Voice: Call-notes resemble Green Woodpecker's, but 'laughing' song is much less harsh and becomes *progressively deeper and slower*. Drums for long periods in spring.
Habitat: As Green Woodpecker, but also occurs locally in deciduous mountain forests up to tree limit. Less often in coniferous woods. Map 212.

GREEN WOODPECKER *Picus viridis*   **Plate 69**
Du – Groene specht   Fr – Pic vert
Ge – Grünspecht   Sw – Gröngöling
Identification: 12" (31cm). Large, strong-billed, full-winged and relatively small-tailed woodpecker; conspicuously bigger than any pied woodpecker. Plumage *yellow-green above*, with conspicuous *pale yellow rump*, pale olive to yellowish-green below, with long *crimson crown, nape and hind-neck, black face-mask and 'moustache'* and pale-barred primaries. Male's 'moustache' has crimson centre. Juvenile lacks black face and has duller plumage, pale-spotted above and darkly close-barred on head and body. Flight outline bulky; action flapping, then 'shooting' with long wing-closures producing deep undulations. Hops and climbs heavily, head up, tail down. Often on ground, after ants. Spanish race *P. v. sharpei* has grey cheeks, neck-sides and breast, recalling Grey-headed, but still shows long red crown. Beware also confusion with female or immature Golden Oriole, which see.
Voice: Loud, far-carrying, ringing laugh. Very seldom drums and then weakly.
Habitat: Deciduous woods, parks, farmlands, commons with scattered trees. Nests in hole bored in trees. Map 213.

BLACK WOODPECKER *Dryocopus martius*   **Plate 69**
Du – Zwarte specht   Fr – Pic noir
Ge – Schwarzspecht   Sw – Spillkråka
Identification: 18" (45cm). *Rook-sized* woodpecker. Plumage *uniformly black*; male with long, slightly crested crimson crown, female duller with crimson restricted to rear crown. Bill pale horn; eyes pale yellow. Flight less regularly undulating than other woodpeckers, recalling Nutcracker.
Voice: Laugh even more manic and higher-pitched than Green, but usually slower and shorter : *chock-choc-choc* or *kwick-wick-wick-wick*; also grating *krukru...* or ringing *krri-krri-krri-krri* and loud whistled *kleea*. Occasional drum very loud.
Habitat: Mature coniferous forest in northern and mountainous regions and in

beech woods. Excavates very large oval nest-hole, sometimes at considerable height. Map 214.

GREAT SPOTTED WOODPECKER *Dendrocopos major*   **Plate 69**
Du – Grote bonte specht   Fr – Pic épeiche
Ge – Buntspecht   Sw – Större hackspett

Identification: 9" (23cm). Commonest and most widespread of tribe, much smaller than Green but twice size of Lesser Spotted. Plumage pied except for *crimson under tail-coverts* on buff-white under-parts, *crimson nape-patch* of male and *crimson crown of immature* of both sexes. Distinguished by bold *white scapular patches on wholly black back* and *unbroken black bar across white cheeks*. Irrupting race *D. m. major* of N. Europe shows distinctly shorter bill and purer white under-parts. Flight outline dominated by relatively large, leaf-shaped wings; action distinctive, with bursts of strong wing-beats and marked undulations. Rarely on ground but visits bird-tables and feeders.
Voice: Call loud, sharp *tchick* or *kik*, more penetrating and more frequently uttered than similar call of Lesser Spotted. Both sexes drum in short, very rapid, abrupt bursts, using resonant dead branch.
Habitat: More a woodland and garden bird than Green, but also in pine woods in north. Map 215.

SYRIAN WOODPECKER *Dendrocopos syriacus*   **Plate 69**
Du – Syrische bonte specht   Fr – Pic syriaque
Ge – Blutspecht   Sw – Balkanspett

Identification: 9" (23cm). Size, shape and behaviour as Great Spotted. Adult *lacks black bar on rear cheeks* but has *longer red nape-patch on male*, whiter forehead, less white on outer-tail feathers and paler red under-tail coverts. Immature suggests Middle Spotted but shows reddish collar and black 'moustache' meeting bill.
Voice: Call softer, less penetrating than Great Spotted: quiet *chig*, also distinctive *kirrook* suggesting Moorhen. Rapid drum lasts longer than Great Spotted.
Habitat: Chiefly around villages and near cultivation. Map 216.

MIDDLE SPOTTED WOODPECKER *Dendrocopos medius*   **Plate 69**
Du – Middelste bonte specht   Fr – Pic mar
Ge – Mittelspecht   Sw – Mellanspett

Identification: 8" (21cm). Slightly smaller than Great Spotted, with weak bill. Plumage pattern similar to Great Spotted and Syrian but distinctly paler on head, with *buff-white face* and slightly crested, *light crimson crown* without black edges. Black mark under cheeks extends past shoulder to form *sharp streaks along buff flanks*; last contrast little with *pale, rose-pink vent* and under tail-coverts; less broadly-panelled white on scapulars. Flight outline and action much as Great Spotted but is more secretive, keeping to crowns of trees. Uses bill more as probe than hatchet.
Voice: Resembles Great Spotted's quick chatter, but is slightly lower in pitch and the first note is usually higher: *ptik-teuk-teuk-teuk-teuk*. In spring has slow, nasal cry, *wait...wait...* repeated in descending or ascending scale. Drums rarely.
Habitat: Usually in hornbeam and beech forest, in high branches. Excavates nest-hole high up in deciduous tree. Map 217.

WHITE-BACKED WOODPECKER *Dendrocopos leucotos*   **Plate 69**
  Du – Witrugspecht   Fr – Pic à dos blanc
  Ge – Weissrückenspecht   Sw – Vitryggig hackspctt
Identification: 10" (25cm). Largest pied woodpecker, with long, powerful bill
and rather long neck. Plumage pattern closer to Lesser than Great Spotted, with
white lower back and rump, *broad white band across wing-coverts*, strongly
white-barred flight feathers but *only partly white rear scapulars*, black-streaked
flanks and pale pink under-tail. Face and crown like Great Spotted but scarlet
crown of male mottled grey and *black band under cheeks not reaching nape*
Immature has scarlet crown, much invaded by black at rear. South European
race *D. l. lilfordi* has black and white-barred lower back and heavier flank-
streaks. Beware confusion with Three-toed, which see. Flight outline larger than
Great Spotted; action slower and more powerful.
Voice: Call quieter and deeper than Great Spotted. Drum powerful and long,
accelerating towards quieter finish; suggests bouncing ping-pong ball.
Habitat: Hilly deciduous woods with plenty of old rotting trees; locally in
dense coniferous forests; around towns in winter. Nests in hole bored in rotted
trees. Map 218.

LESSER SPOTTED WOODPECKER *Dendrocopos minor*   **Plate 69**
  Du – Kleine bonte specht   Fr – Pic épeichette
  Ge – Kleinspecht   Sw – Mindre hackspett
Identification: 5¾" (14cm). Smallest European Woodpecker, *little larger than
Nuthatch* but with stocky build and *fluttering, deeply undulating flight* suggesting Woodlark or short-tailed finch at times. Plumage *barred rather than pied*
(some birds appearing almost white-backed); *lacks red or pink vent*. Crown dull
red in male, brownish-white in female and immature; black mark under cheeks
does not reach nape but extends downwards to become streaks on flanks. Shy and
retiring, keeping to uppermost twigs and branches; more often heard than seen.
Voice: Commonest call *shrill, feeble*, slowly repeated *pee-pee-pee*, recalling
distant Kestrel or Wryneck; also weak *kik* suggesting tired Great Spotted. Drums
frequently, with rather slow, rattling and varying roll lasting longer than Great
Spotted.
Habitat: Old orchards and open woodlands. Map 219.

THREE-TOED WOODPECKER *Picoides tridactylus*   **Plate 69**
  Du – Drieteenspecht   Fr – Pic tridactyle
  Ge – Dreizehenspecht   Sw – Tretåig hackspett
Identification: 8¾" (22cm). Close in size to Great Spotted but is *larger headed*
and rather short-tailed. Plumage black and white but lacks obvious pied or barred
appearance and red marks. Easily distinguished by unique combination of *black
cheeks,* complete *white divide of back* from nape to rump, *barred flanks* and almost
all-black scapulars and wings, latter only flecked white. Crown of male *yellow in
centre*, of female black. Juvenile duskier, with mottled back. Flight and behaviour
recall Lesser Spotted but is often inactive. Occasionally rings trees.
Voice: Call variable, sometimes like Great Spotted, but also soft *kyuk* recalling
Redwing. Drum powerful and long, distinctly slower than Great Spotted.
Habitat: Mountain and arctic forest, with preference for burnt tracts. Nests in
holes bored in trees and telegraph poles. Map 220.

Plate 1

DIVERS

Large, long-bodied diving birds with dagger-like bills; may dive from the surface or sink; run or thrash along the water on take-off. Seldom on land except at the nest. Sexes alike. Immature birds are more scaly above than winter adults.

RED-THROATED DIVER
Map 1 p.30

Silhouette snakier than other divers; head and thin bill often uptilted.
Breeding: Grey head; unmarked back; dark red throat patch.
Winter: Pale face; least contrasting neck pattern; finely speckled back.

BLACK-THROATED DIVER
Map 2 p.30

Bulbous head with straight, rather slender bill carried level.
Breeding: Grey crown, dark face; chequered fore-back.
Winter: Very dark above, white below, with striking white flank-patch.

GREAT NORTHERN DIVER
Map 3 p.31

Large and heavy; dagger-like bill carried level.
Breeding: Black head, dusky bill; chequered upper-parts.
Winter: Broken neck pattern; pale-based bill; dark back, with faint scallop marks in first winter.

WHITE-BILLED DIVER
p.32

Largest diver; head and scissor-shaped bill often uptilted.
Breeding: Like Great Northern but bill ivory; checks on back larger.
Winter: Upper-parts paler than Great Northern, particularly neck; pale scallop marks obvious in first winter.

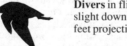

Divers in flight are hunchbacked, with a slight downward droop to the neck and the feet projecting behind.

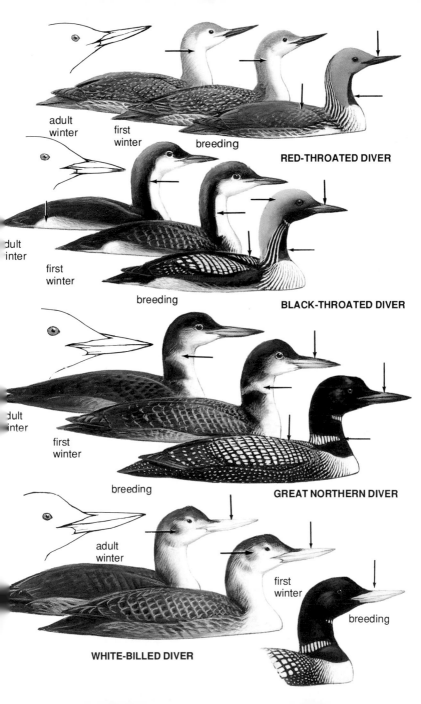

adult winter

first winter

breeding

RED-THROATED DIVER

adult winter

first winter

breeding

BLACK-THROATED DIVER

adult winter

first winter

breeding

GREAT NORTHERN DIVER

adult winter

first winter

breeding

WHITE-BILLED DIVER

Plate 2

GREBES

Grebes are rather duck-like, diving birds with flat, lobed toes, thin neck, and tail-less look. Most have white wing-patches, pointed bills. Sexes alike. May dive from the surface or sink. Flight laboured, with sagging neck.

LITTLE GREBE
Map 4 p.33

Breeding: Small; puffy, dark; light patch on the bill.
Winter: Paler below. Identify by shape and bill.

SLAVONIAN GREBE
Map 7 p.34

Beeding: Buffish head-tufts; rufous-chestnut neck.
Winter: Black and white pattern; straight dark bill; black cap extends down to eye.

BLACK-NECKED GREBE
Map 8 p.34

Breeding: Golden ear-tufts; black neck.
Winter: Like Slavonian Grebe, but greyer neck; upturned bill; black cap extends below eye.

RED-NECKED GREBE
Map 6 p.33

Breeding: Rusty-chestnut neck, white chin and cheek.
Winter: Greyish neck; no white above the eye; yellow-based bill.

GREAT CRESTED GREBE
Map 5 p.33

Breeding: White neck; black 'horns'; rusty neck-frill.
Winter: Satiny white; white above the eye; pinkish bill.

PIED-BILLED GREBE (below)
p.32

Note thick, ungrebe-like 'chicken bill' and puffy white stern. No wing-patch. In breeding plumage, has black throat and ring around the bill.

winter

breeding

Pied-billed Grebe

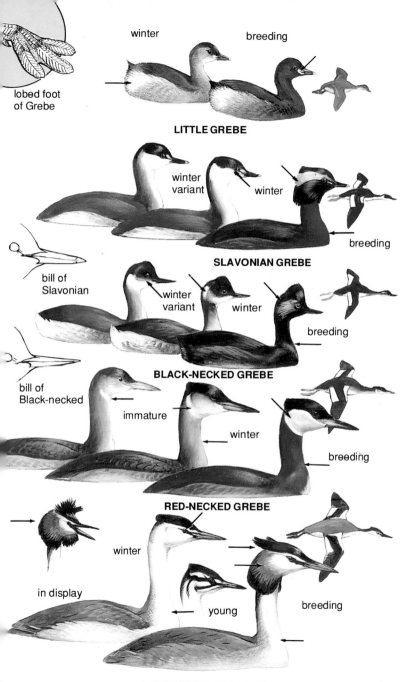

lobed foot
of Grebe

winter

breeding

LITTLE GREBE

bill of
Slavonian

winter
variant

winter

breeding

SLAVONIAN GREBE

bill of
Black-necked

winter
variant

winter

breeding

BLACK-NECKED GREBE

immature

winter

breeding

RED-NECKED GREBE

in display

winter

young

breeding

GREAT-CRESTED GREBE

Plate 3 STORM-PETRELS, FULMAR, SHEARWATERS

Storm-petrels are little dark sea-birds with white rump-patches. They are usually seen skimming or flitting low over the waves, recalling hirundines.
Fulmars and Shearwaters are oceanic, cross-shaped birds that fly with several flaps and a glide, banking on stiff, little-flexed wings over waves.

LEACH'S PETREL Map 14 p.39
Tail with fork (seldom visible). Diagonal grey bar on upper wings; divided white rump-patch. Bounding, erratic flight on angled wings.

WILSON'S PETREL p.38
Square-ended tail; longish legs extending beyond the tail. White rump wraps around body. Bat-like flight on little-angled wings.

STORM PETREL Map 13 p.39
Smallest of tribe; square-ended tail; whitish bar under wing. Flitting flight on rather straight wings.

MANX SHEARWATER Map 11 p.37
Wholly black above, white below. Darker primaries than Little. Gliding and beating flight, with erratic rhythm.

MEDITERRANEAN SHEARWATER Map 12 p.37
Similar to Manx Shearwater but browner above and below, especially west Mediterranean race which may suggest Sooty.

LITTLE SHEARWATER p.38
Smaller, more compact than Manx Shearwater; black crown does not extend below eye. White lining reaches wing tips. Fluttering flight recalls Puffin.

CORY'S SHEARWATER Map 10 p.36
No sharp head pattern; yellowish bill; wholly white under-parts. May or may not have white at the base of the tail. Flight like Fulmar but much lazier on bending wing-tips.

GREAT SHEARWATER p.36
Well-defined dark cap, white cheek, and white patch at base of tail. White underparts smudged under wing and down belly. Flight rather like Manx Shearwater but much more powerful.

FULMAR Map 9 p.35
Bull-necked; stubby bill. Stiff-winged, gliding and beating flight. Light phase: White head; light patch at base of primaries. *Dark phase*: Buffy to smoke-grey head and body; under-wing noticeably darker.

SOOTY SHEARWATER p.37
Dark all over except for whitish linings of under-wings. Flight like Manx but with strong, mechanical wing-beats.

Madeiran (left), Leach's (centre) and Swinhoe's Petrel all have a more or less forked tail, but Madeiran has broadest white rump and widest wing-bar, while Leach's has deepest fork to tail and divided white rump. Swinhoe's instantly identified by dark rump, uniform with upperparts.

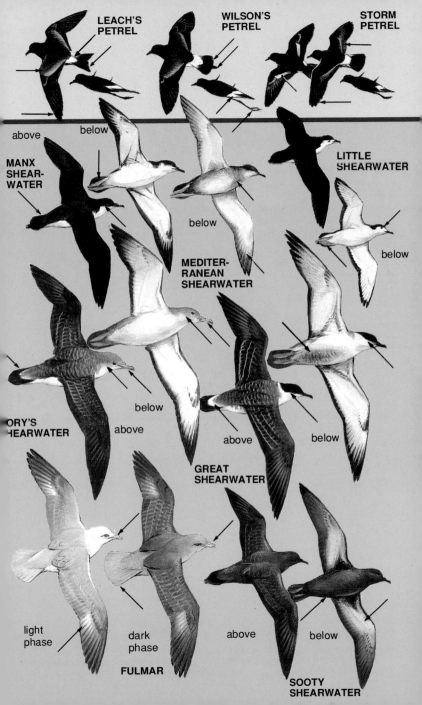

LEACH'S PETREL

WILSON'S PETREL

STORM PETREL

above   below

MANX SHEAR-WATER

LITTLE SHEARWATER

below

MEDITER-RANEAN SHEARWATER

below

CORY'S SHEARWATER

below   above

GREAT SHEARWATER

above   below

FULMAR

light phase   dark phase

above   below

SOOTY SHEARWATER

Plate 4

CORMORANTS

Cormorants are large, blackish water birds, all except Pygmy Cormorant larger than any duck. In flight, their necks are held slightly above the horizontal. They fly in line or V formation, like geese, and stand upright with neck in an S; may strike a "spread-eagle" pose, with wings spread out to dry. They swim low, like divers, but with neck more erect, and hook-tipped bill tilted up at an angle. Sexes alike.

CORMORANT
Map 16 p.40

Large, with heavy bill, pale chin and cheeks. Breeding birds have a white patch on the thighs. Continental birds when breeding have much white on the neck. Immature can be separated from young Shag by larger size, heavier build, and presence of much white on the under-parts.

SHAG
Map 17 p.41

Smaller, thinner-billed and proportionately broader-winged than Cormorant. Adults lack white cheek-patch and when breeding may have a short erect crest. Most immatures much darker on under-parts than young Cormorant.

PYGMY CORMORANT
Map 18 p.41

Smaller, shorter-necked, and shorter-billed than Shag. Tail noticeably longer.

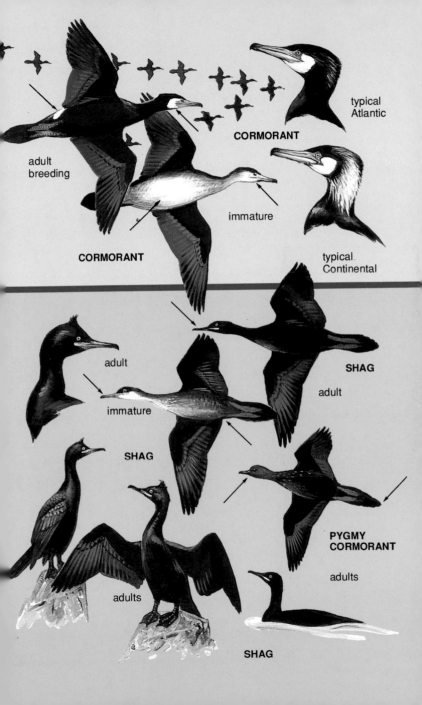

CORMORANT

adult breeding

CORMORANT

immature

typical Atlantic

typical Continental

SHAG

adult

adult

immature

SHAG

PYGMY CORMORANT

adults

adults

SHAG

Plate 5

MISCELLANEOUS LARGE LAKE AND SEA BIRDS

WHITE PELICAN p.41
Very large with huge wingspan. Huge, flat, pouched bill. Extensive
black on primaries and secondaries of under-wing are diagnostic. Feet
reddish. Flies in lines, often at a great height.

DALMATIAN PELICAN Map 19 p.42
Very large. Separated from White Pelican by 'dirtier' white plumage
and by lack of extensive black on under-wing. Feet blackish.

BLACK-BROWED ALBATROSS p.35
Wing span 7 ft. (2 m.). Confused with immature Northern Gannet and
black-backed gulls but general character like huge Fulmar. Note
striking black-white-black under-wing pattern and dark tail. Effortless
flight, recalling Fulmar and Cory's Shearwater.

NORTHERN GANNET Map 15 p.40
Plunges after fish.
Adult: White; pointed tail; golden nape; bold black primaries.
Immature: Dark brown with a pointed tail.
Changing immature: Increasingly white, patched with dark.

WHITE PELICAN

DALMATIAN PELICAN

above

below

BLACK-BROWED ALBATROSS

NORTHERN GANNET

adult

changing immature

immature

Plate 6

LONG-LEGGED MARSH BIRDS
(Bitterns, Herons, Cranes)

 **Herons** (including bitterns and egrets) fly with their necks tucked back to their shoulders.
Cranes and all other large long-legged marshbirds fly with their necks extended.

BITTERN Map 20 p.42
Tawny-brown; barred and mottled. Bill often pointed upwards.

AMERICAN BITTERN p.43
Smaller than Bittern; more streaked, less barred. Lacks black crown
but shows conspicuous black patch on side of neck and much darker
flight feathers.

LITTLE BITTERN Map 21 p.43
Very small; large creamy wing-patch.
Male: Black back.
Female: Brown back.
Juvenile: Brownish; streaked below; streaked wings.

NIGHT HERON Map 22 p.43
Adult: Whitish or pale breast, black back, black crown.
Immature: Brown; whitish spots on back and wings.

GREY HERON Map 27 p.45
Large, pale grey; dark flight-feathers.

PURPLE HERON Map 28 p.46
More slender than Grey Heron; bulging neck and longer feet
conspicuous in flight.
Adult: Darker than Grey, with chestnut neck.
Immature: Sandier.

CRANE Map 118 p.95
Large, grey. Black neck with white cheek-stripe. Drooping feathers
cloak tail.

DEMOISELLE CRANE p.95
Smaller than Crane; black breast, white head-tufts.

BITTERN

AMERICAN BITTERN

juvenile

NIGHT HERON

juvenile

LITTLE BITTERN

adult

juvenile

adult

adult

adult

GREY HERON

PURPLE HERON

adult

adult

CRANE

DEMOISELLE CRANE

Plate 7

LONG-LEGGED MARSH BIRDS
(Herons, Spoonbill, Glossy Ibis, Flamingo, Storks)

LITTLE EGRET Map 25 p.44
Small, white; yellow feet, slender black bill.

GREAT WHITE EGRET Map 26 p.45
Large, white; dark or blackish feet, yellow on bill.

CATTLE EGRET Map 24 p.44
Small; looks white; heavy 'jowl'. Buffish plumes, reddish legs and bill
when breeding; plumes lost after breeding, when bill and legs become
yellowish or dusky.

SQUACCO HERON Map 23 p.44
Adult: Sandy-brown on ground but white-winged in flight. Legs pink
when breeding, dull greenish at other times.
Juvenile: Striped breast.

SPOONBILL Map 32 p.47
Large; uniquely spatulate, long bill.
Adult: White; blackish bill. In summer has pendant crest.
Juvenile: Pinkish bill; black wing-tips.

GLOSSY IBIS Map 31 p.47
Dark glossy body; long decurved bill.

GREATER FLAMINGO p.47
Bright crimson on wings; very long neck and red legs; bent bill.

WHITE STORK Map 30 p.46
White, with much black on wings.

BLACK STORK Map 29 p.46
Black, with white belly.

White Stork　　　　**Flamingo**　　　　**Black Stork**

breeding

LITTLE EGRET

breeding

GREAT WHITE
EGRET

breeding

n-breeding

CATTLE
EGRET

breeding

non-breeding

juvenile

adults

SQUACCO HERON

adult

SPOONBILL

juvenile

GLOSSY IBIS

GREATER FLAMINGO

WHITE STORK

BLACK STORK

Plate 8

SWANS AND GEESE
(See also Plate 9)

BEWICK'S SWAN   Map 34 p.49
Most goose-like swan, with shortest neck and rounded head giving
gentle expression.
Adult: Rounded patch on bill yellow, pattern variable.
Immature: Dingy; bill dull flesh at base.

WHOOPER SWAN   Map 35 p.49
Noticeably larger and gawkier than Bewick's, with flatter crown and
longer bill.
Adult: Yellow patch on bill more extensive than Bewick's and points
forward.
Immature: Larger than Bewick's Swan; longer neck.

MUTE SWAN   Map 33 p.49
Largest swan, with usually curved neck; does not bugle.
Adult: Bill orange, with a black basal knob.
Immature: Bill flesh, black at base without the prominent knob.

SNOW GOOSE   p.52
Typical *Anser* form but occurs in two colour phases.
Adult: White, with black primaries in the wings; in blue phase, only
head and upper neck white.
Immature: Dingier; bill dark; in blue phase, head dusky.

BARNACLE GOOSE   Map 42 p.53
White face obvious above black chest and neck.

CANADA GOOSE   Map 41 p.53
Largest goose. Black neck but light chest; white chin and cheek-patch.

BRENT GOOSE   Map 43 p.53
Small white neck-bar difficult to see on black neck, lacking in
immature.
Dark-bellied form: Looks uniformly dark. Usually E. and S. British
coasts.
Pale-bellied form: Chest contrasts with pale belly. In Britain mainly
west, especially Ireland.

RED-BREASTED GOOSE   p.54
Broad white flank-stripe; harlequin head pattern and chestnut breast.

juv.

adult

BEWICK'S

juv.

adult

WHOOPER

juv.

adult

MUTE

MUTE SWAN

WHOOPER SWAN

BEWICK'S SWAN

adult

SNOW GOOSE

SNOW GOOSE blue phase

SNOW GOOSE

white phase

CANADA GOOSE

BARNACLE GOOSE

juvenile

RED-BREASTED GOOSE

BRENT GOOSE

light-bellied form

dark-bellied form

Plate 9

SWANS AND GEESE IN FLIGHT
(See also plate 8)

Most swans and geese travel in line or V formation.

BRENT GOOSE   Map 43 p.53
Smallest, most duck-like goose; black head, neck and chest and dark upper-wing.
Pale-bellied form: Light whitish underbody.
Dark-bellied form: Dark underbody, appearing uniform with chest at distance.

BARNACLE GOOSE   Map 42 p.53
Bright grey upper-wing; white face on black neck and chest.

CANADA GOOSE   Map 41 p.53
Largest and longest-necked goose. Black neck 'stocking' contrasts with light chest.

BEWICK'S SWAN   Map 34 p.49
Most goose-like swan, with silent flight; neck shorter than Whooper.

WHOOPER SWAN   Map 35 p.49
Long, straight head and neck; silent flight.

MUTE SWAN   Map 33 p.49
Largest swan, with long, loose neck; 'singing' wing-beats.

SNOW GOOSE   p.52
Shape and flight like Pink-footed.
White phase: All white except for black primaries.
Blue phase: All dusky-blue except for white head and fore-neck.

BRENT GOOSE
light-bellied form

dark-bellied form

below

BARNACLE GOOSE

above

above

CANADA GOOSE

BEWICK'S SWAN

adults

WHOOPER SWAN

white phase

adults

SNOW GOOSE

blue phase

adult

MUTE SWAN

Plate 10

GREY GEESE
(See also Plate 11)

The best place in Europe to study geese is the New Grounds of the Wildfowl and Wetlands Trust, at Slimbridge in England. Captive examples of all birds shown on this plate can be studied there and during winter many can be seen in a wild state. The first Director of the Trust, the late Sir Peter Scott, guided the preparation of these goose plates.

Grey Geese with ORANGE legs

WHITE-FRONTED GOOSE
Map 38 p.51

Adult shows white forehead above bill and variable blotches on belly but both are lacking in immature.
Russian race: Pink bill, grey-brown upper-parts.
Greenland race: Orange-yellow bill; olive-brown upper-parts. Winters mostly in western isles of Scotland and Ireland.

LESSER WHITE-FRONTED GOOSE
Map 39 p.51

Smaller, nimbler than White-fronted; wing-tips extend past tail. Stubby pink bill; yellow eye-ring, even in immature; white forehead more extensive than White-fronted.

BEAN GOOSE
Map 36 p.50

Brownest of grey geese, with long dark head and neck. Orange-yellow bill, with variable black markings.

Grey Geese with PINK legs

PINK-FOOTED GOOSE
Map 37 p.50

Smaller, more dainty than Greylag or Bean. Small dark head on rather short dark neck. Pink bill, with black base.

GREYLAG GOOSE
Map 40 p.51

Largest, palest and most grey of grey geese; black speckles on belly.
Western race: Orange-yellow bill.
Eastern race: Pink bill; broad, light feather tips on upper-parts produce pale-barred appearance.

juv.

adult

WHITE-FRONTED

Greenland form

LESSER WHITE-FRONTED

BEAN

adult

juvenile

GREENLAND WHITE-FRONTED GOOSE

WHITE-FRONTED GOOSE

adult

BEAN GOOSE

adult

juvenile

LESSER WHITE-FRONTED GOOSE

PINK-FOOTED GOOSE

eastern form

western form

GREYLAG GOOSE

PINK-FOOTED

western

eastern

GREYLAG

Plate 11

CHIEFLY GREY GEESE IN FLIGHT
(See also Plate 10)

For the most part, grey geese on the wing all look very similar and it requires much experience to separate them at a distance. Their voices (below) are useful clues. White-fronted and Pink-footed more agile in flight, particularly when landing, than Bean and Greylag.

WHITE-FRONTED GOOSE Map 38 p.51
Fore-wing brownish. At close range, adult shows white forehead and black blotches across the belly. Greenland race looks darker (but beware effect of light).
Voice: Musical, high-pitched, usually disyllabic, sometimes trisyllabic: *kow-lyow* or *lyo-lyok* etc.

BEAN GOOSE Map 36 p.50
Dark neck; rather brown with little fore-wing contrast.
Voice: Reedy and bassoon-like *ung-unk*, not unlike lower notes of Pink-footed Goose. Relatively silent.

PINK-FOOTED GOOSE Map 37 p.50
Dark head but quite striking blue-grey fore-wing and pale chest.
Voice: Musical *ung-unk*, higher than Bean Goose. Sometimes *king-wink*, or often repeated *wink-wink-wink*.

GREYLAG GOOSE Map 40 p.51
Rather large; pale head and strikingly pale grey fore-wing.
Voice: Loud *aahng-ung-ung*, or *gaahnk*, very like farmyard goose.

RED-BREASTED GOOSE p.54
Smallest and blackest goose, with nimblest flight. White side-stripes contrast with black belly; rufous chest.

WHITE-FRONTED GOOSE

below

adults

above

immature below

BEAN GOOSE

below

above

PINK-FOOTED GOOSE

above

below

above

below

GREYLAG GOOSE

below

RED-BEASTED GOOSE

Plate 12

SURFACE-FEEDING DUCKS
(Marshes and Ponds – see also Plate 19 & 21)

These ducks spring directly from the water when taking flight.

MALLARD Map 49 p.58
Male: Green head; white neck-ring; purplish-brown breast.
Female: Some orange on bill; whitish tail.

PINTAIL Map 50 p.59
Long-necked and -tailed.
Male: Needle tail; dark head above white chest.
Female: Grey bill; slender pointed tail.

GADWALL Map 47 p.57
Shorter head than Mallard. White inner speculum in flight.
Male: Grey body; black stern, pale tertials.
Female: Orange-sided bill.

WIGEON Map 46 p.56
Round-headed.
Male: Chestnut head; buff crown. Grey body with pinkish breast.
Female: Short, blue-grey bill.

SHOVELER Map 52 p.60
Long-billed, stocky-bodied.
Male: Green head, white chest, chestnut flanks.
Female: Blue shoulders may show.

MANDARIN p.55
Rather large head, long tail; white stern.
Male: Orange 'side-whiskers'; orange 'sails'.
Female: White mark around the eye; white chin.

TEAL Map 48 p.58
Smallest and most compact surface-feeding duck.
Male: Grey with a dark head and horizontal white stripe above the wing.
Female: White stripe at tail base.

GARGANEY Map 51 p.59
Longer bill than Teal.
Male: White stripe on dark head; pale grey flanks.
Female: From Teal by lined face, greyer wings; obscure speculum.

MARBLED DUCK p.61
Dappled plumage; shaggy head; dark smudge through eye; whitish tail.

MALLARD ♂ ♀

PINTAIL ♂ ♀

GADWALL ♂ ♀

WIGEON ♂ ♀
grey form
rusty form

SHOVELER ♂ ♀

MANDARIN ♂ ♀

TEAL ♂ ♀

GARGANEY ♂ ♀

MARBLED DUCK ♂

Plate 13

DIVING DUCKS
(Goldeneyes, Pochards etc. – see also Plate 20 & 22)

Diving ducks (ducks of open water and sea) patter along the surface when taking flight. Surface-feeding ducks (Plate 12) spring directly up from the water.

GOLDENEYE
Map 62 p.67

Chunky, triangular head on sloping body.
Male: Round white spot before eye on green head.
Female: Brown head; white collar; grey body; white on wing visible when swimming.

BARROW'S GOLDENEYE
p.66

Large, with more mane on head than Goldeneye.
Male: White crescent by bill on purple head; blacker above than Goldeneye.
Female: Very similar to Goldeneye (see text).

FERRUGINOUS DUCK
Map 55 p.62

Longer bill and less round head than Tufted.
Male: Deep mahogany; white under tail-coverts.
Female: Duller but still shows white stern.

SCAUP
Map 57 p.63

Broad bill on large head; deep broad body.
Male: Blue bill; black fore-parts; pale back; black stern. "Black at both ends, white in the middle".
Female: Sharply defined white patch at base of bill.

TUFTED DUCK
Map 56 p.62

Rather short bill, round head, compact.
Male: Black with white flanks; thin drooping crest.
Female: Suggestion of a crest; white restricted or absent at base of bill but occasionally obvious under tail (see text).

POCHARD
Map 54 p.61

Rather long bill, oval head, fat chest
Male: Chestnut head; black chest ahead of pale grey body.
Female: Buff mark around eye and base of bill; blue band on bill.

RED-CRESTED POCHARD
Map 53 p.61

Long bill, deep head on quite long neck.
Male: Red bill, almost orange head and white flanks.
Female: Pale cheek; from female Common Scoter by paler plumage; white wing-patch; red on bill.

GOLDENEYE

BARROW'S GOLDENEYE

FERRUGINOUS DUCK

SCAUP

winter

breeding

TUFTED DUCK

POCHARD

RED-CRESTED POCHARD

Plate 14

DIVING DUCKS AT SEA
(Scoters – see also Plate 20 & 22)

Scoters are chunky, robust sea-ducks, with dark plumage. They pack and fly closely, passing in lines or arrow-shaped formations.

VELVET SCOTER   Map 61 p.66
Largest scoter, with white secondaries forming bold patches in flight.
Male: Black body; lower bill yellow.
Female: Light face-spots.

SURF SCOTER   p.66
Size between Velvet and Common; eider-like bill.
Male: Black body; white patches on upper head and bill and nape.
Female: Light face-spots.

COMMON SCOTER   Map 60 p.65
Smallest scoter, with obvious bill knob in male.
Male: All black; restricted orange patch on bill.
Female: Dark body; dark crown contrasts with light cheeks.

Scoters fly in line or V formation

Velvet

Surf

Common

♂

♀ imm.

VELVET SCOTER

♂

♀ 1st winter

SURF SCOTER

♂

♀ 1st winter ♂

COMMON SCOTER

Velvet   Surf   Common

Diving ducks (sea and bay ducks) pack or raft on water, skitter when taking wing.

Plate 15

DÌVING DUCKS AT SEA
(Eiders – see also Plate 20 & 22)

Eiders are the largest sea-ducks, with strikingly "reversed" plumage patterns in most males and important differences in bill and head structure and pattern.

EIDER
Map 58 p.63

Male: White above; black below and on head cap.
Female: Brown; heavily barred. See diagram below.

KING EIDER
p.63

Male: Head and fore-parts whitish; rear two-thirds black. Frontal shield orange.
Female: Less angular and less coarsely marked than Eider. See diagram below.

STELLER'S EIDER
p.64

Much the smallest eider, with shortest bill.
Male: White head; chestnut under-parts; black spot on side of breast.
Female: Uniformly dusky. See diagram below.

SPECTACLED EIDER
p.243

Male: White "goggles" on greenish head; white back; black upper-parts.
Female: Brown with a suggestion of "goggles".

Eider   **King Eider**   **Steller's Eider**

Female Eiders can be told by their bills; long and sloping in the Eider, with a long lobe extending to the forehead; stubbier in the King Eider, with less lobing; no obvious lobes in the Steller's.

EIDER

KING EIDER

STELLER'S EIDER

SPECTACLED EIDER

Plate 16

SHELDUCKS
(See also Plate 19, 20, 21 & 22)

SHELDUCK   Map 45 p.55
Goose-like form but duck-like bill. Green-black and white with
chestnut belt encircling body. Male has knob on red bill; female lacks
knob.

RUDDY SHELDUCK   Map 44 p.55
Orange-chestnut body; pale head. Male has narrow black neck-ring,
lacking in female.

DIVING DUCKS AT SEA
(Small species)

LONG-TAILED DUCK   Map 59 p.65
Needle tail; dark wings and tail.
Male in summer: White face-patch on mainly dark upper-parts.
Male in winter: Pretty pied pattern.
Female in summer: Light neck patch below dark head.
Female in winter: White, dark-spotted face below dark cap.

HARLEQUIN   p.64
Male: Slate and white harlequin pattern, rusty flanks.
Female: Dark brown; three light face spots.

BUFFLEHEAD   p.243
Tiniest sea-duck, recalls Goldeneye but with white blaze on head.
Male: White blaze reaches crown and nape.
Female: White blaze restricted to rear cheeks.

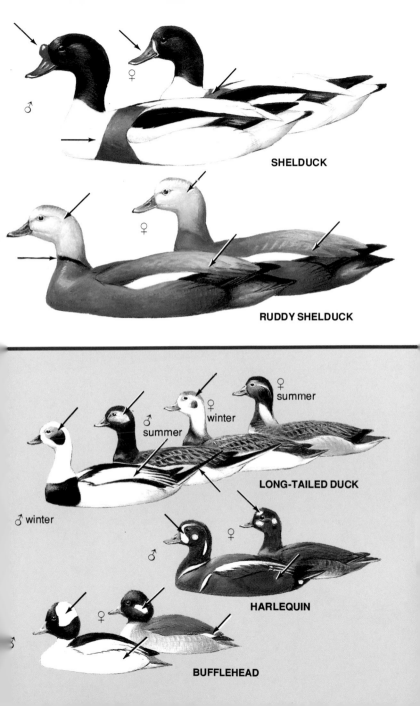

SHELDUCK

♂

♀

RUDDY SHELDUCK

♀

LONG-TAILED DUCK

♂ summer

♀ winter

♀ summer

♂ winter

HARLEQUIN

♂

♀

BUFFLEHEAD

♂

♀

Plate 17

SAW-BILLS
(See also Plate 19 & 21)

Saw-bills (mergansers) are stream-lined, fish-eating ducks, with slender spike-like bills with toothed mandibles. They swim low in the water.

GOOSANDER
Map 65 p.68

Largest saw-bill; rarely at sea.
Male: Long white body; black back; dark head; red bill.
Female: Crested rufous head; sharply-defined throat and neck.

RED-BREASTED MERGANSER
Map 64 p.67

Rangiest saw-bill; most marine of tribe.
Male: White collar; chestnut breast-band; wispy crest.
Female: Crested rufous head; blended throat and neck.

SMEW
Map 63 p.67

Small but boldly patterned; rarely at sea.
Male: White, patterned with black; white crest.
Female: Grey with a chestnut cap; white cheeks; short bill.

HOODED MERGANSER
p.243

Small and dark.
Male: Fan-shaped black and white crest may be raised or lowered.
Two black bars in front of brown flanks.
Female: Dusky, with full loose tawny crest.

STIFF-TAILS

Stiff-tails are small dumpy ducks, with swollen bills and long tails that are often cocked.

WHITE-HEADED DUCK
Map 66 p.69

Male: Dark body; white head; blue bill (in summer).
Female: Light cheek crossed by sharp dark line.

RUDDY DUCK (see also Plate 18)
p.68

Male in summer: Chubby, with ruddy body, white cheeks black cap, blue bill.
Male in winter: Grey with white cheeks, dark cap, dark bill.
Female: Similar to winter male but with dull dark line on cheek.

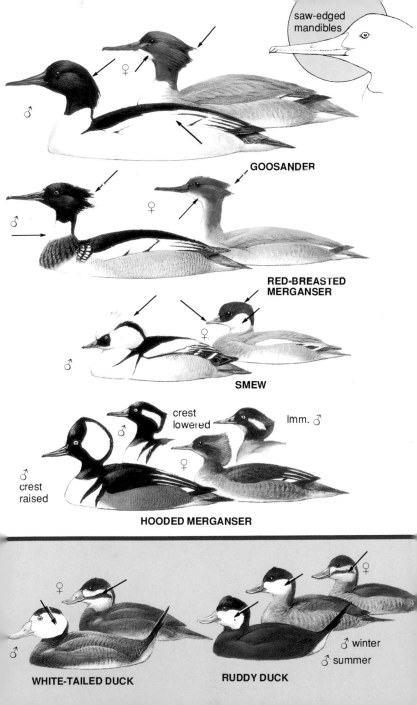

saw-edged mandibles

GOOSANDER

♂ ♀

RED-BREASTED MERGANSER

♂ ♀

SMEW

♂ ♀

crest raised
crest lowered
♂
Imm. ♂
♀

HOODED MERGANSER

♀ ♂
WHITE-TAILED DUCK

♀
♂ winter
♂ summer
RUDDY DUCK

Plate 18

VAGRANT WATERFOWL
(Mostly from North America)

Note: Only males are shown in flight.

BLACK DUCK p.58
Sooty brown with paler head, metallic violet wing-patch. Flashing
white wing linings in flight. Sexes similar.

RUDDY DUCK (see also Plate 17) p.68
Male in summer: Ruddy; white cheek, black cap, blue bill.
Male in winter: Greyish; white cheek, dark cap.
Female: Dark line across pale buffy cheek.

RING-NECKED DUCK p.62
Male: High-crowned head, white band on bill; vertical white mark in
front of the pale grey flanks.
Female: Indistinct light face-patch; white eye-ring and white ring on
bill.

BLUE-WINGED TEAL p.60
Male: White crescent on face, black and white stern.
Female: Pale face-spot near base of bill; bill longer and cheeks plainer
than female Garganey's.

BAIKAL TEAL p.57
Male: Creamy cheek with a dark circular pattern.
Female: White spot near bill; broken supercilium and shadow of
male's facial pattern.

AMERICAN WIGEON p.56
Male: Pinkish brown body; grey head with a dark green ear-patch and
a white crown.
Female: Differs from female Wigeon by greyer, more streaked head
and usually whiter borders on the tertials.

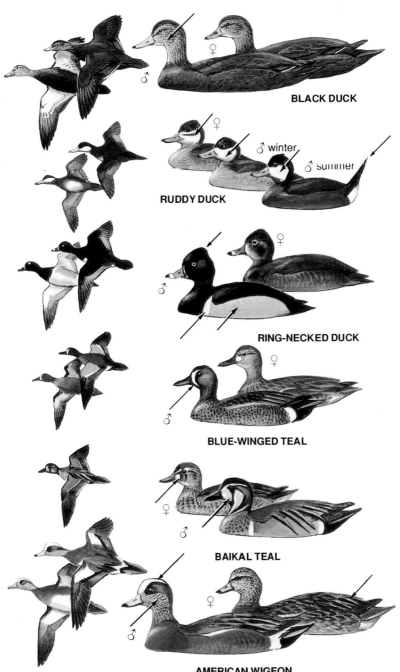

BLACK DUCK

RUDDY DUCK
♀
♂ winter
♂ summer

RING-NECKED DUCK
♂
♀

BLUE-WINGED TEAL
♀
♂

BAIKAL TEAL
♀
♂

AMERICAN WIGEON
♂
♀

Plate 19

DUCKS IN FLIGHT FROM ABOVE
(See also Plate 12, 16, 17 & 21)

Note: Only males are analysed below. For females, see text.

SHELDUCK Map 45 p.55
Black, white and chestnut pattern.

RUDDY SHELDUCK Map 44 p.55
Cinnamon colour; large white fore-wing patches.

MALLARD Map 49 p.58
Dark head, neck-ring, dark breast; two white borders to purple-blue speculum.

BLACK DUCK p.58
Blackish with paler head: speculum lacks pale borders.

PINTAIL Map 50 p.59
Lengthy fore and aft, with needle tail; dark head; dull speculum.

WIGEON Map 46 p.56
Large white wing panels; grey back.

SHOVELER Map 52 p.60
Long bill; white sides to back; blue wing-panels.

GADWALL Map 47 p.57
Grey-brown; white patch on inner speculum.

GARGANEY Map 51 p.59
Small; white head line; bluish wing-panels.

TEAL Map 48 p.58
Small; dark head; wide light fore-border to green speculum.

SMEW Map 63 p.67
White head and inner wing; black outer wing.

GOOSANDER Map 65 p.68
Cylinder shape; dark head; white scapulars and inner wing.

RED-BREASTED MERGANSER Map 64 p.67
Less bulky than Goosander; dark head and chest band; dark back and white inner wing.

Saw-bills (Smew, Goosander and Red-breasted Merganser) fly with bill, head, neck and body held in a horizontal line.

RUDDY
SHELDUCK

SHELDUCK

MALLARD

BLACK
DUCK

PINTAIL

WIGEON

SHOVELER

GARGANEY

GADWALL

TEAL

GOOSANDER

SMEW

RED-BREASTED MERGANSER

Plate 20

DUCKS IN FLIGHT FROM ABOVE
(See also Plate 13, 14, 15, 16 & 22)

Note: Only males are analysed below. Some females have similar wing patterns. See text.

TUFTED DUCK Map 56 p.62
All black; white wing-bar.

SCAUP Map 57 p.63
Pale grey back; white wing-bar.

FERRUGINOUS DUCK Map 55 p.62
Mahogany; white wing-bar.

POCHARD Map 54 p.61
Dark red head; pale grey back and wing-bar.

RED-CRESTED POCHARD Map 53 p.61
Red head; broad white stripe extends nearly length of wing.

GOLDENEYE Map 62 p.67
Large white squares on inner wing; dark head on short neck. Wings whistle in flight.

LONG-TAILED DUCK (Winter) Map 59 p.65
Dark unpatterned wings; much white on head and body.

HARLEQUIN p.64
Stocky with small bill; slaty with harlequin pattern.

KING EIDER p.63
Black back; whitish fore-parts; white fore-wings.

EIDER Map 58 p.63
White back; white fore-wings; black belly.

VELVET SCOTER Map 61 p.66
Black body; white secondaries form obvious patches.

SURF SCOTER p.66
Black body; white patches on head.

COMMON SCOTER Map 60 p.65
All black.

TUFTED DUCK

♂

♀

SCAUP

♀

FERRUGINOUS DUCK

♂

RED-
CRESTED
POCHARD

♀

POCHARD

♂

♀

GOLDENEYE

♂

♀

LONG-TAILED
DUCK

♂

♀

HARLEQUIN

♂

KING
EIDER

♀

EIDER

♂

♀

VELVET SCOTER

♀

SURF SCOTER

♂

COMMON SCOTER

♀

Plate 21

DUCKS OVERHEAD
(See also Plate 12, 16, 17 & 19)

Note: Only males are analysed below. For females, see text.

SHELDUCK — Map 45 p.55
Chestnut breast-band around white under-body. Black stripe down the belly.

RUDDY SHELDUCK — Map 44 p.55
Cinnamon body; white wing-linings.

MALLARD — Map 49 p.58
Dark head and chest; white neck-ring; pale belly.

BLACK DUCK — p.58
White wing linings contrast with dusky body.

PINTAIL — Map 50 p.59
Small dark head; long thin neck; white breast; needle tail.

WIGEON — Map 46 p.56
Clean-cut white belly, grey flanks; dark pointed tail.

SHOVELER — Map 52 p.60
Long, spoon-like bill. Dark head and belly separated by white breast.

GADWALL — Map 47 p.57
White belly; white inner speculum.

GARGANEY — Map 51 p.59
Small; dark fore-parts; white band on face; pale under-parts. Blackish leading edge to under-wing.

TEAL — Map 48 p.58
Small size; dark head before white belly.

SMEW — Map 63 p.67
All-white below, except on edges of wing and tail.

GOOSANDER — Map 65 p.68
Cylinder shape; dark head; white body; white wing-linings.
Female's head contrasts sharply with neck.

RED-BREASTED MERGANSER — Map 64 p.67
Slimmer than Goosander, with a dark breast-band.
Female's head merges into neck.

SHELDUCK

RUDDY SHELDUCK

♂

MALLARD
♀
♂

♂

BLACK DUCK

PINTAIL
♂
♀

WIGEON
♂
♀

SHOVELER
♂
♀

GARGANEY
♂
♀

TEAL
♂
♀

GADWALL
♂
♀

SMEW
♀
♂

GOOSANDER
♂
♀

RED-BREASTED MERGANSER
♂
♀

Plate 22

DUCKS OVERHEAD
(See also Plate 13, 14, 15, 16 & 20)

Note: Only males are analysed below. For females, see text.

TUFTED DUCK — Map 56 p.62
Black head and chest; white flanks and bar showing through wing.

SCAUP — Map 57 p.63
Similar to Tufted but much bulkier, with duller flanks.

FERRUGINOUS DUCK — Map 55 p.62
Mahogany fore-parts and flanks framing white belly; bright white bar
shows through wing. White under tail-coverts.

POCHARD — Map 54 p.61
Chestnut head; black breast contrasts with light belly.

RED-CRESTED POCHARD — Map 53 p.61
Rufous head; bold white flank-patches on black under-parts.

GOLDENEYE — Map 62 p.67
Blackish wing-linings contrast with white secondaries; white body.

LONG-TAILED DUCK — Map 59 p.65
Uniform dark wings; dark breast-band separates white head and belly.

HARLEQUIN — p.64
Uniform dark wings; rufous sides; harlequin head-pattern.

KING EIDER — p.63
White chest; black belly; blunt head.

EIDER — Map 58 p.63
White chest; black belly; pointed head.

VELVET SCOTER — Map 61 p.66
Black body; white patch on the secondaries.

SURF SCOTER — p.66
Black body; white on head and bill; dull flight-feathers.

COMMON SCOTER — Map 60 p.65
Black body; silvery flight-feathers.

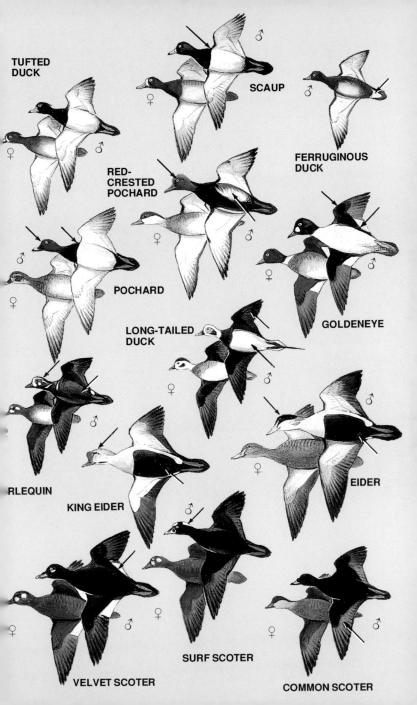

TUFTED DUCK

♀

♂

SCAUP

♂

FERRUGINOUS DUCK

RED-CRESTED POCHARD

♀

♂

♂

♀

POCHARD

♂

♀

GOLDENEYE

LONG-TAILED DUCK

♀

♂

RLEQUIN

♂

♀

KING EIDER

EIDER

♀

♂

♀

VELVET SCOTER

SURF SCOTER

♂

COMMON SCOTER

Plate 23

VULTURES

GRIFFON VULTURE   Map 73 p.73
Long, broad wings; short, dark, squared tail. Pale neck-ruff; pale lines
along under wing.

BLACK VULTURE   Map 74 p.73
Size of Griffon, but with more massive bill, dark neck-ruff and more
wedged-shaped tail. Looks all black.

LAMMERGEIER   Map 71 p.72
Rather falcon-like on the wing; long, narrow, often angled wings and
long, diamond-shaped tail. Rusty body; rusty-buff head with
projecting 'moustaches'.

EGYPTIAN VULTURE   Map 72 p.72
Smaller than other vultures. Long black and white wings and
wedge-shaped white tail. Long, thin bill; yellow face. Juvenile all dark.

GRIFFON VULTURE

BLACK VULTURE

LAMMERGEIER

EGYPTIAN VULTURE

EGYPTIAN VULTURE

LAMMERGEIER

GRIFFON VULTURE

BLACK VULTURE

Plate 24

HARRIERS AND KITES
(See also Plate 25)

Harriers have small heads, long bodies, long wings and long tails.

MARSH HARRIER
Map 76 p.74

Largest in genus, with broadest wings.
Male: Grey only on wings and tail; rufous with streaks below.
Female: Dark brown; pale buff crown and throat; no white on rump.
Juvenile: Similar to female, or with head nearly all dark.

MONTAGU'S HARRIER
Map 79 p.75

Slimmer than Hen Harrier.
Male: Dusky-grey; black bars across upper secondaries; greyish rump; rusty streaks on under-parts.
Female: Face marks whiter and rump-patch slightly narrower than Hen.
Juvenile: Deep rufous underparts.

HEN HARRIER
Map 77 p.74

Largest of three pale-rumped (ring-tailed) species.
Male: Grey, with a clear white rump-patch; no black bar across secondaries on upper wing.
Female & juvenile: Brown, streaked; barred tail; bold white rump-patch.

PALLID HARRIER
Map 78 p.74

Male: Paler than Hen Harrier, with a white breast; indistinct rump-patch; no black wing-bar.
Female: Best distinguished from Montagu's Harrier by even bolder face marks and dark undersurface to secondaries.
Juvenile: Paler below than Montagu's; dark 'boa' mark around neck.

Kites are rather similar in shape to harriers, but have notched or forked tails.

BLACK KITE
Map 68 p.71

Dusky; slightly forked tail.

RED KITE
Map 69 p.70

Rich rusty; streaked; with a pale head; deeply forked tail.

BLACK-SHOULDERED KITE
p.70

Black shoulders; white tail.

juvenile

♀

MARSH HARRIER

♂

♀

juvenile

♂

MONTAGU'S HARRIER

♀

♂

juvenile

HEN HARRIER

♂

♀

PALLID HARRIER

BLACK KITE

RED KITE

BLACK-SHOULDERED KITE

Plate 25

HARRIERS AND KITES IN FLIGHT
(See also Plate 24)

Harriers have long wings, long tails and long bodies. Their wings are not as pointed as those of falcons and their flight is more languid and gliding, usually low over the ground. When gliding, their wings (especially the three smaller species) are usually held in a shallow V.

MARSH HARRIER Map 76 p.74
Male: Dark back, contrasting with pale grey wing areas and tail.
Female: Dark; pale crown and shoulders.

MONTAGU'S HARRIER Map 79 p.75
Male: Dark bar across secondaries; pale greyish rump.
Female: From Hen Harrier by slimmer build, slightly smaller rump-patch and broad pale band across all under-secondaries.

HEN HARRIER Map 77 p.74
Male: White rump. From below, dark tips to secondaries form obvious trailing edge to wing.
Female: Streaked brown; bold white rump, and barred under-secondaries forming dark patch near body.

PALLID HARRIER Map 78 p.74
Male: Even paler than Hen; lacks dark trailing bar on wing.
Female: From Montagu's by very dark secondaries and coverts on under-wing. See diagram.

Left, Underwing patterns of (*above*) female Montagu's and (*below*) female Pallid Harrier. Note much darker, less barred appearance of Pallid's secondaries

Kites are rather similar in shape to harriers, but have notched or forked tails. They are buoyant gliders, making great use of their flexible tails. When gliding, their wings are usually held level.

RED KITE Map 69 p.70
Rusty; deeply forked tail; distinctive wing pattern with bold white patches on primaries.

BLACK KITE Map 68 p.71
Dusky; slightly forked tail; nearly uniform wings below. Note: Can be confused with some dark Marsh Harriers.

MARSH HARRIER ♀

MARSH HARRIER ♂

MONTAGU'S HARRIER ♀

MONTAGU'S HARRIER ♂

HEN HARRIER

RED KITE

BLACK KITE

Plate 26

BUZZARDS AND HAWKS
(See also Plates 27 and 31)

Buzzards have heavy bodies and short wide tails. When gliding and particularly wheeling or soaring, wings are usually held raised.

ROUGH-LEGGED BUZZARD
Map 84 p.77
Dark sides to belly; whitish tail with a dark terminal band. May be paler in the far north. Often hovers.

BUZZARD
Map 83 p.76
Variable. Usually dark with blotched or barred under-parts, showing pale band under breast. Tail usually as shown, sometimes almost unbarred cinnamon.

HONEY BUZZARD
Map 67 p.70
Head smaller and more projecting, tail longer than Buzzard's. Tail has broad black, unevenly spaced bands near base and at tip.

LONG-LEGGED BUZZARD
p.77
Tail pale cinnamon, usually unbarred; base sometimes whitish.

Accipiters (bird hawks) have small heads, short wings and long tails.

SPARROWHAWK
Map 81 p.76
Male: Small; under-parts closely barred with red-brown.
Female: Larger than male; under-parts closely barred with grey.

GOSHAWK
Map 80 p.75
Adult: Like a very large Sparrowhawk; grey bars; dark cheek; white supercilium. White under-tail coverts are prominent. Sexes alike. Adults may be very pale in the far north or in mixed British population.
Juvenile: Brown, streaked; pronounced supercilium.

LEVANT SPARROWHAWK
Map 82 p.76
Smaller even than male Sparrowhawk. Diagram shows the differences in head pattern between a Sparrowhawk (*left*) and a Levant Sparrowhawk (*right*).

pale

ROUGH-LEGGED
BUZZARD

typical

BUZZARD

dark
phase

pale
phase

adult

typical

HONEY
BUZZARD

LONG-
LEGGED
BUZZARD

immature

adult

♂

♀

adult

GOSHAWK

SPARROWHAWK

Plate 27

BUZZARDS AND SMALL EAGLES OVERHEAD
(See also Plate 26)

Buzzards are bulky, with broad wings and broad tails. They soar and wheel high in the open sky. Certain of the eagles are similar in outline to buzzards but usually have proportionately longer wings.

BUZZARD   Map 83 p.76
Variable; usually dark, short-necked; secondaries and tail usually with numerous narrow bars.

ROUGH-LEGGED BUZZARD   Map 84 p.77
Dark belly; whitish tail with broad black band at tip; black 'wrist-patches' on pale under-wing.

HONEY BUZZARD   Map 67 p.70
Head more projecting; tail longer than Buzzard's, with broad black bands near the base. Note complete barring of all flight-feathers.

LONG-LEGGED BUZZARD   p.77
Tail pale rusty, usually without bars; rufous wing-linings.

BONELLI'S EAGLE   Map 90 p.80
Much larger and longer-tailed than Buzzard.
Adult: Silky-white under-parts; dark wing-linings and tail band.
Juvenile: Dark-edged rufous wing-linings; barred tail.

BOOTED EAGLE   Map 89 p.80
Buzzard size, but longer tail.
Light phase: White wing-linings; dark flight feathers.
Dark phase: Dark; pale at base of primaries and tail.

SHORT-TOED EAGLE   Map 75 p.73
Large and long-winged. White under-parts and under-wings usually contrast strikingly with dark upper breast. Some lack dark breast-band.

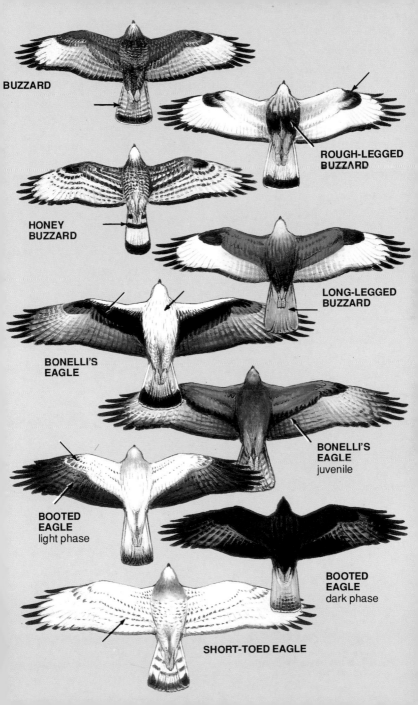

BUZZARD

ROUGH-LEGGED BUZZARD

HONEY BUZZARD

LONG-LEGGED BUZZARD

BONELLI'S EAGLE

BONELLI'S EAGLE juvenile

BOOTED EAGLE light phase

BOOTED EAGLE dark phase

SHORT-TOED EAGLE

Plate 28

EAGLES
(See also Plate 29)

Eagles are relatively huge, usually with long and broad, well-fingered wings and ample tails. Like buzzards, they fly high but show much more majestic flight actions.

GOLDEN EAGLE
Map 88 p.79

Much larger than Buzzard, with much heavier bill. Adult all dark with golden feathers on head and hind-neck. See overhead pattern of adult and immature on Plate 29.

WHITE-TAILED EAGLE
Map 70 p.72

Adult: More bulky than Golden Eagle; entire head pale, bill yellow, tail white. See overhead flight patterns of adult and immature on Plate 29.

STEPPE EAGLE
p.79

Smaller than Golden Eagle.
Adult: Almost uniform dark brown, often with a rusty-yellow patch on the nape; gape extends back to rear of eye.
Juvenile: *Cafe-au-lait* coloured, with two pale wing-bars in flight (not shown).

IMPERIAL EAGLE
Map 87 p.79

Close in size and appearance to Golden Eagle but pale crown of the adult may be almost whitish in some birds. Usually some pure white feathers on scapulars. Spanish form has conspicuous white shoulders.

LESSER SPOTTED EAGLE
Map 85 p.78

Smallest of genus in Europe. Similar to Spotted Eagle but less heavily built, with narrower wings. Immature far less spotted than Spotted Eagle.

SPOTTED EAGLE
Map 86 p.78

Medium-sized.
Adult: Very dark throughout, usually with white visible on the upper tail-coverts.
Immature: Copious large whitish spots form pale bands on wing, also white V at base of tail.

Head on silhouettes show gliding attitude.

GOLDEN EAGLE

adult

WHITE-TAILED EAGLE

adult

adult

STEPPE EAGLE

adults

adult
Spanish form

adult

eastern form

IMPERIAL EAGLE

adult

adult

LESSER SPOTTED EAGLE

immature

immature

SPOTTED EAGLE

Plate 29

EAGLES AND OSPREY OVERHEAD
(See also Plate 28)

GOLDEN EAGLE Map 88 p.79
Much larger than Buzzard, with projecting head, long 'fingered' wings
and ampler tail.
Immature: 'Ringed' tail with white base; large white patches along
bases of primaries and outer secondaries.
Adult: Almost uniformly dark. Seen from above, golden feathers on
head and wing-coverts are diagnostic.

WHITE-TAILED EAGLE Map 70 p.72
Distinguished from Golden by its shorter, more wedge-shaped tail,
huge bill and vulturine wing-shape.
Adult: White tail; pale head.
Immature: Paler than Golden Eagle, often streaked with white and
brown on the under-parts.

OSPREY Map 91 p.81
White head, clear white belly; long and loose wings show black
'wrist-patches'.

Spotted Eagle immature (after P.J. Hayman)
Note: All head-on silhouettes show gliding, not soaring attitudes.

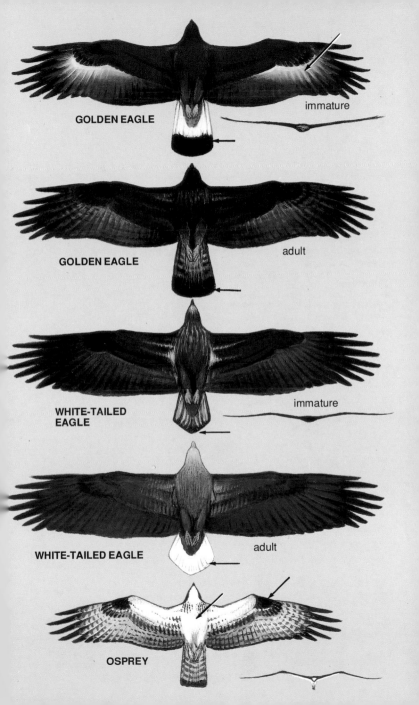

GOLDEN EAGLE immature

GOLDEN EAGLE adult

WHITE-TAILED EAGLE immature

WHITE-TAILED EAGLE adult

OSPREY

Plate 30

FALCONS
(See also Plate 31)

Falcons have rather large heads, broad
shoulders, long pointed wings, longish tails.

KESTREL
Map 93 p.82

Male: Spotted, rufous back; grey tail ends in black band.
Female: Barred rufous upper-parts and tail.

LESSER KESTREL
Map 92 p.81

Smaller and more gregarious than Kestrel; no spots on the back; blue
wing-coverts; white wing-linings.

MERLIN
Map 95 p.82

Male: Smallest of all falcons; dark blue-grey back; streaked rusty
under-parts.
Female: Close to Kestrel in size; dark brown above; boldly banded tail.

PEREGRINE
Map 100 p.85

Adult: Slate back; whitish breast; heavy black 'moustache'.
Immature: Brown, streaked below; heavy 'moustache'.

LANNER
Map 97 p.84

Buff cap; dark brown back.

SAKER
Map 98 p.84

Pale, whitish head; brown back and wings.

HOBBY
Map 96 p.83

Like small, slight Peregrine; streaked under-parts; rufous 'trousers';
white neck-patch.

ELEONORA'S FALCON
p.83

Longer-winged and -tailed than other falcons, with slow flight.
Dark phase: Black with yellow feet.
Pale phase: Suggests small immature Peregrine or large Hobby, but
'moustache' narrower and belly rustier.

RED-FOOTED FALCON
Map 94 p.82

Male: Slaty but with silvery primaries; red feet; rusty under
tail-coverts.
Female: Rusty crown and belly; barred grey back.
Juvenile: Like Hobby but browner above (see text).

KESTREL

LESSER KESTREL

MERLIN

juvenile

adult

PEREGRINE

LANNER

SAKER

juvenile

adults

pale form
adult

juvenile

♀

adults

♂

juvenile

adult

dark form

HOBBY

**ELEONORA'S
FALCON**

**RED-FOOTED
FALCON**

Plate 31

FALCONS AND ACCIPTERS OVERHEAD
(See also plates 26 and 30)

Falcons have long, pointed wings, long tails. Their wing-strokes are strong, rapid but usually shallow.

GYRFALCON
Map 99 p.84

Grey phase: Larger than Peregrine; broader bases and blunter tips to wings; less contrasting face pattern.
White phase: Can look as white as Snowy Owl.

MERLIN
Map 95 p.82

Smaller than Kestrel; darker, more compact, with dashing flight.

PEREGRINE
Map 100 p.85

Falcon shape; face pattern; size near Crow.

HOBBY
Map 96 p.83

Like small, slim Peregrine, but tail shorter; wings more Swift-like.

RED-FOOTED FALCON
Map 94 p.82

Shape suggests both Kestrel and Hobby.
Male: Very dark; red feet; rusty under tail-coverts.
Female: Rusty wing-linings, unmarked rusty belly, banded tail.

KESTREL
Map 93 p.82

Hovers habitually. Small, slim; black band near tip of the tail.

ELEONORA'S FALCON
p.83

Pale form: Striped rusty under-parts; all dark wings.
Dark form: All dark, with pale feet.

LESSER KESTREL
Map 92 p.81

Seldom hovers. Tail slightly wedge-shaped; white wing-linings.

Accipiters (bird hawks) have short, rounded wings and long tails. In flight they alternate several rapid wing-beats with a short glide; they also soar.

GOSHAWK
Map 80 p.75

Very large, with more projecting head, deeper chest and more bulging inner wing than Sparrowhawk. Under-parts barred with grey; conspicuous white under tail-coverts. Note: Immature streaked below.

SPARROWHAWK
Map 81 p.76

Under-parts barred with rusty (male) or grey-brown (female and immature).

LEVANT SPARROWHAWK
Map 82 p.76

Pale underwing; broad black wing-tips.

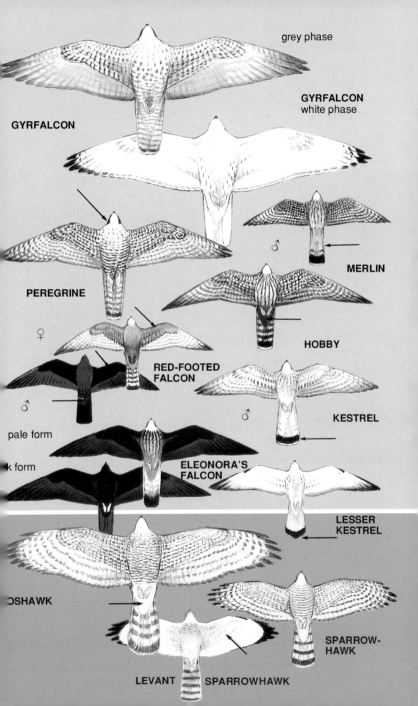

grey phase

GYRFALCON
white phase

GYRFALCON

MERLIN ♂

PEREGRINE

♀

HOBBY

♂ **RED-FOOTED
FALCON**

KESTREL ♂

pale form

k form **ELEONORA'S
FALCON**

**LESSER
KESTREL**

OSHAWK

**SPARROW-
HAWK**

LEVANT SPARROWHAWK

Plate 32

GAME BIRDS
(See also Plate 33)

PHEASANT — Map 110 p.90
Very long pointed tail.
Male: Richly coloured; usually white neck-ring.
Female: Large, tawny-brown.

BLACK GROUSE — Map 104 p.87
Lyre-shaped or notched tail.
Male: Blackcock; glossy black; white wing-bar.
Female: Greyhen; large, orange- and rufous-brown.

CAPERCAILLIE — Map 105 p.87
Broad fan tail.
Male: Huge size; dusky colouration.
Female: Very large, brown.

HAZEL GROUSE — Map 101 p.85
Partridge size; fan tail with wide black band. Colour phases vary from rufous to grey, tending towards rufous in south parts of range, grey in the north.

Pheasant   **Black Grouse**   **Capercaillie**

Display postures differ in male gamebirds
See also illustrations of other game-birds on Plate 33.

PHEASANT

♂

PHEASANT

♀

PHEASANT

♀

BLACK GROUSE
(Greyhen)

BLACK GROUSE
(Blackcock)

♂

♀ **CAPER-
CAILLIE**

HAZEL GROUSE

♂

CAPERCAILLIE

Plate 33

GAME BIRDS
(See also Plate 32)

RED GROUSE Map 102 p.86
Dark rufous plumage; dark wings and tail. Female less rufous, more barred.

PTARMIGAN Map 103 p.86
Winter: White, with black tail.
Summer: White wings; grey or brown body; black tail.

WILLOW GROUSE Map 102 p.86
Winter: From male Ptarmigan, see line drawing below.
Summer: Rufous; white wings; black tail.
Occurs at lower altitudes than Ptarmigan.

GREY PARTRIDGE Map 108 p.89
Orange head; mottled upper-parts; rufous tail. Male with a dark horseshoe patch on the underparts.

QUAIL Map 109 p.90
Small; sandy brown; striped head.

ANDALUSIAN HEMIPODE p.91
Quail-like; bright rufous patch on the breast; bold spots on sides of breast.

Red legs, uniform backs and rufous tails (conspicuous only in flight) characterize the following three *Alectoris* partridges. They are best separated by their neck patterns.

RED-LEGGED PARTRIDGE Map 107 p.88
Necklace black, breaking into profuse short streaks. Beware frequent hybrids with Chukar.

ROCK PARTRIDGE Map 106 p.88
Necklace black, clean-cut. See also Chukar (below and p.88).

BARBARY PARTRIDGE p.89
Necklace red-brown, with white spots; grey face.

male, winter

Willow Grouse and Ptarmigan   **Chukar**
Note the black face-patch on the male (not female) Ptarmigan in winter. Both sexes of Willow Grouse lack this, but have thicker bills.

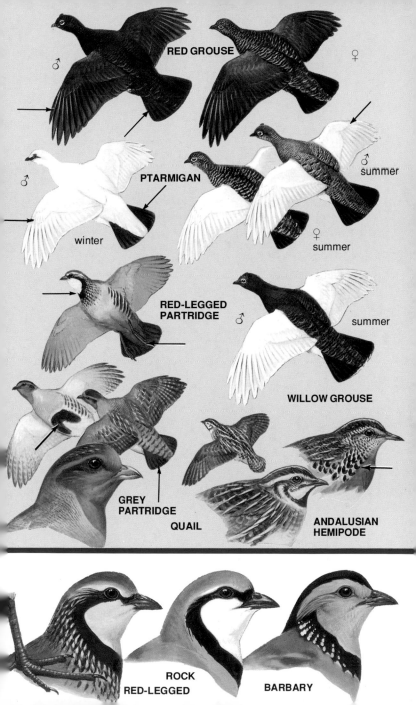

RED GROUSE ♂ ♀

PTARMIGAN ♂ winter

♂ summer

♀ summer

RED-LEGGED PARTRIDGE ♂

summer

WILLOW GROUSE

GREY PARTRIDGE

QUAIL

ANDALUSIAN HEMIPODE

ROCK

RED-LEGGED

BARBARY

Plate 34

RAILS AND CRAKES
(Small chicken-like, marsh birds)

WATER RAIL Map 111 p.91

Adult: Long red bill; barred flanks; white or cream under tail.
Juvenile: Dusky, with mottled under-parts.

CORNCRAKE Map 115 p.93

Rusty-red wings; yellowish bill. Yellowish-buff below, heavily
marked above.

LITTLE CRAKE Map 113 p.92

Male: Slaty breast; green legs; red spot on bill.
Female: Buffish breast; greenish legs; red spot on bill.

SPOTTED CRAKE Map 112 p.92

Suggests a short-billed Water Rail. Note buff under tail-coverts,
greenish legs, red base of bill.

BAILLON'S CRAKE Map 114 p.93

Slaty breast; no red on bill; legs brownish-flesh; bold bars on flanks.
Dark upper-parts are narrowly marked with white.

SORA p.244

Adult: Black face and throat. White under-tail coverts.
Immature: Buff-breasted; lacks full black throat-patch.

WATER RAIL

adult

juvenile

SORA

adult

1st
autumn

CORNCRAKE

♂

♀

LITTLE CRAKE

♂

SPOTTED CRAKE

BAILLON'S CRAKE

♂

Plate 35

MOORHEN, COOTS, PURPLE GALLINULE
(Duck-like swimmers)

COOT   Map 117 p.94
Adult: Slate grey with a white bill and white forehead shield.
Juvenile: From Moorhen by larger size, no white on under-tail coverts.
Chick: Orange-red on head.

CRESTED COOT   p.94
Similar to Coot but with red knobs (often inconspicuous) above the
forehead.

PURPLE GALLINULE   p.94
Deep purplish-blue; very large red bill; red legs.

ALLEN'S GALLINULE   p.245
Adult: Dark green and blue; red bill and legs.
Immature: Smaller, sandier than Moorhen, with reddish legs.

MOORHEN   Map 116 p.93
Adult: Red bill; white flank-stripe and white under-tail.
Juvenile: Brownish with yellowish-green bill.
Chick: Red on forehead.

Coots skitter on takeoff

lobed foot of coot

juvenile

adults

adult

COOT

chick

CRESTED
COOT

adult

adult

PURPLE
GALLINULE

juvenile

ALLEN'S
GALLINULE

adults

juvenile

MOORHEN

chick

Plate 36
BUSTARDS, SANDGROUSE, STONE CURLEW

Bustards are large-bodied, long-legged and -striding birds of open plains.
Sandgrouse are plump, dove-like desert birds with pointed tails. Only males are shown (see texts for females).
The **Stone Curlew** is a heavily built wader of large fields and plains.

GREAT BUSTARD   Map 120 p.97
Male: Very large; head and neck pale grey (no black). Much white on the wing.
Female: Smaller, lacks the rusty breast-band.

LITTLE BUSTARD   Map 119 p.96
Male: Black and white neck pattern; shows much white in flight.
Female: Streaked brown head and neck.

HOUBARA BUSTARD   p.96
Silhouette recalls hen Turkey. Both sexes have long black feathers drooping down the sides of the neck. Far less white on wing than other bustards.

BLACK-BELLIED SANDGROUSE   p.141
Large black belly and primaries. Tail less elongated than in other sandgrouse.

PIN-TAILED SANDGROUSE   p.141
White belly and under-wings; rusty breast-band; long needle-pointed tail.

PALLAS'S SANDGROUSE   p.142
Small black belly; whitish wing-linings; long needle-pointed tail.

STONE CURLEW   Map 124 p.98
Hunched attitude; large pale eyes; broad contrasting bars on the wings.

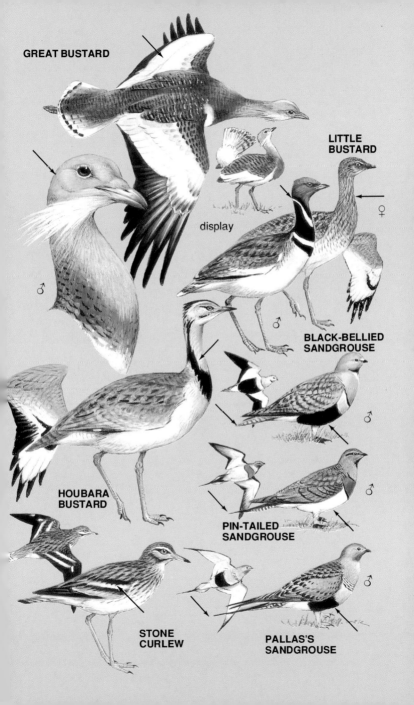

GREAT BUSTARD

LITTLE BUSTARD

display

♀

♂

♂

BLACK-BELLIED SANDGROUSE

♂

HOUBARA BUSTARD

PIN-TAILED SANDGROUSE

♂

STONE CURLEW

PALLAS'S SANDGROUSE

♂

Plate 37

PLOVERS

Plovers are wading birds, more compactly built and thicker-necked than most sandpipers, with pigeon-like bills and large eyes. Unlike most sandpipers, plovers run in short stops and starts. Sexes alike.

GREY PLOVER
Map 131 p.103

In flight, shows bold white wing-bar. From beneath, shows diagnostic black axillaries in wing-pits.
Summer: Black below; speckled silvery above, white rump, barred tail.
Winter: Stout shape; speckled grey above, whitish below.

GOLDEN PLOVER
Map 130 p.103

In flight, shows no strong wing-bar. From beneath, fully whitish wing-lining diagnostic.
Summer: Black below, speckled gold above; broad white flank-stripe. Southern form less black below.
Winter: Less stout than Grey Plover; golden-brown above; dark rump.

AMERICAN GOLDEN PLOVER
p.102

Second smallest of golden plovers, with narrow wings. In flight, shows dusky wing-lining.
Summer: Slighter build than Golden Plover; underbody solid black, lacking dividing white flank-stripe.
Winter: Less golden above than Golden Plover. Immature wholly mottled below. Calls include *klee-e-eet* like Lapwing.

PACIFIC GOLDEN PLOVER
p.102

Smallest of golden plovers, with proportionately longest legs; shares dusky wing-lining with American Golden Plover.
Summer: More golden above but less black below than American Golden Plover.
Winter: More golden above than American Golden; toes extend beyond tail. Calls include *dlu-eep* like Spotted Redshank.

winter

juvenile

breeding

GREY PLOVER

southern

winter

northern

GOLDEN PLOVER

breeding

juvenile

breeding

juvenile

PACIFIC GOLDEN PLOVER

breeding

AMERICAN GOLDEN PLOVER

Plate 38

RINGED PLOVERS, PRATINCOLES

RINGED PLOVER   Map 127 p.100
Small; single band across the breast; yellow-orange legs; yellow on
the base of bill. Long white wing-bar.

LITTLE RINGED PLOVER   Map 126 p.100
Smaller than Ringed Plover; flesh-coloured legs; white line above
black over forehead; yellow ring around eye. No wing-bar.

KENTISH PLOVER   Map 128 p.101
Smaller and paler than Ringed Plover; black on sides of breast only;
blackish legs; unbroken supercilium. White wing-bar.

KILLDEER   p.101
Larger than Ringed Plover. Two black breast-bands; long orange rump
and tail. Long white wing-bar.

CASPIAN PLOVER   p.245
Larger than Ringed, with long wings and legs. Male's rufous chest
bordered black below. Smaller than Greater Sand Plover.

GREATER SAND PLOVER   p.101
Larger than Ringed and Caspian with long legs and proportionally
large bill. Male has black face and rufous chest.

DOTTEREL   Map 129 p.102
White stripe over the eye and across the breast; russet flanks; black
belly. No wing-bar.

COLLARED PRATINCOLE   Map 125 p.99
Rather tern-like; forked tail, light throat-patch. In flight, shows white
rump, wings with rufous linings and pale trailing edges.

BLACK-WINGED PRATINCOLE   p.99
Like Collared Pratincole but black beneath wings which lack pale
trailing edges.

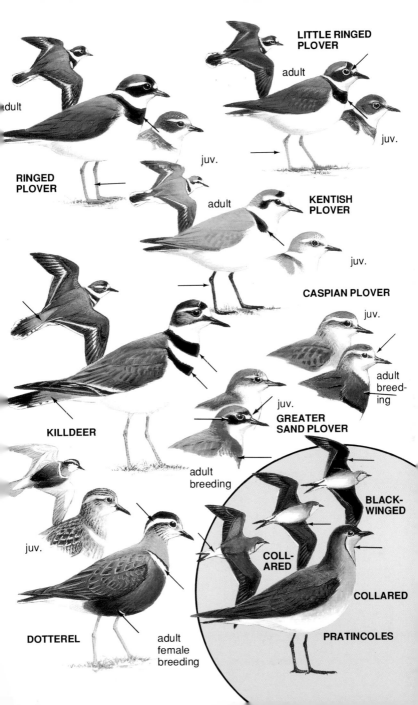

LITTLE RINGED PLOVER

adult

juv.

RINGED PLOVER

adult

juv.

KENTISH PLOVER

adult

juv.

CASPIAN PLOVER

juv.

adult breeding

KILLDEER

juv.

GREATER SAND PLOVER

adult breeding

BLACK-WINGED

COLLARED

juv.

DOTTEREL

adult female breeding

COLLARED PRATINCOLES

Plate 39

LARGE PLOVERS, TURNSTONE, COURSER

SOCIABLE PLOVER p.104
Black crown; white supercilia join in V on nape; dark belly-patch.
Bold black primaries contrast with white secondaries; white rump.

SPUR-WINGED PLOVER p.104
Strikingly black and white except for grey-brown back.

WHITE-TAILED PLOVER p.105
White tail, dusky chest, conspicuously black and white wings.

LAPWING Map 132 p.105
Long wispy crest; black upper breast; iridescent back. White-tipped
black wings have white lining.

TURNSTONE Map 156 p.121
Complex flight pattern diagnostic.
Breeding: Tortoiseshell back; distinctive harlequin face.
Winter: Dusky breast-band; orange legs.

CREAM-COLOURED COURSER p.99
Sandy; bold eye-stripes; long creamy legs. Dark underwings
distinctive.

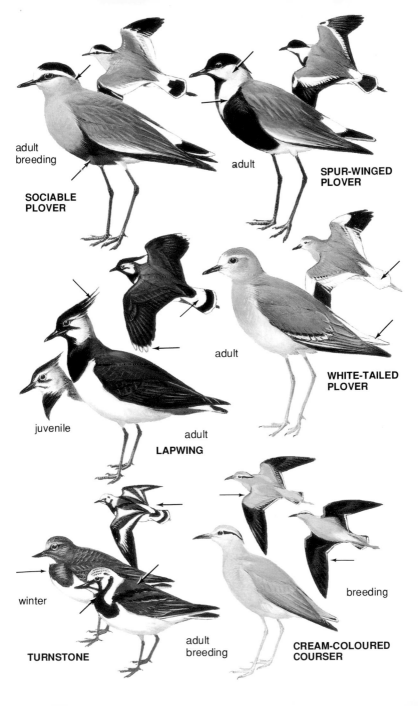

adult
breeding

**SOCIABLE
PLOVER**

adult

**SPUR-WINGED
PLOVER**

adult

juvenile

adult

LAPWING

**WHITE-TAILED
PLOVER**

winter

adult
breeding

TURNSTONE

breeding

**CREAM-COLOURED
COURSER**

Plate 40

PLOVERS AND TURNSTONE IN FLIGHT
(See also Plates 37, 38, 39)

RINGED PLOVER — Map 127 p.100
Prominent wing-bar; dark tail with long white borders.

LITTLE RINGED PLOVER — Map 126 p.100
From Ringed Plover by voice and lack of wing-bar.

KENTISH PLOVER — Map 128 p.101
Sandy-brown above; broad white wing-bar and sides of tail.

GREY PLOVER — Map 131 p.103
Summer: Black under-parts; white wing-bar and rump.
Winter: Black axillaries show in picture of wing.

GOLDEN PLOVER — Map 130 p.103
Summer: Black on under-parts; no white on rump.
Winter: Lack of strong pattern above and below. White axillaries and wing lining.

DOTTEREL — Map 129 p.102
White face; dark under-parts and dull wing lining; belly paler in winter.

LAPWING — Map 132 p.105
Black and white; very broad, rounded wings.

TURNSTONE — Map 156 p.121
Harlequin pattern.

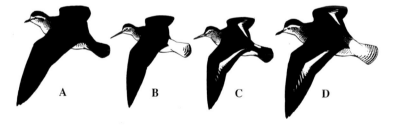

Basic Flight Patterns
A. No wing stripe, no tail pattern, e.g. Dotterel. .
B. No wing stripe, white rump and tail, e.g. Green Sandpiper..
C. Wing stripe, dark rump and tail, e.g. Common Sandpiper.
D. Wing stripe, white rump and tail, e.g. Grey Plover.

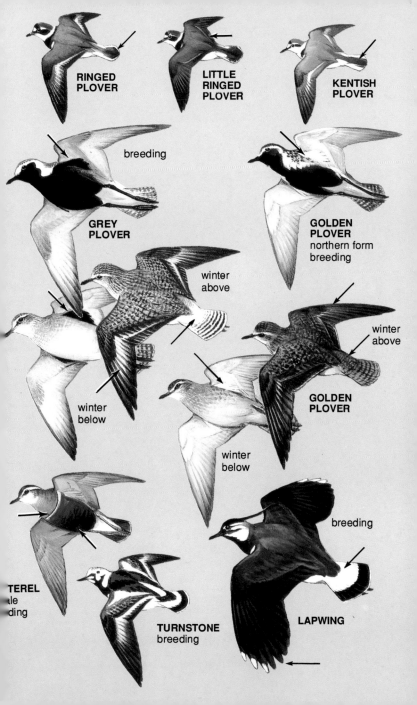

RINGED PLOVER

LITTLE RINGED PLOVER

KENTISH PLOVER

breeding

GREY PLOVER

GOLDEN PLOVER
northern form
breeding

winter above

winter below

winter below

GOLDEN PLOVER

winter above

TEREL
ale
ding

TURNSTONE
breeding

breeding

LAPWING

Plate 41

PHALAROPES

Sandpiper-like birds with lobed toes, equally at home wading or swimming. When feeding, they often spin like tops, rapidly dabbling at the disturbed water. The tubby Red-necked and Grey Phalaropes are largely sea-going.

RED-NECKED PHALAROPE
Map 157 p.121

Breeding: Rufous-red neck and dusky chest contrast with white throat; male duller.
Winter: Grey with strongly striped back.

GREY PHALAROPE
Map 158 p.122

Breeding: Rufous below; white cheeks; male duller.
Winter: Grey with unstriped back.

WILSON'S PHALAROPE
p.121

Breeding: Long bill, strong facial pattern, chestnut and black neck-stripe.
Winter: From other phalaropes by white rump and lack of wing-bar.

breeding

RED-NECKED PHALAROPE

winter

juvenile

winter

♂ breeding

♀ breeding

winter

GREY PHALAROPE

juvenile

winter

♂ breeding

d foot
alarope

♀ breeding

winter

WILSON'S PHALAROPE

juvenile

winter

♂ breeding

Plate 42

LARGE WADERS
(See also Plate 50, 51 & 52)

AVOCET Map 123 p.98
Very long, upturned bill; black and white head and back.

OYSTERCATCHER Map 121 p.97
Large size; black head and back; deep orange-red bill.

BLACK-WINGED STILT Map 122 p.97
Black above; white below; very long pink legs. Both sexes can have
black or white crowns.

BLACK-TAILED GODWIT Map 145 p.114
Tall-standing, with long straight bill.
Summer: Chestnut breast; bars on flanks; black tail-band.
Winter: Grey; black tail-band.

BAR-TAILED GODWIT Map 146 p.115
Dumpier than Black-tailed Godwit, with shorter legs and upturned bill.
Summer: Fully rufous below; barred tail.
Winter: Grey-brown; barred tail.

TEREK SANDPIPER p.120
Upturned bill, short yellow legs; blackish on scapulars. Bobs its tail.

CURLEW SANDPIPER p.110
Summer: Deep rusty; decurved bill, white rump.
Juvenile: Grey-brown with decurved bill, white rump.

CURLEW Map 148 p.116
Very long decurved bill; no stripes on crown.

WHIMBREL Map 147 p.115
Shorter decurved bill than Curlew; stripes on crown; bars on flanks.

SLENDER-BILLED CURLEW p.115
Bill length close to Whimbrel's, but crown more like Curlew's. Note
heart-shaped spots on body-sides.

OYSTERCATCHER

AVOCET

BLACK-
WINGED
STILT

nter

BAR-TAILED
GODWIT

winter

LACK-
AILED
ODWIT

breeding

REK
NDPIPER

breeding

SLENDER-
BILLED
CURLEW

CURLEW

breeding

juvenile

WHIMBREL

CURLEW
SANDPIPER

Plate 43

LONG-BILLED SNIPE-LIKE WADERS AND KNOT
(See also Plate 51)

WOODCOCK Map 144 p.114
Stout; long bill; barred crown; barred under-parts.

SNIPE Map 142 p.113
Long straight bill; striped crown and mantle; barred flanks; white belly.

GREAT SNIPE Map 143 p.113
Larger and shorter-billed than Snipe; barred overall below.

JACK SNIPE Map 141 p.113
Smaller than Snipe, with shorter bill; centre of crown dark; bold stripes on 'velvet' back.

Tails of snipes

Snipe   Great Snipe   Jack Snipe

Note that bold white sides of Great Snipe are more barred in immature

LONG-BILLED DOWITCHER p.113
Dowitchers have long white wedge up the back, snipe-like bill and rather short legs. They are most readily distinguishable by voice. The Long-billed is much the more likely of the two.
Juvenile: Grey-brown, with rather even pale fringes to upper-parts; black tail-bars denser than on Short-billed.
Winter: Grey; dense tail-bars.
Voice: Single thin *keek*.

SHORT-BILLED DOWITCHER p.113
Bill length overlaps with Long-billed.
Juvenile: Buff-brown, with distinctive uneven fringes to upperparts; black tail-bars more open than on Long-billed.
Winter: Grey; open tail-bars.
Voice: Staccato *tu-tu-tu*; see also text.

KNOT Map 133 p.106
Relatively short bill, stout but lengthy body and short legs; in flight, long white wing-bar and barred rump.
Breeding: Rufous under-parts.
Winter: Grey; light scaly feather edgings.
Juvenile: Grey-brown, with pinkish chest; black bars inside pale fringes of upperpart feathers.

WOODCOCK

SNIPE

GREAT SNIPE

JACK SNIPE

juvenile

winter

LONG-BILLED DOWITCHER

juvenile

SHORT-BILLED DOWITCHER

feeding posture

juvenile

winter

breeding

KNOT

Plate 44

LARGE SANDPIPERS
(called shanks)

SPOTTED REDSHANK Map 149 p.116
Longer-billed and -legged than Redshank; white wedge up back but dusky wings.
Adult summer: Looks blackish; rather dark reddish legs.
Adult winter: Much paler and greyer than Redshank; bright red legs.

REDSHANK Map 150 p.117
White inner primaries and secondaries diagnostic. Quite long orange-red legs; reddish base to bill.

GREENSHANK Map 152 p.118
Long greenish legs; white rump and wedge up the back.

GREATER YELLOWLEGS p.118
Shape of Greenshank, but legs bright yellow. Larger than Lesser Yellowlegs; bill longer and slightly upturned; leg joints more prominent.
Voice: 3-note whistle, *whew-whew-whew*, or *dear! dear! dear!*.

LESSER YELLOWLEGS p.118
Bright yellow legs; white rump; smaller than Greater Yellowlegs; finer bill.
Voice: *Yew* or *yu-yu* (lower, less forceful than the clear triplet of Greater Yellowlegs).

winter

breeding

SPOTTED REDSHANK

REDSHANK

GREENSHANK

GREATER YELLOWLEGS

LESSER YELLOWLEGS

Plate 45

SMALLER SANDPIPERS

WOOD SANDPIPER Map 154 p.119
Slender; a bit paler and browner than Green Sandpiper; legs paler,
yellowish at times. Underwings mottled.

GREEN SANDPIPER Map 153 p.119
Dark above, with a square white rump; legs dull greenish. Underwings
completely dark.

SOLITARY SANDPIPER p.119
Like Green Sandpiper, sharing dark underwing but with dark (not
white) rump and whiter 'spectacle'.

MARSH SANDPIPER Map 151 p.117
Like a small, delicate Greenshank, with very slender legs, needle-like
bill. White wedge up the back extends as far as in Greenshank.

STILT SANDPIPER p.111
Shaped like very small Greenshank but rather heavy bill droops
slightly. White rump does not extend up the back. When breeding,
heavily barred, with rusty cheek-patch.

WOOD
SANDPIPER

GREEN
SANDPIPER

SOLITARY SANDPIPER

winter

breeding

MARSH SANDPIPER

winter

breeding

STILT SANDPIPER

Plate 46

RUFFS AND NORTH AMERICAN SANDPIPERS

RUFF Map 140 p.112
Male (Ruff) much larger than female (Reeve); both show insignificant
wing-bar but white lateral tail coverts catch eye.
Male spring: Extraordinary ruff; very variable in colour.
Male autumn/winter: Scaly on upper-parts; brownish, often with white
face and pale chest.
Female: Rather like male in autumn but lacks pale head.

UPLAND SANDPIPER p.116
Small head, short bill, shoe-button eye, thin neck, long tawny tail.

BUFF-BREASTED SANDPIPER p.111
Under-parts rich buff; small head; yellow legs; beware confusing
juvenile Ruff. In flight, whitish under-wing contrasts with buff body.

PECTORAL SANDPIPER p.109
Suggests small Reeve in flight; more Dunlin-like on ground. Sharp
division between streaked breast and white belly.

SHARP-TAILED SANDPIPER p.109
Suggests Pectoral Sandpiper, but no sharp separation of streaks
between the breast and scalloped belly in summer adult. In autumn,
juvenile has bright tawny breast with streaks confined to the sides.

ads
breeding
les

RUFF

winter
♂

♀
Reeve

**BUFF-BREASTED
SANDPIPER**

**UPLAND
SANDPIPER**

juvenile

**PECTORAL
SANDPIPER**

**SHARP-TAILED
SANDPIPER**

adult
breeding

Plate 47

SANDPIPERS

COMMON SANDPIPER
Map 155 p.120

Bobbing tail action and fluttered wing beats distinctive. White wedge behind the smudge on side of breast; white wing-bar and barred sides to tail.

SPOTTED SANDPIPER
p.120

Teeters like Common Sandpiper, but tail shorter.
Adult breeding: Thrush-like spots; pale, black-tipped, bill.
Winter: Like Common Sandpiper, but breast cleaner white in the centre, no streaking. Wing-coverts barred pale grey.

DUNLIN
Map 138 p.110

Rather long, slightly drooped bill distinctive.
Adult breeding: Rusty back, black patch on belly.
Winter: Unpatterned grey-brown face and upper-parts, greyish wash across the breast.
Juvenile: Buff-brown on back, fully streaked below, unlike other *Calidris* sandpipers and stints.

SANDERLING
Map 134 p.106

Sanderlings chase retreating waves on sand beaches like clockwork toys. Short bill.
Breeding: Rusty above and on breast; white belly.
Winter: Grey and white, black shoulders.
Juvenile: Grey back with heavy speckles.

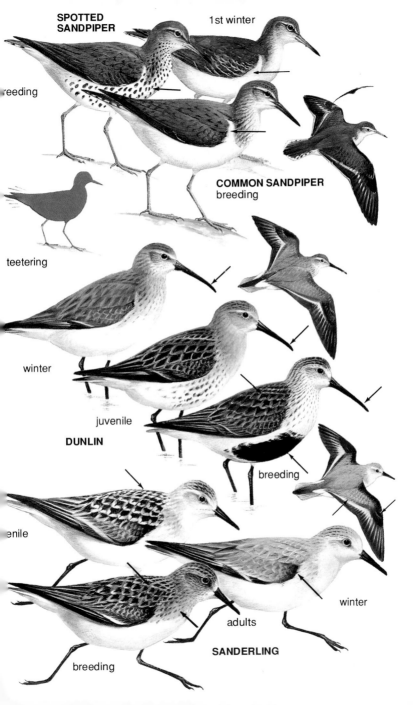

SPOTTED SANDPIPER

1st winter

breeding

teetering

COMMON SANDPIPER
breeding

winter

juvenile

DUNLIN

breeding

juvenile

adults

winter

breeding

SANDERLING

Plate 48

STINTS AND PURPLE SANDPIPER
(See also Plate 52)

Stints, the smallest *Calidris* sandpipers, are difficult to separate. First note leg colour: typically black on Little, Broad-billed, Rufous-necked and typically pale, even yellowish on Temminck's, Long-toed, Purple.

LITTLE STINT
Map 135 p.107

Smallest regular wader, sometimes common in autumn. Very small, straight bill; blackish legs; outer tail-feathers grey.
Juvenile: Foxy-red, with white Vs on back.
Winter: Plainer, grey and white.
Breeding: Rusty crown and upper-parts, with yellowish V high on back.

TEMMINCK'S STINT
Map 136 p.107

Legs shorter and body longer than Little Stint; no V on back; outer tail-feathers pure white. Legs olive or brownish grey. In summer, buff-olive back has strong black blotches on scapulars.

BROAD-BILLED SANDPIPER
Map 139 p.111

Long, broad-based, bent-tipped bill; double supercilium over eye. Stripes on back recall Snipe.

LONG-TOED STINT
p.246

Closely resembles Least Sandpiper but toes even longer, with central toe exceeding bill, and gait slower. Dark head and obvious supercilium; white Vs on back of juvenile recall Little Stint.

RED-NECKED STINT
p.246

Closely resembles Little but body longer and legs shorter.
Juvenile: Similar to dull Little Stint but Vs on back less obvious, wing-coverts and tertial edges greyer.
Winter: Best distinguished from Little Stint by shape and call.
Breeding: Variably rusty head and upper breast; black-spangled upper-parts, grey wing-coverts.

PURPLE SANDPIPER
Map 137 p.110

Rock-loving; always dark and portly.
Winter: Slaty, with yellowish legs and base of bill.
Breeding: Paler head; rusty feather-edges on back.

juvenile

winter

breeding

LITTLE STINT

juvenile

breeding

TEMMINCK'S STINT

juvenile

breeding

bill above

BROAD-BILLED SANDPIPER

juvenile

breeding

winter

LONG-TOED STINT

juvenile

winter

breeding

variant breeding

RED-NECKED STINT

PURPLE SANDPIPER

breeding

winter

Plate 49

SMALL SANDPIPERS FROM NORTH AMERICA

All have dark grey or blackish legs except Least Sandpiper which has typically yellowish legs.

WHITE-RUMPED SANDPIPER p.108
Larger than stints. Has long wings overlapping tail and slightly decurved end to bill; note white rump low over tail.
Voice: Mouse-like *jeet*, like scraping of two flints.

BAIRD'S SANDPIPER p.108
Size and shape close to White-rumped but bill straight; note black rump and buffier, browner upper-parts.

LEAST SANDPIPER p.108
Smallest stint, with very fine bill and least marked wing-bar of all. Plumage noticeably dark even on lores; V on back of juvenile thin and indistinct. See text for separation from Long-toed Stint.

SEMIPALMATED SANDPIPER p.107
Greyish-brown; typically short thick bill. See text for separation from other stints.
Voice: Distinctive *chewp* or *chirrup*.

WESTERN SANDPIPER p.246
Largest stint, with longest bill of all, thicker at base and distinctly drooped at tip. Very rusty in summer but greyish in winter. Autumn juveniles with shorter bills virtually indistinguishable from Semipalmated Sandpiper.
Voice: Distinctive thin *jeet*.

winter

breeding

WHITE-RUMPED SANDPIPER

juvenile

breeding

BAIRD'S SANDPIPER

winter

juvenile

LEAST SANDPIPER

breeding

winter

juvenile

breeding

SEMIPALMATED SANDPIPER

♂ immature

♀ winter

juvenile

breeding

WESTERN SANDPIPER

♀ breediing

Plate 50

LARGE WADERS IN FLIGHT
(See also Plate 42)

AVOCET   Map 123 p.97
White, marked black above; thin upturned bill and trailing legs.

BLACK-WINGED STILT   Map 122 p.97
Wings black above and below; white body and tail; extremely long
trailing pink legs.

OYSTERCATCHER   Map 121 p.97
White wing-bars and rump contrast with black upper-parts; orange bill.

WHIMBREL   Map 147 p.115
Both Whimbrel and Curlew are brown with whitish rumps, but
Whimbrel is smaller and neater. Bent-tipped bill; broad stripes on the
crown, and barred flanks.
Voice: Far-carrying whinny or titter.

CURLEW   Map 148 p.116
Very long decurved bill; no bold stripes on the crown.
Voice: Far-carrying statement of name.

BAR-TAILED GODWIT   Map 146 p.115
White rump; barred greyish tail; no wing-bar; long, slightly upturned
bill.

BLACK-TAILED GODWIT   Map 145 p.114
Bold white wing-bar and rump; broad black tail-band. Very long bill.

Oystercatchers

AVOCET

BLACK-WINGED
STILT

OYSTERCATCHER

WHIMBREL

CURLEW

BAR-TAILED
GODWIT

BLACK-TAILED
GODWIT

Plate 51

MEDIUM-SIZED WADERS IN FLIGHT
(See also Plate 43)

SNIPE Map 142 p.113
Long bill, usually held downwards; pointed wings with white trailing edges; zig-zags in long escape flight, calling harshly.

GREAT SNIPE Map 143 p.113
Slightly bulkier than Snipe, with shorter bill held up. White-edged, black panel along wing centre; more white on corners of tail than Snipe; flies off low in short escape flight; usually silent.

JACK SNIPE Map 141 p.112
Smaller than Snipe, with noticeably shorter bill; no white on pointed tail; rises silently, with less zig-zagging, and quickly returns to ground.

WOODCOCK Map 144 p.114
Bulky; long bill; rounded wings; dead-leaf colour; flies off low in escape flight through trees.

DOWITCHER (both species) p.113 and 246
Snipe-like bill; long narrow white wedge up the back; white on rear edge of wing. Best distinguished by call.

REDSHANK Map 150 p.117
Broad white band on rear edge of wing; white rump.

GREENSHANK Map 152 p.118
Long white wedge up back to the shoulders; no white wing-stripe.

SPOTTED REDSHANK Map 149 p.116
Winter pattern similar to Greenshank, but inner flight feathers more barred.

GREEN SANDPIPER Map 153 p.119
Very dark above; white rump; blackish under-wing.

WOOD SANDPIPER Map 154 p.119
From Green Sandpiper by less dark upper-parts, hence less contrasting rump, and paler mottled under-wing.

TEREK SANDPIPER p.120
Broad white trailing edge to inner wing recalls Redshank but back and rump uniformly grey.

CREAM-COLOURED COURSER p.99
Pale sandy; dark primaries and wing-linings. Feet trail behind tail.

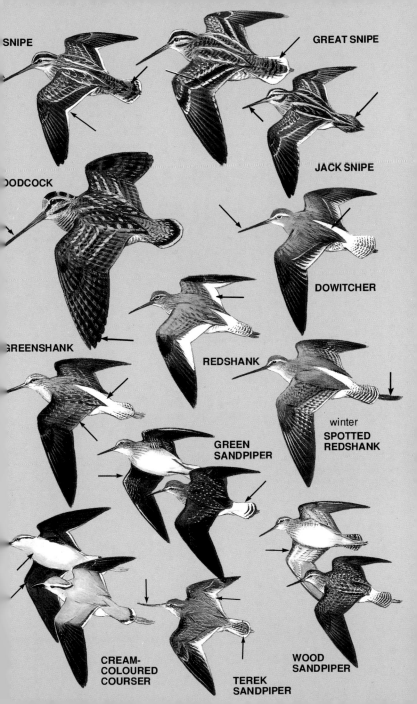

SNIPE

GREAT SNIPE

JACK SNIPE

WOODCOCK

DOWITCHER

GREENSHANK

REDSHANK

winter
SPOTTED
REDSHANK

GREEN
SANDPIPER

CREAM-
COLOURED
COURSER

TEREK
SANDPIPER

WOOD
SANDPIPER

Plate 52

WADERS IN FLIGHT

DUNLIN Map 138 p.110
Autumn: Brownish-grey; near size of Sanderling, but darker with less
conspicuous wing-bar.

PURPLE SANDPIPER Map 137 p.110
Winter: Slaty; white lateral tail-coverts and marks on inner wing.

KNOT Map 133 p.106
Winter: Stocky but long-winged; greyish with lightly barred rump and
grey tail.

CURLEW SANDPIPER p.110
Autumn: Suggests grey Dunlin but with rump entirely white.

SANDERLING Map 134 p.106
Winter: Pearly-grey; has most conspicuous wing-bar of any small
wader.

COMMON SANDPIPER Map 155 p.120
Identify by very shallow, fluttered wing-beats and stiffly bowed
wing-set when gliding. Wing-bar conspicuous.

LITTLE STINT Map 135 p.107
Juvenile: Very small; narrow but lengthy wing-bar; grey sides to tail.

TEMMINCK'S STINT Map 136 p.107
From Little Stint by duskier colour; white sides to tail.

RED-NECKED PHALAROPE Map 157 p.121
Juvenile: Striped back; bold wing-bars, and jet black centre to rump.

GREY PHALAROPE Map 158 p.122
Winter: Sanderling-like, but smaller and tubbier, with slightly less
contrasting wing-bar.

PECTORAL SANDPIPER p.109
Dark brown, with only a trace of a wing-bar; tail pattern between
Dunlin and Ruff.

STONE CURLEW Map 124 p.98
Long-bodied and -winged. Bold double white wing-bars.

RUFF Map 140 p.112
Insignificant wing-bar, but striking oval white patches almost join at
base of tail. Ruffed males in spring look dark- and full-chested.

DUNLIN

winter

PURPLE SANDPIPER

KNOT
winter

autumn

CURLEW SANDPIPER

winter

SANDERLING

COMMON SANDPIPER

LITTLE STINT

juvenile

juvenile

RED-NECKED PHALAROPE

GREY PHALAROPE

winter

TEMMINCK'S STINT

PECTORAL SANDPIPER

STONE CURLEW

♀
Reeve

RUFF

♂
spring

Plate 53

SKUAS

Skuas are dark, hawk-like seabirds which pursue other birds in a piratical manner. All immatures show white wing-flashes. Breeding adults of the three smaller species have elongated central tail-feathers (see drawing below). Arctic and Pomarine Skuas occur in light, intermediate and dark phases; their tail points are sometimes broken off. Immatures have stubbier central tail-feathers and are difficult to separate.

GREAT SKUA   p.124
Largest and most heavily built; dark ruddy-brown; large wing-flashes;
blunt tail.

ARCTIC SKUA   Map 159 p.123
Medium-sized; most variable plumage pattern; pointed central
tail-feathers.

POMARINE SKUA   p.123
Second largest, and most gull-like in shape; broad wing-bases;
scalloped flanks and under-wings; blunt (and partially twisted) central
tail-feathers.

LONG-TAILED SKUA   Map 160 p.124
Smallest and lightest; narrow wings; complete white collar on
hind-neck; no wing-flashes on adult; very long, flexible, pointed
central tail-feathers.

Arctic

Long-tailed

Pomarine

Tails of adult skuas

GREAT SKUA

ARCTIC SKUA
light phase

ARCTIC SKUA
dark phase

intermediate phase

ARCTIC SKUA

juvenile

juvenile

dark phase

breeding

light phase
POMARINE SKUA

LONG-TAILED SKUA

juvenile

Plate 54   ADULT GULLS

In identifying gulls, look particularly at wing patterns and note leg colours. All birds shown here are adults. The dark-headed species lose their hoods in winter.

GREAT BLACK-BACKED GULL   Map 170 p.131
Large size; black back and wings; flesh-coloured legs.

LESSER BLACK-BACKED GULL   Map 167 p.130
Size of Herring Gull; legs usually yellow or orange.
Northern forms: Dark (blackish or black back).
Southern form: Paler (dark grey back).

GLAUCOUS GULL   Map 169 p.131
Size of Great Black-backed Gull; white primaries; heavy angular head and bill.

ICELAND GULL   p.130
Size of Herring Gull, but head rounder and bill smaller; long white primaries.

IVORY GULL   p.132
Size of Common Gull; all white; black legs.

HERRING GULL   Map 168 p.130
Commonest large gull. Grey back and wings; black and white wing-tips; legs flesh (yellow in southern form).

COMMON GULL   Map 166 p.129
Smaller than Herring Gull; round head; greenish-yellow bill and legs.

KITTIWAKE   Map 171 p.132
Smaller than Common Gull. Solid black, 'dipped in ink' wing-tips; black legs.

AUDOUIN'S GULL   Map 165 p.128
Size between Herring and Common. Red bill with a black band, olive legs; black outer primaries contrast with pale grey wings.

LITTLE GULL*   Map 162 p.126
Smallest gull. The rounded wings are dusky below. Dark hood in summer.

SABINE'S GULL*   p.127
Smaller than Kittiwake. Black outer primaries; white triangle in wing; forked tail. Slaty head in summer.

BLACK-HEADED GULL*   Map 163 p.127
Commonest small gull. Long wedge of white on leading primaries; dusky under surface to outer wing; red bill and legs. Dark hood in summer.

MEDITERRANEAN GULL*   Map 161 p.125
Mainly white wings; extensive black hood in summer.

SLENDER-BILLED GULL   Map 164 p.128
Wings as Black-headed Gull, but head white. Bill long and drooping.

* Adults in winter lose their dark heads, which then resemble those of immatures (see Plate 55).

GLAUCOUS

GREAT
BLACK-BACKED

ICELAND

LESSER
BLACK-BACKED

HERRING

IVORY

COMMON

KITTIWAKE

below
winter

SABINE'S

above

winter

LITTLE
breeding

AUDOUIN'S

breeding

SLENDER-
BILLED

winter

BLACK-HEADED

MEDITERRANEAN

breeding

Plate 55

IMMATURE GULLS

Identifying immature gulls needs great care. They take from two to five years to assume adult plumage. Their successive plumages are best studied in a handbook such as The Birds of the Western Palearctic.

GREAT BLACK-BACKED GULL　　　　　　　　Map 170 p.131
Large size; more contrast between chequered back and pale under-parts than in young Herring Gull.

LESSER BLACK-BACKED GULL　　　　　　　Map 167 p.130
Very similar at first to young Herring Gull; almost uniform but wings and fore body darker; identification easier as birds grow older. See text.

GLAUCOUS GULL　　　　　　　　　　　　Map 169 p.131
First winter: Buffish, with 'waved' marks and paler primaries; striking black tip to bill.
Second winter: Very white throughout.
Iceland Gull has similar sequence of plumages but marks less 'waved', more spotted.

HERRING GULL　　　　　　　　　　　　　Map 168 p.130
First winter: Mottled muddy-brown;; northern birds with paler inner primaries than Lesser Black-backed.
Second winter: Whiter, with tail broadly black.

COMMON GULL　　　　　　　　　　　　　Map 166 p.129
From second-winter Herring Gull by narrower, sharper black band on the tail, smaller size, shorter bill.

KITTIWAKE　　　　　　　　　　　　　　Map 171 p.132
Dark diagonal 'zig-zag' band across wing; black hind-collar.

BLACK-HEADED GULL　　　　　　　　　　Map 163 p.127
Whitish outer primaries already obvious. Narrow black tail-band.

SABINE'S GULL　　　　　　　　　　　　　　p.125
Already shows adult's bold 'triangular' wing pattern; light flight; forked tail.

MEDITERRANEAN GULL　　　　　　　　　Map 161 p.125
From Black-headed Gull by stubbier bill, darker eye-patch, blackish (not whitish) leading primaries. From Common Gull by narrower tail-band and paler midwing panel.

LITTLE GULL　　　　　　　　　　　　　Map 162 p.126
Wing pattern as in immature Kittiwake but much smaller; wings more rounded; dark cap; lacks black bar on the nape.

GLAUCOUS
first winter

GREAT
BLACK-BACKED

second winter

GLAUCOUS
second winter

LESSER
BLACK-BACKED

first winter

second winter

HERRING

HERRING

COMMON

KITTIWAKE

BLACK-HEADED

SABINE'S

MEDITERRANEAN

LITTLE

Lower six species all first winter

Plate 56

RARE OR VAGRANT GULLS

GREAT BLACK-HEADED GULL   p.125
Large size; black band on big yellow bill; long flat forehead; black
band across white primaries.

LAUGHING GULL   p.126
Adult: Dark mantle blends into the black wing-tips. Black hood lost in
winter.
First winter: Dusky with contrasting white rump and white rear edge
of wing.

BONAPARTE'S GULL   p.127
At all ages, primaries white below, with black trailing edge.
Adult: Like small Black-headed but with thinner black bill.
First winter: Dark trailing edge on wing, and dark diagonal bar.

ROSS'S GULL   p.132
At all ages, rather long graduated tail.
Breeding adult: Tinged with pink below; narrow black necklace;
dusky wing-linings; delicate black bill; no black on wing-tips.
Winter adult: Loses most of pink tone and necklace.
First winter: Kittiwake-like pattern, but lacks neck collar.

RING-BILLED GULL   p.129
Size between Herring and Common but bill heavy.
Adult: Yellowish or pale greenish legs; black ring encircling bill.
First winter: Tail-band narrower than Herring and usually (but not
always) well-defined.

FRANKLIN'S GULL   p.126
Smaller, more compact than Laughing. Beware confusion with
immature Mediterranean.
Adult: Dusky mantle and inner wings contrast with white-black-white
wing-tips. Black hood lost in winter.
First winter: From Laughing by darker head-cap, paler inner primaries
and cleaner under-wing and body.

GREAT BLACK-HEADED GULL

lt
eding

adult winter

LAUGHING GULL

first winter

adult breeding

first winter

adult winter

adult winter

first winter

BONAPARTE'S GULL
dult reeding

ROSS'S GULL

first winter

adult winter

RING-BILLED GULL

adult

adult breeding

adult breeding

first winter

FRANKLIN'S GULL

Plate 57

TERNS

Terns are more slender in build, narrower of wing and more graceful in flight than gulls. Their bills are more slender and sharply pointed, usually held downward towards the water, especially when feeding. Tails are usually forked. Most terns are grey above and white below, with black caps in summer. See also Plate 59.

GULL-BILLED TERN Map 172 p.133
Stout, stubby almost gull-like black bill. Greyish rump and tail, latter only moderately forked.

SANDWICH TERN Map 174 p.134
Whitest of common terns, with shaggy cap. Long slender black bill has yellow tip, as though 'dipped in mayonnaise'.

CASPIAN TERN Map 173 p.133
Largest tern with heavy scarlet bill and gull-like flight. Dusky underside of primaries; cap streaked much of the year.

COMMON TERN Map 175 p.135
Adult breeding: Bill orange-red with a black tip. From above, note dark outer primaries contrasting with the paler grey of rest of the wing. From beneath, dark outer primaries contrast with the semi-transparent inner primaries.
Juvenile: White forehead; dark 'shoulders'.

ROSEATE TERN p.134
Looks as white as Sandwich, with similar but lighter silhouette.
Adult breeding: Rather short wings but longest tail-streamers of all. Bill largely black.
Juvenile: Paler 'shoulders' than Common; flecking on wings recalls Sandwich but wing tips pale.

ARCTIC TERN Map 176 p.135
Looks smaller-headed than Common, with even more buoyant flight.
Adult breeding: Greyer below than Common Tern; bill blood-red to the tip. From above, primaries show less contrast than Common. When overhead, flight-feathers translucent with well-defined border of black on the tips of the primaries.
Juvenile: Similar to Common Tern but shows sharp black border to primaries like adult, and much whiter secondaries.

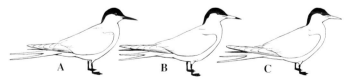

A Roseate Tern. Whitest of the three; tail extends well beyond short wings.
B Common Tern. Tail does not extend beyond the wing-tips.
C Arctic Tern. Greyer than Common Tern, with slightly longer tail and shorter legs.

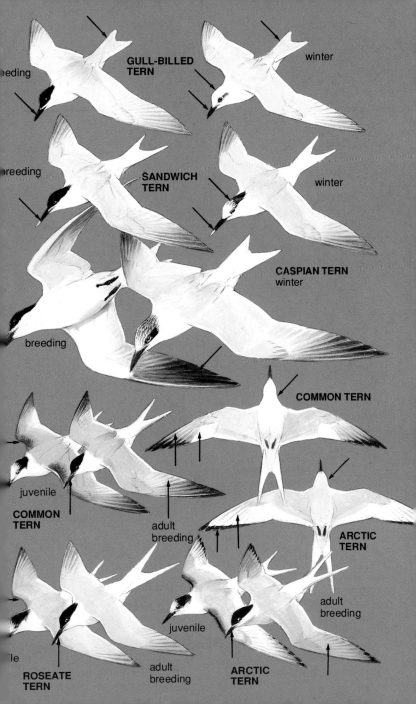

GULL-BILLED TERN

breeding

winter

breeding

SANDWICH TERN

winter

breeding

CASPIAN TERN
winter

COMMON TERN

juvenile

COMMON TERN

adult breeding

ARCTIC TERN

adult breeding

le

ROSEATE TERN

adult breeding

juvenile

ARCTIC TERN

Plate 58

TERNS

With the exception of the Little Tern, the species shown on this plate are 'marsh terns'.

WHISKERED TERN
Map 178 p.137

Adult breeding: Dusky underparts; white cheek.
Winter: Larger and paler than Black Tern; less black on the nape.
Mantle, rump and tail are nearly uniform pale grey. For juvenile, see text.

LITTLE TERN
Map 177 p.137

Smallest European sea tern with quickest wing-beats of all.
Adult breeding: Yellow bill with black tip; white forehead. Black outer primaries.
Juvenile: Black fore-edge of wing.

BLACK TERN
Map 179 p.137

Adult breeding: Black head and body; grey wings and tail; white wing-lining.
Winter: From White-winged Black Tern by dusky patch on the side of the neck. No contrast between grey mantle, rump and tail.
Juvenile: Black 'yoke' across top of back and fore wings.

WHITE-WINGED BLACK TERN
Map 180 p.138

Adult breeding: Black body and head; white upper wing-coverts; white rump and tail; black wing-lining.
Winter: Like Black Tern, but lacks the dark smudge on side of the neck. Unlike Whiskered or Black Tern, white rump contrasts strongly with grey mantle.
Juvenile: Dark brown 'saddle' between mainly pale wings.

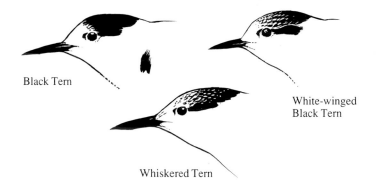

Black Tern

White-winged Black Tern

Whiskered Tern

Heads of Marsh Terns in Winter

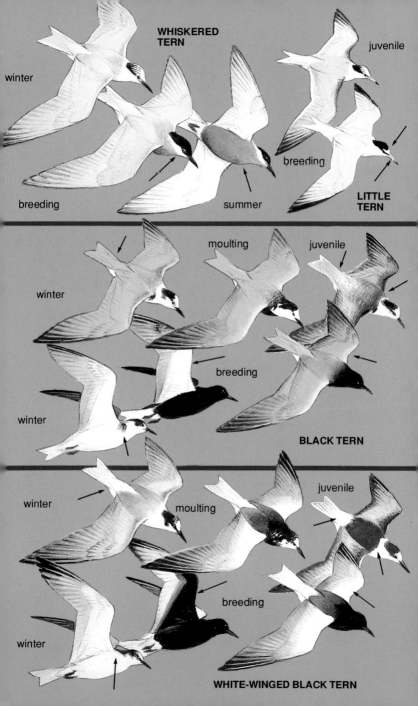

WHISKERED TERN

winter

juvenile

breeding

summer

breeding

LITTLE TERN

winter

moulting

juvenile

winter

breeding

BLACK TERN

winter

moulting

juvenile

winter

breeding

WHITE-WINGED BLACK TERN

Plate 59

HEADS OF TERNS

The bills and head patterns of terns are key identification features. In the breeding season, all terns have black caps. By late summer, they begin to acquire the white foreheads typical of winter plumage.

BLACK TERN
Map 179 p.137
Breeding: Black bill and head.
Winter: 'Pied' head (see text).
White-winged Black Tern similar but bill stubbier and crown in winter less black; see Plate 58 and text.

WHISKERED TERN
Map 178 p.137
Breeding: Wine-red bill, white cheeks, dusky throat and breast.
Winter: Bill darker (note dagger-like shape) and crown speckled.

LITTLE TERN
Map 177 p.137
Breeding: Yellow bill with black tip; white forehead and eyebrow.
Juvenile: Bill darker and crown dusky, speckled.

COMMON TERN
Map 175 p.135
Breeding: Orange-red bill with black tip.
Winter: Bill darker; black patch from eye around the nape.

ARCTIC TERN
Map 176 p.135
Breeding: Blood-red bill without black tip; note more rounded crown than Common.
Winter: Similar to Common Tern.

ROSEATE TERN
p.134
Breeding: Fine bill mostly black; some have considerable red at the base.
Winter: More slender bill than Common Tern.

GULL-BILLED TERN
Map 172 p.133
Breeding: Stout, black bill.
Winter: Black ear-patch; speckled nape.
Juvenile: Gull-like, due to restricted ear-patch.

SANDWICH TERN
Map 174 p.134
Breeding: Crested; black bill with yellow tip.
Winter: Similar, with large white forehead.

CASPIAN TERN
Map 173 p.133
Breeding: Huge, dagger-like scarlet bill; slight crest.
Winter: Dusky tip to bill; streaked forehead and crown.

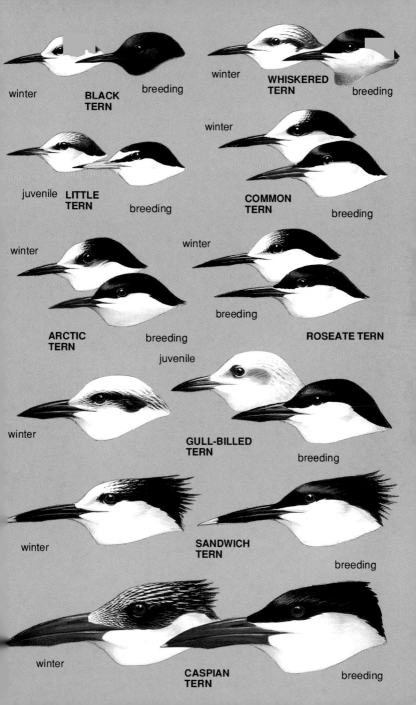

winter
BLACK TERN
breeding

winter
WHISKERED TERN
breeding

juvenile **LITTLE TERN**
breeding

winter
COMMON TERN
breeding

winter
ARCTIC TERN
breeding
juvenile

winter
ROSEATE TERN
breeding

winter
GULL-BILLED TERN
breeding

winter
SANDWICH TERN
breeding

winter
CASPIAN TERN
breeding

Plate 60

VAGRANT TERNS

These terns are strays from the western Atlantic or from the shores of western or northern Africa.

FORSTER'S TERN p.136

Frostier primaries than Common Tern's; bill more orange; tail greyer. In autumn and winter, both adults and immatures have a black mask through the eye and ear (but not around the nape).

ROYAL TERN p.248

Large but slimmer, more crested than Caspian Tern, with less deep, more orange bill. For most of the year, forehead clean white; non-breeding Caspian Tern has streaked forehead and crown.

LESSER CRESTED TERN p.134

About size of Sandwich Tern but with rich orange-yellow bill and more deeply forked tail.

SOOTY TERN p.136

Black above, white below; white forehead.
Immature: Dark brown; back spotted with white.

BRIDLED TERN p.248

Greyer on the back than Sooty Tern. Note the white collar or 'bridle' and whiter tail.

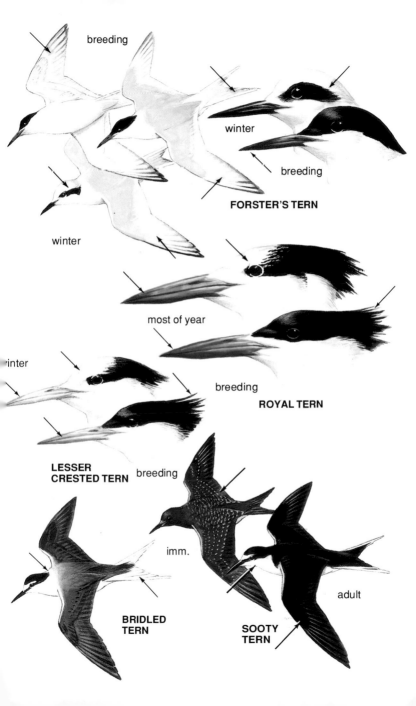

breeding

winter

FORSTER'S TERN

winter

breeding

winter

most of year

breeding

ROYAL TERN

inter

**LESSER
CRESTED TERN** breeding

imm.

**BRIDLED
TERN**

**SOOTY
TERN**

adult

Plate 61

AUKS

Auks are bustling black and white seabirds with stubby necks. They have a whirring flight, and a straddle-legged look when about to land. (See also Plate 62).

RAZORBILL
Map 182 p.139
Long, pointed tail; clean flanks.
Adult: Deep bill with white marks on heavy head.
Immature: Smaller bill, with curved ridge.

BRÜNNICH'S GUILLEMOT
p.139
Thicker-billed than Guillemot, with clean flanks.
Summer: Light mark along gape.
Winter: Dark cap to below the eye; lacks line across cheeks.

GUILLEMOT
Map 181 p.138
More slender-billed than Brünnich's and Razorbill, with streaked flanks.
Summer: Dark head; on some, striking spectacle or 'bridle'.
Winter: Black line across white cheek.

The **Great Auk** (inset, bottom left) was a large, flightless auk which frequented islands in the North Atlantic. The last known pair was killed in Iceland in 1844.

immature

breeding

RAZORBILL   winter

winter

BRÜNNICH'S GUILLEMOT

breeding

GUILLEMOT

winter

GUILLEMOT

breeding

BRÜNNICH'S

"bridled"
form

breeding

RAZORBILL

breeding

**GREAT
AUK**

Plate 62

AUKS

Most **auks** have an erect posture when on their nesting ledges by the sea (See also Plate 61).

Puffin   Razorbill   Guillemot   Black Guillemot

LITTLE AUK   p.140
Starling-size; stubby bill; 'neckless' form; dark underwing. Rapid wing-beats suggest wader.

BLACK GUILLEMOT   Map 183 p.140
Smaller, more compact than large auks.
Breeding: Black body; pointed bill; large oval white wing-patches. Feet and inside of mouth orange-red.
Winter: Mottled off-white body; large white wing-patches less contrasting.

PUFFIN   Map 184 p.140
Smaller, more compact than larger auks, with large bill and head; dusky underwing not as dark as Little Auk.
Breeding: Triangular, brightly-coloured bill; whitish cheeks.
Winter: Triangular bill, dusky cheeks.
Immature: Smaller bill, even duskier cheeks.

winter

winter

breeding

LITTLE AUK

winter

winter

breeding

breeding

BLACK GUILLEMOT

winter

breeding

immature

breeding

winter

PUFFIN

adults
summer

**BLACK
GUILLEMOT**

breeding

PUFFIN
breeding

LITTLE AUK

breeding

Plate 63

PIGEONS AND DOVES

The terms 'pigeon' and 'dove' are loosely used and often interchangeable. For the most part, 'pigeon' refers to the larger species, 'dove' to the smaller.

WOODPIGEON Map 187 p.143
Largest of family; white neck-patch on adult; white wing-patches, long banded tail.

ROCK DOVE Map 185 p.142
White rump; two bold black wing-bars; white underwings. The various feral and racing pigeons are descendants of this species and many still closely resemble it, in both form and plumage.

STOCK DOVE Map 186 p.143
Smaller, more compact than Woodpigeon; short black bars on the secondaries; light grey panels on upper-wings and rump; grey under-wing.

TURTLE DOVE Map 189 p.144
Smallest common European dove; scaled rufous back; long, deeply rounded, white-rimmed tail.

RUFOUS TURTLE DOVE p.144
Larger than Turtle Dove, close in size to Collared; heavy flight; edges of wing coverts whiter than Turtle Dove; hind-neck brown, not grey. Tail markings vary (see text).

LAUGHING DOVE p.144
Smaller than Turtle Dove, with proportionately longer tail; chequered black and rusty patch on the lower neck; dusky-blue wing panels. Restricted to S.E. Balkans and Turkey.

COLLARED DOVE Map 188 p.143
Larger than Turtle Dove, with longer, less rounded tail; black collar; white on outer half of under-tail.

Feral pigeons (descended from the Rock Dove) show a great variety of colour and pattern.

WOODPIGEON

ROCK DOVE

STOCK DOVE

RUFOUS TURTLE DOVE

TURTLE DOVE

LAUGHING DOVE

COLLARED DOVE

Plate 64

OWLS
(See also Plate 65)

Mainly nocturnal birds of prey with silent flight. Large headed, with facial discs and large eyes facing front.

SHORT-EARED OWL Map 201 p.151
Buffy-brown; strongly mottled and streaked, especially on breast; dark patches emphasise yellow eyes. Long, narrow wings jerked upwards in slow flight.

BARN OWL Map 191 p.147
Heart-shaped or roundish 'monkey' face; dark eyes; no breast streaks. Light flight, with frequent slow hover.
Light-breasted race: White below.
Dark-breasted race: Tawny below.

SCOPS OWL Map 192 p.147
Very small; plumage variable, mainly dull grey and rusty-brown. Erects short 'ears' on small head when alarmed. Long wings; rather dashing flight.

LONG-EARED OWL Map 200 p.150
Smaller than Short-eared; strictly nocturnal on territory; heavily and uniformly streaked below; amber eyes. Erects long 'ears' when alarmed; broader wings than Short-eared but flight similar.

SNOWY OWL Map 194 p.148
Large; white with dark bars; big yellow eyes; recalls Buzzard in flight. Male less barred than female; almost pure white when old.

EAGLE OWL Map 193 p.147
Huge; rusty, with streaks and bars; orange eyes; prominent 'ears'. Shallow wing-beats give fast flight.

SHORT-EARED OWL

dark-breasted race

light-breasted race

BARN OWL

SCOPS OWL

LONG-EARED OWL

SNOWY OWL

EAGLE OWL

Plate 65

OWLS
(See also Plate 64)

Most **owls** are nocturnal and therefore seldom seen well unless discovered at their daytime roosts or on passage. It is particularly important to learn their voices, which are described in the text. None of the following species has 'ear-tufts'.

LITTLE OWL   Map 197 p.149
Small, squat but with long legs; heavily spotted; often active by day; undulating flight.

TENGMALM'S OWL   Map 202 p.151
From Little Owl by larger head, broad 'eyebrows' on whiter face, more heavily outlined facial discs; strictly nocturnal; direct flight. Chocolate-brown juvenile unmistakable.

TAWNY OWL   Map 198 p.149
Stockily built; rufous or grey plumage; streaked breast; direct flight. Note large black eyes.

HAWK OWL   Map 195 p.148
Heavy black facial 'frames'; barred under-parts, long tail; recalls Sparrowhawk in flight.

PYGMY OWL   Map 196 p.148
Hawfinch-size; small-headed; cocks its tail; undulating flight.

URAL OWL   Map 199 p.150
Very large with long, graduated tail; buff-brown, streaked; unlined face; recalls Buzzard in flight. Note small dark eyes.

GREAT GREY OWL   p.150
Huge, grey; large round head, with concentric lines around face; small yellow eyes. Note black chin with white 'moustache'. Very slow flight.

LITTLE OWL

juvenile

adult

TENGMALM'S OWL

grey phase

rufous phase

TAWNY OWL

HAWK OWL

PYGMY OWL

URAL OWL

GREAT GREY OWL

Plate 66

HOOPOE, ROLLER, BEE-EATERS, KINGFISHERS

HOOPOE Map 210 p.156
Bold black and white barring across wings and tail; erectile fan-like
crest. Recalls butterfly in flight.

ROLLER Map 209 p.155
Blue-green head and breast; chestnut back. Vivid violet-blue flight
feathers catch eye in crow-like flight.

BLUE-CHEEKED BEE-EATER p.155
Long green body and tail streamers; red and yellow throat; touch of
blue on face; coppery underwing.

BEE-EATER Map 208 p.155
Long, blue under-body but short tail streamers; yellow throat; chestnut
and yellow above; pale rufous underwing.

PIED KINGFISHER p.155
Black and white; striped head and banded breast.

BELTED KINGFISHER p.155
Large with strong bill and bushy crest. Male has single broad grey
chest-band; female has additional lower rufous breast-band.

KINGFISHER Map 207 p.154
Small, stumpy; brilliant blue-green back; warm rufous under-parts.

HOOPOE

ROLLER

BLUE-
CHEEKED
BEE-EATER

BEE-EATER

PIED
KINGFISHER

♂

BELTED
KINGFISHER

KINGFISHER

Plate 67

CUCKOOS

CUCKOOMap 190 p.146
Grey head and upper breast; barred under-parts.
Rufous phase of female: Rare; barred above and below.

GREAT SPOTTED CUCKOOp.145
Crested, with very long tail; heavily spotted above, creamy below.
Immature: Black cap, rufous panel on outer wing.

YELLOW-BILLED CUCKOOp.146
Yellow lower mandible; large white tail-spots; chestnut panel on
primaries.

BLACK-BILLED CUCKOOp.146
All black bill, small dull tail-spots; no chestnut on wing.

rufous phase
(♀ only)

CUCKOO

adult

EAT SPOTTED CUCKOO

immature

YELLOW-BILLED CUCKOO

BLACK-BILLED CUCKOO

under-tail patterns

Plate 68

NIGHTJARS

All **nightjars** share falcon-like silhouette, but in poor light at dawn and dusk, their silent flight is a characteristic mix of stiff wing-beats and loose glides. Difficult to find on ground except when resting on road or path.

NIGHTJAR
Map 203 p.152

'Dead leaf' or 'bark' camouflage above, closely barred below.
Voice: Churring song after dark; call soft nasal *goo-ek*, recalling frog.

RED-NECKED NIGHTJAR
p.152

Larger and longer-tailed than Nightjar with rustier upper-parts, especially on nape, and more white on the throat.
Voice: Male utters incessantly repeated *kutuk-kutuk-kutuk......*, recalling steam engine.

EGYPTIAN NIGHTJAR
p.152

Smaller, paler, sandier than Nightjar, with no obvious white marks on wings and tail.
Voice: Nightjar-like, rapidly repeated *kour*, sounding hollow.

COMMON NIGHTHAWK
p.249

Smaller, darker, greyer than Nightjar and less crepuscular; slightly forked tail and bold white bands across long pointed wings and tail.
Voice: Nasal '*peent*' (not yet heard in Europe).

NIGHTJAR

RED-NECKED NIGHTJAR

EGYPTIAN NIGHTJAR

COMMON NIGHTHAWK

Plate 69 WOODPECKERS AND WRYNECK

All these species are more often heard than seen, particularly in breeding season when they use drumming to announce presence. Facial, back and ventral patterns are important to their separation.

GREAT SPOTTED WOODPECKER   Map 215 p.158
Commonest of family; large white scapular patches, black crown and full bar across lower face. Juvenile has red crown. Note red vent and unmarked underbody. Drums frequently but rapid roll short.

SYRIAN WOODPECKER   Map 216 p.158
Like Great Spotted, but white face lacks complete cross-bar. Drum roll longer.

MIDDLE SPOTTED WOODPECKER   Map 217 p.158
Resembles juvenile Great Spotted, but black face marks not joined; red cap lacks black border. Note pink, not red, vent and streaked flanks. Drum roll weak, infrequent.

LESSER SPOTTED WOODPECKER   Map 219 p.159
Sparrow-size with barred back. Note pale vent and streaks on underbody. Drum roll rather slow, rattling.

WHITE-BACKED WOODPECKER   Map 218 p.159
Largest of pied woodpeckers; white lower back separates strongly barred wings. Note pink vent and streaked flanks. Drum roll strong but accelerates in faint ending.

BLACK WOODPECKER   Map 214 p.157
Crow-size; black. Male has fully red crown; female red on rear crown only. Drum roll long and powerful.

THREE-TOED WOODPECKER   Map 220 p.159
White-centred or -barred back; barred flanks; black cheeks. Male has yellow cap. Drum roll longer and slower than Great Spotted.

GREY-HEADED WOODPECKER   Map 212 p.157
Grey head with isolated narrow black 'moustaches'; olive-greenish back. Only the male has the red cap. Juvenile like female. Drum roll frequent, louder than Green. Laugh more musical than Green.

GREEN WOODPECKER   Map 213 p.157
Dark face with joined dark 'moustache'; greenish back contrasts with yellowish rump. Juvenile spotted. Drums infrequently; roll long but surprisingly faint.

WRYNECK   Map 211 p.156
Long barred tail; Nightjar-like plumage. Call suggests falcon.

Lesser Spotted	Middle Spotted	Great Spotted	White-backed

juvenile

♂

MIDDLE
SPOTTED

♀

♂

GREAT
SPOTTED

SYRIAN

LESSER
SPOTTED

♂

♀

♂

WHITE-BACKED

BLACK

♂

THREE-TOED

♀

♂

juvenile

♂

GREY-HEADED

GREEN

WRYNECK

Plate 70

LARKS

Streaked, mainly brown ground-birds which sing in the air. They somewhat resemble pipits (Plate 72) because of their whitish outer tail-feathers, but are mostly heavier, with broader wings and tails.

SKYLARK   Map 225 p.163
Commonest of family, with short crest and white edges to rear wing and on longish tail.

WOODLARK   Map 224 p.162
From Skylark by short tail without white sides; supercilia meet on nape; black and white mark on wing-edge.

CRESTED LARK   Map 223 p.162
Long spikey crest; short tawny-edged tail; buff lining to rounded wings.

SHORE LARK   Map 226 p.163
Adult 'horned'; black patches on face and breast; yellow throat. Immature lacks 'horns' but shows similar facial marks.

THEKLA LARK   p.162
Very like Crested Lark, crest less spikey, neck and breast more boldly marked; grey lining to wings.

CALANDRA LARK   Map 221 p.160
Largest lark breeding in Europe. Thick heavy bill; black neck-patch. In flight, shows whitish rear edges to dark under-wings.

SHORT-TOED LARK   Map 222 p.161
Small; pale sandy or grey with clear breast; small neck-spot. Note complete cloaking of primaries by tertials.

LESSER SHORT-TOED LARK   p.161
Even smaller than Short-toed; grey-brown; finely streaked breast. Note clear extension of primaries beyond tertials.

WHITE-WINGED LARK   p.160
Rusty crown; large white wing-patches. Beware confusion with Snow Bunting.

BLACK LARK   p.161
Large male all black, in winter 'scaled' with white. Female noticeably smaller; recalls Calandra but lacks white trailing edge to wing.

DUPONT'S LARK   p.160
Thin curved bill and long legs, giving upright stance; conspicuous eye-stripe; no white in wings.

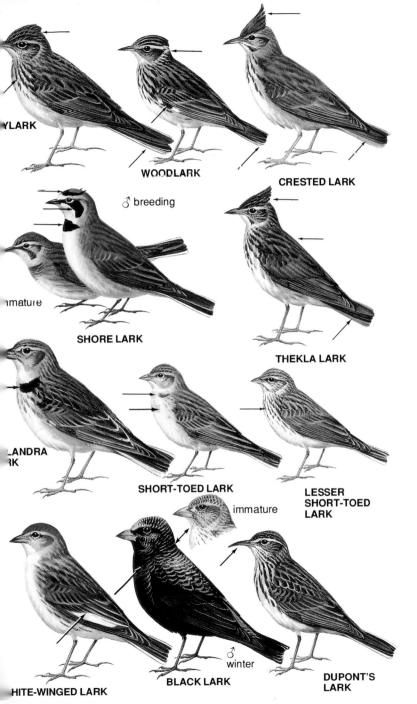

YLARK

WOODLARK

CRESTED LARK

♂ breeding

immature

SHORE LARK

THEKLA LARK

LANDRA RK

SHORT-TOED LARK

LESSER SHORT-TOED LARK

immature

♂ winter

WHITE-WINGED LARK

BLACK LARK

DUPONT'S LARK

Plate 71 SWIFTS, MARTINS AND SWALLOWS

Swifts are swallow-like, but structurally distinct, with a flat skull and all four toes pointing forward. Flight very rapid, 'twinkling', sailing between spurts, with narrow wings often stiffly bowed.

SWIFT Map 204 p.153
Almost completely blackish; short forked tail; small white throat.

PALLID SWIFT Map 205 p.153
Slightly bulkier and paler than Swift; dark outer primaries and wing-pits; broader white throat; dark eye-patch. Flies more slowly.

ALPINE SWIFT Map 206 p.154
Very large; dark breast-band separates white throat and belly, suggesting giant Sand Martin. Powerful flight.

WHITE-RUMPED SWIFT p.154
Much smaller and slimmer than Swift; longer tail forks; narrow white rump. Breeds only in southern Spain. Smaller scale than above.

LITTLE SWIFT p.154
Smallest, most compact of family; square tail; wide, deep white rump. Scale as White-rumped Swift.

Swallows are sparrow-sized birds characterized by slim, stream-lined form and graceful flight. Long, pointed wings; short bills with wide gapes; tiny feet.

HOUSE MARTIN Map 231 p.165
Velvet-black upper-parts interrupted by white rump; white under-parts.

SWALLOW Map 229 p.164
Deeply forked tail with narrow streamers; red face and dark breast-band; pale under tail-coverts.

RED-RUMPED SWALLOW Map 230 p.165
Tail streamers shorter, less narrow, than Swallow. Buff nape and rump; pale throat and underbody ending in dark under tail-coverts.

SAND MARTIN Map 227 p.164
Uniformly brown upper-parts; broad band across breast interrupts white underbody.

CRAG MARTIN Map 228 p.164
Brown upper-parts; no breast-band on dull under-parts; square tail with white spots when spread.

| Swallow | House Martin | Red-rumped Swallow | Sand Martin |

PALLID SWIFT

SWIFT

WHITE-RUMPED SWIFT

LITTLE SWIFT

ALPINE SWIFT

HOUSE MARTIN

SWALLOW

RED-RUMPED SWALLOW

SAND MARTIN

CRAG MARTIN

Plate 72

PIPITS

Pipits are streaked brown ground-birds with white, or whitish, outer tail-feathers and long claws. They may suggest larks (Plate 70) but are more slender, and wag their tails like wagtails to which they are closely related. Calls are important to identification.

MEADOW PIPIT Map 234 p.167
Commonest of family; usually olive, streaked above and below. Note thin shrill *weesk* or *tseep* call, often repeated, and long hind claw.

TREE PIPIT Map 233 p.167
Slightly larger than Meadow Pipit, with buffer colour, less streaked flanks and pinker legs. Note short hoarse *dzeez* call and short hind claw.

ROCK PIPIT Map 236 p.168
Strictly coastal except when migrating. Dark legs; greyish outer tail-feathers; little marked head except in Scandinavian form. Note *weest* call, more emphatic than Meadow.

WATER PIPIT Map 237 p.168
Breeds in mountains but descends to freshwater marshes in winter; shares dark legs with Rock. White outer tail-feathers.
Breeding: Pinkish unstreaked breast; greyish upper-parts.
Winter: White supercilium; streaked whitish breast.
Call similar to Rock.

TAWNY PIPIT Map 232 p.166
Slim, with long legs and tail.
Adult: Tawny unstreaked breast.
Immature: More streaked than adult; beware confusion with Richard's.
Note calls which recall House Sparrow and Yellow Wagtail.

RICHARD'S PIPIT p.165
Largest of family, with stout legs and very long hind claw; heavily streaked breast and back. Note shouted *schreep* call and pre-landing hover.

RED-THROATED PIPIT Map 235 p.168
Best separated from Meadow and Tree by streaked rump and thin, lengthy *pseeze* call.
Breeding: Variable brick-red throat.
Winter: From Meadow Pipit by usually rustier plumage and blacker, heavier streaks.

PECHORA PIPIT p.167
Shortest tail of family. Strong white back stripes and wing-bars; buffy outer tail-feathers difficult to see. Note short hard *pwit* call.

OLIVE-BACKED PIPIT p.166
Recalls Tree but rather olive back little streaked. Note white supercilium and spot behind ear-coverts. Note call which recalls both Tree and Red-throated.

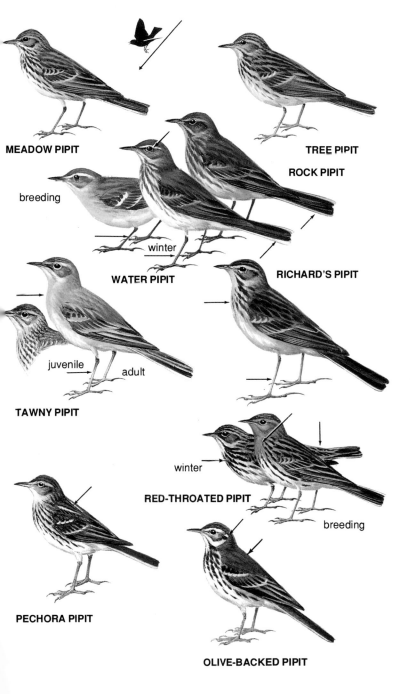

MEADOW PIPIT

TREE PIPIT

ROCK PIPIT

breeding

winter

WATER PIPIT

RICHARD'S PIPIT

juvenile   adult

TAWNY PIPIT

winter

RED-THROATED PIPIT

breeding

PECHORA PIPIT

OLIVE-BACKED PIPIT

Plate 73

WAGTAILS

Wagtails are boldly patterned ground-birds, more slender and much longer-tailed than pipits. Some pipits and all wagtails wag their tails. See further analysis of wagtail species and subspecies on Plate 74.

YELLOW/BLUE-HEADED WAGTAIL   Map 238 p.169
All forms show yellow under-parts and olive-green back when adult; under-parts less yellow in juveniles.
Yellow Wagtail: Yellow and olive head in male and female.
Blue-headed Wagtail: Blue-grey cap and cheeks; white supercilium in male.
Note high *dzeep* call.

PIED/WHITE WAGTAIL   Map 240 p.170
No yellow in any plumage.
Pied Wagtail: Black back and rump; black cap and bib joined.
White Wagtail: Grey back and rump; black cap and bib separated.
Note disyllabic *chizzick* call.

GREY WAGTAIL   Map 239 p.169
Yellow under-tail, grey back in all plumages; tail longer than other wagtails.
Breeding: Male has black throat.
Note high-pitched, ringing *tzi-zist* call.

CITRINE WAGTAIL   p.169
Adult recalls Yellow, immature Pied.
Male: Yellow head; black hind-collar before grey back.
Female: Browner, duller above; lacks black hind-collar.
Immature: Difficult to separate from palest Blue-headed Wagtail; see text.
Note strident *tsreep* call, usually harsher than Yellow.

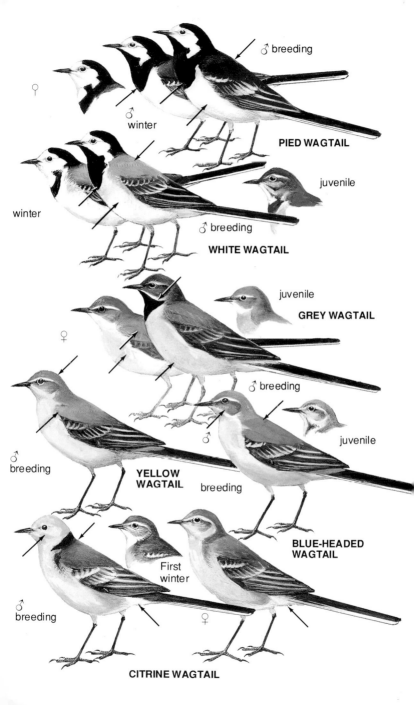

♀

♂ breeding

♂ winter

PIED WAGTAIL

winter

juvenile

♂ breeding

WHITE WAGTAIL

juvenile

GREY WAGTAIL

♀

♂ breeding

♂

♂ breeding

YELLOW WAGTAIL

breeding

juvenile

BLUE-HEADED WAGTAIL

♂ breeding

First winter

♀

CITRINE WAGTAIL

Plate 74   **HEADS OF WAGTAILS**

WHITE WAGTAIL GROUP *Motacilla alba*   Map 240 p.170
Distinguished by lack of yellow or olive in plumage.

PIED WAGTAIL
M.a. yarrelli. Back and rump black (male) or very dark (female).
Black cap and black bib are joined in adults. Breeds in British Isles
and adjacent shores of Continent.

WHITE WAGTAIL
M.a. alba. Clean grey back and rump. Black cap and
black bib separated. Breeds on the Continent.

GREY WAGTAIL *Motacilla cinerea*   Map 239 p.169
Distinguished by grey back, bold white wing-bar (showing through
wing), yellow underparts.
Male breeding: Black throat.
Female and male in winter: Whitish throat.

YELLOW WAGTAIL GROUP *Motacilla flava*   Map 238 p.169
Distinguished by olive-green back; yellow under-parts.

YELLOW WAGTAIL
M.f. flavissima. Yellow and olive heads. Breeds in the British Isles, a
few on adjacent shores of the Continent.

BLUE-HEADED WAGTAIL
M.f. flava. Male breeding: Full white supercilium; yellow throat.
Central Europe (in area not occupied by other races).

SPANISH WAGTAIL
M.f. iberiae: Male breeding: Short white supercilium starting from
eye; white throat. Breeds in Spain and Portugal, races merging in
southern France.

ASHY-HEADED WAGTAIL
M.f. cinereocapilla. Male breeding: Grey crown and cheek; usually no
supercilium; white throat. Italy, Corsica, Sardinia, Sicily, Albania.

GREY-HEADED WAGTAIL
M.f. thunbergi. Male breeding: Grey crown, blackish cheek; no
supercilium; yellow throat. Central and northern Scandinavia.

BLACK-HEADED WAGTAIL
M.f. feldegg. Male breeding: Black cap and cheek; no supercilium;
yellow throat. Louder call.

Note: Systematics of the Yellow Wagtail group are complex. Some authors
classify various forms as distinct species but intergradation occurs where ranges
overlap. Furthermore, mutants resembling other races breed with birds of normal
appearance. Thus birds identical with Sykes's Wagtail *M.f. beema* of Russia
have breed with normal Yellow Wagtails *M.f. flavissima* in England.

PIED

♂ breeding

♀

winter

juvenile

♂ breeding

winter

WHITE WAGTAIL

♂ breeding

♀ breeding

winter

GREY WAGTAIL

juvenile

♂ breeding

winter

YELLOW

♂ breeding

♂ breeding

winter

SPANISH

BLUE-HEADED WAGTAIL

Y-HEADED

♂ breeding

GREY-HEADED

♂ breeding

BLACK-HEADED

Plate 75

WHEATEARS

Wheatears are ground-loving birds of open country, often flying up to perches and then showing distinctive black and white patterns on tail; all have white rumps. See examples of patterns on plate.

NORTHERN WHEATEAR
Map 255 p.177

Commonest of family, widespread on passage.
Breeding male: Grey back; black mask.
Female and winter: Brown above, buff below.

BLACK-EARED WHEATEAR
Map 256 p.178

Breeding male: Pale whitish or sandy back but black scapulars and wings.
Female and winter: Buff back; indistinct supercilium; orange-buff chest band.

DESERT WHEATEAR
p.179

Recalls Black-eared Wheatear but scapulars pale like back; mainly black tail. Breeding male has wholly black throat joined to wings.

ISABELLINE WHEATEAR
p.176

Sandy-grey above, with palest wings of all wheatears; tail largely black; large bill and long legs, showing thighs. Look for diagnostic whitish under-wing. Beware confusion with pale Greenland Wheatear; see text.

PIED WHEATEAR
p.177

Breeding male: Black back and throat, white crown.
Female and winter: Duller than Black-eared, with pale tips to upperpart feathers.

BLACK WHEATEAR
Map 257 p.179

Largest of family. Wholly black head and body.

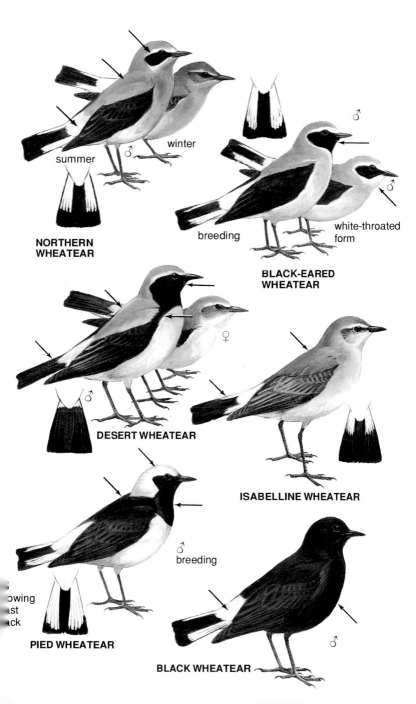

summer

winter

♂

**NORTHERN
WHEATEAR**

♂

♂
white-throated
form

breeding

**BLACK-EARED
WHEATEAR**

♀

♂

DESERT WHEATEAR

ISABELLINE WHEATEAR

♂
breeding

owing
st
ck

PIED WHEATEAR

♂

BLACK WHEATEAR

Plate 76

ROBINS, CHATS, NIGHTINGALES

Robins, Stonechats and Whinchats show themselves well but **Bluethroats** and the **Nightingales** skulk in dense cover. Rump and tail patterns are important to identification.

ROBIN
Map 247 p.173

Epitome of tribe.
Adult: Orange face and breast, redder in British race.
Juvenile: Spotted and barred.

STONECHAT
Map 254 p.176

Male: Black head; white half-collar above rusty breast; white rump in breeding plumage.
Female: Dark brown, with suggestion of male's pattern.
Eastern race distinctive, with pale supercilium and throat; bold pale rump. See text.

WHINCHAT
Map 253 p.175

White stripes outline dark cheeks; white patches by tail base. Male has orange throat and breast; female and juvenile buffier below.

BLUETHROAT
Map 250 p.174

Shows pale supercilium and orange patches by tail base.
Male: Blue throat with red or white spot.
Female: U-shaped necklace around white throat.

NIGHTINGALE
Map 249 p.173

Rufous-brown back; broad chestnut tail; plain breast.

THRUSH NIGHTINGALE
Map 248 p.173

Greyer above, with less chestnut in tail; mottled breast.

juvenile

ROBIN

adult

♂ winter

Eastern race

♀

adults

♂ breeding

STONECHAT

♂

♀

WHINCHAT

♂ breeding

red-spotted form

♀

BLUETHROAT

♂ breeding

white-spotted form

NIGHTINGALE

THRUSH NIGHTINGALE

Plate 77
REDSTARTS, BLUETAIL, ROCK THRUSHES

The **redstarts** and **Rock Thrush** share bright rusty rumps and tails and perch in the open, like **Blue Rock Thrush**. The **Red-flanked Bluetail** skulks but has a distinctive call.

BLACK REDSTART
Map 251 p.175

Male: Black with white panel on wings.
Female: Dirty grey with dull wings.

REDSTART
Map 252 p.175

Male: Grey crown and back, white forehead, black bib; orange underparts.
Female: Brown above, buff below.

RED-FLANKED BLUETAIL
p.174

Male: Deep blue above and on tail; orange flanks.
Female: Dusky with clouded chest emphasizing white throat, pale eye-ring; orange flanks.
Note short hard calls.

ROCK THRUSH
Map 258 p.179

Male: Blue head, white back, orange under-parts.
Female: Mottled and barred.

BLUE ROCK THRUSH
Map 259 p.180

Male: Slaty blue head and body.
Female: Dusky above; barred and spotted below.

BLACK REDSTART

REDSTART

RED-FLANKED BLUETAIL

ROCK THRUSH
breeding

BLUE ROCK THRUSH

Plate 78

THRUSHES

BLACKBIRD Map 261 p.182
Male: All black, with yellow bill and eye-ring.
Female: Dark brown, with lightly streaked throat.

RING OUZEL Map 260 p.181
Black, with white crescent on breast; pale feather-edges on wings.

FIELDFARE Map 262 p.183
Grey head and rump; rusty back; heavy breast spotting.

SONG THRUSH Map 263 p.183
Brown, with spotted under-parts; buff wing-linings.

MISTLE THRUSH Map 265 p.184
Larger, greyer than Song; bolder, rounder spots; white wing-linings
and tail-corners.

REDWING Map 264 p.184
Reddish flanks and wing-linings; cream supercilium and surround to
cheeks.

WHITE'S THRUSH p.180
Bold 'scaly' pattern above and below; black and white wing-linings.

DUSKY THRUSH p.182
Black breast-bands; pale supercilium and dark cheeks. Dusky and
Naumann's Thrushes intergrade; they are races of same species.

NAUMANN'S THRUSH p.182
Rusty breast; rusty wings.

BLACK-THROATED THRUSH p.183
Hood and bib contrast with white under-parts. Black-throated and
Red-throated are races of same species.

RED-THROATED THRUSH p.183
Rufous supercilium, throat and breast.

SIBERIAN THRUSH p.180
Male: Slate-black, with striking white supercilium.
Female: Grey-brown, with pale supercilium, and mottles below.

AMERICAN ROBIN p.185
Brick-red below; grey back and blackish head; broken eye-ring.

EYE-BROWED THRUSH p.182
Grey upper breast; rusty sides; pale supercilium.

BLACKBIRD

♂ ♀

RING OUZEL

♂

FIELDFARE

SONG THRUSH

MISTLE THRUSH

REDWING

RARE THRUSHES

'HITE'S

DUSKY

BLACK-THROATED

♂

1st winter

SIBERIAN

♂

♀

AMERICAN ROBIN

♂

NAUMANN'S

♂

RED-THROATED

♂

EYE-BROWED

Plate 79

SWAMP WARBLERS
NO STREAKS ON THE BACK

Field Marks and Habitat

Song

REED WARBLER
Brown above; buffish-white below; only faint supercilium. *Reeds, marshes.*

Map 275 p.190

Phrases repeated 2-3 times: *chirruc-chirruc, jag-jag-jag*, etc.

GREAT REED WARBLER
Very large size; obvious supercilium; strong bill. *Reed-beds.*

Map 276 p.191

Strident *karra-karra, krik-krik, gurk-gurk*, etc.

MARSH WARBLER
More olive above and paler below than Reed Warbler, with shorter bill and pale spectacle round eye. *Wet thickets, ditches by rivers.*

Map 274 p.190

More musical and more varied tempo than Reed Warbler, with canary-like trills, mimicry, etc.

CETTI'S WARBLER
Dark rufous, with pale supercilium and greyish breast; cocks tail. *Dense thickets, bushy ditches.*

Map 266 p.185

Loud abrupt burst, chiefly repetition of *cheweeoo.*

SAVI'S WARBLER
Like large Reed Warbler but tail longer, broader and rounder. *Reed-beds.*

Map 270 p.187

Trill like Grasshopper Warbler but lower, faster, lacking reeling tone.

RIVER WARBLER
Olive-toned above; soft streaks on breast. *Thickets, dense herbage.*

Map 269 p.187

Rapid but quiet *chuff* notes, clearly separated.

WITH STREAKS ON THE BACK

SEDGE WARBLER
Creamy supercilium, tawny rump. *Widespread; from reeds to wet scrub.*

Map 273 p.188

Chatter more varied and hurried than Reed Warbler; includes trills, mimicry.

MOUSTACHED WARBLER
From Sedge Warbler by blacker cap, whiter eye-stripe, rustier back. *Reed-beds, swamps.*

Map 271 p.188

Recalls Reed Warbler but sweeter, includes phrase suggesting Woodlark's *lu-lu-lu-lu.*

GRASSHOPPER WARBLER
Mottled olive-brown upperparts; indistinct supercilium. *Marshy undergrowth, grassy scrub.*

Map 268 p.187

Long reeling trill or buzzing on high note.

AQUATIC WARBLER
Golden-buff crown stripe and supercilium. *Open marshes, sedge.*

Map 272 p.188

Recalls Sedge Warbler but phrases shorter, tempo more even.

FAN-TAILED WARBLER
Heavily streaked; plain face, short, well marked tail. *Marshes, crops.*

Map 267 p.186

Sings in air, lisping *zip..zip..zip* (or *dzeep*).

GREAT REED

REED

MARSH

CETTI'S

SAVI'S

RIVER

SEDGE

MOUSTACHED

GRASSHOPPER

AQUATIC

ZIP ··· ZIP ··· ZIP ··· ZIP ··· ZIP ··· ZIP ···

FAN-TAILED

Plate 80

SCRUB WARBLERS, etc.

Mostly *Sylvia*. With distinctive marks and 'capped' appearance.

Field Marks and Habitat

Song

BLACKCAP
Black cap above eye in male; rufous in female. *Trees with undergrowth.*

Map 290 p.197
Rich warbling phrases; more varied and shorter than Garden Warbler.

ORPHEAN WARBLER
Black cap surrounds white eye. *Open woodland, orchards, groves.*

Map 285 p.196
Mellow thrush-like warble; phrases repeated 4-5 times.

SARDINIAN WARBLER
Black cap surrounds eye; red eye-ring; flanks grey; cocks tail. *Dry scrub in open country or wood.*

Map 284 p.195
Recalls Whitethroat, but longer, with staccato *cha-cha-cha-cha.*

WHITETHROAT
White throat, rusty fringes on wing; pale legs. *Bushes, bramble patches.*

Map 288 p.197
Short, scratchy, urgent chatter, often from display-flight.

LESSER WHITETHROAT
Dark mask, dull wings; dark legs. *Tall hedgerows, shrubbery.*

Map 287 p.196
Unmusical rattling on one note, often from high song-post.

RÜPPELL'S WARBLER
Black throat; white moustache in male. *Rocky scrub in Aegean.*

p.195
Like Sardinian Warbler; notes interspersed with loud pulsating rattle.

SPECTACLED WARBLER
Like small Whitethroat with shorter tail; white eye-ring; pinker breast. *Dry scrub around Mediterranean.*

Map 282 p.194
Short and Whitethroat-like; quieter, without grating notes.

SUBALPINE WARBLER
Orange breast; pale moustache; red eye-ring in male. *Bushes, wood edges and glades.*

Map 283 p.194
Recalls Sardinian Warbler and Linnet; lacks hard scolding notes.

DARTFORD WARBLER
Dark vinous breast; cocked tail. *Gorse, low scrub etc.*

Map 281 p.194
Musical chatter with liquid notes; recalls Whitethroat.

MARMORA'S WARBLER
Dark slaty breast in male. *Low scrub in W. Mediterranean.*

p.193
Resembles Dartford Warbler, but less harsh.

BARRED WARBLER
Barred breast; wing-bars at all ages. *Thorny thickets, bushes.*

Map 286 p.196
Resembles poor Blackcap; more rapid, scratchier and briefer phrases.

RUFOUS BUSH ROBIN
Rufous; bold supercilium; large fan tail. *Gardens, groves around Mediterranean.*

Map 246 p.172
Musical, disjointed, some phrases recalling Skylark and thrush.

BLACKCAP

ORPHEAN WARBLER

SARDINIAN WARBLER

♂

WHITETHROAT

LESSER WHITETHROAT

RÜPPELL'S WARBLER

♀ ♂

♀ ♂

SPECTACLED WARBLER

SUBALPINE

MARMORA'S WARBLER

♂ ♂ ♂

♂

DARTFORD WARBLER

♂

brown-backed race

adult

rufous race

BARRED WARBLER

RUFOUS BUSH ROBIN

immature

Plate 81 **LEAF WARBLERS**

Field Marks and Habitat Voice

WILLOW WARBLER
Map 296 p.201

'Cleaner' than Chiffchaff, with more
distinct supercilium, long wings and
(usually) pale legs. *Bushes, small trees.*

Liquid musical cascade; downscale ending in sad-sweet flourish. Call soft, almost disyllabic *houeet.*

CHIFFCHAFF
Map 295 p.201

'Dirtier' than Willow Warbler, with more
distinct eye-ring, darker bill and (usually)
dark legs. Eastern races paler, often showing
long wing-bar and then suggesting Greenish
Warbler. *Trees; bushes on migration.*

Deliberately repeated *chiff-chaff-chiff-
chiff- chaff* delivered from high song-post.
Call short *huit.*

ARCTIC WARBLER
Map 292 p.198

Strong bill; long supercilium; wing-bar; pale
legs. *Arctic forests.*

Short, high trill *ziz-ziz-ziz.* Call husky
tsssp.

GREENISH WARBLER
Map 291 p.197

Weak bill, long supercilium; short wing-bar;
dark legs. *Forests, coppices.*

Loud, high-pitched jingle merging into a
trill or gabble. Call sharp *see-wee.*

YELLOW-BROWED WARBLER
p.199

Long supercilium; two wing bars, lower
emphasized by dark band. *Deciduous
canopies.*

Call sharp *see-veest,* recalling Coal Tit.

BONELLI'S WARBLER
Map 293 p.200

Pale head; greenish wings; yellow rump.
Pine forest, cork groves.

Loose trill on the same note, flatter than
Wood Warbler. Call drawn-out *doo-eee.*

WOOD WARBLER
Map 294 p.201

Bold supercilium; yellow throat; white
belly. *Hanging woodlands and deciduous
forest.*

Repeated notes on one pitch, accelerating
into a dry trill. Call sharp *zip.*

TREE WARBLERS

ICTERINE WARBLER
Map 279 p.192

Striking wing panel; long wings; bluish
legs. *Woods with undergrowth in N.E. and
C. Europe.*

Pleasing jumble of notes, each repeated;
some discordant, many mimic other song-
birds. Musical call.

MELODIOUS WARBLER
Map 280 p.193

No striking wing panel; short wings;
brownish legs. *Woods and scrub in S.W.
Europe.*

Prolonged warbling chatter, faster than Icterine. House Sparrow-like call.

OLIVE-TREE WARBLER
Map 278 p.192

Big bill; pale patch on wing. *Olive groves,
oaks.*

Louder, slower, deeper than relatives, recalling Great Reed Warbler.

OLIVACEOUS WARBLER
Map 277 p.191

Long bill; short wings; mousy. *Open damp
woods and scrub.*

Vigorous but slow chatter, at times recalling Reed Warbler.

GARDEN WARBLER
Map 289 p.197

Unmarked, brownish. *Woods, hedges,
thickets.*

Mellow babble, suggesting Blackcap but
longer, less varied.

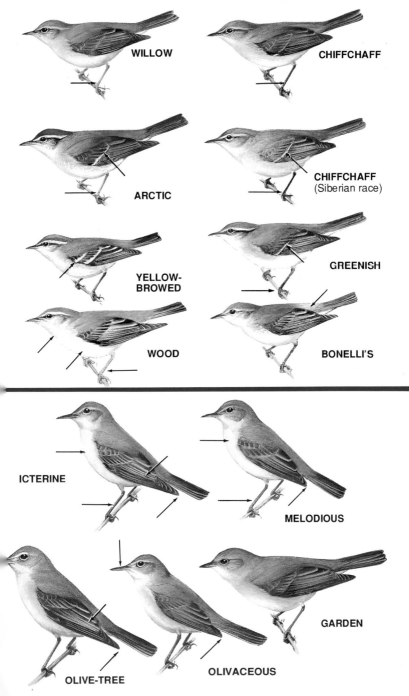

WILLOW

CHIFFCHAFF

ARCTIC

CHIFFCHAFF
(Siberian race)

YELLOW-
BROWED

GREENISH

WOOD

BONELLI'S

ICTERINE

MELODIOUS

OLIVE-TREE

OLIVACEOUS

GARDEN

Plate 82

RARE WARBLERS

Mostly vagrants from Asia.

LANCEOLATED WARBLER   p.186
Smallest of genus; heavily streaked back and breast.

PALLAS'S GRASSHOPPER WARBLER   p.186
Recalls Sedge Warbler; pale supercilium; heavily streaked back;
rufous rump shading into dark tail with dull white tip. Juvenile has
lightly streaked buffy breast.

BLYTH'S REED WARBLER   p.189
Greyer-olive than Reed Warbler; fine bill; short dull spectacle like
Marsh; clicking call.

BOOTED WARBLER   p.192
Smallest of genus; short wings; fine bill; whitish supercilium under
dark crown smudge.

RADDE'S WARBLER   p.200
Larger and more olive than Willow Warbler; strong bill; long, very
conspicuous supercilium; creamy under-parts end in rufous-buff vent;
stout yellowish legs.

DUSKY WARBLER   p.200
Smaller than Radde's Warbler; more grey-brown, with finer bill,
rustier supercilium; harsh call and constantly flicked wings.

PADDYFIELD WARBLER   p.189
Short-winged and long-tailed; paler and more sandy-rufous above than
Reed Warbler, with short, fine bill, whitish supercilium with dark
outline; clicking call.

DESERT WARBLER   p.195
Very pale, sandy; base of bill, eyes and legs pale yellow; white outer
tail-feathers. Spreads and raises tail.

PALLAS'S WARBLER   p.199
Striped crown suggests Firecrest, but otherwise plumage pattern like
Yellow-browed Warbler, except for pale patch on lower back; call
softer than Yellow-browed.

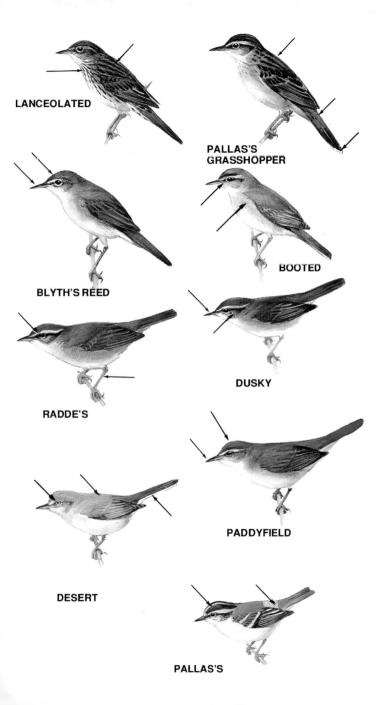

LANCEOLATED

PALLAS'S GRASSHOPPER

BLYTH'S REED

BOOTED

RADDE'S

DUSKY

DESERT

PADDYFIELD

PALLAS'S

Plate 83

GOLDCRESTS, DIPPER, WREN, CREEPERS AND NUTHATCHES

GOLDCREST   Map 297 p.202
Tiny; black-bordered, orange or yellow crown-stripe. Eye emphasized
by diffuse pale ring.

FIRECREST   Map 298 p.203
From Goldcrest by strong black eye-stripe and white supercilium;
bronze 'shoulders'.

DIPPER   Map 242 p.171
Portly, often bobs; dark with white 'bib'; short cocked tail.

WREN   Map 243 p.171
Tiny, rotund, reddish-brown; tail usually cocked.

TREECREEPER   Map 316 p.210
Slender, with fine, curved bill; streaked brown above, with rusty
rump; silvery-white below. Sibilant calls.

SHORT-TOED TREECREEPER   Map 317 p.211
Nearly identical with Treecreeper, but supercilium less distinct and
flanks more brownish. Separable on loud call, recalling Coal Tit.

WALLCREEPER   Map 315 p.210
Large crimson patches on very rounded wings; recalls butterfly in
flight.

NUTHATCH   Map 313 p.209
Stumpy; short tail; sharp bill; blue-grey above; rufous below.
Scandinavian form whiter below. Note Nuthatches climb down trees
head first.

KRÜPER'S NUTHATCH   p.208
Bold, dark rufous patch on the breast. Asia Minor; breeds on Greek
islands.

CORSICAN NUTHATCH   p.209
Small; white stripe over the eye; cap black in male, slate in female.
Corsica.

ROCK NUTHATCH   Map 314 p.209
Larger, paler and more upright than Nuthatch; longer bill; no tail
spots. Balkans, Greece.

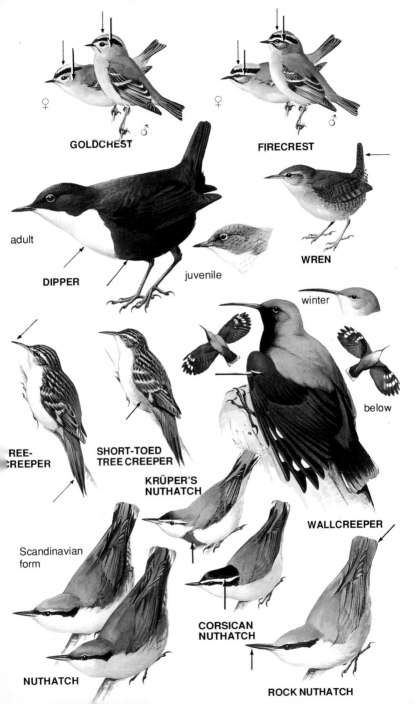

GOLDCREST

♀ ♂

FIRECREST

♀ ♂

WREN

adult

DIPPER

juvenile

winter

below

REE-
CREEPER

**SHORT-TOED
TREE CREEPER**

**KRÜPER'S
NUTHATCH**

WALLCREEPER

Scandinavian
form

NUTHATCH

**CORSICAN
NUTHATCH**

ROCK NUTHATCH

Plate 84

FLYCATCHERS AND WAXWING

Flycatchers are small birds which sit upright while waiting for passing insects. They frequently flick their tails upwards.
Waxwings are sleek, crested, Starling-size brown birds, usually seen in flocks.

PIED FLYCATCHER   Map 302 p.204
Breeding male: Black and white, large white wing-patch. In winter, male is similar to the female.
Female: Brown back; white wing-patch similar to male's.

SEMI-COLLARED FLYCATCHER   p.204
Breeding male: From Pied Flycatcher by presence of upper white wing-bar and partial collar.

COLLARED FLYCATCHER   Map 301 p.204
Breeding male: Full white collar and pale grey rump; large white wing-patch extends along whole wing.

SPOTTED FLYCATCHER   Map 299 p.203
Grey-brown back; streaked breast; wing marks restricted to pale edges of larger feathers.

RED-BREASTED FLYCATCHER   Map 300 p.204
Male: Orange-red throat; grey cheek.
Female: Buffish breast.
Both show pale eye-ring and white patches on tail base.

WAXWING   Map 241 p.170
Long crest; yellow tip on tail; scarlet spines on secondaries.

PIED
FLYCATCHER

♀ ♂ breeding

SEMI-COLLARED
FLYCATCHER

♂ breeding

COLLARED
FLYCATCHER

♂ breeding

SPOTTED
FLYCATCHER

WAXWING

RED-BREASTED
FLYCATCHER

♀ ♂

Plate 85

SHRIKES

Shrikes are hook-billed songbirds which behave like little hawks, catching insects, mice and small birds. All adults have black masks.

RED-BACKED SHRIKE
Map 320 p.212
Male: Grey crown; chestnut back.
Female: Rusty back; barred breast.

WOODCHAT SHRIKE
Map 323 p.214
Adult: Large white scapular-patches; chesnut crown; white rump.
Juvenile: Thickly barred; trace of scapular-patch.

LESSER GREY SHRIKE
Map 321 p.213
Black forehead. Stubbier bill than Great Grey Shrike; more upright
pose; longer wings.

GREAT GREY SHRIKE
Map 322 p.213
Light grey forehead; white supercilium; much white on the scapulars.
Longer bill than Lesser Grey Shrike; longer tail but shorter wings.

MASKED SHRIKE
p.214
From Woodchat Shrike by white forehead, black crown and rump;
reddish flanks.

ISABELLINE SHRIKE
p.212
Sandy, with wholly rufous tail and pale patch at base of primaries.

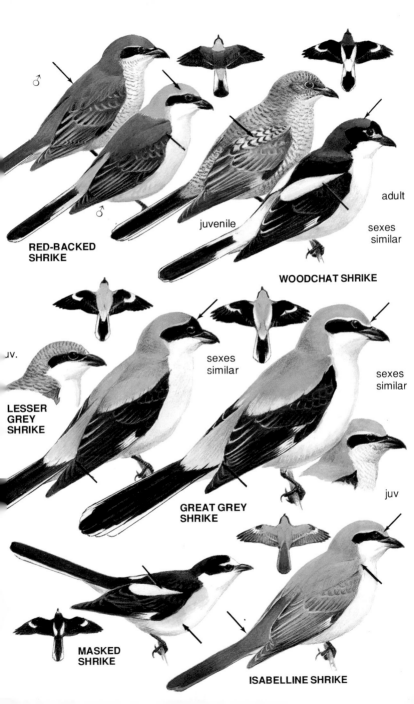

RED-BACKED SHRIKE

juvenile

WOODCHAT SHRIKE

adult

sexes similar

jv.

LESSER GREY SHRIKE

sexes similar

sexes similar

GREAT GREY SHRIKE

juv

MASKED SHRIKE

ISABELLINE SHRIKE

Plate 86

TITS

Small birds with stubby bills; extremely active, often hanging upside down in their busy search for food. Most true tits (*Parus*, first three rows) have black bibs, white cheeks and black or dark caps. In true tits, sexes are similar.

GREAT TIT   Map 312 p.208
Black bib extends to full stripe on the belly.

COAL TIT   Map 310 p.207
White spot on the nape; double white wing-bar.

BLUE TIT   Map 311 p.208
Blue cap; yellowish under-parts.

MARSH TIT   Map 305 p.206
Glossy black cap; small bib; no light panel on wing. Explosive disyllabic call.

WILLOW TIT   Map 307 p.206
Dull black cap; light panel on wing formed by pale tertial edges; long white cheeks. Distinctive multisyllabic buzzing call. Scandinavian form much paler, with grey back.

AZURE TIT   p.208
White cap; white under-parts; much white on the wing.

SOMBRE TIT   Map 306 p.206
As large as Great Tit; drab, with large bill and bib.

SIBERIAN TIT   Map 308 p.207
Brown cap; large bib; 'dusty' appearance.

CRESTED TIT   Map 309 p.207
Crested; 'bridled' face.

BEARDED TIT   Map 303 p.205
Male: Drooping black 'moustaches' on blue-grey head.
Female: No 'moustaches'; sandy-brown.
Note very long, graduated tail and black vent.

LONG-TAILED TIT   Map 304 p.205
Black and white crown-stripes; pinkish hues; very long tail.

PENDULINE TIT   Map 318 p.211
Smaller than Blue Tit. Black mask through the eyes; rusty back; long thin call.

GREAT

COAL

BLUE

MARSH

WILLOW
northern form

AZURE

SOMBRE

SIBERIAN

CRESTED

BEARDED
♀

LONG-TAILED
northern form

PENDULINE

Plate 87

SMALLER CROWS, JAYS, ORIOLE AND STARLINGS

MAGPIE Map 326 p.215
Pied pattern; long tail.

NUTCRACKER Map 327 p.216
Brown with white flecks; white under tail-coverts; black-based, white-tipped tail.

AZURE-WINGED MAGPIE p.215
Grey-blue wings and tail; black cap. Spain, Portugal.

CHOUGH Map 329 p.216
Curved red bill; red legs. See also Plate 88.

ALPINE CHOUGH Map 328 p.216
Shorter yellow bill; red legs. See also Plate 88.

JAY Map 324 p.214
Pinkish-brown, with white rump and black tail; blue and white patches on wings.

SIBERIAN JAY Map 325 p.215
Dusty grey-brown; rufous on wings and tail.

GOLDEN ORIOLE Map 319 p.211
Male: Bright yellow, with black wings and tail.
Female: Greenish above; whitish below, finely streaked.

SPOTLESS STARLING p.219
Black; spots lacking in summer and only small in winter. Spain, Portugal, Sardinia, Sicily, Corsica.

STARLING Map 335 p.218
Iridescent, with fine spots above at all seasons and large white spots below in winter.
Juvenile: Grey-brown, lacking obvious marks.

ROSE-COLOURED STARLING p.219
Shorter-billed than Starling, with dull pink body, black 'hood' and black wings.
Juvenile: Sandy, with yellow bill, pale rump and light edges to wing-feathers.

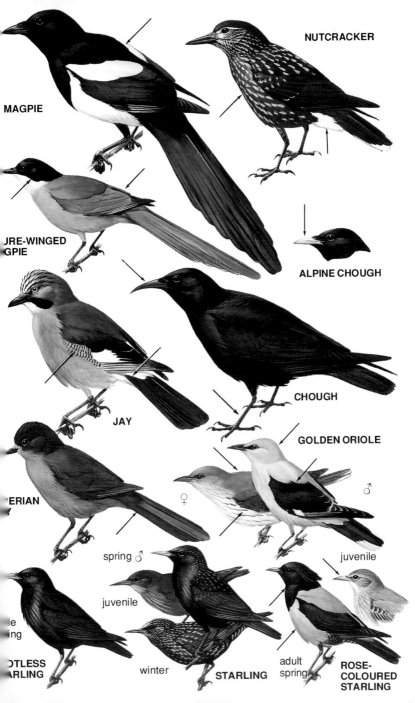

MAGPIE

NUTCRACKER

AZURE-WINGED MAGPIE

ALPINE CHOUGH

JAY

CHOUGH

IBERIAN

GOLDEN ORIOLE

♀

♂

spring ♂

juvenile

juvenile

SPOTLESS STARLING

winter

STARLING

adult spring

ROSE-COLOURED STARLING

Plate 88

THE CROW FAMILY

CHOUGH Map 329 p.216
Thin red bill; broad, well-fingered wings.

ALPINE CHOUGH Map 328 p.216
Shorter yellow bill; less broad and fingered wings.

HOODED CROW Map 333 p.217
Grey back, wing-lining and belly; black hood.

CARRION CROW Map 332 p.217
All black; moderately thick bill. Only flocks in late autumn.

JACKDAW Map 330 p.217
Small; short bill, grey nape; pale grey eyes. Gregarious.

ROOK Map 331 p.217
Bare face patch, pale bill; shaggy 'trousers'. Gregarious.
Juvenile: Similar to Carrion Crow but bill more slender.

RAVEN Map 334 p.218
Very large; massive bill, shaggy throat, wedge-shaped tail.

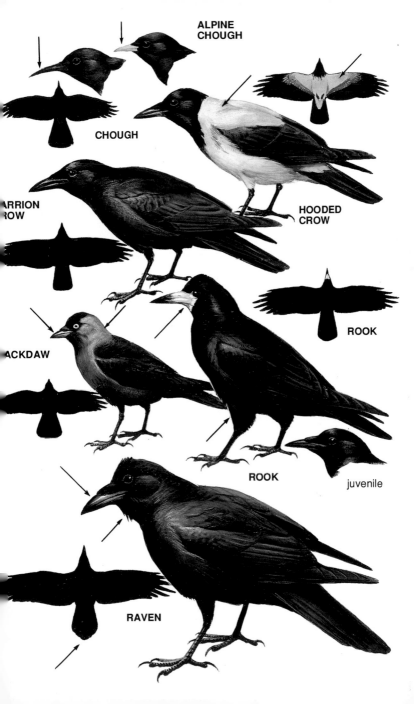

ALPINE
CHOUGH

CHOUGH

HOODED
CROW

CARRION
CROW

HOODED
CROW

JACKDAW

ROOK

ROOK

juvenile

RAVEN

Plate 89

FINCHES

Finches (and buntings) have stout bills, adapted for seed cracking. Three types of bills exist within the group; that of the Hawfinch, Bullfinch and Pine Grosbeak thick and rounded in outline; the more ordinary canary-like bill of most finches (and buntings); and that of the crossbills, the mandibles of which are crossed at the tips.

HAWFINCH   Map 356 p.230
Parrot-like with massive bill and head; white wing-bands; short tail.

CHAFFINCH   Map 341 p.223
Double white wing-bars; white sides to long tail. Male has blue-grey crown, pinkish cheeks and breast.

BRAMBLING   Map 342 p.223
Narrow white rump above black tail; orange chest and 'shoulders'. Male in summer has black head and back.

GOLDFINCH   Map 346 p.225
Red and white face; broad yellow band across wing.

GREENFINCH   Map 345 p.224
Male: Green; large yellow wing- and tail-patches.
Female: Duller; less yellow wing-patches.

CITRIL FINCH   Map 344 p.224
Unstreaked; greyish nape; dull green wing-bars.

SISKIN   Map 347 p.225
Male: Black crown and chin; yellow wing-bar, rump and tail-patches.
Female: Streaked white underparts.

SERIN   Map 343 p.223
Stumpy form; stubby bill; heavily streaked except for yellow breast and rump in male. Most finches have a strongly undulating flight.

TRUMPETER FINCH (below)   p.228
Stubby orange-pink bill; no obvious plumage marks but distinctive 'toy trumpet' call.

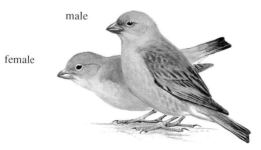

male

female

HAWFINCH

♂

CHAFFINCH

♂

♀

BRAMBLING

♂ breeding

♂ winter

♀

GOLDFINCH

sexes similar

♂

♀

GREENFINCH

sexes similar

CITRIL FINCH

SISKIN

♂

♀

SERIN

♂

♀

Plate 90

FINCHES

The **Linnet**, **Twite** and **redpolls** are small finches with converging appearances; important to remember that Linnets are the commonest and most widespread, but all have distinctive calls.

BULLFINCH
Map 355 p.230

Black cap; stubby bill; white rump above long black tail.
Male: Rose-red breast.
Female: Warm pinkish-brown breast.

LINNET
Map 348 p.225

Male: Red forehead and breast; uniform chestnut back; no black on the chin.
Female: Streaked, grey head; more streaked and browner back.
Twittering calls.

REDPOLL
Map 350 p.226

Red forehead; black chin; buff wing-bars in Lesser but whiter in paler Mealy from N. Europe. Males have pink breasts. Metallic, chittering call.

ARCTIC REDPOLL
Map 351 p.227

From Redpoll by shorter bill, looser and much frostier plumage; unstreaked white rump; fully white wing-bars. Similar call to Redpoll.

TWITE
Map 349 p.226

Rich buff with black streaks and paler wing-bars than Linnet; yellow bill in winter. Male has pinkish rump, like Redpoll. Typical call hoarse and distinctly nasal.

SCARLET ROSEFINCH
Map 353 p.229

Male: Rosy-carmine head, breast and rump; uniform wings.
Female: Yellowish-brown, streaked; round head with bold dark eye; two pale wing-bars.

PINE GROSBEAK
Map 354 p.229

Male: Largest European breeding finch. Rosy-grey, with stubby bill, long tail; two white wing-bars on black wings.
Female: Golden-brown and grey; white wing-bars as male.

CROSSBILL
Map 352 p.227

Male: Dull red with dark wings and tail; fully crossed mandibles.
Female: Yellowish-grey; dark wings and tail.

PARROT CROSSBILL
p.228

Very stout bill. See text for discussion and **Scottish Crossbill**.

TWO-BARRED CROSSBILL
p.227

Male: Carmine with two white wing-bars; crossed mandibles on fine bill.
Female: Yellowish-olive, strongly streaked; white wing-bars as male.

BULLFINCH

MEALY

LINNET

ARCTIC REDPOLL

REDPOLL

TWITE

SCARLET ROSEFINCH

PARROT CROSSBILL

PINE GROSBEAK

CROSSBILL

TWO-BARRED CROSSBILL

Plate 91

SPARROWS, ACCENTORS AND BUNTINGS

HOUSE SPARROW   Map 336 p.220
Male: Grey crown; black bib.
Female: Plain dingy breast, dull supercilium.
Former Italian race now considered hybrid between House and
Spanish Sparrow; has chestnut crown.

SPANISH SPARROW   Map 337 p.220
Male: Chestnut crown; heavy black streaks on back and flanks.
Female: Similar to House Sparrow but with faint streaks on flanks.

TREE SPARROW   Map 338 p.220
Black cheek-spot; chestnut crown.

ROCK SPARROW   Map 339 p.221
Pale; striped crown; white tail-spots; indistinct yellow spot on the
breast.

DUNNOCK   Map 244 p.172
Streaked brown above; grey face and breast; thin bill.

ALPINE ACCENTOR   Map 245 p.172
Chestnut splashed flanks; spotted white throat; black and white
wing-bars.

RUSTIC BUNTING   Map 363 p.236
Breeding male: Black and white head; rusty breast-band and nape.
Winter: Retains trace of summer head and breast pattern.
Short, ticking call.

SNOW BUNTING   Map 358 p.233
Large white wing-patches; head washed with buff. In summer, male
has white head and black back.
Rippling call.

SNOWFINCH   Map 340 p.221
From Snow Bunting by grey head and black chin. Strictly alpine.

LAPLAND BUNTING   Map 357 p.232
Breeding male: Black face and chest; white 'zig-zag' mark before
rusty nape.
Female and winter male: Rusty nape.
Immature: Light crown stripe.
Ticking call.

REED BUNTING   Map 364 p.237
Breeding male: Black head and bib; white moustache stripe and collar.
Female: Blackish border to cheeks reaches bill; creamy moustache.
Plaintive call.

HOUSE SPARROW

♂

♀

TREE SPARROW

sexes
similar

♂

"ITALIAN" SPARROW

♂

SPANISH SPARROW

sexes
similar

**ROCK
SPARROW**

...nter

sexes similar

DUNNOCK

sexes similar

**ALPINE
ACCENTOR**

...eeding

**RUSTIC
BUNTING**

♀

♂

SNOW BUNTING

sexes similar

SNOWFINCH

...mature

♂ breeding

LAPLAND BUNTING

♂
breeding

♀

**REED
BUNTING**

Plate 92

BUNTINGS

CORN BUNTING Map 366 p.238
Large; streaked; big bill; no white on the tail.

LITTLE BUNTING p.236
Rufous crown and cheeks, boldly outlined in black; pale eye-ring.

ROCK BUNTING Map 361 p.234
Black stripes on grey head; buffish-orange belly; long tail below deep
rufous rump.

ORTOLAN BUNTING Map 362 p.235
Olive head and breast; yellow moustache, throat and eye-ring.
Immature: Streaked; pink bill; pale eye-ring.

CRETZSCHMAR'S BUNTING p.235
From Ortolan Bunting by rusty throat, blue-grey head.
Immature: Resembles immature Ortolan Bunting.

YELLOWHAMMER Map 359 p.233
Always yellowish, with rufous rump.

CIRL BUNTING Map 360 p.234
Male: Black throat below black and yellow face.
Female: From Yellowhammer by olive-brown rump.

BLACK-HEADED BUNTING Map 365 p.238
Male: Black hood; yellow below; rufous back.
Female: Unstreaked below; bright yellow under tail-coverts; long,
deep bill.

YELLOW-BREASTED BUNTING p.236
Male: Black face; dark chestnut bar across yellow under-parts; bold
white upper wing-bar recalls Chaffinch.
Female: Strongly striped head.

RED-HEADED BUNTING p.260
Male: Red head and breast; greenish above, yellow below.

PINE BUNTING p.233
Male: White crown and cheeks; chestnut throat-patch.

MEADOW BUNTING p.260
Male: Dark chestnut crown, rear cheeks and breast-band; white
supercilium; black 'moustache'.

BLACK-FACED BUNTING p.259
Male: Dark grey face; dull yellow under-parts.

CINEREOUS BUNTING p.235
Male: Dull yellow head; greyish body and nape.

LITTLE

ROCK

sexes
similar

CORN

sexes
similar

♂

ORTOLAN

CRETZSCHMAR'S

♀ ♂
breeding

imm.

♂

YELLOWHAMMER

CIRL

♀ ♂

♀ ♂

BLACK-HEADED

YELLOW-BREASTED

♀ ♂
breeding

♀ ♂
breeding

RED-HEADED ♂   PINE ♂   MEADOW ♂   BLACK-FACED ♂   CINEREOUS ♂

Plate 93

VAGRANT WOOD WARBLERS FROM NORTH AMERICA

Unrelated to the Old World Warblers. Shown opposite are the most frequently recorded strays. At least a dozen others have been recorded only one, two or three times in Britain and Europe. For these see Accidentals, also *A Field Guide to the Rare Birds of Britain and Europe* by I. Lewington, P. Alström and P. Colston, or *A Field Guide to the Birds of Eastern and Central North America* by R.T. Peterson.

BLACKPOLL WARBLER   p.231
Breeding male: Striped grey with black cap, white cheeks.
Autumn: Olive; dull yellow below, faintly streaked, two white wing-bars. Usually pale yellowish legs.

BLACK-AND-WHITE WARBLER   p.256
Striped lengthwise with black and white, particularly on crown. Creeps along trunks and branches of trees.

YELLOW-RUMPED WARBLER   p.231
Note bright yellow rump, also yellow patches on crown and before the wing.

AMERICAN REDSTART   p.257
Male: Black with bright orange patches on wings and tail.
Female: Olive-brown with yellow patches on wings and tail.

NORTHERN PARULA   p.231
Bluish with a yellow breast and a dull greenish patch on the back. Dark breast-band of male lacking in female.

NORTHERN WATERTHRUSH   p.258
Thrush-like, walks along water edges teetering its tail. Striped below; creamy or buff supercilium.

RED-EYED VIREO (below)   p.222
Unrelated to wood warblers, vireos have bills with a more curved ridge and a slight hook. The Red-eyed is the most likely vireo, occurring in autumn. Note grey cap contrasting with strong black-bordered white eyebrow stripe. Eye may be dull red (adult) or brown (immature).

adult

immature

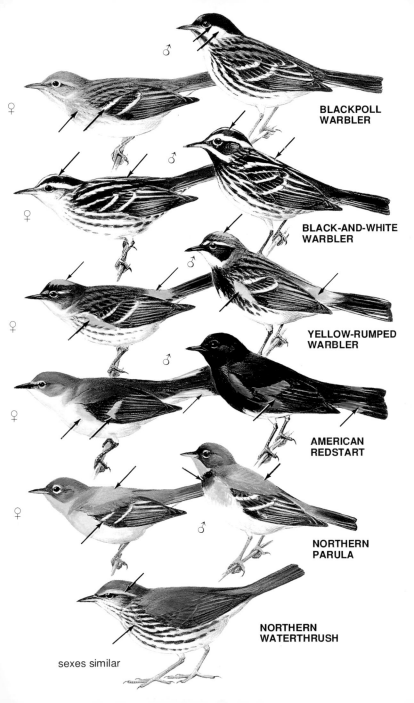

♂

♀

**BLACKPOLL
WARBLER**

♂

♀

**BLACK-AND-WHITE
WARBLER**

♂

♀

**YELLOW-RUMPED
WARBLER**

♀

**AMERICAN
REDSTART**

♀

♂

**NORTHERN
PARULA**

**NORTHERN
WATERTHRUSH**

sexes similar

Plate 94

VAGRANT SONGBIRDS FROM NORTH AMERICA

Ten accidental strays are shown here. Fifteen other closely-related species (icterids, tangers, thrushes and sparrows) have also been recorded but are not included here. They are currently best illustrated and described in *A Field Guide to the Rare Birds of Britain and Europe* by I. Lewington, P. Alström and P. Colston.

NORTHERN (BALTIMORE) ORIOLE   p.239
Male: Unmistakeable in summer. Flame-orange and black, with black head. Immature male has less black on the head and whitish throat.
Female: Olive-brown above, burnt orange-yellow below, two white wing-bars. Immature may have pale throat.

SCARLET TANAGER   p.258
Breeding male: Flaming scarlet with black wings and tail.
Male winter: Dull greenish above, yellowish below; dark wings.
Female: Similar to winter male but less dark in the wings.

GREY-CHEEKED THRUSH   p.181
Dull grey-brown. From Swainson's Thrush by greyish cheek and less conspicuous eye-ring.

SWAINSON'S THRUSH   p.181
Spot-breasted thrush; buffy on the breast and cheeks. Note conspicuous buff eye-ring.

BOBOLINK   p.261
In autumn ochre-buff, with striped crown; can recall Quail.

AMERICAN ROBIN   p.185
Brick red breast, dark grey back, yellow bill, striped throat.

SONG SPARROW   p.259
Recalls Dunnock but related to bunting; dark malar stripe and spot on brest centre.

FOX SPARROW   p.259
Larger than House Sparrow; rufous and grey, with chestnut tail.

DARK-EYED JUNCO   p.259
Grey hood, white belly, pale bill. Note flashing white outer tail-feathers.

WHITE-THROATED SPARROW   p.232
Note clean-cut white throat and striped crown. Polymorphic; may have black and white, or black and tan, head stripes.

WHITE-CROWNED SPARROW   p.259
From White-throated by pale bill, lack of yellow in supercilium and white throat.

INDIGO BUNTING   p.261
Breeding male: All blue.
Autumn: Tan, breast paler with indistinct streaks.

ROSE-BREASTED GROSBEAK   p.238
Male: Black head; pale bill; rose breast. In winter like female.
Female: Heavy grosbeak bill, striped crown, dark cheek patch. Yellow or pink wing-linings.

NORTHERN ORIOLE

imm.

♂ breeding

SCARLET TANAGER

♂ breeding

♀

♀ breeding

GREY-CHEEKED THRUSH

SWAINSON'S THRUSH

winter

AMERICAN ROBIN

FOX SPARROW

NG ARROW

typical

autumn

BOBOLINK

d

WHITE-THROATED SPARROW

adult

DARK-EYED JUNCO

TE-OWNED ARROW

♀

♂

♂ moulting

♀ winter

♂ breeding

INDIGO BUNTING

♂ autumn

ROSE-BREASTED GROSBEAK

Plate 95

SOME INTRODUCED BIRDS
(See also Plate 96)

Many alien species have been introduced, or have escaped into Britain and western Europe. Although most often they were doomed to failure, some, such as those shown here and on Plate 96, have become feral.

ROSE-RINGED PARAKEET p.145
Slim, long-tailed, green parrot, with hooked red bill. Male has narrow ring on the neck.

BLACK FRANCOLIN p.89
Male: Black-bodied, grouse-like bird with white speckles, white cheek-patch and a broad chestnut collar.
Female: Brown, with close bars.

PHEASANT Map 110 p.90
See Plate 32 and caption.

GOLDEN PHEASANT p.90
Male: Unmistakable, with scarlet under-parts, golden crest, scalloped head-dress and rump.
Female: Similar to female Pheasant but curved tail longer, more strongly barred.

LADY AMHERST'S PHEASANT p.91
Male: Unmistakable, with a scalloped head-dress, white under-parts, barred white tail.
Female: Similar to female Golden Pheasant (see text).

Note: The birds shown on this plate vary in scale. See text for measurements.

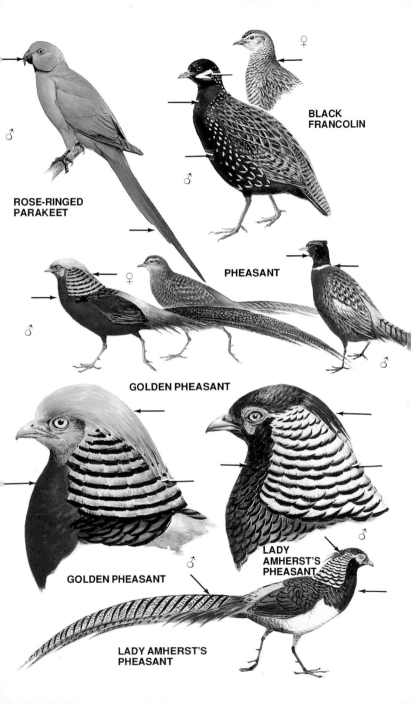

ROSE-RINGED
PARAKEET

BLACK
FRANCOLIN

PHEASANT

GOLDEN PHEASANT

GOLDEN PHEASANT

LADY
AMHERST'S
PHEASANT

LADY AMHERST'S
PHEASANT

Plate 96

MORE INTRODUCED BIRDS

AVADAVAT p.221
Male: Red with white speckles
Female: Grey with red bill and rump.

COMMON WAXBILL p.222
Tiny, finely-barred dark finch, with red bill, white cheeks and red
belly. Immature has white bill.

WOOD DUCK p.55
Male: Bizarre face pattern, swept-back crest, and rainbow iridescence
are unique.
Female: Dull-coloured; dark crested head; note large white eye-patch;
beware confusion with Mandarin.

CANADA GOOSE Map 41 p.53
See Plates 8 and 9 and text.

EGYPTIAN GOOSE p.54
Goose-like; buffish with chocolate eye- and lower breast-patches.

BAR-HEADED GOOSE p.52
Silvery grey; two black bars on back of white head.

AVADAVAT

COMMON WAXBILL

WOOD DUCK

♂ in eclipse
(autumn)

**CANADA
GOOSE**

BAR-HEADED GOOSE

EGYPTIAN GOOSE

LARKS: Alaudidae

Mostly streaked brown, ground-haunting and -nesting birds, with flapping flight and running gait. Songs well developed, often delivered high in air. Sexes similar except in Black Lark. Small *Calandrella* species may suggest finch or bunting.

DUPONT'S LARK *Chersophilus duponti*   **Plate 70**
  Du – Dupont's leeuwerik   Fr – Sirli de Dupont
  Ge – Dupont-Lerche   Sw – Dupontlärka
Identification: 7½" (19cm). Highly terrestrial, secretive lark; brown plumage relieved by *pale eye-ring and supercilium*, intricate *scaling of back*, deeply streaked chest and white edges to tail. Rarely on wing except in high song-flight ending in *spectacular plunge*, followed by characteristic *swift run* to dense ground-cover. Stance slim and erect, often on low plants.
Voice: Song recalls Linnet; short, musical and nasal, most distinctive phrase *dzee-too-see*. Calls whistling *hoo-ee* and Greenfinch-like *dweej*.
Habitat and Range: Semi-desert with wild thyme, scrub, etc. Breeds S., C. and NE. Spain; vagrant elsewhere around W. Mediterranean.

CALANDRA LARK *Melanocorypha calandra*   **Plate 70**
  Du – Kalanderleeuwerik   Fr – Alouette calandre
  Ge – Kalanderlerche   Sw – Kalanderlärka
Identification: 7½" (19cm). Large, stocky uncrested lark, with *heavy bill* and *large 'triangular' wings*. Plumage basically well-streaked brown above, off-white below, relieved by *yellowish-horn bill*, bold *black half-collar on neck-sides* above sparse streaks. Under-wings appear *almost black with bright white trailing edges*; white sides to tail. Juvenile buffier, with incomplete neck-patches. Flight free and powerful, more buoyant than Skylark. Walk and run confident. Beware all congeners, which see.
Voice: Song recalls Skylark but louder, more melodious, with frequent interjections of nasal call *kleetra* producing jingling Corn Bunting-like quality; usually delivered in high circle, with long terminal dive.
Habitat: Stony wastelands, farmlands and steppes. Nests on ground. Map 221.

WHITE-WINGED LARK *Melanocorypha leucoptera*   **Plate 70**
  Du – Witvleugelleeuwerik   Fr – Alouette leucoptère
  Ge – Weissflügellerche   Sw – Vitvingad lärka
Identification: 7" (17.5cm). Form between Skylark and Calandra, with relatively longer tail than latter. Streaked tawny upper-parts, noticeably *chestnut on crown, ear-coverts and wing-coverts*, contrast with *strikingly white under-parts*, with streaks restricted to chest-sides and flanks. In flight, upper-wing has *black primaries and bases to secondaries* contrasting with *broad white trailing edge*; under-wing shows white coverts. White tail-edges and outer web of longest primary also catch eye. Female duller, with streaked brown crown. Flight like Skylark but gait as Calandra.
Voice: Calls not well known, seemingly like Skylark but higher-pitched.
Habitat and Range: Mainly grass-steppe in home range. Passes through, occasionally winters in E. Romania; also vagrant across Europe S. to Malta, W. to Britain and NW. to Finland.

BLACK LARK *Melanocorypha yeltoniensis*　　　　　**Plate 70**
　Du – Zwarte leeuwerik　　　　　Fr – Alouette nègre
　Ge – Mohrenlerche　　　　　Sw – Svartlärka
Identification: 8½" (21cm) male; 7½" (19cm) female. Largest European lark, with similar form to Calandra. Male basically *black* except for *yellow-horn bill*; in fresh plumage, wide *off-white or buff tips over head and body*. Female basically black-brown above and dull white below; pale tips on head and back, off-white narrow supercilium and wing-covert edges, and black patches and spots particularly on chest sides and flanks create more typical lark pattern. Juvenile less marked below than female. *No bold white marks on wings and tail* but rump can look pale. Flight and gait as Calandra.
Voice: Calls not well known; recordings indicate sharp clear monosyllable.
Habitat and Range: Grass or bush steppe, often near water, also in deserts, invading cultivation and road-sides in winter. Winter vagrant from C. Asia to C. Europe and North Sea coast.

SHORT-TOED LARK *Calandrella brachydactyla*　　　　　**Plate 70**
　Du – Kortteenleeuwerik　　　　　Fr – Alouette calandrelle
　Ge – Kurzzehenlerche　　　　　Sw – Korttålärka
Identification: 5½" (14cm). Small, Linnet-like lark, with *short pointed bill*, capped rather than crested head and *wing-points almost fully cloaked* by *tertials*. Plumage little marked but, close-to, dark cap, *dark patch between neck and breast-side*, dark centres to scapulars and median coverts catch eye. Flight pattern lacks pale trailing edge to wing, but black outer and white outermost tail-feathers obvious. S. European race *C. b. brachydactyla* sandy-rufous above, with chestnut cap; vagrants of Asian race *C. b. longipennis* duller and darker, grey-brown above, with heavier bill. Some adults and juveniles lack visible neck patches, being apparently only streaked on sides of breast. Flight fast, with finch-like undulations and sweep over ground. Gait jerky, recalling pipit.
Voice: Song simple, about eight high-pitched twittering notes repeated at short intervals; long-sustained and given in characteristic high, *steeply rising and falling* flight. Short dry *tchi-tchirrp*, recalling House Sparrow; in alarm, drawn-out *tee-oo*.
Habitat: Open sandy or stony wastes, dry mud-flats with *Salicornia*, steppes and fields. Nests on ground. Map 222.

LESSER SHORT-TOED LARK *Calandrella rufescens*　　　　　**Plate 70**
　Du – Kleine Kortteenleeuwerik　　　　　Fr – Alouette pispolette
　Ge – Stummellerche　　　　　Sw – Dvärglärka
Identification: 5½" (14cm). Close in size and form to Short-toed but with more sparrow-like character and distinctive voice. Plumage patterned like Short-toed but more heavily streaked; S. European races *C. r. apetzii* (Spain) and *heinei* (Volga delta eastwards) respectively browner and greyer. Best distinguished by *copiously, finely streaked breast* and *wing-points protruding beyond tertials*. Flight and gait much as Short-toed. Needs care in identification.
Voice: Song more developed and continuous than Short-toed, mixing melodic phrases with mimicry and twitters, delivered from *rising spiral or high circling, almost level* flight. Characteristic call short, hard *prrit*, recalling Lapland Bunting more than Short-toed.

Habitat and Range: Prefers dry edges of marshes or lagoons, marginally as Short-toed. Breeds in S. and E. Spain, wandering to S. W. C. and N. Europe (including Britain).

CRESTED LARK *Galerida cristata*   Plate 70

Du – Kuifleeuwerik   Fr – Cochevis huppé
Ge – Haubenlerche   Sw – Tofslärka

Identification: 6¾" (17cm). Quite large, deep-bellied lark with *rather long, slightly decurved bill,* long upstanding *spike-like crest* and relatively short tail. Plumage rather uniform, with sandy- to grey-brown upper-parts and creamy-buff under-parts, less strongly streaked than Skylark except on breast. Juvenile pale-spotted above, with shorter crest. Flight outline characterised by *broad, rounded wings* and *square tail*; pattern lacks pale trailing edges but shows buff outer tail-feathers and *glowing orange-buff under-wing.* Flight action rather heavy and flapping, developing marked undulations. Portly walk or run, with characteristic shuffle when feeding.

Voice: Song loud and clear but less musical and shorter-phrased than Skylark, delivered from perch or in flight. Usual call shrill, liquid *klee-tree-weeoo,* rising and falling, often interjected into song.

Habitat: Generally flat grassy or arid country; often near habitation, dusty mule-tracks, roadsides, etc. Nests on ground. Map 223.

THEKLA LARK *Galerida theklae*   Plate 70

Du – Thekla Leeuwerik   Fr – Cochevis de Thékla
Ge – Theklalerche   Sw – Lagerlärka

Identification: 6¼" (15.5cm). Close in form and appearance to Crested but with *shorter bill,* more *fan-like crest,* slimmer build and longer legs. Plumage less uniform than Crested, with more prominent streaks on upper-parts, distinctly *heavier spots on breast and lower cheeks,* and rufous rump. In flight, shows *brown-grey under-wing,* which may even look silvery. Perches on plants more than Crested.

Voice: Song more mellow than Crested, with longer pauses. Usual call soft fluted *doo-dee-doo-deee* or *tu-tweeoo,* lower-pitched than Crested.

Habitat and Range: Prefers broken inclines and interfaces between open and vegetated ground, occurring within and above range of Crested. Resident in S. and E. Iberia, Balearics and adjacent France.

WOODLARK *Lullula arborea*   Plate 70

Du – Boomleeuwerik   Fr – Alouette lulu
Ge – Heidelerche   Sw – Trädlärka

Identification: 6" (15cm). Rather small but stocky lark with *fine bill,* rounded crest, *broad rounded wings* and *short square tail.* Plumage generally buff-brown above, well streaked and strikingly relieved by conspicuous *white supercilia joining on nape,* rufous cheeks, *pale-tipped black primary- coverts*; clean cream below, with sharply streaked breast. Flight outline blunt-winged and short-tailed; pattern lacks white trailing edges to wings and tail but may show white tips on outer feathers. Flight action distinctive, with loose erratic wing-beats producing hesitant undulations and wavering track. Steps lightly; habitually perches in trees.

Voice: Song sweet and musical, with deliberate phrases interspersed with liquid trill *lu-lu-lu-lu* and *tee-oo*, delivered from perch or in flight. Flight-call clear, lilting *lit-loo-eet* or *toolooeet*.
Habitat: Edges of woods, hillsides with a few trees, sandy heaths, etc. Winters in fields. Nests on ground. Map 224.

SKYLARK *Alauda arvensis*   **Plate 70**
    Du – Veldleeuwerik   Fr – Alouette des champs
    Ge – Feldlerche   Sw – Sånglärka
Identification: 7" (17.5cm). Commonest, most widespread lark of region, typifying family but with *relatively longer tail* than other species. Head, breast and upper-parts brown, boldly streaked and contrasting with buff-white under-parts; close-to, short crest, pale fore-face and pale flight-feather margins catch eye. Juvenile has 'pepper and salt' spotted plumage. Flight outline dominated by long wings and tail which show respectively *obvious white trailing edges and outer feathers*; action quite strong but uneven, with bursts of wing-beats and 'shoots' with closed wings producing hesitant, undulating progress (but see song-flight). Gait free, even-paced walk, varied by run and shuffle.
Voice: Song high-pitched, slightly jangled but brilliantly musical outpouring, long sustained, particularly in ascending, hovering and descending flight. Calls variable, commonest rippled *chir-r-up*; beware overlap with other larks.
Habitat: Moors, fields, marshes, sand-dunes. Nests on ground. Map 225.

SHORE LARK *Eremophila alpestris*   **Plate 70**
    Du – Strandleeuwerik   Fr – Alouette hausse-col
    Ge – Ohrenlerche   Sw – Berglärka
    N. Am – Horned Lark
Identification: 6½" (16cm). Medium-sized elegant lark with Skylark-like form except for proportionally shorter bill and even longer tail; adult male has *thin 'horns'* above eyes. Plumage pinkish-brown above, softly streaked off-white below; easily distinguished from all but Temminck's Horned by *pale yellow face and throat* and *bold black cheeks and breast-band*. Juvenile spotted above, with face-marks obscured (as in winter adult). Flight outline most streamlined of larks; pattern cryptic except for noticeably *dark under-side to white-sided tail*; action light, recalling large pipit. Gait often fast, with high-stepping walk, shuffle and run.
Voice: Song tinkling and warbling; includes long drawn-out note suggesting Corn Bunting. Calls pipit- or wagtail-like, thin *tseep* and rippling *tsee-sirrp* or *tsee-ree*.
Habitat: Winters on coast on shingle strands, salt-marshes and adjacent stubble fields. Breeds above tree limit in dry tundra. Map 226.

MARTINS AND SWALLOWS: Hirundinidae

Slim, streamlined form and graceful flight are distinctive. Forked tails, long pointed wings and short bills with very wide gapes. Plumage basically dark above and pale below except in Crag Martin. Insect food caught in flight. Sexes similar. Build mud nests on rocks or buildings (except Sand Martin).

SAND MARTIN *Riparia riparia* Plate 71

Du – Oeverzwaluw   Fr – Hirondelle de rivage
Ge – Uferschwalbe   Sw – Backsvala
N. Am – Bank Swallow

Identification: 4¾" (12cm). Smallest, slightest European hirundine, with barely forked tail. *Earth-brown head-cap, upper-parts and breast-band* contrast with white under-parts. Flight outline slight, with dark wings flickering in weak fluttering action. Much more localised than other hirundines, feeding chiefly over water. Crag Martin larger, with different under-part pattern and rather slow flight.

Voice: Song weak twitter. Contact call dry *tchrrip*, in alarm short *brrit*.

Habitat: Open country with ponds, rivers, etc. Nests socially, in tunnels bored in sand- and gravel-pits, river banks, cliffs. Map 227.

CRAG MARTIN *Ptyonoprogne rupestris* Plate 71

Du – Rotszwaluw   Fr – Hirondelle de rochers
Ge – Felsenschwalbe   Sw – Klippsvala

Identification: 5¾" (14.5cm). Thick-set hirundine, largest of family in Europe but with proportionately *shortest, almost square tail*. Plumage dingy, dusky-brown above, buff below with little contrast and *no breast-band*; close-to, shows *almost black under-wing coverts*, dirty vent and *white spots near tip of spread tail*. Flight outline stocky and action least energetic of family, with much *level, slow gliding*.

Voice: Song throaty twitter. Call weak, quiet *tchrri* or *prrit*.

Habitat: Mountain gorges, inland and coastal cliffs. Builds half-cup mud nest in rock cleft or on cliff-face. Map 228.

SWALLOW *Hirundo rustica* Plate 71

Du – Boerenzwaluw   Fr – Hirondelle de cheminée
Ge – Rauchschwalbe   Sw – Ladusvala
N. Am – Barn Swallow

Identification: 7½" (19cm). Commonest, most widespread hirundine, with *longest and narrowest tail-streamers of family*. Sheeny *dark blue upper-parts and lower throat-band* enclose chestnut-red face and throat and contrast with *creamy-white under-parts*; tail white-spotted at base. Juvenile much duller, with pale gape. Flight swooping and graceful, with easy fluent wing-beats. Gregarious, nesting in scattered groups around farms.

Voice: Song pleasant weak, sometimes confident twittering warble. Calls include high *tswit, tsee-tsewit*, becoming rapid twitter in excitement, and *splee-plink* in alarm.

Habitat: Farmland, especially with stock; settlements in open country. Builds open mud and straw nest on rafters or ledges in cow sheds, stables, etc, locally in chimneys. Map 229.

RED-RUMPED SWALLOW *Hirundo daurica*   **Plate 71**
Du – Roodstuitzwaluw   Fr – Hirondelle rousseline
Ge – Rötelschwalbe   Sw – Rostgumpsvala

Identification: 7" (18cm). Form close to Swallow, but has *blunter wing-tips*, more wide-set and *less wire-like tail streamers* and relatively *lethargic flight*. Dark sheeny blue upper-parts strikingly interrupted by chestnut nape and *pale rufous rump*; warm buff under-parts lack dark face and breast-band of Swallow but end in *black vent and under tail-coverts*. Black tail lacks spots.

Confusion species: At distance, best distinguished from Swallow by less elegant, flatter, slower flight; close-to, head appears capped, not all dark. Beware however rare hybrids of Swallow x House Martin.

Voice: Song short, sweet, twittering warble, less vehement than Swallow. Flight-call distinctive, rather quiet *chew-ic* or *quitsch*, recalling House Sparrow; in alarm, harsh *keer*.

Habitat: Sea and inland cliffs, less partial to cultivated areas than Swallow, but in flat country usually frequents bridges and buildings. Builds nest like House Martin's, but with spout-shaped entrance, in caves, cleft rocks, under bridges, also buildings etc. Map 230.

HOUSE MARTIN *Delichon urbica*   **Plate 71**
Du – Huiszwaluw   Fr – Hirondelle de fenêtre
Ge – Mehlschwalbe   Sw – Hussvala

Identification: 5¼" (13cm). Compact hirundine with *well forked tail lacking streamers*; only one with *pure white rump*. Breeding plumage blue-black on head-cap, back, wings and tail; white below, including feathered legs and feet. Flight action less swooping, more fluttering and level than Swallow and often at greater height. Sociable at all times, nesting in colonies.

Voice: Song soft, sweet chirping twitter. Contact call clear, merry *tchirrip* or *tchichirrip*; in alarm, shrill *tseep*.

Habitat: Like Swallow but adapted to nesting on buildings, even entering towns and cities; locally still breeds on cliffs. Mud nest cupped under eaves and fully enclosed, with entrance hole at top. Map 231.

PIPITS AND WAGTAILS: Motacillidae

Terrestrial birds, running and walking briskly. Pipits are brown and streaked, with white or whitish outer tail-feathers; less slender than wagtails. Sexes similar. Ground nesting. Wagtails are very slender, strongly patterned, with long tails, slender bills and slender legs. Sexes dissimilar. Ground, cranny or rock nesting.

RICHARD'S PIPIT *Anthus novaeseelandiae*   **Plate 72**
Du – Grote Pieper   Fr – Pipit de Richard
Ge – Spornpieper   Sw – Större piplärka

Identification: 7" (17.5cm). Large, heavy, long-tailed and particularly long-legged pipit, with very long hind-claws. Plumage recalls Skylark, being basically brown above and buffish-white below, with *heavy streaks* on upper-parts and breast. Distinction from Blyth's and immature Tawny never easy but close-to, *pale lores* giving plain face, complete pale surround to cheeks, *heavy malar stripe* and *strong rounded streaks on breast* are useful clues, while *loud 'shouted' call* rules out Tawny. For further distinctions from Blyth's, see Accidentals. Flight powerful, with rapid surge after take-off and deep undulations over long distance; often hovers before landing, like Skylark. Has strutting walk and loping run, with large feet noticeably lifted. Solitary.

Voice: Most characteristic call explosive, initially stuttered, then loud, stressed *shreep* or *sh-rout*, given during take-off; also short monosyllables, *cherp*.

Habitat and Range: Wet grasslands, marshy steppes and rice fields. Annually on passage, or in winter, Heligoland, S. Spain and British Isles; vagrant elsewhere in Europe.

TAWNY PIPIT *Anthus campestris*   **Plate 72**
  Du – Duinpieper   Fr – Pipit rousseline
  Ge – Brachpieper   Sw – Större piplärka

Identification: 6½" (16.5cm). Noticeably lengthy, slim wagtail-like pipit. Adult *pale, almost uniform* sandy above, pale sandy to cream below, with fewer characters than other large pipits. Close-to, shows *dark loral streak and 'moustache'* joining in front of eye, dull malar stripe and vestigial streaks on sides of breast, *dark median coverts* and pale whitish wing-bars, brighter ochre rump and yellowish legs. Immature much darker than adult, with streaked upper-parts and darker malar stripe and streaks across breast; suggests both Richard's and Blyth's but distinguished by finer bill, legs and feet, short hind-claw and voice. Flight and gait wagtail-like, former lacking powerful bounds of larger species.

Voice: Song repeated, metallic *chivee, chivee, chivee*, usually from high, then parachuting flight. Calls most varied of all pipits; commonest drawn-out *tsweep*, recalling Yellow Wagtail, brief *chup* and sparrow-like *chirrup*.

Habitat: Wastelands, with sand and scrub, in winter also frequents cultivated land. Nests in depression, sheltered by vegetation. Map 232.

OLIVE-BACKED PIPIT *Anthus hodgsoni*   **Plate 72**
  Du – Indische Boompieper   Fr – Pipit sylvestre
  Ge – Waldpieper   Sw – Sibirisk piplärka

Identification: 5¾" (14.5cm). Size and form close to Tree Pipit but with apparently 'receding chin' and deep chest; 'pumps' tail in most exaggerated wag of tribe. Upper-parts *pale green-olive* with *only vestigial back streaks* but bright wing-bars; under-parts white with evenly spread *large black spots on breast and flanks*. Head well marked with black-edged, *buff, then white supercilium* and usually white and black marks on rear cheeks. Flight and gait like Tree Pipit.

Voice: Calls include quiet *tsee* and loud, strident *teaze* in alarm, recalling Redwing.

Habitat and Range: Usually edges and glades of taiga. Vagrants from Asia to W. Europe (including Britain) often enter coastal woods.

TREE PIPIT *Anthus trivialis* **Plate 72**
Du – Boompieper   Fr – Pipit des arbres
Gc – Baumpieper   Sw – Trädpiplärka
Identification: 6" (15cm). Quite small, elegant pipit, with slimmer rear body than Meadow, from which best distinguished by *strong call*. Plumage warm-toned brown above and buff below; close-to, distinguished from Meadow and Red-throated by deeper bill, broader supercilium, noticeably pale eye-ring, paler, more obvious wing-bars, *boldly spotted breast but only finely streaked flanks* and distinctly *pale pink legs* with short hind claw. Flight action stronger and gait more deliberate than Meadow. Tail-wag slight and gentle.
Voice: Song loud and musical, increasingly confident but decelerating trill, ending in canary-like *seea-seea-seea*; uttered in spiralling, then parachuting descent to perch (unlike Woodlark which plunges into ground cover). Commonest call strong, high-pitched buzzing *teez* or *skeeze*; in alarm, breeding bird gives chinked *zip*.
Habitat: Heaths, clearings in woods, hillsides, fields with scattered trees and bushes. Nests under bracken, in long grass, etc. Map 233.

PECHORA PIPIT *Anthus gustavi* **Plate 72**
Du – Petsjora-Pieper   Fr – Pipit de la Petchora
Ge – Petschorapieper   Sw – Tundrapiplärka
Identification: 5¾" (14.5cm). Small, quite compact but slim pipit, with fine bill, shortish tail and *distinctive call*. Plumage basically buff above and white below, with *copious streaks on back and rump* and densely streaked breast and flanks isolating clean belly; close to, distinguished by *buffish-white stripes on back*, bright *white double wing-bar*, buffish-white outer tail-feathers, and lack of obvious malar streaks. Flight silhouette and action suggests short-tailed, juvenile Meadow. Difficult to flush from dense ground cover.
Voice: Commonest call diagnostic stony, hard *pwit* or *p(r)it*, usually repeated.
Habitat and Range: Usually on edge of tundra near taiga. Vagrant from N.E. Europe and Asia to W. and C. Europe (including Britain).

MEADOW PIPIT *Anthus pratensis* **Plate 72**
Du – Graspieper   Fr – Pipit farlouse
Ge – Wiesenpieper   Sw – Ängspiplärka
Identification: 5¾" (14.5cm). Rather small but dumpy ground-haunting pipit; commonest and most widespread of tribe. Best distinguished by *voice* as plumage lacks striking field marks, being olive or brown above, well streaked except on rump, and buff to grey-white below, fully spotted and streaked on breast and flanks. Close-to, *indistinct face pattern*, dull double wing-bar, white outer tail-feathers, *pale brown legs* and long hind-claw give useful clues. Flight action erratic, with uneven bursts of wing-beats giving hesitant progress. Gait most creeping of tribe. Occasionally wags tail.
Voice: Song thin piping, tinkling trill, lacking *loud terminal flourish of Tree*; song-flight similar to Tree but also sings from ground. Commonest call thin, shrill *weesk* or *tseep*, almost hysterically repeated in alarm; breeding birds and some migrants utter quiet *chip*.
Habitat: Moors, dunes, rough pastures; in winter prefers marshes, cultivated land, sea coasts. Nests on ground. Map 234.

RED-THROATED PIPIT *Anthus cervinus*   **Plate 72**
Du – Roodkeelpieper   Fr – Pipit à gorge rousse
Ge – Rotkehlpieper   Sw – Rödstrupig piplärka
Identification: 5¾" (14.5cm). Rather small pipit but plumper than Meadow.
Breeding adult unmistakable with *rusty-red to orange fore-face, throat and
breast*, pale lines on back and *boldly streaked rump*. Winter adult and immature
far less distinctive, with pale olive through tawny to brown upper-parts, heavily
streaked overall, and pale buff to white under-parts, *heavily spotted on breast
and flanks*; close-to, well-marked face (recalling Tree) and buff under tail-
coverts helpful. Flight form and action like Tree.
Voice: Song intermediate in phrasing and quality between Tree and Meadow.
Commonest calls thin hissing and piercing *peese* or *peez-eez*, with noticeable
pulse of volume in longer version, and full, abrupt *teu* or *chwit*.
Habitat: Swampy tundra, marshes and moist cultivated land, usually with
dwarf vegetation, often near coast. Nests on ground. Map 235.

ROCK PIPIT *Anthus petrosus*   **Plate 72**
Du – Oeverpieper   Fr – Pipit maritime
Ge – Strandpieper   Sw – Skärpiplärka
Identification: 6½" (16cm). Bulky maritime pipit, with rather long bill, strong
legs and rather broad tail. Winter adult and immatures of both races have *dark
plumage and legs*; olive-toned and softly streaked above, dirty-buff and heavily
and *broadly streaked below*, with indistinct face-pattern except for pale eye-
ring, dull wing-bars and *dull greyish to buff outer tail-feathers*. Breeding adults
of western (island) races similar but Scandinavian Rock Pipit *A. p. littoralis* has
paler, brighter pattern recalling Water Pipit, with bluish tinge to head, *paler
supercilium and wing-bars*, restricted streaks along sides of creamy or pinkish
breast and flanks and paler but not white outer tail-feathers. Flight action lacks
hesitancy of Meadow.
Voice: Song loud, sometimes musical, sometimes tinkling, with strong terminal
trill, given in 'flapping', less parachuting flight. Call sibilant *feest* or *weesp*, less
squeaky than Meadow; breeding birds utter metallic *tchip*.
Habitat: Rocky shores, cliffs and offshore islands, also wintering along hard
mud coasts near breeding stations. Nests in crevices. Map 236.

WATER PIPIT *Anthus spinoletta*   **Plate 72**
Du – Waterpieper   Fr – Pipit spioncelle
Ge – Wasserpieper   Sw – Vattenpiplärka
Identification: 6½" (16cm). Size and form as Rock but strictly montane in
breeding season. Winter adult and immature much paler and cleaner than Rock,
with *strong whitish supercilium*, grey-brown upper-parts, bright whitish wing-
bars, *light body-streaks* mainly confined to breast and *white outer tail-feathers*.
Breeding adult most colourful of all pipits, with *bluish-grey head* relieved by
white supercilicum and *peachy throat*; breast and body marks restricted to faint
flank lines. For Buff-bellied (formerly American Water), see Acidentals. Flight
and gait as Rock but often markedly timid; perches freely on trees and bushes.
Voice: Call less loud than Rock.
Habitat: Mountain slopes and rocks above treeline, descending in winter to wet
meadows and watercress beds, also sheltered estuarine waters. Map 237.

YELLOW WAGTAIL (and other races) *Motacilla flava*   **Plate 73, 74**
Yellow Wagtail *M. f. flavissima*
 Du – Engelse Gele Kwikstaart   Fr – Bergeronnette flavéole
 Ge – Englische Schafstelze   Sw – Engelsk gulärla
Blue-headed Wagtail *M. f. flava*
 Du – Gele Kwikstaart   Fr – Bergeronnette printaniére
 Ge – Schafstelze   Sw – Gulärla
Identification: 6½" (16cm). Quite slender, long-tailed, long-legged; wags tail less than Pied and Grey. Plumage varies between sexes; variations in races, hybrids and mutants create many pitfalls. Typical breeding male *green-backed* above, with two yellow-white bars on coverts of almost black wings, and *yellow below*. Races best separated by head patterns of males: Yellow Wagtail *M. f. flavissima* of British Isles and adjacent European coasts has *yellow head with greenish crown and cheeks*, Blue-headed *M. f. flava* of central Europe has *bluish crown, white supercilium, bluish-grey cheeks and white chin*; other forms are portrayed on Pl. 74. Winter male and females of all races duller, rather brown-backed and often paler yellow below. Racial differentiation much more difficult but female Yellow shows at least yellow tinge to supercilium. Juveniles of all races resemble females but have distinctive buff on throat and brown breast-bib, with Yellow again showing yellow in pale head marks. Beware hybrids resembling extra-limital races and brown or bluish and white mutants suggesting immature Citrine Wagtail. Flight bounding, like large pipit. Walks and runs.
Voice: Song simple, repeated *tsip-tsip-tsipsi*. Commonest call loud musical *tsweep*, also more grating *tsirr*.
Habitat: Typically near water, in marshes, meadows but also in cereals. Nests in depression under grass or crop. Map 238.

CITRINE WAGTAIL *Motacilla citreola*   **Plate 73**
 Du – Citroenkwikstaart   Fr – Bergeronnette citrine
 Ge – Zitronenstelze   Sw – Citronärla
Identification: 6½" (16cm). Form and flight similar to Yellow Wagtail but tail rather longer. Plumage always *bluish or slate on back*, with two strikingly *white bars on wing-coverts*. Breeding male easily identified by *canary-yellow head and neck* contrasting with *black hind-collar*. Female and winter male much less distinctive, resembling dark Yellow from in front but with almost white vent producing look of White from behind. Immature very like grey mutant Yellow but distinguished close-to by *pale buff forehead, fore-supercilium* and breast-band, *white rear supercilium* reaching round pale-spotted cheeks, extensive *grey flanks* and *lack of yellow vent*; even more than adult, resembles White Wagtail from behind. Bobs head and wags tail less than other wagtails.
Voice: Call harsh *sweep* or *dzzeep*, recalling Tree Pipit.
Habitat and Range: In Asia near fresh water in open country and bushy areas, whence vagrant to S., C., W. and N. Europe (including Britain); has hybridised in Finland and Sweden; now breeds in Lithuania.

GREY WAGTAIL *Motacilla cinerea*   **Plate 73, 74**
 Du – Grote Gele Kwikstaart   Fr – Bergeronnette des ruisseaux
 Ge – Gebirgstelze   Sw – Forsärla
Identification: 7½" (19cm). Longest, slimmest wagtail, with *almost incessant*

tail-wag. Distinguished at any season from all other yellow-bodied wagtails by *pale blue-grey back,* greenish-yellow rump and *very long tail*. Narrow whitish supercilium, mostly white throat and brilliant yellow under-body in all plumages; breeding male also has white moustachial streak above *black throat-bib*; juvenile has under-parts buffish except vent. Flight most bounding or shooting of family, with 'whipping' tail and diagnostic *broad white band along mid-wing,* transparent from below. Gait tripping; looks relatively short-legged. Rather solitary except at roosts.

Voice: Song brief repetitive, staccato trill, initially recalling Wren. Commonest call high-pitched, metallic stuttered *tzitzi,* more clipped than other wagtails.

Habitat: Shallow streams in hill country, but also lowlands, woodland streams, sewage-farms and cultivated land, particularly in winter. Nests in holes in walls, bridges, banks, etc. Map 239.

PIED WAGTAIL and WHITE WAGTAIL *Motacilla alba*   Plate 73, 74
Pied Wagtail *M.a. yarrellii*

Du – Rouwkwikstaart	Fr – Bergeronnette d'Yarrell
Ge – Trauerbachstelze	Sw – Engelsk sädesärla

White Wagtail *M.a. alba*

Du – Witte kwikstaart	Fr – Bergeronnette grise
Ge – Bachstelze	Sw – Sädesärla

Identification: 7" (17.5cm). Commonest and bulkiest wagtail, with shorter tail than Grey. Black crown contrasts with *long white forehead*; wings black, with white tips to median coverts, white margins to greater coverts and tertials; tail black with white edges. Plumage truly pied only in adult male Pied *M.a. yarrellii* of Britain which has *black back and rump*; adult male White *M.a. alba* of Europe has *black nape separated from breast* and *pale grey back and rump*. Racial distinction of female, immature and winter male less easy: Pied can have dusky or grey back, White may hide grey rump. Winter adult retains only black crescent on breast, looking much whiter-headed. Juvenile much swarthier and browner than adult; lacks pale forehead and shows dull supercilium, dark cheeks and blackish necklace. Flight outline most chesty of wagtails; action more energetic and bounding than Yellow. Walks with exaggerated head bob, also runs. Migrants less gregarious than Yellow, except at roost.

Voice: Song jaunty twitter, more developed in White than Pied. Commonest call lively *tchizzick*; in alarm, sharp *tchik*.

Habitat: Farms, open country and towns. Often, but not always, near water. Nests in holes in buildings, rocks etc. Map 240.

WAXWINGS: Bombycillidae

WAXWING *Bombycilla garrulus*   Plate 84

Du – Pestvogel	Fr – Jaseur boréal
Ge – Seidenschwanz	Sw – Sidensvans
N. Am – Bohemian Waxwing	

Identification: 7" (17.5cm). Plump, starling-like passerine with unmistakable ample *pointed crest* and short tail. Plumage mainly dull brown above and pinkish-buff below, relieved by *black eye-stripe and bib*, almost black flight-feathers margined yellow and white and *'spiked' wax-red on secondaries*, grey rump, chestnut vent and *yellow-tipped black tail*. Immature lacks wax 'spikes'; juvenile pale-faced and softly streaked on belly and flanks. Flight outline and action recall Starling but both less dart-like. Often tame, with acrobatic berry-feeding habits suggesting Crossbill.

Voice: Song quiet, variably pitched twitter, including weak trill *zhreee*, also used as call.

Habitat: Breeds in open glades of northern coniferous and birch woods. Winters in more open country, seeking berried fruit in hedges and gardens. Map 241.

DIPPERS: Cinclidae

DIPPER *Cinclus cinclus*   **Plate 83**
   Du – Waterspreeuw   Fr – Cincle plongeur
   Ge – Wasseramsel   Sw – Strömstare

Identification: 7" (17.5cm). Portly and aquatic, with character of both thrush and wren; *'bobs' spasmodically* on sturdy legs and often cocks tail. Large *white breast* shines out from otherwise dark adult plumage, blackish in tone except for chestnut chest in most British birds *C.c. gularis*. Juvenile slate above, mottled dusky and white below. Iberian race *C. c. atroventer* has almost black belly. Flight low, whirring but rapid, following stream courses. Gait powerful, allowing bird to walk or plunge into fast-flowing water; swims down to obtain food from stream-bed, using feet and wings. Usually solitary and sedentary.

Voice: Song (nearly all year) succession of short, high grating explosive notes and liquid warble. Call short *zit*; in alarm, metallic *clink*.

Habitat: Swift hill streams; occasionally visits river gravels and coasts in winter. Builds large globular nest in crevices under waterfalls, bridges, banks; invariably by running water. Map 242.

WRENS: Troglodytidae

WREN *Troglodytes troglodytes*   **Plate 83**
   Du – Winterkoning   Fr – Troglodyte
   Ge – Zaunkönig   Sw – Gärdsmyg
   N. Am – Winter Wren

Identification: 3¾" (9.5cm). Tiny, plump, extremely active and pugnacious little bird with *fine decurved bill*, short round wings and *short, often cocked tail*. Plumage rufous-brown, with thin pale supercilium and *close-barred wings and flanks*. Flight low and direct on whirring wings. Forages *mouse-like* on ground and hunts insects warbler-like in foliage.

Voice: Astonishingly powerful song (almost all year) long, breathless stream of strident but not unmusical notes and trills. Call loud, stony *tit-tit-tit*, becoming harsh *churr....* in alarm.

Habitat: Almost ubiquitous in low cover or rock shelter but commonest in woods and gardens. Builds globular nest in hedges, hay-ricks, holes in trees, banks or buildings. Map 243.

ACCENTORS: Prunellidae

Rather drab and sparrow-like in appearance, but with slender bills. They have a distinctive shuffling gait, warbler-like flight in smaller species, unobtrusive habits and brief, high-pitched jingling songs. Sexes similar. Bush or rock nesting.

DUNNOCK *Prunella modularis*   Plate 91
    Du – Heggemus   Fr – Accenteur mouchet
    Ge – Heckenbraunelle   Sw – Järnsparv

Identification: 5¾" (14.5cm). Rather featureless, inconspicuous but often confiding passerine, with *dark thin bill* preventing confusion with sparrow. *Head and neck slate or purplish-grey* (brighter in male), with brownish crown and cheeks, upper-parts rich brown streaked black, under-parts dusky with dark rufous flank-streaks. Flight outline and action recall warbler but gait distinctive, with characteristic *slow creep* or shuffle. Feeds on ground close to cover, often flicking one or both wings.

Voice: Song (almost all year) hurried, weak but pleasant jingle, much shorter and less powerful than Wren; distinctive call high, peeping *tseep*, also high trill.

Habitat: Wood edges, coppices, hedges, garden bushes. Nests in bushes, evergreens, wood-piles. Map 244.

ALPINE ACCENTOR *Prunella collaris*   Plate 91
    Du – Alpenheggemus   Fr – Accenteur alpin
    Ge – Alpenbraunelle   Sw – Alpjärnsparv

Identification: 7" (17.5cm). Larger, plumper montane relative of Dunnock, with stronger bill and legs. Plumage more brightly coloured; distinctive marks are *black-spotted chin and throat*, irregular double white wing-bar enclosing obvious, almost *black band across greater coverts*, broad *chestnut streaks on flanks*, pale buff tips to tail-feathers and coral-red legs. Flight rather lark-like. Feeds in open, sometimes in small flocks.

Voice: Song pleasant, sustained, rapid warble, from ground or brief display flight. Calls lark-like; trilling *tchir-rip* and throaty *churrg*.

Habitat: Rocky mountain slopes, up to snow-line. Winters lower. Nests in holes among rocks or vegetation. Map 245.

ROBINS, CHATS AND THRUSHES: Turdidae

Mostly colourful or strongly patterned, rather upstanding passerines. Bills fairly slender. Tails mostly square-ended, often cocked or held up. Sexes similar in robins, nightingales and spotted thrushes, but markedly dissimilar in most other species. Thrushes build substantial cup nests in bushes, trees, rocks.

RUFOUS BUSH ROBIN *Cercotrichas galactotes*   Plate 80
    Du – Rosse Waaierstaart   Fr – Agrobate roux
    Ge – Heckensänger   Sw – Trädnäktergal

Identification: 6" (15cm). Slim, long-legged chat, with rather thrush-like attitudes. Quickly recognised by *long, chestnut fan-tail, boldly tipped black and white*. Western race *C. g.galactotes* has all upper-parts foxy red-brown; eastern race *C. g. syriacus* (so-called Brown-backed Warbler) has chestnut confined to rump and tail, remainder of upper-parts grey-brown. Both have *bold creamy supercilium* and sandy under-parts. Behaviour much bolder than warblers; perches conspicuously on bushes and ground, with wings drooped, long tail fanned and jerked vertically.

Voice: Song very musical but disjointed and varying in volume, recalling Skylark in some short phrases. Sings from prominent perch, telegraph wires, etc., and in slow, descending display-flight. Call a hard *teck*.

Habitat: Gardens, vineyards and olive groves. Nests in prickly-pear hedges and palm bushes. Map 246.

ROBIN *Erithacus rubecula* **Plate 76**
   Du – Roodborst   Fr – Rougegorge
   Ge – Rotkehlchen   Sw – Rödhake

Identification: 5½" (14cm). Rather small, plump, round-headed, neckless chat; commonest and most widespread of tribe. Adult basically olive-brown above and off-white below, with *reddish-orange fore-face and breast*, margined with grey. Juvenile lacks red breast, being strongly mottled pale buff on dark brown; distinguished from young Redstart by dark brown, not chestnut tail; from Nightingale by smaller size, buffier under-parts and same difference in tail colour. Flight flitting; hops. Confiding behaviour (and exposure of characteristic jaunty attitudes) restricted to redder-breasted British race *E. r. melophilus*; usually shy in Europe.

Voice: Song (all year) varied but well pronounced series of short, high-pitched warbles, at longer intervals in winter. Calls include persistent, often fast repeated *tic*, weak *tsip* or *tsissip* and thin, plaintive *tseee*.

Habitat: Woods with undergrowth, gardens, hedges, coppices, etc. Nests in holes or crannies in walls, banks, trees, hedge-bottoms, ivy, tin cans, etc. Map 247.

THRUSH NIGHTINGALE *Luscinia luscinia* **Plate 76**
   Du – Noordse Nachtegaal   Fr – Rossignol progné
   Ge – Sprosser   Sw – Näktergal

Identification: 6½" (16cm). Form and behaviour as Nightingale but plumage duller, with *tail no brighter than rufous-brown* and *soft brownish mottling on breast* emphasising pale throat.

Voice: Song like Nightingale but often lacks classic crescendos in otherwise louder, more pealed performance. Calls higher-pitched, more clipped than Nightingale.

Habitat: Dense and damp thickets, particularly alder and birch, and in swampy undergrowth. Nesting habits like Nightingale's. Map 248.

NIGHTINGALE *Luscinia megarhynchos* **Plate 76**
   Du – Nachtegaal   Fr – Rossignol philomèle
   Ge – Nachtigall   Sw – Sydnäktergal

Identification: 6½" (16cm). Quite large, Robin-like but relatively long-tailed chat; rather featureless but with *remarkable song*. Plumage uniform warm brown above, with *bright chestnut upper tail-coverts and tail* obvious in flight; brownish-white below. Juvenile resembles young Robin but distinguished by greater bulk, paler under-parts and chestnut tail; from Redstart by larger size, and less bright, not shivered tail. Behaviour like Robin but flight freer, more sweeping. Skulks in cover, usually solitary.

Voice: Song vehement, loud and musical, with repeated notes and phrases of which most characteristic are deep, bubbling *chook-chook-chook* and slow *piu-piu-piu* rising to pealing crescendo; delivered day and night, usually from hidden perch. Calls include liquid *wheet*, loud *tac*, soft, clipped *tuc* and in alarm harsh *kerr*.

Habitat: Deciduous lowland woods, moist thickets, tangled hedges. Nest well hidden near ground in brambles, nettles etc. Map 249.

BLUETHROAT *Luscinia svecica*   **Plate 76**
Du – Blauwborst   Fr – Gorgebleue
Ge – Blaukehlchen   Sw – Blåhake

Identification: 5½" (14cm). Size and form like Redstart but with relatively shorter tail frequently spread and flirted. Conspicuous *basal chestnut panels on tail* diagnostic at all ages. Breeding male has large bright *shiny blue throat-patch*, separated from lower breast by black and chestnut bands; patch spotted red-chestnut in Red-spotted race *L. s. svecica* of Scandinavia, and white in White-spotted form *L. s. cyanecula* of C. and S. Europe. Winter males doubtfully separable as coloured spots and most of blue throat are lost. Females and immatures not racially distinguishable since all show whitish throat, streaked with black on sides and across *irregular necklace or breast-band* and rarely marked with blue or chestnut traces. Juvenile more streaked than Robin. Flight usually low and darting, ending in swoop to base of cover.

Voice: Song, very musical and varied, in parts faintly resembling Nightingale and Woodlark, but much higher-pitched, weaker and less rich; introduces sharp, high note like striking metal triangle, also cricket-like sound. Sings (often at dusk) from perch and in zig-zag flight. Calls sharp *tac*, soft *wheet* and guttural *turrc*.

Habitat: Swampy thickets and heaths, tangled hedges, etc. Breeds close to ground among birch, willow and juniper scrub; uses such habitat even in high mountains, but in W. Central Europe and above Arctic Circle, often in lowlands. Map 250.

RED-FLANKED BLUETAIL *Tarsiger cyanurus*   **Plate 77**
Du – Blauwstaart   Fr – Rossignol à flancs roux
Ge – Blauschwanz   Sw – Blåstjärt

Identification: 5½" (14cm). Rather small chat with form and flight recalling both Redstart and Robin. Male has *cobalt blue and grey upper-parts*, relieved by variable white supercilium, and *cream-white throat* and under-parts, splashed *bright rufous-orange on flanks*. Female and immature male share bluish rump and tail and orange flanks but have olive-brown upper-parts, *whitish eye-ring* and *white throat* emphasized by clouded breast. Juvenile like young Robin.

Voice: Song distinctive, recalling thrush: 6-7 clear notes, with early dip in pitch and distinct fall at end: *whew-wee-whew-wee-wee-wellu-it*; uttered day and night, usually from tree-top. Calls include short, almost quacked note from wintering birds, Robin-like *tick-tick* from vagrants, *weep* from breeding birds.

Habitat and Range: Dense, damp pine or spruce forests. Nests on ground. Now probably established as summer visitor to eastern Finland; has bred Estonia. Vagrant from Russia and Asia to N., C., W. and S. Europe (including Britain).

BLACK REDSTART *Phoenicurus ochruros*   **Plate 77**
Du – Zwarte Roodstaart   Fr – Rougequeue noir
Ge – Hausrotschwanz   Sw – Svart rödstjärt
Identification: 5½" (14cm). Both sexes at all ages share form, flickering *rusty tail and rusty rump* with Redstart. Male of western race *P. o. gibraltariensis* in Europe *sooty black* and grey, with *white panel on innermost flight-feathers* obvious on old birds. Female and immature dirty grey; always darker than Redstart, lacking buff under-parts. Vagrant eastern races have rufous under-body contrasting with dark breasts. Actions like Redstart but bolder, perching upright on buildings, telegraph wires and rocks when slightly sturdier build shows, while flight is slightly heavier.
Voice: Song short and rapidly uttered, with simpler and less musical phrase than Redstart, interspersed with curious spluttering, hissing notes; sings from prominent high perch or roof-top. Calls include short *tsip*, scolding *tucc-tucc* and rapid rattle in alarm.
Habitat: Cliffs, buildings, rocky slopes, occasionally vineyards, etc. Breeds in holes in walls, rocks, buildings. Map 251.

REDSTART *Phoenicurus phoenicurus*   **Plate 77**
Du – Gekraagde Roodstaart   Fr – Rougequeue à front blanc
Ge – Gartenrotschwanz   Sw – Rödstjärt
Identification: 5½" (14cm). Slim, long-tailed chat; *constantly flickers bright rusty tail from rusty rump*. Breeding male has *black face and throat*, emphasised by white forehead, *bluish-grey crown and back, and orange-chestnut breast* and flanks; face and throat made hoary by pale fringes after autumn moult. Female and immature greyish-brown above, with pale eye-ring, buffish-white below. Vagrants of S. W. Asian race *P. p. samamisicus* have whitish patch along innermost flight-feathers. Juvenile mottled like young Robin but already shows bright rump and tail; much paler than Black Redstart. Actions like Robin but flight light, even floating, trailing tail. Rather shy.
Voice: Song short pleasing jingle of hurried, Robin-like notes, fading to feeble twitter. Calls rather tremulous *whee-tic-tic*, liquid *wheet* very like note of Willow Warbler, and clear *tooick*.
Habitat: Woodlands, parks, heaths with bushes and old trees, occasionally ruins. Nests in holes in trees, stone walls, sheds, etc. Map 252.

WHINCHAT *Saxicola rubetra*   **Plate 76**
Du – Paapje   Fr – Traquet tarier
Ge – Braunkehlchen   Sw – Buskskvätta
Identification: 5" (12.5cm). Small and rakish, with short tail; recalls Stonechat but distinguished at all seasons by prominent *pale supercilium over dark face-patch*, white basal patches on tail and less upright pose. Male striking, with *black-brown crown and cheeks* divided by broad *white supercilium*, further emphasized by *white 'moustache'*, white patch high on wing and warm orange-buff throat and breast. Female and immature paler, with sandier plumage, buff supercilium and smaller wing-patch. Juvenile lacks wing-patch. Actions like Stonechat but more sociable, often in loose parties.
Voice: Song brief, rather metallic but pleasing warble, recalling Redstart but

lacking terminal twitter; uttered from bush-top, occasionally in flight. Call short *tic-tic* or *tu-tic-tic*, also clicks and churrs.

Habitat: Commons, marshes, railway embankments, open country, with a few bushes, bracken, gorse, etc. On passage also in cultivated fields. Nests in coarse grass, often at foot of small bush, or large plant. Map 253.

STONECHAT *Saxicola torquata*   Plate 76

Du – Roodborsttapuit   Fr – Traquet pâtre
Ge – Schwarzkehlchen   Sw – Svarthakad buskskvätta

Identification: 5" (12.5cm). Small, *round-headed, upright* chat. Breeding males of western races in Europe have distinctive *black head and throat*, emphasized by *white half-collar*, black-brown upper-parts and tail, relieved by white line on inner wing and white mottles on rump, and *orange-chestnut breast* fading into white under-body; in autumn, duller above and even more warmly coloured below. Female and immature far less distinctive but still dark-headed, lacking pale supercilium, and ruddy below, unlike Whinchat. Vagrants of eastern races, particularly *S. t. maura* of Siberia, have similar form but more contrasting plumage, but with variable pale supercilium and throat; can be confused with Whinchat, but distinguished by *large, orange to white rump* and *black wing-pit*. Flight low and whirring. When alert, jerks wings and tail; breeding birds scold vociferously.

Voice: Song consists of irregular, rapidly repeated double notes, not unlike Dunnock's. Sings from elevated perch or in 'dancing' song-flight. Calls persistent scolding *wheet, tsack-tsack*, like hitting two stones together, also clicking note similar to Whinchat's.

Habitat: As Whinchat, but usually more fond of gorse-clad commons and of coastal areas. Map 254.

ISABELLINE WHEATEAR *Oenanthe isabellina*   Plate 75

Du – Isabeltapuit   Fr – Traquet isabelle
Ge – Isabellsteinschmätzer   Sw – Isabellastenskvätta

Identification: 6½" (16.5cm). Second largest wheatear, with long head, broad wings, *long legs*, rather short tail and *almost uniform appearance*. Distinguished from palest immatures of Greenland Wheatear *O. o. leucorrhoa* by tiny hook on bill-tip, *black lores* (speckled in female and immature), *much paler and broader edges to wing-coverts and inner flight-feathers,* short but broad white rump and *broad black band on tail* (more than half length, with less central extension towards rump than Northern Wheatear). *Creamy wing lining* (lacking even speckled coverts) diagnostic. Flight outline shows broad wings and full but not long tail; action more floating than Northern Wheatear. Runs more than other wheatears; also often stands higher, showing thighs when alert.

Voice: Song long, rich, lark-like cadence, unlike other wheatears. Call loud *cheep* or *weep*, also whistling *wheet-whit.*

Habitat and Range: Usually in steppe, barren plains, or lower slopes of bare hills; shows preference for sandy locations in winter. Breeds N.E. Greece and European Turkey. Vagrant elsewhere in E., C., W. and N. Europe (including Britain).

Northern Wheatear in flight

NORTHERN WHEATEAR *Oenanthe oenanthe*   **Plate 75**
  Du   Tapuit   Fr – Traquet motteux
  Ge – Steinschmätzer   Sw – Stenskvätta
Identification: 5¾-6¼" (14.5-16cm). Medium-sized chat, often prominently perched; commonest of tribe in north. In flight, contrast of *white rump* and basal tail-patches with *black centre and terminal band to tail* catch eye; under-wing speckled black on coverts. Breeding male has *blue-grey crown and back*, broad white supercilium, black ear-coverts and wings, and buffish to white under-parts. Winter male, female and immature show brown crown and back, duller but still strong supercilia, partly black or brown ear-coverts and wings, and buffier under-parts; a few birds are noticeably paler, especially below. Greenland race *O. o. leucorrhoa* which passes through W. Europe is larger and more richly coloured below but many intermediate birds not safely identifiable. Flight outline less compact than smaller chats and action more fluent, bird flitting low across ground and then bouncing onto perch, often to 'bob' and wave tail. Hops and runs.
Confusion species: Beware variant Northerns which can resemble relatives, particularly pale Greenland (suggesting Isabelline), rufous immature (Black-eared) and dull immature (Pied).
Voice: Song brief, somewhat lark-like warble, combining musical notes and wheezy rattle. Calls hard *chack* and *wheet-chack...*; in alarm, plaintive *weep*.
Habitat: Downs, moors, hilly pastures, cliff-tops, dunes. Nests in holes in walls, rabbit warrens, stone heaps, etc. Map 255.

PIED WHEATEAR *Oenanthe pleschanka*   **Plate 75**
  Du – Bonte Tapuit   Fr – Traquet pie
  Ge – Nonnensteinschmätzer   Sw – Nunnestenskvätta
Identification: 5¾" (14.5cm). Looks longer-tailed and shorter-legged than Northern Wheatear. Plumage pied only in male, with *grey-white crown and shawl* and cream-white rump, tail patches and under-parts below breast contrasting strikingly with otherwise black plumage. In winter, crown sullied earth-brown and inner wing-feathers pale-margined. Female and immature difficult to identify but show *black wing-lining* (ruling out Northern) and have duskier head,

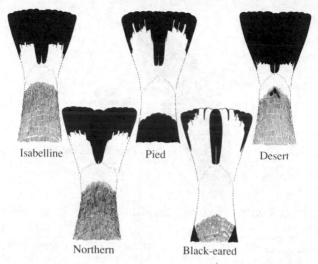

Isabelline *Pied* *Desert*

Northern *Black-eared*

Rump and tail patterns of five wheatear species drawn from specimens of
males in the British Museum (Natural History)

chest and back than Black-eared, with diagnostic *pale back spots and scales* in
first autumn (see figure for typical tail pattern). Prone to feed shrike-fashion
from low perch.

Voice: Song very brief, variable musical phrase, repeated at intervals. Call
harsh *zack*.

Habitat and Range: 'Soft' coastal cliffs in Europe, elsewhere stony barrens,
rocky hillsides with a few bushes. Nests in holes. Summer visitor, breeding
coastal Romania and Bulgaria. Vagrant to W., C. and N. Europe (including Britain).

BLACK-EARED WHEATEAR *Oenanthe hispanica*   **Plate 75**
    Du – Blonde Tapuit   Fr – Traquet oreillard
    Ge – Mittelmeersteinschmätzer   Sw – Medelhavstenssskvätta

Identification: 5¾" (14.5cm). Looks rounder-headed, longer-tailed and shorter-legged than Northern Wheatear. Body plumage of western race *O. h. hispanica* (W. Mediterranean east to N. Italy) sandiest, wings blackest and *black
tail-marks least extensive* of tribe (see figure above). Males dimorphic, with
either just black eye-patch or full black face and throat, and *black scapulars*
'narrowing' back; some breeding males look virtually white on back and body.
Female and immature resemble Northern but, close-to, distinguished by *indistinct supercilium*, black wing-lining and tail pattern. Eastern race *O. h. melanoleuca* (E. Mediterranean) confusing, with most males white-backed and females
and immatures distinctly duller, even grey-brown above. Perches readily on
plants and trees.

Confusion species: Most immatures of western race can be separated from

Pied by sandy-rufous upper-parts (lacking pale marks) and sandy-buff chest-band. Immatures of eastern race similar to Pied in colour but upper-parts unmarked, while chest usually shows orange-toned band.
Voice: Song rapid, high-pitched *schwer, schwee, schwee-oo*, from perch or circling display flight. Call muffled *check*, followed by plaintive whistle from breeding bird.
Habitat: Open or lightly wooded arid country and stony mountain slopes. Usually breeds in holes among rocks, walls, etc. Map 256.

DESERT WHEATEAR *Oenanthe deserti*   **Plate 75**
  Du – Woestijntapuit   Fr – Traquet du désert
  Ge – Wüstensteinschmätzer   Sw – Ökenstenskvätta
Identification: 5½" (14cm). Rather small wheatear; buffiest of tribe, with virtually *all-black tail*. Male recalls black-throated form of Black-eared but distinguished by less distinct supercilium, duller, less variable sandy- to grey-buff upper-parts (including scapulars) and breast, and less black wings (usually retaining pale margins on inner feathers even when worn). Has *small white rump* and apparently short tail lacking central 'T' extension of all other wheatears. Female and immature suggest Isabelline but easily separated by much smaller size, dumpy build, *black wing-lining* and small dull buffish rump.
Voice: Call rather plaintive, soft whistle.
Habitat and Range: Barren and rocky or sandy wastes; in winter also in cultivated areas near barren ground. Vagrant from Africa, Asia to S., W., C. and N. Europe (including Britain).

BLACK WHEATEAR *Oenanthe leucura*   **Plate 75**
  Du – Zwarte Tapuit   Fr – Traquet rieur
  Ge – Trauersteinschmätzer   Sw – Svart stenskvätta
Identification: 7" (17.5cm). Largest wheatear of region, with big head and deep chest. Easily identified by slightly glossy *black plumage*, relieved only by white rump, vent and long basal tail patches. Female and immature usually duller, with brown tinge to black plumage. Flight noticeably buoyant. Beware lack of white crown on some White-crowned Black Wheatears (see Accidentals).
Voice: Song brief but rich warble, comparable with Blue Rock Thrush. Anxiety-note *pee-pee-pee*.
Habitat: Rocky deserts, sea cliffs and mountainous regions. Nests in holes among rocks, frequently screening entrance with a little wall of pebbles. Map 257.

ROCK THRUSH *Monticola saxatilis*   **Plate 77**
  Du – Rode Rotslijster   Fr – Merle de roche
  Ge – Steinrötel   Sw – Stentrast
Identification: 7½" (19cm). Noticeably upright thrush-like, montane chat, with *short chestnut tail* loosely swung or flickered. Breeding male colourful, with *pale slate-blue head,* neck and mantle, *white blaze on back,* blackish wings and *chestnut-orange under-parts and under-wing.* In winter, fresh buffish fringes obscure pattern. Female similar to winter male, some with trace of white on back, all with paler *scaled and barred under-parts.* Juvenile like female but noticeably pale spotted from nape to rump. Flight thrush-like; long wings make

tail look even shorter. Solitary, running away from disturbance and diving into rocks to hide.
Voice: Song clear, fluted warble, from perch and brief vertical display-flight. Call medium-pitched *chack, chack.*
Habitat: Breeds in open rocky regions and among trees at 1,700-8,000ft. (500-2,700m.). Map 258.

BLUE ROCK THRUSH *Monticola solitarius*   Plate 77
Du – Blauwe Rotslijster   Fr – Merle bleu
Ge – Blaumerle   Sw – Blåtrast
Identification: 8" (20cm). Form even more thrush-like than Rock Thrush due to much longer tail and less upright stance. At distance, dark plumage recalls Blackbird. Close-to, breeding male unmistakeably *slate-blue*, almost black on back, wings and tail; in winter, faintly scaled buff. Female and juvenile dark *dusky-brown, spotted and scaled buff-white*; close-to, some females show bluish tinge. Flight and behaviour like Rock Thrush but longer tail always obvious.
Voice: Song loud and fluty, in short deliberate phrases recalling Blackbird. Calls include hard *tchuck*, plaintive *tsee* and characteristic liquid *uit-uit* suggesting Nuthatch.
Habitat: Rocky desert regions and bare mountainsides down to sea level. Nests in crevices in rocks, cliffs and buildings. Map 259.

WHITE'S THRUSH *Zoothera dauma*   Plate 78
Du – Goudlijster   Fr – Grive dorée
Ge – Erddrossel   Sw – Guldtrast
Identification: 10¾" (27cm). Largest thrush reaching region; form recalls Mistle Thrush but tail proportionately shorter. Plumage *rich golden-brown, boldly scaled with black* crescents on head and body. In flight, *under-wing boldly banded black and white* and long, uppertail-coverts show pale, unmarked patch. Flight heavy, soon becoming deeply undulating, recalling Green Woodpecker. Shy, haunting dense cover.
Voice: Exceptionally silent for thrush but may *churr*.
Habitat and Range: Normally in deep forest with heavy undergrowth. Vagrant from Asia to C., W., N. and S. Europe (including Britain).

SIBERIAN THRUSH *Zoothera sibirica*   Plate 78
Du – Siberische Lijster   Fr – Merle sibérien
Ge – Sibirische Drossel   Sw – Sibirisk trast
Identification: 9" (22.5cm). Rakish thrush; size and form as Song Thrush. Male slaty-black, with *bold white supercilium, white belly-centre and barred vent;* in overhead flight, shows conspicuous *white bands on underwing* and white tail-corners. Female and immature share last two marks but are dusky-brown above and buffish-white below, with strong *buff supercilium* and chequered face, breast and flanks. Flight and behaviour apparently as *Turdus* thrush.
Voice: Calls include gruff squawk and soft *zit* recalling Song Thrush.
Habitat and Range: Normally in damp forest. Vagrant from E. Asia to S., W., C. and N. Europe (including Britain).

SWAINSON'S THRUSH *Catharus ustulatus*   **Plate 94**
Du – Dwerglijster   Fr – Grive petite
Ge – Zwergdrossel   Sw – Beigekindad skogstrast
Identification: 7½" (19cm). Only three-quarters size of Song Thrush; may suggest Nightingale. Upper-parts *dull olive* with faintly russet tinge; shows obvious *buff eye-ring and speckles on cheek* and blackish spots on buff neck and breast, fading out on *olive-brown flanks*; rest of under-parts dull white. Underwing dull brown, with pale cream band along centre. Flight more flitting than Song Thrush. Occasionally cocks and slowly lowers tail. Skulks like somewhat similar Grey-cheeked Thrush, which see.
Voice: Calls emphatic *whit* and high-pitched *queep*.
Habitat and Range: Normally lowland coniferous forest; migrants seek out damp thickets. Vagrant from N. America to W., C. and E. Europe (including Britain).

GREY-CHEEKED THRUSH *Catharus minimus*   **Plate 94**
Du – Grijswangdwerglijster   Fr – Grive à joues grises
Ge – Grauwangendrossel   Sw – Gråkindad skogstrast
Identification: 7½" (19cm). Slightly bulkier and longer-legged than Swainson's, with similar plumage pattern, but, close-to, distinguished by colder, *dark olive-grey upper-parts*, far more indistinct, whitish eye-ring (sometimes incomplete or missing), finely mottled *grey and off-white cheeks*, more defined malar spots and cold *ochre-grey breast and flanks*. Not known to cock tail.
Voice: Call long, rather nasal *wheu* or *quee-a*, quite unlike Swainson's but close to Veery.
Habitat and Range: As Swainson's but more northerly distribution in N. America apparently reflected in its arrival only to N. and W. Europe (including Britain).

RING OUZEL *Turdus torquatus*   **Plate 78**
Du – Beflijster   Fr – Merle à plastron
Ge – Ringdrossel   Sw – Ringtrast
Identification: 9½" (24cm). Size close to Blackbird but form slighter and more rakish, with longer wings. Male dull blackish with broad *white crescent across breast* and thin *white margins on flight-feathers*; in winter, *pale-scaled* on lower body. Female dark brown, with narrower, barred breast-crescent and more pale scales at all seasons. Juvenile lacks crescent and scales; looks like heavily spotted and barred Blackbird. In Alpine and eastern races, white margins of flight-feathers form striking panel; in winter, their plumage is heavily scaled greyish-white on scapulars and below. Flight rapid, hurtling up and down cliffs. Shy and nervous, often hiding in rocks. Pied Blackbirds sometimes show white on breast but lack pale wing-panel.
Voice: Song poorly developed; mixes double or treble notes *tcheru*, *tchivi* and *ti-cho-o* (repeated 3- 4 times) with pauses and chuckles. Calls include diagnostic rattling *tac-tac-tac* (often extended into chatter), pipe, chuckle and trills.
Habitat: Hilly moorlands and mountains, usually above 1,000ft (300m.). Breeds among heather, juniper, rocks, often by track or stream; also within tree limit on Continent. Map 260.

BLACKBIRD *Turdus merula*   **Plate 78**
Du – Merel   Fr – Merle noir
Ge – Amsel   Sw – Koltrast
Identification: 10" (25cm). Commonest, most widespread thrush; sturdy with long tail frequently raised and fanned on landing. Male *all black* with *bright orange-yellow bill and eye-ring*; in first winter, more dusky with dark bill. Beware occasional albinistic morphs. Female dark brown above, paler, more rufous below, with speckled whitish chin. Juvenile like female but more rufous and strongly mottled. Flight fast but erratic due to varying rhythm of wing-beats. Hops and runs. Sociable and noisy.
Voice: Song rich, mellow, melodious warble, with fluted notes but often with weak, chuckled ending; does *not* repeat phrases, unlike Song Thrush. Calls loud and varied; in alarm, anxious *tchook*; when mobbing, persistent *tchink, tchink, tchink* (often in group chorus), and when flushed, screeching hysterical chatter.
Habitat: Farmland, woods, gardens, town parks and squares etc. Nests in hedges, wood-piles, sheds etc. Map 261.

EYE-BROWED THRUSH *Turdus obscurus*   **Plate 78**
Du – Vale Lijster   Fr – Grive obscure
Ge – Weissbrauendrossel   Sw – Gråhalsad trast
Identification: 8½" (21.5cm). Rakish, Redwing-like, with unique combination of *grey upper-breast* and *orange-buff sides to breast and flanks*. Upper-parts olive-brown, with smoky-grey head marked with *long white supercilium*, dark eye-stripe and 'moustache' and *white throat*; under-wing pale grey and belly white. Female and immature duller than male, with browner, less cleanly patterned head and paler buff breast and flanks. Actions recall Redwing, of which adult in poor light may suggest Eye-browed.
Voice: Calls include pipit-like *tlip*, soft *tchuck* and in alarm, loud *kewk*.
Habitat and Range: Mixed forest and fringe woods. Vagrant from E. Asia to all Europe (including Britain).

DUSKY THRUSH and **NAUMANN'S THRUSH** *Turdus naumanni* **Plate 78**
Dusky Thrush *T. n. eunomus*
Du – Bruine Lijster   Fr – Grive à ailes rousses
Ge – Rostflügeldrossel   Sw – Svartfläckig bruntrast

Naumann's Thrush *T. n. naumanni*
Du – Naumann's Lijster   Fr – Grive de Naumann
Ge – Naumannsdrossel   Sw – Rödfläckig bruntrast
Identification: 9" (22.5cm). Rather stocky, with stout bill; longer-winged and -tailed than Redwing. Plumage shows diagnostic combination of *broad pale supercilium* and *rufous-chestnut on and under wings and on rump*. Dusky Thrush *T.n. eunomus* from N. Siberia distinguished by contrast of cream supercilium with *dark rear cheeks*, pale half-collar and *black-splashed under-parts*, always showing gorget and sometimes second lower half-band. Naumann's Thrush *T.n. naumanni* from S.E. Siberia distinguished by *dull pink-red mottling of under-parts* and *red-chestnut tail*. Intermediate birds occur. Flight outline plump like Song, flight action and gait can recall Fieldfare.
Voice: Calls include *swer(k)-swer(k)-swer(k)* and *kvereg* in alarm and *spirr* in flight, last with piercing Starling-like tone.

Habitat and Range: Normally in broken or fringe forest. Both races wander from Asia to most of Europe (including Britain), with individual home latitudes reflected in occurrences.

BLACK-THROATED THRUSH and   **Plate 78**
RED-THROATED THRUSH *Turdus ruficollis*
Black-throated Thrush *T. r. atrogularis*
   Du – Zwartkeellijster   Fr – Grive à gorge noire
   Ge – Schwarzkehldrossel   Sw – Svarthalsad taigatrast

Red-throated Thrush *T. r. ruficollis*
   Du – Roodkeellijster   Fr – Grive à gorge rouge
   Ge – Rotkehldrossel   Sw – Rödhalsad taigatrast
Identification: 9¼" (23cm). Size and form like Blackbird but shorter-tailed; behaviour and plumage pattern recall Fieldfare. Plumage of male distinctly dark-throated and -breasted, with brown upper-parts and contrasting *dull white under-body* and rufous-buff under-wing. Black-throated *T. r. atrogularis* of E. Russia to central Siberia has *black breast* and *black-brown tail*; Red-throated *T. r. ruficollis* of SE. Siberia has *dull red breast and tail*. Female and immature of both races lack dark throats and breasts, showing instead spotted malar stripes and scalloped or spotted breasts, but have diagnostic tail colours. Flight action over long distance recalls Fieldfare. Rather upright on ground, making long hops.
Voice: Calls include throaty *which-which-which*, softer than Blackbird's chuckle, and thin *see* in flight, like Redwing.
Habitat and Range: Normally in sparse or open forest, wintering in open country. Vagrant from Russia and Asia to most of Europe (including Britain), most records being of Black-throated.

FIELDFARE *Turdus pilaris*   **Plate 78**
   Du – Kramsvogel   Fr – Grive litorne
   Ge – Wacholderdrossel   Sw – Björktrast
Identification: 10" (25cm). Rakish, long-tailed, noisy thrush, only slightly smaller than Mistle; often locally, commonest winter thrush of open country. Adult plumage colourful, with *pale grey head*, rusty-yellow, black-spotted throat and breast, *chestnut back*, and blackish wings; *grey rump contrasts with almost black tail*; black chevrons on flanks and *white under-wing* and belly. Immature duller, less contrasting. Flight outline loose and long-tailed, action also loose but without deep undulations of Mistle. Markedly gregarious.
Voice: Song at best weak string of chuckles, whistles, squeaks and calls. Commonest call aggressive-sounding cackle *tchak-tchak-tchak......*
Habitat: Winters in open country, seeking food in fields and along hedges. Breeds usually colonially near clearings or margins of woods, particularly in birch, occasionally on buildings and haystacks; on ground above tree limit. Map 262.

SONG THRUSH *Turdus philomelos*   **Plate 78**
   Du – Zanglijster   Fr – Grive musicienne
   Ge – Singdrossel   Sw – Taltrast
Identification: 9" (22.5cm). Commonest medium-sized, short-tailed thrush,

with brown upper-parts, *buff wing-lining* and strongly *spotted under-parts*. Western peripheral races suffused olive above, buff below; European race greyer-toned above, with much cleaner ground below. Distinguished from Mistle and Fieldfare by much smaller size, uniform upper-parts and yellowish-buff ground to breast and flanks; from Redwing by lack of prominent supercilium, chestnut flanks and under-wing. Flight outline most compact of tribe; action fast, with more constant wing-beats than large thrushes. Often feeds in open, spasmodically hopping and running. Gregarious only on migration.

Voice: Song loud and musical, with short, varied *phrases repeated 2-4 times*, between brief pauses. Calls include loud *tchuck*, or *tchick*, repeated rapidly as alarm; flight-call a soft *sip* (shorter than Redwing's call).

Habitat: Among human habitation, parks, woods and hedges. Nests in bushes, hedges, ivy, etc., occasionally in buildings. Map 263.

REDWING *Turdus iliacus*   **Plate 78**
   Du – Koperwiek   Fr – Grive mauvis
   Ge – Rotdrossel   Sw – Rödvingetrast

Identification: 8¼" (21cm). Smallest common thrush, with form resembling Song Thrush. Plumage pattern strong, with rather dark brown upper-parts and basically white under-parts relieved by *long creamy supercilium contrasting with dark cheeks*, pale throat and cheek surround, splashed and streaked rather than spotted breast and flanks, *rufous-chestnut flanks and under-wing* and white patch by vent. Flight outline and action most Starling-like of tribe, and fastest. Distant or poorly lit bird could be confused with Eye-browed and Dusky Thrushes, which see.

Voice: Song varies greatly locally; a repeated phrase of 4-6 fluty notes, rising and falling, typically *trui-trui-trui-troo-tri*, followed by a weak, warbling subsong. Calls include distinctive thin *see-ip* or *seeze* (often heard from night migrants), harsh *chittuc* and abrupt *kewk*.

Habitat: Winters in open country near woods. Nests on tree stumps, woodstacks, in trees or bushes, on ground, etc., in light woods, marshy localities, often on edges of Fieldfare colonies. Map 264.

MISTLE THRUSH *Turdus viscivorus*   **Plate 78**
   Du – Grote Lijster   Fr – Grive draine
   Ge – Misteldrossel   Sw – Dubbeltrast

Identification: 10½" (26cm). Second largest and fullest-tailed thrush, distinguished from Song by much larger size, lengthier shape, *greyish-olive-brown upper-parts*, boldly and *irregularly-spotted under-parts* and taller stance. Juvenile strongly pale-spotted. Shares bright white wing-lining with Fieldfare but readily distinguished by more uniform upper-parts, buffish not rusty breast and *whitish corners to longer, paler tail*. Flight outline longest of common thrushes, with bulky body 'tailing off', action strong and buoyant with longer, more regular wing closures than Fieldfare, producing deep undulations. Sociable at times but never gregarious. Juvenile may suggest White's Thrush, which see.

Voice: Song loud, somewhat Blackbird-like, but lacks mellowness and variety, repeating short, rather similar phrases. Sings in all weathers, from tree-tops. Calls include dry, rasping chatter and hard *tuc-tuc-tuc*.

Habitat: Large gardens, orchards, woods. Nests in bare fork in tree. Small flocks roam open country and fields in autumn. Map 265.

AMERICAN ROBIN *Turdus migratorius*   **Plate 78**
Du – Roodborstlijster   Fr – Merle migrateur
Ge – Wanderdrossel   Sw – Vandringstrast
Identification: 10" (25cm). Largest N. American thrush, with character and actions close to Blackbird. Plumage dark blackish-grey above, *brick-red below* and on under-wings, relieved by yellow bill, *broken white eye-ring*, white, black-streaked chin and throat, white vent and tail corners. Flight over long distance recalls Fieldfare.
Voice: Calls harsh, scolding, recalling Blackbird.
Habitat and Range: Normally woods, thickets and around human habitation. Vagrant from N. America to W., N., C. and S. Europe (including Britain).

WARBLERS: *Sylviidae*

Warblers are small, active insectivorous birds, with slender bills. Many confusingly devoid of distinctive markings; plumages wear rapidly, adding to difficulty in identification. Call-notes often rather similar. Songs and behaviour diagnostically important. Usually nest in low vegetation on or near ground, or (in *Acrocephalus*) in reeds. Sexes similar, except in *Sylvia*. For convenience, tribes can be divided into four groups – swamp warblers (*Cettia, Cisticola, Locustella, Acrocephalus*), tree warblers (*Hippolais*), scrub warblers (*Sylvia*), and leaf warblers (*Phylloscopus*) – but habitat preferences frequently overlap. Scrub warblers rather long-tailed. Goldcrest and Firecrest (*Regulus*) are minute arboreal birds related to leaf warblers but also recalling tits in behaviour; adults have brilliant streak of colour on crown; sexes nearly similar; tree-nesting.

CETTI'S WARBLER *Cettia cetti*   **Plate 79**
Du – Cetti's Zanger   Fr – Bouscarle de Cetti
Ge – Seidensänger   Sw – Cettisångare
Identification: 5½" (14cm). Quite large, Dunnock-shaped, very skulking warbler, with *unmistakeable song* and full and rounded *tail often cocked*. Upperparts *dark rufous-brown*, relieved only by indistinct whitish supercilium (like Wren); under-parts greyish-white, with brownish flanks and brown-barred under tail-coverts. Flight outline compact, action whirring in straight dashes between cover.
Voice: Song (usually from bird hidden in dense vegetation) *very loud, abrupt burst* of short phrases, repeating particularly *cheweeoo* but with varying emphasis and at long intervals. Calls include explosive *pex*, loud *chee*, short *twic*, soft *huit* and churring alarm note, like Wren.
Habitat: Low, tangled vegetation, usually near water, ditches, swamps, reedbeds. Nest well hidden in low vegetation. Map 266.

FAN-TAILED WARBLER Cisticola juncidis Plate 79
Du – Waaierstaartrietzanger Fr – Cisticole des joncs
Ge – Cistensänger Sw – Grässångare
Identification: 4" (10cm). Noticeably small, skulking warbler, with stubby tail and *unmistakeable song* given from sustained *undulating song-flight*. Plumage basically buff above and on sides of body, buff- to greyish-white below; sharply streaked black on crown and *broadly splashed black on mantle* (not rump), wings and tail. From below, tail boldly tipped black and white on outer feathers; face plain, with *pale cream to whitish eye-ring*. May suggest young Sedge or Aquatic Warbler, but is much smaller, without clear supercilium.
Voice: Song simple, with penetrating, rasping *dzeep* or *zreep* note uttered with *each upward bound* of high (c.10 m) territorial flight. Call *tew*.
Habitat: Wet and dry localities, grain fields, rough grassy plains, marshes. Builds deep purse-shaped nest suspended in rushes, long grass, growing corn, or dense herbage. Map 267.

PALLAS'S GRASSHOPPER WARBLER Locustella certhiola Plate 82
Du – Siberische Snor Fr – Locustelle de Pallas
Ge – Steifenschwirl Sw – Starrsångare
Identification: 5¼" (13cm). Largest streaked member of skulking tribe occurring in region, with plumage pattern and buff ground recalling Sedge as much as Grasshopper. Head shows dark, streaked crown and *pale buff-white supercilium* and eye-ring; *grey-buff nape and shawl* contrast with heavily streaked back; *rusty rump* obvious above cross-barred, *dark-ended tail,* with narrow white tips forming *pale rim*. Under-parts greyish-buff, but creamy with streaked breast in juvenile. Dark primary coverts may show in flight, when long, round-winged, broad-rumped and fan-tailed outline and fluttering action distinctive. Creeps and *runs*.
Voice: Call sharp disyllabic *chir-chirr*.
Habitat and Range: Damp meadows with long grass and in rank undergrowth. Winters in rice fields, reeds, swamps. Vagrant from C. Asia, Siberia to C., N. and W. Europe (including Britain).

LANCEOLATED WARBLER Locustella lanceolata Plate 82
Du – Temminck's Rietzanger Fr – Locustelle lancéolée
Ge – Strichelschwirl Sw – Träsksångare
Identification: 4½" (11cm). Smallest member of tribe, with *pipit-like appearance*; skulks in grass tufts. Plumage recalls Grasshopper but darker-, browner-toned, with *sharp and heavy streaks above* and particularly on *well defined gorget* below whitish chin and throat; supercilium and eye-ring indistinct. Fan-tail may appear pointed in immature. May flush into short whirring flight, suggesting long-tailed Wren, but normally stays within ground cover, creeping, walking and running like tiny mouse.
Voice: Call as Pallas's Grasshopper but sharper, slightly lower-pitched.
Habitat and Range: Rank vegetation and reeds bordering water, wet meadows and overgrown marshes. Vagrant from NE. Russia, Asia to N., C., W. and S . Europe (including Britain).

GRASSHOPPER WARBLER *Locustella naevia* Plate 79

Du – Sprinkhaanrietzanger Fr – Locustelle tachetée
Ge – Feldschwirl Sw – Gräshoppsångare

Identification: 5" (12.5cm). Rather small, lithe and *markedly fan-tailed* warbler, with distinctive *reeling song*. Plumage variable, with yellowish-buff to dull olive-brown ground to upper-parts, chest and flanks; *subdued streaks* most obvious on crown, back and wings, least so on under-parts. Supercilium indistinct, eye-ring narrow but bright. Tail faintly barred; may appear pale-rimmed but *lacks darkening feather-ends* of Pallas's Grasshopper. Flight outline long, with round wings and trailing fan-tail; action whirring and fluttering, with occasional twitch of tail. Creeps, walks and runs with great agility, threading its way through tangled vegetation. When most brightly patterned, can resemble Pallas's Grasshopper; when least so, Savi's.

Voice: Song fast, dry, incessant reeling, with mechanical but slightly muffled tone and ventriloquial effect (due to bird turning head to direct song over wide arc); uttered day or night. Calls short *twhit* or *pitt* and *chik*, merging into chatter in alarm.

Habitat: Undergrowth in marshes, water-meadows, dry heaths, hedgerows, etc. Nest well concealed on or near ground in long grass, rushes, undergrowth. Map 268.

RIVER WARBLER *Locustella fluviatilis* Plate 79

Du – Krekelzanger Fr – Locustelle fluviatile
Ge – Schlagschwirl Sw – Flodsångare

Identification: 5" (12.5cm). Size and form close to Grasshopper but slightly deeper-chested and shorter-tailed. Plumage *unstreaked*, dark greyish- to olive-brown above and off-white below, with *soft blurred streaks or mottles from throat to breast*, clouded flanks and white-tipped, brown under tail-coverts. Immature more rufous above and buffier below, with only faint breast mottles. Behaviour as Grasshopper but less skulking.

Voice: Song recalls Grasshopper Warbler's, but notes are softer and *slower*, with rhythmic 'chuffing' quality recalling distant steam-engine running at high speed; ends with 4-5 quiet *zwee* notes. Often sings from exposed bush-top under trees. Call low, harsh.

Habitat: Moist localities, also often in woodland thickets, or tangled herbage and bramble patches in open ground, or in forest glades, including pine. Nests on or close to ground, in moist undergrowth. Map 269.

SAVI'S WARBLER *Locustella luscinioides* Plate 79

Du – Snor Fr – Lucustelle luscinioïde
Ge – Rohrschwirl Sw – Vassångare

Identification: 5½" (14cm). Quite large, sleek, warbler with broad, rounded tail, at first sight suggesting Reed Warbler but with song recalling Grasshopper. Plumage *unstreaked and rather uniform* dark tawny to rufous-brown above, brownish-white below, with more rufous breast, flanks and under-tail (last showing whitish tips in some). Supercilium indistinct but pale eye-ring may catch eye; legs dark, reddish-brown (usually pink in Grasshopper). Actions as Grasshopper but less skulking, singing from reed-head.

Voice: Song like Grasshopper but tone more buzzing than reeling, due to lower-pitched, faster notes; can be confused with noise made by Bush Cricket; often preceded by low ticking notes which accelerate into trill. Calls include surprising *ching-ching*, like Great Tit, quiet, persistent *tswik* and scolding chatter. **Habitat:** Swamps, with wet *Phragmites* reed-beds. Nest well concealed among thick tangle of dead reeds and sedges. Map 270.

MOUSTACHED WARBLER *Acrocephalus melanopogon*   Plate 79

Du – Zwartkoprietzanger   Fr – Lusciniole à moustaches
Ge – Tamariskensänger   Sw – Kaveldunsångare

Identification: 5" (12.5cm). Rather small, fine-billed; Wren-like, with *short rounded tail often cocked,* but leggy. Plumage pattern and colours recall bright Sedge; close-to, distinguished by *almost black crown,* bold always *white supercilium* (usually ending squarely at nape), *rusty nape and back,* latter with sharp black streaks. Face shows darker cheeks and whiter throat than Sedge, latter contrasting more with fully rufous sides to breast and flanks. Flight outline differs from Sedge in shorter, more rounded wings and narrower, more rounded tail. Skulks except when singing.
Voice: Song recalls Reed Warbler but jauntier and less harsh, with distinctive crescendo of clear notes recalling Nightingale. Calls include soft but penetrating *trrrt* and harsher *tac-tac-tac*; run into scolding rattle in alarm.
Habitat: Reed-beds and swamps particularly with bulrushes. Nests in reeds or low bushes above shallow water. Map 271.

AQUATIC WARBLER *Acrocephalus paludicola*   Plate 79

Du – Waterrietzanger   Fr – Phragmite aquatique
Ge – Seggenrohrsänger   Sw – Vattensångare

Identification: 5" (12.5cm). Size as Sedge but form differs in slimmer appearance and more graduated, *spiky tail.* Plumage suggests sandy Sedge but Aquatic has *yellower, even golden ground* over which heavy black lines create *'tiger stripes'*, emphasizing *pale central crown-stripe and long supercilium* and continuing as streaks on rump and upper tail-coverts (tawny and only faintly marked on Sedge). Adult shows sparse, thin streaks on sides of breast and fore-flanks; much paler (even greyer) in worn plumage than autumn juvenile. Lores always pale; legs orange-yellow (greyish in most Sedge). Behaviour as Sedge but more skulking, often feeding at ground level.
Confusion species: Juvenile Sedge, showing cream-buff centre to crown and bright legs, frequently mistaken for Aquatic.
Voice: Song suggests Sedge but more lethargic, with shorter stanzas and constant tempo; mixes trills with piped *dee-dee-dee.* Call *tucc,* deeper-toned than Sedge.
Habitat: As Sedge Warbler, but prefers open marshes with low vegetation, sedge, etc. Nests near ground. Map 272.

SEDGE WARBLER *Acrocephalus schoenobaenus*   Plate 79

Du – Rietzanger   Fr – Phragmite des joncs
Ge – Schilfrohrsänger   Sw – Sävsångare

Identification: 5" (12.5cm). Rather small but robust, inquisitive warbler; commonest and most widespread streaked member of tribe. Adult dull grey-brown above, but distinguished from Reed (with which it often occurs) by blackish-edged crown, *bold whitish supercilium* and rather indistinct streaks on back. Rump 'glows' tawny; under-parts off-white with rufous sides to breast and rear flanks; legs greyish-brown. Juvenile noticeably brighter, with generally buffier plumage, pale creamy central crown-stripe, small dark spots on breast and paler, brighter buff legs. At all ages *dark lores* give bird frowning expression (unlike plain-faced look of Aquatic). Flight outline compact, with shorter tail than *Phylloscopus* and *Sylvia* warblers, often depressed; action strong but rather fluttering. Hops.

Voice: Song distinctive, being loud, *remarkably varied in tempo* and full of mimicry; hectic mix of trills, churrs and musical notes contains characteristic accelerating chatter which turns into more tuneful chant. Sings from perch or short vertical display-flight. Calls include explosive *tuc*, stuttered rattle and harsh *churr*.

Habitat: Reed-beds and lush vegetation near water, swampy thickets, crops. Builds untidy nest in low, dense vegetation. Map 273.

PADDYFIELD WARBLER *Acrocephalus agricola*   **Plate 82**
Du – Veldrietzanger   Fr – Rousserolle isabelle
Ge – Feldrohrsänger   Sw – Fältsångare

Identification: 5" (12.5cm). Size as Reed Warbler but has shorter, slighter bill, proportionately shorter, more rounded wings and longer tail. Plumage variable in tone with pale sandy-buff to orange-rufous upper-parts (wearing duller) and warm buff and white under-parts. Unlike any small unstreaked relative, *dusky edge to crown* emphasises *whitish supercilium* and lower eye-crescent. Flight and behaviour as Reed but also recalls chat, flicking and cocking tail.

Voice: Song recalls Marsh, with quick tempo, rich mimicry but lacking harsh notes. Calls include quiet *tschik* and harsh *chek-chek*.

Habitat and Range: Normally in dense vegetation and reeds beside lakes and marshes, breeding in S. Russia and Bulgaria. Vagrant from there or Asia to E., N., C., and W. Europe (including Britain).

BLYTH'S REED WARBLER *Acrocephalus dumetorum*   **Plate 82**
Du – Blyth's Kleine Karekiet   Fr – Rousserolle des buissons
Ge – Buschrohrsänger   Sw – Bussksångare

Identification: 5" (12.5cm). Size as Reed but has finer bill, shorter, rounder wings and relatively longer tail; often adopts *'banana' posture*. Plumage when fresh most grey-olive toned of tribe, with *pale 'bulging' fore-supercilium* and eye-ring; dull, *markedly uniform wings*, and noticeably white under-parts. Immature appearance overlaps with Marsh and dull Reed but shows structural differences and short supercilium. Legs average darker, greyer than relatives. Flight and behaviour as Reed but wing-beats noticeably more whirring. Identification requires close scrutiny; calls helpful.

Voice: Song recalls, and even excels, Marsh; is exceptionally loud, musical and long, with steady tempo (every phrase repeated at least 5 or 6 times) and brilliant mimicry. Calls include hard *tack* and softer *tchik* much closer to Marsh than Reed.

Habitat and Range: Unlike Reed, equally at home in thickets and wood edges as in reed-beds; frequently seen in canopy foliage. Breeds in S. Finland and

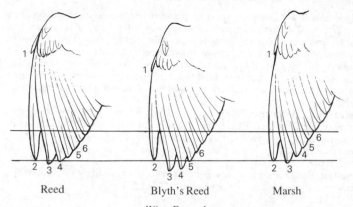

Reed   Blyth's Reed   Marsh

Wing Formulae
Note comparative length of second primary and also depth of notch on inner web

Baltic States, visits Sweden (has bred); vagrant from there and Asia to C. and W. Europe (including Britain).

MARSH WARBLER *Acrocephalus palustris*   **Plate 79**
Du – Bosrietzanger   Fr – Rousserolle verderolle
Ge – Sumpfrohrsänger   Sw – Kärrsångare
Identification: 5" (12.5cm). Size as Reed but has slightly shorter bill, higher rear crown, *more pear-shaped body* and longer wings. Plumage when fresh *greenest-toned* of small relatives, with pale fore-supercilium and eye-ring forming 'spectacle', *white throat contrasting with clouded breast,* pale tips to primaries (emphasizing long wing-point), clear *cream to white under-body* and pale legs providing distinctions from Reed. Immature appearance overlaps with Blyth's Reed and Reed but plumage colder, while legs usually paler, more straw or pink; best distinguished by calls (see below). Flight and behaviour as Reed.
Voice: Song exceptionally *musical* and varied, with changing tempo and mix of trills, harsh notes and runs into *astonishing mimicry* (even of tropical species learnt in winter quarters). Calls include loud, repeated *tchuc,* quiet *tuc* or *stit,* stuttering *tic-tirric* or *st-t-t-t-t,* all unlike Reed, and soft *churr.*
Habitat: Dense, low vegetation in ditches, thickets, stream banks, osier-beds, crops, often near water. Builds untidy nest, supported by 'handles' woven around low vegetation. Map 274.

REED WARBLER *Acrocephalus scirpaceus*   **Plate 79**
Du – Kleine Karekiet   Fr – Rousserolle effarvatte
Ge – Teichrohrsänger   Sw – Rörsångare
Identification: 5" (12.5cm). Quite small but robust warbler, with quite long bill recalling *Hippolais,* commonest of small unstreaked members of tribe: no obvious plumage character but has *distinctive voice.* Plumage brown, usually with *rusty tone especially on flanks and rump,* relieved only by indistinct buff fore-

supercilium and eye-ring, pale whitish throat and belly, dark centres to tertials and buff under tail-coverts. Immature brighter than adult, with tawny, even orange tinge to upper-parts. Flight outline shows wing and depressed tail of equal length; action rather laboured. Hops. Skulks except when singing.
Confusion species: Particularly in dull, greyish eastern race *A. s. fuscus*, Reed can be mistaken for Marsh and Blyth's Reed; in bright, 'glowing' juvenile plumage, may also suggest Paddyfield. Best separated by harshest call and least marked head of quartet; see also other species.
Voice: Song predominantly *chattering*, with harsh phrases *chirruc-chirruc*, *jag-jag-jag*, etc. repeated 2-3 times and interspersed with mimicry; sounds fussy and gruff compared with exuberant outpouring of Sedge. Calls include low *churr*, harsh *skar* or *tchar* in alarm (with *z* sound to some ears).
Habitat: Reed-beds and waterside vegetation; in parts of Europe also found in cultivated land away from water. Breeds colonially, suspending nest in reeds or bushes. Map 275.

GREAT REED WARBLER *Acrocephalus arundinaceus* **Plate 79**
Du – Grote Karekiet   Fr – Rousserolle turdoïde
Ge – Drosselrohrsänger   Sw – Trastsångare
Identification: 7½" (19cm). Large, heavy warbler, with *stout bill*, angular head, *round, ample tail* and strong legs. Plumage as Reed but easily distinguished by size, *usually bold cream supercilium*, emphasized by dark loral streak, and white throat-jowl. Flight outline long and bulky, particularly when tail spread before landing; plunges headlong and heavily into reeds. Hops; stands up thrush-like on ground.
Voice: Song loud, harsh and *prolonged chatter, audible over great distance*; comprises series of grating notes repeated 2-3 times: *karra-karra, gurk-gurk-gurk, krik-krik, karra.....* and so on. Calls include harsh *chack*, deep churring croak and shrike-like chatter in alarm.
Habitat: Breeds colonially, building suspended nest like Reed Warbler, in reeds bordering open water, on river banks, clay-pits. Map 276.

OLIVACEOUS WARBLER *Hippolais pallida* **Plate 81**
Du – Vale Spotvogel   Fr – Hypolaïs pâle
Ge – Blassspötter   Sw – Eksångare
Identification: 5¼" (13cm). Rather pot-bellied warbler, with *long bill*, flat or peaked crown and relatively *short wings* whose points form about ¼ of their folded length (falling short of or at end of upper tail-coverts). Plumage *olive-grey to brown* above, dull white below; indistinctly marked by short dull whitish supercilium, paler eye-ring, dull buff-white edges to tertials and inner secondaries not forming obvious panel and dull buff wash from sides of breast along flanks to under tail. Immature may show buffier rump. Western race *H. p. opaca* of Spain larger and more olive-toned than grey to brown eastern races. Bill length emphasized by pale pink to straw lower mandible; face looks plain due to pale lores. Flight outline shows round wings; action laboured and fluttering. Hops, often flicking tail downwards when feeding.
Confusion species: Garden Warbler lacks long bill and head marks; Booted Warbler much smaller, and finer- and shorter-billed, with dusky mark over

supercilium; Melodious also smaller and shorter-billed, typically green and yellow but beware washed-out bird in autumn.
Voice: Song vigorous rapid babble of musical, chattering and harsh choked notes repeated in even tempo. Call *tec* or *click* not distinctive; also sparrow-like chatter.
Habitat: Cultivated areas and gardens, with trees and bushes. Nests in bushes, hedges, etc., but sometimes in palm trees. Map 277.

BOOTED WARBLER *Hippolais caligata*   Plate 82

Du – Russische Spotvogel   Fr – Hypolaïs russe
Ge – Buschspötter   Sw – Gråsångare

Identification: 4½" (11cm). Smallest, most confusing of short-winged *Hippolais* warblers, with noticeably *short, fine bill*, more rounded head and rather square tail; form recalls *Phylloscopus* or small *Sylvia*. Plumage like Olivaceous but close-to, distinguished by usually *dusky smudge over supercilium*, narrow dusky line through eye and narrow whitish edges to tail; upper-parts tone varies, with many looking browner-olive than Olivaceous, while under-parts can look buffier on flanks and silvery-whitish elsewhere. Flight outline and action also recall *Phylloscopus*. Skulks, liking lower cover than larger relatives.
Voice: Song fast and chattering, mix of babbles, chirrups and *shrek, shrek* notes, all given in short phrases. Calls include *click* and softer *zett,zett,zett-zett.*
Habitat and Range: Usually in bushy regions or cultivation, locally in semi-desert scrub. Breeds W. Russia, vagrant from there and Asia to all Europe (including Britain) but not S.

OLIVE-TREE WARBLER *Hippolais olivetorum*   Plate 81

Du – Griekse Spotvogel   Fr – Hypolaïs des oliviers
Ge – Olivenspötter   Sw – Olivgulsångare

Identification: 6" (15cm). Largest of *Hippolais* warblers, with strikingly *big, dagger-like bill*, long wings and stout legs and feet. Upper-parts brownish-grey, darker than other European *Hippolais* and relieved by buffish-white supercilium, bright white eye-ring, dusky lores and cheeks and *patch of whitish edges on tertials and inner secondaries* (except on worn adult). Under-parts dusky-white, with dusky wash on sides of breast or on breast, flanks and vent. Legs usually dark, even slate. Flight outline bulky, recalling Great Reed Warbler, as does action. Hops. Most skulking of tribe.
Voice: Song loud, more raucous than other *Hippolais*, with repeated short phrases recalling Great Reed. Call hard *tuc* or *tack.*
Habitat: Frequents thorn scrub, olive and oak woods, keeping well out of sight. Nests in fork of branch. Map 278.

ICTERINE WARBLER *Hippolais icterina*   Plate 81

Du – Spotvogel   Fr – Hypolaïs ictérine
Ge – Gelbspötter   Sw – Härmsångare

Identification: 5¼" (13cm). Commonest and most widespread member of tribe in Europe. Long-billed, quite stout, perky warbler, with *peaked crown* and relatively *long wings* whose points form about a third of their folded length (falling at or beyond end of upper tail-coverts). Plumage typically olive-green above and lemon-yellow below, with short yellow supercilium, bright eye-ring and pale lores giving plain look to face. Best field marks are striking *yellow wing-panel* (formed by fringes to tertials and inner secondaries) and *blue-grey legs*. In dull adult and immature, upper-parts are greyer, with thinner whitish wing-panel, and under-parts less strongly yellow. Flight outline shows distinctly longer wings than small relatives, with flowing wing-beats. Hops, foraging clumsily through foliage with confident manner. Frequently raises crown feathers when excited.

Voice: Song loud, varied and long sustained; quality recalls Marsh Warbler; contains nasal *geea* note unique to species and much mimicry. Calls include diagnostic trisyllablic *deederoid* or *tete-lu-eet*, Chiffchaff-like *hooeet*, generic *tec* and *churr* in alarm.

Habitat: Gardens, parks and cultivated land, but also found in woods, thickets and hedges. Builds snug nest in shrubs, hedges, etc. Map 279.

MELODIOUS WARBLER *Hippolais polyglotta* Plate 81
Du – Orpheusspotvogel Fr – Hypolaïs polyglotte
Ge – Orpheusspötter Sw – Polyglottsångare

Identification: 5" (12.5cm). Somewhat smaller S.W. European counterpart of Icterine; differs in *shorter bill*, rounder crown and *much shorter, rounded wings*. Plumage pattern and colours similar to Icterine but slightly browner above and often distinctly *richer yellow below*, with usually only pale shade rather than panel on wing, and *brownish legs*. Immature much paler below, with yellow often reduced to only pale suffusion. Flight outline shows short rounded wings, producing fluttering action. Behaviour as Icterine.

Confusion species: Worn adult confusing, with bleached plumage suggesting both Olivaceous and Booted; occasional, much browner immatures may be mistaken for unstreaked *Acrocephalus* warblers.

Voice: Song like Icterine but differs in slower start, then more hurried delivery of more chattering, less imitative notes; frequently contains distinctive *krrrr* recalling House Sparrow, also used as call.

Habitat: Similar to Icterine, but more often in lush vegetation near water. Builds snug nest in bushes, rarely in trees. Map 280.

MARMORA'S WARBLER *Sylvia sarda* Plate 80
Du – Sardijnse Grasmus Fr – Fauvette sarde
Ge – Sardengrasmücke Sw – Sardinisk sångare

Identification: 4¾" (12cm). Size and form as Dartford Warbler but slightly shorter-tailed. Male has upper-parts dark slate-grey, with *almost black face, wings and tail*; under-parts paler *dusky-grey*, dark even on belly; base of bill bright orange or red; eye-ring scarlet. Female and immature browner above, juvenile noticeably whiter below. Behaviour as Dartford.

Voice: Song short-phrased, simple series of notes, often beginning with clear *heet, churee, churee, churee, churee*; lower-pitched than Dartford, recalls Sardinian Warbler. Calls include short, subdued, disyllabic *churu*, sharp *tzig* and in alarm soft *trrt*.

Habitat and Range: Restricted to dry scrub, often among rocky country. Resident in E. coastal Spain, W. Mediterranean islands; vagrant to W. Europe (including Britain).

DARTFORD WARBLER *Sylvia undata* Plate 80
Du – Provence-Grasmus Fr – Fauvette pitchou
Ge – Provencegrasmücke Sw – Provencesångare

Identification: 5" (12.5cm). Small, perky warbler with *long, narrow tail, often cocked and flicked*. Looks all-dark at distance but close-to, male has *slate-grey head* shading to *dark brown upper-parts*, dull *reddish-brown under-parts* with white spotted chin and throat (when fresh) and white belly; base of bill yellowish, eye-ring red. Female duller above and below, with greyer back. Immature much browner above and buffier below. Flight outline long, with *jerking tail*; action weak and whirring; bird rarely rises above cover. Hops. Raises crown feathers. Forms small groups in winter. Skulks in dense, dry vegetation, particularly gorse.

Voice: Song short, hard but musical chatter with occasional liquid notes; recalls Whitethroat as does dancing song-flight. Calls include harsh, drawn-out *chaihrr-er*, used to scold, and *tak*, extended into rattle.

Habitat: Open commons with heather and gorse, dwarf oak, cistus-covered hillsides, etc. Nests in scrub near ground. Map 281.

SPECTACLED WARBLER *Sylvia conspicillata* Plate 80
Du – Brilgrasmus Fr – Fauvette à lunettes
Ge – Brillengrasmücke Sw – Glasögonsångare

Identification: 5" (12.5cm). Form and plumage strongly recall Whitethroat but noticeably smaller, with proportionately shorter tail. Male has grey head and shawl round neck, with *almost black face* and *obvious white eye-ring*, ochre-brown back, *vividly red-chestnut wings* with dark alula and tertial centres, grey-brown rump and tail, last with white outer tail-feathers. Under-parts show striking white throat, pink breast and buffish-white under-parts; base of bill and *legs bright orange-straw*. Female and particularly immature duller, with grey areas suffused brownish but with bright rufous wing-panels like Whitethroat. Flight outline and action like small Whitethroat. Hops, often cocking tail. See also Subalpine.

Voice: Song short and high-pitched, with fluted notes leading into chatter; from perch or dancing song-flight. Calls include very dry, clear rattle *zerrrrr*, suggesting Wren.

Habitat: Chiefly in *Salicornia* on coastal flats and (often with Dartford Warbler) in low scrub. Nests in low bush. Map 282.

SUBALPINE WARBLER *Sylvia cantillans* Plate 80
Du – Baardgrasmus Fr – Fauvette passerinette
Ge – Weissbartgrasmücke Sw – Rödstrupig sångare

Identification: 4¾" (12cm). Size recalls Dartford but form suggests small Whitethroat. Male distinctive, with *blue-grey head and upper-parts*, darker wings and white-edged tail; narrow but conspicuous *white 'moustache'* contrasts with *pinkish-chestnut throat, breast and flanks*; white belly and red eye-ring may show. Female duller, less bluish above and more rusty-orange below, but usually shows white 'moustache' and also *white outer eye-ring*. Immature confusing, often browner above; may lack 'moustache' but always shows whitish eye-ring. Legs pale brown. Best distinguished from Spectacled by basically grey-brown wings with only buff fringes and less distinct dark centres to tertials and coverts. Flight and behaviour like small Whitethroat but lifts tail frequently; has habit of 'looking back over shoulder' before taking cover.

Voice: Song quite clear and slow, with varied 'bouncing' and chattering phrases; quality quite pleasing compared with Sardinian, can recall Linnet. Sings from bush or in song-flight. Calls include hard but quiet *tec* or *tett*, sometimes repeated or run into dry rattle, and in high alarm, bubbled rattle *prrrrt*, suggesting Crested Tit.

Habitat: Low bushes and thickets, often with scattered trees; also in open woodland glades and along stream banks. Nests in thick bushes. Map 283.

SARDINIAN WARBLER *Sylvia melanocephala*   **Plate 80**
Du – Kleine Zwartkop   Fr – Fauvette mélanocéphale
Ge – Samtkopfgrasmücke   Sw – Sammetshätta

Identification: 5¼" (13cm). Small, rather scrawny warbler, with longish, graduated tail. Both sexes look 'fierce' due to *red-brown eye-ring*. Male has *black hood* contrasting with *white chin and throat*, dark grey upper-parts, sides to breast and flanks and blackish, conspicuously white-edged tail. Female duller, with grey-brown cap to head and dirty brown-grey upper-parts and flanks. Immature browner than female, with brown eye-ring. *Bobbing flight* and restless behaviour recall Whitethroat but more skulking. Cocks tail.

Voice: Song rapid gabble of musical whistles and harsh notes including *trr-trr*. Calls include *explosive, loud staccato cha-cha-cha-cha*, like rapidly wound wooden rattle, and loud, hard *tsek* or *treek, treek*.

Habitat: Dry, fairly open bushy scrub, thickets, pine and evergreen oak woods, etc. Nests in low bushes and undergrowth. Map 284.

RÜPPELL'S WARBLER *Sylvia rueppelli*   **Plate 80**
Du – Rüppell's Grasmus   Fr – Fauvette masquée
Ge – Maskengrasmücke   Sw – Svarthakad sångare

Identification: 5½" (14cm). Size and form close to Whitethroat. Male has *long black hood and bib*, with conspicuous *white 'moustache'*, clean grey upper-parts, black, white-edged tail and *peach-white under-parts*. Female duller with, at most, blackish throat but also showing indication of white 'moustache'. Immature like female but throat always clean, while wings have buffish-brown covert and tertial fringes. Eye-ring and legs reddish-brown. Actions and behaviour as Whitethroat.

Voice: Song like Sardinian but not so loud and with 'rhythmic' pulse in gabble, often delivered from *Greenfinch-like display flight*. Calls include sparrow-like rattle.

Habitat and Range: Breeds in bushes among low scrub with rocky outcrops. Summer visitor, breeding Aegean region. Vagrant elsewhere in S., E., N. and W. Europe (including Britain).

DESERT WARBLER *Sylvia nana*   **Plate 82**
Du – Woestijngrasmus   Fr – Fauvette naine
Ge – Wüstengrasmücke   Sw – Ökensångare

Identification: 5" (12.5cm). Form Whitethroat-like but much smaller and paler. Spiky bill has dark tip and yellowish base; narrow white ring around *pale yellow eye*. Pale sandy grey-brown upper-parts, with ochre fringes to tertials,

rusty rump and *rusty-brown tail with bold white edges*; pale whitish under-parts, with buff flanks and *pale yellow legs*. Markedly terrestrial; flight usually low. Has distinctive habit of spreading and raising tail.
Voice: Call short trill; alarm note rattling.
Habitat and Range: Normally in bushy steppes. Vagrant from S. Asia to all of Europe (including Britain).

ORPHEAN WARBLER *Sylvia hortensis*   Plate 80
Du – Orpheusgrasmus   Fr – Fauvette orphée
Ge – Orpheusgrasmücke   Sw – Mästersångare

Identification: 6¼" (15.5cm). Noticeably large, lengthy warbler, with strong bill and ample breast. May suggest Sardinian but easily separated by *dull blackish head-cap* merging into grey mantle, *pale straw eye* (in fully adult birds) and *buff, not grey, flanks*. Female slightly and immature much browner than male, immature with dark eye. Flight outline and action may suggest small thrush. Hops; notably arboreal.
Voice: Song variable, recalling Ring Ouzel in Iberia but Blackbird or Nightingale in Greece due to differing combinations of loud mellow notes. Call sharp *tak*.
Habitat: Wooded districts, orchards, scrub, citrus and olive groves. Nests in bushes, low branches. Map 285.

BARRED WARBLER *Sylvia nisoria*   Plate 80
Du – Gestreepte Grasmus   Fr – Fauvette épervière
Ge – Sperbergrasmücke   Sw – Höksångare

Identification: 6¼" (15.5cm). Largest warbler of tribe, with *stout but pointed bill* on peaked head, robust body, rather *long full tail* and strong legs. At all ages in fresh plumage, has *double whitish wing-bar, pale tertial tips and fringes* and white corners to tail. Adult *barred with dark crescents below* but these much less distinct in female; immature merely dappled on flanks. Male ashy grey-brown above, whitish below; female faintly grey-brown above; both have *pale yellow eyes*. Immature greyish- to dun-brown above and buffier below, with brown eye. Flight shrike-like; often flicks tail. Skulks in dense cover.
Voice: Song recalls Blackcap or Garden Warbler but shorter-phrased and scratchier in tone; includes rattling *tcharr, tcharr* or *trrrrr-tt-t*, also used as call in addition to hard *tchack* and *churr*.
Habitat: Thorny thickets, bushy commons and hedges, clearings in woods, etc. Usually nests in thorn-bushes. Map 286.

LESSER WHITETHROAT *Sylvia curruca*   Plate 80
Du – Braamsluiper   Fr – Fauvette babillarde
Ge – Klappergrasmücke   Sw – Ärtsångare

Identification: 5¼" (13cm). Slighter and more compact than Whitethroat with *distinctive song*. Systematics complex, with western breeding race intergrading with larger eastern form in Balkans; Siberian *S. c. blythi* accepted as vagrant, large and small steppe forms also reported from Britain. All types distinguished from Whitethroat by *blackish mask on ear-coverts* (least obvious in small steppe form), trace of pale supercilium, greyish or dun-brown upper-parts (palest in far eastern birds), *lack of vivid chestnut wings* (but occasionally showing ginger-buff fringes to tertials in far eastern birds), and dark legs. Flight outline differs from Whitethroat in shorter, less broad tail; action more flitting. Except in brief song period, keeps within cover.

Voice: Song begins with subdued 'far off' warbling chatter, becomes louder, 'nearer' unmusical rattle recalling Cirl Bunting; delivered from thick cover or tree top, not from song-flight. Call short *tett*, with Blue Tit-like scold *chay-de-de-de* also given by Balkan birds.

Habitat: As Whitethroat, though usually in taller, denser vegetation, with more trees. Map 287.

WHITETHROAT *Sylvia communis*   **Plate 80**
   Du – Grasmus   Fr – Fauvette grisette
   Ge – Dorngrasmücke   Sw – Törnsångare
Identification: 5½" (14cm). Medium-sized, rather long-tailed warbler, with often raised crest and tail, giving perky look. Male has *pale grey cap* contrasting with *white throat*, brown back, *conspicuously chestnut wings*, pinkish-buff under-parts and dusky *white-edged tail*. Winter male and female less grey on head and less pink on breast. Immature rather bright warm brown on head and back. Legs pale reddish-brown. Beware indistinct whitish eye-ring suggesting smaller relatives. Flight outline noticeably long, sometimes loose-tailed; action flitting. Restless, darting in and out of cover.

Voice: Song vigorous, *urgent chatter*, delivered from bush, wire or dancing song-flight. Calls include repeated *check*, harsh *whett, whett, whett* and scolding *tcharr* or *chairr.*

Habitat: Fairly open country with bushes, brambles, gorse, nettle-beds. Nests near ground in low vegetation. Map 288.

GARDEN WARBLER *Sylvia borin*   **Plate 81**
   Du – Tuinfluiter   Fr – Fauvette des jardins
   Ge – Gartengrasmücke   Sw – Trädgårdssångare
Identification: 5½" (14cm). Medium-sized, *plump* warbler, with *stout bill* and rather *round head*. Plumage *featureless*, with olive-tinged grey-brown upper-parts and paler buff-white under-parts; at some angles, faintly paler lores and eye-patch make eye look dark and large. Distinguished from female and immature Blackcap by lack of dark cap. Flight form quite bulky; action flitting but strong, recalling Robin. Secretive, keeping well hidden except when tending fledged young.

Voice: Song *charming, babble* of quiet mellow notes, lacking strong terminal phrase of Blackcap and diagnostically *longer sustained.* Calls include Blackcap-like *cheek, cheek*, low harsh *tchurr-r-r* and distinctive but faint *whit.*

Habitat: Woods with abundant undergrowth, thickets, bushy commons with bramble patches, overgrown hedges, fruit bushes. Nests in low bushes and brambles. Map 289.

BLACKCAP *Sylvia atricapilla*   **Plate 80**
   Du – Zwartkop   Fr – Fauvette à tête noire
   Ge – Mönchsgrasmücke   Sw – Svarthätta
Identification: 5½" (14cm). Size and form as Garden but looks flatter-headed, with sharper bill. Male has short *glossy black crown-cap*, female and immature

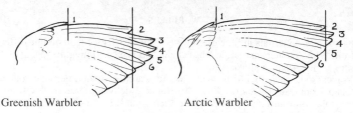

Greenish Warbler   Arctic Warbler

Wing Formulae
Greenish has longer first primary and shorter second primary than Arctic

have less obvious *red-brown caps*. Rest of plumage greyer than Garden, particularly on head, nape and fore under-parts; female somewhat browner below than male, and immature rustier above and yellow-tinged below. Flight outline and action as Garden but less secretive. Frequently winters in Europe; uses garden feeders.

Voice: Song remarkably rich, *chortling warble,* less sustained than Garden but more varied with louder melancholy, fluted ending. Calls include emphatic *tac, tac,* rapidly repeated in alarm, and scolding *churr.*

Habitat: Woodland glades with undergrowth, overgrown hedges, fruit bushes. Nests in brambles, honeysuckle, evergreens, etc. Map 290.

GREENISH WARBLER *Phylloscopus trochiloides*   **Plate 81**
   Du – Grauwe Fitis   Fr – Pouillot verdâtre
   Ge – Grüner Laudsänger   Sw – Lundsångare
Identification: 4¼" (10.5cm). Size and structure close to Chiffchaff; systematics complex, may be conspecific with Green (treated here as species, see Accidentals), and Two-barred Greenish (reported from Britain and Holland, treated here as E. Asian race). Pale greyish-olive above, dull white below; spiky bill with orange-flesh base; *long yellowish supercilium* (often turning up at nape); dusky eye-stripe; short, narrow *straight whitish wing-bar* on outer greater coverts (in fresh plumage); bright greenish fringes on inner wing and *dusky legs.* E. Asian race, *P. t. plumbeitarsus* has second whitish bar on median coverts, sometimes faint yellowish tinge on fore under-parts, and even darker legs. Flicks wings open.

Confusion species: N. Asian races of Chiffchaff can be taken for Greenish, but their supercilia always short and wing-bars longer but less distinct; Arctic Warbler is larger, with yellowish-brown legs and different wing formula (see diagram) and call.

Voice: Song short, high and loud, beginning with rapidly repeated call note, merging into a gabbled Wren-like trill. Call shrill but cheerful *chee-wee.*

Habitat: Very varied; occurs up to 11,000ft (3,300m.); deciduous or coniferous woodlands, coppices, orchards, etc. Nests on or near ground, not necessarily with undergrowth, occasionally in low stone walls. Map 291.

ARCTIC WARBLER *Phylloscopus borealis*   **Plate 81**
   Du – Noordse Boszanger   Fr – Pouillot boréal
   Ge – Nordischer Laubsänger   Sw – Nordsångare
Identification: 4¾" (12cm). Size close to Wood Warbler; structure like rather short-tailed Willow Warbler but with strong bill and long wing-points. Bright olive-green above, grey-white below, with *long white supercilium* (often turning

up on nape but can be shortened by wear), white eye-crescents, dusky eye-stripe; *one indistinct and one distinct white wing-bar* in fresh plumage (often one and occasionally both lost with wear); yellow-orange base to bill and *bright straw legs*. Flicks wings and tail. Flight usually dashing. Greenish Warbler slighter, with dusky legs and different call.

Voice: Song distinctive, fast, reeling trill, recalling both Cirl Bunting and Tree Pipit. Calls distinctive, including husky *tssp*, hard *zik* and chatter like Lesser Whitethroat.

Habitat: Usually in lush undergrowth near water, but also in birch and coniferous woods. Nests on ground. Map 292.

PALLAS'S WARBLER *Phylloscopus proregulus*   **Plate 82**

Du – Pallas' Boszanger	Fr – Pouillot de Pallas
Ge – Goldhähnchenlaubsänger	Sw – Kungsfågelsångare

Identification: 3¾" (9.5cm). Smallest *Phylloscopus* reaching Europe, with size, plumage pattern and behaviour recalling both Yellow-browed Warbler and Firecrest. Distinguished from former by *yellow forehead, supercilium and central crown-stripe*, emphasised by *blackish-green sides to crown and eye-stripe*, brighter green upper-parts, and *double yellow wing-bar* emphasized by blackish bands. Diagnostic *primrose-yellow* (or yellow and white) *patch on lower back* difficult to see except when bird flicks wings open or hovers. Actions recall Firecrest more than Yellow-browed.

Voice: Song remarkably powerful trill with many pure, canary-like notes. Call soft but shrill, rising *weesp* or *tooweep*, more prolonged than Yellow-browed, sometimes recalling Chiffchaff.

Habitat and Range: Mainly in tree-tops, nesting in birch, conifer and mixed forest. Vagrant from Asia to N., W., C., S and E. Europe (including Britain).

YELLOW-BROWED WARBLER *Phylloscopus inornatus*   **Plate 81**

Du – Bladkoninkje	Fr – Pouillot à grands sourcils
Ge – Gelbbrauenlaubsänger	Sw – Taigasångare

Identification: 4" (10cm). Size between Goldcrest and Chiffchaff but form typically phylloscopine except for rather short tail. Plumage basically greenish above and whitish below, strikingly relieved by noticeably *long cream supercilium*, dusky eye-stripe, *whitish double wing-bar* emphasised by blackish bands, *bold white tips and edges to tertials* and secondaries and yellowish under tail-coverts. Some birds show faint pale divide on crown and yellowish wash on rump (but both marks nowhere near as obvious as on Pallas's). Very active, with fast flight more confident that Goldcrest; regularly fly-catches and occasionally hovers.

Confusion species: Except close-to, Pallas's may hide its specific features. Yellow-browed also subject to confusing plumage variation, with mounting reports in W. Europe of S.W. Asian race *P. i. humei* (regarded as separate species by some authors), distinguished by dark bill, much duller, greyer upper-parts, usually only one wing-bar and reduced tertial marks.

Voice: Song undistinguished, repeating short high, thin yet buzzing phrases. Calls frequently with high, piercing *seeveest* or *tsweest*, recalling Coal Tit but with rising inflection. Call of S.W. Asian race *tseelu* or *tissyip*, with downward inflection.

Habitat and Range: Normally taiga, often in willows and in winter in scrub. Asian vagrant to most parts of Europe, especially northern countries in autumn. Some may winter Portugal or attempt to do so as far north as Britain.

RADDE'S WARBLER *Phylloscopus schwarzi*   **Plate 82**
  Du – Radde's Boszanger   Fr – Pouillot de Schwarz
  Ge – Bartlaubsänger   Sw – Videsångare
Identification: 5" (12.5cm). Size as Wood Warbler but with almost tit-like bill (in male), short points to rounded wings and *stout legs and feet*. Brown, or oily-olive above, cream, washed yellow-brown and olive below, with bright orange base to bill, *long deep cream supercilium* (reaching nape), almost black eye-stripe, *orange-buff under tail-coverts* and *bright straw legs*. Flight heavier and more direct than other *Phylloscopi*, showing broad rump and tail. Skulks in ground cover. Arctic Warbler without wing-bars also lacks colourful under-parts; Dusky Warbler is smaller, greyer, with darker legs.
Voice: Calls infrequently with nervous *twit-twit* and nasal, slightly slurred *chrep*.
Habitat and Range: Chiefly arboreal, but also skulks in undergrowth. Vagrant from Asia to C., N. and W. Europe (including Britain).

DUSKY WARBLER *Phylloscopus fuscatus*   **Plate 82**
  Du – Bruine Boszanger   Fr – Pouillot brun
  Ge – Dunkellaubsänger   Sw – Brunsångare
Identification: 4½" (11cm). Size as largest Chiffchaff, with spiky bill. Creeps through ground cover; *constantly flicks wings open* and *calls loudly*. Greyish-brown above, dingy white, washed buff below, with bright flesh base to bill, *long rusty-white supercilium* (reaching nape), dusky eye-stripe and *brown legs*. Flight as Chiffchaff but 'scuttles' between cover.
Confusion species: Dull N. Asian races of Chiffchaff usually arboreal, with dark bill and different call; Radde's Warbler larger, usually olive-toned and pale-legged.
Voice: Calls frequently, with hard, *clicking chak* or *chek*.
Habitat and Range: Usually feeds on ground in damp localities. Vagrant from Asia to C., N. and W. Europe (including Britain).

BONELLI'S WARBLER *Phylloscopus bonelli*   **Plate 81**
  Du – Bergfluiter   Fr – Pouillot de Bonelli
  Ge – Berglaubsänger   Sw – Bergsångare
Identification: 4½" (11.5cm). Size slightly larger than Willow Warbler with more tit-like bill and rounder head. Head and back greyish olive-brown, with *indistinct whitish supercilium* and pale mottled cheeks (creating rather plain face), *wings noticeably yellowish-green* on feather fringes, contrasting with back, and *silky-white under-parts*. Long *rump yellowish in adult* (but difficult to see); frequently shows patch of yellow at carpal joint (but other *Phylloscopi* may exhibit similar mark). In eastern race *P. b. orientalis* of Balkans, tertials are sharply fringed whitish. Base of bill pinkish, legs grey-brown. Flight form and action slightly heavier than Willow. Beware confusion with adult Chiffchaff in head moult.
Voice: Song short, sweet, slow trill on same note, *swee-wee-wee-wee-wee-wee*; suggests start of Wood Warbler's song or distant Cirl Bunting or Lesser White-

throat. Calls include soft, fully disyllabic *hou-eet*, short *chee,chee* and, in eastern race, loud, hard *tsiep* or *chip*, recalling young House Sparrow.
Habitat: Dense foliage of trees. Locally in dry pine or deciduous forests, open cork oak groves, or even scattered vegetation up to tree limit in mountains. Nests on ground under trees. Map 293.

WOOD WARBLER *Phylloscopus sibilatrix* Plate 81

Du – Fluiter Fr – Pouillot siffleur
Ge – Waldlaubsänger Sw – Grönsångare

Identification: 5" (12.5cm). Largest of European *Phylloscopus* warblers, with *long, pointed wings* often drooped below relatively short tail. Plumage pattern much more developed than Willow Warbler or Chiffchaff, with bright *yellowish-green upper-parts* and white under-parts relieved by *pale sulphur-yellow supercilium, throat and breast*, dusky-green eye-stripe, bright yellowish fringes to tertials, inner secondaries and greater coverts, orange base to bill and yellowish- to grey-brown legs.
Voice: Has two songs; piping *piu*, repeated 5-20 times, and slowly repeated *stip* accelerating to 'shivering' grasshopper-like trill *stip, stip, stip, stip-stip-stip-shreeeee*. Sings while moving among tree foliage and in flight. Calls include liquid *piu* and soft *whit, whit, whit*.
Habitat: Deciduous woods with light ground cover: also found in coniferous forests in C. Europe. Nests on ground among light undergrowth, usually in beech or oak woods. Map 294.

CHIFFCHAFF *Phylloscopus collybita* Plate 81

Du – Tjiftjaf Fr – Pouillot véloce
Ge – Zilpzalp Sw – Gransångare

Identification: 4¼" (11cm). Size and form close to Willow Warbler but with smaller-looking bill, rounder head and slightly *shorter, more rounded wings* (see diagram); best distinguished by *onomatopaeic song*. Systematics complex, with three races breeding in Europe and at least one vagrant from Asia. Plumage darkest, brownest above in S.W. Europe, palest above in Fenno-Scandia and palest below in Siberia. Typical W. European bird *P. c. collybita* dingy olive-brown above, buffish-white with yellowish wash below, relieved by *almost wholly black bill*, short indistinct yellowish supercilium, *whitish eye-ring* and usually *dark grey-brown legs*. Juvenile much yellower below but still dingier than young Willow. In autumn, Siberian race *P. c. tristis* shows much sharper, buff-white supercilium, *long, curving pale wing-bar*, whiter under-parts and *black legs*; frequently confused with Greenish Warbler. Flight more fluttering than Willow and behaviour less dashing. *Drops and wags tail* while feeding. Beware worn or moulting adult suggesting Bonelli's, which see.
Voice: Song begins with quiet chitter, develops into irregularly ordered diagnostic *chiff, chiff, chaff, chiff, chaff........* Calls vary: European birds give less disyllabic *hweet* than Willow Warbler, loud *twit* and subdued *tsiff-tsiff-tsiff*; Siberian and Fenno-Scandian races utter more urgent *peet* or *cheep*, suggesting distressed young chicken.
Habitat: More arboreal than Willow Warbler. Usually nests just above ground in brambles, evergreens, etc., in light woods and bushy commons. Winters in fairly open vegetation. Map 295.

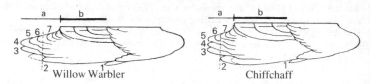

Willow Warbler   Chiffchaff

Wing Formulae
Willow Warbler: 2nd primary longer than 7th
Chiffchaff: 2nd equal or shorter than 7th. Note relative lengths of a and b pro-
portions of wings. Dotted lines show possible range in position of 2nd pri-
mares (After Scott and Grant)

WILLOW WARBLER *Phylloscopus trochilus*   **Plate 81**
Du – Fitis   Fr – Pouillot fitis
Ge – Fitis   Sw – Lövsångare
Identification: 4¼" (11cm). Small, slender *Phylloscopus* warbler, with longer-
looking bill, flatter head and slightly longer wings than Chiffchaff; most abundant summer visitor to northern Europe, with *sweet, sad song*. Plumage less
variable than Chiffchaff and always cleaner-toned, with brighter olive-toned
upper-parts, paler whiter under-parts; relieved by bright orange base to bill,
longer, cleaner supercilium and usually *pale brown legs*. Rare vagrants resembling N.Asian race *P. t. yakutensis* are greyer above, washed-out below; much
paler than Siberian Chiffchaff. Juvenile often very yellow below, suggesting
green and yellow *Hippolais* warbler. Flight light and flitting, acrobatic when
feeding and chasing aggressively after other passerines; flicks wings and tail.
Precise wing formula shown in diagram.
Voice: Song most beautiful of tribe; liquid musical cadence with fast start,
slight drop in pitch, pause then pick up to final tender, dying phrase *sooeet-
sooeetoo*. Call almost disyllabic *hooeet*, weaker, softer, more extended than
Chiffchaff.
Habitat: Less arboreal than Chiffchaff, more fond of low vegetation. Nests on
ground in open bushy localities. Map 296.

GOLDCREST *Regulus regulus*   **Plate 83**
Du – Goudhaantje   Fr – Roitelet huppé
Ge – Wintergoldhähnchen   Sw – Kungsfågel
Identification: 3½" (9cm). Smallest bird in Europe, yet hardy enough to be
resident in woods from Baltic southwards; *plump form* combines features of
Phylloscopus warbler and small *Parus* tit, with *tiny spiky bill* on relatively large
head. Plumage basically dull olive-green above, dull whitish-buff below, strikingly relieved by sheeny *orange* (male) *or yellow (female) crown-centre with
black borders*, pale greyish patch round *dark eye*. Double white wing-bar
banded black particularly across bases of secondaries, and yellowish-white tips
and fringes to inner flight feathers, and red-brown legs. Juvenile lacks crown
marks. Flight form tubby, with 'stick' tail; action fast and flitting, *hovers persistently*. Small hops produce 'creeping' gait. Roams with tits in winter; often
tame. Best distinguished from Firecrest by lack of white supercilium and black
eye-stripe.

Voice: Song very high-pitched, with silvery tinkling twitter *stit-it-stir-ti* rapidly repeated 3-4 times before louder terminal flourish. Call persistent shrill *sree-sree-sree* or *zee-zee-zee*, much less pronounced than Firecrest.
Habitat: Coniferous or mixed woods; in winter also in hedges and undergrowth. Builds suspended nest, usually under tip of branch of conifer (but rarely in pine). Map 297.

FIRECREST *Regulus ignicapillus*   Plate 83
Du – Vuurgoudhaantje   Fr – Roitelet à triple-bandeau
Ge – Sommergoldhähnchen   Sw – Brandkronad kunsfågel

Identification: 3½" (9cm). Size, form and behaviour as Goldcrest but easily distinguished even at distance by cleaner, brighter appearance, with noticeably greener back and '*shining' white under-parts*. Head beautifully decorated by *red* (male) *or yellow* (female) *crown-centre with black borders*, golden forehead, *bold white supercilium* contrasting with *black eye-stripe*, and greyish rear cheeks; side of neck and shoulder shows golden-orange patch. Juvenile's crown marks rudimentary.
Voice: Song less developed than Goldcrest, with accelerating high but monotonous double notes on same pitch. Calls variable, some indistinguishable from Goldcrest but slowly repeated *zit* and stressed *zeet* are distinctive.
Habitat: As Goldcrest, but less partial to coniferous woods and more often in low undergrowth, bushy swamps, bracken, etc. Builds suspended nest in coniferous or deciduous trees, bushes, creepers, etc. Map 298.

FLYCATCHERS: Muscicapidae

Like North American tyrant flycatchers (see Accidentals), Old World flycatchers are usually seen perched *upright* on vantage points, from which they make short, erratic flights after passing insects. Bills broad at the base. Sexes similar only in Spotted. Hole or tree nesting.

SPOTTED FLYCATCHER *Muscicapa striata*   Plate 84
Du – Grauwe Vliegenvanger   Fr – Gobe-mouche gris
Ge – Grauschnäpper   Sw – Grå flugsnappare

Identification: 5½" (14cm). Most ubiquitous flycatcher, with lengthiest form and characteristic upright, watchful posture; often flicks wings and tail. Adult ashy-brown above, *spotted on crown*; whitish below, *softly streaked on breast*. Juvenile initially short-tailed, heavily *spotted with white overall*. Beware confusing thin pale edges to wing feathers with fully white patches and bars of *Ficedula* species. Hawks passing insects with rapid, agile flight, often planing back to same perch. Rather solitary except after breeding and on migration.
Voice: Song hardly developed, usually thin hasty *sip-sip-see-sitti-see-see*. Calls include thin grating *tzee* and rapid *tzee-tuc-tuc*.
Habitat: Gardens, parks, edges of woods. Nests on or in buildings, against tree trunks, behind creepers, etc. Map 299.

RED-BREASTED FLYCATCHER *Ficedula parva*   **Plate 84**
Du – Kleine Vliegenvanger   Fr – Gobe-mouche nain
Ge – Zwergschnäpper   Sw – Mindre flugsnappare
Identification: 4½" (11.5cm). Smallest, most agile flycatcher, often sitting with drooping wings and flicking and *cocking tail*. Easily distinguished by *bold white basal patches on blackish tail*. Adult male suggests tiny Robin, with greyish head and *bright reddish-orange bib*; female and immature lack bib but have *narrow whitish eye-ring*. Upper-parts dun-brown, under-parts buffish-white. Shy when breeding but migrants make conspicuous sallies in air or to ground, flying 'tightest circles' of tribe. Often feeds like warbler in foliage.
Voice: Song opens like Pied Flycatcher or Willow Warbler, ends like Redstart with quicker, descending trill. Calls include short *tek* or *tssk*, brisk *zeek*, clear *teelu* in alarm and quiet chatter.
Habitat: Usually deciduous forests; on passage, also in open cultivation. Nesting habits like Pied, but also builds open nest against tree trunk. Map 300.

SEMI-COLLARED FLYCATCHER *Ficedula semitorquata*   **Plate 84**
Du – Balkanvliegenvanger   Fr – Gobe-mouche à demi-collier
Ge – Halbringschnäpper   Sw – Balkanflugsnappare
Identification: 5" (12.5cm). Size, form, behaviour and habitat as Pied and Collared. Adult male when breeding intermediate in appearance and voice, only certainly distinguished by combination of *white half-collar* and *white tips of median coverts*. Winter male, female and immature virtually indistinguishable from Collared but tail white-edged as Pied.
Voice: Song like Pied but weaker and higher-pitched.
Range: Breeds sparsely in Balkans.

COLLARED FLYCATCHER *Ficedula albicollis*   **Plate 84**
Du – Withalsvliegenvanger   Fr – Gobe-mouche à collier
Ge – Halsbandschnäpper   Sw – Halsbandsflugsnappare
Identification: 5" (12.5cm). Size, form, behaviour and habitat as Pied. Adult breeding male distinguished by larger white forehead, *complete white collar*, larger white blaze on tertials and longer white wing-bar, *greyish-white rump* and virtually all-black tail. Close-to, winter male, female and immature may show greyer upper-parts than Pied, with pale nape, *long, bold, white wing-bar* creating (when folded) bulging mark by primary coverts, and pale rump.
Voice: Song unlike Pied, rather short, 'squeezed out' squeaky *tsee-tsee-tsee-sui-see*. Calls include loud *eehlp* in alarm and quiet *click*. Map 301.

PIED FLYCATCHER *Ficedula hypoleuca*   **Plate 84**
Du – Bonte Vliegenvanger   Fr – Gobe-mouche noir
Ge – Trauerschnäpper   Sw – Svartvit flugsnappare
Identification: 5" (12.5cm). Relatively shorter-tailed than Spotted and Red-breasted; most widespread of three similar species, particularly in N. Europe. Easily distinguished from Spotted by *bold white wing-bar and tertial edges*. Adult male when breeding truly pied: *jet-black above* except for *small white forehead*, wing marks and tail edges; pure white below; in winter like female but retains pale forehead. Female and immature dun-brown above, buffish-white below, with smaller wing marks and trace of dull 'moustache' on throat. Separ-

ation of paler females from Semi-collared and Collared often impossible. Behaviour much as Spotted but keeps more to cover, seldom hunts twice from same perch and often feeds on ground; constantly flirts wings and tail.

Voice: Song quite loud, sprightly, high *zee-it, zee-it, zee-it* interspersed with musical notes and Redstart-like trill. Calls include metallic *whit*, anxious *phweet*, persistent *tic* or *wheetic* and explosive *tschist*.

Habitat: Usually deciduous woods and gardens, often near water, also in coniferous forests. Nests in holes in trees, walls, nest-boxes. Map 302.

BABBLERS: Timaliidae

BEARDED TIT *Panurus biarmicus*   **Plate 86**

Du – Baardmees   Fr – Mésange à moustaches
Ge – Bartmeise   Sw – Skäggmes

Identification: 6½" (16cm). 'Pheasant-tailed' and tit-like bird; normally restricted to reedbeds. Plumage mainly bright, warm tawny-buff, streaked *white and black over wings* and along flight feathers. Adult male beautiful, with pale *bluish-grey hood*, conspicuous *drooping black 'moustache'* and conspicuous *black under tail-coverts*. Female paler, with tawny-buff head and vent; immature distinctive, with dark blackish back and white throat. Bill bright orange-straw. Flight fast and whirring, trailing tail. Acrobatic in reeds and on ground, where it prances with raised tail like babbler. Highly sociable.

Voice: Song twittering. Calls include distinctive twanging *tching*, scolding *p'whut*, squeaky *cheeu*, etc.

Habitat: Extensive and secluded reed-beds. Nests low down near edge of wet reed-bed. Erupting birds enter weeds and deciduous bushes. Map 303.

LONG-TAILED TITS: Aegithalidae

LONG-TAILED TIT *Aegithalos caudatus*   **Plate 86**

Du – Staartmees   Fr – Mésange à longue queue
Ge – Schwanzmeise   Sw – Stjärtmes

Identification: 5½" (13cm), tail 3" (7.5cm). Tiny, almost ball-shaped tit with *long, straight tail* which 'whips' in flight. Plumage basically *black, white and pink* but tones softened by loose feathers and varying by race. British and S.W. European forms have bold *blackish eye-stripe* on white head; Northern *A. c. caudatus* has *pure white head*. Flight whirring and 'bouncing'. Highly acrobatic and sociable, moving about in processions.

Voice: Song infrequent, mix of rapid *see-see-sui* and calls which include distinctive low *tupp*, repeated trilling *tsirrup* and weak *tzee-tzee-tzee*.

Habitat: Thickets, bushy heaths, coppices, hedgerows; also woods in winter. Builds ovoid mossy, lichen-covered nest, usually in gorse, thorn or bramble bushes, occasionally well up in trees. Map 304.

TITS: Paridae

Small, plump, short-billed birds, very acrobatic when feeding. Most tits roam in mixed bands in winter. Appearances either colourful or rather drab but often with dark cap. Sexes generally similar. Nest in holes.

MARSH TIT *Parus palustris*   Plate 86
Du – Glanskopmees   Fr – Mésange nonnette
Ge – Sumpfmeise   Sw – Entita

Identification: 4½" (11cm). Scarce, local tit, sharing small size and basic plumage pattern with Willow Tit. Separated at distance only by *distinctive voice* and close-to by *glossy* black crown, shorter white cheeks, smaller black bib, *uniform wings* and square tail.

Confusion species: Willow Tit, from which worn adult and juvenile may be indistinguishable.

Voice: Deep, nasal *tchair* and scolding *chick-adeedee* may suggest other tits but loud *pitchew* or *piti-chewee* diagnostic. Song varies from a repeated *tsip* note to four- or five-note phrases such as *pitchaweeoo*.

Habitat: Misnamed as no particular fondness for marshes, being mainly sedentary in deciduous or mixed woods, rarely reaching gardens. Nests in tree holes. Map 305.

SOMBRE TIT *Parus lugubris*   Plate 86
Du – Rouwmees   Fr – Mésange lugubre
Ge – Trauermeise   Sw – Balkanmees

Identification: 5½" (14cm). Scarce specialised tit; largest of black-capped species with form and flight recalling Great Tit. Distinguished by *strong bill*, long *dull brownish-black crown* (chocolate-toned in female), large black bib and pale-edged tertials forming wing-panel like Willow Tit. Siberian Tit geographically separated; Marsh and Willow Tits much smaller.

Voice: Distinctive *sirrah,* harsh *zweet-zweet*, rich chattering *chur-r-r*. Song rather buzzing in tone, with repeated *chip* and *churr* notes and more developed *cheeu-cheeu* ...... and *tr-wiu tr-wiu* ...... phrases.

Habitat: Mixed woods of plains and mountain slopes, often near rocks. Nests in tree holes, rarely rocks. Map 306.

WILLOW TIT *Parus montanus*   Plate 86
Du – Matkopmees   Fr – Mésange boréale
Ge – Weidenmeise   Sw – Talltita

Identification: 4½" (11cm). Status and appearance as Marsh Tit but larger-headed, with distinctive voice. Separated close-to by *dull, sooty* black crown, *long buff-washed cheeks* (reaching nape), larger black bib, *thin whitish edges to tertials* and innermost secondaries (forming pale panel in fresh plumage) and round-ended tail. Northern race *P. m. montanus* of Fenno-Scandia grey-backed, with pure white cheeks; other races intermediate. Beware confusion with Marsh, particularly in worn plumage when Willow's wing-panel may be lost.

Voice: Nasal buzzing *eez-eez-eez* diagnostic; very thin *zi-zi-zi* and loud *chay* less distinctive. Quiet warbling song includes Nightingale-like *chu, chu, chu* and Wood Warbler-like *piu, piu, piu*.

Habitat: Fond of damp ground, lake sides; roves more widely than Marsh Tit. Excavates nest cavities in rotted alder, birch, willow, etc. Map 307.

SIBERIAN TIT *Parus cinctus*   **Plate 86**
    Du – Bruinkopmees   Fr – Mésange lapone
    Ge – Lapplandmeise   Sw – Lappmes

Identification: 5¼" (13cm). Size close to Great Tit with similar lengthy tail, but has *remarkably fluffy* appearance. *Dusky-brown crown and nape*, slightly rufous-brown upper-parts and flanks and *large ragged sooty-black bib* contrast with long white cheeks and greyish-white under-body. Juvenile noticeably neater and less 'dusty' than adult. Flight outline and action as Great.

Voice: Song fast, thin purring *chee-urr, chee-urr* .... Commonest call fast *tee-tee, tayee, tayee*, recalling Willow but with hoarse final notes not so drawn out.

Habitat: Almost exclusively in birch and coniferous forests. Nests in old woodpecker holes, or excavates holes in soft dead trees. Map 308.

CRESTED TIT *Parus cristatus*   **Plate 86**
    Du – Kuifmees   Fr – Mésange huppée
    Ge – Haubenmeise   Sw – Tofsmes

Identification: 4½" (11cm). Form like Blue Tit but has diagnostic *pointed crest*. Head basically whitish with *black-speckled crest*, narrow black eye-stripe extending around cheeks and complete narrow black collar joining black bib; upper-parts warm greyish-brown, under-parts whitish with buff flanks. Flight outline and action as Blue. Sometimes seeks food on tree trunks. Less sociable than other tits.

Voice: Song fast repeated trisyllabic *seeh-burrurrlt, seeh-burrurrlt*..... Calls include purring or bubbling trill as in last section of song, deeper-toned than Long-tailed Tit, also thin *tzee-tzee-tzee*.

Habitat: Usually pinewoods, but also mixed woods and thickets. Nests in holes in decayed trees, fence posts, etc. Map 309.

COAL TIT *Parus ater*   **Plate 86**
    Du – Zwarte Mees   Fr – Mésange noire
    Ge – Tannenmeise   Sw – Svartmes

Identification: 4½" (11cm). Marginally smallest tit in Europe, with large head but narrow tail. Only black-crowned tit with *bold white patch from rear crown to nape* and *double white wing-bar*; clean white cheeks contrast with crown and black bib and upper breast. Upper-parts grey, with strong olive tone in British race *P. a. britannicus*; under-parts dull white, with buff wash on flanks strongest in European forms. Adult of Irish race *P. a. hibernicus* and all juveniles have yellowish cheeks and under-parts. Flight outline includes straightest tail of tribe; action fast, whirring and darting. Wanders less than Great or Blue, usually staying within woods.

Voice: Song clear, repeated *seetoo* or *seetoooee*, more rapid and less strident than similar notes of Great Tit. Calls include clear, thin *tsui* or *tsee-eet* and short twitter, also scolding *chi-chi-chich* and thin *sissi-sissi-sissi*. Some notes very like Goldcrest's.

Habitat: Prefers conifers but will enter deciduous woods and gardens. Nests in holes in banks and tree stumps, usually near ground. Map 310.

BLUE TIT *Parus caeruleus*   **Plate 86**
Du – Pimpelmees   Fr – Mésange bleue
Ge – Blaumeise   Sw – Blåmes
Identification: 4½" (11cm). Commonest, tamest and most ubiquitous tit. Shares green-blue upper-parts, single white wing-bar and yellow under-parts with Great Tit, but instantly separated by smaller size, *white head decorated by blue crown*, thin *black eye-stripe* and small black bib, and *wholly blue tail*. Juvenile duller, with yellowish cheeks. Flight action fluttering. Acrobatic. Azure Tit is larger, with wholly white crown and under-parts.
Voice: Song high *tsee-tsee*, followed by long trill. Varied call-notes, *tsee-tsee-tsee-tsit*, etc. and harsh, scolding *chur-r-r*.
Habitat: As Great Tit. Map 311.

AZURE TIT *Parus cyanus*   **Plate 86**
Du – Azuurmees   Fr – Mésange azurée
Ge – Lasurmeise   Sw – Azurmes
Identification: 5¼" (13cm). Quite large, rather long-tailed tit; mainly blue above and white below, with *white head* except for dark eye-stripe, *broad white inverted V on wing* and bright white edges to tail. Juvenile greyer above, even on crown. Flight outline lengthy but action as Blue.
Voice: Call-note recalls Long-tailed Tit's low *tsirr*; in alarm, loud *tcherpink*.
Habitat and Range: Wanders west from Russia to all but S. Europe, frequenting particularly waterside willows and bushes in reedbeds.

GREAT TIT *Parus major*   **Plate 86**
Du – Koolmees   Fr – Mésange charbonnière
Ge – Kohlmeise   Sw – Talgoxe
Identification: 5½" (14.5cm). Largest common tit; shares yellow under-parts with Blue Tit but instantly separated by larger size, *black head with triangular white cheeks*, full *black bib extending down body centre* and bright white tail-edges. Juvenile duller-headed, with yellowish cheeks. Flight less fluttering than smaller tits, suggesting warbler.
Voice: Song consists of two- or three-syllable variations on familiar, ringing *teechew-teechew-teechew*, and occasional mimicry. Calls most varied of tits but Chaffinch-like *tsink, tsink* diagnostic.
Habitat: Mixed woods, hedges, gardens. Nests in holes in trees, walls, drainpipes, nest-boxes, etc. Map 312.

NUTHATCHES: Sittidae

Nuthatches recall tiny woodpeckers, having strong bills and large feet, but climb trees (or rocks) upwards or downwards, without using their tail as a prop. Loud, far-carrying, ringing voices. Sexes similar. Hole nesting.

KRÜPER'S NUTHATCH *Sitta krueperi*   **Plate 83**
Du – Krüpers Boomklever   Fr – Sittelle de Krüper
Ge – Türkenkleiber   Sw – Krüpers nötväcka
Identification: 5" (12.5cm). Smallest of three nuthatches inhabiting S.E. Europe but with typical form of tribe. Plumage basically blue-grey above and whit-

ish below; face rather pale relieved by *glossy black crown-patch* (not reaching nape), white supercilium, black loral stripe and dusky eye-stripe; *breast boldly patched dark rufous.*
Voice: Song shrill, yodelling trill, suggesting loud Blue Tit. Calls brief *puit*, harsher *shwee*, recalling Greenfinch, and in flight short *jek*, like Brambling.
Habitat and Range: Found chiefly in outer foliage of conifers (Asia Minor). Breeds Greek Islands.

CORSICAN NUTHATCH *Sitta whiteheadi*   **Plate 83**
   Du – Zwartkopboomklever   Fr – Sittelle corse
   Ge – Korsikanischer Kleiber   Sw – Korsikansk nötväcka
Identification: 4 ¾" (12cm). Smallest nuthatch in Europe, confined to Corsica where only representative of tribe. Plumage blue-grey above and wholly whitish below; *strongly lined head* with black crown and eye-stripe in male and slate-grey crown and dusky eye-stripe in female isolating conspicuous, *long white supercilium.*
Voice: Song clear and accelerating *dewdewdewdewdew-di-di-di-di-di*. Calls include Jay-like nasal scold *chay-chay-chay.....*, weak trilling *pupupupu*, louder nasal *pooi* and thin trilling *tsi-tsi-tsi*.
Habitat and Range: Confined to mountain forests and groves (particularly of chestnut) in Corsica. Makes nest holes in rotting trees.

NUTHATCH *Sitta europaea*   **Plate 83**
   Du – Boomklever   Fr – Sittelle torchepot
   Ge – Kleiber   Sw – Nötväcka
Identification: 5½" (14cm). Active, tree-climbing passerine, with pointed *chisel-bill* and noticeably *short tail*, not used as support. Colourful, with blue-grey upper-parts relieved by *long black eye-stripe* turning down neck and *white marks on end of tail*. Under-parts mainly *pale reddish-buff* in W. European forms but *mostly white* in Fenno-Scandian and N. Russian race; upper flanks and vent splashed chestnut in all birds. Flight outline compact, with relatively large wings; action fast-flapping, progress darting. Crouches while climbing in any direction, even downwards. Hammers at nuts wedged in cracks.
Voice: Song loud, ringing whistling trill, including loud *tui*, long *chi-chi-chi-chi*, *qui-qui-qui*, etc. Far-carrying calls include ringing metallic *chwit, chwit, chwit*, repeated *tsit*, shrill trilling *tsirr* and in alarm excited *twett-twett-twett*.
Habitat: Old deciduous trees in woods, parks, gardens. Nests in holes in trees, occasionally in walls, nest-boxes, etc., plastering entrance hole and crevices with mud. Map 313.

ROCK NUTHATCH *Sitta neumayer*   **Plate 83**
   Du – Rotsklever   Fr – Sittelle des rochers
   Ge – Felsenkleiber   Sw – Klippnötväcka
Identification: 5½" (14cm). Largest nuthatch, due to proportionately longer bill and legs and less crouched posture. Plumage pattern and colour much as northern race of Nuthatch but all tones look faded except for long black eye-stripe; distinguished by uniformly *buffish rear under-parts* (lacking chestnut dappling under tail) and wholly *grey tail*. Actions as Nuthatch but more prone to upright hops.

Voice: Extremely vocal, paired birds *constantly calling* to each other with very varied vocabulary. Song trilling *zee-a,zee-a,zee-a*, then descending into further trill with terminal flourish. Calls include Jay-like screeches, loud whistles and other emphatic notes.

Habitat: Rocky gorges, mountainsides, cliffs. Breeds in caves and crannies in rocks, plastering entrance with mud, to form short funnel. Map 314.

WALLCREEPERS: Tichodromadidae

WALLCREEPER *Tichodroma muraria*   **Plate 83**

Du – Rotskruiper   Fr – Tichodrome échelette
Ge – Mauerläufer   Sw – Murkrypare

Identification: 6½" (16cm). Spectacular, rock-climbing bird with long de-curved bill. *Broad, rounded wings* – often flicked open when bird moves and *splayed like butterfly in flight* – display *brilliant crimson* on coverts and bases of flight-feathers, contrasting with otherwise black feathers except for *double row of large white spots on outer primaries*. Rest of plumage dusky-grey, with black lower face and breast in summer, becoming grey-white in winter, and white-cornered, grey-tipped, black tail. Juvenile like winter adult but brownish, with straighter bill. Seeks food on rock-faces and old stone and wooden buildings.

Voice: Clear, piping *zee-zee-titi-zwee*, in rising cadence.

Habitat: High rocky ravines, earth cliffs, ruins, mostly from about 6,000ft (2,000m.) to snowline; descends in winter to rocky valleys and foothills. Breeds in deep crevices. Map 315.

TREECREEPERS: Certhiidae

Small, restless, mouse-like birds, with long, slender, decurved bills and cryptic plumage. Usually seen creeping up tree trunks. Sexes similar. Nest in crevices.

TREECREEPER *Certhia familiaris*   **Plate 83**

Du – Kortsnavelboomkruiper   Fr – Grimpereau des bois
Ge – Waldbaumläufer   Sw – Trädkrypare

Identification: 5" (12.5cm). Small, slim, rather mouse-like bird, with thin *de-curved bill* and graduated *stiff tail* used as prop when climbing trees. Upper-parts brown, finely streaked white and buff, relieved by *complete white supercilium*, two buff-white wing-bars (lower visible in flight); under-parts silvery-white, with rear flanks and vent usually clean on northern race *C. c. familiaris* but often sullied or buff-washed in southern and western forms. Long hind-claw visible at close range (but length difficult to judge in field). Flight light and flitting, con-tributing with obscure plumage to always unobtrusive presence. Gait hopping but appears to creep when climbing (always upwards in spurts) on trunks and branches and then flying to base of next tree. Often with tits in winter. See also Short-toed Treecreeper.

Voice: Generally *thin and sibilant*. Song weak, high-pitched *tsee-tsee-tsizzi-tsee*, starting slowly and accelerating. Commonest call similarly toned *tsee* or *tsit*.

Habitat: Woods, parks, gardens with large trees. Nests behind loose bark, in split trees, behind ivy, etc. In C. and S. Europe, prefers mountain woodlands and avoids lowlands. Map 316.

SHORT-TOED TREECREEPER *Certhia brachydactyla* Plate 83
Du – Boomkruiper Fr – Grimpereau des jardins
Ge – Gartenbaumläufer Sw – Trädgårdsträdkrypare

Identification: 5" (12.5cm). No trustworthy difference in form from Tree-creeper, though bill often appears bent down at end, but *voice distinctive*. Close-to, separated with care by duller, more irregularly streaked upper-parts and particularly *short, dull supercilium* (most obvious behind eye), more contrasting rump and duller under-parts, looking *dirty and brownish on rear flanks and vent*, and white spots on ends of inner primaries. Flight and behaviour as Treecreeper.

Voice: Generally *quite loud and tit-like*. Typical song rhythmic but short *teet, teet, teeteroititt*; commonest calls high, shrill, penetrating *zeet*, recalling Dun-nock, and loud, emphatic *teet*, often repeated and suggesting Coal Tit.

Habitat: Gardens, parks, coppices, avoiding heavy woodlands. In C. and S. Europe, Treecreeper usually restricted to mountains and regions above 3,000ft (900m.), whereas Short-toed occurs from 5,000ft (1500m.) to sea level. Map 317.

PENDULINE TITS: Remizidae

PENDULINE TIT *Remiz pendulinus* Plate 86
Du – Buidelmees Fr – Mésange rémiz
Ge – Beutelmeise Sw – Pungmes

Identification: 4¼" (11cm). Small, tit-like bird with fine bill and narrow tail. Far less noticeable than true tits, but adult easily distinguished by pale *greyish-white head and throat with broad black mask, contrasting chestnut back* and buffish-white under-parts. Juvenile mainly pale ash-brown, lacking mask but already showing warm brown back. Flight and behaviour tit-like.

Voice: Soft plaintive *tsee* or *seeou* distinctive, recalling Robin; also conversational *tsi-tsi-tsi*.

Habitat: Marshy localities, thickets, along dykes, etc., locally in dry regions. Builds ovoid nest with funnel-shaped entrance, suspended in outer twigs of bush or tree (occasionally as high as 6-7m) and in reeds. Map 318.

ORIOLES: Oriolidae

GOLDEN ORIOLE *Oriolus oriolus* Plate 87
Du – Wielewaal Fr – Loriot
Ge – Pirol Sw – Sommargylling

Identification: 9½" (24cm). Rather large, somewhat thrush-like bird with long wings and lengthy tail. Male unmistakable; *bright yellow with mainly black wings and tail*, latter boldly cornered with yellow. Female and juvenile *yellow-ish-green above*, with darker wings and tail; *greyish to white below*, with light streaks. Flight action fluent, rapid but undulating; regains tree cover with char-acteristic upward sweep. Rather secretive, staying hidden in tree canopies but

call far-carrying. Green Woodpecker similarly coloured to female but much heavier and broader-winged.
Voice: Diagnostic loud, *fluted* whistle *weela-weeo*; harsh *chr-r-r* in alarm, also swears like Jay.
Habitat: Essentially arboreal; woods, well-timbered parks, old orchards, riverine trees. Nest usually slung between horizontally forked branch. Map 319.

SHRIKES: Laniidae

Strikingly patterned, with hook-tipped bills and hawk-like behaviour. Usually perch watchfully upright on conspicuous vantage points, fanning their rather long tails. Prey often impaled on thorn-bush 'larders'. Call-notes are harsh, but songs surprisingly musical. Sexes nearly similar, except Red-backed. Bush or tree nesting.

ISABELLINE SHRIKE *Lanius isabellinus*   **Plate 85**

Du – Isabelklauwier   Fr – Pie-grièche isabelle
Ge – Isabellwürger   Sw – Isabellatörnskata

Identification: 6¾" (17cm). Size and form as Red-backed, with which formerly considered conspecific, but is slightly longer-tailed. Two races, W. Asian *L. i. phoenicuroides* and E. Asian *L. i. isabellinus*, occur, requiring great care in separation from Red-backed with which western birds hybridise. Typically, adult male *phoenicuroides* has distinctive *rufous crown*, white supercilium, black face-mask, *grey-brown mantle*, small white patch at base of primaries and *strongly rufous rump and tail*. Male *isabellinus* is noticeably *more pallid*, with less striking head pattern, only vestigial primary mark and *paler sandy-rufous rump and tail*. Females often similar but immatures lack head pattern; distinguished from Red-backed by *pale bill*, paler, plainer mantle, *only faint barring on under-parts* and cinnamon rump and tail, with *rufous colour also showing on under-side*.
Voice: Harsh *shaak*, like Red-backed.
Habitat and Range: Open country with scrub, cultivation. Vagrant from Asia to Europe (including Britain).

RED-BACKED SHRIKE *Lanius collurio*   **Plate 85**

Du – Grauwe Klauwier   Fr – Pie-grièche écorcheur
Ge – Neuntöter   Sw – Törnskata

Identification: 6¾" (17cm). Commonest shrike of region, with strong, slightly hooked bill, long- and loose-tail and upright stance. Male colourful and strongly patterned, with *chestnut back* separating *pale blue-grey crown and rump*, broad *black eye-stripe* contrasting with white throat, pinkish-white under-body, and *black tail, white-sided particularly at base*. Female dull rufous-brown above, buffish-white, closely barred with brown crescents below, and dark but less white-edged tail. Immature like female but more rufous and close-barred above; tail may be rufous above but is always greyish below. Flight outline lengthy; action fast and direct; may glide and hover when hunting along hedge but usually pounces on prey from perch. Impales small birds and insects on thorn 'larders' more often than other shrikes. Occasional Red-backeds with red upper tails cause serious confusion with Isabelline.

Voice: Song quite musical, often prolonged and ventriloquial warble interspersed with buzzing notes and mimicry; recalls loud Garden Warbler. Call harsh *shack* or *chee-uk*.
Habitat: Bushy commons, uncut hedges, thickets, old quarries. Nests in bushes, small trees, bramble patches. Map 320.

LESSER GREY SHRIKE *Lanius minor*   Plate 85

Du – Kleine Klauwier   Fr – Pie-grièche à poitrine rose
Ge – Schwarzstirnwürger   Sw – Svartpannad törnskata

Identification: 8" (20cm). Smaller than Great Grey, with proportionately slightly shorter bill, much longer primaries forming *long wing-point*, and shorter tail. Plumage pattern of adult differs in *broad black forehead* (less evident in female), *lack of white supercilium* or scapular edge, and *broad white patch on outer wing*. Immature in first winter lacks black forehead; juvenile has *yellowish-buff* plumage, only finely barred above and below, with dull brownish-black wings and tail. Flight outline less lengthy than Great Grey; action powerful, not undulating like Great Grey; hovers frequently. Perched stance often more upright than Great Grey.
Confusion species: Beware variations of Great Grey: S. European birds have pinkish breasts like Lesser Grey; vagrants from W. Asia lack white supercilia. Structure always important to distinction of these species.
Voice: Song like Woodchat but tempo slower. Calls harsh scold and *kviell*.
Habitat: Fairly open cultivated country with scattered trees and bushes, roadsides, commons, etc. Nests fairly high in trees – even up to 60ft (18m); often in loosely scattered colonies. Map 321.

GREAT GREY SHRIKE *Lanius excubitor*   Plate 85

Du – Klapekster   Fr – Pie-grièche grise
Ge – Raubwürger   Sw – Varfågel
N. Am – Northern Shrike

Identification: 9½" (24cm). Boldest, largest and longest-tailed shrike of region, with striking grey, black and white plumage but short primaries, forming only *stubby wing-point* falling short of upper tail-coverts. At all ages, N. European race *L. e. excubitor* distinguished from Lesser Grey by *longer, less stubby bill*, wholly grey crown, *narrow white supercilium*, black eye-patch, *long white edge to scapulars,* long *narrow white bar across wing* (appearing 'broken' when folded) and bolder white tips to tertials and tail. Female usually faintly 'waved' brown on breast. Juvenile browner above and duller below, with brown crescents on breast and flanks. S. European race *L. e. meridionalis* has *duskier upper-parts* with shorter broader white wing-bar, and pink flush below. Asian steppe race *L. e. pallidirostris* looks washed-out, with pale bill and incomplete face marks. Flight outline lengthy, with large head and long graduated tail obvious: action strong, with bursts of wing-beats producing 'rocketing' progress ending in steep upward glide to prominent perch; hovers. Tail frequently waved or fanned. Pounces down from perch onto small birds, mice, lizards and insects.
Voice: Song subdued and slow, repeating both harsh and musical notes. Calls include characteristic *shek-shek*, sometimes prolonged into Magpie-like rattle, and grating *jaaeg* or *vaaech* in alarm or anger.
Habitat: Less fond of open country for breeding than other shrikes, northern

birds liking clearings in taiga. In winter, heaths, hedges and wood edges. Nest site varied, occasionally in high trees, usually in thorn bushes. Usually resident but northern birds winter far to south, while steppe race vagrant from Asia to W. Europe (including Britain). Map 322.

WOODCHAT SHRIKE *Lanius senator* Plate 85
Du – Roodkopklauwier   Fr – Pie-grièche à tête rousse
Ge – Rotkopfwürger   Sw – Rödhuvad törnskata

Identification: 7" (17.5cm). Rather big-headed shrike, intermediate in size between Lesser Grey and Red-backed. Pied adult easily distinguished by *chestnut crown and nape*, white scapulars dividing black back and wings, and *white rump*; female duller than male. Immature resembles Red-backed but is less rufous, with *pale spotted scapulars*, pale bar across base of primaries and pale mottled rump. Mediterranean Islands race *L. s. badius* lacks wing-bar. Flight and behaviour as Lesser Grey.

Voice: Song attractive, sustained musical warble, mixed with harsh notes and mimicry. Calls recall Lesser Grey but include frequent House Sparrow-like chatter.

Habitat: Dry open country, olive groves, orchards, bushy commons, occasionally large woods. Nests in trees of all sizes. Map 323.

MASKED SHRIKE *Lanius nubicus* Plate 85
Du – Maskerklauwier   Fr – Pie-grièche masquée
Ge – Maskenwürger   Sw – Masktörnskata

Identification: 6¾" (17cm). Smallest, slimmest shrike of region, with *narrow tail*, pied upper-parts and wings and *rufous flanks*. Male also differs from Woodchat in *bold white forehead* and supercilium, *black crown and rump* and more conspicuous white edges to tail. Female duskier, with less rufous flanks. Immature greyer and barred; lacks rufous flanks but already shows pale supercilium and scapulars. Flight like Red-backed but lighter, even more agile. Keeps to cover, seldom adopting open perch.

Voice: Song slow, uneven, grating subdued monotone of scratchy notes. Commonest call distinctive harsh but plaintive *keer*.

Habitat and Range: Olive groves, gardens and lightly wooded country. Nests fairly high in trees. Summer visitor to Turkey, Greece and S. Yugoslavia; irregular Bulgaria. Vagrant elsewhere in S. and W. Europe.

CROWS: Corvidae

The largest of the perching birds, with black or boldly patterned plumage. Longish, powerful bills. Gruff voices. Sexes similar. Tree, cliff or hole nesting.

JAY *Garrulus glandarius* Plate 87
Du – Vlaamse Gaai   Fr – Geai des chênes
Ge – Eichelhäher   Sw – Nötskrika

Identification: 13½" (34cm). Broad-winged, colourful crow, often heard before seen. Round head shows erectile, black and white streaked crown, pale blue eye and *short black 'moustache'*; body pinkish-brown, paler below, contrasting with *black-barred blue primary coverts* and white-patched black flight-feathers; *rump and vent white, isolating black tail*. Flight laboured, with bursts of *irregular deep wing-beats* below body line. Hops and leaps. Shy but cunning, usually in dense cover but 'thieving' around houses with gardens; often in small noisy parties.

Voice: Diagnostic call penetrating, raucous *skraaak*, sometimes in chorus, also other harsh and subdued chuckling, clicking and mewing notes.

Habitat: Rarely far from trees. Usually nests in well-secluded woods. Map 324.

SIBERIAN JAY *Perisoreus infaustus* **Plate 87**
Du – Taiga Gaai   Fr – Mésangeai imitateur
Ge – Unglückshäher   Sw – Lavskrika

Identification: 12" (30cm). Smallest crow, with *small pointed bill*, fluffy plumage and relatively longer tail than Jay. *Fox-red wing-patches, under wing-coverts, rump and sides of tail* conspicuous in flight. Crown and nape dull sooty-brown; wings, back, centre tail-feathers and under-parts mouse-grey, flanks and under tail-coverts rufous. Retiring and usually silent in breeding season, otherwise perky and confident, snatching food from humans in winter. Agile in clinging to tips of pine branches to reach cones. Flight action mixes quick bursts of wing-beats with glides.

Voice: Cheerful *kook, kook*, and raucous *chair*, also *whisk-ee* and Buzzard-like mewing notes.

Habitat: Thick northern coniferous and birch woods, resorting to logging camps and villages in winter. Usually nests in spruce or pine, on branch close to trunk. Map 325.

AZURE-WINGED MAGPIE *Cyanopica cyana* **Plate 87**
Du – Blauwe Ekster   Fr – Pie-bleue
Ge – Blauelster   Sw – Blåskata

Identification: 13½" (34cm). Slimmest crow, with rather broad wings, *very long, graduated tail* and *distinctive voice*. Easily recognised by *jet black head-cap* extending below eyes and to nape, *pale blue wings* with black inner webs to primaries, and pale blue tail. Back and rump brownish-grey, under-body buffish except for white throat. Actions recall Magpie but flight less fluttering, with *floating glide*. Confident and perky, roaming about in noisy bands except in breeding season.

Voice: Commonest call querulous *zhree*, with rising inflection, also harsh *kraa, kwink-kwink-kwink* and clear *kwee*.

Habitat and Range: Gardens, orchards, olive and eucalyptus groves and particularly ilex and pine woods. Breeds in scattered groups, building open nest, usually in fork of pine, ilex, poplar or oak. Resident in C. and S. Spain, Portugal.

MAGPIE *Pica pica* **Plate 87**
Du – Ekster   Fr – Pie bavarde
Ge – Elster   Sw – Skata

Identification: 18" (45cm). Medium-sized crow with *proportionately longest tail of tribe*, diamond shaped when fully spread. Plumage *unmistakably pied*, with scapulars, flanks and belly and primaries (except tips) white and remaining feathers black, glossed blue, green and purple especially on tail. Flight action unbalanced, with *irregular bursts of wing-beats* and short glides. Often in small parties, occasionally forms larger gatherings in winter and spring.

Voice: Loud, rapid, laughing *chak-chak-chak-chak*, also various not unmusical chattering and piping notes when breeding.

Habitat: Farmlands and open country, entering towns in recent years. Builds *domed nest* in tall trees, thorn bushes, hedgerows, wood edges, even bramble-patches. Map 326.

NUTCRACKER *Nucifraga caryocatactes* Plate 87

Du – Notenkraker Fr – Casse-noix moucheté
Ge – Tannenhäher Sw – Nötkråka

Identification: 12½" (32cm). Quite small crow with *long but strong bill* and in flight oddly upslanted body, *large rounded wings* and relatively short tail. Uniquely in family, dark brown facial and body plumage copiously *spotted with white*, while conspicuous *white under tail-coverts and rim to under-tail* form diagnostic flight characters. Flight action unsteady, like Jay. Often in small parties, except when breeding. Perches on tree-tops.

Voice: Harsh *kror*, loud, rasping *krair*, often repeated fairly quickly 4-6 times, and Jay-like *skraaak*. In breeding season various croaks, clicks and mewing notes.

Habitat: Mainly coniferous forests in mountainous regions, also deciduous woods in winter and open country during westward eruptions. Breeds in conifers. Map 327.

ALPINE CHOUGH *Pyrrhocorax graculus* Plate 87, 88

Du – Alpenkauw Fr – Chocard à bec jaune
Ge – Alpendohle Sw – Alpkaja

Identification: 15" (38cm). Size and form close to Chough but with *much shorter and straighter bill*, less fingered primaries and relatively *longer tail*. Plumage black, only faintly glossed blue. *Bill pale yellow at all ages*. Flight and behaviour much as Chough.

Voice: Less noisy than Chough but commonest calls distinctive, with clear, piercing, whining *tsi-eh* or *chirrish* and rolling *krrrree* (both with strange 'electronic' resonance) not matched by Chough.

Habitat: Mountains. Does not normally descend to lowlands, nor occur on sea coasts. Nests in cleft rocks and in ruins. Map 328.

CHOUGH *Pyrrhocorax pyrrhocorax* Plate 87, 88

Du – Alpenkraai Fr – Crave à bec rouge
Ge – Alpenkrähe Sw – Alpkråka

Identification: 15½" (39cm). Size noticeably larger than Jackdaw, with *long thin curved bill* and rather raptorial outline in soaring flight due particularly to widely separated upcurved primaries. Plumage glossy blue-black, with strikingly *red bill and legs* in adult, orange bill in juvenile. Flight free, buoyant and, frequently, dramatically tumbling. Walks and hops.

Voice: Most distinctive call long, rather merry, high-pitched *chweeaw* or *chee-aah* recalling young Jackdaw but much more memorable; also onomatopoeic *chuff* and strangely gull-like *kwuk-uk-uk*.

Habitat: Mountains, but never at highest altitudes attained by Alpine Chough, and locally cliffs and rocky outcrops near sea. Nests in cleft rocks, cliff ledges, caves. Map 329.

JACKDAW *Corvus monedula* **Plate 88**

Du – Kauw Fr – Choucas des tours
Ge – Dohle Sw – Kaja

Identification: 13" (33cm). Smallest common crow, with rather short pointed bill and portly, jaunty mien. Plumage basically black, with *white to pale grey eye*, deep *grey shawl* and dusky under-body noticeable close-to. Obviousness of shawl varies between individuals and races, with Scandinavian and E. European birds having more silvery nape, latter showing obvious white patches either side of neck. Flight action powerful and fast, *rather pigeon-like*, occasionally tumbling like Chough. Gait quick, with waddling walk and hop. Gregarious, often with Rooks and Starlings. Noisy, especially in flock chorus.

Voice: Unmistakable *chak* and, when excited, chattering *chaka-chaka-chack*; also *kya* and widely varying breeding calls.

Habitat: Farmlands, parks, cliffs, old buildings. Nests sociably in holes in trees, buildings, cliffs, occasionally in burrows. Map 330.

ROOK *Corvus frugilegus* **Plate 88**

Du – Roek Fr – Corbeau freux
Ge – Saatkrähe Sw – Råka

Identification: 18" (46cm). Large crow, with *long pointed bill, bare whitish face* (in adult), *usually peaked crown* and loose thigh feathers like '*baggy trousers*'; most gregarious of family throughout year. Plumage totally black, with *strong violet gloss* catching sunlight more than any other crow. Juvenile duller, with fully feathered black face but always longer thinner bill than Carrion Crow. Flight outline shows longer, narrower and more fingered wings and more graduated tail than Carrion Crow; action more elegant, with faster, deeper wingbeats and more skilful glide and soar; flocks 'straggle' to roosts.

Voice: Distinctive *kaaa* or *aargh*, gruff but less harsh than Carrion Crow; many other calls include Raven-like croak and gull-like *ki-ook*.

Habitat: Prefers agricultural areas with some trees. Nests and roosts *in tree-top colonies*. Map 331.

CARRION CROW and HOODED CROW *Corvus corone* **Plate 88**

Carrion Crow *C. c. corone*
Du – Zwarte Kraai Fr – Corneille noire
Ge – Rabenkrähe Sw – Svartkråka

Hooded Crow *C. c. cornix*
Du – Bonte Kraai Fr – Corneille mantelée
Ge – Nebelkrähe Sw – Grå kråka

Identification: 18½" (47cm). Second largest and most widespread crow of region. Similar to Rook but with much *stouter bill always feathered at base and decurved at tip*, flatter head, slightly shorter wing and slightly shorter, not so rounded tail; thighs feathered but not as cloaked as Rook. Plumage of Carrion Crow *C. c. corone* all-black, with only moderate blue iridescence difficult to detect in field; Hooded Crow *C. c. cornix* of Ireland and N.W. Britain and *C. c.*

Flight-silhouettes of Raven and the Carrion and Hooded Crow

sardonius of S.E. Europe have respectively grey and buff-grey cloak and waist-coat. Races interbreed freely, producing various intergrades. Flight action slower, lazier than Rook, with *steady wing-beats*. When breeding, strictly in territorial pairs, but gathers at roosts and in autumn flocks. Often seen at carrion.
Voice: Distinctive harsh, croaking *kraa*, repeated 3-4 times; also querulous, repeated *keerk* and muffled metallic *konk*.
Habitat: Farmland, moors, sea-shores, even town parks. Usually nests in trees, occasionally on cliffs. Maps 332 and 333.

RAVEN *Corvus corax*   **Plate 88**
   Du – Raaf   Fr – Grand corbeau
   Ge – Kolkrabe   Sw – Korp
Identification: 25" (63cm). Huge majestic crow; larger than Buzzard, with *massive bill*, shaggy throat, long wings and *diamond-shaped tail*; distinctive *deep and resonant voice*. Plumage black, with silvery iridescence. Flight powerful, recalling large raptor, with measured but driving wing-beats; often soars and glides; markedly aerobatic when courting, turning half-over and tumbling. Walks and hops. Shy and wary; where common, forms small flocks.
Voice: Repeated, deep *prruk*; deep *koo-rook*, tooting note like old-fashioned motor horn, and high metallic *tok*; many other croaking and clucking notes.
Habitat: Frequents and breeds on cliffs, mountains, also in trees. Map 334.

STARLINGS: Sturnidae

Stocky birds, with long pointed bills, short tails. Jaunty, garrulous and very active. Feed on open ground. Sexes similar. Hole nesting.

STARLING *Sturnus vulgaris*   **Plate 87**
   Du – Spreeuw   Fr – Etourneau sansonnet
   Ge – Star   Sw – Stare
Identification: 8½" (21cm). *Dart-like flight silhouette* derives from long, sharp bill, pear-shaped head and body, pointed wings, and short tail. Plumage

blackish, glossed bronze-green and purple; *closely speckled white in winter*, particularly on female. Bill of adult dusky in winter, lemon-yellow in spring; strong legs reddish-brown. Juvenile mouse-brown, with whitish throat and blackish bill and legs. Flight direct, rapid. Occurs in huge flocks in autumn and winter, roosting in noisy throngs on city buildings, woods and reedbeds.

Voice: Call harsh descending *tcheeer*. Song long and rambling, comprising clear whistles, clicks, rattles, chuckles and excellent mimicry, delivered from exposed perch.

Habitat: Equally at home in town or open country. Breeds in holes in trees, buildings, thatches, nest-boxes, etc., or holes in ground in barren areas. Map 335.

SPOTLESS STARLING *Sturnus unicolor* **Plate 87**

Du – Zwarte Spreeuw Fr – Etourneau unicolore
Ge – Einfarbstar Sw – Svartstare

Identification: 8½" (21cm). Form, behaviour and flight like Starling but close-to, longer lanceolate feathers on throat and around neck may show on male. At distance, indistinguishable from Starling but, close-to, breeding male is obviously *blacker*, with more even, more purple gloss, *no spots* and *pink legs*; female duller. In winter, adults greyish-black; females particularly speckled with small, arrow-shaped white spots. Juvenile darker than Starling.

Voice: Louder and shriller than Starling's; notably whistling *seeooo*.

Habitat and Range: Usually in small colonies on cliffs and in towns and villages, locally in wooded regions and around isolated farms. Nests in holes in trees, cliffs, ruins, under eaves, etc. Resident in Spain, Portugal, Corsica, Sardinia, Sicily. Vagrant Greece.

ROSE-COLOURED STARLING *Sturnus roseus* **Plate 87**

Du – Rose Spreeuw Fr – Martin roselin
Ge – Rosenstar Sw – Rosenstare

Identification: 8½" (21cm). Form and behaviour similar to Starling but noticeably shorter-billed. Adult unmistakable, *rose-pink with glossy, black crested head, neck, wings and tail*. Bill orange-yellow in summer, brown in winter; legs pink. Juvenile lacks crest but much paler than Starling, with sandy-brown upperparts, dark, pale-fringed wings, dark tail, whitish under-parts, *yellowish bill* and *pinkish* legs; in flight, shows *pale rump* and dark patches under wing. Gregarious, even when nesting; mixes freely with Starling, particularly when feeding among cattle. Beware occasional biscuit-coloured juvenile Starling.

Voice: Flight note shorter, somewhat less harsh than Starling; feeding flocks maintain rapid, high-pitched chatter, louder though less varied than Starling.

Habitat and Range: Open country, agricultural land, cliffs, steppes. Breeds in holes among stones on open ground, and in walls or wood-stacks. Passage in Greece, breeding irregularly in SE. Europe, west to Hungary and Italy and occurring in summer and autumn erratically westwards over rest of Europe to British Isles, Iceland.

SPARROWS: Passeridae

Thick-billed, sturdy little birds, mainly without bright colours. Sexes dissimilar in House and Spanish, similar in other species. Nest in holes, trees, buildings or rocks.

HOUSE SPARROW *Passer domesticus*   Plate 91

Du – Huismus	Fr – Moineau domestique
Ge – Haussperling	Sw – Gråsparv

Identification: 5¾" (14.5cm). Perhaps the most familiar urban bird. Male distinguished by *dark grey crown,* chestnut nape, *black throat and breast* and whitish cheeks. Female and juvenile nondescript, dull brown above and dusty white below, with faintly pale supercilium and buff wing-bars but no distinctive marks. Male of hybrid House × Spanish Sparrow (formerly regarded as separate subspecies, so-called Italian) brighter in breeding plumage, with rich chestnut crown, whiter cheeks and under-parts. Gregarious, commensal. Flight finch-like but more direct, on whirring wings. See also Tree and Spanish Sparrows.
Voice: Garrulous and varied. Loud *cheep, chissis* and various grating, twittering and chirping notes.
Habitat: Built-up areas and cultivated land, seldom far from human habitation. Nests in holes, or crevices in buildings, ivy, ricks, etc. Map 336.

SPANISH SPARROW *Passer hispaniolensis*   Plate 91

Du – Spaanse Mus	Fr – Moineau espagnol
Ge – Weidensperling	Sw – Spansk sparv

Identification: 5¾" (14.5cm). Bolder-looking than House Sparrow. Male has rich *chestnut-red crown*, very white cheeks, conspicuous *black throat* extending onto *black-splashed and -streaked breast and flanks* and *black-streaked back*. Female and juvenile resemble House Sparrow but some show stronger lines on back and faint streaks along flanks. Behaviour and flight as House Sparrow but much more often seen away from buildings.
Voice: Full contralto *chup* and other notes resembling House Sparrow's, but all are higher in tone.
Habitat: Not restricted to houses, preferring bushy woods, roadside trees and forests. Breeds colonially and singly, building untidy straw nests in branches of wayside or forest trees, foundations of occupied or unoccupied nests of storks, eagles, etc., and in old martins' nests. Map 337.

TREE SPARROW *Passer montanus*   Plate 91

Du – Ringmus	Fr – Moineau friquet
Ge – Feldsperling	Sw – Pilfink

Identification: 5½" (14cm). Smallest, most compact sparrow; sexes alike. Distinguished by combination of rich *chocolate-brown crown,* striking *black spot* on clean white cheeks and almost complete *white collar*. Rare hybrids with House Sparrows confusing; may show grey crown centre and dusky cheek smudge. Shyer than House Sparrow; often tightly flocked and localised in weedy fields.
Voice: Higher-pitched and more abrupt than House Sparrow: short metallic

chik or *chop*, repeated *chit-tchup* and rapid twittering *tiwi-twit-iwit*. Unmistakable flight call *tek, tek*.
Habitat: In W. Europe, more rural than House Sparrow, wintering in weedy fields. In south and eastern countries, occurs around houses and in the north on tundra. Nests in holes in trees (particularly pollarded willows), nest-boxes, haystacks, etc., but also in houses in S. and E. Europe. Map 338.

ROCK SPARROW *Petronia petronia*   **Plate 91**
  Du – Rotsmus   Fr – Moineau soulcie
  Ge – Steinsperling   Sw – Stenfink
Identification: 5½" (14cm). Stocky, pale sparrow, with short tail. Head pattern most obvious feature, with grey-brown crown centre, *dark brown crown sides, long deep cream supercilium* reaching nape and dark cheeks. *White spots on tips of tail-feathers* conspicuous, particularly in flight. Under-parts faintly mottled with pale brown lines; pale yellow spot on throat visible only when close and raising head. Juvenile paler, lacks throat spot. Flight strong, with deep wing-beats.
Voice: Characteristic, squeaky *pey-i*, recalling Goldfinch. Varied chipping notes recall House Sparrow.
Habitat: High rocky mountain slopes, stony ground, ruins, etc., also in dry river-beds and arid farmlands; seldom among houses though sometimes among trees. Nests in crevices in rocks and trees. Map 339.

SNOWFINCH *Montifringilla nivalis*   **Plate 91**
  Du – Sneeuwvink   Fr – Niverolle
  Ge – Schneefink   Sw – Snöfink
Identification: 7" (17.5cm). Finch-like montane sparrow. Wing and tail pattern recalls Snow Bunting but, close-to, male easily distinguished by *grey head* with *black throat*, uniformly *chocolate-brown back and rump* and greyish to cream wash on under-parts. Bill black in spring, yellowing in winter; legs black. Female and particularly juvenile duller, with less white on wings and tail. Perches upright, jerking tail nervously. Often tame.
Voice: Harsh *tswik*. Song, in nuptial flight and when perched, repeated *sitticher-sitticher* and rapid trill.
Habitat: Bare mountain-tops above 6,000ft (1,800m.), lower in winter. Visits mountain huts and ski camps. Nests in rock crevices, walls, under eaves, etc. Map 340.

WAXBILLS: Estrildidae

Very small, finch-like birds, with narrow tails and stubby red bills when adult. Live close together. Grass nesting. European presence due to escapes.

COMMON WAXBILL *Estrilda astrild*   **Plate 96**
  Du – Sint Helena-fazantje   Fr – Astrild ondulé
  Ge – Wellenastrild   Sw – Helenaastrild
Identification: 3¾" (9.5cm). Tiny, finch-like, but with quite long, narrow graduated tail. At all ages, *finely barred* dark brown on crown, body, wings and

tail; shows *whitish cheeks* and crimson belly. Adult has conspicuous *wax-red bill and stripe through eye*; immature's bill blackish. Flight light, with whirring wing-beats and narrow tail. Nearly always in ground cover; flocks close-packed.
Black-rumped Waxbill *E. troglodytes*, easily distinguished by *almost black rump and tail*, is probably also feral in Iberia.
Voice: Call short, buzzing *tzuk-ut*.
Habitat and Range: Normally in bushy grassland of Africa but feral birds now in Portugal and Spain frequent thickets and rushes.

AVADAVAT *Amandava amandava*   **Plate 91**
  Du – Tijgervink   Fr – Bengali rouge
  Ge – Tigerfink   Sw – Tigerfink
Identification: 4" (10cm). Tiny, short-tailed seed-eater from India, much favoured by cage-bird trade. Breeding male unmistakable; all *crimson, finely speckled on wings and under-parts with small white spots*; wings, belly and tail darker. Winter male, female and immature brown above and pale buff-white below, with blackish lores, greyish throat and breast, dull yellow belly, and *crimson only on rump*. Juvenile lacks red rump but has double buff wing-bar. Bill coral-red but initially blackish-brown in juvenile; eye red. Flight and behaviour like waxbill.
Voice: Song soft but high-pitched continuous twitter. Call series of high-pitched chirps.
Habitat and Range: Usually near water or human settlement. Escaped birds now firmly established as feral breeding species in central Spain.

VIREOS: Vireonidae

RED-EYED VIREO *Vireo olivaceus*   **Plate 93**
  Du – Roodoogvireo   Fr – Viréo aux yeux rouges
  Ge – Rotaugenvireo   Sw – Rödögd vireo
Identification: 5" (12.5cm). Size and form much as *Hippolais* warbler but with much stouter hooked bill, strong legs and relatively shorter tail. Adult greyish olive-green above, whitish below, with *blue-grey crown, conspicuous black-bordered white supercilium,* red eye and dusky wings and tail. Immature has dull crown and brown eye. Legs blue. Flight action recalls warbler but outline more compact. Keeps within foliage, moving heavily.
Voice: Vagrants call with striking nasal *chway*.
Habitat and Range: Normally in deciduous trees. Vagrant from N. America to W. Europe (including Britain).

FINCHES: Fringillidae

Large family of diverse seed-eating song-birds, with undulating flight. Plumage often brightly coloured, particularly in males. Bill shapes adapted to food source, usually strong with thick bases. For convenience, tribes can be divided into three main groups – large finches (*Fringilla, Carpodacus, Pyrrhula*), small finches (*Serinus,* most *Carduelis*), crossbills (*Loxia*) – but a few are highly individual. Calls important to quick distinction of small species. Nest in trees, bushes or on ground.

CHAFFINCH *Fringilla coelebs*   **Plate 89**

Du – Vink   Fr – Pinson des arbres
Ge – Buchfink   Sw – Bofink

Identification: 6" (15cm). Commonest and most widespread finch, with proportionately longest tail of tribe. At all times, distinguished by *bold double white wing-bar* and *white outer tail-feathers*. Male colourful, with *slate-blue crown and nape*, chestnut mantle, greenish rump and *pink under-parts*, tinged brown in British race *F. c. gengleri* but noticeably clean on Continental form *F. c. coelebs*. Female and immature relatively dull, pale olive-brown above, dusky-white below, cleanest on Continental form. Flight outline lengthy; action light with bursts of wing-beats interspersed with wing closures, producing undulating progress. Except in breeding season, gregarious, often with other finches; sexes often in separate flocks.

Voice: Song brief, accelerating vigorous cascade of c. 12 notes, ending in flourish *choo-ee-o*; varies locally. Calls include loud, repeated *chwink*, more plaintive *wheet*, short *chwit* and in flight subdued *chewp*.

Habitat: Farmlands with hedges, woods, commons, gardens. Nests usually fairly low, in bush or tree. Map 341.

BRAMBLING *Fringilla montifringilla*   **Plate 89**

Du – Keep   Fr – Pinson du nord
Ge – Bergfink   Sw – Bergfink

Identification: 5¾" (14.5cm). Chaffinch-like but with conspicuous though narrow *oval white rump* and shorter, more forked *black tail*. Basic plumage pattern similar to Chaffinch but wing-bars and body plumage always warmer-toned. Breeding male has *black head and mantle*, bold *orange shoulder patch and breast*; in winter, head and mantle fringed brownish. Female and immature less distinctive but distinguished by *dusky stripes on crown*, buffier wing marks and under-parts and dark tail. Flight outline more compact than Chaffinch; action lighter, more erratic. Except in breeding season, highly gregarious, often joining other finches. Bullfinch has wider white rump and is much heavier bird.

Voice: Song grating, monotonously repeated *dzweea*, recalling Greenfinch and interspersed with a few very weak chipping notes. Calls include metallic *tsweep* and muttered *tchuc*, often repeated rapidly in flight.

Habitat: Winters in beech woods, and farmlands. Breeds chiefly in birch, but also in conifers, usually on outskirts of wood. Map 342.

SERIN *Serinus serinus*   **Plate 89**

Du – Europese Kanarie   Fr – Serin cini
Ge – Girlitz   Sw – Gulhämpling

Identification: 4½" (11cm). Smallest true finch of region, with *stubby bill* and *bright yellow rump* in adult. Male *distinctly greenish*, strongly striped on back and flanks, with yellow forehead, supercilium and fore under-parts and pale yellow double wing-bar. Female duller, with browner back and greyer under-parts. Immature much duller, with brown streaks on buff ground; lacks yellow rump. Flight outline very compact; action fast, undulating. Sociable; markedly terrestrial.

Confusion species: Siskin, which see; also escaped Canary, *S. canaria* which is larger, with longer tail, greyer upper-parts and yellower under-body, and Yellow-fronted Canary (Green Singing Finch) *S. mozambicus*, which is same size, with black face-marks and fully yellow under-parts.

Voice: Song diagnostic, *rapid, prolonged, hissing jingle,* interspersed with trills; delivered from high perch or Greenfinch-like song flight. Calls include quick, dry twitter in flight, *si-twi-twi-twi* or *tillil-lit*, hard, Wren-like *chit-chit-chit* and liquid *tsooeet* in alarm.

Habitat: Parks, gardens, vineyards, etc. Nests in trees, vines, small bushes. Map 343.

CITRIL FINCH *Serinus citrinella* Plate 89

Du – Citroensijs Fr – Venturon montagnard
Ge – Zitronenzeisig Sw – Citronsiska

Identification: 5" (12.5cm). Small montane finch, with *greyish shawl* and *unstreaked under-parts in adult*. Male greenish on back, faintly streaked; greenish-yellow on face, under-parts, rump and on median and broad tips of greater coverts, last forming *dull bar across blackish wings*. Female duller, with less yellow face, greyer breast and heavier back streaks. Immature greyish-brown, with yellowish face and under-parts, fully streaked above and below. Corsican race *S. c. corsicana* rusty on mantle and paler yellow below. Flight outline longer than Serin but action light, giving dancing progress. Sociable.

Voice: Song mixes Siskin-like creaking notes and Goldfinch-like musical twitters, often during circling flight. Calls include plaintive *tsi-i*, metallic *chwick*, and flight twitter.

Habitat: Mountains with scattered conifers and open rocky ground; above 5,000ft (1,500m.) in summer, lower in winter. Corsican race nests down to sea level. Nests in conifers. Map 344.

GREENFINCH *Carduelis chloris* Plate 89

Du – Groenling Fr – Verdier
Ge – Grünling Sw – Grönfink

Identification: 5¾" (14.5cm). Stocky, big-headed, fork-tailed finch, with *pale pinkish bill* and bold *golden basal patches on tail*. Male pale yellowish-olive-green, with brighter yellow face, belly, rump and bold *golden bases to primaries*. Female duller, less green and with less clean yellow marks. Immature browner, streaked above and below, with dull wings. Flight outline chunky; action strong and undulating. Beware confusing juvenile with *Carpodacus* finches.

Voice: Song Canary-like twitter, mixed with calls, given from perch or bat-like flight round territory. Breeding season call prolonged nasal *dzwee-e*. Calls include repeated short *chup* (somewhat recalling Crossbill), *teu* and soft twitter *chi-chi-chi-chi-chit*, less metallic than Linnet.

Habitat: Gardens, shrubberies, farmlands. Nests in hedges, bushes and small trees, particularly evergreens. Map 345.

GOLDFINCH *Carduelis carduelis*   **Plate 89**
Du – Putter   Fr – Chardonneret
Ge – Stieglitz   Sw – Steglits
Identification: 5" (12.5cm). Graceful, *slender-billed*, fork-tailed finch, with undulating, *dancing flight* and *distinctive calls*. Adult highly decorated, with *scarlet-white-black head*, black wings blazed with *long gold panel,* white rump and black tail. Immature has greyish-buff head, back and chest, with dull streaks. Sociable, often in family parties and flocks on autumn thistles.
Voice: Song Canary-like twitter, based on unmistakable liquid *sw12t-witt-witt-witt* call. Other calls include soft *ah-i* in alarm and rather harsh *geez*.
Habitat: Gardens, orchards, cultivated land. Forages for thistle-seed in wastelands and roadsides during autumn and winter. Nests in trees, usually near tip of branch; occasionally in hedges. Map 346.

SISKIN *Carduelis spinus*   **Plate 89**
Du – Sijs   Fr – Tarin des aulnes
Ge – Zeisig   Sw – Grönsiska
Identification: 4¾" (12cm). Small, slender-billed, rather dumpy but very active finch, with *golden-yellow bar across black-banded wings*, greenish-yellow rump and *golden-yellow sides to black-tipped tail*. Male has *black crown* and chin, contrasting with diffuse *yellow supercilium and face*, greenish cheeks and softly streaked *greyish-green back*, greenish-yellow breast and fore-flanks merging with white belly and vent, flanks and under tail-coverts *sharply streaked black*. Female and occasional dull male greyer above and whiter below; lack black crown but are noticeably more streaked and lined over breast and flanks. Immature appreciably browner than female, with even heavier streaking above and below. Flight outline more compact than Redpoll; action fast and bouncing. Highly acrobatic when feeding, birds swarming at food source and indulging in occasional mass flights. Often with Redpolls.
Confusion species: Serin even smaller, with stubby bill and twittering call; Citril Finch larger, with longer tail and under-parts only softly streaked in juvenile and unstreaked in adult.
Voice: Song long, rapid nasal twitter, often terminating in striking wheeze; given from perch and song-flight. Calls include diagnostic drawn-out, clear but sad *tsy-zi, spey-i* or *dlee-u*, in flight wheezy *tsooeet* and dry *kettekett*.
Habitat: Alder, coniferous woods, birch and uncut hedges. Nests high in conifers, usually at extremity of branch. Map 347.

LINNET *Carduelis cannabina*   **Plate 90**
Du – Kneu   Fr – Linotte mélodieuse
Ge – Hänfling   Sw – Hämpling
Identification: 5¼" (13cm). Commonest, most widespread small finch, with dark grey bill and on adult *white edges to primaries and outer tail-feathers* forming bright panels. Breeding male has *pale grey head* and white throat, with *pale crimson crown-patch and breast* and bright *chestnut-brown mantle.* Winter male much duller, often with no visible red. Female and immature even duller, with close-streaked, dun-brown appearance, buffier in juvenile which has diffuse wing-bars. Legs flesh brown. Flight outline compact but longer-tailed than

Redpoll; action fast and undulating. Gregarious for most of year. Linnet presents many traps for unwary observer; see particularly Twite and Redpoll.
Voice: Song very varied, pleasant musical twitter, mixing pure and nasal notes; given from prominent perch, sometimes in chorus. Flight-note rapid twitter; alarm call *tsooeet*.
Habitat: Open country with hedges; in winter roams in large flocks over waste ground, farmlands, marshes. Breeds sociably, in gorse, thickets and hedges, occasionally in marram grass and heather. Map 348.

TWITE *Carduelis flavirostris*   **Plate 90**
Du – Frater   Fr – Linotte à bec jaune
Ge – Berghänfling   Sw – Vinterhämpling
Identification: 5½" (14cm). Shape and appearance like large immature Linnet but with longer tail, cleaner, more buffish, less dun tone to plumage, and almost *black legs in adult*. Close-to, distinguished by *yellow bill in winter,* warm *buff face and throat*, stronger, less diffuse streaking above and below, less obvious white fringes on primaries and *more defined buff-white double wing-bar*. Male has *pink rump*. Flight and behaviour as Linnet.
Voice: Song more chattering than twittering, with curious hoarse, twanging quality. Diagnostic call *hoarse, nasal chweet* or *tweit*; constant twitter from flocks.
Habitat: Breeds sociably on moors and high wastelands, nesting in heather, occasionally bushes and walls. In winter roams in flocks over coastal regions, fields, marshes, etc. Map 349.

REDPOLL *Carduelis flammea*   **Plate 90**
Du – Barmsijs   Fr – Sizerin flammé
Ge – Birkenzeisig   Sw – Gråsiska
Identification: 4¾"-6" (12-15cm). Compact finch, with streaked grey-brown plumage, *bright crimson fore-crown* and *black chin* in adult. Systematics are complex, with at least three races regularly mixing in winter quarters; appearances vary by size and in paleness of plumage, especially on rump. Lesser Redpoll *C. f. cabaret* of Britain and Alps smallest and brownest, with least noticeable *pale buff wing-bars* and almost *concolorous rump*. Mealy Redpoll *C. f. flammea* of Fenno-Scandia somewhat larger than Lesser; with greyest plumage relieved by *white wing-bars* and *greyish-white streaked rump*. Greenland Redpoll *C. f. rostrata largest* and darkest, with *strong bill*, clean wing-bars and *heavy 'zebra' stripes* on flanks. All males 'drenched' red or rose on breast, particularly when breeding. Juvenile lacks red crown but already shows sharp wing-bars. Gregarious.
Voice: Song sustained mix of flight calls and buzzing trill, delivered in flight. Flight call rapid, sustained twitter *chut-chut-chut...,* with curiously broken notes and metallic echo; also plaintive *tsooeet* in alarm and Greenfinch-like *djuee*.
Habitat: Copses, shrubberies, preferably of birch, then alder and willow; in northern forests, chiefly deciduous; also rocky outcrops above tree-line in mountainous areas and on tundra. Nests, often sociably, in birch, alder, willow or juniper. Map 350.

ARCTIC REDPOLL   *Carduelis hornemanni*   **Plate 90**
Du – Witstuitbarmsijs   Fr – Sizerin blanchâtre
Ge – Polarbirkenzeisig   Sw – Snösiska

Identification: 5¼" (13cm). Size and shape as Mealy Redpoll but with even smaller bill, slightly longer tail, always *frosty-looking,* loose plumage with *pure white rump* on adult. Looks 'ghostly' compared to Mealy, adult distinctly paler on back which looks black-and-white lined, with conspicuous pure white wing-bars, tertial edges and tail-fringes, and *much whiter below,* with *sparser streaks on sides of breast and flanks* (none visible on under tail-coverts). Head may be tinged buff like Mealy but breast paler pink in breeding plumage. Immature more heavily marked, with faint streaks invading rump; appearance overlaps with palest Mealy. Flight and behaviour as Redpoll but often markedly terrestrial.

Voice: As Redpoll but flight twitter slower, with almost disyllabic notes. Other calls include *cherp,* like House Sparrow.

Habitat: Overlaps with northern Redpolls but does not interbreed, usually in more open or marshy tundra, nesting in dwarf birch and tussocks of upper latitudes. Map 351.

TWO-BARRED CROSSBILL   *Loxia leucoptera*   **Plate 90**
Du – Witbandkruisbek   Fr – Bec-croisé à ailes blanches
Ge – Bindenkreuzschnabel   Sw – Bändelkorsnäbb
N. Am – White-winged Crossbill

Identification: 6¼" (15.5cm). Form differs from Crossbill in slighter bill, smaller head and slimmer body. All plumages show *bold double white wing-bar,* bright white tertial tips and *black-spotted white under-tail coverts.* Adult male more rose-red than Crossbill with blacker back, wings and tail; female lighter yellow and more streaked; juvenile dusky-brown, more finely streaked, with narrower but still striking wing-bars. Legs black. Flight and behaviour as Crossbill but less gregarious. Beware exceptional Crossbill with prominent wing-bars.

Voice: Song rich, varied and quite long-phrased; recalls Siskin but contains loud trills. Calls weaker, thinner and dryer-toned than Crossbill: *kip-kip* or *chiff-chiff,* more liquid *peet* or *tweeht,* recalling Canary, and *chut-chut,* recalling Redpoll.

Habitat and Range: As Crossbill, but prefers larch forests. Fluctuating breeding N. Finland, N. Sweden, Norway. Winters Baltic States, sometimes reaching C., N.W. and W. Europe and British Isles.

CROSSBILL   *Loxia curvirostra*   **Plate 90**
Du – Kruisbek   Fr – Bec-croisé des sapins
Ge – Fichtenkreuzschnabel   Sw – Mindre korsnäbb
N. Am – Red Crossbill

Identification: 6½" (16cm). Heavy, somewhat parrot-like, fork-tailed finch, with fully crossed mandibles characteristic of tribe. Plumage pattern of adult rather uniform but juvenile streaked, with faint wing-bars. Adult male *brick-red,* with dark blackish wings and tail emphasizing *bright, pink-toned rump* in flight; young male has orange and red plumage. Female olive-brown with *yellowish rump* and under-body. Juvenile darker, more olive-grey, with initially uncrossed mandibles. Flight outline sparrow-like but heavy bill and tail-fork show well; action powerful, with bounding undulations. Gregarious and tame. Irrupts in late summer every few years, with occasional large invasions being followed by breeding outside normal range.

Confusion species: Beware rare individual with narrow white wing-bars, suggesting Two-barred; separation from Scottish and Parrot Crossbills often impractical.

Voice: Song, at times subdued, a hesitant mix of short trills, creaking, warbling and chipping notes; some phrases recall Greenfinch. Flight call persistent, loud, emphatic *glipp-glipp* or *chip-chip-chip*; other calls include quiet *chuk-chuk*.

Habitat: Coniferous woods, chiefly spruce, but also pine and larch. Dropped, open cones on ground indicate presence. Breeds in conifers. Map 352.

SCOTTISH CROSSBILL *Loxia scotica* Plate 90

Du - Schotse Kruisbek   Fr - Bec-croisé écossais
Ge – Schottischer kreuzschnabel   Sw – Skotsk korsnäbb

Identification: 6½" (16cm). Formerly considered race of Crossbill, now regarded as distinct species resident within forests of northern Scotland, feeding especially on cones of Scots Pine *Pinus sylvestris*. Structure, appearance and voice intermediate between Crossbill and Parrot Crossbill; not safely identifiable except in relict habitat. Studies continuing; not illustrated. Beware recent incursion of breeding Crossbills to north Scottish forests.

PARROT CROSSBILL *Loxia pytyopsittacus* Plate 90

Du – Grote Kruisbek   Fr – Bec-croisé perroquet
Ge – Kiefernkreuzschnabel   Sw – Större korsnäbb

Identification: 6¾" (17cm). Largest crossbill, with *more rounded, parrot-like bill* (lacking obviously crossed mandible tips), *thicker head and bull neck*; looks 'front-heavy'. Plumage as Crossbill, but some males duller red, while all adults have less black wings. *Pale ivory cutting edges* of bill (joining in strong 'S' curve) sometimes visible close-to. In recent years, has become irruptive, even staying to breed or winter in Britain. Beware variation of Crossbill plumage.

Voice: Still under study but song contains possibly specific *cheeler, cheeler* phrase. Some calls undoubtedly slightly stronger, deeper and hollower-sounding than Crossbill: hence very hard *cherk, cherk* (not *chuk, chuk*) in alarm, full *chok* from feeding birds and strong, less ringing *goolp, goolp* or *chup, chup, chup* in flight all sound different.

Habitat and Range: Resident within northern taiga, breeding Finland and Scandinavia, southwards sporadically to E. Germany and wintering in Denmark, rest of Germany and Austria. Vagrants reach W. and S. Europe (including Britain).

TRUMPETER FINCH *Bucanetes githagineus* Plate 89

Du – Woestijnvink   Fr – Bouvreuil githagine
Ge – Wüstengimpel   Sw – Ökentrumpetare

Identification: 5½" (14cm). Stumpy, ground-feeding finch, with *stubby bill* and *distinctive voice*. Plumage rather uniform greyish-brown, with blacker primary and tail feathers noticeably pale-fringed. Breeding male has bright *coral-red bill* and *rosy-pink hue* on fore-face, rump, wings, under-parts and sides of tail. Winter male, female and immature duller, lacking rosy hue and having yellowish bills. Difficult to observe, crouching close to ground or flying away in rapid, undulating flight.

Voice: Song peculiarly nasal, *monotonous buzzing bleat*, recalling toy trumpet. Call harsh *chizz*.

Habitat and Range: Deserts and barren hill country, but often near water sources. Nests in rocky crevices or stone walls. Asiatic and N. African species now breeding S.E. Spain. Visits Malta; vagrant elsewhere in S., N., C. and W. Europe (including Britain).

SCARLET ROSEFINCH *Carpodacus erythrinus*   **Plate 90**

Du – Roodmus   Fr – Roselin cramoisi
Ge – Karmingimpel   Sw – Rosenfink

Identification: 5 3/4" (14.5cm). Rather sparrow-like but quite long- and forked-tailed finch, with *heavy conical bill*. Dark eye obvious in plain face on round head. Male is *rosy-carmine on head, breast and rump*, becoming reddish-brown on rest of upper-parts and whitish on belly; buff tips on median coverts and carmine tips and fringes on greater coverts barely form bars. Young male, female and immature very different, being nondescript with greyish- to olive-brown upper-parts and buffish-white under-parts, relieved by fine, soft streaks most obvious on breast and flanks, and usually indistinct but occasionally bright *whitish double wing-bar*. Flight outline suggests lengthy sparrow but action finch-like, developing undulations. Somewhat sluggish. Beware streaked juvenile Greenfinch, which lacks wing-bars and has yellow tail-edges. See also Pallas's Rosefinch.

Voice: Song short, far-carrying, pure but sharp *switi-sweetoo* or *weeje-wiiweeja*. Call quiet, piping *tiu-eek*, sometimes shortened to *pluip*.

Habitat: In summer, thickets, copses, undergrowth near water. Nests low down, usually in swampy vegetation, locally in dry oak woods. Map 353.

PINE GROSBEAK *Pinicola enucleator*   **Plate 90**

Du – Haakbek   Fr – Dur-bec des sapins
Ge – Hakengimpel   Sw – Tallbit

Identification: 8" (20cm). Large and lengthy finch, with *Bullfinch-like bill* and *double white wing-bar* on blackish wings. Male *deep rose-pink* on head, neck, breast, rump and lower flanks, with distinctive *grey upper flanks* and black-lined back. Female equally distinctive; *golden-brown or grey* where male is pink. Juvenile duller than female, with greyer tones. Flight outline suggests huge bunting or long-tailed thrush but tail is notched; action loose but powerful, soon producing undulations. Sociable in winter; usually very tame.

Voice: Song fast, crystal-clear series of whistled and occasional twanging notes. Calls include strongly fluted *tee-tee-tew* or *peelee-jeeh, peeleeju* and, in alarm, musical *cheevli-cheevli*.

Habitat: Northern mixed and coniferous woods. Usually nests in conifer. Map 354.

BULLFINCH *Pyrrhula pyrrhula*   **Plate 90**
Du – Goudvink   Fr – Bouvreuil pivoine
Ge – Gimpel   Sw – Domherre

Identification: 5¾"-6¼" (14.5-15.5cm). Stubby-billed, large-headed, bull-necked finch with *black fore-face and cap,* single broad *whitish wing-bar* on black wings and *white rump* above long, square-cut black tail. Male striking, with *bright rose-red under-parts* and *bluish-grey upper-parts*; female much duller and more uniform, with grey-brown upper-parts and pinkish-brown under-parts. Juvenile like female but lacks black cap until first moult. Northern race *P. p. pyrrhula* distinctly larger, deeper-billed and brighter than S. and W. European forms; female looks cleaner and 'ghostly'. Flight outline shows round head, full body and long tail; action not fast, with slow undulations. Secretive, seldom far from cover; often in parties in winter.

Voice: Song very subdued mix of creaking, warbling and call notes, including *djee-ur-ur* and *teek, teek, tioo* phrases. Calls soft, piping but penetrating *wheeb* or *pew* and downward inflected *pee-u-u*; sound hollower from northern bird.

Habitat: Plantations, thickets, hedgerows, gardens, orchards. Nests in evergreens, garden bushes, hedges. Map 355.

HAWFINCH *Coccothraustes coccothraustes*   **Plate 89**
Du – Appelvink   Fr – Gros-bec
Ge – Kernbeisser   Sw – Stenknäck

Identification: 7" (17.5cm). Second largest and much the stockiest native finch of region, with *huge bill,* bull neck and *short tail. Head rufous-tawny, with black lores and throat* emphasizing bill which is gun-metal blue in spring but pale horn in winter; nape grey, contrasting with *rich brown back*; wings blue-black crossed by *broad buff-white covert panel,* tail brown with *white terminal band*; under-parts pale pinkish-brown, white on vent. Female duller, less rufous on crown and grey on secondaries. Juvenile yellowish-brown on head and breast, with broken covert panel and spotted and barred flanks. Flight outline front-heavy with relatively long wings and short tail; action powerful and undulating; capable of steep ascents and dives in display flight. Bold white patches on wings visible from above and particularly below. Walks with waddle and hops powerfully. Extremely wary; forms flocks in winter, ground-feeding in woods.

Voice: Song seldom heard because given from tree-top perch: halting *teek, teek, tur-whee-whee.* Calls include loud explosive *ptik, ptik-it* or *pix,* thin Blackbird-like *tzeeip* or *srree,* and harsh *chi,* recalling Spotted Flycatcher.

Habitat: Chiefly arboreal; mixed woodlands (particularly with beech and hornbeam), parks, orchards. Nests in tree-top, or on low horizontal branch, or against trunk, often in scattered groups. Map 356.

NEW WORLD WARBLERS: Parulidae

Size, form and behaviour are much as leaf warblers, but similarities stem from evolutionary convergence, not close relationship. Plumages intricately patterned; brilliantly coloured in breeding males, but usually duller and less distinctive in winter, females and immatures. Calls sharp and often clicking. Vagrant across North Atlantic (see Accidentals for others).

NORTHERN PARULA *Parula americana*   **Plate 93**
Du – Blauwe Zanger   Fr – Paruline à collier
Ge – Meisensänger   Sw – Messångare
Identification: 4 1/2" (11.5cm). Very small, almost Goldcrest-sized, with notched tail and remarkably coloured plumage in adult. *Head, wings and upperparts bluish,* relieved by dark face, *broken white eye-ring,* bronze-green mantle and *double white wing-bar*; under-parts *yellow from chin to breast,* white elsewhere, with black and rufous mark across upper breast in male. Immature less bluish above, and, like female, lacks breast-mark.
Voice: Call short *chick.*
Habitat and Range: Usually in mature, often riverine woods but vagrants use deciduous bushes. Vagrant from N. America to N. Europe (including Britain).

YELLOW-RUMPED (MYRTLE) WARBLER   **Plate 93**
Dendroica coronata
Du – Geelstuitzanger   Fr – Paruline à croupion jaune
Ge – Kronwaldsänger   Sw – Gulgumpad skogssångare
Identification: 5" (12.5cm). Slightly larger and relatively longer-tailed than Willow Warbler. Shows diagnostic combination of *yellow patches* on crown and by shoulder and *white throat* in breeding adult, and *bright yellow rump* and *white spots near end of tail* in all plumages. Breeding male has *black face with white eye-ring,* grey-streaked back, *black breast and fore-flanks* (forming inverted 'V' on under-parts), double white wing-bar and white under-parts. Winter male and female duller, with grey-brown back and breast and more streaked under-parts. Immature rather different, with browner head, back and buffier under-parts relieved by tiny buff crown-patch, narrow pale eye-ring, cream throat, fuller flank-streaks and only dull yellow or orange patch by shoulder.
Voice: Call sharp *check,* surprisingly loud for size of bird; also sharp, thin *tsi.*
Habitat and Range: Usually in conifers but vagrants enter deciduous trees and bushes. Vagrant from N. America to W. Europe (including Britain).

BLACKPOLL WARBLER *Dendroica striata*   **Plate 93**
Du – Zwartkopzanger   Fr – Paruline rayée
Ge – Streifenwaldsänger   Sw – Vitkindad skogssångare
Identification: 5" (12.5cm). Size and shape recall Wood Warbler but tail relatively longer; most frequent of tribe to cross Atlantic to Europe, most likely to be seen in immature plumage. Has *double white wing-bar* and *white tail-spots* in all plumages. Breeding male *black-capped, white-cheeked,* well-streaked on mantle, neck sides and flanks, and white-bodied below; winter male and female have pipit-like head pattern. Immature like winter adult but more colourful, with greyish-olive crown and back, *pale yellowish face, breast* and flanks, all *softly streaked*; reliefs restricted to faint pale supercilium, wing-bars and *greyish-white edges to inner flight-feathers* on blackish wings. Beware confusion with Bay-breasted Warbler *D. castanea* (another possible transatlantic vagrant), from which best distinguished by white under tail-coverts and *pale yellow-brown legs.*
Voice: Call abrupt *chi*p or *tsip.*

Habitat and Range: Normally in coniferous forest but wider-spread on migration. Vagrant from N. America to W. Europe (including Britain).

BUNTINGS: Emberizidae

Seed-eating birds with similar bills to finches but longer tails. Include both North American 'sparrows' (see also Accidentals) and Old World buntings, of which most males are brightly coloured. Small species often difficult to separate, particularly from Reed Bunting, but most have ticking calls (see also Accidentals). Nest in trees, bushes, on ground, or in crevices.

WHITE-THROATED SPARROW *Zonotrichia albicollis*   **Plate 94**
　　Du – Witkeelgors   Fr – Bruant à gorge blanche
　　Ge – Weisskehlammer   Sw – Vithalsad sparv
Identification: 6½" (16cm). Sparrow-like, short-necked N. American bunting, as large as and almost as long as Yellowhammer but with more Dunnock-like appearance and behaviour. Body and wings resemble House Sparrow but head pattern different, with dark bill and *sharply edged white throat*, pale central crown-stripe, *dark lateral crown-stripes*, broad pale supercilium and dark cheeks. Typical breeding male has *black and white head stripes*, with diagnostic *bright yellow* spot on *fore-supercilium*. Winter male has duller stripes and may lose yellow spot; female and immature have dark brown and buff head-stripes. Breast and flanks streaked dark brown in immature. Tail dark brown. Flight like European bunting but usually at lower height. Skulks. See other N. American sparrows, particularly White-crowned.
Voice: Calls include hard *chink* and slurred *tseet*.
Habitat and Range: Thickets and low scrub. Vagrant from N. America to W., N., C. and E. Europe, (including Britain).

LAPLAND BUNTING *Calcarius lapponicus*   **Plate 91**
　　Du – Ijsgors   Fr – Bruant lapon
　　Ge – Spornammer   Sw – Lappsparv
Identification: 6" (15cm). Sturdy, lark-like ground bunting, with long wings. Breeding male has *black head, throat, breast and fore-flanks*, interrupted by *yellow-buff band behind eye*, becoming white below cheek and invading fore-flanks. *Nape bright chestnut*, merging with streaked brown upper-parts; wing-coverts chestnut with buff bars. Dark tail white-sided; under-parts white. Winter male has black markings largely covered by buff fringes. Female and immature more nondescript, streaked buffish-brown, with *chestnut wing-coverts* narrowly barred buff-white, and dark stripes or streaks on crown edges, around cheeks, on throat-sides and flanks. Pale crown centre and *pale area round eye* distinctive. Pauses to feed, then *runs* on. Flight lark-like but with blunt head, and flickering beats of long wings obvious. Gregarious.
Confusion species: In brief sighting, can be confused with smaller larks (Lesser Short-toed sharing similar rattle) and immature Snow Bunting (sharing similar short call).
Voice: Song vigorous but musical, not unlike short phrase of Skylark. Call quiet, clear *teu*, usually followed by dry rattling *ticky-tick-tick*.

Habitat: Winters in coastal stubble fields, saltings, coastal moors and along beaches. Breeds in treeless barrens, open tundra and moss-heaths. Map 357.

SNOW BUNTING *Plectrophenax nivalis*   **Plate 91**
Du – Sneeuwgors   Fr – Bruant des neiges
Ge – Schneeammer   Sw – Snösparv
Identification: 6½" (16cm). Large, round-headed ground bunting. Adult easily identified by *black tipped white wings*, this pattern combining with dancing flight to make flying flock look like snow flurry. Breeding male *snow-white*, except for *black saddle, primaries and tail centre*. Breeding female cream-white below, with grey-brown head and upper-parts (including rump), and tawny patches on breast-sides; shows buffish supercilium. In autumn and winter, male and female more similar, with *warm sandy crown, cheek-patch and breast-band*; male's saddle feathers fringed buff. Juvenile grey and buff, dark-streaked above and dark-blotched below, with much reduced white in wings (barely visible in young female). First winter buffier below than female; still shows reduced white in wings. Highly gregarious, forming dense flocks which *creep and run* over ground. Flight free and dancing, birds ascending quickly. Often tame.
Confusion species: Snow Finch has similar wing pattern but ranges not known to overlap; Lapland Bunting approaches appearance of young female.
Voice: Song clear, rapid, musical trill *turi-turi-turi-tetitui*, rather lark-like and given on downward glide from display flight or from perch. Call *soft but musical ripple*, with terminal emphasis, diagnostic; also loud *tsweet*, plaintive *teup* and ringing *teu*.
Habitat: Winters along sea-shores and open coastal regions, occasionally inland downs and fields. Nests deep in crevices, in rocky or mountainous regions. Map 358.

PINE BUNTING *Emberiza leucocephalos*   **Plate 92**
Du – Witkopgors   Fr – Bruant à calotte blanche
Ge – Fichtenammer   Sw – Tallsparv
Identification: 6½" (16cm). Size and form as Yellowhammer, with similar chestnut rump and voice. Beware hybrids from central Siberia which also stray west but, in pure-blooded birds, *plumage ground white, not yellow*. Breeding male has unmistakable head pattern, with *black-edged white crown and cheeks* and *chestnut eye-stripe and throat-band*. White body speckled chestnut across chest and along flanks. Winter male shows duller head. Female and immature browner, lacking bold white marks on head but differing from Yellowhammer in *buffish-white wing-bars* and sharper throat and breast streaks on fully whitish under-parts. No certain difference in voice from Yellowhammer.
Habitat and Range: Open country with farms and coniferous woods. Vagrant from Siberia to N., C., W. and S. Europe (including Britain).

YELLOWHAMMER *Emberiza citrinella*   **Plate 92**
Du – Geelgors   Fr – Bruant jaune
Ge – Goldammer   Sw – Gulsparv
Identification: 6½" (16cm). Commonest bunting with lengthy silhouette, ending in long, often flirted tail. Both sexes share streaked chestnut back, *chestnut rump*, lemon-yellow under-parts streaked on flanks, and white outer tail-feathers

conspicuous on take-off. Male has *brilliant lemon-yellow, little-marked head* and olive-rufous wash on chest-sides. Female and juvenile much less yellow on head, with more developed facial pattern and streaks on throat and breast. Flight free, less undulating than most finches. Gregarious.

Confusion species: Pine Bunting, which see; Cirl Bunting, from which best distinguished by chestnut rump and voice.

Voice: Song rapid *chi-chi-chi-chi-chi.......chweee*, often translated as 'little-bit-of-bread-and-no-cheese'. Calls include slurred *twitic* and metallic *chip*.

Habitat: Farmlands, roadsides, commons, open country. Breeds on or near ground at foot of hedge, on ditchside, etc. Map 359.

CIRL BUNTING *Emberiza cirlus* **Plate 92**
Du – Cirlgors Fr – Bruant zizi
Ge – Zaunammer Sw – Hächsparv

Identification: 6½" (16cm). Quite slim, relatively compact bunting with *olive-brown rump*. Male unmistakable, with olive-green head decorated by *yellow stripes above and below eye* and *black throat* (last obscured in winter), yellow collar below throat, *olive-green breast-band*, rufous-chestnut scapulars and shoulder patch and yellow under-parts, finely streaked on flanks. Female and juvenile much duller, distinguished from Yellowhammer by more striped head, chestnut on back confined to scapulars, dull rump and *finer streaks on less intensely yellow under-parts*. Elusive, hiding in canopy and in ground cover. Flight as Yellowhammer but tail less obvious.

Voice: Song monotonous, hurried jingle, recalling Lesser Whitethroat. Calls include quiet, weak *sip* and *sissi-sissi-sip* in flight.

Habitat: Tall hedgerows and trees bordering cultivated land or downs; on Continent often on bushy and rocky hillsides. Winters in farmlands, particularly in sheltered stubble. Nests low down in hedge, trees, sometimes on bank sides. Map 360.

ROCK BUNTING *Emberiza cia* **Plate 92**
Du – Grijze Gors Fr – Bruant fou
Ge – Zippammer Sw – Klippsparv

Identification: 6¼" (15.5cm). Slim bunting, with rather long, thin tail often flicked open when feeding on ground. Male *whitish- to ashy-grey on head and upper breast*, with *black lines on crown-sides, through eye* and round cheeks to dark grey bill; looks narrow-headed due to linear pattern. Rest of plumage warm brown, sharply streaked on back, with *white median covert-bar* more striking than buffish tips and fringes to greater coverts and tertials, markedly *rufous rump, chest and flanks*; outer tail-feathers bright white. Female and immature duller, with streaked crown, breast and (slightly) flanks; bill grey like male. Flight like Yellowhammer but outline slighter.

Voice: Song fast, squeaky, varied e.g. *zi-zi-zi-zi-zirr* or *suit wit tell-tellwit drr weeay sit seeay*, last note rising. Calls include weak *zeet* and thin whistled *seeee* or *seea*.

Habitat: Usually rocky mountainsides, often on trees, occasionally at sea level; often descends in winter. Breeds on or near ground. Map 361.

CINEREOUS BUNTING *Emberiza cineracea*   **Plate 92**
Du   Smyrna Gors   Fr – Bruant cendré
Ge – Kleinasiatische Ammer   Sw – Gulgrä sparv
Identification: 6½" (16cm). Size and shape close to Ortolan but with rather longer tail. Male *pale brownish-grey*, with bluish-pink bill, *yellow face, eye-ring and throat* shading into *ash-grey nape and upper breast*, buffish covert- and tertial-edges, whitish under-parts and white outer tail-feathers. Female and immature share yellow throat but are otherwise duller, browner, with pale rufous covert- and secondary-fringes and sharp streaks above and from throat to flanks. Flight and gait as Ortolan. Uncommon and shy.
Voice: Song simple, ringing *deur deur deur-deurdree-do* or *zir-zir-zir-zirdli-zi.* Calls include *kip, kleup* and *chiff.*
Habitat and Range: Dry rocky or stony slopes with scanty vegetation up to tree limit. Breeds Greek islands.

ORTOLAN BUNTING *Emberiza hortulana*   **Plate 92**
Du – Ortolaan   Fr – Bruant ortolan
Ge – Ortolan   Sw – Ortolansparv
Identification: 6¼" (15.5cm). Smaller than Yellowhammer, with shorter tail but more pointed bill. Male has *greenish-grey hood* down to mantle and upper breast, relieved by pale *sulphur-yellow lores, eye-ring and throat*, last interrupted by greenish line extending from breast. Back, rump and wings buff-brown, streaked on mantle and noticeably barred pale across median coverts; tail dark brown with white edges; *body rufous-buff*. Female duller, with streaks on head and breast but still yellowish eye-ring and throat. Bill of adult waxy-pink. Immature browner and more heavily streaked than female but already shows pale eye-ring; *rump greyish-brown*; bill greyish. All show yellow under-wing. Flight outline more compact than Yellowhammer; flight rather pipit-like.
Voice: Song mournful but ringing *swee-swee-swee-swee-drii-drii* or *zeee-zeee-zeu-zeu,* sometimes with notes reversed and always changing in pitch; uttered during circular territorial patrol; ends in multisyllable. Calls include rather weak *zit* like Cirl Bunting, piping *tseu* or *chu* in alarm, muffled *pwit* or *plett* in diurnal flight and clear, metallic *sleea* in nocturnal flight.
Habitat: Open hilly country, often also in lowlands, gardens, scrub. Breeds on or near ground in growing crops or weeds. Map 362.

CRETZSCHMAR'S BUNTING *Emberiza caesia*   **Plate 92**
Du – Bruinkeelortolaan   Fr – Bruant cendrillard
Ge – Grauer Ortolan   Sw – Rostsparv
Identification: 6¼" (15.5cm). Size, shape and plumage pattern as Ortolan but under-wing whitish in all plumages. Voice distinctive. Male has *bright blue-grey hood*, with *rusty face marks and rump*. Female duller, with pale buff, not yellowish throat. Immature buffier than Ortolan, with much warmer, *rufous rump*. Flight and behaviour as Ortolan.
Voice: Song shorter than Ortolan, rather deep *dze-dze-dzree* or *jee-jee-jee-jii* or higher-pitched, sibilant, more musical *wee wee wee wiih*; always ends with single note. Calls include metallic, insistent *styip* or *spit,* sharper than Ortolan.
Habitat and Range: Bare rocky hillsides and semi-desert regions with scattered and stunted vegetation. Nests on ground. Summer visitor, breeding com-

monly in Greece and north to Dalmatia. Vagrant elsewhere in S., E., C., W. and N. Europe (including Britain).

RUSTIC BUNTING *Emberiza rustica*   **Plate 91**

Du – Bosgors   Fr – Bruant rustique
Ge – Waldammer   Sw – Videsparv

Identification: 5¾" (13.5cm). Rather small, secretive bunting with shortish tail and nervous habit of raising crown-feathers. *Silky-white throat and under-parts* in all plumages. Breeding male *black-headed, with broad white stripe be-hind eye* and white spots on rear cheek and nape. *Chest-band and flank spots rufous-chestnut*, like upper-parts and inner wings which are streaked black on mantle and tipped white on wing-coverts, forming double bar; dark, white-edged tail contrasts with rufous rump. Winter male browner on head, with dark malar stripe. Female and juvenile duller than winter male, latter with more irregular chest-marks including dark breast-spot. Flight light, outline lacking trailing tail of larger buntings.

Confusion species: Little Bunting has similar call and clean under-parts but is smaller, with different facial pattern and dull rump.

Voice: Song recalls Dunnock, mournful but mellow *seeoo-see-see-sissioo-see-see*. Calls include rather high-pitched *zit* like Song Thrush, and *tsip-tsip-tsip*.

Habitat: Thickets near water and mixed woods with rank undergrowth. Breeds in grass or low bushes. Map 363.

LITTLE BUNTING *Emberiza pusilla*   **Plate 92**

Du – Dwerggors   Fr – Bruant nain
Ge – Zwergammer   Sw – Dvärgsparv

Identification: 5¼" (13.5cm). Small, skulking bunting, little longer than Lin-net. Narrow, straight tail and wings often flicked, like Dunnock. *Bill fine, trian-gular*; under-parts rather clean white, *finely streaked* in all plumages. Breeding male has *warm foxy head*, with *pale eye-ring, black edges to crown and lower rear cheek* (latter not reaching bill); rest of upper-parts usually rather dull brown, streaked black; tail edged white. Female and juvenile duller but diagnos-tic head pattern discernible. Legs bright pink-brown. Flight most finch-like of buntings, with little tail-flirting.

Confusion species: Easily confused with small Reed Bunting, Pallas's Reed Bunting and Yellow-browed Bunting, which see.

Voice: Song rather quiet and varied, recalling Ortolan and Reed. Call hard, clicked *zik* or *tick*, often repeated.

Habitat and Range: Near water in tundra, valleys with undergrowth and mar-shes. Breeds on ground among willows or dwarf willow scrub. Rare summer visitor, breeding in N. Finland (and eastwards); has bred N. Norway and Sweden. Scarce but regular on passage and occasional in winter in most W. European countries (including Britain).

YELLOW-BREASTED BUNTING *Emberiza aureola*   **Plate 92**

Du – Wilgengors   Fr – Bruant auréole
Ge – Weidenammer   Sw – Gyllensparv

Identification: 5½" (14cm). Smaller and more compact than Yellowhammer, with rather finch-like build. Male distinctive, with *black lower head,* chestnut-brown crown, back, wings and rump, *bright chrome-yellow under-parts* relieved by narrow *chestnut-brown necklace* and upper flank-streaks. Wings boldly splashed *white on leading wing-coverts*, forming patch like Chaffinch, and barred buff across greater coverts. Rather short tail dark brown, with partial white edges. Female may suggest Yellowhammer but head striped like Aquatic Warbler, with blackish lateral crown-stripes, *pale yellow-buff supercilium*, dark rear eye-stripe, pale whitish spot on rear cheeks and dark edge to lower cheeks; under-parts much less marked, with *streaks confined to rear flanks*. Immature like female but usually streaked on breast as well as flanks. Flight outline like small Chaffinch, action less flirting than Yellowhammer. Skulks, except when singing.

Voice: Song more fluted than Ortolan and Lapland, with curious jumping phrases rising in pitch *treeu-treeu-treeu-huhuhu-treea-treea-trip-treeeh.* Calls include short *zipp* or *tik* and soft *trssit.*

Habitat and Range: Open country. In summer, chiefly birch and willow scrub near water, but also on steppes. Nests on ground or in small bushes. Breeds in central Finland. Migrates eastwards; vagrant in C., W. and S. Europe (including Britain).

REED BUNTING *Emberiza schoeniclus* **Plate 91**

Du – Rietgors   Fr – Bruant des roseaux
Ge – Rohrammer   Sw – Sävsparv

Identification: 6¼" (15.5cm). Locally common bunting, with size close to Yellowhammer but for slightly shorter *tail often flirted open* on ground and looking thick-ended in flight, which is characterized by erratic bursts of wing-beats. Breeding male distinctive, with *black head and breast* interrupted by *white 'moustache'* and circled by high, broad *white halter*. Back and wings brown, streaked dark, with rufous lesser wing-coverts, warm buff fringes to coverts and tertials, *greyish-brown rump*, dark brown tail with brilliant white edges flashing in flight. Under-parts greyish-white, finely streaked on upper flanks. Winter male has black head obscured with buff fringes. Female and immature swarthy and less distinctive, with brown cap and cheeks relieved by buffish-white supercilium and cheek-surround; blackish lower edge of cheeks reaches bill; whitish throat interrupted by *obvious black 'moustache'* which joins breast- and flank-streaks. Eastern birds have noticeably larger bills.

Confusion species: Smaller individuals invite confusion with Pallas's Reed (which has greyish lesser coverts, plainer head, paler back lines, paler wing fringes, sometimes paler, white-marked rump, and disyllabic call), Rustic (has whiter under-parts, chestnut streaks on under-parts, rufous rump, short dry call) and Little (separated by pale eye-ring, lower dark edge of chestnut cheeks not reaching bill, straight narrow tail, short dry call).

Voice: Song tinny and repetitive, beginning slowly but ending rapidly, *tseek-tseek-tseek-tississisk.* Calls include loud *tseek*, plaintive *tsiu*, metallic *chink* and in alarm *chit.*

Habitat: Reed-beds, swamps, sewage-farms; locally in farmland which it roams in winter, often in small flocks. Breeds on or near ground in rank vegetation. Map 364.

BLACK-HEADED BUNTING *Emberiza melanocephala*　　**Plate 92**
Du – Zwartkopgors　　　　　　　　Fr – Bruant mélanocéphale
Ge – Kappenammer　　　　　　　　Sw – Svarthuvad sparv
Identification: 6½" (16.5cm). Male unmistakable, with *black head-cap* contrasting with *yellow surround and under-parts*, rufous-brown back, pale rufous rump, blackish wings with pale buff margins to coverts and tertials and blackish tail without white edges. Female and immature rather pale and nondescript; distinctive *unstreaked under-parts* end in pale yellow under tail-coverts; dull rufous tinge to upper-parts, brightest on rump. Flight outline long; action more powerful than Yellowhammer. Beware confusion with Red-headed Bunting (see Accidentals.)
Voice: Song unusually musical and pleasing, opening with *chit* or *sitt* notes and developing into melancholy warbling *siit siit siiteree-siit-siiteeray*. Calls include soft *chup*, short loud *zitt* and quiet *zee*.
Habitat: Open country with scattered woods and undergrowth, olive groves, gardens. Breeds in low vegetation. Map 365.

CORN BUNTING *Miliaria calandra*　　**Plate 92**
Du – Grauwe Gors　　　　　　　　Fr – Bruant proyer
Ge – Grauammer　　　　　　　　　Sw – Kornsparv
Identification: 7" (17.5cm). Largest bunting of region, with stubby bill, round head and chesty body, often dangling tail and, in flight, *trailing legs*. Plumage dull brown above, buff-white below, *heavily streaked overall* except on belly and vent; close-to, pale supercilium and cheek-surround and dark malar stripe and breast-streaks stand out; tail lacks white edges. Flight heavy, rather lark-like at times. Often perches prominently on roadside wires, fence-posts or bushes.
Voice: Song diagnostic, accelerating jingle, with metallic tone suggesting *rattling of keys*. Calls include short rasping *chip*, harsh longer *zeep* and from autumn parties *tip-a-tip*.
Habitat: Open farmlands, roadsides, wastelands, hedges. Nests in long grass, among thistles, in hedge-bottoms, etc. Map 366.

ROSE-BREASTED GROSBEAK *Pheucticus ludovicianus*　　**Plate 94**
Du – Roodborstkardinaal　　　　　Fr – Guiraca à poitrine rose
Ge – Schwarzkopfkernknacker　　　Sw – Brokig kardinal
Identification: 7¼" (18cm). Size and shape close to Corn Bunting but with *larger, conical bill*. Breeding male unmistakable, with *black head and upper-parts,* contrasting with *rose breast and fore-belly* and almost white bill; black wings and tail relieved by bold, *double white wing-bar* on coverts, *white panel at base of primaries;* rose under-wing, *white rump* and white inner webs to flight-feathers; white under-body. Female and immature recall large brown *Carpodacus* finch, with *heavily striped head*, streaked back and under-parts, *double whitish wing-bar* (sometimes worn off) and small whitish panel at base of primaries. Female has orange-yellow under-wing; young male has rose under-wing and rose- and buff-dappled breast. Flight direct over short distance but becomes bounding.
Voice: Call loud, sharp, metallic *peek* or *kik*.
Habitat and Range: Normally deciduous woods and thickets. Vagrants seek berries and seeds. Vagrant from N. America to W., N. and S. Europe (including Britain).

ICTERIDS: Icteridae

NORTHERN (BALTIMORE) ORIOLE *Icterus galbula*   **Plate 94**
 Du – Baltimoretroepiaal   Fr – Oriole du Nord
 Ge – Baltimoretrupial   Sw – Baltimoretrupial

Identification: 7½" (19cm). Size as Starling but with more balanced form due to long tail usually carried above wing-tips. Male has unmistakable *black hood, back, wings and tail*, contrasting with deep *orange on median coverts, rump and under-body, and tail corners*; bold *white wing-bar*. Female and immature much duller, olive-brown on head and upper-parts and less vivid orange below, with *double whitish wing-bar*.

Voice: Call mellow, whistled *kew-li*.

Habitat and Range: Usually in woodland and copses. Vagrant from N. America to W. Europe (including Britain).

ACCIDENTALS

The following notes give the salient features of rare and irregular species. Species recorded in Europe more than about 20-25 times are described in the main text. The geographical origin of each species is shown, followed by the European regions in which it has been reported with some confidence at least once. In instances where the species is most likely to be seen in Europe in immature or winter plumage, this is also described. Alternative names are shown in brackets.

WANDERING ALBATROSS *Diomedea exulans.* Largest ocean-bird, with proportionately longer wings than Black-browed (11ft, 3.3m. wing-span) and feet extending behind tail. Adult *white*, with pink bill and black flight feathers producing *sharply etched wing-tip and trailing edge.* Juvenile *dark brown except for white face and wing lining*; immature increasingly mottled white. Vagrant from southern oceans to W. and S. Europe.

SOUTHERN GIANT PETREL *Macronectes giganteus.* Huge Fulmar-like petrel; size of small albatross (8ft, 2.4m. wing-span) but proportionately much stouter bill, *stumpier body*, shorter, narrower wings and shorter fan-shaped tail. Commoner morph *mottled dusky-grey*, with white head when old; scarcer form white, with body mottled brown. Flight less effortless than true albatross, with frequent flaps and awkward landing and take-off. Vagrant from southern oceans to W. Europe (Britain).

SOFT-PLUMAGED PETREL *Pterodroma mollis.* Small short-billed gadfly petrel, close in size to Manx Shearwater. Grey-brown above, with distinctive *dark 'zig-zag' across wings* (placed as in immature Kittiwake), dark face mask and hood, variable grey on breast (not forming full band on most northern birds), white underparts, and *dusky under-wings* with faint to obvious pale marks along bases of primaries and secondaries and inner lesser wing-coverts. Vagrant to W. Europe, including Britain (race and origin uncertain).

BLACK-CAPPED PETREL *Pterodroma hasitata.* Large gadfly petrel; size between Sooty and Manx Shearwaters. Plumage pattern strongly recalls Great Shearwater; differs in shorter, stouter bill, *white forehead*, broader white collar, usually much *broader white patch above tail* and cleaner white under-parts. Flight bounding, rising and falling. Vagrant from Caribbean to W. Europe (Britain).

BULWER'S PETREL *Bulweria bulwerii.* Rather slender, dark petrel; 25% larger than Leach's and Swinhoe's with noticeably *long, at times wedge-shaped tail* and long, slender wings. Sooty-brown, looking *all-black at distance*, with grey-brown panel on greater coverts. Flight fast, swooping and careening, unlike storm petrels. Vagrant from central Atlantic islands to W. and S. Europe (including Britain).

WHITE-FACED STORM PETREL (**FRIGATE PETREL**) *Pelagodroma marina.* Quite large, close in size to Leach's but shorter-winged. Distinguished by *wholly white under-body and wing-lining*, white forehead extending over eye and round *dark ear-coverts*, dark tail contrasting with *grey rump*, and long legs with feet trailing behind tail. Flight less fluttering, more banking and sideways dancing than common small petrels. Vagrant from central Atlantic islands to W. and C. Europe (including Britain).

SWINHOE'S PETREL *Oceanodroma monorhis.* Easily distinguished from otherwise similar Leach's Petrel by lack of white rump and narrower, more indistinct bar across greater coverts. Bulwer's Petrel is a third larger, with pointed not forked tail. Origin of recent vagrants to British coasts unclear; normally confined to Pacific and Indian Oceans.

RED-BILLED TROPICBIRD *Phaethon aethereus*. Although allied to pelicans, size, form and rapid flight suggest huge tern cum pigeon; wedge-shaped tail ends in *very long whipping white tail-streamers*. Plumage *white*, relieved by red (adult) or yellow (immature) bill, black rear eye-stripe reaching shaggy nape, *black outer primaries* and speckled and barred inner wings and mantle. Vagrant from tropical Atlantic to W. Europe.

RED-FOOTED BOOBY *Sula sula*. Form and size as Brown Booby; occurs in bewildering range of plumages, with only bluish-pink bill, large eye and big *red feet* constant. White morph tinged yellow on head and neck, with black flight-feathers and carpal patch on under-wing; dark morph wholly grey-brown; intermediate morphs usually dark-backed and -winged. Juvenile of all morphs like adult dark morph. Vagrant from tropical Atlantic to N. Europe.

MASKED BOOBY *Sula dactylatra*. Largest booby but 10% smaller than Gannet. Adult white, with *yellow bill, noticeably blackish face*, wholly black flight-feathers, black-splashed tertials and black tail; rear inner wing more broadly banded black than either sub-adult Northern Gannet or adult Cape Gannet; wholly white (not orange) head prevents confusion with Cape Gannet *S. capensis*. Immature like smaller Brown Booby but dark hood is separated from brown back by *white collar*. Vagrant from Caribbean and S. Atlantic to Spain.

BROWN BOOBY *Sula leucogaster*. Gannet-like, plunge-diving sea-bird, 30% smaller than Northern Gannet with proportionately shorter bill and wings but as long tail. At all ages, head, chest, upper-parts, wings and tail *dark chocolate-brown*, contrasting with *white under- body and wing-lining* but last mottled dusky in immature. Bill and legs yellow in adult, greyish in juvenile. Vagrant from tropical Atlantic to S. Europe.

DOUBLE-CRESTED CORMORANT *Phalacrocorax auritus*. Slightly smaller than Cormorant, with proportionately slighter bill and smaller head. Plumage uniform greenish-black, glossy when breeding but unrelieved except for grey bill, *orange-yellow gape and lower face*; juvenile and immature browner, greyish-white on cheeks, fore-neck, breast and (on some) belly. Flight outline as Cormorant but action somewhat lighter. Vagrant from N. America to W. Europe (Britain).

MAGNIFICENT FRIGATEBIRD *Fregata magnificens*. Large (7ft, 2.1m. wingspan), *prehistoric- looking, piratical* sea-bird, with long, slender, hooked bill, much angled narrow wings and *very long, deeply forked tail* (usually held closed). Adult glossy black, with *red inflatable throat-patch in male, white breast in female*; immature has *white head* and most of under-body. Flight sailing, then suddenly skua-like when chasing other seabirds for food. Never settles on water. Vagrant from tropical Atlantic to W. and C. Europe (including Britain).

LEAST BITTERN *Ixobrychus exilis*. Even smaller than Little Bittern, with more rufous plumage particularly on face, hind-neck and on scapulars and greater coverts. Adult shows *pale 'braces' on sides of black back*. Vagrant from N. America to Iceland.

SCHRENCK'S LITTLE BITTERN *Ixobrychus eurhythmus*. Male distinguished from Little Bittern by *dark chestnut cheeks, back and wing- bases*; greyish-buff (not creamy) wing-coverts and lead- coloured flight-feathers; narrow dark streak down centre of throat and upper breast. Legs green (not yellow). Female and immature rufous-brown, finely speckled with pale buff; under- parts buff with heavy streaking. Vagrant from E. Asia to C. and S. Europe.

GREEN-BACKED HERON *Butorides striatus.* Close in size and form to Little Bittern, but with relatively large bill and thick neck; rather crow-like in flight. Adult has black crown, *deep chestnut neck,* dark *bluish upper-parts,* black primaries and tail, grey under-parts and yellowish legs. Immature brown, heavily streaked on breast and spotted white on scapulars and wings. Raises crest and cocks tail in alarm. Vagrant from N. America to W. Europe (including Britain).

CHINESE POND HERON *Ardeola bacchus.* Size and form similar to Squacco Heron. Breeding adult tri-coloured, with *dark red-brown head, neck and breast,* slate-grey back and white wings, tail and under-body. Winter adult and juvenile closely resemble Squacco but back darker brown, with heavier, more contrasting streaking over head, neck and breast. Beware escapes. Vagrant from E. Asia to Norway.

SNOWY EGRET *Egretta thula.* Closely related to Little Egret and similar in size. Breeding adult distinguished by *loose head-crest* of several plumes (only wisp of 2-3 in Little) and typically bright *yellow loral* skin and yellowish rear edges to legs. Winter adult and immature always show *yellowish legs* but beware occasional Little showing similar feature. Vagrant from N. America to Iceland.

WESTERN REEF HERON *Egretta gularis.* Size and form of Little Egret, with similar yellow toes, crest and scapular plumes when breeding. Occurs in several colour phases. Western race *E. g. gularis* is *dark slate-grey* with white chin and throat. Occasional white form very difficult to distinguish from typical white form of Little Egret as both have dark bills and yellow toes, but Reef has slightly thicker, brownish (not black) bill and is more usually seen in coastal waters and estuaries. Eastern race *E. g. schistacea* also has white form but with orange-yellow bill. Vagrant from Africa to S. and C. Europe.

GREAT BLUE HERON *Ardea herodias.* Noticeably larger than Grey Heron. Adult differs distinctly in *dusky pink* neck and *rufous marginal coverts and thighs.* Juvenile less distinctive but shows *rufous spotting* on wing coverts as well as last two marks of adult. Vagrant from N.America to Spain.

BALD IBIS *Geronticus eremita.* Much larger than Glossy Ibis. Black, shaggy plumage, with green, bronze and purple gloss. *Head mainly bare and red*, with decurved red bill. Legs dark red. Approaching extinction in N.W. Africa and W. Asia; formerly accidental in S. Europe.

AFRICAN SPOONBILL *Platalea alba.* Size, form and flight as Spoonbill but adult easily distinguished by *bare red face,* bright *pink legs*, and lack of yellowish foreneck. Vagrant from Africa to S., W. and C. Europe.

LESSER FLAMINGO *Phoenicopterus minor.* Only two-thirds size of Greater Flamingo, with characteristic short-based and *sharply bent-down bill* and shorter, thicker neck. Further distinguished by dark black-tipped, carmine bill and face, and more intensely pink and crimson plumage. Relative compactness shows in flight. Vagrant from N.W. Africa to S. Europe.

FULVOUS WHISTLING DUCK *Dendrocygna bicolor.* Long-necked and -legged, with flight silhouette and action at times suggesting small ibis. Head, neck and under-body bright *orange-chestnut*, with black-margined *cream stripes on flanks* and cream-buff undertail coverts; back brown-black, broadly barred rufous. In flight, *long broad wings look very dark* and white crescent shows over tail and projecting feet. Whistles loudly. Vagrant from tropical Africa to S.W. Europe.

FALCATED DUCK *Anas falcata*. Size close to Gadwall but shape differs in maned head and short stern. Male unmistakable, with *purple-green head elongated by drooping mane* and contrasting with white, black-collared neck, dusky grey body *cloaked by pale grey and black and white scapulars* drooping over white, black-barred and -ended stern. Female and immature recall Gadwall but greyish face less patterned, nape slightly maned, speculum green-black and bill grey. Flight outline noticeably large-headed in male; action recalls large teal. Vagrant from E. Asia to E. and W. Europe.

CANVASBACK *Aythya valisineria*. 10% larger than Pochard with *proportionately longer bill*; noticeably broad-beamed. Plumage similar to Pochard but blackish *bill lacks sub-terminal pale band*, while body paler and duller. Male has blackish crown and face (but beware wet face of diving Pochard). In flight, noticeably pale dusty wings show even less striking central band than Pochard. Vagrant from N. America to NW. Europe.

LESSER SCAUP *Aythya affinis*. Size and head-shape similar to Ring-necked Duck but with flatter back; lacks broad beam of Scaup. Breeding male patterned like Scaup but differs in shorter narrower bill with *tiny black nail*, duller, *purple- and bronze-glossed head* and breast, *coarser vermiculations on back and flanks* and *white wing-bar restricted to secondaries*, not extending onto most primaries as in Scaup. Female and immature recall Scaup or rare white-faced Tufted, only distinguishable by shorter wing-bar. Identification bedeviled by close similarity of *Aythya* hybrids, particularly males of Tufted × Scaup and Tufted × Pochard; certain sight of tiny bill-nail then crucial. Vagrant from N. America to W. Europe (Britain and Ireland).

SPECTACLED EIDER *Somateria fischeri*. Easily distinguished from other eiders by *large, circular, pale eye-patch*. Male has back of head and *forehead pale green*; upperparts yellowish-white; under- parts blackish. Female closely barred brown and black, with greyish-buff head and neck. Vagrant from Siberia to N. Europe. Pl. 15

BUFFLEHEAD *Bucephala albeola*. Tiny duck, no larger than Teal but with outline like Goldeneye. Male has greenish-black head with *deep white 'blaze' from eye to nape*, black back and white neck, scapulars and body; in flight, all but leading edge of inner wing white, forming patch like Goldeneye. Female and immature like Goldeneye but have diagnostic *white band on cheeks* and no neck-collar. Flight light, springing from water. Vagrant from N. America to W., N. and C. Europe (including Britain). Pl. 16

HOODED MERGANSER *Mergus cucullatus*. Slightly longer than Smew, with typical spike-like saw-bill and slim flight-silhouette, but has generally dark appearance. Male is black and white, with *fan-shaped, white, erectile crest*, outlined with black; breast white, with two black bars in front of wing, brownish flanks. Female much smaller and darker than female Goosander and Red-breasted Merganser, with dark head and neck and *prominent, bushy, buff crest*. Vagrant from N. America to N., W. and C. Europe (including Britain). Pl. 17

PALLAS'S FISH EAGLE *Haliaeetus leucoryphus*. Smaller than White-tailed Eagle, with less heavy bill and more agile flight. Adult dark brown, with *buffish- white* *head* and *broad white band across base of tail* (like immature Golden Eagle). Immature resembles White-tailed but under-wing shows striking pale yellowish-brown median under wing- coverts and large pale panel on inner primaries. Legs grey. Vagrant from Russia and Asia to N. and C. Europe.

LAPPET-FACED VULTURE *Torgos tracheliotus*. As large and as dark as Black Vulture, with even more massive bill. Distinguished at short range by *naked pink head and throat*. In flight, adult shows distinctive narrow whitish bar near front of dark under-side of wing, and white thighs and sides of crop. Vagrant from Africa or S.W. Asia to S. Europe.

DARK CHANTING GOSHAWK *Melierax metabates*. Smaller and longer-legged than Goshawk. Grey, with finely barred under-parts and rump; white-tipped blackish tail. Legs and base of bill are *orange*. In flight broad, pale grey wings with *contrasting black tips* and uniform dark grey upper breast are diagnostic. Immature is brown, with paler barred rump and under-parts. Erect stance and long orange legs noticeable when perched. Has clear whistle and piping notes. Vagrant from N.W. Africa to S. Europe.

SWAINSON'S HAWK *Buteo swainsoni*. Close in size, shape and flight to Buzzard but distinguished from latter's pale morphs by *broad brown breast-band*, contrasting with white throat and off-white body, and distinctive *unmarked pale buff under wing-coverts*, contrasting with dusky flight-feathers. Vagrant from N. America to N. Europe.

TAWNY EAGLE *Aquila rapax*. Much smaller and scruffier than Golden or Imperial. Head and body tawny-buff to dull brown, relieved by large pale rump, dark brown flight feathers and dark grey-barred tail. Yellow gape extends to front of yellow eye (not to rear as in Steppe). Juvenile and immature as in Styeppe but lack central white band on under- wing. Vagrant from N. Africa to Spain and Sardinia; also escapes from collections.

AMERICAN KESTREL *Falco sparverius*. Distinctly smaller, shorter-winged and -tailed than Kestrel, with *diagnostic chestnut tail* and in male *blue-grey wings*. Female resembles Kestrel but shares with male *rufous-centred grey crown*, dark 'moustache', second dark bar behind ear-coverts and dark spot on sides of nape. Vagrant from N. America to S., W. and C. Europe (including Britain).

SOOTY FALCON *Falco concolor*. Size between Hobby and Eleonora's but outline close to latter except for shorter tail with slightly *projecting central tail-feathers*. Dimorphic, with adult either almost black, or grey with darker flight-feathers. Juvenile resembles Eleonora's but more blotched on paler under-parts. Flight like Eleonora's but wings usually more angled. Voice suggests Kestrel. Vagrant from N. Africa or S.W. Asia to S. Europe.

BARBARY FALCON *Falco pelegrinoides*. Slightly smaller than Peregrine, with narrower wings making tail look proportionately somewhat longer. Adult recalls Peregrine but distinguished by *rusty collar round nape*, paler upper-parts and *much whiter under-parts and wing-linings*. Juvenile shows narrow rusty-yellow collar and only *thinly streaked under-parts*, unlike Peregrine. Beware confusion with paler Peregrine of Iberia and Lanner, which see. Vagrant from N. Africa or Near East to S. Europe.

SORA *Porzana carolina*. Size and shape close to Spotted Crake but with longer bill and neck, shorter wings. Adult tawnier above than Spotted, with virtually uniform *unmarked wing-coverts*, and greyer below, with fuller flank-barring, few white spots and *striking black face and throat-centre*; juvenile much plainer than Spotted, with *chestnut, black-centered crown*. At all ages, shows *bright white 'fleck'* just behind eye and wholly *greenish-yellow bill*. Vagrant from N. America to W. and N. Europe (including Britain). Pl. 34

ALLEN'S GALLINULE *Porphyrula alleni*. Smaller than Moorhen. Plumage black, glossed bronze- green on upper-parts, reddish-blue on neck and under-parts. *Bill and legs dark red*; frontal *shield green*. Immature sandy, with obvious dark feather-centres on back and scapulars, and whitish centre to neck-front and under-body but *pale buff under-tail*, unlike larger young American Purple. Vagrant from W. Africa to S., C., W. and N. Europe (including Britain). Pl. 35

AMERICAN PURPLE GALLINULE *Porphyrula martinica*. Size and shape of Moorhen but with *much longer, yellow legs*. Brilliant bronze above, purple head and under-parts; *all-white under tail-coverts*; red bill tipped yellow, with pale blue frontal shield. Immature like young Moorhen, but with pure white under tail-coverts and *no white flank-stripe*. Vagrant from N. America to W., N and C. Europe (including Britain).

AMERICAN COOT *Fulica americana*. At all ages, distinguished from Coot and Crested Coot by *divided white patch beneath tail*. Adult has slight reddish bump on upper bill-shield and reddish marks near bill-tip. Vagrant from N. America to W. Europe (including Britain).

SANDHILL CRANE *Grus canadensis*. Noticeably smaller than Crane but with similar form including bushy 'cloak' over tail. Adult *paler grey* than Crane, with much buff on larger wing-coverts and *white cheeks behind red lores and fore-crown*; juvenile mottled buff and brown, *lacking grey wings of Crane*. Vagrant from N. America to W. Europe (including Britain).

ORIENTAL PRATINCOLE *Glareola maldivarum*. Smaller than Collared, with distinctly *shorter, less forked tail*. Plumage combines dark, uniform upper-wing of Black-winged with chestnut-lined under-wing of Collared. Vagrant from S. Asia or India to W. Europe (Britain).

SEMIPALMATED PLOVER *Charadrius semipalmatus*. Similar size and shape to Ringed but, close-to, distinguished by *stubbier bill*, more domed crown with less white above and behind and below eye, *paler edges to wing-coverts*, less strong wing-bar, *rather short, less rufous tail* and more complete webbing between toes. Most safely identified by voice: *strangled, reedy* call *chur-wee* or *chu-weet* and piped *chip, chip*. Vagrant from N. America to W. Europe (including Britain).

LESSER SAND PLOVER *Charadrius mongolus*. Averages 15% smaller than Greater Sand, with shorter, less heavy, *never bulbous bill*, shorter, *usually darker grey legs* and *shorter, harder, less rolling* call *chitik*. In breeding male, face-mask even blacker and breast usually more extensively buff-chestnut. Immature shows *thinner and duller edges to scapulars and wing-coverts*. Wing-bar narrower, particularly on bases of inner primaries. Noticeably larger, longer-tailed and duskier above than Kentish. Vagrant from Asia to N., C. and W. Europe.

CASPIAN PLOVER *Charadrius asiaticus*. 10% larger than Ringed, with *relatively finer bill* and *longer legs and wing-points*. Adult has white face interrupted by dark eye-panel emphasizing *long supercilium*, dusky-brown upper-parts and wings *lacking obvious wing-bar*, white under-body, *grey under-wing* and almost wholly grey tail. Breeding male has *deep rusty breast- band with black lower border*; winter male and female have dusky breast-band. Immature buffish about head with fully *pale-scaled back and wing-coverts*. Flight call short *chep*, often repeated; somewhat recalls Turnstone. Vagrant from Asia to E., S., C., W. and N. Europe (including Britain). Pl. 38

GREAT KNOT *Calidris tenuirostris*. Slightly larger and *more attenuated than Knot*, with proportionately longer bill and wings (tips extending well past tail). Breeding adult uniformly *streaked and splashed black*, with *russet-red restricted to scapulars*. Winter adult similar to Knot but supercilium less formed and breast often bolder-marked. Juvenile distinctive, with paler face and *obvious dark feather-centres on back and scapulars*. In flight, wing-bar less distinct than Knot but *rump and upper tail-coverts almost white,* contrasting more with darker tail. Vagrant from E. Asia to C., W. and N. Europe (including Britain).

WESTERN SANDPIPER *Calidris mauri*. Largest stint, with size over-lapping Semi-palmated and sharing slightly webbed feet. Best distinguished by distinctive *thin, high-pitched* call *cheet* recalling White- rumped Sandpiper, front-heavy build with *long, usually decurved bill*, rather long legs and somewhat short wings. First autumn plumage brighter than Semipalmated with *pale face*, long white supercilium and *rufous upper scapulars* contrasting with grey back and wing-coverts. Vagrant from N. America to W., N. and C. Europe (including Britain). Pl. 49

RED-NECKED STINT *Calidris ruficollis*. Lengthy stint, recalling Little but differing in flatter back, *more attenuated rear body* with fuller vent and *rather short legs*; separated from Semipalmated by unwebbed feet. Best distinguished by distinctive *squeaky* call *treet* and in first autumn plumage by unforked supercilium, greyish ear-coverts, *lack of obvious white V* on mantle, *greyish wing-coverts* and *dull tertial edges*. Breeding adult has *bright orange-red head and neck* and boldly spangled back and scapulars. Vagrant from E. Asia to C., N. and W. Europe (including Britain). Pl. 48

LONG-TOED STINT *Calidris subminuta*. Second smallest stint, sharing with Least dark dappled plumage and *yellowish legs* but having even longer toes. Best distinguished by distinctive *shrill but rolling* call *cherrp* and in first autumn plumage by long *dark head-cap reaching bill*, contrasting with bright supercilium and greyish nape, and bright *rusty brown edges to upper-part feathers*, interrupted by *sharp white V* on mantle. Vagrant from E. Asia to N. and W. Europe (including Britain). Pl. 48

SHORT-BILLED DOWITCHER *Limnodromus griseus*. Closely resembles Long-billed but usually slightly smaller with *shorter bill*. Best distinguished by distinctive rapid, *slightly slurred, usually trisyllabic* call *tururu* or *kut-kut-kut* (suggesting Turnstone), and *dark bars on tail narrower than or no more than equal to white bars*. If retained in first autumn, juvenile tertials and inner wing-coverts show diagnostic *coarse irregular barring*, while breast looks distinctly warm buff. Vagrant from N. America to W., N. and C. Europe (including Britain and Ireland). Pl. 43

ASIATIC DOWITCHER *Limnodromus semipalmatus*. Up to 20% *larger than Long-billed*, closely resembling Bar-tailed Godwit both in shape and plumages but with proportionately deeper-based, straight and blunt- tipped bill. *Lacks obvious pale back-centre* of other dowitchers but shows *much white on under-wing* and pale flecked area across secondaries and inner primaries. Juvenile resembles Short-billed but has *sharp-scaled buff, not notched, fringes to back and tertials* and more streaked breast and barred flanks. *Legs dark grey,* not dull yellowish or green as in other dowitchers. Vagrant from E. Asia to W. Europe.

HUDSONIAN GODWIT *Limosa haemastica.* Size and shape intermediate between Black-tailed and Bar-tailed; plumage pattern closer to former but easily distinguished by narrower and *shorter white wing-bar,* dramatically *black and grey under wing-coverts,* rather narrow white rump and pale rim to black tail. Breeding adult has *greyish head* contrasting with *dark chestnut under-body.* Vagrant from N. America to W. and C. Europe (including Britain).

LITTLE WHIMBREL *Numenius minutus.* Only three-quarters size of Whimbrel, with *shorter, slenderer, less curved bill,* buffier ground to plumage, particularly on *brown-barred wing-lining,* and *dark rump and tail* uniform with back. Beware confusion with dark-rumped races of Whimbrel, and Eskimo Curlew. Calls include trisyllabic soft titter *te-te-te,* rougher *tchew-tchew-tchew* and harsh *keveek-ek* in alarm. Vagrant from Asia to N. and W. Europe (including Britain).

ESKIMO CURLEW *Numenius borealis.* Slightly larger than Little Whimbrel, with relatively longer, *more pointed wings extending well past tail* and shorter legs. Plumage differs in *less contrasting head-stripes,* more cinnamon rather than buff ground, particularly to wing- lining, *more heavily barred breast and flanks,* last with bold Y marks. Virtually extinct; former vagrant from N. America to W. and N. Europe (including Britain).

GREY-TAILED TATTLER *Heteroscelus brevipes.* Size close to Redshank but with shorter legs, while appearance differs in *wholly grey, unpatterned upper-parts, breast and under-wing* contrasting with white supercilium, greyish-white cheeks and throat and white under-body. Immature shows tiny white spots on scapulars, wings and tail-sides. Legs and grooved base to bill yellow. Bobs like *Actitis* sandpiper. Beware confusion with darker, longer-winged Wandering Tattler *H. incanus.* Call disyllabic upslurred *tu- whip,* recalling Ringed Plover. Vagrant from E. Asia to W. Europe (Britain).

WILLET *Catoptrophorus semipalmatus.* Tall, shank-like wader with straight, rather deep bill, thick neck and rather long, thick legs giving *heavy, ungainly appearance.* Looks dull grey at distance but, in flight, unmistakable with *bold white rump* and *broad white wing-bar almost completely surrounded by black on both surfaces.* Legs blue-grey. Call clear *pill-will- willet* or *kip-kip-kip.* Vagrant from N. America to N. and W. Europe.

WHITE-EYED GULL *Larus leucophthalmus.* Sooty-backed gull with *very long, black- tipped red bill,* blackish under-wings, black head and *black lower throat contrasting with white collar,* white broken eye-ring and *yellow legs.* Dark wings have white trailing edge. Immature lacks whitish nape. Slightly larger than Common Gull but narrower-winged. Vagrant from Red Sea to S. Europe.

GREY-HEADED GULL *Larus cirrocephalus.* Slightly larger than Black-headed. Easily identified in breeding plumage by *pale grey head,* red- rimmed, pale yellow eye and dark under-wings. Bill and legs *red.* Breast sometimes peach-tinted. In winter distinguished from Black-headed by pale grey smudge on cheek (not dark cheek-spot) and by eye colour. Black primaries of adult have white at base (and at tip of first primary), forming *light patch across centre of outer wing* – not near leading edge as in Black-headed. Vagrant from Africa to S. Europe.

ROYAL TERN *Sterna maxima*. In flight, resembles large Sandwich due to rather pale plumage and similar but more powerful flight, while *pale primaries except for dusky tips* provide ready separation from Caspian. At rest, suggests small Caspian but *orange bill less deep*, mantle and wings paler grey and *tail longer and distinctly forked*. Except in full breeding plumage, *large forehead white*. Immature has more variegated inner wing than Caspian. Call *krryuk*, deeper, more rolling than Sandwich but less raucous than Caspian. Vagrant from America and W. Africa to S., W. and N. Europe (including Britain). Pl. 60.

ELEGANT TERN *Sterna elegans*. Size between Royal and Lesser Crested but outline differs in *distinctively long, fine and drooping bill* and prominent mane. Plumage resembles Lesser Crested but *under-surface of primaries much darker*; bill yellow to pale orange, often appearing *faded on tip*. Vagrant from America to W. Europe (including Ireland).

ALEUTIAN TERN *Sterna aleutica*. Slightly bulkier and shorter-tailed than Arctic. Breeding adult has *white forehead extending over eye* into black crown, dusky mantle and wings, latter with white 'window' on inner primaries and *dark bar on under-surface of secondaries*; bill and *legs black*. May be confused with Bridled, which see. Commonest call soft whistled, *wader-like multisyllable*. Vagrant from N. Pacific to W. Europe (Britain).

WHITE-CHEEKED TERN *Sterna repressa*. Smaller than Common with general character and breeding plumage suggesting both Arctic and Whiskered. Adult shows distinctive *silvery-white bases to primaries*, grey rump and tail and blackish-red bill. Immature also greyer above than Common, with stronger wing-marks. Vagrant from Red Sea to W. Europe (Britain).

BRIDLED TERN *Sterna anaethetus*. Smaller than Sooty, with *whitish collar* and *greyer back, rump and tail*. Close-to, narrower *white forehead extends behind eye* into black crown. Vagrant from Caribbean or Africa to W. and C. Europe (including Britain). Pl. 60.

LEAST TERN *Sterna antillarum*. Smaller even than Little but with relatively deeper tail-fork and distinctive *harsh squealing* call *zeek* or *zreeeek*. Plumage differs in always grey rump and tail. Vagrant from N. America to W. Europe (Britain).

BROWN NODDY *Anous stolidus*. Except for immature Sooty, only *dark brown tern* to reach Europe and easily distinguished by *wedge-shaped tail*. Adult has *greyish-white crown and nape* in strange reversal of normal tern head-pattern. Flight suggests foraging gull. Beware confusion with small dark skua. Vagrant from warm seas to W., C. and N. Europe.

ANCIENT MURRELET *Synthliboramphus antiquus*. Size 20% larger than Little Auk, with *short, pointed pale bill*. In breeding plumage, most of head black, with white eye-crescents, *white plume* from over eye to nape, *partial 'ruff' of white lines* and dusky upper-parts; in winter and when young, plume and 'ruff' absent. Vagrant from N. Pacific to W. Europe (Britain).

CRESTED AUKLET *Aethia cristatella*. Longer-winged than Little Auk, with *short crest curving forward*, wholly *dusky plumage* and, when breeding, '*red nose*' (small bill) and *narrow white tuft* falling from eye to nape. In winter and when young, bill brownish and crest shorter or lacking. Vagrant from N. Pacific to Iceland.

PARAKEET AUKLET *Cyclorrhynchus psittacula*. Size 10% larger than Little Auk, with more obvious *round, almost upturned bill*. Head, neck and upper-parts dusky, relieved by *red bill* and *white eye and eye- tuft* (last lacking in winter, when bill darkens). Vagrant from N. Pacific to N. Europe.

SPOTTED SANDGROUSE *Pterocles senegallus*. Size and shape as Pin-tailed, with pale plumage relieved at distance only by striking under-wing pattern, with *front half white and rear half fully black*. Close-to, male shows *pale grey head, neck and upper breast*, containing orange cheeks and throat, dusky-buff, pale-spotted scapulars and wing-coverts and *black ventral streak*. Female shows paler orange throat and *heavily black-spotted neck, body and wing-coverts*. Call *quitoo*. Vagrant from N. Africa or Middle East to S. Europe.

MOURNING DOVE *Zenaida macroura*. Smaller than Turtle but with *long, tapering tail* and more direct flight on *whistling wings*. Plumage suggests Collared but darker, especially on grey wings; *tail dun- brown, with black and white tips to graduated feathers*. Close- to, shows black spots on cheek, scapulars and tertials. Vagrant from N. America to W. Europe (including Britain).

AFRICAN MARSH OWL *Asio capensis*. Suggests small dark Short-eared but distinguished by *dark eyes* on paler face, *uniform brown upper-parts, wing- coverts and breast*, blotched under-body and more barred under- surface to secondaries. Vagrant from N.W. Africa to S. Europe.

COMMON NIGHTHAWK *Chordeiles minor*. Smaller, darker and greyer than European nightjars and less crepuscular. Has slightly forked tail and *bold white bands* across very long, pointed wings. Flight much freer than European nightjars, hawking insects in falcon-like manner. Vagrant from N. America to W. Europe (including Britain). Pl. 68.

NEEDLE-TAILED SWIFT *Hirundapus caudacutus*. Large swift, with relatively bulky body, short wings and *very short, square tail*. Plumage sooty, glossed green on crown, wings and tail, relieved by white forehead and throat, *pale greyish-dun patch high on back* and *conspicuous white horse-shoe mark* around broad beam under tail. Flight action includes slow, level planing on slightly bowed wings. Vagrant from E. Asia to E., N., S. and W. Europe (including Britain).

CHIMNEY SWIFT *Chaetura pelagica*. Small, very short- and square-tailed swift, no larger than Little and less robust, with narrower wings. Plumage sooty grey-brown, with *dull buff eye -brow and fore under- parts* and grey under-surfaces to flight feathers. Flight flittering, suggesting hirundine at times; also planes on much bowed wings. Vagrant from N. America to W. Europe (Britain).

PACIFIC SWIFT *Apus pacificus*. Slightly larger and more attenuated than Swift, with even more forked tail. Sooty, with *large white rump contrasting with noticeably black tail*; white throat obvious but pale margins to wing-pit and under-body feathers only show close-to. More rakish in flight than Swift. Vagrant from E. Asia to W. Europe.

SMYRNA KINGFISHER *Halcyon smyrnensis*. Largest kingfisher occurring in S. and E. Europe, with *huge red bill*, rich *chocolate-brown head, upper mantle and under-parts*, splashed white from chin to chest-centre, and *brilliant blue wings and tail*, with paler primary bases and black primary tips showing in flight. Flight action woodpecker-like. Laughs noisily. Vagrant from Near East to S. and E. Europe.

PIED KINGFISHER *Ceryle rudis*. Large, shaggily crested kingfisher, *strikingly pied* on head, upper-parts and tail but with white under-parts, except for *double black breast-band* on male and single one on female. Hovers frequently. Vagrant from Near East to S., E. and C. Europe. Pl. 66.

BELTED KINGFISHER *Ceryle alcyon*. Largest kingfisher occurring in W. Europe, with long black dagger-bill, *dusky-blue head, chest-band and upper- parts* and *white neck-collar and under-parts*. Female has second, lower, chestnut breast-band. Loud, harsh, almost mechanical rattle. Vagrant from N. America to W. and C. Europe (including Britain). Pl. 66.

NORTHERN ('YELLOW-SHAFTED') FLICKER *Colaptes auratus*. Form and behaviour recall Green Woodpecker but 20% smaller. Plumage *grey and brown above*, with red nape-band and *pure white rump*, buff on face, with black 'moustache' on male only; cream below, with *black band on breast* and heavy black spots elsewhere; *under-wing and under-tail golden-yellow*. Flight like Green. Vagrant from N. America to W. Europe.

YELLOW-BELLIED SAPSUCKER *Sphyrapicus varius*. Noticeably smaller and slighter than Great Spotted. Plumage pattern suggests pied woodpecker but, close-to, shows *black-and-white-lined face*, narrow *white panel on wing-coverts* and *close- barred back, flanks and tail*. Male shows red on crown and centre of throat; female has white throat-centre; both have distinctive pale *yellowish belly* between dusky flanks. Rings trees with lines of holes, seeking sap; fly-catches. Vagrant from N. America to W. Europe (including Britain).

EASTERN PHOEBE *Sayornis phoebe*. Size, form and tail-flick recall Spotted Flycatcher. Adult has wholly *dark bill,* domed *dusky head* contrasting with grey upper-parts, with pale margins to tertials, and white under-parts divided by *clouded chest* and fore-belly. Immature less distinctive, but has conspicuous narrow *buffish-white double wing-bar* and yellowish tinge to less clouded under-parts. Call onomatopoeic *fee-bee* or *fee-blee*. Vagrant from N. America to W. Europe (Britain).

ACADIAN FLYCATCHER *Empidonax virescens*. Size close to Pied but with relatively larger bill. Dull greyish-green above, with *conspicuous pale eye-ring* and *double whitish wing-bar*; paler below, with dusky- yellow wash on breast and flanks; distinguished from similar N. American congeners by combination of *white throat and greenish and yellow tones*. Sharp calls distinctive: emphatic *spit-chee* or *wee-see* and thin *peet*. Vagrant from N. America to Iceland.

BAR-TAILED DESERT LARK *Ammomanes cincturus*. Rather small, *bunting-like* lark, with small stubby bill and round head. Plumage *noticeably uniform*: grey- to rufous-buff above, pale rufous to cream white below, with *orange glow on upper- and under-wing and tail-base*; primaries and *tail feathers variably tipped black,* usually strong enough to form inverted T on tail. Vagrant from N. Africa (or Middle East) to S. Europe.

HOOPOE LARK *Alaemon alaudipes*. Quite large but slender lark, with *long, slightly decurved bill* and long legs; at times pipit-like but *recalls Hoopoe in flight*. Pale sandy-grey above with whitish supercilium, *dark eye-stripe and 'moustache'*; dirty white below, with speckled chest; open wings display *two brilliant white bands either side of black flight feathers*; tail largely black, with white edges. Vagrant from N. Africa (or Middle East) to S. Europe.

BIMACULATED LARK *Melanocorypha bimaculata*. 10% smaller than Calandra, with proportionately longer wings and shorter tail; distinguished by narrower, longer neck-patches, inconspicuous *buff trailing edge to less dark wings* and *buff-edged tail with terminal white rim*. Vagrant from Asia to S., W. and N. Europe (including Britain).

TEMMINCK'S HORNED LARK *Eremophila bilopha*. Smaller, shorter-tailed, desert-haunting relative of Shore Lark, with similar 'horns', plumage and behaviour. Differs distinctly in almost uniform *sandy-rufous upper-parts* and *white ground to face and throat*. Vagrant from N. Africa to S. Europe.

TREE SWALLOW *Tachycineta bicolor*. Size between Swallow and Sand Martin. Adult unmistakable with *iridescent blue-green head, shoulders and back* contrasting with *pure white under-parts*. Immature confusing, with olive-brown upper-parts and dull greyish wash over breast. At all ages, high, white lateral coverts make rump appear narrow. Vagrant from N. America to W. Europe (Britain).

CLIFF SWALLOW *Hirundo pyrrhonota*. Form martin-like, with virtually *square tail*, but plumage recalls Red-rumped Swallow. Close-to, shows cream forehead, *dark blue-black cap over chestnut head*, buff collar and upper breast, white-lined, blue-black saddle and wholly *orange rump*. Flight slower than European hirundines, includes characteristic soaring and planing. Vagrant from N. America to W. Europe (Britain).

BLYTH'S PIPIT *Anthus godlewskii*. Size and form like Richard's but with relatively shorter, finer- tipped bill on smaller head and somewhat shorter tail, legs and hindclaw; *longest tertial cloaks primary-tips*. Plumage like paler Richard's or immature Tawny but, close-to, shows clues of dark loral mark, rather short supercilium (not extending into cheek-surround), *pale, spotted hind-neck*, indistinct malar stripe and *sparse triangular spots on breast*, pale upper wing-bars contrasting with *square-cut* black centres to median coverts in adult, and *orange-buff flanks and under tail-coverts*. Flight and gait recall Tawny, not Richard's. Distinctive call harsh *psheeoo*. Vagrant from S.C. Asia to W. and N. Europe (including Britain).

BUFF-BELLIED PIPIT *Anthus rubescens*. Size and form as Rock and Water, with almost white outer tail-feathers and noticeably *buff under-parts narrowly streaked black* overall in adult and immature. Face pattern quite conspicuous, with buff supercilium and in breeding adult almost *white throat*. Vagrant from N. America to W., C. and S. Europe (including Britain).

CEDAR WAXWING *Bombycilla cedrorum*. Distinctly smaller than Waxwing but with similar plumage pattern and behaviour at all ages. Distinguished by *lack of yellow and white wing-marks*, clean *white, not rufous, vent* and under tail-coverts, and yellowish lower flanks and belly. Call like Waxwing but even thinner and more quavering. Vagrant from N. America to W. Europe (Britain).

NORTHERN MOCKINGBIRD *Mimus polyglottos*. Distinctive, somewhat thrush-like passerine, with *long tail flicked from side to side* and curiously slow flight action. Plumage recalls grey shrike since grey-black wings broadly banded white on outer half and double-barred white on inner, and tail black with wide white edges. Easily distinguished by lack of black face mask, and *fine, slightly decurved bill* and *pale yellow eye* set in whitish face. Calls include loud *tchack* and much mimicry. Vagrant from N. America to W. and C. Europe (including Britain).

BROWN THRASHER *Toxostoma rufum.* Size and basic plumage pattern recall scrawny Mistle Thrush but character more like Jay cum babbler, with *long rounded tail often raised and waved.* Red-brown above, with *yellow eye* set in greyish cheeks and *double white wing-bar*; white below, boldly lined with blackish spots. Strong bill rather long and decurved. Vagrant from N. America to W. Europe (Britain).

GREY CATBIRD *Dumetella carolinensis.* Starling-sized but is slender, long-tailed and chat-like. *Slate-grey* with *black cap* and *chestnut-red vent.* Mews like cat. Vagrant from N. America to W. and C. Europe (including Britain).

SIBERIAN ACCENTOR *Prunella montanella.* Size and form as Dunnock. Upper-parts, flight- feathers and flanks as in Dunnock but easily distinguished by Whin-chat-like pattern of *dull black crown, lores and ear- coverts* contrasting with *ochre-buff supercilium* and fore under-parts. Vagrant from N. Asia to S., C. and N. Europe.

BLACK-THROATED ACCENTOR *Prunella atrogularis.* Slightly larger than Siberian Accentor but easily distinguished by *diagnostic black throat and bib* and more lined back. Vagrant from Urals to N. Europe.

SIBERIAN RUBYTHROAT *Luscinia calliope.* Form and flight recall Bluethroat but noticeably larger, often cocking tail. Plumage brown above, creamy below. Breeding male has *iridescent crimson throat,* conspicuous *white supercilium and edge to throat* isolating dark cheeks. Winter male, female and immature lack throat colour but show same striking facial pattern. Vagrant from Asia to S., C. and W. Europe (including Britain).

SIBERIAN BLUE ROBIN *Luscinia cyane.* Form and flight like Robin but with relatively shorter tail and longer, stouter *pale legs*; on ground, can suggest small crake. Male *dark blue above* with *black face and neck side,* silky-white below. Female olive-brown above, often with bluish rump, off-white below, with *mottled breast* and clouded flanks; pale eye-ring. Vagrant from Asia to W. and N. Europe.

WHITE-THROATED ROBIN *Irania gutturalis.* Form and flight as Nightingale. Male has *black face* marked by white supercilium and throat, *slate-grey upper-parts*, black, often cocked tail and contrasting *rufous-orange under-body.* Female relatively dowdy, with olive-brown head and back, pale eye-ring, dusky-buff chest and pale rufous flanks. Loud, bell-like song. Vagrant from S.W. Asia to N., C. and W. Europe (including Britain).

DAURIAN REDSTART *Phoenicurus auroreus.* Size and form as Redstart. Both sexes show *bold, fully white wing-panel on tertials and inner secondaries* (much stronger than in S.W. Asian race of Redstart *P. p. samamiscus*). Male has *long grey crown and shawl*, contrasting with black face and throat, back and wings, rufous under-body, rump and tail. Female and immature brownish-grey, with fully buff under-parts. Vagrant from E. Asia to W. Europe (Britain).

MOUSSIER'S REDSTART *Phoenicurus moussieri.* Short reddish tail and bush-perching habit give impression of cross between Redstart and Stonechat. Male distinguished from other redstarts by combination of *white head-band, half- collar and wing-patch.* Upper-parts and head are black; rump, tail and under-parts orange. Female is grey-brown above, brownish-orange below, usually lacking white wing-patch. Vagrant from N. Africa to S. and W. Europe (including Britain).

GÜLDENSTADT'S REDSTART *Phoenicurus erythrogaster.* Third larger than Black Redstart, with relatively longer wings and shorter tail. Male recalls eastern race of Black Redstart but easily distinguished by *long white crown* (to nape), *large white wing-patch* and *maroon- chestnut tail.* Female and immature suggest large female Redstart but plumage more uniformly grey-buff, with pale greyish fringes to flight-feathers and duller, darker rump and tail. Vagrant from Caucasus to E. Europe.

WHITE-CROWNED BLACK WHEATEAR *Oenanthe leucopyga.* Size and form close to Black Wheatear but both sexes usually show blue sheen on black plumage, while black tail-marks are restricted to central feathers and outer tips so that *rump and tail can appear wholly white.* Diagnostic *white crown* or crown-patch untrustworthy, as absent on many birds. Vagrant from N. Africa or Near East to S. and W. Europe (including Britain).

VARIED THRUSH *Zoothera naevia.* Large thrush, with typical plumage pattern basically similar to American Robin but further decorated by *rufous rear supercilium, double wing-bar* and tertial edges and *black breast- band*; lacks pale eye-ring but has white band across spread flight-feathers. Rare pale morph occurs, as in first vagrant from N. America to W. Europe (Britain).

WOOD THRUSH *Hylocichla mustelina.* Smaller than Song Thrush but largest of smaller N. American thrushes, with *reddish-chestnut head-cap,* bright tawny-brown upper-parts, *obvious white eye-ring* and white under-parts covered in *round black spots.* Flight light and fast. Occasionally runs. Vagrant from N. America to W. Europe (including Britain).

HERMIT THRUSH *Catharus guttatus.* Size and appearance close to Swainson's but easily distinguished by *bright rufous rump and tail* which is frequently cocked and then slowly lowered. Call low *chuck.* Vagrant from N. America to W., N. and C. Europe (including Britain).

VEERY *Catharus fuscescens.* Size and form close to Swainson's Thrush but appearance likely to recall Nightingale due to *warm tawny-brown* upper-parts, almost chestnut tail and *smudged rather than spotted throat and breast.* Pale tips to greater wing-coverts form more obvious bar than on congeners. Call low, down-slurred *phew* or *whee-u.* Vagrant from N. America to W. Europe (Britain).

TICKELL'S THRUSH *Turdus unicolor.* Size close to Redwing. Male mainly *bluish-grey,* with whiter under-body; female and immature *olive-brown above and on breast,* with *speckled throat-sides,* mottled breast, *tawny flanks* and whitish under-body. Under-wing orange- buff. Vagrant from W. Himalayas to C. Europe.

PALE THRUSH *Turdus pallidus.* Rather large thrush easily distinguished by *broad white tail- corners* and *grey or white wing-lining.* Adult male has *dark brownish-grey head, throat and breast,* rich brown upper-parts and *brownish flanks* over white belly and vent. Female and immature browner on head and breast with streaked, white throat; immature shows white tips to greater coverts. Vagrant from E. Asia to C. Europe.

GRAY'S GRASSHOPPER WARBLER *Locustella fasciolata.* Size as Great Reed Warbler but form typical of tribe. Plumage most recalls River or dull Savi's but under-parts differ in diagnostic *rusty-yellow vent and under tail-coverts.* Vagrant from E. Asia to C. and W. Europe.

THICK-BILLED WARBLER *Acrocephalus aedon*. Size as Great Reed Warbler but structure differs noticeably in *short, thick bill on rounded head*, short, rounded wings and *relatively long, tapering tail*. Brown head, back and wings contrast with *rufous rump and tail*. Head lacks supercilium but grey lores and cream eye-ring emphasize eye. Legs blue. Vagrant from E. Asia to W. Europe (Britain).

TRISTRAM'S WARBLER *Sylvia deserticola*. Appearance and form intermediate between Dartford, Spectacled and Subalpine. Male distinguished by combination of *white eye-ring, rufous-edged wings, dark vinous breast* and flanks and *white-edged tail*. Female and immature duller; distinctions from Spectacled and Subalpine not yet studied. Song recalls Dartford but *chit-it* call distinctive. Vagrant from N.W. Africa to S. Europe.

MÉNÉTRIES'S WARBLER *Sylvia mystacea*. Size, form and appearance recall Sardinian and Subalpine Warblers. Male suggests former but distinguished by *less black rear head*, paler grey upper-parts with weakly marked tertials and variable *pink flush on centre of throat, breast and flank*s. Female and immature suggest pale Subalpine, showing less grey head and brighter eye-ring than Sardinian; best distinguished from Subalpine by pale buff, not orange, flanks, much less rufous wings with *weakly marked tertials* and *slate tail contrasting with rump*. Frequent raising and *waving of tail* distinctive. Vagrant from Near East to Portugal.

EASTERN CROWNED WARBLER *Phylloscopus coronatus*. Size as Chiffchaff but plumage pattern combines features of Greenish and Pallas's. *Fully yellow under tail- coverts* contrasting with otherwise whitish under-body are diagnostic. Head shows noticeably dark eye-stripe, long yellow- white supercilium, dusky crown sides and *dull yellowish-olive median stripe* (most obvious from behind). Wing shows whitish bars across greater coverts and (when fresh) median coverts. Vagrant from E. Asia to W. Germany.

GREEN WARBLER *Phylloscopus nitidus*. Size and form as Greenish but greener above, with usually but not always stronger yellow tone to supercilium and yellow tint on one or two wing-bars and to entire under-parts. Pale birds indistinguishable from Greenish. Vagrant from Caucasus to W. Europe (Britain).

RUBY-CROWNED KINGLET *Regulus calendula*. Slightly larger than Goldcrest but with appearance suggesting juvenile of that species. Close-to, easily distinguished by *bright, bold (not diffused) white eye-ring*. Male may show *ruby crown-patch*. Vagrant from N. America to Iceland.

BROWN FLYCATCHER *Muscicapa dauurica*. Slightly larger than Red-breasted Flycatcher, with uniform brown-grey upper-parts and tail and wholly whitish under-parts. Close-to, shows rather long, broad-based bill, with yellowish or pinkish base to lower mandible, *pale lores and eye-ring* emphasizing *large dark eye* and in fresh plumage narrow pale edges to tertials and wing-bar. Call thin *see*. Vagrant from E. Asia to C., N. and W. Europe (including Britain).

MUGIMAKI FLYCATCHER *Ficedula mugimaki*. Slightly larger than Red-breasted. Adult male black above, with contrasting *white rear supercilium, wing panel*, tertial edges and small basal patches on sides of tail; throat, *chest and flanks orange-rufous*, belly white. Female and immature recall Red-breasted but show consistently rufous-buff throat and breast, one or two dull white wing-bars and *no white patches* *in tail*. First year male often has white tail-patches as well as bold white wing-bar. Call a dry, scraping *chirr...* Vagrant from E. Asia to W. Europe (Britain).

RED-BREASTED NUTHATCH *Sitta canadensis*. Form and plumage pattern as Corsican Nuthatch but under-body including throat and cheeks *rufous-chestnut in male*, pinkish-buff in female. Vagrant from N. America to W. Europe (including Britain).

BROWN SHRIKE *Lanius cristatus*. Size and form close to Isabelline but with larger bill and head and longer, more graduated tail. Plumage similar to darker Isabelline but differs in *pale forehead* and white supercilium, *larger black face-mask* and *less rufous rump and tail*. Vagrant from E. Asia to C. and W. Europe (including Britain).

RUFOUS-BACKED (BLACK-HEADED) SHRIKE *Lanius schach*. Size and form close to Great Grey but adult's head pattern resembles Lesser Grey; easily distinguished from both by *orange-buff lower back, scapulars and rump*, dull black wings inconspicuously patched white at base of primaries and long *graduated black, buff-edged tail*. Immature dusky, with barring above and below but reduced facial mask; already shows diagnostic tail-pattern. Vagrant from W.C. Asia to C. Europe.

DAURIAN JACKDAW *Corvus dauuricus*. Size, form and actions as Jackdaw but *dark-eyed*, with more jowl. Pied adult and juvenile unmistakable, with *greyish-white shawl, breast and under-body*; at distance, dark immature indistinguishable from Jackdaw but, close-to, shows only *restricted grey patch behind eye* hardly reaching nape. Vagrant from E. Asia to N. and E. Europe.

DAURIAN (PURPLE-BACKED) STARLING *Sturnus sturninus*. Smaller and noticeably shorter-billed than Starling, with *pale ashy head and breast* merging into *white under-parts*. Dark *iridescent purple and green back, wings and tail* strikingly relieved by *broad white panel along base of flight-feathers*, broad mottled white wing-bar on median coverts and often buff-white rump. Immature brown where adult iridescent, with wholly dark primaries. Vagrant from E. Asia to N. and W. Europe (including Britain).

DEAD SEA SPARROW *Passer moabiticus*. 20% smaller than House Sparrow. Adult male has distinctive *long whitish-yellow-buff supercilium*, dark grey cheeks, whitish 'moustache' leading into *yellow line at side of neck* and small black bib. Female and immature resemble House but may show yellow in dull supercilium. Call high-pitched *trrirp*. Vagrant from Near East to S. Europe.

YELLOW-THROATED VIREO *Vireo flavifrons*. Size and form close to Red-eyed Vireo but much more colourful. *Spectacle and breast bright yellow*, head and upper-parts olive-green, wings blackish with *bold double white wing-bar*, and tertial edges, belly and under tail-coverts white. Confusion possible with slender-billed but similarly patterned Pine Warbler *Dendroica pinus*, also potential vagrant but with white tail spots. Vagrant from N. America to W. Europe (including Britain).

PHILADELPHIA VIREO *Vireo philadelphicus*. Size noticeably smaller than Red-eyed but has characteristic stubby bill of tribe. Head pattern and upper-parts somewhat recall Red-eyed but crown olive and supercilium less sharp and long; distinguished by *yellowish wash from chin to belly and on flanks*. Beware confusion with immature *Phylloscopus* warblers. Vagrant from N. America to W. Europe (Britain).

RED-FRONTED SERIN *Serinus pusillus*. Serin-size, rather dark, stocky finch, with *nearly black head and breast* highlit by *'luminous' orange-red forehead* and *dull orange rump* diagnostic in adult. Juvenile more Serin-like but *face and throat suffused orange- buff*, with dark mottles appearing on head and breast in first winter. Call rippling *drillt-drillt*. Vagrant from Near East to S. Europe.

PALLAS'S ROSEFINCH *Carpodacus roseus*. Slightly longer-tailed than Scarlet Rosefinch, with pale horn bill, white-streaked pink head, pink body and rump, more streaked back and brighter, almost white double wing-bar in male and darker browner, faintly pink-faced and -rumped appearance in female. Immature more heavily streaked below than Scarlet. Call short, subdued whistle. Vagrant from E. Asia to C. and W. Europe (including Britain).

LONG-TAILED ROSEFINCH *Uragus sibiricus*. Redpoll-sized, stubby-billed and extraordinarily long-tailed finch; shape recalls Long-tailed Tit. Plumage *washed-out*, with pale grey or buff ground suffused pink on face and breast (male) and rump (both sexes), *black-and-white-barred wings* and *white-edged, black tail*. Call loud *pee-you-een*. Vagrant from E. Asia to N. Europe.

EVENING GROSBEAK *Coccothraustes vespertina*. Bulkier than Rose-breasted Grosbeak, with almost *Hawfinch-like whitish bill* and shorter tail. Plumage curiously patterned, with *black wings, boldly patched white on inner half*, also at base of primaries in female, and black tail, tipped white in female. *Head, chest and mantle dusky* in male, with *sulphur-yellow forehead and streak over eye*, paler dusky yellow in female; under body sulphur-yellow in male, dull yellow and whitish in female. Flight undulating. Call House Sparrow-like *chirp*. Vagrant from N. America to W. Europe (Britain).

BLACK-AND-WHITE WARBLER *Mniotilta varia*. Small, somewhat Nuthatch-like in *tree-creeping* behaviour, with astonishing *black-and-white striped plumage*. Male has black cheeks and throat; female and immature lack these but show buff fringes on flanks. Beware confusion with male Blackpoll Warbler which lacks white central crown-stripe. Calls weak *tsip* and hard *tik*. Vagrant from N. America to W. Europe (including Britain). Pl. 93.

GOLDEN-WINGED WARBLER *Vermivora chrysoptera*. Small, rather tit-like, with greenish upper-parts and whitish under-parts strikingly decorated with *yellow fore-crown and wing-coverts*, white supercilium and 'moustache' encircling *black cheek-patch* and *black* (male) *or dusky* (female, immature) *bib*. Call *chip*. Vagrant from N. America to W. Europe (Britain).

TENNESSEE WARBLER *Vermivora peregrina*. Slightly smaller and stouter than Willow Warbler. In spring, male's head is grey with white supercilium and yellow eye-ring. Full olive-green upper-parts *brightest on rump*; under tail-coverts *pure white*; broad but indistinct wing- bar. Female and winter male have greenish head and yellowish face, breast and flanks; may recall Arctic Warbler except for dark legs, but green rump and white under tail-coverts remain conspicuous. Call penetrating *zit-zit*, recalling Firecrest. Vagrant from N. America to W. Europe (including Britain).

YELLOW WARBLER *Dendroica petechia*. Small, delicate, with at distance virtually uniform *primrose-yellow plumage*. Distinguished from other N. American warblers with yellow marks, and juvenile Willow Warbler, by *rusty streaks on* *under-parts*, pale yellow double wing-bar and *pale yellow spots on tail-feathers*. Call rather soft *tsep*. Vagrant from N. America to W. Europe (Britain).

CHESTNUT-SIDED WARBLER *Dendroica pensylvanica*. Small, delicate, with long, *often cocked tail* and *very white under-parts*. Adult conspicuously *lined black below eye and chestnut along flanks*; crown and back yellowish-green, emphasized by black eye-stripe and cheek- surround which develops into streaks on back; wings and tail blackish-brown, with double white wing-bar and whitish basal tail-fringes. Immature *ghostly in appearance*, with pale unmarked face, unstreaked back and *unlined under-parts*; has narrow white eye-ring. Call a rather loud *tsick*. Vagrant from N. America to W. Europe (Britain).

BLACK-THROATED BLUE WARBLER *Dendroica caerulescens*. Small but quite long-tailed, with diagnostic *white mark at base of primaries*. Male *blue on crown, back, rump* and wing- coverts, black elsewhere except for contrasting *white underbody*. Female and immature very different, with dark olive upper-parts relieved by *narrow white supercilium* and uniform greenish-yellow under-parts. Call short *chip* or rather soft *tsep*. . Vagrant from N. America to Iceland.

BLACK-THROATED GREEN WARBLER *Dendroica virens*. Smaller than Blackpoll Warbler, with *pale golden-yellow face* framed by black (male) or dusky (female) bib and olive crown and back; *pale cheeks* are diagnostic among N. American vagrants of tribe. Wings and tail blackish, with double white wing-bar; under-parts white below blackish-streaked flanks. Immature has greenish cheeks. Call *tsick*. Vagrant from N. America to C. Europe.

BLACKBURNIAN WARBLER *Dendroica fusca*. Smaller than Blackpoll Warbler, with bright *orange* (male) or *yellowish to orange head* (female) marked with black crown-surround and *black cheeks extending downwards* to break into black streaks on sides of white under- body. Back black or blackish, with *white 'braces'*; wings and tail blackish, with almost white coverts (in male) or double wing-bar (female). Immature very different, closely resembling Black-throated Green but lacks full yellow cheek-surround and has darker yellowish ground to throat, breast and flanks. Call rich *chip*. Vagrant from N. America to W. Europe (Iceland).

CAPE MAY WARBLER *Dendroica tigrina*. Size just under Blackpoll. Shares yellow rump with Magnolia and Yellow-rumped but otherwise *dark or greyish- olive above*, with less striking double white wing-bar and *buff to yellow ear-patch* in winter and immature plumage. Breeding male easily distinguished by *yellow face, patched chestnut* below and behind eye, *white wing-covert panel* and black-streaked yellow body; female duller, lacks chestnut face-patch. Immature differs from adult in *almost unstreaked back* and from Magnolia and Yellow-rumped in duller, *more widely and sharply streaked throat* and under-parts. Calls high nasal *swee-swee-swee* and thin, rather hard *tsip*. Vagrant from N. America to W. Europe (Britain).

MAGNOLIA WARBLER *Dendroica magnolia*. Rather small but long and full-tailed warbler, with *bold white band half-way down tail* (on all but central feathers) and yellow rump and under-parts in all plumages. Breeding male has *blue-grey on crown, white rear supercilium*, black back and wings with almost wholly white wing-coverts, and black-streaked breast and flanks. Female and immature greyish-olive on head and back, with *bright white spectacle*, and almost unstreaked below but showing *narrow grey breast- band*. Call almost disyllabic *dzip or tlep*. Vagrant from N. America to W. Europe (Britain).

AMERICAN REDSTART *Setophaga ruticilla.* Small, *tail-fanning*, wing-drooping warbler, with bold *salmon-orange* (male) *or yellow basal patches on tail* (female). Breeding male black with *orange shoulder-patch, orange band across base of flight-feathers* and white belly. Female and immature mainly olive-brown above and fully white below, with white eye-ring and *yellow patches* by or on blackish flight-feathers and tail; young male *dusky on chest sides*, with more orange-toned patches. Catches flies in butterfly-like flight. Calls high *tseet* and clicking *tsip*. Vagrant from N. America to W. Europe (including Britain). Pl. 93.

OVENBIRD *Seiurus aurocapillus.* Pipit-sized, ground-haunting warbler, with rather thrush-like form and plumage of *plain olive upper-parts* and *black- splashed malar stripe, breast and flanks* standing out on white under-parts. Head decorated with *central rufous-orange stripe with black borders*, pale supercilium and *prominent white eye-ring*. Immature has duller central crown-stripe. Legs pinkish. Raises tail and droops wings. Call loud *tzick* or softer *tseet*. Vagrant from N. America to W. Europe (Britain).

NORTHERN WATERTHRUSH *Seiurus noveboracensis.* Size and form close to Ovenbird but appearance even more pipit-like; behaviour recalls Actitis sandpiper, with horizontal stance, water-edge feeding and *constant teetering of body*. Plumage basically dusky-olive above and yellowish- white below, with *long yellowish supercilium* and *spotted throat, breast and lower body*. Call explosive *peent*, also *chif* and *tsink*. Vagrant from N. America to W. Europe (including Britain). Pl. 93.

COMMON YELLOWTHROAT *Geothlypis trichas.* Small, ground cover-haunting, *tail-cocking* warbler, with greenish-brown upper-parts, wings and tail and yellow-buff under-parts except for pale whitish belly. Male has *broad black mask* from forehead through eye to lower ear coverts, *edged with pale grey* and obscured in winter and immature; female lacks mask, has *pale loral streak* and greenish upper cheek. Legs pinkish-orange. Calls distinctive husky *tchep* and soft, clicking *tep*. Vagrant from N. America to W. Europe (Britain).

HOODED WARBLER *Wilsonia citrina.* Larger than Yellow Warbler and Wilson's but also very yellow below, females and immatures suggesting small Melodious. Spring male has yellow face surrounded by conspicuous *black hood*. Look for *white spots on tail*. Call metallic *chink*. Vagrant from N. America to W. Europe (including Britain).

WILSON'S WARBLER *Wilsonia pusilla.* Small, delicate, with *yellowish-green upper- parts*, wings and tail and *fully yellow under-parts*; lacks tail spots of larger Hooded. Male has *glossy black cap*; female and immature have greenish crown and cheeks with yellow supercilium and eye-ring. Very active. Calls short *tsip* and harsher *chut*. Vagrant from N. America to W. Europe (Britain).

CANADA WARBLER *Wilsonia canadensis.* Largest and darkest of three congeners to cross Atlantic, with distinctly *grey* (male) *or greenish- grey* (female and immature) *upper-parts*, yellow-white spectacle and *black* (male) *or dusky* (female and immature) *spotted necklace* on wholly yellow under-parts. Call *tchip* or *check*, recalling House Sparrow. Vagrant from N. America to Iceland.

SUMMER TANAGER *Piranga rubra.* Slightly longer than Scarlet, with larger bill. Plumage pattern differs distinctly in *dull, hardly contrasting wings and tail*. Breeding male rose-red; winter male, female and immature olive and mustard yellow; all show pale yellow under-wing, Call low *chicky-tuck-tuck* or *chiduduk*. Vagrant from N. America to W. Europe (Britain). Pl. 94.

SCARLET TANAGER *Piranga olivacea*. Size as Crossbill, with stout pointed *whitish bill* and *black* (male) *or blackish wings and tail* contrasting with rest of plumage. Breeding male *scarlet*, winter male, female and immature greenish-yellow (suggesting Greenfinch); all show white under-wing. Call low toneless *keepback* or *chip*, recalling Crossbill and followed by grating *durr*. Vagrant from N. America to W. Europe (including Britain).

RUFOUS-SIDED TOWHEE *Pipilo erythrophthalmus*. Large, sparrow-like, with *long, full tail often raised*. Male black above and on upper breast, with *white belly* and conspicuous *rusty flanks*. Large white edges on outer tail-feathers and wing-feathers. Female and immature brown where male is black. Calls a loud *chewink* or *towhee*, also soft *heu* and sharp *tsit*. Vagrant from N. America to W. Europe (Britain).

LARK SPARROW *Chondestes grammacus*. Rather small N. American sparrow with *chestnut crown-stripes and cheeks* contrasting with *whitish crown-centre, supercilium, eye-crescents*, rear cheek-streak (suggesting Quail), *black 'moustache' and breast-spot*. In flight, shows fan-shaped *black tail with white edges and corners*. Vagrant from N. America to W. Europe (including Britain).

SAVANNAH SPARROW *Ammodramus sandwichensis*. Rather small, relatively short- and notch- tailed N. American sparrow. Plumage essentially brownish-white, with soft streaks above and sharper, heavier ones below; head relieved by *whitish central crown-stripe* and *yellowish lores or supercilium*. Calls thin *tsi* and harder *tsep*. Both continental race *A. s. sandwichensis* and larger paler Sable Island race *A. s. princeps* (so-called Ipswich Sparrow) have crossed Atlantic to W. Europe (Britain).

FOX SPARROW *Zonotrichia iliaca*. Much larger than House Sparrow, with *conspicuous chestnut tail* and bunting-like shape. Upper-parts boldly streaked rufous-brown; under-parts creamy; breast and flanks heavily streaked with rufous-brown. Calls *chik* and a quiet *tsee-eet*. Vagrant from N. America to W., C. and S. Europe (including Britain). Pl. 94.

SONG SPARROW *Zonotrichia melodia*. Size, shape and behaviour recall both bunting and Dunnock; long slightly rounded *tail opened and 'pumped' in flight*. Darker above and more heavily streaked than Savannah, with greyish-buff central crown-stripe, supercilium and neck, *rather rufous wings* and dark brown tail. Breast has *black spot in centre* but immature may lack this. Calls low nasal *tchap* or *tcheck* and high *tsii*. Vagrant from N. America to W. Europe (including Britain). Pl. 94.

WHITE-CROWNED SPARROW *Zonotrichia leucophrys*. Slightly larger and longer-necked than White-throated Sparrow; distinguished by *pinkish-yellow bill*, less clear-cut white throat, *always wholly white or whitish supercilium* and paler back stripes. Calls rather sharp *pzit* and high *tssiep*. Vagrant from N. America to W. and C. Europe (including Britain).

DARK-EYED (SLATE-COLOURED) JUNCO *Junco hyemalis*. Smaller than Tree Sparrow, with bunting-like form. Plumage uniform *dark slate-grey*, except for *pinkish-white bill* and conspicuous *white belly, vent and outer tail-feathers* (last obvious when tail flicked and in flight). Immature similarly patterned but dark *brown*-grey.

Calls clicking twitter and slightly liquid *chek*. Vagrant from N. America to W., C. and S. Europe (including Britain). Pl. 94.

BLACK-FACED BUNTING *Emberiza spodocephala*. Size as Yellow-breasted Bunting, with similar upper-parts but paler under-parts. Male has *olive-grey hood and breast, almost black around bill*; female paler brownish- grey on head, streaked on breast, with indistinct pale supercilium and pale yellow throat. Call soft *tik-tik*. Vagrant from Siberia to C. and N. Europe. Pl. 92.

MEADOW BUNTING *Emberiza cioides*. Size as Yellowhammer, with apparently large head, deep chest and long tail. *Dark-striped head and warm breast isolate large white throat*. Male noticeably *chestnut on crown, rear ear- coverts*, back, rump and *deep chest-band* and flanks; head further marked by *sharp white supercilium*, white moustachial stripe, *narrow black 'whisker'*. Wings buffish- brown, with double buff wing-bar; tail buff-brown, with black webs emphasizing white outer tail-feathers. Female and immature duller, with streaked crown as well as back, less clearly defined chest-band and smudged 'whisker'; beware confusion with Pine Bunting. Call soft *tsik-tsik*. Vagrant from E. Asia to S. and N. Europe.

YELLOW-BROWED BUNTING *Emberiza chrysophrys*. Resembles Little Bunting but larger-billed; breeding male differs in blacker head, with *narrow white crown-stripe, yellow supercilium* and white spot on rear cheek; female and juvenile duller but show yellow in supercilium. Calls as Little Bunting; also soft, shrill whistle. Vagrant from E. Asia to C. and W. Europe (including Britain).

CHESTNUT BUNTING *Emberiza rutila*. Rather short, large-headed bunting. Male *uniformly chestnut on head, chest, back and flank-stripes*, bright yellow on under-body; female and juvenile recall Yellow-breasted Bunting but are rustier above, with less distinct wing-bars. Beware confusion with larger Red-headed Bunting. Call soft *tik- tik*. Vagrant from E. Asia to C., S. and W. Europe.

PALLAS'S REED BUNTING *Emberiza pallasi*. Form like other small buntings but tail proportionately longer, often flicked and fanned, like Reed. Plumages recall Reed but male shows *conspicuously paler back stripes* and *whitish rump*. Female and juvenile more nondescript, with dull head pattern (lacking dark marks of Reed), often heavy, *inverted L marks on lower throat* and *very pale fringes on wing*. Calls include disyllabic *psee-oop* and chirps. Vagrant from E. Asia to W. Europe (including Britain).

RED-HEADED BUNTING *Emberiza bruniceps*. Slightly shorter than Black-headed, but with similar dark tail. Breeding male *rufous-chestnut on most of head and breast*, merging into strongly *greenish, streaked upper-parts* and contrasting with *lemon yellow under-parts and rump*. Female and immature difficult to distinguish from Black-headed but some show diffuse chestnut throat-patch and greenish tinge to back and rump. Calls include *tweet*, *chip* and tinny *ziff*. Beware escaped cage-bird. Vagrant from Asia across Europe. Pl. 92.

DICKCISSEL *Spiza americana*. Size as House Sparrow but with more pointed bill and short, almost pointed tail. Male distinctive, with streaked greyish head marked by *bold yellowish supercilium, white eye-ring*, dusky cheeks and white throat, divided by black line leading into *large black bib*; upper-parts streaked brown, rufous on fore-wing; under-body *yellow at edge of bib*, then greyish. Female and immature much duller, lacking bib and yellow surround; streaked on breast-sides and flanks. Call low *br-r-r-r-rt*, recalling Longtailed Tit. Vagrant from N. America to N. Europe.

BLUE GROSBEAK *Guiraca caerulea*. Smaller, shorter-tailed than Rose-breasted, with *double rufous-buff wing-bar* in all plumages. Male almost *violet blue*, with heavy steely bill and pale-edged wing-feathers. Female and immature buffy-brown, softly streaked above but hardly so below. Occasionally flicks tail. Call sharp *chink*. Vagrant from N. America to N. Europe.

INDIGO BUNTING *Passerina cyanea*. Size and shape as Linnet; much smaller than Blue Grosbeak. Breeding male *deep blue all over*, with almost black wings and tail. Winter male, female and immature *plain brown* above, with pale fringes to wing-coverts forming indistinct double bar in immature; buff-white below with soft streaks on breast and flanks; may show tinge of blue at shoulder and on tail. Calls sharp thin *spit* and loud *pwit*, sometimes repeated. Vagrant from N. America to W. and N. Europe. Pl. 94.

LAZULI BUNTING *Passerina amoena*. Size and shape as Indigo. Breeding male *pale blue on hood, back, rump* and wing-coverts; wings and tail blackish with distinct *double white wing-bar; breast and flanks orange*, under-body white. Winter male, female and immature like Indigo but greyer above and unstreaked below; all show obvious wing- bars. Vagrant from N. America to W. Europe.

BOBOLINK *Dolichonyx oryzivorus*. Stout, like Corn Bunting, with *pointed tail-feathers*. Plumage in autumn basically yellowish-buff, with large *conical orange bill*, bluish lores, *heavily striped head and back* and streaked breast and flanks. Breeding male unmistakable, with *black head* and under-parts, *yellow nape and shawl* and largely *white back*. Call metallic *pink*. Vagrant from N. America to N. and W. Europe (including Britain). Pl. 94.

BROWN-HEADED COWBIRD *Molothrus ater*. Smaller than Starling, with much shorter conical bill; *carries tail up* when walking. Male blackish-brown with *brown hood*; female mouse-grey-brown, with slightly paler throat; immature like female but faintly streaked on breast. Call *chuck*; in flight high, whistled *weeee-titi*. Vagrant from N. America to N. Europe.

COMMON GRACKLE *Quiscalus quiscula*. Conspicuous, like Starling cum Magpie, with long *broadening keel-shaped tail* and sprightly gait. Plumage basically black variably *glossed green, blue and violet*; eyes yellow. Female smaller, less iridescent. Call cackling *chuck* or *chack*. Vagrant from N. America to C. Europe.

YELLOW-HEADED BLACKBIRD *Xanthocephalus xanthocephalus*. Blackbird-size with heavy pointed bill. Male unmistakable: black with *orange-yellow head and breast* showing conspicuous *white wing-patch* in flight. Female smaller and browner, with yellow confined to throat, upper breast and around cheek; lower breast streaked with white; wings wholly dusky brown. Calls low *kruk* or *kack*. Vagrant from N. America to N. and C. Europe.

About the Maps

The red areas represent the birds **breeding range**. The area below the heavy dotted line, or enclosed by it, is the bird's **winter range**. This does not mean that the bird occurs everywhere within these limits, but locally where its proper habitat is available. Additional information is given in the form of a short caption beside each map, along with a cross reference to the major plate on which the species is illustrated and the page reference for its text entry. For example, if the bird's winter range is identical with its breeding range, or if the bird entirely leaves the area, it is so stated, and the dotted line is not used. Thus: 'Resident' (if all the year); 'Partial migrant' (if many but not all individuals leave the northern part of the range in winter); 'Summer visitor' (if the species winters entirely outside Europe). Areas which may be visited on passage between breeding and winter quarters are not mapped. In the few cases where maps are inappropriate, brief information on the range is given in the main text. Further information is welcomed by the authors, who may be contacted c/o HarperCollins*Publishers*.

1 Red-throated Diver
Partial migrant. Vagrant south to Mediterranean islands. Pl. 1; p.30

2 Black-throated Diver
Mainly migrant. Vagrant Faeroes. Pl. 1; p.30

3 Great Northern Diver
Mainly migrant. Has bred Scotland. Vagrant C, E and S Europe. Pl. 1; p.31

4 Little Grebe
Partial migrant. Vagrant Faeroes. Pl. 2; p.33

5 Great Crested Grebe
Partial migrant. Has bred Sicily. Vagrant Iceland. Pl. 2; p.33

6 Red-necked Grebe
Partial migrant. Has bred Holland, France. Vagrant Ireland, Iceland, Spain. Pl. 2; p.33

7 Slavonian Grebe
Partial migrant. Has bred Poland. Vagrant C and SW Europe. Pl. 2; p.34

8 Black-necked Grebe
Partial migrant. Has bred Ireland, Finland, Italy, etc. Breeding areas often changed. Pl. 2; p.34

9 Fulmar
Partial migrant. Vagrant Finland, C and S Europe. Pl. 3; p.35

10 Cory's Shearwater
Nests south of red line. Scarce autumn visitor to Atlantic coasts. Vagrant C Europe. Pl. 3; p.36

11 Manx Shearwater
Partial migrant. Red line encloses colonies. Ranges widely at sea. Vagrant inland. Pl. 3; p.37

12 Mediterranean Shearwater
Partial migrant. Nests south of red line. Has bred Bulgaria. In autumn North Sea north to Scotland, Scandinavia; also Black Sea. Pl. 3; p.37

13 Storm Petrel
Partial migrant. Lines enclose nesting areas. May breed in N Norway. Vagrant inland. Pl. 3; p.39

14 Leach's Petrel
Red line encloses main colonies. Has bred Ireland. Vagrant inland including S Europe. Pl. 3; p.39

15 Northern Gannet
Partial migrant. Red line encloses main colonies. Vagrant Baltic, C Europe, E Mediterranean. Pl. 5; p.40

16 Cormorant
Partial migrant. Has bred Austria, Italy, Estonia. Passage C Europe. Pl. 4; p.40

17 Shag
Winter dispersal area includes N Sea. Vagrant Baltic, inland N and C Europe. Pl. 4; p.41

18 Pygmy Cormorant
Partial migrant. Has bred Italy, Hungary. Vagrant N, C and W Europe. Pl. 4; p.41

19 Dalmatian Pelican
Partial migrant. Vagrant C Europe, Italy. Pl. 5; p.42

20 Bittern
Partial migrant. Has bred Greece. Vagrant Iceland. Pl. 6; p.42

21 Little Bittern
Summer visitor, occasional winter. Vagrant British Isles (has bred), Iceland, N Europe. Pl. 6; p.43

22 Night Heron
Summer visitor. Vagrant British Isles, N Europe. Pl. 6; p.43

23 Squacco Heron
Summer visitor. Has bred Czechoslovakia. Vagrant British Isles, C and N Europe. Pl. 7; p.44

24 Cattle Egret
Partial migrant or (esp. imms.) dispersive. Has bred Italy. Vagrant Britain, C, N and E Europe. Pl. 7; p.44

25 Little Egret
Partial migrant. Has bred Holland, Czechoslovakia; wintered in British Isles. Vagrant C and N Europe. Pl. 7; p.44

26 Great White Egret
Partial migrant. Has bred Switzerland. Vagrant Britain, W and N Europe. Pl. 7; p.45

27 Grey Heron
Partial migrant. Vagrant Iceland. Pl. 6; p.45

28 Purple Heron
Summer visitor. Vagrant British Isles, N Europe. Pl. 6; p.46

29 Black Stork
Mainly summer visitor. Has bred France, Sweden. Vagrant Britain, N Europe. Pl. 7; p.46

30 White Stork
Mainly summer visitor. Some winter in N Spain. Vagrant British Isles, N Europe. Pl. 7; p.46

31 Glossy Ibis
Summer visitor. Has bred Italy, France, Hungary. Vagrant British Isles, N and E Europe. Pl. 7; p.47

32 Spoonbill
Mainly summer visitor. Has bred Denmark, Portugal, Italy, attempted Latvia. Vagrant N and C Europe. Pl. 7; p.47

33 Mute Swan
Partial migrant. Vagrant S Europe. Pl. 8; p.49

34 Bewick's Swan
Winter visitor from N Russia. Vagrant S Europe. Pl. 8; p.49

35 Whooper Swan
Mainly migrant. Has bred Scotland. Vagrant SW Europe. Pl. 8; p.49

36 Bean Goose
Migrant. Vagrant Ireland, Iceland, Greece. Pl. 10; p.50

37 Pink-footed Goose
Migrant. Vagrant E, C and S Europe. Pl. 10; p.50

38 White-fronted Goose
Winter visitor from N Russia, Greenland. Vagrant SW Europe. Pl. 10; p.51

39 Lesser White-fronted Goose
Migrant. Vagrant S, C and W Europe (almost annual in Britain). Pl. 10; p.51

40 Greylag Goose
Partial migrant. Pl. 10; p.51

41 Canada Goose
Partial migrant. Vagrant Iceland and south to Spain. Pl. 8; p.53

42 Barnacle Goose
Winter visitor from high Arctic. Feral breeder in S Sweden, Estonia, Iceland. Passage Baltic, Iceland. Vagrant S and E Europe. Pl. 8; p.53

43 Brent Goose
Winter visitor from high Arctic. Vagrant to most Europe south to Mediterranean. Pl. 8; p.53

44 Ruddy Shelduck
Partial migrant. Vagrant to almost all Europe, including British Isles and Iceland. Pl. 16; p.55

45 Shelduck
Partial migrant. Vagrant Iceland, C Europe. Pl. 16; p.55

46 Wigeon
Partial migrant. Occasionally breeds in Ireland, C, E and S Europe. Pl. 12; p.56

47 Gadwall
Partial migrant. Occasionally breeds in Italy, Norway. Pl. 12; p.57

48 Teal
Partial migrant. Occasionally breeds elsewhere in S Europe. Pl. 12; p.58

49 Mallard
Partial migrant. Breeds irregularly in Sicily. Pl. 12; p.58

50 Pintail
Mainly migrant. Breeds sporadically south to Mediterranean. Pl. 12; p.59

51 Garganey
Summer visitor. Has bred Norway, Ireland. Pl. 12; p.59

52 Shoveler
Partial migrant. Breeds irregularly Portugal. Pl. 12; p.60

53 Red-crested Pochard
Partial migrant. Has bred Italy, Greece, Vagrant British Isles, N Europe. Pl. 13; p.61

54 Pochard
Partial migrant. Vagrant Faeroes. Pl. 13; p.61

55 Ferruginous Duck
Partial migrant. Has bred Italy, Latvia. Pl. 13; p.62

56 Tufted Duck
Partial migrant. Has bred Spain. Pl. 13; p.62

57 Scaup
Mainly migrant. Has bred
Scotland, Denmark. Vagrant
most S Europe. Pl. 13; p.63

58 Eider
Partial migrant. Has bred
Switzerland. Vagrant C, S
and E Europe. Pl. 15; p.63

59 Long-tailed Duck
Mainly migrant. Vagrant C,
S and E Europe. Pl. 16;
p.65

60 Common Scoter
Mainly migrant. Immatures
summer in N Sea. Vagrant
C and SE Europe. Pl. 14;
p.65

61 Velvet Scoter
Migrant. Many moult in
Denmark in July. Vagrant
Iceland, SE Europe.
Pl. 14; p.66

62 Goldeneye
Mainly migrant. Has bred
Yugoslavia, Switzerland.
Pl. 13; p.67

63 Smew
Migrant. Perhaps annual in
Ireland. Vagrant SW
Europe. Pl. 17; p.67

**64 Red-breasted
Merganser**
Partial migrant. Pl. 17;
p.67

65 Goosander
Partial migrant. Has bred Ireland, Yugoslavia. Vagrant SW Europe. Pl. 17; p.68

66 White-headed Duck
Partial migrant. Erratic breeding persists elsewhere in S Europe. Vagrant C Europe. Pl. 17; p.69

67 Honey Buzzard
Summer visitor. Vagrant Ireland, Iceland. Pl. 26; p.70

68 Black Kite
Summer visitor. Has bred Scandinavia. Vagrant British Isles. Pl. 24; p.71

69 Red Kite
Partial migrant. May breed in Latvia. Vagrant Ireland, Finland. Pl. 24; p.70

70 White-tailed Eagle
Mainly resident. Being reintroduced Scotland. Has bred in Denmark *et al*. Vagrant elsewhere W Europe. Pl. 28; p.72

71 Lammergeier
Resident, greatly reduced. Reintroduction in Austria. Pl. 23; p.72

72 Egyptian Vulture
Mainly migrant but some midwinter in S Europe. Vagrant C, N Europe and Britain. Pl. 23; p.72

73 Griffon Vulture
Partial migrant. Vagrant C, N and E Europe and British Isles. Pl. 23; p.73

74 Black Vulture
Resident. Extinct in Romania *et al*. Vagrant C Europe. Pl. 23; p.73

75 Short-toed Eagle
Summer visitor. Vagrant N Europe. Pl. 27; p.73

76 Marsh Harrier.
Partial migrant. Has bred Norway. Vagrant Ireland, Faeroes. Pl. 24; p.74

77 Hen Harrier
Partial migrant. Has bred Denmark, Italy. Vagrant Iceland. Pl. 24; p.74

78 Pallid Harrier
Summer visitor. Has bred Sweden, Germany. Vagrant S, C and W Europe including Britain. Pl. 24; p.74

79 Montagu's Harrier
Summer visitor. Erratic breeder in England. Has bred Greece, Ireland. Pl. 24; p.75

80 Goshawk
Mainly resident. Vagrant Ireland. Pl. 26; p.75

81 Sparrowhawk
Partial migrant. Vagrant Iceland. Pl. 26; p.76

82 Levant Sparrowhawk
Summer visitor. Has bred Hungary. Vagrant little further north and west. Pl. 26; p.76

83 Buzzard
Partial migrant. Pl. 26; p.76

84 Rough-legged Buzzard
Migrant. Vagrant Iceland, Ireland, SW Europe. Pl. 26; p.77

85 Lesser Spotted Eagle
Migrant. Vagrant N, W and S Europe. Pl. 28; p.78

86 Spotted Eagle
Migrant. Has bred Sweden. Few may winter in France, Holland. Vagrant west to British Isles, Portugal. Pl. 28; p.78

87 Imperial Eagle
Partial migrant. Vagrant N, C and W Europe. Pl. 28; p.79

88 Golden Eagle
Mainly resident, extending in E Europe in winter. Has bred in Ireland. Vagrant Holland. Pl. 28; p.79

89 Booted Eagle
Summer visitor. Has wintered in S Europe. Vagrant C and N Euroope. Pl. 27; p.80

90 Bonelli's Eagle
Mainly resident. Vagrant C, E and N Europe. Pl. 27; p.80

91 Osprey
Mainly summer visitor. Has bred in many countries S and C Europe. Vagrant Ireland, Iceland. Pl. 29; p.81

92 Lesser Kestrel
Mainly summer visitor. Vagrant C, N and W Europe including British Isles. Pl. 30; p.81

93 Kestrel
Partial migrant. Vagrant Iceland. Pl. 30; p.82

94 Red-footed Falcon
Summer visitor. Has bred in N Europe and west to France. Annual in Britain. Vagrant Spain, Ireland. Pl. 30; p.82

95 Merlin
Partial migrant. Vagrant Malta. Pl. 30; p.82

96 Hobby
Summer visitor. Vagrant Ireland, Iceland. Pl. 30; p.83

97 Lanner
Mainly resident. Vagrant E, C and SW Europe. Pl. 30; p.84

98 Saker
Partial migrant. Vagrant C and N Europe. Pl. 30; p.84

99 Gyrfalcon
Mainly resident. Winter vagrant to W (including British isles), C and S Europe. Pl. 31; p.84

100 Peregrine
Partial migrant. Has bred Denmark, Belgium. Vagrant Iceland. Pl. 30; p.85

101 Hazel Grouse
Resident. Vagrant Holland. Pl. 32; p.85

102 Red Grouse (A)
Resident in Britain, Ireland.
Willow Grouse (B) Resident in continental Europe. Pl. 33; p.86

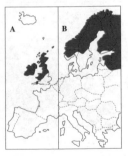

103 Ptarmigan
Resident. Pl. 33; p.86

104 Black Grouse
Resident. Pl. 32; p.87

105 Capercaillie
Resident. Vagrant Belgium, Denmark. Pl. 32; p.87

106 Rock Partridge
Resident. Pl. 33; p.88

107 Red-legged Partridge
Resident. Pl. 33; p.88

108 Grey Partridge
Resident. Pl. 33; p.89

109 Quail
Partial migrant. Has bred Faeroes. Irregular or fluctuating most British Isles, also N Europe. Occasional in winter north to British Isles, Germany. Pl. 33; p.90

110 Pheasant
Resident. Pl. 32; p.90

111 Water Rail
Partial migrant. Pl. 34; p.91

112 Spotted Crake
Mainly summer visitor. Nesting erratic in Scotland, England. Few winter North Sea area. Vagrant Ireland, Iceland. Pl. 34; p.92

113 Little Crake
Mainly summer visitor. Has bred Sicily. Annual in Sweden, Finland. Vagrant W Europe incl. Britain where occasional winter. Pl. 34; p.92

114 Baillon's Crake
Mainly summer visitor, often sporadic. Vagrant north to British Isles, Faeroes, Finland. Pl. 34; p.93

115 Corncrake
Summer visitor. Breeding may persist in N England. Vagrant Iceland. Pl. 34; p.93

116 Moorhen
Partial migrant. Vagrant Iceland. Pl. 35; p.93

117 Coot
Partial migrant. Vagrant Iceland (has bred). Pl. 35; p.94

118 Crane
Migrant. Some winter in NE France. Vagrant Ireland, Iceland. Pl. 6; p.95

119 Little Bustard
Partial migrant. Vagrant British Isles, C and N Europe. Pl. 36; p.96

120 Great Bustard
Mainly resident, extending range in winter. Vagrant to most Europe including Britain. Pl. 36; p.97

121 Oystercatcher
Partial migrant. Has bred Spain. Vagrant to or passage C Europe. Pl. 42; p.97

122 Black-winged Stilt
Mainly summer visitor. Irregular breeder north to N Germany, Britain. Vagrant N Europe. Pl. 42; p.97

123 Avocet
Partial migrant. Vagrant Iceland, Finland. Pl. 42; p.98

124 Stone Curlew
Partial migrant. Formerly bred in Holland. Has wintered in England. Vagrant Ireland, Iceland, N Europe. Pl. 36; p.98

125 Collared Pratincole
Summer visitor. Vagrant British Isles, C and N Europe. Pl. 38; p.99

126 Little Ringed Plover
Summer visitor. Vagrant Ireland. Pl. 38; p.100

127 Ringed Plover
Partial migrant. Has bred Spain. Irregular winter in Greece. Passage S and E Europe. Pl. 38; p.100

128 Kentish Plover
Partial migrant. Has bred England. Vagrant Ireland, S Baltic. Pl. 38; p.101

129 Dotterel
Migrant. Has bred Poland, Czechoslovakia, France, Spain, Wales. Vagrant Ireland, Iceland. Pl. 38; p.102

130 Golden Plover
Partial migrant. Has bred Belgium. Pl. 37; p.103

131 Grey Plover
Winter visitor from north-east. Immatures summer in winter range. Passage C Europe. Vagrant Iceland. Pl. 37; p.103

132 Lapwing
Partial migrant. Breeds in Iceland occasionally. Pl. 39; p.105

133 Knot
Winter visitor. Non-breeders in summer on coasts W Europe. Vagrant E Europe. Pl. 43; p.106

134 Sanderling
Winter visitor. Non-breeders in summer on coasts W Europe. Passage most Europe. Pl. 47; p.106

135 Little Stint
Migrant. Passage most Europe. Few winter north to Britain. Vagrant Iceland. Pl. 48; p.107

136 Temminck's Stint
Migrant. Passage most Europe. Vagrant Ireland, Portugal. Pl. 48; p.107

137 Purple Sandpiper
Partial migrant.
Non-breeders in summer
south to England. Vagrant
C, E and S Europe. Pl. 48;
p.110

138 Dunlin
Partial migrant. Passage all
Europe. Non-breeders in
summer in winter range.
Has bred N France, Hol-
land. Pl. 47; p.110

139 Broad-billed Sandpiper
Summer visitor. Passage
Denmark, Italy eastwards.
Vagrant W Europe
including British Isles.
Pl. 48; p.111

140 Ruff
Mainly migrant. Has bred
Austria. Vagrant Iceland.
Pl. 46; p.112

141 Jack Snipe
Migrant. Vagrant Iceland.
Pl. 43; p.113

142 Snipe
Partial migrant. Has bred
Yugoslavia. Pl. 43; p.113

143 Great Snipe
Summer visitor. May breed
Finland. Passage C Europe.
Vagrant W Europe
including British Isles.
Pl. 43; p.113

144 Woodcock
Partial migrant. Perhaps annual in Iceland. Pl. 43;
p.114

145 Black-tailed Godwit
Mainly migrant. Has bred Faeroes, Spain. Pl. 42; p.114

146 Bar-tailed Godwit
Migrant. Non-breeders in summer on coasts Britain, W Europe. Vagrant Iceland. Rare inland. Pl. 42; p.115

147 Whimbrel
Migrant. Non-breeders in summer on coasts W Europe. Few winter north to British Isles, Denmark. Pl. 42; p.115

148 Curlew
Partial migrant. Has bred Spain. Non-breeders in summer on coasts south to Mediterranean. Pl. 42; p.116

149 Spotted Redshank
Migrant. Non-breeders in summer south to Mediterranean. Pl. 44; p.116

150 Redshank
Partial migrant. Pl. 44; p.117

151 Marsh Sandpiper
Summer visitor. Has wintered in Spain. Vagrant C Europe west to Britain. Pl. 45; p.117

152 Greenshank
Migrant. Non-breeders summer south to Mediterranean. Has bred Ireland. Vagrant Iceland. Pl. 44; p.118

153 Green Sandpiper
Migrant. Has bred SW to Britain, Austria, Italy. Pl. 45; p.119

154 Wood Sandpiper
Summer visitor. Has bred Iceland. Passage west to Ireland. Vagrant Portugal. Pl. 45; p.119

155 Common Sandpiper
Mainly summer visitor. Has bred Holland, Greece. Vagrant Iceland. Pl. 47; p.120

156 Turnstone
Migrant. Non-breeders summer in winter range. Thin passage or vagrant inland. Pl. 39; p.121

157 Red-necked Phalarope
Summer visitor. Irregular breeder in Ireland. Vagrant or passage England, most Europe. Pl. 41; p.121

158 Grey Phalarope
Summer visitor. Few autumn (winter) coasts W Europe. Vagrant elsewhere. Pl. 41; p.122

159 Arctic Skua
Mainly summer visitor. Few winter north to N Sea. Thin passage C Europe, Mediterranean. Pl. 53; p.123

160 Long-tailed Skua
Summer visitor. Passage Britain, Ireland, perhaps Switzerland. Vagrant elsewhere C, E and S Europe. Pl. 53; p.124

161 Mediterranean Gull
Partial migrant. Breeding often sporadic at spots shown. Vagrant N Europe, Ireland. Pl. 54; p.125

162 Little Gull
Mainly migrant. Has nested in Britain, Norway, Germany, Romania. Vagrant Iceland. Pl. 54; p.126

163 Black-headed Gull
Partial migrant. Has bred Greece. Pl. 54; p.127

164 Slender-billed Gull
Partial migrant. Vagrant Britain, Portugal, C and N Europe. Pl. 54; p.128

165 Audouin's Gull
Widely scattered in Mediterranean in winter. Vagrant Portugal, C Europe. Pl. 54; p.128

166 Common Gull
Partial migrant. Has bred Czechoslovakia, Hungary. Pl. 54; p.129

167 Lesser Black-backed Gull
Partial migrant. Has bred E Germany, Poland. Some summer Mediterranean. Pl. 54; p.130

168 Herring Gull
Partial migrant. Has bred Hungary, Czech. Winters coasts, fewer inland, all Europe except where waters freeze. Pl. 54; p.130

169 Glaucous Gull
Partial migrant. Vagrant C, S and E Europe. Pl. 54; p.131

170 Great Black-backed Gull
Partial migrant. Immatures often summer outside breeding range. Vagrant SE Europe. Pl. 54; p.131

171 Kittiwake
Partial migrant, rarely far inland. Vagrant SE Europe north to Baltic. Pl. 54; p.132

172 Gull-billed Tern
Mainly summer visitor. Has bred England. Vagrant Ireland, C and N Europe. Pl. 57; p.133

173 Caspian Tern
Mainly summer visitor. Occasionally breeds in N Sea, Mediterranean. Vagrant to most Europe incl. British Isles. Pl. 57; p.133

174 Sandwich Tern
Partial migrant. Has bred Poland. Vagrant Norway, C Europe. Pl. 57; p.134

175 Common Tern
Mainly summer visitor. Occurs coasts in Italy, Sicily in winter. Pl. 57; p.135

176 Arctic Tern
Summer visitor. Vagrant C and S Europe. Pl. 57; p.135

177 Little Tern
Summer visitor. Vagrant Norway. Pl. 58; p.137

178 Whiskered Tern
Summer visitor. Has bred widely in C Europe. Vagrant British Isles, N Europe. Pl. 58; p.137

179 Black Tern
Summer visitor. Passage, and has bred, Britain and Ireland, Iceland. Vagrant Norway. Pl. 58; p.137

180 White-winged Black Tern
Summer visitor. Has bred west to France, passage in Spain. Vagrant British Isles, N Europe. Pl. 58; p.138

181 Guillemot
Partial migrant, leaving N Baltic. Winters sea south to Spain. Vagrant C and E Europe, Mediterranean. Pl. 61; p.138

182 Razorbill
Partial migrant, leaving N Baltic. Has bred Estonia. Winters sea south to dotted line. Vagrant C Europe. Pl. 61; p.139

183 Black Guillemot
Mainly resident. Winters south to dotted line. Vagrant France, C Europe. Pl. 62; p.140

184 Puffin
Summer visitor to land. Vagrant east to Adriatic, C Europe. Pl. 62; p.140

185 Rock Dove
Resident. Feral domestic birds extend to Arctic Circle. Pl. 63; p.142

186 Stock Dove
Partial migrant. Pl. 63; p.143

187 Woodpigeon
Partial migrant. Has bred Iceland. Pl. 63; p.143

188 Collared Dove
Mainly resident. Has bred Iceland. Pl. 63; p.143

189 Turtle Dove
Summer visitor. Irregular breeder in Ireland. Pl. 63; p.144

190 Cuckoo
Summer visitor. Vagrant Iceland. Pl. 67; p.146

191 Barn Owl
Mainly resident. Vagrant north to Finland. Pl. 64; p.147

192 Scops Owl
Partial migrant. Vagrant British Isles, C and N Europe. Pl. 64; p.147

193 Eagle Owl
Resident. Has bred Belgium. Vagrant Denmark, Holland, Britain. Pl. 64; p.147

194 Snowy Owl
Partial migrant. Range variable. Irregular in Scotland (has bred). Vagrant south to France, Yugoslavia. Pl. 64; p.148

195 Hawk Owl
Partial migrant. Almost annual in Poland. Vagrant south to Britain, Yugoslavia. Pl. 65; p.148

196 Pygmy Owl
Mainly resident. Vagrant Denmark, Holland, Belgium. Pl. 65; p.148

197 Little Owl
Resident. Vagrant Ireland, Sweden. Pl. 65; p.149

198 Tawny Owl
Resident. Pl. 65; p.149

199 Ural Owl
Mainly resident. Vagrant south to Italy. Pl. 65; p.150

200 Long-eared Owl
Partial migrant. Farther north in lemming years. Annual in Iceland, Faeroes. Pl. 64; p.150

201 Short-eared Owl
Partial migrant. Has bred
Ireland, Italy, Bulgaria.
Pl. 64; p.151

202 Tengmalm's Owl
Partial resident. Has bred
Denmark, Belgium. Vagrant
Britain, SW Europe.
Pl. 65; p.151

203 Nightjar
Summer visitor. Vagrant
Iceland. Pl. 68; p.152

204 Swift
Summer visitor. Vagrant Iceland. Pl. 71; p.153

205 Pallid Swift
Summer visitor. Vagrant
Britain, C and N Europe.
Pl. 71; p.153

206 Alpine Swift
Summer visitor. Vagrant
British Isles, C and N
Europe. Pl. 71; p.154

207 Kingfisher
Partial migrant. Vagrant
Norway. Pl. 66; p.154

208 Bee-eater
Summer visitor. Has occa-
sionally bred in Britain and
many countries north to
Sweden. Vagrant Ireland,
Finland. Pl. 66; p.208

209 Roller
Summer visitor. Vagrant north to British Isles, Iceland, regular in Finland. Pl. 66; p.155

210 Hoopoe
Mainly summer visitor. Occasionally breeds Britain, N Europe. Annual Ireland, vagrant Iceland.
Pl 66; p.156

211 Wryneck
Mainly summer visitor. May no longer breed in England, almost established in Scotland. Vagrant Iceland, Ireland. Pl. 69; p.156

212 Grey-headed Woodpecker
Resident. Vagrant Lapland. Pl. 69; p.157

213 Green Woodpecker
Resident. Vagrant Ireland and Finland. Pl. 69; p.157

214 Black Woodpecker
Mainly resident. Pl. 69; p.157

215 Great Spotted Woodpecker
Mainly resident. Vagrant Ireland, Iceland. Pl. 69; p.158

216 Syrian Woodpecker
Mainly resident. Pl. 69; p.158

217 Middle Spotted Woodpecker
Mainly resident. Has bred Holland, Latvia. Vagrant Portugal, Sweden. Pl. 69; p.158

218 White-backed Woodpecker
Resident. Pl. 69; p.159

219 Lesser Spotted Woodpecker
Resident. Pl. 69; p.159

220 Three-toed Woodpecker
Resident. Vagrant Denmark. Pl. 69; p.259

221 Calandra Lark
Mainly resident. Vagrant Britain, C and N Europe. Pl. 70; p.160

222 Short-toed Lark
Summer visitor. Vagrant British Isles, Iceland, C and N Europe. Pl. 70; p.222

223 Crested Lark
Mainly resident. Vagrant Britain, Finland. Pl. 70; p.223

224 Woodlark
Partial migrant. Vagrant Ireland (has bred), Scotland. Pl. 70; p.162

225 Skylark
Partial migrant. Vagrant Iceland. Pl. 70; p.163

226 Shore Lark
Mainly migrant. Has bred Scotland. Vagrant to many parts of Europe. Pl. 70; p.163

227 Sand Martin
Summer visitor. Vagrant Faeroes. Pl. 71; p.164

228 Crag Martin
Partial migrant. May winter in Yugoslavia. Vagrant north to Britain, Finland. Pl. 71; p.164

229 Swallow
Summer visitor. Has bred Iceland, Faeroes. Pl. 71; p.164

230 Red-rumped Swallow
Summer visitor. Vagrant British Isles, C, E and N Europe. Pl. 71; p.165

231 House Martin
Summer visitor. Vagrant Iceland. Pl. 71; p.165

232 Tawny Pipit
Summer visitor. Has bred Switzerland. Annual in England, vagrant north to Iceland. Pl. 72; p.166

233 Tree Pipit
Summer visitor. Annual in Ireland, vagrant to Iceland. Pl. 72; p.167

234 Meadow Pipit
Partial migrant. Pl. 72; p.167

235 Red-throated Pipit
Summer visitor. Passage Europe west to Italy. Vagrant to W Europe including British Isles. Pl. 72; p.168

236 Rock Pipit
Partial migrant. Has bred Iceland. Pl. 72; p.168

237 Water Pipit
Partial migrant. Vagrant Denmark. Pl. 72; p.168

238 Yellow Wagtail
Summer visitor. Has bred Ireland. Vagrant Iceland. Pl. 73; p.169

239 Grey Wagtail
Partial migrant. Vagrant Iceland. Pl. 73; p.169

240 Pied Wagtail
Partial migrant. Pl. 73; p.170

241 Waxwing
Partial migrant. Extends most winters beyond limit shown. Vagrant Iceland, Ireland, Spain. Pl. 84; p.170

242 Dipper
Mainly resident. In winter extends over Finland, Baltic States, reaches Holland. Pl. 83; p.171

243 Wren
Partial migrant. Pl. 83; p.171

244 Dunnock
Partial migrant. Vagrant Iceland. Pl. 91; p.172

245 Alpine Accentor
Partial migrant. Spreads to lower levels in winter. Vagrant north to Britain, N Europe. Pl. 91; p.172

246 Rufous Bush Robin
Summer visitor. Irregular in S France, vagrant to Italy, E and C Europe, British Isles. Pl. 80; p.172

247 Robin
Partial migrant. Annual in Iceland. Pl. 76; p.173

248 Thrush Nightingale
Summer visitor. Vagrant west to Britain, France, Italy. Pl. 76; p.173

249 Nightingale
Summer visitor. Vagrant
Scotland, Ireland, N
Europe. Pl. 76; p.173

250 Bluethroat
Summer visitor. Has bred
Switzerland, Italy. Rare pas-
sage Britain (has bred in
Scotland), vagrant to Ire-
land, Iceland. Pl. 76; p.174

251 Black Redstart
Partial migrant. Has bred
Scotland, Norway. Vagrant
Iceland. Pl. 77; p.175

252 Redstart
Summer visitor. Vagrant Iceland. Pl. 77; p.175

253 Whinchat
Summer visitor. Vagrant
Iceland. Pl. 76; p.175

254 Stonechat
Partial migrant. Has bred
Finland. Vagrant to most N
Europe. Pl. 76; p.176

**255 Northern
Wheatear**
Summer visitor. Pl. 75;
p.177

**256 Black-eared
Wheatear**
Summer visitor. Vagrant
British Isles, C and N
Europe. Pl. 75; p.178

257 Black Wheatear
Resident. Vagrant Britain, N, C and SE Europe. Pl. 75; p.179

258 Rock Thrush
Summer visitor. Vagrant Britain, N Europe. Pl. 77; p.179

259 Blue Rock Thrush
Mainly resident. Vagrant C and N Europe. Pl. 77; p.180

260 Ring Ouzel
Partial migrant. Has bred Denmark, Faeroes. Vagrant Iceland. Pl. 78; p.181

261 Blackbird
Partial migrant. Has bred Iceland. Pl. 78; p.182

262 Fieldfare
Partial migrant. Breeds irregularly in Britain, has bred in Iceland. Pl. 78; p.183

263 Song Thrush
Partial migrant. Vagrant Iceland. Pl. 78; p.183

264 Redwing
Mainly migrant. Has bred SE England, France, Czechoslovakia. Pl. 78; p.184

265 Mistle Thrush
Partial migrant. Vagrant Iceland. Pl. 78; p.184

266 Cetti's Warbler
Mainly resident, vulnerable to hard winters. Has bred in Germany. Vagrant C and N Europe. Pl. 79; p.185

267 Fan-tailed Warbler
Mainly resident, vulnerable to hard winters. Vagrant Britain, Ireland. Pl. 79; p.186

268 Grasshopper Warbler
Summer visitor. Vagrant Iceland. Pl. 79; p.187

269 River Warbler
Summer visitor. Annual Sweden (has bred). Vagrant W to Britain. Pl. 79; p.187

270 Savi's Warbler
Summer visitor. Has bred Sweden. Vagrant Scotland, Ireland, N Europe. Pl. 79; p.187

271 Moustached Warbler
Partial resident. Vagrant Britain (has bred), C Europe. Pl. 79; p.188

272 Aquatic Warbler
Summer visitor. Has bred west to France; passage west to Iberia. Annual in Britain; vagrant to N Europe. Pl. 79; p.188

273 Sedge Warbler
Summer visitor. Vagrant
Iceland. Pl. 79; p.188

274 Marsh Warbler
Summer visitor. Has bred
Spain. Vagrant Scotland,
Faeroes. Pl. 79; p.190

275 Reed Warbler
Summer visitor. Breeds S
Ireland. Has bred Scotland,
Ireland. Vagrant Iceland.
Pl. 79; p.190

**276 Great Reed
Warbler**
Summer visitor. Annual in
Britain. Vagrant Ireland,
Norway. Pl. 79; p.191

**277 Olivaceous
Warbler**
Summer visitor. Vagrant
British Isles, C Europe.
Pl. 81; p.191

**278 Olive-tree
Warbler**
Summer visitor. Vagrant It-
aly, Romania. Pl. 81; p.19

279 Icterine Warbler
Summer visitor. Annual in
Britain, Ireland. Vagrant
Faeroes. Pl. 81; p.192

**280 Melodious
Warbler**
Summer visitor. Annual in
Britain, Ireland. Vagrant C
and N Europe. Pl. 81;
p.193

281 Dartford Warbler
Mainly resident. Vagrant
Ireland, C and E Europe.
Pl. 80; p.194

**282 Spectacled
Warbler**
Mainly summer visitor.
Resident in Malta. Pl. 80;
p.194

**283 Subalpine
Warbler**
Summer visitor. Vagrant
British Isles, C, N and E
Europe. Pl. 80; p.194

**284 Sardinian
Warbler**
Mainly resident. Vagrant
Britain, C, N and E
Europe. Pl. 80; p.195

285 Orphean Warbler
Summer visitor. Vagrant
Britain, C Europe. Pl. 80;
p.196

286 Barred Warbler
Summer visitor. Rare pas-
sage E Britain; vagrant to
Ireland, Iceland. Pl. 80;
p.196

**287 Lesser
Whitethroat**
Summer visitor. Has bred
Ireland. Vagrant Iceland,
Spain. Pl. 80; p.196

288 Whitethroat
Summer visitor. Vagrant Iceland. Pl. 80; p.197

289 Garden Warbler
Summer visitor. Vagrant Iceland. Pl. 81; p.197

290 Blackcap
Partial migrant. Passage to Faeroes, Iceland. Pl. 80; p.197

291 Greenish Warbler
Summer visitor. Has bred Denmark. Migrates east. Vagrant British Isles, C Europe. Pl. 81; p.197

292 Arctic Warbler
Summer visitor. Migrates east. Vagrant British Isles, C and S Europe. Pl. 81; p.198

293 Bonelli's Warbler
Summer visitor. Vagrant British Isles, N Europe. Pl. 81; p.200

294 Wood Warbler
Summer visitor. Vagrant Iceland. Pl. 81; p.201

295 Chiffchaff
Partial migrant. On passage drifts to Iceland. Pl. 81; p.201

296 Willow Warbler
Summer visitor. On passage drifts to Iceland. Pl. 81; p.201

297 Goldcrest
Partial migrant. Has bred
Faeroes; vagrant to
Iceland. Pl. 83; p.202

298 Firecrest
Partial migrant. Has bred
Sweden. Annual in Ireland;
vagrant to N Europe.
Pl. 83; p.203

299 Spotted Flycatcher
Summer visitor. Vagrant
Iceland. Pl. 84; p.203

300 Red-breasted Flycatcher
Summer visitor. Has bred
Norway. Rare passage to
Britain, France, Italy; va-
grant west to Spain, Ireland,
Iceland. Pl. 84; p.204

301 Collared Flycatcher
Summer visitor. Irregular
breeder in Greece. Vagrant
N and W Europe, including
Britain. Pl. 84; p.204

302 Pied Flycatcher
Summer visitor. Passage to
Ireland. Vagrant Iceland.
Pl. 84; p.204

303 Bearded Tit
Wanders in winter. Has
bred Finland. Vagrant
Scotland. Pl. 86; p.205

304 Long-tailed Tit
Partial migrant. Pl. 86;
p.205

305 Marsh Tit
Mainly resident. Vagrant
Ireland. Pl. 86; p.206

306 Sombre Tit
Resident. Vagrant Italy.
Pl. 86; p.206

307 Willow Tit
Mainly resident. Pl. 86;
p.206

308 Siberian Tit
Mainly resident. Vagrant Estonia. Pl. 86; p.207

309 Crested Tit
Mainly resident. Pl. 86;
p.207

310 Coal Tit
Partial migrant in northern
part of range. Pl. 86; p.207

311 Blue Tit
Partial migrant in northern
part of range. Pl. 86; p.208

312 Great Tit
Partial migrant in northern
part of range. Vagrant Iceland. Pl. 86; p.208

313 Nuthatch
Resident. Occasionally breeds in Finland after irruptions. Pl. 83; p.209

314 Rock Nuthatch
Resident. Pl. 83; p.209

315 Wallcreeper
Dispersive in winter, rarely reaching Britain, N Germany, Malta. Pl. 83; p.210

316 Treecreeper
Mainly resident. Vagrant Faeroes. Pl. 83; p.210

317 Short-toed Treecreeper
Mainly resident. Vagrant England, N Europe. Pl. 83; p.211

318 Penduline Tit
Has bred Belgium, Finland. Wanders in winter, has reached Britain. Pl. 86; p.211

319 Golden Oriole
Summer visitor. Has bred Scotland, Norway. Vagrant Ireland, Iceland. Pl. 87; p.211

320 Red-backed Shrike
Summer visitor. Breeds irregularly in Scotland, (formerly?) England. Vagrant Ireland, Iceland. Pl. 85; p.212

321 Lesser Grey Shrike
Summer visitor. Vagrant north to British Isles, N Europe. Pl. 85; p.213

322 Great Grey Shrike
Partial migrant. Vagrant Ireland, Faeroes. Pl. 85; p.213

323 Woodchat Shrike
Summer visitor. Vagrant British Isles, N Europe. Pl. 85; p.214

324 Jay
Partial migrant in northern part of range. Pl. 87; p.214

325 Siberian Jay
Mainly resident. Vagrant C Europe. Pl. 87; p.215

326 Magpie
Resident. Pl. 87; p.215

327 Nutcracker
Mainly resident. Irregularly breeds in Denmark. Siberian race occasionally invades Europe west to Britain, Iberia. Pl. 87; p.216

328 Alpine Chough
Resident. Recorded in S Spain. Vagrant Czechoslovakia. Pl. 87; p.216

329 Chough
Resident. Pl. 87; p.216

330 Jackdaw
Partial migrant. Vagrant Iceland. Pl. 88; p.217

331 Rook
Partial migrant. Vagrant Iceland. Pl. 88; p.217

332 Carrion Crow
Mainly resident. Vagrant N Europe, Poland. Pl. 88; p.217

333 Hooded Crow
Partial migrant. Vagrant Iceland, SW Europe. Pl. 88; p.217

334 Raven
Mainly resident. Pl. 88; p.218

335 Starling
Partial migrant. Pl. 87; p.218

336 House Sparrow
Mainly resident. Has bred Iceland. Line surrounds range of Italian Sparrow. Pl. 91; p.220

337 Spanish Sparrow
Mainly resident. Vagrant Britain, S France. Pl. 91; p.220

338 Tree Sparrow
Partial migrant. Has bred Faeroes. Vagrant Iceland. Pl. 91; p.220

339 Rock Sparrow
Resident. Vagrant Britain, C Europe. Pl. 91; p.221

340 Snowfinch
Resident, rarely to lower levels in winter. Vagrant C Europe, Balearics. Pl. 91; p.221

341 Chaffinch
Partial migrant. Annual in Iceland. Pl. 89; p.223

342 Brambling
Migrant. Has bred Scotland, more often in Holland, Denmark. Annual in Iceland. Pl. 89; p.223

343 Serin
Partial migrant. Has bred England. Vagrant Ireland, Finland. Pl. 89; p.223

344 Citril Finch
Mainly resident, spreading in winter. Has bred Balearics. Vagrant Britain, C Europe. Pl. 89; p.224

345 Greenfinch
Partial migrant. Vagrant
Iceland. Pl. 89; p.224

346 Goldfinch
Partial migrant. Pl. 89;
p.225

347 Siskin
Partial migrant. Has bred
Faeroes. Vagrant Iceland.
Pl. 89; p.225

348 Linnet
Partial migrant. Vagrant
Faeroes. Pl. 90; p.225

349 Twite
Partial migrant. Vagrant S
Europe. Pl. 90; p.226

350 Redpoll
Partial migrant. Has bred
Estonia. Pl. 90; p.226

351 Arctic Redpoll
Mainly migrant. Vagrant
Britain, C and E Europe.
Pl. 90; p.227

352 Crossbill
Mainly resident. After irregular irruptions breeds
more widely, including Ireland. Vagrant Iceland.
Pl. 90; p.227

353 Scarlet Rosefinch
Summer visitor. Has bred Scotland, England, Holland. Vagrant Iceland, S Europe. Pl. 90; p.229

354 Pine Grosbeak
Partial migrant. Vagrant to S and W Europe including Britain. Pl. 90; p.229

355 Bullfinch
Mainly resident. Vagrant Iceland. Pl. 90; p.230

356 Hawfinch
Partial migrant. Balearics in winter. Vagrant Ireland, Faeroes. Pl. 89; p.230

357 Lapland Bunting
Migrant. Has bred Scotland. Annual passage Ireland. Vagrant Iceland and south to Portugal, Italy. Pl. 91; p.232

358 Snow Bunting
Partial migrant. Vagrant to most S European countries. Pl. 91; p.233

359 Yellowhammer
Partial migrant. Vagrant Iceland, Sicily. Pl. 92; p.233

360 Cirl Bunting
Mainly resident. Has bred Hungary. Vagrant Ireland, C Europe. Pl. 92; p.234

361 Rock Bunting
Mainly resident. Range slightly extended in winter. Vagrant Britain, Poland. Pl. 92; p.234

362 Ortolan Bunting
Summer visitor. Thin passage to E Britain. Vagrant Ireland, Iceland. Pl. 92; p.235

363 Rustic Bunting
Summer visitor. Has bred Estonia, Latvia. Vagrant C, S and W Europe, including Britain. Pl. 91; p.236

364 Reed Bunting
Partial migrant. Vagrant Iceland. Pl. 91; p.237

365 Black-headed Bunting
Summer visitor. Vagrant C, N and W Europe including Britain. Pl. 92; p.238

366 Corn Bunting
Mainly resident. Vagrant N Europe. Pl. 92; p.238

Index

Common English names are printed in Roman type. Scientific names are in *italics*. The figures in Roman type refer to the descriptive text pages, those in **bold** type refer to the colour plates and those in *italics* refer to the distribution maps.

Accentor, Alpine 172, **91**, *245*
    Black-throated 252
    Siberian 252
Accipiter brevipes 76, **26**, *82*
    gentilis 75, **26**, **31**, *80*
    nisus 76, **26**, **31**, *81*
Acrocephalus aedon 254
    agricola 189, **82**
    arundinaceus 191, **79**, *276*
    dumetorum 189, **82**
    melanopogon 188, **79**, *271*
    paludicola 188, **79**, *272*
    palustris 190, **79**, *274*
    schoenobaenus 188, **79**, *273*
    scirpaceus 190, **79**, *275*
Actitis hypoleucos 120, **47**, **52**, *155*
    macularia 120, **47**
Aegithalos caudatus 205, **86**, *304*
Aegolius funereus 151, **65**, *202*
Aegypius monachus 73, **23**, *74*
Aethia cristatella 248
Aix galericulata 55, **12**
    sponsa 55, **96**
Alaemon alaudipes 250
Alauda arvensis 163, **70**, *225*
Albatross, Black-browed 35, **5**
    Wandering 240
Alca torda 139, **61**, *182*
Alcedo atthis 154, **66**, *207*
Alectoris barbara 89, **33**
    chukar 88, **33**
    graeca 88, **33**, *106*
    rufa 88, **33**, *107*
Alle alle 140, **62**
Alopochen aegyptiacus 54, **96**
Amandava amandava 222, **91**
Ammodramus sandwichensis 259
Ammomanes cincturus 250
Anas acuta 59, **12**, **19**, **21**, *50*
    americana 56, **18**
    clypeata 60, **12**, **19**, **21**, *52*
    crecca 58, **12**, **19**, **21**, *48*
    discors 60, **18**
    falcata 243
    formosa 57, **18**
    penelope 56, **12**, **19**, **21**, *46*
    platyrhynchos 58, **12**, **19**, **21**, *49*
    querquedula 59, **12**, **19**, **21**, *51*
    rubripes 58, **18**, **19**
    strepera 57, **12**, **19**, **21**, *47*
Anous stolidus 248

Anser albifrons 51, **10**, **11**, *38*
    anser 51, **10**, **11**, *40*
    brachyrhynchus 50, **10**, **11**, *37*
    caerulescens 52, **8**, **9**
    erythropus 51, **10**, *39*
    fabalis 50, **10**, **11**, *36*
    indicus 52, **96**
Anthropoides virgo 95, **6**
Anthus campestris 166, **72**, *232*
    cervinus 168, **72**, *235*
    godlewskii 251
    gustavi 167, **72**
    hodgsoni 166, **72**
    novaeseelandiae 165, **72**
    petrosus 168, **72**, *236*
    pratensis 167, **72**, *234*
    rubescens 251
    spinoletta 168, **72**, *237*
    trivialis 167, **72**, *233*
Apus affinis 154, **71**
    apus 153, **71**, *204*
    caffer 154, **71**
    melba 154, **71**, *206*
    pacificus 249
    pallidus 153, **71**, *205*
Aquila chrysaetos 79, **28**, **29**, *88*
    clanga 78, **28**, **29**, *86*
    heliaca 79, **28**, *87*
    nipalensis 79, **28**
    pomarina 78, **28**, *85*
    rapax 244
Ardea cinerea 45, **6**, *27*
    herodias 242
    purpurea 46, **6**, *28*
Ardeola bacchus 242
    ralloides 44, **7**, *23*
Arenaria interpres 121, **39**, **40**, *156*
Asio capensis 249
    flammeus 151, **64**, *201*
    otus 150, **64**, *200*
Athene noctua 149, **65**, *197*
Auk, Little 140, **62**
Auklet, Crested 248
    Parakeet 249
Avadavat 222, **91**
Avocet 98, **42**, **50**, *123*
Aythya affinis 243
    collaris 62, **18**
    ferina 61, **13**, **22**, *54*
    fuligula 62, **13**, **20**, **22**, *56*
    marila 63, **13**, **20**, *57*

nyroca 62, **13, 20, 22**, *55*
  valisineria 243

Bartramia longicauda 116, **46**
Bee-eater 155, **66**, *208*
  Blue-cheeked 155, **66**
Bittern 42, **6**, *20*
  American 43, **6**
  Least 241
  Little 43, **6**, *21*
  Schrenck's Little 241
Blackbird 182, **78**, *261*
  Yellow-headed 261
Blackcap 197, **80**, *290*
Bluetail, Red-flanked 174, **77**
Bluethroat 174, **76**, *250*
Bobolink 261, **94**
Bombycilla cedrorum 251
  garrulus 170, **84**, *241*
Bonasa bonasia 85, **32**, *101*
Booby, Brown 241
  Masked 241
  Red-footed 241
Botaurus lentiginosus 43, **6**
  stellaris 42, **6**, *20*
Brambling 223, **89**, *342*
Branta bernicla 53, **8, 9**, *43*
  canadensis 53, **8, 9**, *41*
  leucopsis 53, **8, 9**, *42*
  ruficollis 54, **8, 11**
Bubo bubo 147, **64**, *193*
Bubulcus ibis 44, **7**, *24*
Bucanetes githagineus 228, **89**
Bucephala albeola 243
  clangula 67, **13, 20, 22**, *62*
  islandica 66, **13**
Bufflehead 243
Bullfinch 230, **90**, *355*
Bulweria bulwerii 240
Bunting, Black-faced 260, **92**
  Black-headed 238, **92**, *365*
  Chestnut 260
  Cinereous 235, **92**
  Cirl 234, **92**, *360*
  Corn 238, **92**, *366*
  Cretzschmar's 235, **92**
  Indigo 261, **94**
  Lapland 232, **91**, *357*
  Lazuli 261
  Little 236, **92**
  Meadow 260
  Ortolan 235, **92**, *362*
  Pallas's Reed 260
  Pine 233, **92**
  Red-headed 260, **92**
  Reed 237, **91**, *364*
  Rock 234, **92**, *361*
  Rustic 236, **91**, *363*
  Snow 233, **91**, *358*
  Yellow-breasted 236, **92**
  Yellow-browed 260

Burhinus oedicnemus 98, **36, 52**, *124*
Bustard, Great 97, **36**, *120*
  Houbara 96, **36**
  Little 96, **36**, *119*
Buteo buteo 76, **26, 27**, *83*
  lagopus 77, **26, 27**, *84*
  rufinus 77, **26, 27**
  swainsoni 244
Butorides striatus 242
Buzzard 76, **26, 27**, *83*
  Honey 70, **26, 27**, *67*
  Long-legged 77, **26, 27**
  Rough-legged 77, **26, 27**, *84*

Calandrella brachydactyla 161, **70**, *222*
  rufescens 161, **70**
Calcarius lapponicus 232, **91**, *357*
Calidris acuminata 109, **46**
  alba 106, **47, 52**, *134*
  alpina 110, **47, 52**, *138*
  bairdii 108, **49**
  canutus 106, **43, 52**, *133*
  ferruginea 110, **52**
  fuscicollis 108, **49**
  maritima 110, **48, 52**, *137*
  mauri 246, **49**
  melanotos 109, **46, 52**
  minuta 107, **48, 52**, *135*
  minutilla 108, **49**
  pusilla 107, **49**
  ruficollis 246, **48**
  subminuta 246, **48**
  temminckii 107, **48, 52**, *136*
  tenuirostris 246
Calonectris diomedea 36, **3**, *10*
Canvasback 243
Capercaillie 87, **32**, *105*
Caprimulgus aegyptius 152, **68**
  europaeus 152, **68**, *203*
  ruficollis 152, **68**
Carduelis cannabina 225, **90**, *348*
  carduelis 225, **89**, *346*
  chloris 224, **89**, *345*
  flammea 226, **90**, *350*
  flavirostris 226, **90**, *349*
  hornemanni 227, **90**, *351*
  spinus 225, **89**, *347*
Carpodacus erythrinus 229, **90**, *353*
  roseus 256
Catbird, Grey 252
Catharus fuscescens 253
  guttatus 253
  minimus 181, **94**
  ustulatus 181, **94**
Catoptrophorus semipalmatus 247
Cepphus grylle 140, **62**, *183*
Cercotrichas galactotes 172, **80**, *246*
Certhia brachydactyla 211, **83**, *317*
  familiaris 210, **83**, *316*
Ceryle alcyon 250, **66**
  rudis 250, **66**

Cettia cetti 185, **79**, *266*
Chaetura pelagica 249
Chaffinch 223, **89**, *341*
Charadrius alexandrinus 101, **38, 40**, *128*
  asiaticus 245, **38**
  dubius 100, **38, 40**, *126*
  hiaticula 100, **38, 40**, *127*
  leschenaultii 101, **38**
  mongolus 245
  morinellus 102, **38, 40**, *129*
  semipalmatus 245
  vociferus 101, **38**
Chersophilus duponti 160, **70**, *221*
Chettusia gregaria 104, **39**
  leucura 105, **39**
Chiffchaff 201, **81**, *295*
Chlamydotis undulata 96, **36**
Chlidonias hybridus 137, **58, 59**, *178*
  leucopterus 138, **58**, *180*
  niger 137, **58, 59**, *179*
Chondestes grammacus 259
Chordeiles minor 249, **68**
Chough 216, **87, 88**, *329*
  Alpine 216, **87, 88**, *328*
Chrysolophus amherstiae 91, **95**
  pictus 90, **95**
Chukar 88, **33**
Ciconia ciconia 46, **7**, *30*
  nigra 46, **7**, *29*
Cinclus cinclus 171, **83**, *242*
Circaetus gallicus 73, **27**, *75*
Circus aeruginosus 74, **24, 25**, *76*
  cyaneus 74, **24, 25**, *77*
  macrourus 74, **24**, *78*
  pygargus 75, **24, 25**, *79*
Cisticola juncidis 186, **79**, *267*
Clamator glandarius 145, **67**
Clangula hyemalis 65, **16, 20, 22**, *59*
Coccothraustes coccothraustes 230, **89**, *356*
  vespertina 256
Coccyzus americanus 146, **67**
  erythrophthalmus 146, **67**
Colaptes auratus 250
Columba livia 142, **63**, *185*
  oenas 143, **63**, *186*
  palumbus 143, **63**, *187*
Coot 94, **35**, *117*
  American 245
  Crested 94, **35**
Coracias garrulus 155, **66**, *209*
Cormorant 40, **4**, *16*
  Double-crested 241
  Pygmy 41, **4**, *18*
Corncrake 93, **34**, *115*
Corvus corax 218, **88**, *333*
  corone 217, **88**, *332*
  dauuricus 255
  frugilegus 217, **88**, *331*
  monedula 217, **88**, *330*

Coturnix coturnix 90, **33**, *109*
Courser, Cream-coloured 99, **39**
Cowbird, Brown-headed 261
Crake, Baillon's 93, **34**, *114*
  Little 92, **34**, *113*
  Spotted 92, **34**, *112*
Crane 95, **6**, *118*
  Demoiselle 95, **6**
  Sandhill 245
Crex crex 93, **34**, *115*
Crossbill 227, **90**, *352*
  Parrot 228, **90**
  Scottish 228, **90**
  Two-barred 227, **90**
Crow, Carrion 217, **88**, *332*
  Hooded 217, **88**, *332*
Cuckoo 146, **67**, *190*
  Black-billed 146, **67**
  Great Spotted 145, **67**
  Yellow-billed 146, **67**
Cuculus canorus 146, **67**, *190*
Curlew 116, **42, 50**, *148*
  Eskimo 247
  Slender-billed 115, **42**
  Stone 98, **36, 52**, *124*
Cursorius cursor 99, **39**
Cyanopica cyana 215, **87**
Cyclorrhynchus psittacula 249
Cygnus columbianus 49, **8, 9**, *34*
  cygnus 49, **8, 9**, *35*
  olor 49, **8, 9**, *33*

Delichon urbica 165, **71**, *231*
Dendrocopos leucotos 159, **69**, *218*
  major 158, **69**, *215*
  medius 158, **69**, *217*
  minor 159, **69**, *219*
  syriacus 158, **69**, *216*
Dendrocygna bicolor 242
Dendroica caerulescens 257
  coronata 231, **93**
  fusca 257
  magnolia 257
  pensylvanica 257
  petechia 256
  striata 231, **93**
  tigrina 257
  virens 257
Dickcissel 260
Diomedea exulans 240
  melanophris 35, **5**
Dipper 171, **83**, *242*
Diver, Black-throated 30, **1**, *2*
  Great Northern 31, **1**, *3*
  Red-throated 30, **1**, *1*
  White-billed 32, **1**
Dolichonyx oryzivorus 261, **94**
Dotterel 102, **38, 40**, *129*
Dove, Collared 143, **63**, *188*
  Laughing 144, **63**
  Mourning 249

Rock 142, **63**, *185*
Rufous Turtle 144, **63**
Stock 143, **63**, *186*
Turtle 144, **63**, *189*
Dowitcher, Asiatic 246
Long-billed 113, **43**
Short-billed 246, **43**
Dryocopus martius 157, **69**, *214*
Duck, Black 58, **18, 19**
Falcated 243
Ferruginous 62, **13, 20, 22**, *55*
Fulvous Whistling 242
Long-tailed 65, **16, 20, 22**, *59*
Marbled 61, **12**
Ring-necked 62, **18**
Ruddy 68, **17, 18**
Tufted 62, **13, 20, 22**, *56*
White-headed 69, **17**, *66*
Wood 55, **96**
Dumetella carolinensis 252
Dunlin 110, **47, 52**, *138*
Dunnock 172, **91**, *244*

Eagle, Bonelli's 80, **27**, *90*
Booted 80, **27**, *89*
Golden 79, **28, 29**, *88*
Imperial 79, **28**, *87*
Lesser Spotted 78, **28**, *85*
Pallas's Fish 243
Short-toed 73, **27**, *75*
Spotted 78, **28, 29**, *86*
Steppe 79, **28**
Tawny 244
White-tailed 72, **28, 29**, *70*
Egret, Cattle 44, **7**, *24*
Great White 45, **7**, *26*
Little 44, **7**, *25*
Snowy 242
Egretta alba 45, **7**, *26*
garzetta 44, **7**, *25*
gularis 242
thula 242
Eider 63, **15, 20, 22**, *58*
King 63, **15, 20, 22**
Spectacled 243, **15**
Steller's 64, **15**
Elanus caeruleus 70, **24**
Emberiza aureola 236, **92**
bruniceps 260, **92**
caesia 235, **92**
chrysophrys 260
cia 234, **92**, *361*
cineracea 235, **92**
cioides 260
cirlus 234, **92**, *360*
citrinella 233, **92**, *359*
hortulana 235, **92**, *362*
leucocephalos 233, **92**
melanocephala 238, **92**, *365*
pallasi 260
pusilla 236, **92**

rustica 236, **91**, *363*
rutila 260
schoeniclus 237, **91**, *364*
spodocephala 260, **92**
Empidonax virescens 250
Eremophila alpestris 163, **70**, *226*
bilopha 251
Erithacus rubecula 173, **76**, *247*
Estrilda astrild 221, **96**

Falco biarmicus 84, **30**, *97*
cherrug 84, **30**, *98*
columbarius 82, **30, 31**, *95*
concolor 244
eleonorae 83, **30, 31**
naumanni 81, **30, 31**, *92*
pelegrinoides 244
peregrinus 85, **30, 31**, *100*
rusticolus 84, **31**, *99*
sparverius 244
subbuteo 83, **30, 31**, *96*
tinnunculus 82, **30, 31**, *93*
vespertinus 82, **30, 31**, *94*
Falcon, Barbary 244
Eleonora's 83, **30, 31**
Red-footed 82, **30, 31**, *94*
Sooty 244
Ficedula albicollis 204, **84**, *301*
hypoleuca 204, **84**, *302*
mugimaki 254
parva 204, **84**, *300*
semitorquata 204, **84**
Fieldfare 183, **78**, *262*
Finch, Citril 224, **89**, *344*
Trumpeter 228, **89**
Firecrest 203, **83**, *298*
Flamingo, Greater 47, **7**
Lesser 242
Flicker, Northern 250
Yellow-shafted 250
Flycatcher, Acadian 250
Brown 254
Collared 204, **84**, *301*
Mugimaki 254
Pied 204, **84**, *302*
Red-breasted 204, **84**, *300*
Semi-collared 204, **84**
Spotted 203, **84**, *299*
Francolin, Black 89, **95**
Francolinus francolinus 89, **95**
Fratercula arctica 140, **62**, *184*
Fregata magnificens 241
Frigatebird, Magnificent 241
Fringilla coelebs 223, **89**, *341*
montifringilla 223, **89**, *342*
Fulica americana 245
atra 94, **35**, *117*
cristata 94, **35**
Fulmar 35, **3**, *9*
Fulmarus glacialis 35, **3**, *9*

Gadwall 57, **12, 19, 21**, *47*

Galerida cristata 162, **70**, *223*
   theklae 162, **70**
Gallinago gallinago 113, **43, 51**, *142*
   media 113, **43, 51**, *143*
Gallinula chloropus 93, **35**, *116*
Gallinule, Allen's 245, **35**
   American Purple 245
   Purple 94, **35**
Gannet, Northern 40, **5**, *15*
Garganey 59, **12, 19, 21**, *51*
Garrulus glandarius 214, **87**, *324*
Gavia adamsii 32, **1**
   arctica 30, **1**, *2*
   immer 31, **1**, *3*
   stellata 30, **1**, *1*
Gelochelidon nilotica 133, **57, 59**, *172*
Geothlypis trichas 258
Geronticus eremita 242
Glareola maldivarum 245
   nordmanni 99, **38**
   pratincola 99, **38**, *125*
Glaucidium passerinum 148, **65**, *196*
Godwit, Bar-tailed 115, **42, 50**, *146*
   Black-tailed 114, **42, 50**, *145*
   Hudsonian 247
Goldcrest 202, **83**, *297*
Goldeneye 67, **13, 20, 22**, *62*
   Barrow's 66, **13**
Goldfinch 225, **89**, *346*
Goosander 68, **17, 19, 21**, *65*
Goose, Bar-headed 52, **96**
   Barnacle 53, **8, 9**, *42*
   Bean 50, **10, 11**, *36*
   Brent 53, **8, 9**, *43*
   Canada 53, **8, 9**, *41*
   Egyptian 54, **96**
   Greylag 51, **10, 11**, *40*
   Lesser White-fronted 51, **10**, *39*
   Pink-footed 50, **10, 11**, *37*
   Red-breasted 54, **8, 11**
   Snow 52, **8, 9**
   White-fronted 51, **10, 11**, *38*
Goshawk 75, **26, 31**, *80*
   Dark Chanting 244
Grackle, Common 261
Grebe, Black-necked 34, **2**, *8*
   Great Crested 33, **2**, *5*
   Little 33, **2**, *4*
   Pied-billed 32, **2**
   Red-necked 33, **2**, *6*
   Slavonian 34, **2**, *7*
Greenfinch 224, **89**, *345*
Greenshank 118, **44, 51**, *152*
Grosbeak, Blue 261
   Evening 256
   Pine 229, **90**, *354*
   Rose-breasted 238, **94**
Grouse, Black 87, **32**, *104*
   Hazel 85, **32**, *101*
   Red 86, **33**, *102*
   Willow 86, **33**, *102*

Grus canadensis 245
   grus 95, **6**, *118*
Guillemot 138, **61**, *181*
   Black 140, **62**, *183*
   Brünnich's 139, **61**
Guiraca caerulea 261
Gull, Audouin's 128, **54**, *165*
   Black-headed 127, **54, 55**, *163*
   Bonaparte's 127, **56**
   Common 129, **54, 55**, *166*
   Franklin's 126, **56**
   Glaucous 131, **54, 55**, *169*
   Great Black-backed 131, **54, 55**, *170*
   Great Black-headed 125, **56**
   Grey-headed 247
   Herring 130, **54, 55**, *168*
   Iceland 130, **54**
   Ivory 132, **54**
   Laughing 126, **56**
   Lesser Black-backed 130, **54, 55**, *167*
   Little 126, **54, 55**, *162*
   Mediterranean 125, **54**, *161*
   Ring-billed 129, **56**
   Ross's 132, **56**
   Sabine's 127, **54, 55**
   Slender-billed 128, **54**, *164*
   White-eyed 247
Gypaëtus barbatus 72, **23**, *71*
Gyps fulvus 73, **23**, *73*
Gyrfalcon 84, **31**, *99*

Haematopus ostralegus 97, **42, 50**, *121*
Halcyon smyrnensis 249
Haliaeetus albicilla 72, **28, 29**, *70*
   leucoryphus 243
Harlequin 64, **16, 22**
Harrier, Marsh 74, **24, 25**, *76*
   Hen 74, **24, 25**, *77*
   Montagu's 75, **24, 25**, *79*
   Pallid 74, **24**, *78*
Hawfinch 230, **89**, *356*
Hawk, Swainson's 244
Hemipode, Andalusian 91, **33**
Heron, Chinese Pond 242
   Great Blue 242
   Green-backed 242
   Grey 45, **6**, *27*
   Night 43, **6**, *22*
   Purple 46, **6**, *28*
   Squacco 44, **7**, *23*
   Western Reef 242
Heteroscelus brevipes 247
Hieraaetus fasciatus 80, **27**, *89*
   pennatus 80, **27**
Himantopus himantopus 97, **42, 50**, *122*
Hippolais caligata 192, **82**
   icterina 192, **81**, *279*
   olivetorum 192, **81**, *278*
   pallida 191, **81**, *277*
   polyglotta 193, **81**, *280*
Hirundapus caudacutus 249

Hirundo daurica 165, **71**, *230*
   pyrrhonota 251
   rustica 164, **71**, *229*
Histrionicus histrionicus 64, **16**, **22**
Hobby 83, **30**, **31**, *96*
Hoopoe 156, **66**, *210*
Hoplopterus spinosus 104, **39**
Hydrobates pelagicus 39, **3**, *13*
Hylocichla mustelina 253

Ibis, Bald 242
   Glossy 47, **7**, *31*
Icterus galbula 239, **94**
Irania gutturalis 252
Ixobrychus eurhythmus 241
   exilis 241
   minutus 43, **6**, *21*

Jackdaw 217, **88**, *330*
   Daurian 255
Jay 214, **87**, *324*
   Siberian 215, **87**, *325*
Junco hyemalis 259, **94**
Junco, Dark-eyed 259, **94**
   Slate-coloured 259, **94**
Jynx torquilla 156, **69**, *211*

Kestrel 82, **30**, **31**, *93*
   American 244
   Lesser 81, **30**, **31**, *92*
Killdeer 101, **38**
Kingfisher 154, **66**, *207*
   Belted 250, **66**
   Pied 250, **66**
   Smyrna 249
Kinglet, Ruby-crowned 254
Kite, Black-shouldered 70, **24**
   Black 71, **24**, **25**, *68*
   Red 71, **24**, **25**, *69*
Kittiwake 132, **54**, **55**, *171*
Knot 106, **43**, **52**, *133*
   Great 246

Lagopus lagopus 86, **33**, *102*
   mutus 86, **33**, *103*
Lammergeier 72, **23**, *71*
Lanius collurio 212, **85**, *320*
   cristatus 255
   excubitor 213, **85**, *322*
   isabellinus 212, **85**
   minor 213, **85**, *321*
   nubicus 214, **85**
   schach 255
   senator 214, **85**, *323*
Lanner 84, **30**, *97*
Lapwing 105, **39**, **40**, *132*
Lark, Bar-tailed Desert 250
   Bimaculated 251
   Black 161, **70**
   Calandra 160, **70**, *221*
   Crested 162, **70**, *223*
   Dupont's 160, **70**
   Hoopoe 250

Lesser Short-toed 161, **70**
Shore 163, **70**, *226*
Short-toed 161, **70**, *222*
Temminck's Horned 251
Thekla 162, **70**
White-winged 160, **70**
Larus argentatus 130, **54**, **55**, *168*
   atricilla 126, **56**
   audouinii 128, **54**, *165*
   canus 129, **54**, **55**, *166*
   cirrocephalus 247
   delawarensis 129, **56**
   fuscus 130, **54**, **55**, *167*
   genei 128, **54**, *164*
   glaucoides 130, **54**
   hyperboreus 131, **54**, **55**, *169*
   ichthyaetus 125, **56**
   leucophthalmus 247
   marinus 131, **54**, **55**, *170*
   melanocephalus 125, **54**, *161*
   minutus 126, **54**, **55**, *162*
   philadelphia 127, **56**
   pipixcan 126, **56**
   ridibundus 127, **54**, **55**, *163*
   sabini 127, **54**, **55**
Limicola falcinellus 111, **48**, *139*
Limnodromus griseus 246, **43**
   scolopaceus 113, **43**
   semipalmatus 246
Limosa haemastica 247
   lapponica 115, **42**, **50**, *146*
   limosa 114, **42**, **50**, *145*
Linnet 225, **90**, *348*
Locustella certhiola 186, **82**
   fasciolata 253
   fluviatilis 187, **79**, *269*
   lanceolata 186, **82**
   luscinioides 187, **79**, *270*
   naevia 187, **79**, *268*
Loxia curvirostra 227, **90**, *352*
   leucoptera 227, **90**
   pytyopsittacus 228, **90**
   scotica 228, **90**
Lullula arborea 162, **70**, *224*
Luscinia calliope 252
   cyane 252
   luscinia 173, **76**, *248*
   megarhynchos 173, **76**, *249*
   svecica 174, **76**, *250*
Lymnocryptes minimus 112, **43**, **51**, *141*

Macronectes giganteus 240
Magpie 215, **87**, *326*
   Azure-winged 215, **87**
Mallard 58, **12**, **19**, **21**, *49*
Mandarin 55, **12**
Marmaronetta angustirostris 61, **12**
Martin, Crag 164, **71**, *228*
   House 165, **71**, *231*
   Sand 164, **71**, *227*
Melanitta fusca 66, **14**, **20**, **22**, *61*

nigra 65, **14, 20, 22**, *60*
perspicillata 66, **14, 20, 22**
Melanocorypha bimaculata 251
  calandra 160, **70**, *221*
  leucoptera 160, **70**
  yeltoniensis 161, **70**
Melierax metabates 244
Merganser, Hooded 243, **17**
  Red-breasted 67, **17, 19, 21**, *64*
Mergus albellus 67, **17, 19, 21**, *63*
  cucullatus 243, **17**
  merganser 68, **17, 19, 21**, *65*
  serrator 67, **17, 19, 21**, *64*
Merlin 82, **30, 31**, *95*
Merops apiaster 155, **66**, *208*
  superciliosus 155, **66**
Micropalama himantopus 111, **45**
Miliaria calandra 238, **92**, *366*
Milvus migrans 71, **24, 25**, *68*
  milvus 71, **24, 25**, *69*
Mimus polyglottos 251
Mniotilta varia 256, **93**
Mockingbird, Northern 251
Molothrus ater 261
Monticola saxatilis 179, **77**, *258*
  solitarius 180, **77**, *259*
Montifringilla nivalis 221, **91**, *340*
Moorhen 93, **35**, *116*
Morus bassanus 40, **5**, *15*
Motacilla alba 170, **73, 74**, *240*
  cinerea 169, **73, 74**, *239*
  citreola 169, **73**
  flava 169, **73, 74**, *238*
Murrelet, Ancient 248
Muscicapa dauurica 254
  striata 203, **84**, *299*

Neophron percnopterus 72, **23**, *72*
Netta rufina 61, **13, 20, 22**, *53*
Nighthawk, Common 249, **68**
Nightingale 173, **76**, *249*
  Thrush 173, **76**, *248*
Nightjar 152, **68**, *203*
  Egyptian 152, **68**
  Red-necked 152, **68**
Noddy, Brown 248
Nucifraga caryocatactes 216, **87**, *327*
Numenius arquata 116, **42, 50**, *148*
  borealis 247
  minutus 247
  phaeopus 115, **42, 50**, *147*
  tenuirostris 115, **42**
Nutcracker 216, **87**, *327*
Nuthatch 209, **83**, *313*
  Corsican 209, **83**
  Krüper's 208, **83**
  Red-breasted 255
  Rock 209, **83**, *314*
Nyctea scandiaca 148, **64**, *194*
Nycticorax nycticorax 43, **6**, *22*

Oceanites oceanicus 38, **3**

Oceanodroma castro 39
  leucorhoa 39, **3**, *14*
  monorhis 240
Oenanthe deserti 179, **75**
  hispanica 178, **75**, *256*
  isabellina 176, **75**
  leucopyga 253
  leucura 179, **75**, *257*
  oenanthe 177, **75**, *255*
  pleschanka 177, **75**
Oriole, Baltimore 239, **94**
  Golden 211, **87**, *319*
  Northern (Baltimore) 239, **94**
Oriolus oriolus 211, **87**, *319*
Osprey 81, **29**, *91*
Otis tarda 97, **36**, *120*
Otus scops 147, **64**, *192*
Ouzel, Ring 181, **78**, *260*
Ovenbird 258
Owl, African Marsh 249
  Barn 147, **64**, *191*
  Eagle 147, **64**, *193*
  Great Grey 150, **65**
  Hawk 148, **65**, *195*
  Little 149, **65**, *197*
  Long-eared 150, **64**, *200*
  Pygmy 148, **65**, *196*
  Scops 147, **64**, *192*
  Short-eared 151, **64**, *201*
  Snowy 148, **64**, *194*
  Tawny 149, **65**, *198*
  Tengmalm's 151, **65**, *202*
  Ural 150, **65**, *199*
Oxyura jamaicensis 68, **17, 18**
  leucocephala 69, **17**, *66*
Oystercatcher 97, **42, 50**, *121*

Pagophila eburnea 132, **54**
Pandion haliaetus 81, **29**, *91*
Panurus biarmicus 205, **86**, *303*
Parakeet, Rose-ringed 145, **95**
Partridge, Barbary 89, **33**
  Grey 89, **33**, *108*
  Red-legged 88, **33**, *107*
  Rock 88, **33**, *106*
Parula americana 231, *93*
Parula, Northern 231, **93**
Parus ater 207, **86**, *310*
  caeruleus 208, **86**, *311*
  cinctus 207, **86**, *308*
  cristatus 207, **86**, *309*
  cyanus 208, **86**
  lugubris 206, **86**, *306*
  major 208, **86**, *312*
  montanus 206, **86**, *307*
  palustris 206, **86**, *305*
Passer domesticus 220, **91**, *336*
  hispaniolensis 220, **91**, *337*
  moabiticus 255
  montanus 220, **91**, *338*
Passerina amoena 261

cyanea 261, **94**
Pelagodroma marina 240
Pelecanus crispus 42, **5**, *19*
   onocrotalus 41, **5**
Pelican, Dalmatian 42, **5**, *19*
   White 41, **5**
Perdix perdix 89, **33**, *108*
Peregrine 85, **30, 31**, *100*
Perisoreus infaustus 215, **87**, *325*
Pernis apivorus 70, **26, 27**, *67*
Petrel, Black-capped 240
   Bulwer's 240
   Frigate 240
   Leach's 39, **3**, *14*
   Madeiran 39
   Soft-plumaged 240
   Southern Giant 240
   Storm 39, **3**, *13*
   Swinhoe's 240
   White-faced Storm 240
   Wilson's 38, **3**
Petronia petronia 221, **91**, *339*
Phaethon aethereus 241
Phalacrocorax aristotelis 41, **4**, *17*
   auritus 241
   carbo 40, **4**, *16*
   pygmeus 41, **4**, *18*
Phalarope, Grey 122, **41, 52**, *158*
   Red-necked 121, **41, 52**, *157*
   Wilson's 121, **41**
Phalaropus fulicarius 122, **41, 52**, *158*
   lobatus 121, **41, 52**, *157*
   tricolor 121, **41**
Phasianus colchicus 90, **32**, *110*
Pheasant 90, **32**, *110*
   Golden 90, **95**
   Lady Amherst's 91, **95**
Pheucticus ludovicianus 238, **94**
Philomachus pugnax 112, **46, 52**, *140*
Phoebe, Eastern 250
Phoenicopterus minor 242
   ruber 47, **7**
Phoenicurus auroreus 252
   erythrogaster 253
   moussieri 252
   ochruros 175, **77**, *251*
   phoenicurus 175, **77**, *252*
Phylloscopus bonelli 200, **81**, *293*
   borealis 198, **81**, *292*
   collybita 201, **81**, *295*
   coronatus 254
   fuscatus 200, **81**
   inornatus 199, **81**
   nitidus 254
   proregulus 199, **82**
   schwarzi 200, **82**
   sibilatrix 201, **81**, *294*
   trochiloides 198, **81**, *291*
   trochilus 202, **81**, *296*
Pica pica 215, **87**, *326*
Picoides tridactylus 159, **69**, *220*

Picus canus 157, **69**, *212*
   viridis 157, **69**, *213*
Pigeon, Feral 142, **63**, *185*
   Wood 143, **63**, *187*
Pinicola enucleator 229, **90**, *354*
Pintail 59, **12, 19, 21**, *50*
Pipilo erythrophthalmus 259
Pipit, Blyth's 251
   Buff-bellied 251
   Meadow 167, **72**, *234*
   Olive-backed 166, **72**
   Pechora 167, **72**
   Red-throated 168, **72**, *235*
   Richard's 165, **72**
   Rock 168, **72**, *236*
   Tawny 166, **72**, *232*
   Tree 167, **72**, *233*
   Water 168, **72**, *237*
Piranga olivacea 259
   rubra 258, **94**
Platalea alba 242
   leucorodia 47, **7**, *32*
Plectrophenax nivalis 233, **91**, *358*
Plegadis falcinellus 47, **7**, *31*
Plover, American Golden 102, **37**
   Caspian 245, **38**
   Golden 103, **37, 40**, *130*
   Greater Sand 101, **38**
   Grey 103, **37, 40**, *131*
   Kentish 101, **38, 40**, *128*
   Lesser Sand 245
   Little Ringed 100, **38, 40**, *126*
   Pacific Golden 102, **37**
   Ringed 100, **38, 40**, *127*
   Semipalmated 245
   Sociable 104, **39**
   Spur-winged 104, **39**
   White-tailed 105, **39**
Pluvialis apricaria 103, **37, 40**, *130*
   dominica 102, **37**
   fulva 102, **37**
   squatarola 103, **37, 40**, *131*
Pochard 61, **13, 22**, *54*
   Red-crested 61, **13, 20, 22**, *53*
Podiceps auritus 34, **2**, *7*
   cristatus 33, **2**, *5*
   grisegena 33, **2**, *6*
   nigricollis 34, **2**, *8*
Podilymbus podiceps 32, **2**
Polysticta stelleri 64, **15**
Porphyrio porphyrio 94, **35**
Porphyrula alleni 245, **35**
   martinica 245
Porzana carolina 244, **17**
   parva 92, **34**, *113*
   porzana 92, **34**, *112*
   pusilla 93, **34**, *114*
Pratincole, Black-winged 99, **38**
   Collared 99, **38**, *125*
   Oriental 245
Prunella atrogularis 252

   collaris 172, **91**, *245*
   modularis 172, **91**, *244*
   montanella 252
Psittacula krameri 145, **95**
Ptarmigan 86, **33**, *103*
Pterocles alchata 141, **36**
   orientalis 141, **36**
   senegallus 249
Pterodroma hasitata 240
   mollis 240
Ptyonoprogne rupestris 164, **71**, *228*
Puffin 140, **62**, *184*
Puffinus assimilis 38, **3**
   gravis 36, **3**
   griseus 37, **3**
   puffinus 37, **3**, *11*
   yelkouan 37, **3**, *12*
Pyrrhocorax graculus 216, **87, 88**, *328*
   pyrrhocorax 216, **87, 88**, *329*
Pyrrhula pyrrhula 230, **90**, *355*

Quail 90, **33**, *109*
Quiscalus quiscula 261

Rail, Water 91, **34**, *111*
Rallus aquaticus 91, **34**, *111*
Raven 218, **88**, *333*
Razorbill 139, **61**, *182*
Recurvirostra avosetta 98, **42, 50**, *123*
Redpoll 226, **90**, *350*
   Arctic 227, **90**, *351*
Redshank 117, **44, 51**, *150*
   Spotted 116, **44, 51**, *149*
Redstart 175, **77**, *252*
   American 258, **93**
   Black 175, **77**, *251*
   Daurian 252
   Güldenstadt's 253
   Moussier's 252
Redwing 184, **78**, *264*
Regulus calendula 254
   ignicapillus 203, **83**, *298*
   regulus 202, **83**, *297*
Remiz pendulinus 211, **86**, *318*
Rhodostethia rosea 132, **56**
Riparia riparia 164, **71**, *227*
Rissa tridactyla 132, **54, 55**, *171*
Robin 173, **76**, *247*
   American 185, **78**
   Rufous Bush 172, **80**, *246*
   Siberian Blue 252
   White-throated 252
Roller 155, **66**, *209*
Rook 217, **88**, *331*
Rosefinch, Long-tailed 256
   Pallas's 256
   Scarlet 229, **90**, *353*
Rubythroat, Siberian 252
Ruff 112, **46, 52**, *140*

Saker 84, **30**, *98*
Sanderling 106, **47, 52**, *134*

Sandgrouse, Black-bellied 141, **36**
   Pallas's 142, **36**
   Pin-tailed 141, **36**
   Spotted 249
Sandpiper, Baird's 108, **49**
   Broad-billed 111, **48**, *139*
   Buff-breasted 111, **46**
   Common 120, **47, 52**, *155*
   Curlew 110, **52**
   Green 119, **45, 51**, *153*
   Least 108, **49**
   Marsh 117, **45**, *151*
   Pectoral 109, **46, 52**
   Purple 110, **48, 52**, *137*
   Semipalmated 107, **49**
   Sharp-tailed 109, **46**
   Solitary 119, **45**
   Spotted 120, **47**
   Stilt 111, **45**
   Terek 120, **51**
   Upland 116, **46**
   Western 246, **49**
   White-rumped 108, **49**
   Wood 119, **45, 51**, *154*
Sapsucker, Yellow-bellied 250
Saxicola rubetra 175, **76**, *253*
   torquata 176, **76**, *254*
Sayornis phoebe 250
Scaup 63, **13, 20**, *57*
   Lesser 243
Scolopax rusticola 114, **43, 51**, *144*
Scoter, Common 65, **14, 20, 22**, *60*
   Surf 66, **14, 20, 22**
   Velvet 66, **14, 20, 22**, *61*
Seiurus aurocapillus 258
   noveboracensis 258, **93**
Serin 223, **89**, *343*
   Red-fronted 256
Serinus citrinella 224, **89**, *344*
   pusillus 256
   serinus 223, **89**, *343*
Setophaga ruticilla 258, **93**
Shag 41, **4**, *17*
Shearwater, Cory's 36, **3**, *10*
   Great 36, **3**
   Little 38, **3**
   Manx 37, **3**, *11*
   Mediterranean 37, **3**, *12*
   Sooty 37, **3**
Shelduck 55, **16, 19, 21**, *45*
   Ruddy 55, **16, 19, 21**, *44*
Shoveler 60, **12, 19, 21**, *52*
Shrike, Black-headed 255
   Brown 255
   Great Grey 213, **85**, *322*
   Isabelline 212, **85**
   Lesser Grey 213, **85**, *321*
   Masked 214, **85**
   Red-backed 212, **85**, *320*
   Rufous-backed 255
   Woodchat 214, **85**, *323*

Siskin 225, **89**, *347*

Sitta canadensis 255
   europaea 209, **83**, *313*
   krueperi 208, **83**
   neumayer 209, **83**, *314*
   whiteheadi 209, **83**

Skua, Arctic 123, **53**, *159*
   Great 124, **53**
   Long-tailed 124, **53**, *160*
   Pomarine 123, **53**

Skylark 163, **70**, *225*

Smew 67, **17, 19, 21**, *63*

Snipe 113, **43, 51**, *142*
   Great 113, **43, 51**, *143*
   Jack 112, **43, 51**, *141*

Snowfinch 221, **91**, *340*

Somateria fischeri 243, **15**
   mollissima 63, **15, 20, 22**, *58*
   spectabilis 63, **15, 20, 22**

Sora 244, **17**

Sparrow, Dead Sea 255
   Fox 259, **94**
   House 220, **91**, *336*
   Lark 259
   Rock 221, **91**, *339*
   Savannah 259
   Song 259, **94**
   Spanish 220, **91**, *337*
   Tree 220, **91**, *338*
   White-crowned 259
   White-throated 232, **94**

Sparrowhawk 76, **26, 31**, *81*
   Levant 76, **26**, *8*

Sphyrapicus varius 250

Spiza americana 260

Spoonbill 47, **7**, *32*
   African 242

Starling 218, **87**, *335*
   Daurian 255
   Purple-backed 255
   Rose-coloured 219, **87**
   Spotless 219, **87**

Stercorarius longicaudus 124, **53**, *160*
   parasiticus 123, **53**, *159*
   pomarinus 123, **53**
   skua 124, **53**

Sterna albifrons 137, **58, 59**, *177*
   aleutica 248
   anaethetus 248, **60**
   antillarum 248
   bengalensis 134, **60**
   caspia 133, **57, 59**, *173*
   dougallii 134, **57, 59**
   elegans 248
   forsteri 136, **60**
   fuscata 136, **60**
   hirundo 135, **57, 59**, *175*
   maxima 248, **60**
   paradisaea 135, **57, 59**, *176*
   repressa 248
   sandvicensis 134, **57, 59**, *174*

Stilt, Black-winged 97, **42, 50**, *122*

Stint, Little 107, **48, 52**, *135*
   Long-toed 246, **48**
   Red-necked 246, **48**
   Temminck's 107, **48, 52**, *136*

Stonechat 176, **76**, *254*

Stork, Black 46, **7**, *29*
   White 46, **7**, *30*

Streptopelia decaocto 143, **63**, *188*
   orientalis 144, **63**
   senegalensis 144, **63**
   turtur 144, **63**, *189*

Strix aluco 149, **65**, *198*
   nebulosa 150, **65**
   uralensis 150, **65**, *199*

Sturnus roseus 219, **87**
   sturninus 255
   unicolor 219, **87**
   vulgaris 218, **87**, *335*

Sula dactylatra 241
   leucogaster 241
   sula 241

Surnia ulula 148, **65**, *195*

Swallow 164, **71**, *229*
   Cliff 251
   Red-rumped 165, **71**, *230*
   Tree 251

Swan, Bewick's 49, **8, 9**, *34*
   Mute 49, **8, 9**, *33*
   Whooper 49, **8, 9**, *35*

Swift 153, **71**, *204*
   Alpine 154, **71**, *206*
   Chimney 249
   Little 154, **71**
   Needle-tailed 249
   Pacific 249
   Pallid 153, **71**, *205*
   White-rumped 154, **71**

Sylvia atricapilla 197, **80**, *290*
   borin 197, **81**, *289*
   cantillans 194, **80**, *283*
   communis 197, **80**, *288*
   conspicillata 194, **80**, *282*
   curruca 196, **80**, *287*
   deserticola 254
   hortensis 196, **80**, *285*
   melanocephala 195, **80**, *284*
   mystacea 254
   nana 195, **82**
   nisoria 196, **80**, *286*
   rueppelli 195, **80**
   sarda 193, **80**
   undata 194, **80**, *281*

Synthliboramphus antiquus 248

Syrrhaptes paradoxus 142, **36**

Tachybaptus ruficollis 33, **2**, *4*

Tachycineta bicolor 251

Tadorna ferruginea 55, **16, 19, 21**, *44*
   tadorna 55, **16, 19, 21**, *45*

Tanager, Scarlet 259

Summer 258, **94**
Tarsiger cyanurus 174, **77**
Tattler, Grey-tailed 247
Teal 58, **12, 19, 21**, *48*
　Baikal 57, **18**
　Blue-winged 60, **18**
Tern, Aleutian 248
　Arctic 135, **57, 59**, *176*
　Black 137, **58, 59**, *179*
　Bridled 248, **60**
　Caspian 133, **57, 59**, *173*
　Common 135, **57, 59**, *175*
　Elegant 248
　Forster's 136, **60**
　Gull-billed 133, **57, 59**, *172*
　Least 248
　Lesser Crested 134, **60**
　Little 137, **58, 59**, *177*
　Roseate 134, **57, 59**
　Royal 248, **60**
　Sandwich 134, **57, 59**, *174*
　Sooty 136, **60**
　Whiskered 137, **58, 59**, *178*
　White-cheeked 248
　White-winged Black 138, **58**, *180*
Tetrao tetrix 87, **32**, *104*
　urogallus 87, **32**, *105*
Tetrax tetrax 96, **36**, *119*
Thrasher, Brown 252
Thrush, Black-throated 183, **78**
　Blue Rock 180, **77**, *259*
　Dusky 182, **78**
　Eye-browed 182, **78**
　Grey-cheeked 181, **94**
　Hermit 253
　Mistle 184, **78**, *265*
　Naumann's 182, **78**
　Pale 253
　Red-throated 183, **78**
　Rock 179, **77**, *258*
　Siberian 180, **78**
　Song 183, **78**, *263*
　Swainson's 181, **94**
　Tickell's 253
　Varied 253
　White's 180, **78**
　Wood 253
Tichodroma muraria 210, **83**, *315*
Tit, Azure 208, **86**
　Bearded 205, **86**, *303*
　Blue 208, **86**, *311*
　Coal 207, **86**, *310*
　Crested 207, **86**, *309*
　Great 208, **86**, *312*
　Long-tailed 205, **86**, *304*
　Marsh 206, **86**, *305*
　Penduline 211, **86**, *318*
　Siberian 207, **86**, *308*
　Sombre 206, **86**, *306*
　Willow 206, **86**, *307*
Torgos tracheliotus 244

Towhee, Rufous-sided 259
Toxostoma rufum 252
Treecreeper 210, **83**, *316*
　Short-toed 211, **83**, *317*
Tringa erythropus 116, **44, 51**, *149*
　flavipes 118, **44**
　glareola 119, **45, 51**, *154*
　melanoleuca 118, **44**
　nebularia 118, **44, 51**, *152*
　ochropus 119, **45, 51**, *153*
　solitaria 119, **45**
　stagnatilis 117, **45**, *151*
　totanus 117, **44, 51**, *150*
Troglodytes troglodytes 171, **83**, *243*
Tropicbird, Red-billed 241
Tryngites subruficollis 111, **46**
Turdus iliacus 184, **78**, *264*
　merula 182, **78**, *261*
　migratorius 185, **78**
　naumanni 182, **78**
　obscurus 182, **78**
　pallidus 253
　philomelos 183, **78**, *263*
　pilaris 183, **78**, *262*
　ruficollis 183, **78**
　torquatus 181, **78**, *260*
　unicolor 253
　viscivorus 184, **78**, *265*
Turnix sylvatica 91, **33**
Turnstone 121, **39, 40**, *156*
Twite 226, **90**, *349*
Tyto alba 147, **64**, *191*

Upupa epops 156, **66**, *210*
Uragus sibiricus 256
Uria aalge 138, **61**, *181*
　lomvia 139, **61**

Vanellus vanellus 105, **39, 40**, *132*
Veery 253
Vermivora chrysoptera 256
　peregrina 256
Vireo flavifrons 255
　olivaceus 222, **93**
　philadelphicus 255
Vireo, Philadelphia 255
　Red-eyed 222, **93**
　Yellow-throated 255
Vulture, Bearded *see* Lammergeier
　Black 73, **23**, *74*
　Egyptian 72, **23**, *72*
　Griffon 73, **23**, *73*
　Lappet-faced 244

Wagtail, Pied 170, **73, 74**, *240*
　Citrine 169, **73**
　Grey 169, **73, 74**, *239*
　White 170, **73, 74**, *240*
　Yellow 169, **73, 74**, *238*
Wallcreeper 210, **83**, *315*
Warbler, Aquatic 188, **79**, *272*
　Arctic 198, **81**, *292*

Barred   196, **80**, *286*
Black-and-white   256, **93**
Black-throated Blue   257
Black-throated Green   257
Blackburnian   257
Blackpoll   231, **93**
Blyth's Reed   189, **82**
Bonelli's   200, **81**, *293*
Booted   192, **82**
Canada   258
Cape May   257
Cetti's   185, **79**, *266*
Chestnut-sided   257
Dartford   194, **80**, *281*
Desert   195, **82**
Dusky   200, **81**
Eastern Crowned   254
Fan-tailed   186, **79**, *267*
Garden   197, **81**, *289*
Golden-winged   256
Grasshopper   187, **79**, *268*
Gray's Grasshopper   253
Great Reed   191, **79**, *276*
Green   254
Greenish   198, **81**, *291*
Hooded   258
Icterine   192, **81**, *279*
Lanceolated   186, **82**
Magnolia   257
Marmora's   193, **80**
Marsh   190, **79**, *274*
Melodious   193, **81**, *280*
Ménétries's   254
Moustached   188, **79**, *271*
Olivaceous   191, **81**, *277*
Olive-tree   192, **81**, *278*
Orphean   196, **80**, *285*
Paddyfield   189, **82**
Pallas's   199, **82**
Pallas's Grasshopper   186, **82**
Radde's   200, **82**
Reed   190, **79**, *275*
River   187, **79**, *269*
Rüppell's   195, **80**
Sardinian   195, **80**, *284*
Savi's   187, **79**, *270*
Sedge   188, **79**, *273*
Spectacled   194, **80**, *282*
Subalpine   194, **80**, *283*
Tennessee   256
Thick-billed   254
Tristram's   254
Willow   202, **81**, *296*
Wilson's   258
Wood   201, **81**, *294*

Yellow-browed   199, **81**
Yellow-rumped (Myrtle)   231, **93**
Yellow   256
Waterthrush, Northern   258, **93**
Waxbill, Common   221, **96**
Waxwing   170, **84**, *241*
   Cedar   251
Wheatear, Black   179, **75**, *257*
   Black-eared   178, **75**, *256*
   Desert   179, **75**
   Isabelline   176, **75**
   Northern   177, **75**, *255*
   Pied   177, **75**
   White-crowned Black   253
Whimbrel   115, **42, 50**, *147*
   Little   247
Whinchat   175, **76**, *253*
Whitethroat   197, **80**, *288*
   Lesser   196, **80**, *287*
Wigeon   56, **12, 19, 21**, *46*
   American   56, **18**
Willet   247
Wilsonia canadensis   258
   citrina   258
   pusilla   258
Woodcock   114, **43, 51**, *144*
Woodlark   162, **70**, *224*
Woodpecker, Black   157, **69**, *214*
   Great Spotted   158, **69**, *215*
   Green   157, **69**, *213*
   Grey-headed   157, **69**, *212*
   Lesser Spotted   159, **69**, *219*
   Middle Spotted   158, **69**, *217*
   Syrian   158, **69**, *216*
   Three-toed   159, **69**, *220*
   White-backed   159, **69**, *218*
Wren   171, **83**, *243*
Wryneck   156, **69**, *211*

Xanthocephalus xanthocephalus   261
Xenus cinereus   120, **51**

Yellowhammer   233, **92**, *359*
Yellowlegs, Greater   118, **44**
   Lesser   118, **44**
Yellowthroat, Common   258

Zenaida macroura   249
Zonotrichia albicollis   232, **94**
   iliaca   259, **94**
   leucophrys   259
   melodia   259, **94**
Zoothera dauma   180, **78**
   naevia   253
   sibirica   180, **78**